INTELLIGENT INFORMATION PROCESSING III

T0138015

IFIP – The International Federation for Information Processing

IFIP was founded in 1960 under the auspices of UNESCO, following the First World Computer Congress held in Paris the previous year. An umbrella organization for societies working in information processing, IFIP's aim is two-fold: to support information processing within its member countries and to encourage technology transfer to developing nations. As its mission statement clearly states,

> *IFIP's mission is to be the leading, truly international, apolitical organization which encourages and assists in the development, exploitation and application of information technology for the benefit of all people.*

IFIP is a non-profitmaking organization, run almost solely by 2500 volunteers. It operates through a number of technical committees, which organize events and publications. IFIP's events range from an international congress to local seminars, but the most important are:

• The IFIP World Computer Congress, held every second year;
• Open conferences;
• Working conferences.

The flagship event is the IFIP World Computer Congress, at which both invited and contributed papers are presented. Contributed papers are rigorously refereed and the rejection rate is high.

As with the Congress, participation in the open conferences is open to all and papers may be invited or submitted. Again, submitted papers are stringently refereed.

The working conferences are structured differently. They are usually run by a working group and attendance is small and by invitation only. Their purpose is to create an atmosphere conducive to innovation and development. Refereeing is less rigorous and papers are subjected to extensive group discussion.

Publications arising from IFIP events vary. The papers presented at the IFIP World Computer Congress and at open conferences are published as conference proceedings, while the results of the working conferences are often published as collections of selected and edited papers.

Any national society whose primary activity is in information may apply to become a full member of IFIP, although full membership is restricted to one society per country. Full members are entitled to vote at the annual General Assembly, National societies preferring a less committed involvement may apply for associate or corresponding membership. Associate members enjoy the same benefits as full members, but without voting rights. Corresponding members are not represented in IFIP bodies. Affiliated membership is open to non-national societies, and individual and honorary membership schemes are also offered.

INTELLIGENT INFORMATION PROCESSING III

IFIP TC12 International Conference on Intelligent Information Processing (IIP 2006), September 20-23, Adelaide, Australia

Edited by

Zhongzhi Shi
Institute of Computing Technology, Chinese Academy of Sciences
China

K. Shimohara
ATR Network Informatics Laboratories
Japan

D. Feng
University of Sydney
Australia

 Springer

Intelligent Information Processing III

Edited by Z. Shi, K. Shimohara and D. Feng

p. cm. (IFIP International Federation for Information Processing, a Springer Series in Computer Science)

ISSN: 1571-5736 / 1861-2288 (Internet)

ISBN: 13: 978-1-4419-4273-9
Printed on acid-free paper

eISBN: 10: 0-387-44641-9
eISBN: 13: 978-0-387-44641-7

9 8 7 6 5 4 3 2 1
springer.com

Contents

Chapter 6. Expert Systems

Chapter 7. Image Processing

Chapter 8. Natural Language Processing

Welcome Address

Dear Colleagues,

Welcome to the 4th IFIP International Conference on Intelligent Information Processing. On behalf of the organizers, we welcome all scientists and practitioners who are interested in Intelligent Information Processing around the world and who have come to participate in this event. As the world proceeds quickly into the Information Age, it encounters both successes and challenges, and it is well recognized nowadays that Intelligent Information Processing provides the key to the Information Age and to mastering many of these challenges. Intelligent Information Processing supports the most advanced productive tools that are said to be able to change human life and the world itself. However, the path is never a straight one and every new technology brings with it a spate of new research problems to be tackled by researchers; as a result we are not running out of topics; rather the demand is ever increasing. This conference provides a forum for engineers and scientists in academia, university and industry to present their latest research findings in all aspects of Intelligent Information Processing.

As scientists, professors, engineers, entrepreneurs, or government officials all over the world, it is our task to understand the technology and explore effective ways to apply it in the Information Age. This is the motivation of IIP2006.
Dear Colleagues,

M. Stumptner
M. Bramer
T. Ishida
Conference Chairs

Greetings from Program Committee

Dear colleagues and friends:

First of all, we would like to extend to you our warmest welcome and sincere greetings on behalf of the Technical Program Committee of the IFIP International Conference on Intelligent Information Processing, IIP2006, Adelaide.

This is the 4th IFIP International Conference on Intelligent Information Processing. We received over 120 papers, of which 52 papers are included in this program as regular papers and 14 as short papers. We are grateful for the dedicated work of both the authors and the referees, and we hope these proceedings will continue to bear fruit over the years to come. All papers submitted were reviewed by several referees.

A conference such as this cannot succeed without help from many individuals who contributed their valuable time and expertise. We want to express our sincere gratitude to the program committee members and referees, who invested many hours for reviews and deliberations. They provided detailed and constructive review reports that will significantly improve the papers included in the program.

We are very grateful to have the sponsorship of the following organizations: IFIP TC12, International Federation of Automatic Control, Chinese Association of Artificial Intelligence, Australian Computer Society and support by the University of South Australia.

We hope all of you enjoy this diverse and interesting Pro rogram.

Zhongzhi Shi
K. Shimohara
D. Feng
Program Chairs

The Organizations of the Conference

General Chairs

M. Stumptner(Australia)   M. Bramer(UK)   T. Ishida (Japan)

Program Chairs

Z. Shi (China)   K. Shimohara (Japan)   D. Feng (Australia)

PC Committee

N. Bredeche (France)
P. Chen (USA)
H. Chi (China)
H. Dai(Australia)
E. Durfee (USA)
B. Faltings (Switzerland)
I. Futo (Hungary)
N. Gibbins (UK)
F. Giunchiglia (Italy)
V. Gorodetski (Russia)
J. Hendler (USA)
L. Kagal(USA)

D. Leake (USA)
J. Lee (Korea)
D. Lin (Canada)
J. Liu (Hong Kong)
L. Liu (USA)
R. Lu (China)
J. Ma (UK)
R. Meersman (Belgium)
H. Motoda (Japan)
M. Musen (USA)
G. Osipov (Russia)
Y. Peng (USA)

M. Sasikumar (India)
R. Studer (Germany)
R. Sun (USA)
S. Willmott (Spain)
X. Yao (UK)
J. Yang(Korea)
P. Yu (USA)
Eric Yu (Canada)
C. Zhang (Australia)
N. Zhang (Hong Kong)
Y. Zhong (China)
Z. Zhou(China)

Referees List

Nicolas Bredeche	Hiroshi Motoda
Liang Chang	Gulisong Nansierding
Huisheng Chi	Jiarui NI
Honghua Dai	Yun Peng
E. Durfee	Filip Perich
D. Feng	Lirong Qiu
Xin Geng	Markus Stumptner
V. Gorodetski	Yongmei Tan
Xiaoshu Hang	Yiqing Tu
Yanxiang He	Jiaqi WANG
Jun Hu	Jing Wang
Warren JIN	Maoguang Wang
Shimohara Katsunori	Chengqi Zhang
Jaeho Lee	Jung-Jin Yang
Chunsheng LI	Min-Ling Zhang
Gang Li	Sulan Zhang
Lei Li	Zhiyong Zhang
Li LI	Yanchang ZHAO
Ling Liu	Yixin Zhong
Xudong LU	Zhi-hua Zhou
Jiewen Luo	Ling Zhuang
J. Ma	Xingquan Zuo

Keynote Speech

Keynote Speaker: Colin Fyfe

Title: Data Mining through visualization

Biography: Professor Colin Fyfe is an active researcher in Artificial Neural Networks, Genetic Algorithms, Artificial Immune Systems and Artificial Life having written over 250 refereed papers, several book chapters and two books.
He is a member of the Editorial Board of the International Journal of Knowledge-Based Intelligent Engineering Systems and an Associate Editor of International Journal of Neural Systems. He currently supervises 6 PhD students and has acted as Director of Studies for 16 PhDs (all successful) since 1998. 9 former PhD students now hold academic posts including one other Professor and one Senior Lecturer. He is a member of the Academic Advisory Board of the International Computer Science Conventions group and is a Committee member of the EU-funded project, EUNITE - the European Network of Excellence on Intelligent Technologies for Smart Adaptive Systems. He has been Visiting Researcher at the University of Strathclyde, 1993-94, at the Riken Institute, Tokyo, January 1998 and at the Chinese University of Hong Kong, 2000 and Visiting Professor at the University of Vigo, Spain, the University of Burgos, Spain, and the University of Salamanca, Spain.

Keynote Speaker: Javaan Singh Chahl

Title: Autonomous Systems—Biologically Inspired Subsystems

Abstract:
Biology is an inspiration for almost all work on autonomous systems. The earliest work on Artificial Intelligence considered the task to be one of functionally replicating the human brain. Since then it has become clear that there is a need to consider lower organisms, due to the extreme complexity and ethical issues surrounding work on humans. Indeed, working with mammals in general is questionable from a technical perspective. Mammals typically have billions of neurons, as opposed to the tens of thousands in arthropods (insects, crabs, etc.). Behavior of mammals is correspondingly more complex, state dependent and irreproducible. Despite the reduced complexity of arthropods, the autonomous capabilities of the simplest, still far outstrips that of any technical artifact.

For some years we have been using the behavior and sensory systems of arthropods as an inspiration for new autonomous systems capability. Some of the techniques developed have included an alternative sun compass for NASA operations on Mars, means of operating small-unmanned aerial vehicles near the ground for DARPA, and new technology for maintaining level flight in extremely small UAVs for the US Air force. To demonstrate these new concepts it has been necessary to automate platforms carrying sensors that have never been used in a navigation avionics suite.

The experience and outcomes (including many videos) of our research program over the last five years will be presented, with a detailed description of the subsystems and underpinning biological principles.

Biography: Dr Javaan Chahl is a Senior Research Scientist with the Defence Science and Technology, and an adjunct Senior Researcher with the University of South Australia's KES centre. Dr Chahl completed his Engineering degree in 1991 at the University of Newcastle, specializing in Computer Engineering. In 1992 he completed a Graduate Diploma in Neuroscience at the Australian National University, where he studied the applications of neural networks to motion sensitive machine vision systems. In 1996 he completed his doctorate in Neuroscience at the Australian National University, in which he developed a number of different algorithms for controlling vehicles using optical flow. During this time he also developed and patented a new class of reflective surfaces that allow low distortion panoramic imaging. In 1996 he was appointed Post Doctoral Fellow in the Australian National University, studying the application of optical flow and panoramic vision systems to aircraft control. In

1999 he joined the Defence Science and Technology Organisation as a Research Scientist in Weapons Systems Division. Since then he has lead a technical team developing control systems for aircraft based on optical flow and other sensors. In 2002 he was promoted to Senior Research Scientist. Dr Chahl is author of over 35 full-length papers in the fields of computer vision, optics and insect behavior. In addition his work has lead to 5 international patents. He has been principle investigator on contracts with DARPA, NASA, and AFOSR mainly in the area of UAV technologies. In 2001 he was co-recipient of the "Australasian Science Prize".

Keynote Speaker: Zhongzhi Shi

Title: Semantic Web Services

Abstract: Semantic Web techniques apply knowledge representation techniques in a distributed environment. In order to overcome the current deficiencies of the Web service technology stack Semantic Web Services are under going to research and develop to facilitate the higher automation of service discovery, composition, invocation, and monitoring in an open, unregulated, and dynamic environment. In this talk I will give a brief history of Semantic Web Services, in particular focused on service discovery and composition for the emerging concept of Semantic Web Services. Dynamic Description Lgic (DDL) proposed by the Key Laboratory of Intelligent Information Processing, Institute of Computing Technology, Chinese Academy of Sciencestheir, is adopted as a logic foundation of Semantic Web Services. Through DDL we implement service discovery and composition. Finally, I will point out some interesting areas for future research, in particular those related to the Semantic Web Services application area.

Biography: Zhongzhi Shi is a Professor at the Institute of Computing Technology, the Chinese Academy of Sciences, leading the Research Group of Intelligent Science. His research interests include intelligence science, multiagent systems, semantic Web, machine learning and neural computing. Professor Shi has published 10 monographs, 11 books and more than 350 research papers in journals and conferences. He has won a 2nd-Grade National Award at Science and Technology Progress of China in 2002, two 2nd-Grade Awards at Science and Technology Progress of the Chinese Academy of Sciences in 1998 and 2001, respectively. He is a senior member of IEEE, member of AAAI and ACM, Chair for the WG 12.2 of IFIP. He serves as Vice President for Chinese Association of Artificial Intelligence.

TEAMS IN MULTI-AGENT SYSTEMS

Bevan Jarvis, Dennis Jarvis, Lakhmi Jain

Bevan.Jarvis@postgrads.unisa.edu.au
Jarvis.Dennis@gmail.com
Lakhmi.Jain@unisa.edu.au
KES Group, School of Electrical and Information Engineering, University of South Australia

Abstract: Multi-agent systems involve agents interacting with each other and the
               environment and working to achieve individual and group goals. The
               achievement of group goals requires that agents work together within teams. In
               this paper we first introduce three philosophical approaches that result from
               different answers to two key questions. Secondly we consider three theoretical
               frameworks for modelling team behaviour. Next we look at two agent
               implementation models. Finally, we consider one of those implementation
               models – JACK Teams – and place it in the context of the philosophical debate
               and the theoretical frameworks.

Key words: Intelligent agents, Teams, Multi-agent systems

1.   INTRODUCTION

Multi-agent systems are of research interest in philosophy, artificial intelligence and cognitive science. There are two approaches to modelling MAS behaviour – by explicit specification of individual behaviours or by relying on emergent behaviours. In the latter case, collective activity may not always be easily derivable.

Two key issues emerge. First is the question of whether teams should be explicitly modelled, as constructs constraining individual behaviour. Koestler's description of holons [12] represents a positive answer to this question. Assuming an individual-oriented approach, a second issue arises of whether individual-oriented intention suffices to explain collective

Please use the following format when citing this chapter:

Jarvis, B., Jarvis, D., Jain, L., 2006, in IFIP International Federation for Information Processing, Volume 228, Intelligent Information Processing III, eds. Z. Shi, Shimohara K., Feng D., (Boston: Springer), pp. 1–10.

intentionality – as proposed by Bratman [4] – or, as argued by Searle [15], a separate type of intention is required that is oriented towards the group and is not reducible to individual-oriented intention.

The different approaches are reflected in different theoretical frameworks for multi-agent teaming. Holonics [6] is an interpretation of Koestler's ideas. Cohen and Levesque's Joint Intention theory [5] follows Searle by defining joint intentions that are held by the team as a whole. In the SharedPlans theory of Grosz et al. [9, 10], individual-oriented and collective-oriented intention are respectively represented by means of the mental attitudes "intend to" (perform an action) and "intend that" (a proposition becomes true).

Both the Joint Intention theory and the SharedPlans theory have provided the basis for a number of successful implementations. Perhaps the most noted of these is the team-oriented programming (TOP) framework, exhibited in the TEAMCORE system of Pynadath et al. [13], which combines elements of both theories.

JACK Teams [2] is here represented as an agent-based implementation of the holonics model. The defining concept in JACK Teams may be described as providing an agent with the capability to delegate roles and to accept role obligations. An agent can thus be at once part of a greater whole (a group serving another agent) and a self-contained entity, capable of coordinating its own groups. This is essentially the definition of a holon [6].

It will be useful to consider the sources of an individual agent's intentions, which we identify as desires, obligations and norms. Desires belong to the agent. Obligations arise from an agent's agreement with another agent to perform an action or role – they are the result of delegations or contracts. Norms represent the (in human terms often tacit) agreement of agents in a group to follow certain rules. Desires are thus individual-oriented, obligations are oriented to one other individual, and norms are group-oriented.

In sections 2 and 3 we look more closely at the philosophical viewpoints of Searle and Bratman and the related theoretical frameworks developed by Cohen and Levesque and by Grosz and her collaborators. In section 4 we selectively overview some implementations of team behaviour. We conclude by discussing JACK Teams, placing it in the context of the philosophical debate and the theoretical frameworks. While having been developed separately from the philosophical and theoretical models we discuss, JACK Teams still appears to find a natural place among them.

2.   THE PHILOSOPHY OF TEAMS

As mentioned above, two key issues in describing team behaviour are whether the focus of attention is on teams or individuals, and (assuming the latter) how to represent collective intention. At the philosophical level this results in three distinct approaches. The team-centric view inspired by Koestler is that teams can be both parts of larger (or at least not smaller) teams and coordinate smaller teams. From the individual-centric viewpoint, there are two approaches, represented here by Bratman and Searle. Bratman's view is that collective intention can be described by referring to individual intention in combination with other mental attitudes. Searle's opposing view is that collective intention cannot be so reduced.

2.1   Holons and the Janus Effect

Koestler [6] coined the word 'holon' to denote an entity which is both a collection of parts and a part of a greater entity. For example, a human organ is an organised collection of cells and is also a part of the human body. Holons can be part of other holons, forming hierarchies – or heterarchies – called 'holarchies'. The 'Janus effect' denotes the two-sided nature of a holon within a holarchy: facing upwards it has the form of a dependent part, while facing downwards it appears to be a self-contained whole.

Teams are holons in that they are made up of individuals and are also part of a larger organisation. Teams can also be part of other teams, and so the team structure of an organisation is, in the general case, a holarchy.

Koestler in fact does not distinguish between individuals and teams. Rather, he seeks to capture the essence of system behaviour in terms of a holarchy.

2.2   Bratman and Shared Intention

In a series of papers (collected in [4]), Bratman develops his notion of shared intention. This is intention of the group, but comprises a public, interlocking web of intentions of individuals. The interlocking web aspect reflects the fact that an individual's intentions are achieved through hierarchies of plans and subplans that must be meshed with those of other cooperating individuals. The public nature of the web of intentions is established by invoking common knowledge. (Common knowledge is the knowledge by each individual in a group of an infinite set of propositions of the form "I know that X", "I know that you know that X", "I know that you know that I know that X", and so on. A detailed study is provided by Fagin, et al. [8]. It has a close analogue in mutual belief.)

2.3   Searle and Collective Intentionality

Searle contends that in addition to individual intentionality there is collective intentionality, which latter is expressed, by each individual, as "we intend" [15]. Collective intentionality is, he states, "a biologically primitive phenomenon that cannot be reduced to or eliminated in favor of something else." Searle further claims that individual intention plus mutual belief, or any alternative to mutual belief that he has seen, does not in fact result in collective intention. This claim appears incompatible, however, with the logical requirements of the theoretical frameworks discussed below, which rely on common knowledge.

2.4   Norms and Obligations

We follow Dignam et al. [7] in distinguishing between norms and obligations. Norms are held by a group or community, and no individual is identified as the instigator. Obligations involve just two parties (individuals or groups regarded as individuals). One party instigates the obligation, which is held by the other. Using Bratman's terminology [3], both norms and obligations are pro-attitudes (similar to desires), and only in the event that they are accepted and the individual in some way commits to them do they become conduct-controlling pro-attitudes (intentions).

Norms are rules of behaviour – prescriptions or proscriptions – that are understood and enforced within a group or community. Norms include mores, taboos, faux pas and commonly agreed ways of doing things. Some norms are codified as laws. Penalties for breaking a norm range from the extreme – execution or ostracism from the community or group – to minor or none at all – shame, or the knowledge that one has caused insult or injury. Punishments may even take subtle forms such as not being invited to receive some benefit, and it is quite possible for a person not to realise that he or she has been so penalised. These punishments are sanctioned by the group, implicitly or otherwise.

Obligations are most readily explained by referring to delegation. Consider that Adam asks or requires Belinda to act in a particular way (i.e. to perform a role or a task), and Belinda, through agreement or coercion, decides (commits, and therefore feels obligated) to so act. In the case of delegation, the behaviour asked of Belinda is part of a plan coordinated by Adam. Obligations per se allow for punishment only on a limited, individual level. If, for example, Belinda does not behave as agreed, Adam has the option not to rely on her in the future. Any further action that Adam might take is subject to social norms. Obligations in which one or both parties are groups or organisations, however, often involve contracts.

Contracts are one way to enable punishment for not fulfilling obligations. They require that a third person or entity (representing the community or group) may be called upon to arbitrate and decide punishment if the agreement is broken. Contractual obligations exist in the context of a norm (codified in a set of laws) that prescribes that people in general should adhere to contracts.

3.   THEORETICAL FRAMEWORKS FOR TEAMS

3.1   Holonics

In general terms, holonics is the application of Koestler's ideas to the design of multi-agent systems. The objective is to attain in designed systems the benefits that holonic organisation provides to living organisms and societies. These benefits are: stability in the face of disturbance; adaptability and flexibility to change; and efficient use of resources [6].

A noted application is Holonic Manufacturing Systems (HMS). In HMS it is desired that behaviour be explicitly specified: unpredicted emergent behaviour is generally unwelcome in a manufacturing environment.

In the holonics model, a holon has behaviours that are coordinated from above and also specifies behaviours of subsidiary holons. Additionally, it may have behaviours as an individual entity.

3.2   Joint Intentions

In [5], Cohen and Levesque establish that joint intention cannot be defined simply as individual intention with the team regarded as an individual. This is because after the initial formation of an intention, team members may diverge in their beliefs and hence in their attitudes towards the intention. Instead, Cohen and Levesque generalise their own definition of intention. First they present a definition of individual persistent goal and, in terms of this, individual intention. Both definitions use the notion of individual belief. Next, they define precise analogues of these concepts – joint persistent goal and joint intention – by invoking mutual belief in place of individual belief. The definition of joint persistent goal additionally requires each team member to commit to informing other members – to the extent of the team's mutual belief – if it comes to believe that the common goal has been achieved, becomes impossible or is no longer relevant. The result is that, while a team is not an individual, nevertheless joint intention is – at least in definition – similar to individual intention.

In Cohen and Levesque's theory, then, a team with a joint intention is a group that shares a common objective and a certain shared mental state [5]. In particular, joint intentions are held by the team as a whole.

3.3   SharedPlans

In Grosz and Sidner's SharedPlans model [10], two intentional attitudes are employed: "intending to" (do an action) and "intending that" (a proposition will hold). The former is individual-oriented intention, while the latter represents intention directed toward group activity. Additionally, shared intentions are described along with mutually known partial plans to achieve those intentions. Agents are said to have a SharedPlan to do α just in case they hold: (1) individual intentions that the group perform α; (2) mutual belief of a (partial) plan to do α; (3) beliefs about individual or group plans for the sub-acts in the plan to do α; (4) intentions that the selected agents or subgroups succeed in performing their designated sub-acts; and (5) subsidiary commitments to group decision-making aimed at completing the plan to do α.

Grosz and Hunsberger [9] claim to reconcile the two approaches to teams that we have ascribed to Bratman and Searle (to the extent of the disagreement about whether or not group-oriented intention is reducible to individual intention). They provide the "Coordinated Cultivation of SharedPlans" (CCSP) model, which, while relying solely on individual intention, captures the essential properties argued for in accounts that require group-oriented intention [9]. CCSP also provides a general architecture for collaboration-capable agents.

4.   IMPLEMENTATIONS OF TEAMS IN MULTI-AGENT SYSTEMS

Two important architectures for building intelligent agents are Production Systems and the Belief-Desire-Intention (BDI) model [17].

In the Production System model, agent behaviour is coded by specifying rules that are invoked through variable binding and forward chaining.

In the BDI model, individual agents are specified which each have their own beliefs, desires, intentions (desires to which the agent has committed), and plans to carry out their intentions. In practice, commitment to intentions is handled internally to the execution engine, while desires (or goals) are implicit in the events that the agent declares it has plans to handle. Thus, coding a BDI agent consists predominantly in specifying plans and initial beliefs.

In this section we consider two implementation models of team behaviour. Team Oriented Programming (TOP) is an agent-based model that combines ideas from the Joint Intentions and SharedPlans theoretical frameworks described in the previous section. It is implemented in the Production System model. JACK Teams is also agent-based, through extending BDI, but represents an implementation of the Holonics framework.

4.1   JACK Teams

JACK Teams [2] is an extension of JACK [1], which is an implementation of the BDI model of intelligent agency. JACK itself is implemented as an extension of Java, giving it the power of a complete (and well known) computer language.

JACK Teams extends JACK by allowing the definition of agent plans in terms of roles that unspecified agents may perform, and by providing a mechanism by which roles can be matched to agents that have plans to handle them. Importantly, the delegating agent does not require the details of those plans. By way of example, Adam may ask Belinda to buy some anchovies for the pizza he wants to make, but does not need to know whether she will buy them from the local grocer or at the supermarket. All he requires (in the JACK Teams model) is for Belinda to say she has a plan for buying anchovies. Of course, Adam is free to tighten the role specification.

JACK Teams allows for belief propagation, through the notion of team belief connections. The connection is strictly one-to-one, between the coordinating agent and the agent performing a role. The flow of beliefs may be directed either upwards – synthesising the beliefs of an agent into those of the agent whose role it is performing – or downwards – allowing an agent performing a role to inherit beliefs from the coordinating agent.

JACK Teams also separates team structure (the structure needed to perform a plan) from organisational structure. In fact, it has nothing to say about the latter – although appropriate restrictions may be specified if desired.

An agent in JACK Teams is best interpreted as an extension of an ordinary agent such that it can communicate with other (similarly enhanced) agents about the roles that it requires or can fulfil. JACK Teams thus provides a mechanism whereby an individual agent can establish a group that is to some extent committed to the obligations (roles) that it prescribes. The fact that all individuals are so enhanced establishes a powerful mechanism for describing team structures.

A JACK Teams agent is clearly a holon. It performs plans at the behest of other agents, and it coordinates groups to perform its own plans. Since it as extension of an ordinary BDI agent, it also has its own private plans.

4.2   Team Oriented Programming

The Team Oriented Programming framework (TOP) is an attempt to simplify the process of building robust, flexible agent teams [13]. Each potential team member is required to have a functional interface that describes its capabilities, specifying the tasks it can perform, input and output parameters for each task, and constraints on input parameters. TOP has an explicit "team layer", a level of abstraction at which the programmer specifies: the organisational hierarchy of agents for achieving team goals; the team goals; the team procedures for achieving team goals (including initiation and termination conditions); and coordination constraints between agents executing joint activities.

The TEAMCORE [13] (and the more recent Machinetta [14]) implementation of TOP is implemented as wrappers or proxies for agents defined using the production system-based architecture Soar. TEAMCORE is an extension of STEAM [16]. Teamwork knowledge in STEAM consists of three classes of domain-independent rules: coherence preserving, monitor and repair, and selectivity-in-communication. In TEAMCORE, this domain-independent knowledge is encapsulated within wrapper agents, separating it from the possibly heterogeneous domain-level agents.

5.   JACK TEAMS IN CONTEXT

We now look more closely at and seek to place JACK Teams in context with the philosophical positions and theoretical frameworks mentioned in this paper. We focus on JACK Teams because it occupies a unique philosophical position. As an extension of JACK it is based on previous work done by Bratman that provided the philosophical basis for BDI. At the same time it presents an implementation of Koestler's notion of holon.

JACK Teams was developed in response to a requirement to model team structures within organisations – specifically, military organisations. In this context the holonic approach, with its emphasis on explicit specification of behaviour, provides a mechanism for specifying standard military procedures.

The contribution of JACK Teams may be summarised by saying that it gives an agent the capability to reason about and coordinate the delegated behaviour of other agents. If a normal BDI agent represents a member of the species *homo actor* ("man the doer"), then a JACK Teams agent is *homo delegator*. From this apparently simple extension there emerges a powerful device for specifying heterarchies of delegation and obligation.

JACK Teams is firmly on the side of explicit representation of MAS behaviour. Moreover, the engine that matches roles with agents willing to perform them may be said to provide a form of mutual belief for the group, making cooperation possible. This puts it on the side of Bratman.

There is a clear distinction in JACK Teams between private intentions and intentions that are expressed by specifying roles to be filled. These respectively mirror the formulations "intend to" and "intend that" of Grosz et al. Also, there is a clear recognition of the importance of plans in mutual activity. These considerations indicate a concordance with the SharedPlans framework.

In addition, failure by an agent in a role will be detected by the coordinating agent. The latter will either handle the failure or cascade it up the delegation hierarchy (or heterarchy). It is in this manner that JACK Teams implements the communication of plan outcomes to interested parties, analogously to the communication requirement of the Joint Intentions framework.

The mechanism of belief propagation, mentioned above, provides to JACK Teams a form of mutual belief. Although this mutuality is strictly between the agent performing a role and the coordinating agent, the beliefs could be further propagated by either party.

In itself, JACK Teams does nothing towards implementing norms. However, if needed, norms could be implemented in the design of particular systems. One approach would be to implement norms as beliefs, which could be propagated throughout the group.

6.   CONCLUSION AND FUTURE DIRECTIONS

In this paper we have contextualised research into the modelling of team behaviour in multi-agent systems, by considering philosophical and theoretical issues and by briefly describing two implementations.

We have also categorised JACK Teams, which, while closely connected to the holonics model, yet appears to correspond well with the work of Grosz et al., and includes an important feature of Cohen and Levesque's model.

One direction for future research would be to investigate the implementation of norms in JACK Teams. One suggested approach [11] uses explicit team contracts that specify required behaviour of each member of a task team as well as synchronisation requirements between members.

Team contracts can be said to provide agents with an expression of joint intention.

Also of interest is the problem of incomplete information. By way of example, in the operation of agent-controlled unmanned aerial vehicles (UAVs) there may be periods when communication is impossible or is deliberately not used. All the theoretical frameworks discussed assume perfect communication. It would thus become necessary to revisit this assumption.

REFERENCES

1. AOS: JACK Intelligent Agents: JACK Manual, Release 5.0, Agent Oriented Software, Pty Ltd (2005)
2. AOS: JACK Intelligent Agents: JACK Teams Manual, Release 5.0, Agent Oriented Software, Pty Ltd (2005)
3. Bratman, M. E.: Intention, Plans, and Practical Reason, Harvard University Press (1987)
4. Bratman, M.E.: Faces of Intention, Cambridge University Press (1999)
5. Cohen, P.R. and Levesque, H.J.: Teamwork, Technical Report 503, SRI International (1991)
6. Deen, S.M. (ed.): Agent-Based Manufacturing: Advances in the Holonic Approach, Springer-Verlag (2003)
7. Dignum, F., Kinny, D., and Sonenburg, L.: From Desires, Obligations and Norms to Goals, in Cognitive Science Quarterly, 2(3-4) (2002) 407-430
8. Fagin, R., Halpern, J.Y., Moses, Y., and Vardi, M.Y.: Reasoning About Knowledge, The MIT Press (1995)
9. Grosz, B.J. and Hunsberger, L.: The Dynamics of Intention, in Collaborative Activity, Conference on Collective Intentionality IV, Siena (2004)
10. Grosz, B.J. and Sidner, C.L.: Plans for Discourse, in Cohen, P.R., Morgan, J. and Pollack, M.E, eds, Intentions in Communication, The MIT Press (1990)
11. Jarvis, D., Jarvis, J., Rönnquist, R. and Fletcher, M.: Provision of Robust Behaviour in Teams of UAVs – A Conceptual Model, paper to be presented at the 1st SEAS DTC Technical Conference, Edinburgh (2006)
12. Koestler, A.: The Ghost in the Machine, Arkana (1967)
13. Pynadath, D.V., Tambe, M., Chauvat, N. and Cavedon, L.: Toward Team-Oriented Programming, in Intelligent Agents VI: Agent Theories, Architectures and Languages, Springer-Verlag (1999)
14. Scerri, P., Pynadath, D.V., Schurr, N., Farinelli, A., Gandhe, S. and Tambe, M.: Team Oriented Programming and Proxy Agents, in Proceedings of the 1st International Workshop on Programming Multiagent Systems (2004)
15. Searle, J.R.: The Construction of Social Reality, Free Press (1997)
16. Tambe, M.:Towards flexible teamwork, in Journal of Artificial Intelligence Research, 7 (1997) 83-124
17. Wooldridge, M.: Reasoning About Rational Agents, The MIT Press (2000)

THE LINK BETWEEN AGENT COORDINATION AND COOPERATION

Angela Consoli[1], Jeffrey Tweedale[2] and Lakhmi Jain[1]

(1) Knowledge-Based Intelligent Engineering Systems Centre, School of Electrical and Information Engineering University of South Australia.
angela.consoli@unisa.edu.au
(2) Airborne Mission Systems, Defence, Science and Technology Organisation, Adelaide.

Abstract: Agent coordination is the ability to manage the interdependencies of activities between agents while agent cooperation is the process used for an agent to voluntarily enter a relationship with another to achieve a system derived goal. We describe and show the concepts of Coordinative Cooperation and Cooperative Coordination using examples. These concepts demonstrate the ability for intelligent agents to distinguish between cooperation from coordination and vice-versa. Both concepts can be integrated into a process, using a cognitive cycle to explain the interaction between coordination and cooperation. Furthermore, this paper will discuss how the coordination/cooperation loop is initialised and can be affected by Coordinative and Cooperative events. We recommend suggestions on how these concepts can be designed and implemented in a multiagent system (MAS) and introduce AC^{3}M, which is a prototype of this cognitive loop.

Keywords: Multi-agent, coordination and cooperation.

1   Introduction and Motivation

Multi-agent systems (MASs) enlist in a variety of formats and architectures that exploit specific behaviours and reasoning. These behaviours and reasoning can be compared to the study of Classical Management Theory. A pioneer in Classical Management Theory, Taylor (1947) describes and defines the cornerstone principles of management. These principles include the theory of Research and Analysis, training, cooperation and coordination. He considers Research and Analysis in terms

Please use the following format when citing this chapter:

Consoli, A., Tweedale, J., Jain, L., 2006, in IFIP International Federation for Information Processing, Volume 228, Intelligent Information Processing III, eds. Z. Shi, Shimohara K., Feng D., (Boston: Springer), pp. 11–19.

of time management studies and functional analysis that are generally conducted prior to implementing new or improved work processes [1]. Training is a conducted after the implementation to allow for workers to correctly utilities the new process. However, it is coordination and cooperation that are considered as the functions or set procedures that allow for smooth learning during training [1]. Therefore, it is these two functions that we suggest are subjects that are open to further automation.

This paper contains four sections. The section 2 introduces the concepts of the personification of agents and the definitions of agent coordination and cooperation. Section 3 describes the concept of a cognitive loop that exists between coordination and cooperation. These concepts are known as Coordinative Cooperation and Cooperative Coordination. Section 4 describes the implementation of these concepts and followed by a discussion of a prototype of this cognitive loop.

2   Coordination and Cooperation of Agents

2.1   Personification of Agents

The development of agents has seen a shift from autonomous goal-setting agents to MASs that are responsive to and reason with other agents. The personification of agents has allowed the development of intelligent agents to facilitate human-computer interaction that emulates human behaviour. In this way, intelligent agents are provided with more social abilities. Personification increases trustworthiness and credibility of an agent. It also increases user's engagement, for example a learning environment [2]. Personification of agents can be seen as the *coherent believable, stable and typical cluster of traits and attitudes that are reflected in the agent's behaviour* [3].

Bratman (1990) considers that Practical Reasoning is an extension of the personification of agents. He acknowledges that the practical reasoning in agents is the weighting conflicts of competing options, where each is determined from an agent's desires, values, cares and beliefs [4].

Rao and Georgeff (1995) define BDI agents where the *beliefs* are represented as information that is updated by means of actions. An agent's *desires* are its motivational state, and *intentions* are the agent's deliberative component [5]. Wooldridge (2002) further extends the BDI framework by including practical reasoning algorithms plus the concepts of conventions, commitments and plans [6].

2.2   Agent Coordination

The term coordination has been used in explaining concepts in the areas of psychology, sociology, biology, management, finance and information technology

[7], [8]. A working definition is *the act of managing interdependencies between activities performed to achieve a goal* [9].

Agent coordination provide coherency and focus to a MAS. Coherency is important as it aids an agent or MAS to behave and act desirably as a unit [11]. Coherency ensures agents do not conflict, waste effort and squander resources while trying to accomplish their required objectives. The process of coordination enables agents to focus on the task being performed. This unified approach to task decomposition assists the MAS to complete the common goal [10].

2.3   Agent Cooperation

A universally accepted definition of cooperation is *acting together with a common purpose* [12]. Cooperation can result from two specific influences; explicit and implicit influences of norms and values. The former is the influence from either a leader or referee. The latter is the influence is from the norms and values that are common between actors [13].

When an autonomous agent enters a relationship with another agent voluntarily, it is said to be cooperating. An agent will generally acquire a goal of another if there is some positive motivational outcome [14], [15].

Wooldridge and Jennings (1999) highlight two major assumptions required for agent cooperation to succeed. Firstly, because cooperation can fail, an adequate contingency plan is required and agents must initiate the social processes. Agents are required to start interaction processes that will instantiate and help accomplish cooperation [14].

2.4   Coordinative Cooperation

Swarts (2004) argues that coordination is based on two events: the ratification of a proposal and the revision and subsequent ratification of proposals [16]. Like contracts, any form of revision must be met with full and voluntary agreement with all parties. Such agreement is shown as cooperation. The quality of coordination depends on a group's ability to not only communicate and store their ideas, but also to share these ideas with others [16]. The latter event can be seen as Coordinative Cooperation. A working definition would be:

"... The act of managing interdependencies of actors or objects such that an actor/object will voluntarily enter a relationship with another actor/object and adopt the goal of that actor/object for the common purpose of achieving a common goal.. "

For Coordinative Cooperation to be recognised, an event occurs where agents are coordinated into tasks. This event is known as a *Coordinative Event* and is defined as an action that has resulted from coordination.

2.5   Coordinative Cooperation

The assumption of the research focuses on the integration of coordination and cooperation in either order and postulates that the same logic is used in either process. Therefore a working definition of Cooperative Coordination is:

"... When an agent voluntarily enters into a relationship with and adopts the goal of another agent such that the interdependencies between the agents' activities are managed to achieve the goal... "

Using Tulken's (2001) approach to cooperation, cooperative coordination can therefore be pre-empted by two important cooperative characteristics (the explicit influence of a leader and the implicit influence of norms and values). Like Coordinative Cooperation, Cooperative Coordination possesses a certain event that must occur for coordination to be recognised. This event is known as a *Cooperative Event*. In this case, a cooperative event is defined as an action that has resulted from cooperation.

The main difference between Cooperative Coordination and Coordinative Cooperation is hierarchy. In addition, the assumption for both concepts is the requirement that cooperation is voluntary. If this assumption is then broadened and cooperation fails, then the voluntary relationship can also fail. It is mandatory that cooperation must continue until it can be reached and based on this argument, the same approach can be applied in forming voluntary relationships.

3   Implementation

3.1   Defining a Formal Model of Coordinative Cooperation

This research has progressed sufficiently to define a model capable of improving Coordinative Cooperation and Cooperative Coordination using the same approach as Wooldridge and Jennings (2001) when implementing Practical Reasoning in agents. Consider the following: a group of agents where a Coordinative Event has occurred.

Table 1: Algorithm of Coordinative Cooperation

```
1     Algorithm: Coordinative Cooperation
2
3     get the plan through getPlan(AG+)
4     Coordinate the first agent through Allocate(AG+, ag(1), CE)
5
6     while not succeeded(Pl) and getEvent(CE)
7
8         if D(ag(1), ag(n)) then /*Same Norms */
9           if I(ag(1), ag(n)) then /* Same Values */
10            if Committed(ag(1), ag(n), Pl) then
11               /* Voluntarily agreed, thus cooperation */
12               ag(role) = getAgentRole(ag(n))
13               /* Enter agent into Cooperation element & remove
14               from set of agents*/
15               ag(n) → CA
16               ag(n) = ag(n+1)
17            end if
18          end if
19        end if
20
21    end while
```

There are six important steps to this algorithm. Firstly is the function **getPlan()**, where this function retrieves the plan specific for the leader agent. The second point is the function **Allocate()**. This is where the coordination occurs and sets the Coordinative Event. Thirdly is **getEvent()** where this function flags whether the Coordinative Event is still activated. Once cooperation has been achieved, the Coordinative Event is then empty.

Fourthly are the functions **D()** and **I()**. These functions determine if the desires and intentions of the leader and another agent are the same. Once these are found to be the same, the function **Committed()** is then called. This function will determine if the agent will voluntarily agree to the plan of the leader agent. If this function returns true, then it can be said that agent n has voluntarily agreed, thus is cooperating. Therefore agent n is given its role by the function **getAgentRole()** which is based on their desires and intentions and then placed into the set *CA*, or Cooperative Agents. Finally **succeeded()** will be set to true once all agents have been placed into the set *CA*. This indicates that cooperation has been achieved as all agents have voluntarily agreed to the plan of the lead agent, *Ag* .

The same approach can be used with Cooperative Coordination. This algorithm also uses the same functions as Coordinative Cooperation, but there are differences. The main difference is that the function **Allocate()** is used once cooperation has been established. This function is also used for all agents, not just for one as in the case of Coordinative Cooperation. However, the concept of cooperation is the same; all agents must have returned true on the function **Committed()**.

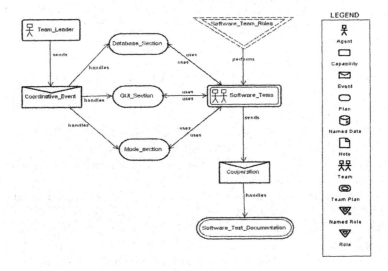16 IIP 2006

3.2 Using JACK™

To show these two algorithms working, a development environment can be used. The development environment JACK™ allows intelligent agents to be developed and implemented within a multiagent system. The difference between JACK™ and other agent-oriented software is the ability to use events, plans and teams to model a MAS, but more importantly, it can use an agent's BDI in making decisions on these events, plans and capabilities. Therefore, Coordinative Events as well as the team's plan can be represented. Consider the case of Coordinative Cooperation using the algorithm defined:

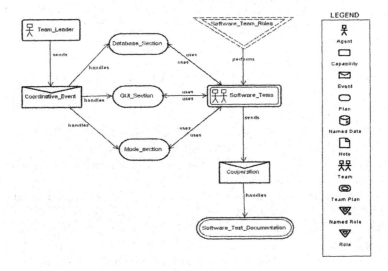

Figure 1. Coordinative Cooperation using JACK™ – Overview

4 AC³M – Modeling Agent Cooperation and Coordination

The concepts discussed have been implemented into a prototype called AC³M. This model uses the algorithm described and JACK™ design architecture to the concepts. Figure 2 demonstrates Cooperative Coordination. Consider a meeting of people/agents that are needed to be formed to solve a specific goal. There is a lead person/agent where this leader needs each person/agent due to their specific role and expertise that they possess. When an agent agrees to cooperate, a line is drawn from the **Team Leader Agent** to an agent. This indicates a cooperative event has occurred. A line will then be drawn from the agent to their expertise, indicating that they have been coordinated to that task. The same logic occurs for Coordinative Cooperation; however in that case, when an agent agrees to cooperate, a line will be extended from the agent to the task, indicating cooperation has occurred.

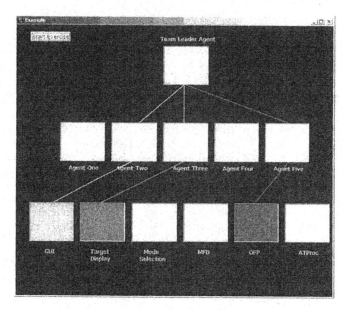

Figure 2. Cooperative Coordination in AC^{3}M

5   Conclusion and Future Works

Coordination and cooperation are two abilities that can be used to assist each other, although they are commonly treated separately and allowed to compete, causing gridlock or system failure. The concepts of Coordinative Cooperation and Cooperative Coordination occur in everyday life for all forms of life. Combining both concepts into a single agent can help in the further development of intelligent agents but more importantly, in the development of systems that can emulate the human society.

The concepts of Coordinative Cooperation and Cooperative Coordination can be broadened by merging the two concepts into one. The concept of a coordination/cooperation loop has been used to demonstrate these principles in the AC^{3}M prototype. This system can also be integrated into JACK™ so the beliefs, desires and intentions of agents can be incorporated to determine when coordination and cooperation are satisfied.

Acknowledgements

I wish to extend my gratitude to the RADSIM team at BAE Systems Australia for not only their unconditional support, but for providing me the inspiration in establishing these concepts. I would also like to thank the KES working group at UniSA for their inspirational and somewhat stimulating conversation on all matter concerning agents.

References

1. Taylor, F.: The Principles of Scientific Management, New York, Harper and Raw (1947).
2. van Mulken, S., Andre, E., Muller, J.P.: The Persona Effect: How Substantial Is It? In: Johnson, H., Nigay, L. and Roast, C. (eds.): Proceedings of HCI'98 - Human Computer Interaction - People and Computers XIII, Springer-Verlag (1998) 53-66
3. Castelfranchi, C., de Rosis, F.,Falcone, R.: Social Attitudes and Personalities in Agents, In: Proceedings of AAAI Fall Symposium on Socially Intelligent Agents, AAAI Press, Cambridge, Massachusetts, United States of America, (8-10 November 1997) 16-21
4. Bratman, M.E.: What is Intention?, In: Intentions in Communications, MIT Press, Cambridge, MA (1990) 15-32
5. Rao, A. S., Georgeff, M. P.: BDI Agents: from theory to practice, In: Proceedings of the First International Conference on Multi-Agent Systems, San Francisco, The MIT Press, (1995) 384-389
6. Wooldridge, M.: An Introduction to Multiagent Systems, Chichester, John Wiley and Sons (2002)
7. Wang, Z., Tianfield, H., Jiang, P.: A Framework for Coordination in Multi-Robot Systems, In: Proceedings of INDIN 2003 – IEEE International Conference on Industrial Informatics, (2003) 483-489
8. Borgoff, UM, Bottini, P, Mussio, P., Pareschi, R.: A Systematic Metaphor of Multi-Agent Coordination in Living Systems, In: Proceedings of ESM'96 – 10th European Simulation Multiconference, Budapest, Hungary, (2-6th June 1996) 245-253
9. Malone, T.W., Crowston, K.: What Is Coordination Theory and How Can It Help Design Cooperative Work Systems? In: Proceedings of CSCW'90 – Conference on Computer-Supported Cooperative Work, Los Angeles, California, United States of America, (1990) 357-370
10. Denti, E., Omicini, A., Ricci, A.: Coordination Tools for the Development of Agent-Based Systems, In: Trappl, R (ed): Proceedings of EMCSR 2002 – 16th European Meeting on Cybernetics and Systems Research, Austrian Society of Cybernetic Studies, Vienna, Austria, (2-5 April 2002) 671-676
11. McBurney, P., Parsons, S.: Engineering Democracy in Open Agent Systems, In: Omicini, A., Petta, P. and Pitt, J (eds): Proceedings of ESAW 2003 – 4th International Workshop on Engineering Societies in the Agents World IV, Lecture Notes in Artificial Intelligence, Springer-Verlag, London, UK, (October 29-31 2003) 66-80
12. Hua, Z.: Study of Multi-Agent Cooperation, In: Proceedings of Third International Conference on Machine Learning and Cybernetics, vol. 5, IEEE, Shanghai, China, (August 2004) 3014-3017
13. Tulken, H.: Economic Theory and International Cooperation on Climate Change Issues, In: Proceedings of International Climate Policy after COP6 – Workshop on Frontiers in

International Climate Policy Research, University of Hamburg, Germany, (September 24-25 2001)

14. Wooldridge, M.: The Cooperative Problem-Solving Process, Journal of Logic and Computation, vol. 9, no. 4, (1999) 563-592

15. D'Inverno, M., Luck, M.: Understanding Agent Systems, Springer-Verlag, Heidelberg (2004)

16. Swarts, J.: Cooperative Writing: Achieving Coordination Together and Apart, In: Proceedings of 22nd Annual International Conference on Design of Communication – The Engineering of Quality Documentation, ACM Press, Memphis, Tennessee, United States of America (2004) 83-89

CLASSIFICATION OF INTELLIGENT AGENT NETWORK TOPOLOGIES AND A NEW TOPOLOGICAL DESCRIPTION LANGUAGE FOR AGENT NETWORKS

Hao Lan Zhang, Clement H.C. Leung and Gitesh K. Raikundalia
School of Computer Science and Mathematics, Victoria University

haolan@sci.vu.edu.au, Clement.Leung@vu.edu.au, Gitesh.Raikundalia@vu.edu.au

Abstract: Topological theory of intelligent agent networks provides crucial information about the structure of agent distribution over a network. Agent network topologies not only take agent distribution into consideration but also consider agent mobility and intelligence in a network. Current research in the agent network topology area adopts topological theory from the distributed system and computing network fields without considering mobility and intelligence aspects. Moreover, current agent network topology theory is not systematic and relies on graph-based methodology, which is inefficient in describing large-scale agent networks. In this paper, we systematically classify the agent network topologies and propose a new description language called *Topological Description Language for Agent networks* (TDLA), which incorporates the mobility and intelligence characteristics in an agent network.

Key words: Agent network topology, intelligent agent, topological description language

Please use the following format when citing this chapter:

Zhang, H., Leung, C.H.C., Raikundalia, G.K., 2006, in IFIP International Federation for Information Processing, Volume 228, Intelligent Information Processing III, eds. Z. Shi, Shimohara K., Feng D., (Boston: Springer), pp. 21–31.

1.   INTRODUCTION

The term *Agent network topology* is derived from mathematical topological theory and this concept overlaps with topological theory in data communication and distributed systems areas.

Applications of multi-agent systems have been arising in many areas. This situation has led to a set of important research problems concerning how an agent network should be designed to perform efficiently and effectively. Thus, we have to consider designing an appropriate network topology before a network, such as an agent network, is actually constructed. Agent network topology analysis enhances agent communication efficiency of an agent network and provides efficient mobility and intelligence to the network.

Existing topological theory in information technology field has been mainly applied to data communication and distributed systems areas for many years and the theory has made some extraordinary contributions. However, as an emerging discipline, the topological theory in multi-agent systems is still preliminary. Existing topological theory cannot fulfil the needs of agent network because an agent network has its specific characteristics, which include: *i*) mobility, *ii*) intelligence, and *iii*) flexibility. The research direction of agent network topology needs to follow these three characteristics. Therefore, this paper classifies the current agent network topologies and analyses the mobility of each topology. We also suggest a new method, called *Topological Description Language for Agent network (TDLA)*, to quantify agent network topologies.

2.   RELATED WORK

Intelligent agent technology, such as multi-agent application, is often considered as a sub-discipline of Distributed Artificial Intelligence (DAI). Research on topological theory in digital network and distributed systems areas including DAI has been carried out (e.g. [1] [2]).

Much work in distributed system and digital network areas can apply to intelligent agent areas, including topological theory. Nelson Minar [2] classifies distributed system topologies into three general and basic categories, including centralized, decentralized, and hybrid topologies. The topological theory developed in Minar's work is not systematic and lacks comprehensive analysis of topological theory. However, it provides some basic ideas about the classification of simple distributed networks and is helpful to the development of topological theory in multi-agent systems.

After the proposal of Small-world theory and its application to complex networks [3] [4] [5], the development of topological theory soon spreads to complex agent networks [6] [7]. Most of the related work in the field emphasises the application of specific topologies, such as Small-world topology or Scale-free topology, to agent networks. This work does not raise the issue of classification of agent networks, which limits the research in gaining comprehensive understanding of agent networks. Thus, this paper clarifies current agent network topological theory.

In our previous research work, we have conducted a performance analysis based on three agent topologies in a newly proposed multi-agent-based architecture [8] called *Agent-based Open Connectivity for Decision Support System (AOCD)*.

3. AGENT NETWORK TOPOLOGIES CLASSIFICATION

Agent network topology theory is a crucial area in terms of developing an appropriate agent network infrastructure for a specific organization. We systematically classify agent network topologies into two main categories, which are: simple agent network topology and complex agent network topology.

3.1 Classification of Simple Agent Network Topologies

In the real world, a network for an industry organization is complex and specific. However, a complex network can be divided into several simple topologies. For instance, Local Area Network (LAN) theory generally defines four basic topologies [1] [9], which include star topology, bus topology, ring topology, and tree topology. Many organizational LAN applications in the field are basically the combinations of these four basic topologies. Based on the traditional topological theory of LAN, Minar [2] suggests four basic simple topologies and two hybrid topologies in evaluating distributed systems topologies. In the multiagent area, we classify the simple agent network topologies into the following categories.

➤ **Centralized agent network topology:**

Figure 1. Centralized Topology

Our definition of centralized agent network topology is: a topology has a central agent and only this central agent is connected with other agents over the network. There is no direct connection between any two agents except with the central agent, as shown in Figure 1. A star-like topology is one of the common cases of centralized topology. The total connections in simple centralized topology is:

$$c = v - 1 \tag{1}$$

where c denotes the total connections and v denotes as the total number of agent over a network including the central agent.

In centralized agent network topology, the central agent is vital to the network. However, the central agent has very inefficient mobility. Total connection of a topology is one of the coefficient facts of agent network mobility. We have the following equation to define the connection-based coefficient of agent network mobility:

$$m_{co} = \frac{1}{\sum_i (Totalconnection / import) \times m_i}$$

where m_{co} is the connection-degree coefficient of mobility, m_i denotes the mobility of an individual agent, *import* denotes the importance of an agent that is measured by the number of connections to the agent. These variables will be used in the following topologies in this section. Therefore, the connection-based coefficient of centralized agent network mobility is:

$$m_{co} = \frac{1}{\sum_{i=1}^{v} ((v-1)/a_i) \times m_i} \tag{2}$$

where a_i is the number of connections for an individual agent. The variables c, v, and a_i will also be used in the following topologies in this section.

➤ **Peer-to-peer agent network topology:**

There are two categories in Peer-to-peer agent network topology: one is fully connected peer-to-peer topology and another is partially connected peer-to-peer topology.

(a) Fully connected   *(b) Partially connected*

Figure 2. Peer-to-peer agent network topology

In Peer-to-peer agent network topology, each agent has direct connection(s) with other node(s) over a network, as shown in Figure 2. In fully connected peer-to-peer topology, each agent has connections with all the other agents over a network. In partially connected peer-to-peer topology, each agent has at least one connection with another agent over a network and the maximum connections is smaller than c. In fully connected peer-to-peer topology, if v denotes the number of agents over a network, then c is given by exhausting all combinations of choosing any two agents:

$$c = \binom{v}{2} = \frac{v(v-1)}{2} \qquad 1 \le v < \infty \tag{3}$$

The connection-based coefficient of fully connected peer-to-peer agent network mobility is:

$$m_{co} = \frac{1}{\sum_{i=1}^{v} (v(v-1)/2a_i) \times m_i} \tag{4}$$

➤ **Broadcasting agent network topology:**

We define the broadcasting agent network topology as follows: all the agents are connected through a common media and there is no direct connection between any of the two agents, as shown in Figure 3. Bus topology is a typical broadcasting agent network topology.

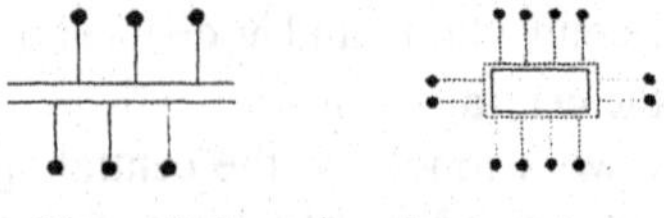

Figure 3. Broadcasting topology

In broadcasting agent network topology, every agent has same role in the network (unlike in centralized agent network topology, the central agent has a more important role than other agents) and there is no direct connection between any of two agents. The total connections in broadcasting topology is:

$$c = v \tag{5}$$

The connection-based coefficient of broadcasting agent network mobility is:

$$m_{cn} = \frac{1}{\sum_{i=1}^{v} (v / a_i) \times m_i} \tag{6}$$

➤ **Closed-loop agent network topology:**

In closed-loop agent network topology, a network forms a loop and each agent connects exactly to two other agents. In the case of removing connections between any two agents, a closed-loop topology will turn into a linear topology.

(a) Simple Ring   (b) Dual Ring   (c) Anomalous closed loop

Figure 4. Closed-Loop topology

As shown in Figure 4 (a) and (b), simple ring and dual ring topologies are the typical closed-loop topologies. Based on our definition, Figure 4 (c) is also a closed-loop topology. The total connections in closed-loop topology is:

$$c = v \tag{7}$$

The connection-based coefficient of closed-loop agent network mobility is:

$$m_{cn} = \frac{1}{\sum_{i=1}^{v} (v / a_i) \times m_i} \tag{8}$$

➤ **Linear agent network topology:**

In linear agent network topology, all agents are distributed in a linear form in sequential order and there is no loop in the network. Each agent is connected to two neighbour agents except the two end agents that are only connected to only one neighbour agent.

(a) Simple Linear   (b) Dual linear   (c) Anomalous linear

Figure 5. Linear topology

In many cases, this topology is regarded as inefficient because the communication between two end agents is extremely inefficient. However, in some cases it appears to be efficient such as in a pipelining process.

The total connections in linear topology is:

$$c = v - 1 \tag{9}$$

The connection-based coefficient of linear agent network mobility is:

$$m_{cn} = \frac{1}{\sum_{i=1}^{v} ((v - 1) / a_i) \times m_i} \tag{10}$$

➤ **Hierarchical agent network topology:**

In hierarchical agent network topology, an agent is the basic unit and a number of agents form a group, which is connected to an upper level agent. In hierarchical agent network topology, an agent is not connected to other agents except to its upper level agent.

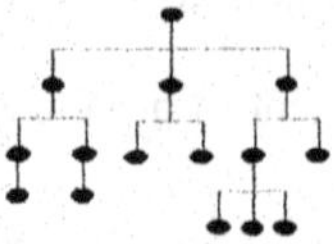

Figure 6. Hierarchical topology

A recursive method can be used to determine if a topology is a hierarchical topology by starting from the end points, which has no lower level agent connected. We define a very important characteristic of hierarchical topology: there is no loop in a hierarchical topology. The total connections in hierarchical topology is:

$$c = v - 1 \tag{11}$$

The connection-based coefficient of hierarchical agent network mobility is:

$$\tag{12}$$

$$m_{co} = \cfrac{1}{\sum_{i=1}^{v} ((v-1)/a_i) \times m_i}$$

Hybrid agent network topology is an important concept in traditional topological theory, which combines two or more simple agent network topologies. Technically speaking, a hybrid agent network topology is still a simple agent network topology compared to complex network topologies from a large-scale point of view. Therefore, a hybrid agent network topology still belongs to the simple agent network topology category.

A hybrid agent network cannot describe an overall complex network in a specific and efficient way, but it explains a complex network in a simple way and it is efficient to a limited scale. A hybrid agent network topology can be a combination of any two or more simple agent network topologies such as a closed loop topology and a simple centralized topology, etc. Hybrid network topology eliminates the difficulties of concurrent control, which mainly plagues centralised topology. Our study shows that hybrid topology offers superior performance in agent-based systems [8]. Nevertheless, simple agent network topological theory (including hybrid topology) can only describe a limited scale of agent networks in a simple way. Hence, current topological theory in the multi-agent field adopts more complex topological theory such as Small-world topology and Scale-free topology to describe a large-scale complex network.

3.2   Classification of Complex Agent Network Topologies

Traditional topological theory is insufficient to describe a complex network such as a multi-agent system. This is because current complex networks emphasise the relationships between nodes and traditional topological theory is unable to define the relationships between nodes and describe an overall view of the network efficiently.

In these circumstances, the topological theory for a complex network is required to provide more abstract descriptions. Current topological theory classifies networks into four major categories:

➤ **Regular Network Topology**

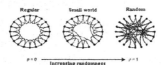

Figure 7. Overview of three complex network topologies (Watt and Strogatz, 1998)

In a regular network, nodes (agents) are distributed in order and the connections between nodes are based on certain constraints. For example, the wiring process is based on finding neighbour agents within the shortest distance. Figure 7 shows an overview of regular network, small-world network and random network [3]. We will explain the transformation process shown on this Figure in the small-world section.

Regular network topology can describe simple networks but it is incapable of describing complex networks efficiently. Generally, regular network topology is limited to describe static networks.

➤ **Random Network Topology**

Random network topology is based on random graph theory, which is described by Paul Erdós and Alfréd Rényi in 1959 [10]. In such a network, the connections between two nodes (agents) are generated randomly.

Considering a graph with vertices contained in a set X, as a binary relation $R \subset X \times X$ by defining R as: $(a,b) \in R$ if there is an edge between a and b. On the contrary, each symmetric relation R on $X \times X$ gives rise to a graph on X. A random graph is a graph R on an infinite set X satisfying the following properties [11]: *i*) R is irreflexive. *ii*) R is symmetric. *iii*) Given any $n+m$ elements $a_1,....,a_n,b_1,....,b_m \in X$ there is $c \in X$ such that $c \in X$ is related to $a_1,..., a_n$, and c is not related to $b_1,..., b_m$.

Based on random graph theory, a random network topology can describe a large-scale complex network. It is more realistic than regular network in describing the real-world complex networks such as multi-agent systems. However, the limitation of random network topology theory is the difficulty of predicting, monitoring and controlling a network. For most agent-based systems this is unacceptable because most of the implemented agent-based systems require a high degree of monitoring and controlling. Therefore, Small-world network topology is suggested.

➤ **Small-World Network Topology**

As we introduced in the previous sections, a regular network topology is easier to monitor and control but it is inefficient in describing a real-world complex network. Oppositely, random network topology has a high degree of disorder, which increases the difficulties of operations over the network such as agent search, agent matching, etc.

In the real world, the connection topology is treated as either completely regular or completely random. It is somewhere between these two extreme cases and it is defined by Watts and Strogatz as the Small-world topology [3]. As shown in Figure 7, p denotes the probability of randomness when an agent is connecting with other agents. When p is 0, a network is wired completely in order. When p is 1, a network is wired completely randomly. For $0 < p < 1$, a network is in Small-world topology scope.

Small-world network theory enables the possible control or monitoring over the network especially in some critical areas of a network through observing and adjusting the probability p.

Small-world concept is becoming important in multi-agent systems, in which agents are often considered as nodes. It is difficult to use simple or regular agent network topology to describe an overall view of a large multi-agent system. Small-world topology could efficiently describe the conceptual view of a complex agent network. However, Small-world topology still lacks the ability to adapt to a dynamic environment. In other words, Small-world topology is not an ideal solution for the networks that are constantly changing. Therefore, Scale-free topology is suggested.

➢ **Scale-free Network Topology**

The three topologies we discussed in the previous sections are basically static and homogeneous, and peak at an average value and decay. Such networks are called *exponential networks* [12]. However, recent research in the field of complex networks indicates that a number of large-scale complex networks including the Internet, WWW, and metabolic networks, are scale-free and the vertices over such a network are not homogeneous.

Barabási and Albert [13] suggest a scale-free network topology, in which a network is allowed to change network connections dynamically and the nodes (agents) on the network are inhomogeneous. The generation scheme of a scale-free network can be summarized into two major steps [12]:

1) **Growth:** Start with a small number (m_0) of nodes; at every time step, a new node is introduced and is connected to $m \le m_0$ existing nodes.

2) **Preferential attachment:** The probability p_i that a new node will be connected to node i (one of the m existing nodes) depends on the degree k_i of node i. As a result, $p_i = k_i / \sum_j k_j$, where degree k_i is the edges number of a node.

Scale-free network topology is considered as the most suitable topology for multi-agent based systems taking high-degree mobility of agent network into account. As we know, one of the most important characteristics of an agent network is that it requires high-degree mobility. To support such a high-degree mobility, a network topology needs the ability of adapting to the dynamic environment and that is the advantage of scale-free topology compared with the other three static topologies.

Similar to simple agent network topologies, complex agent network topologies are based on graph theory, which is inefficient in describing a large-scale network. An analysis of a network topology is often based on the provided network graph and sometimes lacks precise measurements on each agent. Moreover, the existing agent network topologies are incapable of providing much detailed information of each agent and its relationship with other agents on a network, which increases the difficulty of the operations, such as searching or matching, over a network. Thus, we suggest a description language for agent network topology, called *Topological Description Language for Agent networks – TDLA*.

3.3   A Topological Description Language for Agent networks (TDLA)

Topological Description Language for Agent networks consists of three major sections. These three sections are: *i*) *Individual Agent Description (IAD). ii) Main Agent-groups Description (MAD). iii) Overall Agent-network Description (OAD)*.

In the IAD section, the description emphasises the information about each agent on a network. The content of IAD includes (*i*) degree of links (the number of links connected to an agent), (*ii*) extensibility, which indicates whether an agent allows new connections to be attached and how many connections can be attached, (*iii*) local address, which is essential for grouping agents by location or generating actual geographic map, (*iv*) attachment probability and (*v*) routing table, which stores the information of connected agents to the described agent.

As shown in Figure 8, an example of an IAD expression for the circled agent is as follows. The attachment probability indicates the probability of the selected agent to be attached by other agents. The assumptions are: (*a*) the nominated node is allowed to attach a maximum of 10 agents, and (*b*) there are 50 vacant attachments are available in the overall network.

Figure 8. IAD for Individual Agent

Table 1. IAD Routing Table

Connected Agent Address
138.77.201.38
138.77.201.37
138.77.202.1

(1) Degree of links: 3   (2) Local address: 138.77.201.20
(3) Extensibility: $MC - DL = 7$ (MC: Maximum Connections, DL: Degree of Links)
(4) Attachment probability: $\text{Individual Extensibility} \left/ \sum_{i=1}^{n}(MC - DL)i \right.$ (13)
     where n is the total number of agents and the individual extensibility is the current agent's extensibility. The result in this case is: $7/50 = 0.14$.
(5) Routing table: See Table 1.

In the MAD section, the description provides network information based on a group of local agents. A large-scale agent network is usually divided into a number of sub networks (or groups). The information provided by MAD describes the information of main sub networks. MAD information includes (*i*) total agent number in a group, (*ii*) total number of links in a group, (*iii*) main group selection criteria, (*iv*) possible root(s) nomination, (*v*) loop detection in a group and (*vi*) context within an overall network. The criteria for grouping a number of agents are various, which are based on real cases. The geographic area indication is one of the common criteria for selecting a number of agents as the main agent group. If an agent has much more maximum connection capacity than other agents, this agent normally is nominated as root of the group. In some cases, there is no agent nominated as root. It occurs when the maximum-connection capacity of each agent over a network is equal. To further explain the MAD, we use the previous example and suppose the circled part is a main group of agents as shown in Figure 9.

Figure 9. MAD for a main agent-group   *Figure 10*. OAD for overall agent network

The MAD is expressed as following.
(*1*) Total number of agents: 6   (*2*) Total number of links in the group: 6
(*3*) Main group selection criteria: geography-based in Melbourne/Australia
(*4*) Root nomination: 138.77.201.20. (*5*) Loop detection: No loop in the group
(*6*) Context: main entrance of the state of Victoria.

In the OAD section, the general information of network is provided, which includes (*i*) the diameter of the network, (*ii*) total agent number and (*iii*) info of main agent groups. The diameter of the network is $D = \max_{(i,j)} d(i,j)$, where i and j represent two agents. In other words, the longest path between two agents is the diameter of the network. Using the previous example in Figure 10 to explain the OAD expressions:
(*1*) Diameter of the network: 9   (*2*) Total agent number: 12
(*3*) Main agent group info: Total group number: 2
      Group 1: (Root nomination: 138.77.201.20)
            (Group selection criteria: based in Melbourne)
      Group 2: (Root nomination: no root)
            (Group selection criteria: geography-based in Brisbane)

Given the descriptions provided by IAD, MAD and OAD, a network generator is able to automatically determine the capability of the network, the preferable area to attach new agents, the topology category (or the combination of topologies) that the network most likely belongs to and the mobility of each agent. In principle, the agent that has a lower degree of connections is likely to have more mobility. TDLA offers the intelligent capability of generating an agent network by using statistical results provided by its three sections.

4.   CONCLUSION AND FUTURE WORK

Topological theory in agent networks is an important but somehow underdeveloped research area. In this paper, we classify agent network topologies based on two major categories: simple agent network and complex agent network. In general, we can view a complex agent network as an assemblage of several simple agent networks. However, the difficulties arise when we distinguish the partially connected peer-to-peer network with other simple agent networks. Moreover, existing agent network topologies are graph-based, which are unable to provide detailed information of each agent and its relationship with other agents on a network. Therefore, the Topological Description Language for Agent networks is particularly valuable. The significance of this paper is that it makes a systematic treatment in clarifying and organising the current topological theory in multi-agent field. The proposed TDLA is efficient in constructing agent networks and performing tasks, such as searching and inserting agents in a network. Future work will mainly focus on: (i) experimental design for performance analysis of agent network, and (ii) implementation of TDLA in newly proposed *AOCD* architecture.

REFERENCES

1.   T. C. Piliouras, *"Network Design: Management and Technical Perspective"* (2nd ed.), pp.141-196. Published by CRC Press LLC, Printed in U.S.A., 2005.
2.   N. Minar, "Distributed system topologies," 2002, retrieved on July 2005 from http://www.openp2p.com/lpt/a/1461.
3.   D. J. Watts and S.H. Strogatz, *"Collective dynamics of 'small world' networks"*, Nature, vol.393, pp.440-442, June 1998.
4.   D.J. Watts, *"Small Worlds: The Dynamics of Networks between Order and Randomness"*, Princeton University Press, Part I, 1999.
5.   S.H. Strogatz, *"Exploring complex networks"*, Nature, Vol 410, pp.268-276, March 2001.
6.   C. Aguirre, J. Martinez-Munoz, F. Corbacho, and R. Huerta, "Small-World Topology for Multi-Agent Collaboration", In *Proceedings of the 11th International Workshop on Database and Expert Systems Applications*, pp. 231-235, 2000.
7.   X. Jin and J. Liu, "Agent Network Topology and Complexity", In *Proceedings of AAMAS'03*, Australia, July 2003.
8.   H. L. Zhang, C.H.C. Leung, G. K. Raikundalia, "Performance Analysis of Network Topology in Agent-based Open Connectivity Architecture for DSS", In *Proceedings of AINA2006*, Vol.2, pp. 257-261, Vienna, Austria, 2006.
9.   P. Miller and M. Cummins, *"LAN Technologies Explained"*, pp. 6-9. Published by Butterworth-Heinemann, Printed in U.S.A. 2000.
10.   P. Erdós and A. Rényi, "On the evolution of random graphs", *publ. Math. Inst. Hung. Acad. Sci.* vol 5, pp. 17-60, 1959.
11.   B. Bollobás, *"Random Graphs (2nd Edition)"*, 2001, Published by Cambridge University Press.
12.   X. F. Wang and G. Chen, *"Complex Networks: Small-World, Scale-Free and Beyond"*, IEEE Circuits and systems Magazine, 2003.
13.   A-L. Barabási, and R. Albert. *"Emergence of scaling in random networks"*, Science, vol. 286, pp.509-512, Oct. 1999.

REACTIVE (RE) PLANNING AGENTS IN A DYNAMIC ENVIRONMENT

Debdeep Banerjee, Jeffrey Tweedale
KES Centre, University of South Australia, Mawson Lakes, Australia, Debdeep.Banerjee@unisa.edu.au. Airborne Mission Systems Baranch, Defence Science and Technology Organisation Edinburgh, South Australia, Australia, Jeffrey.Tweedale@dsto.defence.gov.au .

Abstract: Intelligent agents are powerful tools for complex and dynamic problems. Belief Desire Intension (BDI) is one of the most popular agent architectures for reactive goal directed agents. Planning is intrinsic for intelligent behaviour. But planning from first principle is costly in terms of computation time and resources. BDI agents retain their reactive property by avoiding planning from real-time planning by using predefined plan library designed by agent designers. BDI agents look for a plan in the library to achieve their goals. If the agent could find a plan it fails to achieve the goal. It would be useful to have some real-time look ahead planning capability within BDI framework. In this paper we have proposed an architecture that includes (re) planning in BDI agents. The proposed architecture describes how to integrate a real-time planner with replanning capability in the current BDI architecture. Replanning capability is important for reactive behaviour.

Key words: BDI agent, AI planning

1.   INTRODUCTION

Intelligent software agents are powerful tools in today's modern software systems. They have been deployed in complex and dynamic hostile environment and even in unknown environments. Research in intelligent agents is very active and progressive. According to Russell and Norvig [14]

Please use the following format when citing this chapter:

Banerjee, D., Tweedale, J., 2006, in IFIP International Federation for Information Processing, Volume 228, Intelligent Information Processing III, eds. Z. Shi, Shimohara K., Feng D., (Boston: Springer), pp. 33–42.

"An agent can be anything that perceives its environment through sensors prior to acting upon the environment through actuators". Wooldridge defines an agent as "a computer system capable of autonomous action in a given environment in order to meet its design objectives" [1]. Jennings adds four main properties to these definitions which are: autonomy, reactivity, pro-activity and social ability [2]. Another important aspect to consider is its environment that an agent operates [14]. The agent's characteristics and capabilities also depend on the environment, because agent has to interact with its environment. Agent's environment has been divided between Static and Dynamic environment, fully Observable and partially Observable environment, Continuous and Discrete environment, Deterministic and Non-deterministic environment. There are mainly three common categories of architectures used to design intelligent agents: the Brooks subsumption architecture [17], Bratmans' Belief-Desires-Intension (BDI) architecture [4] and the layered model [18]. The BDI model was derived from the model of human practical reasoning system [4] based on rational agents that conduct actions that will help it achieve its goals. Practical reasoning is used to decide what to do (deliberation) and how to do it (means-end-analysis) [1].

Planning is intrinsic for any intelligent behaviour. Humans tend to plan most events they contribute to in the real world. The planning process may not always be visible, especially when those actions require routine skills, rule based tasks and procedures performed by subject matter experts. Humans' (re) use the rules, skills and knowledge stored in memory (plans that need to be embodied into agents) to achieve tasks they may have previously encountered [16]. We tend to plan for situations that are new, complex or critical. Planning is a costly process in the terms of time and computation. The motivation for Intelligent Agents is to personify human capabilities, so they can be used in place of humans and how they achieve the given goal by acting rationally in their environment. The main part of a rational act is that of practical reasoning. So the planning is the part of the practical reasoning as it describes a set of actions to achieve a goal [4].

This paper is organized in four parts. Section two describes the problems relating to planning in BDI architecture and the motivation of the proposed architecture. Next section describes the proposed architecture and section four contains the research methodology. Section five concludes the paper with the future directions.

2.   MOTIVATION

BDI agents use a plan library or predefined set of plans, instead of planning from first principle [3]. When an agent commits to an intension, it looks through its plan library for feasible plan, which is executed in order to achieve the goal. If the plan fails and a suitable alternative can't be identified then the agent fails to achieve the goal [3]. The main bottleneck of most BDI architectures is the plan library. Library agents are predominantly deterministic in nature, because all of its behaviour is hard coded into the library. The knowledge about how to achieve a specific task must be explicitly captured as plans in the library by the designer, prior to run-time. If the agent's environment is static, or partially dynamic and deterministic, then the above approach is efficient. In most cases the real environment is dynamic and non-deterministic. In this case it becomes extremely challenging for agent designer to write task specific plans for every possible situation. In this case a generic approach must be to guide the agent towards a possible solution.

Bratman used practical reasoning to construct his BDI architecture [4] when computer hardware had primitive capabilities with limited computational power. Modern computers enable designers to write larger and more complex agents. It also allows designers to relax some of the original resource constraint. Ideally an intelligent rational agent should be able do decide what to do and how to do it in a particular situation. The agent is designed to do a specific task (such as monitoring the communication network and fault diagnosis). Artificial Intelligent agents only need to decide how to achieve its goals by using knowledge about the environment and knowledge about its capabilities and measures. Within this process the agent should identify any sub-tasks to be achieved given the goal and suitable plans to achieve them. To succeed, autonomous agents must have a planning component capable of synthesizing its own course of actions from within the environment it resides.

There are agent architectures (such as RETSINA [19], PROPICE [20], CYPRESS [21], INTERRAP [22], TAIPE [23] etc.) that incorporate a planning component as part of the agent architecture. These systems implement different architecture to incorporate the planning module. Our proposed architecture extends the BDI agent architecture with online planning capabilities which will be handled within main BDI loop rather than accessed as an external component.

3.   A FLEXIBLE PLANNING ARCHITECTURE FOR BDI AGENTS

To provide reactive behaviour to the BDI agents a new architecture has been proposed (Fig 2). This architecture is an extension of the BDI architecture (Fig 1) as Wooldridge described in [3]. Two main modifications have been made in this architecture compare to the previous architecture.

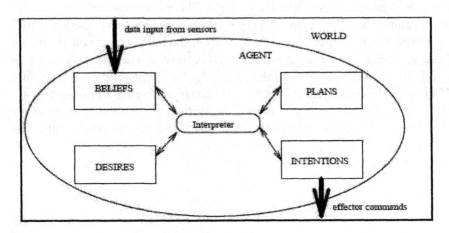

Figure 1. BDI Agent Architecture

The agent interpreter module has been extended by introducing a new State Change Monitor and a Sub Goal Deliberation module. The plan library of the previous architecture has been replaced by the Planning module. The purpose of these changes is to provide an agent means to react in a dynamic environment by reacting to the changes that occurs dynamically within that environment.

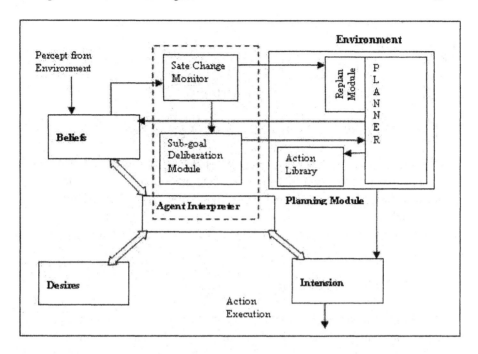

Figure 2. (Re) Planning Agent Architecture

3.1 The Planning module

To overcome the problems of the restricted plan library an online planning module has been introduced in the place of the plan library. The planning module consists of three sub-modules.

3.1.1 Action Library

It contains the actions that an agent can perform. Every action has preconditions and effects. These actions can be modeled as plans without any sub-plans. The practical implementation of the actions can be in different abstraction levels. This level of abstraction depends on the problem.

3.1.2 Planner

This can be any planner that will take the initial state, goal state and a set of action and synthesis a sequence of executable actions. Type of planner can depend on the problem domain.

3.1.3   Replanning Module

It is responsible for repairing or refining a failed plan. The output of the replanning module can be an abstract plan or a partial plan or even a total plan depends on the particular replanning strategy chosen.

3.2   The Extensions of the Agent Interpreter

To be reactive an agent should identify the changes in the environment that has an effect on its behavior. Then agent should decide what it should do to deal with the changes and how it can still achieve its goal. To provide this reactive deliberation capability Sate Change Monitor and Sub-goal Deliberation Module has been proposed as an extension of the agent interpreter.

3.2.1   Sate Change Monitor

It monitors the state of the world. It checks that if environment changes in such a way that it would make the some goal state true or assumptions of planning (conjunction of the preconditions of the actions) false. There can be two types of reactions from the state change monitor. Firstly it needs to identify when the goal is already been achieved or goal can not be achieved, then it stops the planning process and notify the Sub-goal Deliberation Module. Secondly when it identifies that some action preconditions of the plan become false it invokes the replanning module. Then the replanning module tries to repair the current plan. Using the State Change Monitor, we can separate the situation where we would need a new plan and where we need to repair the plan. Until the goal state is achieved or goal state become unachievable agent should try to achieve the goal.

3.2.2   Sub-goal Deliberation

It defines a goal sate for the agent by considering the current environment and agent's desires. It would take current world state and agent's desires as input and produce a desired goal state for the agent. It forwards the goal state to the planner. The Sub-goal Deliberation module can be implemented differently for different domains and can contain domain knowledge. Sub-goal Deliberation Module provides the goal state for planning. For goal state synthesis different approaches, such as decision theoretic approach, case-based approach, knowledge base, hierarchical task network approach etc, can be incorporated. The Sub-goal Deliberation module can be designed as per the type of the environment and the problem. The level of the granularity of the goals is proportional to the dynamic nature of the problem.

This architecture will provide reactivity to the agent situated in a dynamic environment. Agent can handle the changes in the environment by monitoring the state of the world. This architecture is flexible and extensible. Different types of reactive domains (for example robot soccer, UAV, UT etc.) can be encoded by choosing different sub goal formulation methods in Sub-goal Deliberation module. Next section discusses the methodologies involved in developing the architecture discussed above.

4.   METHODOLOGY

In the proposed agent architecture the extension of the agent interpreter would provide the method of Sub-goal Deliberation and the planning module would provide the means-end analysis. We divide the problem in three main parts. The first is designing the Sate Change Monitor module. The second is to provide a real-time planning module with replanning capability and third will be the modeling the Sub-goal Deliberation process.

For the first problem we need to design a module that will identify when a plan fails. There are two possibilities, the goal state has already been achieved by other agents or the goal state become unachievable and some precondition become false due to some changes in the environment. In the first case the State Change Monitor should send a notification to the Sub-goal Deliberation module for new goal deliberation and for the latter case it invokes the replanning sub module of the planning module. To implement a State Change Monitor we need to implement an execution monitoring module that checks if the plan is still consistent with the current world after execution of each action. To check consistency it will check if all the preconditions of the actions that are still to be executed at the next step are true and the goal is still achievable but not achieved yet [14].

For the planning module we assume the environment is fully observable. To incorporate the planning module we need to find a common representation of the actions between the chosen planner and the agent architecture. There are similarities between the BDI architecture and HTN (Hierarchical Task Network) based planning [5]. A wrapper can be created that maps the BDI agent syntax to the HTN based planner syntax similar to [6]. For replanning capabilities we can implement a replanning module on top of the planner. There are different options exist for replanning. First option would be introducing replanning algorithm [8, 9] which can start replanning by backtracking from the point where the plan fails and choose alternative path. Replanning can also be done by plan refinement technique where in the case of a failed plan refinement technique replaces the failed actions with the alternate actions [10, 11]. In the dynamic environment the environment changes very fast. An agent situated in this dynamic environment needs to react to these changes. For this highly reactive behaviour agent may not need to synthesis a full plan for achieving goal. This reactivity can be achieved by incorporating anytime algorithm based planner [7]. In anytime based planner a planner can be interrupted at anytime and planner always have some executable plan as the result [7, 8]. The main problem in this kind of planner is to guarantee the quality of the resultant plan. On the other hand genetic algorithm [12, 13] can also be implemented so at any point of time agent can have an executable plan.

The Sub-goal Deliberation module can be compared to the plan library of the BDI agent architecture. It can contain the domain specific knowledge in the form of predefined task decomposition. Only difference would be instead of producing an executable plan it will produce abstract level tasks as sub goals. We can incorporate different strategies, such as decision theoretic approach, case-based approach, knowledge-based approach, for Sub-goal Deliberation. Sub-goal Deliberation process can be modeled as planning problem that will generate abstract sequence of tasks and the planning module can be seen as action scheduling problem for instantiating those tasks.

5.   CONCLUSION

The current BDI model's main bottleneck is the plan library. If the agent fails to find a plan in its plan library it fails to achieve the goal. This is not desirable in most real world situations. The agent must adapt to the current situation. Since most of the real world environment is complex and highly dynamic it is nearly impossible for an agent designer to write predefined plan for every possible situations. The proposed architecture introduced online planning with replanning capability in BDI agent architecture. This architecture can use the domain knowledge for Sub-goal Deliberation and provide flexibility for different types of dynamic domains. This architecture can also be extent in the cases where the environment is not fully observable and changes frequently in random manner.

The implementation phase has four main steps. The first step is to find a common representation of the planning problem between the planner and the agent architecture. We will use JACK as our BDI implementation. JACK [15] is a BDI based commercial strength multi-agent based software development framework based on JAVA. It is developed by the Agent Oriented Software.

JACK provides a high performance, lightweight implementation of BDI architecture. It is an agent oriented programming extension of JAVA. The second step would be interfacing a external planner with the JACK agent or incorporating an planning algorithm within JACK. The next step would be implementing a State Change Monitor in context of JACK system. Last step would be to extend the planner with some replanning or anytime algorithm for reactivity. Different replanning algorithm can implemented and compared based on the performance.

REFERENCE

1. M. Wooldridge: *Reasoning about Rational Agents*, The MIT Press, London (2000)
2. M. Wooldridge, N.R. Jennings: *Intelligent agents- theory and practice*, Knowledge Engineering Review, 10 (2), (1995)
3. Wooldridge, M: *Practical Reasoning with Procedural Knowledge- A Logic of BDI Agents with Know-How*, in Proceedings of the International Conference on Formal and Applied Practical Reasoning, Springer-Verlag, Berlin (1996)
4. Bratman ME: *Intentions, Plans and Practical Reason*, Harvard University Press: Cambridge, MA (1987)
5. Lavindra de Silva and Lin Padgham: *A Comparison of BDI Based Real-Time Reasoning and HTN Based Planning*. In Proceedings of the 17th Australian Joint Conference on Artificial Intelligence, Cairns, Australia, (Dec 2004)
6. Lavindra de Silva, Lin Padgham: *Planning on Demand in BDI Systems*. International Conference on Automated Planning and Scheduling, Monterey, California, (June 2005)
7. N. Hawes: *Anytime planning for agent behaviour*, In Proceedings of the 12th Workshop of PLANSIG, (2001)157-166
8. Hawes. N: *An anytime planning agent for computer game worlds*. In Workshop on Agents in Computer Games at The 3rd International Conference on Computers and Games (CG'02), Edmonton, Canada, (2002) 1-14
9. G. Boella, R. Damiano: *A replanning algorithm for a reactive agent architecture*. In D. Scott, editor, Artificial Intelligence: Methodology, Systems, and Applications, *LNCS 2443*, Springer Verlag, (2002) 183-192
10. Roman van der Krogt and Mathijs de Weerdt: *Plan Repair using a Plan Library*, BNAIC, (2005) 284-259
11. Roman van der Krogt, Mathijs de Weerdt: *Plan Repair as an Extension of Planning*. ICAPS,(2005) 161-170
12. C. H. Westerberg, J. Levine: *GenPlan- Combining genetic programming and planning*. In Proc. of the 19th Workshop of the UK Planning and Scheduling Special Interest Group (PLANSIG), (2000)
13. L. Spector: *Genetic programming and AI planning systems*, Proceedings of the twelfth national conference on Artificial intelligence, Seattle, Washington, United States, (1994)
14. S. J. Russell, P. Norvig: *Artificial Intelligence- A Modern Approach*. Prentice Hall, 2nd edition, (2003)
15. A. Hodgson, N. Howden, R. Rönnquist and A. Lucas: Jack intelligent agents -- summary of an agent infrastructure. In 5th International Conference on Autonomous Agents (2001)
16. Rasmussen, J: Information processing and human machine interaction: An approach to cognitive engineering, New York, North Holland (1986).

17. R. A. Brooks: *How to build complete creatures rather than isolated cognitive simulators.* In K. VanLehn (ed.), Architectures for Intelligence, Lawrence Erlbaum Assosiates, Hillsdale, NJ (1991) 225-239

18. J. P. Mller and M. Pischel: *The Agent Architecture InteRRaP: Concept and Application.* Technical Report RR-93-26, DFKI Saarbrucken, (1993)

19. M. Paolucci, D. Kalp, A. Pannu, O. Shehory and K. Sycara: *.A planning component for RETSINA agents";* Lecture Notes in Artitcial Intelligence, Intelligent Agents VI, Springer (2000).

20. O. Despouys and F. F. IngrandF: *Propice-Plan: Toward a Unified Framework for Planning and Execution.* In European Conference on Planning (ECP), 278-293, 1999[1]

21. D. Wilkins, K. Myers, J. Lowrance, and L. Wesley: *Planning and reacting in uncertain and dynamic environments,* Journal of Experimental and Theoretical Artificial Intelligence (7) (1995) 972-978.

22. K. Fischer, J.P. Muller and M. Pisschel. *Unifying control in a layered agent architecture,* Agent Theory, Architecture and Language Workshop, Montreal (1995)

23. E. H. Durfee, M. Huber, M. Kurnow and J. Lee, *TAIPE: Tactical Assistants for Interaction Planning and Execution,* First International Conference on Autonomous Agents (Agents'97) (1997).

REASONING ABOUT ACTIONS, KNOWLEDGE AND NORMATIVE ABILITY

XIANWEI LAI[1, 3], SHANLI HU[1, 2], ZHENGYUAN NING[3, *]

[1] *Dept. of Computer Science and Technology, Fuzhou University, Fuzhou 350002, China*
xianweilai@163.com
[2] *Laboratory of Computer Science, Chinese Academy of Sciences, Beijing 100080, China*
husl@fzu.edu.cn
[3] *College of Computer and Information, Fujian Agriculture and Forestry University, Fuzhou 350002, China*
ningzhy@126.com
* The Contact Author

Abstract: The past five years have witnessed an explosion of interest in the use of cooperation logics for reasoning about multi-agent systems. Since the development of ATL, there are many multi-agent cooperation logics developed as an extension to ATL. The cooperation logic called the Normative Alternating-time Temporal Epistemic Logic（NATEL）is developed to extend ATL. Four key contributions have been made. Firstly, the strong and unrealistic assumption of the other two extended cooperation logics of ATL (ATEL, NATL*) that different agents are not allowed to control the same actions have been done away with. Secondly, functions that involved actions are given in more detail, so that the relations between actions and knowledge, actions and agents, actions and states can be researched in depth and separately. Thirdly, actions, knowledge and normative ability can be represented in the object language other than only in the underlying semantics. Lastly, since actions, knowledge and normative ability are taken into account at the same time, the expressive power and flexibility of NATEL are much richer than the other two extended cooperation logics of ATL.

Key words: **ATL, multi-agent systems, cooperation logic, knowledge, actions**

Please use the following format when citing this chapter:

Lai, X.-W., Hu, S.-L., Ning, Z., 2006, in IFIP International Federation for Information Processing, Volume 228, Intelligent Information Processing III, eds. Z. Shi, Shimohara K., Feng D., (Boston: Springer), pp. 43–52.

1 INTRODUCTION

The past five years have witnessed an explosion of interest in the use of cooperation logics for reasoning about multi-agent systems. There are three main cooperation logics developed: first, the Alternating-time Temporal Logic (ATL) [6], [7], where $<<G>>$ is used as a cooperation modality (parameterized path quantifier), and formula $<<G>>$ φ expressing that agents in coalition G can cooperate to ensure that φ holds, that is coalition G have a winning strategy for φ; second, Coalition Logic (CL) [8], [9] where formula $[G]$ φ expressing that coalition G is able to achieve in one move an outcome where φ is true, and formula $[G^*]\varphi$ asserting that coalition G can achieve φ at some point in the future; third, the Coalition Logic for Propositional Control (CL-PC) [10], where by controlling the propositional atoms, an agent or any coalition he is in can determine what it will achieve. Among these cooperation logics developed, ATL which replaces path quantifiers of CTL by cooperation modalities has received particular attention. Over the last three years, cooperation logics like ATEL (which takes knowledge into account) [11], [12], [13] and NATL* (which takes normative ability into account) [14] have been developed to extend ATL in different ways. They can express properties like additional constrains on actions and common knowledge that ATL can not.

There are problems unresolved in these cooperation logics. Firstly, it is a common approach in these extended cooperation logics but obviously too strong and unpractical an assumption that different agents are not allowed to control the same actions. That is, each agent is associated with a set of actions that he can execute, and it is assumed that these sets of actions are pairwise disjoint because they are owned by different agents. Now let us consider an example where the coalition of agents is a family, surely, members in this coalition share a common action 'turn on the TV' when they have had supper. So, it is obvious that a coalition logic which allows different agents to control the same actions needs to be developed. And this leads to the first effort our paper makes.

Secondly, the ability of agents to cooperate to execute actions (what actions an agent or a coalition of agents can perform) and how this relates to their ability to reach certain states of affairs (the effects of actions) are worth investigated separately, but neither ATL nor its extended cooperation logics (ATEL, NATL*) has adopted such an approach. Regarding this, paper [15] provides two logic modules to achieve the separate investigating effect. Although this approach seems clear and the soundness and completeness of the axiom systems of both of the two logic modules are easier to gained and proved, it seems the two abilities mentioned above can be investigated in more detail within a unified model.

Lastly, to make good use of these ideas of extension and combine these extended cooperation logics will form a unified cooperation logic whose expressive power and flexibility are much richer than its ancestors. Modalities of knowledge (comes from epistemic logic) and function of normative ability (to deal with real problems, there are additional constraints on the actions that may be performed in any given state) are investigated together. Since unification creates links between these two approaches which had not been connected before, it is desirable to explore the relations between them even if no old questions can be answered and no new questions arise.

2 UNIFIED MODEL

Compositions of multi-agent systems can be modeled by the following unified model where a state transition results from choices made by the system components and the environment. This unified model (namely, Action-based Normative Alternating Epistemic Transition Systems) is a straightforward extension of the Action-based Alternating Transition Systems (AATSs) used by Wiebe van der Hoek [13]. It combines the main components of [13], [14], [15], and at the same time contains components of our own. It is the semantic structures to our cooperation logic (NATEL).

Definition 1. (UNIFIED MODEL)

A unified model for the semantics to NATEL is a (n+12)-tuple

$M = <S, Ag, P, At, \sim_1, ..., \sim_n, T_{at}, T_{ct}, T_{la}, T_{lc}, T_{st}, T_{ls}, \tau, \pi>$, with the following components:

- S is a finite, non-empty set of states;
- $Ag = \{1, ..., n\}$ is a finite, non-empty set of agents;
- P is a finite, non-empty set of atomic propositions;
- $At = At_1 \cup ... \cup At_n$ is the finite, non-empty set of all actions, where each agent $i \in Ag$ is associated with a finite, non-empty set At_i of possible actions; different agents can perform the same action, i.e., for each i, $j \in Ag$, and $i \neq j$, it may be true that $At_i \cap At_j \neq \phi$; then we define an action tuple as $\alpha = <t_1, ..., t_k>$, where t_i is the action chosen by agent i, $1 \leq k \leq n$, and for any agent i, she can choose nothing (t_i is null) or choose a common action($i \neq j$, but $t_i = t_j$); so that the assumption that different agents can not execute the same actions which obviously does not fit human commonsense understanding of the world has been done away with.
- $\sim_i \subseteq S \times S$ is an epistemic accessibility relation for each agent $i \in Ag$. Each $\sim_i$ must be an equivalence relation;

- T_{ai}: $Ag \rightarrow At$ is a function that assigns to each agent $i \in Ag$ one action from At. Under this definition, it is assumed that the action assigned to the agent is controlled by this agent;
- T_{ci}: $2^{Ag} \rightarrow 2^{At}$ is a function that assigns to each coalition $G \subseteq Ag$ a subset of actions from At. Under this definition, it is assumed that the subset of actions assigned to the coalition of agents are controlled by this coalition;
- T_{ta}: $At \rightarrow Ag$ is a function that assigns to each action $t \in At$ one agent from Ag. It provides us with convenience to find the agent who is exactly controlling this action.
- T_{tc}: $At \rightarrow 2^{Ag}$ is a function that assigns to each action $t \in At$ a subset of agents from Ag. It provides us with convenience to find the coalition of agents who is exactly controlling this action;
- T_{st}: $S \rightarrow 2^{At}$ is a function that assigns to each state $s \in S$ a subset of actions from At. This function provides us with convenience to find the actions that can be executed in certain states;
- T_{ts}: $At \rightarrow 2^{S}$ is a function that assigns to each action $t \in At$ a subset of states from S. This function provides us with convenience to find the states in which this action can be executed;
- $\tau : (S \times U_a) \rightarrow S$ is a state transition function that defines the state τ (s, α) that would result by the performance of α from state s; U_a (defined afterwards) given here is the set of all possible sets of complex actions (also defined afterwards);
- $\pi : S \rightarrow 2^{P}$ is an interpretation function, which gives the set of primitive propositions satisfied in each state: if $p \in \pi(s)$, then proposition p is true in state s.

2.1 Actions

Actions play a key role in this unified model. When deciding 'who should achieve what in which way', the explicit representation of actions helps us to figure out how can agents obtain some state of affairs.

As shown in the unified model, At is the set of all actions. Bringing in the operators of propositional dynamic logic, a complex action can be defined as [15]: $\alpha ::= t | \neg \alpha | \alpha \wedge \alpha | \alpha ; \alpha | \alpha$ '|' $\alpha | \alpha * | \varphi ?$, where the connectives have the usual interpretation, $t \in At$, and φ is a formula of NATEL which will be defined later. Removing all of the connectives within a complex action there will be atomic actions left, and we denote the set of all of these atomic actions A_α. The set of all possible sets of complex actions is expressed as U_a, and a set of complex actions is $u_a \subseteq U_a$. An action tuple for a coalition of agents G is $\langle t_1, t_2, ..., t_k \rangle$, where $t_i \in At_i$, for each $i \in G$. Action tuple is the same as joint action which has been defined in ATEL and NATL*.

2.2 Actions and Agents

The ability of agents to cooperate to execute actions (what actions an agent or a coalition of agents can perform) and how this relates to their ability to reach certain states of affairs (the effects of actions) are worth investigated separately, but neither ATL nor its extended cooperation logics (ATEL, NATL*) has adopted such an approach [15]. As we know, the relation between actions and agents is complex: an action can be controlled by many different agents (that is, group action and common action), and an agent can control many different actions (that is, each agent $i \in Ag$ is associated with a finite, non-empty set At_i of possible actions). Regarding this, several functions (T_{at}, T_{ct}, T_{ta}, T_{tc}, T_{st}, T_{ts}) concerning the relation between agents and actions are given in detail to investigate the relationship in depth. When deciding 'who should achieve what in which way', these functions help us to figure out what actions an agent or a coalition of agents can perform, and help us to find out the agent or coalition of agents who is exactly controlling a single action.

It must be emphasized that by defining 'for each $i,j \in Ag$, and $i \neq j$, it may be true that $At_i \cap At_j \neq \phi$ ', we can allow different agents to control the same action. This differs with the approaches taken by ATEL and NATL*.

2.3 Actions and States

Since the relation between actions and agents has been investigated in depth in last sub-section, we will research the relation between actions and states below.

As shown in the unified model, there are two functions. The first function, $T_{st}: S \rightarrow 2^{At}$ can help us to find the actions that can be executed in certain states. The second function, $T_{ts}: At \rightarrow 2^{S}$ can help us to find the states in which this action can be executed. Besides, these functions bring us convenience to define strategy and strategy tuple below [13], [14]. A strategy for an agent $i \in Ag$ is a function: $\sigma_i: S \rightarrow At_i$, which must satisfy the legality constraint that $\sigma_i(s) \in T_{st}(s)$. A strategy tuple for a coalition $G = \{a_1, ..., a_k\} \subseteq Ag$ is $\sigma_G = <\sigma_1, ... , \sigma_k>$, one for each agent $a_i \in G$. The set of all strategy tuples is denoted as Σ_G. An infinite sequence of states can be defined as $\lambda = s_0, s_1, ...$; given $u \in \mathbb{N}$, $\lambda[u]$ is the component indexed by u in λ. The set of all infinite sequence of states is denoted as $comp(s, \sigma_G) = \{\lambda \mid \lambda[0]=s$ and $\forall u \in \mathbb{N}: \lambda[u+1] \in \{\tau(\sigma_G, \lambda[u])\}\}$. Strategy tuple is the same as strategy profile, and infinite sequence of states is the same as computation (run) which have been defined in ATEL and NATL*. As to the effects of actions (to bring about states of affairs), it can be expressed as $[\alpha]\varphi$. We will leave this to section 3.

2.4 Knowledge

It is useful to bring knowledge into our framework since it helps us to do away with the strong and unrealistic assumption that agents know everything about the state of the system [13].

As shown in the unified model, $\sim_i$ is an epistemic accessibility relation for each agent $i \in Ag$, and it represents indistinguishable states to agent i. The accessibility relations of a coalition of agents $G \subseteq Ag$ is denoted by $\sim_G^E = (\bigcup_{i \in G} \sim_i)$. The transitive closure of $\sim_G^E$ is denoted by $\sim_G^C$. The relation between actions and knowledge is bidirectional, since certain knowledge is required when agents want to execute actions properly, and after executing actions knowledge may be added to.

2.5 Normative Ability

The normative ability $\eta : At \rightarrow 2^S$ is a function that defines a set of additional constraints on the actions that may be performed in any given state [14]. So that if $s \in \eta(t)$, then the normative ability η forbids action t from being performed when the system is in state s.

The relation between function T_{ts} and function η is worth investigated. Since function T_{ts} defines whether or not an action can be executed in the context of the unified model, and function η defines additional constraints on this actions, the requirement is that: $\forall t \in At: (S \setminus T_{ts}(t)) \subseteq \eta(t)$. The operation of implementing the normative ability is thus an update on the unified model.

3 NATEL

Taking advantage of [13], [14], [15], the cooperation logic called the Normative Alternating-time Temporal Epistemic Logic (NATEL) is developed to extend ATL. It is the main contribution of us that actions, knowledge and normative ability can be represented in the object language at the same time other than only in the underlying semantics.

The syntax and semantics of NATEL are given as follows:

Definition 2. (THE SYNTAX OF NATEL)

The formal syntax of NATEL is given by the BNF grammar as:

$\varphi ::= $ true   (truth constant)

|p (primitive propositions)

|$\neg\ \varphi$ (negation)

|$\varphi \wedge \varphi$ (conjunction)

| $[\eta : \alpha\ ]\varphi$ (effect of actions)

| $<<\eta : G>> \alpha$ (what actions a coalition of agents can perform)

| $<<\eta : G>> O\ \varphi$ (in the next state, cooperative ability)

| $<<\eta : G>> \Box\ \varphi$ (now and forever more, cooperative ability)

| $<<\eta : G>> \varphi u \varphi$ (until, cooperative ability)

| $K_i \varphi$ (agent i knows φ)

| $E_G \varphi$ (everyone in coalition G knows φ)

| $C_G \varphi$ (it is common knowledge to everyone in the coalition G that φ)

In this definition, $p \in P$ is a propositional variable, α is a complex action, η is a symbol denoting the normative ability, and $G \in U_G$ is a set of agents.

As shown in the definition of syntax of NATEL, the syntax of ATL is extended by actions, knowledge and normative ability. For example, by $[\eta : \alpha\ ]\varphi$, one can express the property of the effect of actions within the context of the normative ability η. Similarly, by $<<\eta : G>> O\ \varphi$, one can express the property of what the coalition of agents G can enforce to be true in the next state within the context of the normative ability η.

Definition 3. (THE SEMANTICS OF NATEL)

According to the unified model, the semantics of NATEL are given as follows:

$M, s \vDash$ true;

$M, s \vDash p$ iff $p \in \pi(s)$ (where $p \in P$);

$M, s \vDash \neg\ \varphi$ iff $M, s \nvDash \varphi$;

$M, s \vDash \varphi \wedge \psi$ iff $M, s \vDash \varphi$ and $M, s \vDash \psi$;

$M, s \vDash [\eta : \alpha\ ]\varphi$ iff for all states $\tau(s, \alpha\ )$, it will be true that $M, \tau(s, \alpha\ ) \vDash \varphi$ within the context of the normative ability η ;

$M, s \vDash <<\eta : G>> \alpha$ iff for the set of all of the atomic actions of the complex action α, it is true that $A_\alpha \subseteq (T_{ct}(G) \cap T_{st}(s))$ within the context of normative ability η ;

$M, s \vDash <<\eta : G>> O\ \varphi$ iff $\exists\ \sigma_G \in \Sigma_G$, such that $\forall \lambda \in$ comp(s, σ_G), we have $M, \lambda\ [1] \vDash \varphi$ within the context of the normative ability η ;

$M, s \vDash <<\eta : G>> \Box\ \varphi$ iff $\exists\ \sigma_G \in \Sigma_G$, such that $\forall \lambda \in$ comp(s, σ_G), we have $M, \lambda\ [u] \vDash \varphi$ for all $u \in \mathbb{N}$ within the context of the normative ability η ;

$M, s \vDash <<\eta : G>> \varphi u \psi$ iff $\exists\ \sigma_G \in \Sigma_G$, such that $\forall \lambda \in$ comp(s, σ_G), there exist some $u \in \mathbb{N}$ such that $M, \lambda\ [u] \vDash \psi$, and for all $0 \le v < u$, we have $M, \lambda\ [v] \vDash \varphi$ within the context of the normative ability η ;

$M, s \vDash K_i \varphi$ iff for all s' such that $s \sim_i s$': $M, s' \vDash \varphi$;

$M, s \vDash E_G \varphi$ iff for all s' such that $s \sim_G^E s$': $M, s' \vDash \varphi$;

$M, s \vDash C_G \varphi$ iff for all s' such that $s \sim_G^C s'$: $M, s' \vDash \varphi$.

The other connectives ("$\vee$", "$\rightarrow$", "$\leftrightarrow$") can be defined by $\neg$, $\wedge$, and $<<\eta : G>> \Diamond \ \varphi$ is shorthand for $\neg <<\eta : G>> \Box \neg \ \varphi$.

Due to limit of space, a sound and complete axiom system for the cooperation logic (NATEL) is left to our next paper.

4 A CASE STUDY

Our example is a circuit model that consisting of some wire, a lamp (L), two switches (K_1, K_2), two electrical sources (U_1, U_2), either switch K_1 or switch K_2 is turned on will make the lamp lighted. When both switches are turned on, the electrical current will pass directly through K_1 and K_2, and it leads to a clash. According to the circuit model and the unified model, the sets of states, agents, actions, atomic propositions are given as follows. $S =$ $\{s_0, s_1, s_2, s_3\}$, in which s_0 stands for K_1-off and K_2-off, s_1 stands for K_1-off and K_2-on, s_2 stands for K_1-on and K_2-off, s_3 stands for K_1-on and K_2-on; Ag $= \{1, 2\}$; $At = \{$1-on-K_2, 1-off-K_2, 2-on-K_2, 2-off-K_2, 12-on-K_1, 12-off-$K_1\}$; $P = \{K_1$-off, K_2-off, K_1-on, K_2-on$\}$. K_1 can be turned on or turned off either by 1 or 2; K_2 can be turned on or turned off only by the cooperation of both 1 and 2. The actions 1-on-K_2 and 1-off-K_2 can only be executed by agent 1, 2-on-K_2 and 2-off-K_2 can only be executed by agent 2, 12-on-K_1 and 12-off-K_1 are the actions that are allowed to be executed by different agents 1 and 2. The relations between actions and agents, actions and states can be researched separately through functions involved actions. We give some examples of functions to show the relation between agents and actions here. $T_{at}(1)=\{$1-on-K_2, 1-off-K_2, 12-on-K_1, 12-off-$K_1\}$,$T_{at}(2)=\{$2-on-K_2, 2-off-K_2, 12-on-K_1, 12-off-$K_1\}$; $T_{ct}(\{1, 2\})=\{$1-on-K_2, 1-off-K_2, 2-on-K_2, 2-off-K_2, 12-on-K_1, 12-off-$K_1\}$; $T_{ta}($1-on-$K_2)=1$, $T_{ta}($2-on-$K_2)=2$; $T_{tc}($12-on-$K_1)=\{1, 2\}$. They bring us convenience to find the coalition of agents which is exactly controlling certain actions. Action 1-on-K_2 is fully controlled by 1, action 2-on-K_2 is fully controlled by 2, and action 12-on-K_1 is only fully controlled by the coalition of 1 and 2.

In order to avoid the situation of clash (that is, s_3), it is forbidden that both K_1 and K_2 are turned on at a given time. This additional constrain can be expressed by the follow normative ability.

$$\eta(\alpha) = \begin{cases} s_0, & \text{if } \alpha = 1\text{-on-}K_2 \wedge 2\text{-on-}K_2 \wedge 12\text{-on-}K_1 \\ s_1, & \text{if } \alpha = 12\text{-on-}K_1 \\ s_2, & \text{if } \alpha = 1\text{-on-}K_2 \wedge 2\text{-on-}K_2 \end{cases}$$

This normative ability ensures that: when K_1-off and K_2-off, action 1-on-$K_2 \wedge 2$-on-$K_2 \wedge 12$-on-K_1 is forbidden to be executed; when K_1-off and K_2-

on, action 12-on-K_1 is forbidden to be executed; when K_2-off and K_1-on, action 1-on-K_2 ∧ 2-on-K_2 is forbidden to be executed.

Since NATEL takes actions, knowledge and normative ability into account at the same time, its expressive power and flexibility are much richer than the other two extended cooperation logics of ATL. It can express properties like: M, s_0 ⊨ [η : 1-on-K_2 ∧ 2-on-K_2] (K_1-off ∧ K_2-on); its intended interpretation is that operating within the context of the normative ability η, executing action 1-on-K_2 and 2-on-K_2 at the same time in state s_0 can bring about state s_1. This shows the effect of actions; M, s_0 ⊨ <<η : G>> ○((K_1-off ∧ K_2-on) ∨ (K_1-on ∧ K_2-off)); Its intended interpretation is that operating within the context of the normative ability η, in state s_0 the coalition of agent 1 and agent 2 has the ability to bring about state s_1 or s_2 (the next states of s_0). This shows the ability of coalitions.

In a word, we allow different agents to control the same actions and give functions that involved actions in more detail so that we can investigate the relations between actions and knowledge, actions and agents, actions and states separately. Furthermore, actions, knowledge and normative ability are represented in the object language other than only in the underlying semantics to improve the expressive power and flexibility of NATEL.

5 CONCLUSIONS

There are several efforts we have made in this paper. Firstly, different agents are allowed to control the same actions. It do away with the strong and unrealistic assumption of the other two extended cooperation logics of ATL (ATEL, NATL*), so our approach is better. Secondly, functions that involved actions are given in more detail, so that we can research the relations between actions and knowledge, actions and agents, actions and states in depth and separately. Thirdly, a unified model has been given. It combines the main components of [13], [14], [15], and at the same time includes components of our own. Lastly, a cooperation logic called NATEL has been developed as an extension to ATL. As a result, actions, knowledge and normative ability can be represented in the object language other than only in the underlying semantics. And since it takes actions, knowledge and normative ability into account at the same time, its expressive power and flexibility are much richer than the other two extended cooperation logics of ATL. In the 1990s, BDI (belief, desire, intention) was developed to represent the cognitive structure of agents [1]. We have done some work in this area too [2], [3], [4], [5]. It will be a wonderful attempt to combine our existing work in BDI and NATEL, and investigate the relations between them.

ACKNOWLEDGEMENTS

This paper is supported by the National Natural Science Foundation of China under Grant No. 60373079, No. 60573076; and supported by the Foundation of the Chinese Academy of Sciences under Grant No. SYSKF0505.

REFERENCES

1. P. R. Cohen, H. J. Levesque.: Intention is choice with commitment, Artificial Intelligence, Vol 42 (1990) 213-261
2. Shanli Hu, Chunyi Shi.: The computational complexity of dynamic programming algorithm for combinatorial auctions. Proceedings of 2002 International Conference on Machine Learning and Cybernetics IEEE Vol 1 (2002.11) 266-268
3. Shanli Hu, Chunyi Shi and Xiuduan Fang.: The rationality of agents and the weak realism constraint for intentions. Proceedings of 2003 International Conference on Machine Learning and Cybernetics IEEE Vol 4 (2003.11) 2000-2003
4. Shanli Hu, Chunyi Shi.: Twin-subset semantic model for intention. Proceedings of 2003 International Conference on Machine Learning and Cybernetics IEEE Vol 1 (2003.11) 2004-2008
5. Shanli Hu, Chunyi Shi.: A dynamic model of multi-agent system. Proceedings of 2004 International Conference on Machine Learning and Cybernetics IEEE Vol 1 (2004.8) 183-187
6. R. Alur, L. de Alfaro, T. A. Henzinger, S. C. Krishnan, F. Y. C. Mang, S. Qadeer, S. K. Rajamani, and S. Ta_siran.: MOCHA user manual. University of Berkeley Report, 2000
7. R. Alur, T. A. Henzinger, and O. Kupferman.: Alternating-time temporal logic. Journal of the ACM, Vol 49, No. 5 (2002.9) 672–713
8. M. Pauly.: Logic for social software. PhD thesis, University of Amsterdam (2001)
9. M. Pauly.: A modal logic for coalitional power in games. Journal of Logic and Computation, Vol 12, No. 1 (2002) 149–166
10. W. van der Hoek, M. Wooldridge.: On the logic of cooperation and propositional control. Artificial Intelligence, Vol 64, No. 1-2 (2005) 81–119
11. W. van der Hoek M. Wooldridge.: Model Checking Cooperation, Knowledge, and Time - A Case Study. In Research in Economics, 57(3) (2003.9) 235-265
12. W. van der Hoek, M. Wooldridge.: Cooperation, Knowledge, and Time: Alternating-time Temporal Epistemic Logic and its Applications. In Studia Logica, 75(1) (2003.10) 125-157
13. W. van der Hoek, M. Roberts, and M. Wooldridge.: Knowledge and Social Laws. In Proceedings of the Fourth International Joint Conference on Autonomous Agents and Multi-Agent Systems (AAMAS-05), Utrecht, the Netherlands (2005.7)
14. M. Wooldridge, W. van der Hoek.: On obligations and normative ability: towards a logical analysis of the social contract. Journal of Applied Logic, Vol 3 (2005) 396-420,
15. L. Sauro, J. Gerbrandy, W. van der Hoek, and M. Wooldridge.: Reasoning about action and cooperation. To be presented on Proceedings of the Fifth International Joint Conference on Autonomous Agents and Multi-Agent Systems (AAMAS-06), Hakodate, Japan (2006.5)

APPLYING QUANTUM ALGORITHM TO SPEED UP THE SOLUTION OF HAMILTONIAN CYCLE PROBLEMS

VIDYA RAJ C.
Assistant Professor
Dept. of Computer Science & Engineering
The National Institute of Engineering
Mysore – 570008, Karnataka, India

DR. M.S. SHIVAKUMAR
Principal
The National Institute of Engineering
Mysore – 570008, Karnataka, India

Abstract: Quantum computing is an important field of research that applies concepts of quantum physics to building more efficient computers. Although only rudimentary quantum computers have been built so far, many researchers believe that quantum computing has great potential and the quantum computers can efficiently perform some tasks which are otherwise not feasible on a classical computer. The Hamiltonian cycle problem is to determine whether a given graph has a Hamiltonian cycle or not. This problem belongs to the class of NP-complete problems, widely believed to intractable or hard on classical computers. Design of faster-than-classical quantum algorithms for important algorithmic problems has been an interesting intellectual adventure and achievement all along and their existence keeps being one of the key stimuli to those trying to overcome enormous technology problems to build (powerful) quantum computers. In this paper, we have used undirected graphs with varied number of vertices and we have shown how to determine the existence of a Hamiltonian cycle in a given graph. We have also illustrated how quantum search can be applied to obtain the solution of the Hamiltonian cycle problem much faster than the classical approach.

Key words: quantum computers, quantum algorithm, qubit, Hamiltonian cycle

Please use the following format when citing this chapter:

Vidya, R.C., Shivakumar, M.S., 2006, in IFIP International Federation for Information Processing, Volume 228, Intelligent Information Processing III, eds. Z. Shi, Shimohara K., Feng D., (Boston: Springer), pp. 53–61.

1.   INTRODUCTION

The current drive towards increasing speed and miniaturization of computers leads modern technology towards the subatomic domain - quantum computing - where strange quantum behavior takes over from familiar classical notions.   Quantum computation touches upon the foundations of computer science, since quantum computers appear to violate the modern Church-Turing thesis [7]. Quantum computers can perform certain hard tasks, much faster than classical computers.

1.1   Quantum Computation

Quantum computing is a new, more powerful model of computing based on quantum mechanics. The basic variable used in quantum computing is a qubit, represented as a vector in a two dimensional complex Hilbert space where $|0>$ and $|1>$ form a basis in the space. The difference between qubits and bits is that a qubit can be in a state other than $|0>$ or $|1>$ whereas a bit has only one state, either 0 or 1. It is also possible to form linear combination of states, often called superposition.

The state of a qubit can be described by $|\Psi> = \alpha|0> + \beta|1>$ where, the numbers α and β are complex numbers. The special states $|0>$ and $|1>$ are known as computational basis states. We can examine a bit to determine whether it is in the state 0 or 1 but we cannot directly examine a qubit to determine its quantum state, that is values of α and β. When we measure a qubit we get either the result 0, with probability $|\alpha|^2$ or the result 1, with probability $|\beta|^2$, where $|\alpha|^2 + |\beta|^2 = 1$, since the probabilities must sum to one.

Consider the case of two qubits. In two classical bits there would be four possible states, 00, 01, 10 and 11. Correspondingly, a two qubit system has four computational basis states denoted $|00>$, $|01>$, $|10>$ and $|11>$. A pair of qubits can also exist in a superposition of these four states, so the quantum state of two qubits involves associating a complex coefficient, sometimes called amplitude, with each computational basis state, which is given as

$$|\Psi> = \alpha_{00}|00> + \alpha_{01}|01> + \alpha_{10}|10> + \alpha_{11}|11>$$

The logic that can be implemented with qubits is quite distinct from Boolean logic, and this is what has made quantum computing exciting by opening new possibilities [8].

1.2   Quantum Algorithms

Quantum Algorithms introduce a new paradigm of computation such as quantum superposition, quantum entanglement and promises to provide results that cannot be achieved by classical computers. Shor's factoring algorithm and Grover's search algorithm are examples of new algorithms that provide tremendous speedups over their classical counterparts [1][2][6].

In this paper, we would like to use Grover's search algorithm that can provide quadratic speedup, which is considerable when N is large over their classical counterparts.

Suppose we are given a map containing many cities, and wish to determine the shortest route passing through all the cities on the map. A simple algorithm to find this route is to search all possible routes through the cities, keeping a running record of which route has the shortest length. On a classical computer, if there are N possible routes, it takes O(N) operations to determine the shortest route using this method. But quantum search algorithm enables this search method to be sped up substantially, requiring only O($\sqrt{N}$) operations[9][10]. The quantum search algorithm in general can be applied far beyond the route finding example just described to speed up many (though not all) classical algorithms that use search heuristics. Thus given a search space of size N, and no prior knowledge about the structure of information in it, if we want to find an element of search space satisfying a known property, then this problem requires approximately N operations, but the quantum search algorithm allows it to be solved using approximately $\sqrt{N}$ operations[1][2].

1.3   NP – Complete Problems

In complexity theory, the NP-complete problems are the most difficult problems in NP ("non-deterministic polynomial time") in the sense that they are the ones most likely not to be in P. Formally, a decision problem C is NP-complete if it is complete, it is in NP and it is NP-hard, i.e. every other problem in NP is reducible to it[8].

Some well-known problems that are NP-complete when expressed as decision problems are Hamiltonian Cycle problem, Traveling salesman problem, Subgraph isomorphism problem, Graph coloring problem, Boolean satisfiability problem(SAT) etc.

2.   HAMILTONIAN CYCLE PROBLEM

In   graph theory, the Hamiltonian cycle problem is a problem of determining whether a Hamiltonian cycle exists in a given graph. The graph may be directed or undirected. The problem of searching for Hamiltonian cycles, or circuits in a given graph is known to be NP-complete, that is, non-determinant in a classical computer, and always polynomial in a massively parallel processor. Ability to solve such problems might benefit many areas, including the layout of integrated circuits. The Hamiltonian cycle problem is a special case of the traveling salesman problem, the exact solution to this problem may be found as a Hamiltonian circuit with minimum total weight[3]. Once all Hamiltonian circuits are identified, it is easy to calculate weight using an ordinary computer to choose the minimum.

2.1 Problem Definition

Let $G = (V, A)$ be a graph in which $V = \{v_1, v_2 \ldots v_n\}$ is the set of n vertices, and A is the set of m arcs (v_i, v_j). A Hamiltonian cycle (or circuit) in G is a permutation (s_i) of the vertices such that (v_s, v_{s+1}) belongs to A for $i = 1, 2, \ldots, n-1$. Also (v_{sn}, v_{s1}) must belong to A to close the circuit.

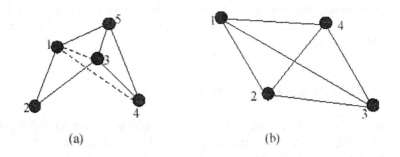

(a)   (b)

Figure 1. Examples of Hamiltonian circuits

Let us consider the above two circuits which characterizes the presence or absence of Hamiltonian circuits. Figure 1a, is a Hamiltonian circuit 1-2-3-4-5-1. Examples of circuits that are not Hamiltonian are 1-2-3-5-1 and 1-2-3-5-4-5-1 because the first leaves out node 4 while the second visits node 5 twice. Figure 1b is characterized by several Hamiltonian circuits: 1-2-3-4-1; 1-2-4-3-1; 1-3-2-4-1; each can be walked backwards, for example: 1-4-3-2-1.

2.2 Classical Approach

A typical algorithm to solve Hamiltonian circuit classically is to perform a search through all possible orderings of the vertices:
1. Generate each possible orderings (v_1, v_2, ..., v_n) of vertices
2. For each ordering, check to see whether it is a Hamiltonian cycle for the graph.
   If not, continue checking the orderings.

Since there are $n^n = 2^{n \log n}$ possible orderings of the vertices which must be searched, this algorithm requires $O(p(n)2^{n[\log n]})$ operations to check for the existence of a Hamiltonian cycle. The polynomial factor p(n) which is predominant due to the implementation of the oracle. This algorithm is deterministic and succeeds with probability [2]. This approach works well for smaller numbers of vertices, but grows exponentially with n, the number of vertices [4].

2.3 Quantum Approach

Nielsen and Chuang began the process of finding Hamiltonian circuits using a quantum computer. On a quantum computer it is possible to estimate the number of solutions much more quickly than is possible on a classical computer by combining the Grover iteration with the phase estimation technique based on quantum Fourier transform [2]. And this is referred to as quantum counting. This allows us to decide whether or not a solution exists, depending on whether the number of solutions is zero, or non-zero.

Let m ≡ [log n], the search space for the algorithm be represented by a string mn qubits, with each block of m qubits being used to store the index to a single vertex with n bits. Therefore, we can write the computational basis state as $|v_1, v_2,..,v_n>$, where each $|v_i>$ is represented by the approximate string of m qubits, for a total of nm qubits.

The oracle is a unitary operator, O, defined by its action on the computational basis:

$|x>|q> \xrightarrow{O} |x>|q \text{ XOR } f(x)>$ where $|x>$ is the index register, the oracle qubit $|q>$ is a single qubit which is flipped if $f(x) = 1$ and it is unchanged otherwise, XOR denotes modulo addition 2.

The oracle for the search algorithm must apply the transformation:

$$O|v_1,v_2,..,v_n> = \begin{cases} |v_1,v_2,..,v_n> & \text{if } v_1,v_2,....,v_n \text{ is not a Hamiltonian cycle} \\ -|v_1,v_2,..,v_n> & \text{if } v_1,v_2,...v_n \text{ is a Hamiltonian cycle} \end{cases}$$

This oracle is easy to design and implement if the description of the graph is known. Applying this oracle, the quantum algorithm require $O(p(n)2^{n[\log n]/2})$ operations to determine whether a Hamiltonian cycle exists. Due to the implementation of the oracle, the polynomial $p(n)$ becomes the overhead which is predominant. But the dominant effect is in determining the resources required for computation which is the exponent in $2^{n[\log n]/2}$. By repeating the algorithm several times (say r) the probability of error can be reduced from 1/6 to $1/6^r$

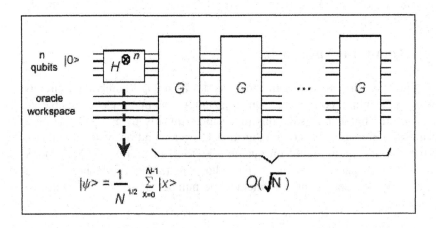

Figure 2. Schematic circuit of Grover search algorithm[2]

2.4   Performance Comparison

The Table 1 given below compares the linear search with quantum search techniques. The comparisons are based on the number of operations required to search the list of N items and the number of operations required to determine the existence of a Hamiltonian in the given circuit. Table 2, gives the performance of classical and quantum search algorithms with respect to the number of vertices & utilization of computational resources.

Table 1. Comparison of classical and quantum search algorithms

Algorithm	Classical search (linear)	Quantum search
Executes on	Classical computer	Quantum computer
Uses	Bits	Qubits
Operations to search N items	$O(N)$	$O(\sqrt{N})$
Operations to determine the existence of a HC	$O(p(n)2^{n[\log n]})$	$O(p(n)2^{n[\log n]/2})$

Table 2. Performance of classical and quantum search algorithms with respect to the number of vertices & utilization of computational resources

No. of Vertices	Classical search resources required for computation $2^{n[\log n]}$	Quantum search resources required for computation $2^{n[\log n]/2}$
2	1.52	1.23
3	2.69	1.64
4	5.30	2.29
5	11.27	3.36
6	25.43	5.04
7	60.36	7.77
8	149.57	12.23
9	384.85	19.62
10	1024.0	32.0
20	68073969.9	8250.69
100	1.61×10^{60}	1.26×10^{30}

The figure shown below is the graphical representation of the performance analysis of the classical and quantum algorithms in terms of the number of vertices and the amount of computational resources required. It can be seen that the resources required for computing the existence of Hamiltonian remains almost same for both classical and quantum algorithms when the number of vertices happen to be very small. However, as the number of vertices increase tremendously, quantum search takes over the classical in terms of speed.

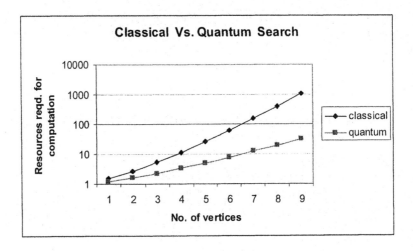

Figure 3. Graphical representation of performance of classical Vs. quantum algorithm

3.   CONCLUSION

In this paper, we studied and analyzed undirected graphs and we were able to apply classical search techniques to find out the existence of Hamiltonian cycle in it. Later we applied Grover's quantum search algorithm to find the solution to the problem of Hamiltonian cycle, using the smallest possible number of applications of oracle. Hamiltonian cycle problem is a NP-complete problem, and by performing exhaustive searches over the set of possible solutions, it would result in a considerable speedup over classical solutions.

ACKNOWLEDGEMENTS

We would like to thank all the authors of various papers and publishers for giving us enough information on this emerging area of computing. Our thanks are due to our institute, "The National Institute of Engineering, Mysore" for all the encouragement and support rendered.

REFERENCES

1. Grover L.K, A Fast Quantum mechanical Algorithm for Database Search, In proceedings of the 28th Annual ACM Symposium on the Theory of Computing, pp. 212-219, quant-ph/9605043, (1996).

2. Nielsen M and Chaung I, Quantum Computation and Quantum Information, Cambridge University press, Cambridge, United Kingdom (2000).

3. G. Johnson, A shortcut through time The path to the quantum computer, Vintage Books, (2003).

4. S. Martello, Hamiltonian Circuits in a Directed Graph, ACM Trans. Math. Software, Vol. 9, No. 1, pp. 131-138, (1983).

5. Burger, John Robert, Quantum Algorithm Processors to Reveal Hamiltonian, arXiv:cs/0508116, 08/ (2005).

6. P. W. Shor, Polynomial-time algorithms for prime factorization and discrete logarithms on a quantum computer, SIAM J. Computing 26, (1997).

7. Deutch, D., Quantum Theory, the Church-Turing Principle, and the Universal Quantum Computer, proc. Roy. Soc. Lond. A400, (1985).

8. M.R. Garey and D.S. Johnson, Computers and Intractability: A Guide to the Theory of NP-Completeness, W.H. Freeman and company, (1995).

9. L.K. Grover, Quantum mechanics helps in searching for a needle in a haystack, Phys. Rev. Lett., 78, pp. 325-328 (1979).

10. Peter W. Shor, Progress in quantum algorithms, MIT, Sept.(2005).

MODEL CHECKING FOR REAL-TIME TEMPORAL, COOPERATION AND EPISTEMIC PROPERTIES *

Zining Cao

Department of Computer Science and Engineering
Nanjing University of Aero. & Astro., Nanjing 210016, China
caozn@nuaa.edu.cn

Abstract   In this paper, we introduce a real-time temporal knowledge logic, called *RTKL*, which is a combination of real-time temporal logic and knowledge logic. It is showed that temporal modalities such as "always in an interval", "until in an interval", and knowledge modalities such as "knowledge in an interval" and "common knowledge in an interval" can be expressed in such a logic. The model checking algorithm is given. Furthermore, we add cooperation modalities to *RTKL* and get a new logic *RATKL*, which can express not only real-time temporal and epistemic properties but also cooperation properties. The model checking algorithm for *RATKL* is also given.

Keywords: Real-time temporal logic, knowledge logic, cooperation, model checking

1.   Introduction

The field of multi-agent systems has recently become interested in the problem of verifying complex systems. In *MAS*, modal logics representing concepts such as knowledge, belief, and intention. Since these modalities are given interpretations that are different from the ones of the standard temporal operators, it is not straightforward to apply existing model checking tools developed for $LTL\backslash CTL$ temporal logic to the specification of *MAS*. The recent developments of model checking *MAS* can broadly be divided into streams: in the first category standard predicates are used to interpret the various intensional notions and these are paired with standard model checking techniques based on temporal logic. Following this line is [12] and related papers. In the other category we can place techniques that make a genuine attempt at extending the model checking techniques by adding other operators. Works along these lines include [3, 10] and so on.

* This work was supported by the National Science Foundation of China under Grant 60473036.

Please use the following format when citing this chapter:

Cao, Z., 2006, in IFIP International Federation for Information Processing, Volume 228, Intelligent Information Processing III, eds. Z. Shi, Shimohara K., Feng D., (Boston: Springer), pp. 63–72.

Real-time is sometimes an important feature of software system. To describe the property of real-time *MASs,* one should express not only real-time temporal temporal but also epistemic property. In this paper, we present a real-time temporal knowledge logic *RTKL,* which is an extension of knowledge by adding real-time temporal modalities. Although its syntax is very simple, we can express the property such as "always in an interval", "until in an interval", "knowledge in an interval", "common knowledge in an interval" and etc. We also studied the model checking algorithm for *RTKL.* To express the cooperation property, we extend *RTKL* to *RATKL* and give its model checking algorithm.

The rest of the paper is organized as follows: In Section 2, we present a real-time temporal knowledge logic *RTKL,* give its syntax, semantics. Furthermore, we give the model checking algorithm. In Section 3, we add cooperation modalities to *RTKL,* and get a new logic *RATKL.* The model checking algorithm for *RATKL* is also given. The paper is concluded in Section 4.

2.   Real-Time Temporal Epistemic Logic *RTKL*

In this section, we introduce a real-time temporal knowledge logic *RTKL,* which can express the epistemic property and real-time behaviour in *MAS.*

Syntax of *RTKL*

The well form formulas of *RTKL* are defined as follows.

Definition 1 The set of formulas in *RTKL,* called L^{RTKL}, is given by the following rules:

(1) If $\varphi \in$ atomic formulas set Π, then $\varphi \in L^{RTKL}$.

(2) If $\varphi \in$ proposition variables set V, then $\varphi \in L^{RTKL}$.

(3) If $\varphi \in L^{RTKL}$, then $\neg\varphi \in L^{RTKL}$.

(4) If $\varphi, \psi \in L^{RTKL}$, then $\varphi \wedge \psi \in L^{RTKL}$.

(5) If $\varphi, \psi \in L^{RTKL}$, then $\bigcirc\varphi, []\varphi, \varphi U\psi \in L^{RTKL}$. Intuitively, $\bigcirc$ means next, $[]$ means always and U means until.

(6) If $\varphi, \psi \in L^{RTKL}$, then $[]_{[i,j]}\varphi, \varphi U_{[i,j]}\psi \in L^{RTKL}$. Intuitively, $[]_{[i,j]}\varphi$ means that φ holds in the interval $[i,j]$. $\varphi U_{[i,j]}\psi$ means there is $k \in [i,j]$, such that ψ holds at time k and φ holds in the interval $[0,k]$.

(7) If $\varphi \in L^{RTKL}$, then $K_a\varphi, E_\Gamma\varphi, C_\Gamma\varphi \in L^{RTKL}$, where $a \in Agent$, $\Gamma \subseteq \Sigma$. Intuitively, $K_a\varphi$ means that agent a knows φ. $E_\Gamma\varphi$ means that every agent in Γ knows φ. $C_\Gamma\varphi$ means that φ is a common knowledge by every agent in Γ.

Using *RTKL,* we can express various of real-time knowledge properties. For example, $K_a[]_{[i,j]}\varphi$ means that agent a knows φ always holds in the interval $[i,j]$. $[]_{[i,j]}K_a\varphi$ means that in the interval $[i,j]$, agent a always knows

φ holds. $\langle\rangle C_\Gamma\varphi$ means eventually, φ is the common knowledge of group Γ, where $\langle\rangle\psi \stackrel{def}{=} \neg[]\neg\psi$.

Semantics of *RTKL*

We will describe the semantics of *RTKL*, that is, a formal model that we can use to determine whether a given formula is true or false.

Definition 2 (Models) Given a set of agents $A = \{1, ..., n\}$, a temporal epistemic model (or simply a model) is a tuple $S = (Q, T, \sim_1, ..., \sim_n, V)$, where

Q is the set of the global states for the system (henceforth called simply states);

$T \subseteq Q \times Q$ is a total binary (successor) relation on G;

$\sim_a \subseteq Q \times Q$ ($a \in A$) is an epistemic accessibility relation for each agent $a \in A$ defined by $s \sim_a s'$ iff $l_a(s) = l_a(s')$, where the function $l_a: Q \to L_a$ returns the local state of agent a from a global state s; obviously $\sim_a$ is an equivalence relation;

$V : Q \to 2^{PV_K}$ is a valuation function for a set of propositional variables PV_K such that $true \in V(s)$ for all $s \in Q$. V assigns to each state a set of propositional variables that are assumed to be true at that state.

We can now turn to the definition of semantics of *RTKL*.

Computations. A computation in M is a possibly infinite sequence of states $\pi = (s_0, s_1, ...)$ such that $(s_i. s_{i+1}) \in T$ for each $i \in N$. Specifically, we assume that $(s_i, s_{i+1}) \in T$ iff $s_{i+1} = t(s_i, act_i)$, i.e., s_{i+1} is the result of applying the transition function t to the global state s_i, and an action act_i. In the following we abstract from the transition function, the actions, and the protocols, and simply use T, but it should be clear that this is uniquely determined by the interpreted system under consideration. Indeed, these are given explicitly in the example in the last section of this paper. In interpreted systems terminology a computation is a part of a run; note that we do not require s_0 to be an initial state. For a computation $\pi = (s_0, s_1, ...)$, let $\pi[k] = s_k$, and $\pi_k = (s_0, ..., s_k)$, for each $k \in N$. By $\Pi(s)$ we denote the set of all the infinite computations starting at s in M.

Definition 3 Semantics of *RTKL*

$[[p]]_S = \{q \mid p \in \pi(q)\};$

$[[\neg\varphi]]_S = Q - [[\varphi]]_S;$

$[[\varphi \wedge \psi]]_S = [[\varphi]]_S \cap [[\psi]]_S;$

$[[\bigcirc\varphi]]_S = \{q \mid \text{for all computations } \pi \in \Pi(q), \text{ we have } \pi[1] \in [[\varphi]]_S.\};$

$[[[]\varphi]]_S = \{q \mid \text{for all computations } \pi \in \Pi(q) \text{ and all positions } m \geq 0, \text{ we}$ have $\pi[m] \in [[\varphi]]_S.\};$

$[[\varphi U \psi]]_S = \{q \mid$ for all computations $\pi \in \Pi(q)$, there exists a position $m \geq 0$, such that $\pi[m] \in [[\psi]]_S$ and for all positions $0 \leq k < m$, we have $\lambda[k] \in [[\varphi]]_S.\}$;

$[[[]_{[i,j]}\varphi]]_S = \{q \mid$ for all computations $\pi \in \Pi(q)$ and all positions $i \leq m \leq j$, we have $\pi[m] \in [[\varphi]]_S.\}$;

$[[\varphi U_{[i,j]}\psi]]_S = \{q \mid$ for all computations $\pi \in \Pi(q)$, there exists a position $i \leq m \leq j$, such that $\pi[m] \in [[\psi]]_S$ and for all positions $0 \leq k < m$, we have $\lambda[k] \in [[\varphi]]_S.\}$;

$[[K_a \varphi]]_S = \{q \mid$ for all $r \in [[\varphi]]_S$ and $r \in \sim_a (q)$ with $\sim_a (q) = \{q' \mid (q, q') \in \sim_a\}\}$

$[[E_\Gamma \varphi]]_S = \{q \mid$ for all $r \in [[\varphi]]_S$ and $r \in \sim_\Gamma^E (q)$ with $\sim_\Gamma^E (q) = \{q' \mid (q, q') \in \sim_\Gamma^E\}\}$, here $\sim_\Gamma^E = (\cup_{a \in \Gamma} \sim_a)$.

$[[C_\Gamma \varphi]]_S = \{q \mid$ for all $r \in [[\varphi]]_S$ and $r \in \sim_\Gamma^C (q)$ with $\sim_\Gamma^C (q) = \{q' \mid (q, q') \in \sim_\Gamma^C\}\}$, here $\sim_\Gamma^C$ denotes the transitive closure of $\sim_\Gamma^E$.

Formally, given a model S, we say that φ is satisfiable in S, and write $S, q \models \varphi$, if $q \in [[\varphi]]_S$ for some q in Q.

Model Checking for *RTKL*

In this section we give a model checking algorithm for *RTKL*. The model checking problem for *RTKL* asks, given a model S and a *RTKL* formula φ, for the set of states in Q that satisfy φ. In the following, we denote the desired set of states by $Eval(\varphi)$.

For each φ' in $Sub(\varphi)$ do

    case $\varphi' = p : Eval(\varphi') := Reg(p)$

    case $\varphi' = \neg\theta : Eval(\varphi') := Eval(true) - Eval(\theta)$

    case $\varphi' = \theta_1 \wedge \theta_2 : Eval(\varphi') := Eval(\theta_1) \cap Eval(\theta_2)$

    case $\varphi' = \bigcirc\theta : Eval(\varphi') := Pre(Eval(\theta))$

    case $\varphi' = []\theta :$

        $Eval(\varphi') := Eval(true)$

        $\rho_1 := Eval(\theta)$

        repeat

            $Eval(\varphi') := Eval(\varphi') \cap \rho_1$

            $\rho_1 := Pre(Eval(\varphi')) \cap Eval(\theta)$

        until $\rho_1 = Eval(\varphi')$

    case $\varphi' = \theta_1 U \theta_2 :$

        $Eval(\varphi') := Eval(false)$

        $\rho_1 := Eval(\theta_1)$

        $\rho_2 := Eval(\theta_2)$

        repeat

            $Eval(\varphi') := Eval(\varphi') \cup \rho_2$

            $\rho_2 := Pre(Eval(\varphi')) \cap \rho_1$

$$\text{until } \rho_1 = Eval(\varphi')$$

case $\varphi' = []_{[i,j]}\theta$:

    $k := j$

    $Eval(\varphi') := Eval(true)$

    while $k \neq 0$ do

        $k := k - 1$

        if $k \geq i$ then $Eval(\varphi') := Pre(Eval(\varphi')) \cap Eval(\theta)$

        else $Eval(\varphi') := Pre(Eval(\varphi'))$

    end while

case $\varphi' = \theta_1 U_{[p,q]}\theta_2$:

    $k := j$

    $Eval(\varphi') := Eval(false)$

    while $k \neq 0$ do

        $k := k - 1$

        $Eval(\varphi') := Pre(Eval(\varphi') \cup Eval(\theta_2)) \cap Eval(\theta_1)$

    end while

case $\varphi' = K_a\theta$: $Eval(\varphi') := \{q \mid Img(q, \sim_a) \subseteq Eval(\theta)\}$

case $\varphi' = E_\Gamma\theta$: $Eval(\varphi') := \cap_{a\in\Gamma} Eval(K_a\theta)$

case $\varphi' = C_\Gamma\theta$:

    $Eval(\varphi') := Eval(true)$

    repeat

        $\rho := Eval(\varphi')$

        $Eval(\varphi') := \cap_{a\in\Gamma}(\{q | Img(q, \sim_a) \subseteq Eval(\theta)\} \cap \rho)$

    until $\rho = Eval(\varphi')$

end case

return $Eval(\varphi)$

The algorithm uses the following primitive operations:

(1) The function Sub, when given a formula φ, returns a queue of syntactic subformulas of φ such that if φ_1 is a subformula of φ and φ_2 is a subformula of φ_1, then φ_2 precedes φ_1 in the queue $Sub(\varphi)$.

(2) The function Reg, when given a proposition $p \in \Pi$, returns the set of states in Q that satisfy p.

(3) The function Pre, when given a set $\rho \subseteq Q$ of states, returns the set of states q such that from q the next state to lie in ρ. Formally, $Pre(\rho)$ contains state $q \in Q$ such that $(q, s) \in T_t$ where $s \in \rho$.

(4) The function $Img : Q \times 2^{Q\times Q} \rightarrow Q$, which takes as input a state q and a binary relation $R \subseteq Q \times Q$, and returns the set of states that are accessible from q via R. That is, $Img(q, R) = \{q' \mid qRq'\}$.

(5) Union, intersection, difference, and inclusion test for state sets. Note also that we write $Eval(true)$ for the set Q of all states, and write $Eval(false)$ for the empty set of states.

Partial correctness of the algorithm can be proved induction on the structure of the input formula φ. Termination is guaranteed since the state space Q is finite. The cases where $\varphi' = K_a\theta$, $\varphi' = E_\Gamma\theta$ and $\varphi' = C_\Gamma\theta$ simply involve the computation of the Img function at most $|Q|^2$ times, each computation requiring time at most $O(|Q|^2)$. Furthermore, real-time CTL model checking algorithm can be done in polynomial time. Hence the above algorithm for $RTKL$ requires at most polynomial time.

Proposition 1 The algorithm given in the above terminates and is correct, i.e., it returns the set of states in which the input formula is satisfied. Furthermore, the algorithm costs at most polynomial time on $|Q|$.

3.   Adding Cooperation Modalities to $RTKL$

To express the cooperation property in open systems, Alur and Henzinger introduced alternating-time temporal logic ATL in [2], which is a generalisation of CTL. The main difference between ATL and CTL is that in ATL, path quantifies are replaced by cooperation modalities. For example, the ATL formula $\langle\langle\Gamma\rangle\rangle \bigcirc \varphi$, where Γ is a group of agents, expresses that the group Γ can cooperate to achieve a next state that φ holds. Thus, we can express some properties such as "agents 1 and 2 can ensure that the system never enters a fail state". An ATL model checking systems called $MOCHA$ was developed [1]. In MAS, agents are intelligent, so it is not only necessary to represent the temporal properties but also necessary to express the mental properties. For example, one may need to express statements such as "if it is common knowledge in group of agents Γ that φ, then Γ can cooperate to ensure ψ". To represent and verify such properties, a temporal epistemic logic $ATEL$ was presented in [10]. This logic extended ATL with knowledge modalities such as "every knows" and common knowledge. In this section, we extend $RTKL$ by adding cooperation modalities and get a new logic $RATKL$, which can express real-time temporal, cooperation and knowledge properties. Furthermore, a model checking algorithm for $RATKL$ was given.

Syntax of $RATKL$

Definition 4 The set of formulas in $RATKL$, called L^{RATKL}, is given by the following rules:

(1) If $\varphi \in$ atomic formulas set Π, then $\varphi \in L^{RATKL}$.

(2) If $\varphi \in$ proposition variables set V, then $\varphi \in L^{RATKL}$.

(3) If $\varphi \in L^{RATKL}$, then $\neg\varphi \in L^{RATKL}$.

(4) If $\varphi, \psi \in L^{RATKL}$, then $\varphi \wedge \psi \in L^{RATKL}$.

(5) If $\varphi, \psi \in L^{RATKL}$, $\Gamma \subseteq \Sigma$, then $\langle\langle\Gamma\rangle\rangle \bigcirc \varphi$, $\langle\langle\Gamma\rangle\rangle[]\varphi$, $\langle\langle\Gamma\rangle\rangle\varphi U\psi \in L^{RATKL}$.

(6) If $\varphi, \psi \in L^{RATKL}$, $\Gamma \subseteq \Sigma$, then $\langle\langle\Gamma\rangle\rangle[]_{[i,j]}\varphi$, $\langle\langle\Gamma\rangle\rangle\varphi U_{[i,j]}\psi \in L^{RATKL}$.

(7) If $\varphi \in L^{RATKL}$, then $K_a\varphi$, $E_\Gamma\varphi$, $C_\Gamma\varphi \in L^{RATKL}$, where $\Gamma \subseteq \Sigma$.

Semantics of *RATKL*

Definition 5 A model S of *RATKL* is a concurrent game structure $S = (\Sigma, Q, \Pi, \pi, e, d, \delta, \sim_a$ here $a \in \Sigma)$, where

(1) Σ is a finite set of agents, in the following, without loss of generality, we usually assume $\Sigma = \{1, ..., k\}$.

(2) Q is a finite, nonempty set, whose elements are called possible worlds or states.

(3) Π is a finite set of propositions.

(4) π is a map: $Q \rightarrow 2^\Pi$, where Π is a set of atomic formulas.

(5) e is an environment: $V \rightarrow 2^Q$, where V is a set of proposition variables.

(6) For each player $a \in \Sigma = \{1, ..., k\}$ and each state $q \in Q$, a natural number $d_a(q) \geq 1$ of moves available at state q to player a. We identify the moves of player a at state q with the numbers $1, ..., d_a(q)$. For each state $q \in Q$, a move vector at q is a tuple $\langle j_1, ..., j_k \rangle$ such that $1 \leq j_a \leq d_a(q)$ for each player a. Given a state $q \in Q$, we write $D(q)$ for the set $\{1, ..., d_1(q)\} \times ... \times \{1, ..., d_k(q)\}$ of move vectors. The function D is called move function.

(7) For each state $q \in Q$ and each move vector $\langle j_1, ..., j_k \rangle \in D(q)$, a state $\delta(q, j_1, ..., j_k)$ that results from state q if every player $a \in \Sigma = \{1, ..., k\}$ choose move j_a. The function is called transition function.

(8) $\sim_a$ is an accessible relation on Q, which is an equivalence relation.

The definition of computation of a concurrent game structure is similar to the case of Kripke structure. In order to give the semantics of *RATKL*, we need to define strategies of a concurrent game structure.

Strategies and their outcomes. Intuitively, a strategy is an abstract model of an agent's decision-making process; a strategy may be thought of as a kind of plan for an agent. By following a strategy, an agent can bring about certain states of affairs. Formally, a strategy f_a for an agent $a \in \Sigma$ is a total function f_a that maps every nonempty finite state sequence $\lambda \in Q^+$ to a natural number such that if the last state of λ is q, then $f_a(\lambda) \leq d_a(q)$. Thus, the strategy f_a determines for every finite prefix λ of a computation a move $f_a(\lambda)$ for player a. Given a set $\Gamma \subseteq \Sigma$ of agents, and an indexed set of strategies $F_\Gamma = \{f_a \mid a \in \Gamma\}$, one for each agent $a \in \Gamma$, we define $out(q, F_\Gamma)$ to be the set of possible outcomes that may occur if every agent $a \in \Gamma$ follows the corresponding strategy f_a, starting when the system is in state $q \in Q$. That is, the set $out(q, F_\Gamma)$ will contain all possible q-computations that the agents Γ can "enforce" by cooperating and following the strategies in F_Γ. Note that the "grand coalition" of all agents in the system can cooperate to uniquely determine the future state of the system, and so $out(q, F_\Sigma)$ is a singleton. Similarly, the set $out(q, F_\emptyset)$ is the set of all possible q-computations of the system.

We can now turn to the definition of semantics of *RATKL*. We omit the definition of $[[p]]_S$, $[[\neg\varphi]]_S$, $[[\varphi \wedge \psi]]_S$, $[[K_a\varphi]]_S$, $[[E_\Gamma\varphi]]_S$, $[[C_\Gamma\varphi]]_S$ since they are given in Definition 3.

Definition 6 Semantics of *RATKL*

$[[\langle\langle\Gamma\rangle\rangle \bigcirc \varphi]]_S = \{q \mid$ there exists a set F_Γ of strategies, one for each player in Γ, such that for all computations $\lambda \in out(q, F_\Gamma)$, we have $\lambda[1] \in [[\varphi]]_S.\}$

$[[\langle\langle\Gamma\rangle\rangle[]\varphi]]_S = \{q \mid$ there exists a set F_Γ of strategies, one for each player in Γ, such that for all computations $\lambda \in out(q, F_\Gamma)$ and all positions $i \geq 0$, we have $\lambda[i] \in [[\varphi]]_S.\}$

$[[\langle\langle\Gamma\rangle\rangle\varphi U\psi]]_S = \{q \mid$ there exists a set F_Γ of strategies, one for each player in Γ, such that for all computations $\lambda \in out(q, F_\Gamma)$, there exists a position $i \geq 0$, such that $\lambda[i] \in [[\psi]]_S$ and for all positions $0 \leq j < i$, we have $\lambda[j] \in [[\varphi]]_S.\}$

$[[\langle\langle\Gamma\rangle\rangle[]_{[i,j]}\varphi]]_S = \{q \mid$ there exists a set F_Γ of strategies, one for each player in Γ, such that for all computations $\lambda \in out(q, F_\Gamma)$ and all positions $i \leq m \leq j$, we have $\lambda[m] \in [[\varphi]]_S.\}$

$[[\langle\langle\Gamma\rangle\rangle\varphi U_{[i,j]}\psi]]_S = \{q \mid$ there exists a set F_Γ of strategies, one for each player in Γ, such that for all computations $\lambda \in out(q, F_\Gamma)$, there exists a position $i \leq m \leq j$, such that $\lambda[m] \in [[\psi]]_S$ and for all positions $0 \leq k < m$, we have $\lambda[k] \in [[\varphi]]_S.\}$

Intuitively, $\langle\langle\Gamma\rangle\rangle \bigcirc \varphi$ means that group Γ can cooperate to ensure φ at next step; $\langle\langle\Gamma\rangle\rangle[]\varphi$ means that group Γ can cooperate to ensure φ always holds; $\langle\langle\Gamma\rangle\rangle\varphi U\psi$ means that group Γ can cooperate to ensure φ until ψ holds; $\langle\langle\Gamma\rangle\rangle[]_{[i,j]}\varphi$ means that group Γ can cooperate to ensure φ always holds in the interval of $[i, j]$; $\langle\langle\Gamma\rangle\rangle\varphi U_{[i,j]}\psi$ means that group Γ can cooperate to ensure φ until ψ holds in the interval of $[i, j]$. For example, a *RATKL* formula $\langle\langle\Gamma_1\rangle\rangle \bigcirc \varphi \wedge \langle\langle\Gamma_2\rangle\rangle[]_{[i,j]}\psi$ holds at a state exactly when the coalition Γ_1 has a strategy to ensure that proposition φ holds at the immediate successor state, and coalition Γ_2 has a strategy to ensure that proposition ψ holds at the current and all future states between time i and j.

Model Checking for *RATKL*

In the following, we give a model checking algorithm for *RATKL*. We denote the desired set of states by $Eval(\varphi)$. The case of p, $\neg\varphi$, $\varphi \wedge \psi$, $K_a\varphi$, $E_\Gamma\varphi s$, $C_\Gamma\varphi$ can be computed similarly in the algorithm for *RTKL*, so we do not give the procedure for these modalities. The main difference between *RTKL* and *RATKL* is that temporal modalities are replaced by alternating-time temporal modalities, so the model checking algorithm for *RATKL* is similar to the algorithm for *RTKL* except that the function $Pre(\rho)$ is replaced by the function $CoPre(\Gamma, \rho)$.

For each φ' in $Sub(\varphi)$ do

case $\varphi' = \langle\langle\Gamma\rangle\rangle \bigcirc \theta : Eval(\varphi') := CoPre(\Gamma, Eval(\theta))$
case $\varphi' = \langle\langle\Gamma\rangle\rangle []\theta :$
  $Eval(\varphi') := Eval(true)$
  $\rho_1 := Eval(\theta)$
  repeat
    $Eval(\varphi') := Eval(\varphi') \cap \rho_1$
    $\rho_1 := CoPre(\Gamma, Eval(\varphi')) \cap Eval(\theta)$
  until $\rho_1 = Eval(\varphi')$
case $\varphi' = \langle\langle\Gamma\rangle\rangle\theta_1 U \theta_2 :$
  $Eval(\varphi') := Eval(false)$
  $\rho_1 := Eval(\theta_1)$
  $\rho_2 := Eval(\theta_2)$
  repeat
    $Eval(\varphi') := Eval(\varphi') \cup \rho_2$
    $\rho_2 := CoPre(\Gamma, Eval(\varphi')) \cap \rho_1$
  until $\rho_1 = Eval(\varphi')$
case $\varphi' = \langle\langle\Gamma\rangle\rangle []_{[i,j]}\theta :$
  $k := j$
  $Eval(\varphi') := Eval(true)$
  while $k \neq 0$ do
    $k := k - 1$
    if $k \geq i$ then $Eval(\varphi') := CoPre(\Gamma, Eval(\varphi')) \cap Eval(\theta)$
    else $Eval(\varphi') := CoPre(\Gamma, Eval(\varphi'))$
  end while
case $\varphi' = \langle\langle\Gamma\rangle\rangle\theta_1 U_{[p,q]}\theta_2 :$
  $k := j$
  $Eval(\varphi') := Eval(false)$
  while $k \neq 0$ do
    $k := k - 1$
    $Eval(\varphi') := CoPre(\Gamma, Eval(\varphi') \cup Eval(\theta_2)) \cap Eval(\theta_1)$
  end while
end case
return $Eval(\varphi)$

The algorithm uses the function $CoPre$. When given a set $\Gamma \subseteq \Sigma$ of players and a set $\rho \subseteq Q$ of states, the function $CoPre$ returns the set of states q such that from q, the players in Γ can cooperate and enforce the next state to lie in ρ. Formally, $CoPre(\Gamma, \rho)$ contains state $q \in Q$ if for every player $a \in \Gamma$, there exists a move $j_a \in \{1, ..., d_a(q)\}$ such that for all players $b \in \Sigma - \Gamma$ and moves $j_b \in \{1, ..., d_b(q)\}$, we have $\delta(q, j_1, ..., j_k) \in \rho$.

Similar to the case of *RTKL*, we have the following proposition:

Proposition 2 The algorithm given in the above terminates and is correct. Furthermore, it costs at most polynomial time on $|Q|$.

4.   Conclusions

Recently, there has been growing interest in the logics for representing and reasoning temporal and epistemic properties in multi-agent systems [3, 6, 9–12]. In this paper, we present a real-time temporal knowledge logic *RTKL*, which is a succinct and powerful language for expressing complex properties. In [8], Halpern and Moses also presented and study some real-time knowledge modalities such as ϵ-common knowledge C_G^ϵ, $\langle\rangle$-common knowledge $C_G^{\langle\rangle}$ and timestamped common knowledge C_G^T. It is easy to see that all these modalities can be expressed in *RTKL*, for example, $C_G^{\langle\rangle} \Leftrightarrow \langle\rangle C_G$ and $C_G^T \Leftrightarrow []_{[T,T]} C_G$. Moreover, the approach to model checking *RTKL* is studied. We further extend *RTKL* by adding cooperation modalities. The logic *RATKL* can express not only real-time and knowledge properties, but also cooperation properties. The model checking algorithm for *RATKL* is given. It is also hopeful to apply such *RTKL* and *RATKL* logics and these model checking algorithms to verify the correctness of real-time protocol systems.

References

[1] R. Alur, L. de Alfaro, T. A. Henzinger, S. C. Krishnan, F. Y. C. Mang, S. Qadeer, S. K. Rajamni, and S. Tasiran, MOCHA user manual, University of Berkeley Report, 2000.

[2] R. Alur and T. A. Henzinger. Alternating-time temporal logic. In Journal of the ACM, 49(5): 672-713.

[3] M. Bourahla and M. Benmohamed. Model Checking Multi-Agent Systems. In Informatica 29: 189-197, 2005.

[4] E. M. Clarke, J. O. Grumberg, and D. A. Peled. Model checking. The MIT Press, 1999.

[5] H. van Ditmarsch, W van der Hoek, and B. P. Kooi. Dynamic Epistemic Logic with Assignment, in AAMAS05, ACM Inc, New York, vol. 1, 141-148, 2005.

[6] N. de C. Ferreira, M. Fisher, W. van der Hoek: Logical Implementation of Uncertain Agents. Proc. EPIA-05, LNAI 3808, pp536-547.

[7] R. Fagin, J. Y. Halpern, Y. Moses, and M. Y. Vardi. Common knowledge revisited, Annals of Pure and Applied Logic 96: 89-105, 1999.

[8] J. Y. Halpern and Y. Moses. Knowledge and common knowledge in a distributed environment. J ACM, 1990, 37(3): 549-587.

[9] W. van der Hoek and M. Wooldridge. Model Checking Knowledge, and Time. In Proceedings of SPIN 2002, LNCS 2318, 95-111, 2002.

[10] W. van der Hoek and M. Wooldridge. Cooperation, Knowledge, and Time: Alternating-time Temporal Epistemic Logic and its Applications. Studia Logica, 75: 125-157, 2003.

[11] M. Kacprzak, A. Lomuscio and W. Penczek. Verification of multiagent systems via unbounded model checking. In Proceedings of the 3rd International Conference on Autonomous Agents and Multiagent Systems (AAMAS-04), 2004.

[12] M. Wooldridge, M. Fisher, M. Huget, and S. Parsons. Model checking multiagent systems with mable. In Proceedings of the First International Conference on Autonomous Agents and Multiagent Systems (AAMAS-02), 2002.

PROBABILISTIC APPROXIMATION UNDER INCOMPLETE INFORMATION SYSTEMS

Yucai Feng, Wenhai Li, Zehua Lv and Xiaoming Ma
Department of Computer Science,
Huazhong University of Science and Technology,
Wuhan 430074, Hubei, China,

lwhaymail@21cn.com

Abstract   By applying the probability estimation of the unavailable attributes derived from the available attributes to the neighborhood system, the suited degree of each neighbor to a given object is depicted. Therefore, the neighborhood space with guaranteed suited precision is obtained. We show how to shrink the rule search space via VPRS model for this space, and also, we will prove the incredibility degree of decision class is guaranteed by the two-layer thresholds.

Keywords: threshold, approximation, neighborhood system, probabilistic, rough set

1.   Introduction

Classical rough sets theory [1] is too rigid to be applied to the real-life environment due to the requirement that all the characters of an object in the system are available [2]. Kryszkiewicz [4] extended the rough set approximation method in incomplete information systems through the tolerance relation with the "missing values" semantics. Slowinski [5] and Stefanowski [6] used similarity relation instead of indiscernibility relation to express the "absent values" semantics. Furthermore, the latter defined a "tolerance class" under the hypothesis that an equivalent probability was associated with each element among such values. The variable precision rough set model [7] classified the objects, probably bearing a family of misclassification(based on a β threshold) in the graduation layer [9-11].

Our research gives a probabilistic angle of view to incomplete values while generating the approximations: the distribution of "missing" or "absent" values is quantificationally taken into account when the relevant neighborhood is generated, to achieve which the guarantee of the covering quality is elucidated by a granulation threshold λ. After this, a symmetric graduation threshold β is proposed to satisfy predefined certainty requirements. The (λ, β) threshold pair includes the certain defined lines which are applied to qualify the approximation regions with the price of controllable imprecision.

Please use the following format when citing this chapter:

Feng, Y., Li, W., Lv, Z., Ma, X., 2006, in IFIP International Federation for Information Processing, Volume 228, Intelligent Information Processing III, eds. Z. Shi, Shimohara K., Feng D., (Boston: Springer), pp. 73–80.

2.   Rough sets preliminaries

An information system AS is a pair (U, A, V, f) where $U \neq \emptyset$ is a non empty set of objects and A is a non empty set of attributes. For $\forall c \in A$ under $f : U \rightarrow V_c$, V_c is the domain of c and $V = \bigcup \{V_c : \forall c \in A\}$. For any $B \subseteq A$, an indiscernibility relation $IND(B)$ is defined with $IND(B) = \{(x, y) \in U \times U : \forall c_i \in B, c_i(x) = c_i(y)\}$. $U/IND(B)$(or U/B) is the family of all the equivalence classes of the indiscernibility relation $IND(B)$ with U.

For any non empty subset of objects $X \subseteq U$, the $B - lower$, $B - upper$ approximations and $B - boundary$ are defined with $X_B = \bigcup \{Y \in U/B | Y \subseteq X\}$, $X^B = \bigcup \{Y \in U/B | Y \cap X \neq \emptyset\}$, $Bn(X) = X^B \setminus X_B$ apart. The $B - lower$ is also called positive region, while the supplement of the $B - upper$ is also called negative region.

A decision information system DS is an information system while $A = C \bigcup \{d\}$ and $d \notin C$, here d is called decision and C is called condition attribute set. Any decision rule is represented as:

$$\sigma = \wedge_{c_j \in B}(c_j(a_i) = v) \rightarrow (d(a_i) = w), \tag{1}$$

where $c_j \in B \subseteq C$, and v and w are the corresponding attribute values of $a_i \in U$ respectively. Here, the left side of the implication is noted by s and t on the opposite. Let $[s]$ denote the set of the objects in DS satisfying s and $[t]$ for t accordingly. A decision rule with $s \rightarrow t$ is certain if and only if $[s] \subseteq [t]$. Otherwise, possible decision rules in the inconsistent decision information system can be induced from the upper approximation of a decision class expressed in t.

3.   Probabilistic Approximation Space

AS is an incomplete information system when some values are not available, and the unavailable values are denoted by " $*$ ". The approximate relations are proposed mainly based on two hypothetical semantics for the unknown values. The lower and upper approximations are derived from the cover of relation τ instead of the indiscernibility class. The cover in a neighborhood system (U, IC) is defined as:

$$C = \bigcup \{I(x) | \forall_{x \in U, y \in I(x)}(y \tau x)\}, \tag{2}$$

in which, accordingly, $I(x)$ denotes the neighborhood of x and τ denotes the relation defined in the information system. The tolerance and similarity approach are proposed in terms of a different explanation for the unavailable values. The key concept of tolerance approach is the tolerance class. Tolerance class denoted by $I_B(x)$ of any object $x \in U$ is induced from the tolerance relation T_B which is reflexive and symmetric, but not necessarily transitive relation and obeys a "missing value" hypothesis[4]. Given an information system AS and a subset of attributes $B \subseteq A$ is defined as:

$$\forall_{x,y \in U \times U}(T_B(x, y) \Leftrightarrow \forall_{c_j \in B}(c_j(x) = c_j(y) \vee c_j(x) = * \vee c_j(y) = *)), \tag{3}$$

where for each object the binary relation T_B identifies a tolerant class $I_B(x) = \{y \in U | T_B(x, y)\}$, and consequently, the $B - lower$ and $B - upper$ of an object set are

$X_B^T = \{x \in U | I_B(x) \subseteq X\}$ and $X_T^B = \{x \in U | I_B(x) \cap X \neq \emptyset\} = \bigcup\{x \in X | I_B(x)\}$ respectively.

The non-symmetric similarity relation is similar with the tolerance relation except that the former is a partial order on the set U under an "absent value" hypothesis[5, 6]. Homoplastically, for a given information system AS and a subset of attributes $B \subseteq A$, the similarity relation S_B is defined as:

$$\forall_{x,y \in U \times U}(S_B(x,y) \Leftrightarrow \forall_{c_j \in B}(c_j(x) = * \vee c_j(x) = x_j(y))). \qquad (4)$$

Consequently, similarity class $R_B(x)$ and converse similarity class $R_B^{-1}(x)$ of object $x \in U$ with respect to B are defined as $R_B(x) = \{y \in U | S_B(y,x)\}$ and $R_B^{-1}(x) = \{y \in U | S_B(x,y)\}$. $B - lower$ and $B - upper$ are $X_B^S = \{x \in U | R_B^{-1}(x) \subseteq X\}$ and $X_S^B = \bigcup\{x \in X | R_B(x)\}$ separately.

Most of the approximation methods are built based on both relations mentioned above. Furthermore, many quantitative and qualitative extensions[8] are applied to the above relations. Among the proposed methods of the incomplete information system, the unbending matching of either tolerance or similarity relation cannot control the inflation of the neighborhood, which results in the bilateral expansion of the $B - boundary$. All these induce the inefficiency of the reducing search space. From the perspective of the probability [12] of the unknown attribute value for two given objects x and y, the tolerance relation supports that any attribute value is suited iff all the available values are suited, while the valued tolerance relation regulates the possibility of the "missing value" followed by an equiprobable distribution hypothesis throughout the domain. Nevertheless, the probability of $c_j(y)$ matching $c_j(x)$ on any $c_j \in B$ with $c_j(x) = * \vee c_j(x) = *$ held is intuitively higher than $c_j(y) = 1/|V_c|$ when the available values are all suited.

DEFINITION 1 *Given $c_j \in B$ and $x, y \in U$ in an incomplete information system AS, if $c_j(x) \in V_c$ and $c_j(y) = *$, the probability of $c_j(y)\Re c_j(x)$ ($\Re$ represents the matching of y to x on c_j) denoted by $P^\vDash(c_j)$ is relative to the cardinality of all the suited attributes $|\{\forall c_j | c_j(x)\Re c_j(y) \in V_c\}|$ independently.*

Obviously, AS is in tolerance relation when $P^\vDash(c_j) = 1$ and $\Re$ denotes " $=$ " and it is in valued tolerance relation while $P^\vDash(c_j) = 1/|V_c|$. Definition 1 is given to depict the suited possibility of two objects on unknown attributes relevant to the cardinality percentage of the available suited attributes, and the unknown attributes are independent from each other.

PROPOSITION 2 *Given a neighborhood system (U, IC), the expected function of any two objects $x, y \in U$ can be expressed by the percentage of suited attributes:*

$$P(x\tau y) = \prod_{\substack{c_j(x) = * \vee c_j(y) = * }}^{\forall c_j \in B} P^\vDash. \qquad (5)$$

For the neighborhood system in Proposition 2, the mapping combination of x and y on c_j has three possible cases due to the unavailable values. When $c_j(y) = c_j(x) \neq *$, the matching of y to x on c_j is certain, so the percentage of $|\{c_j(y) = c_j(x) \neq *\}|$ to $|C|$ represents the conditional probability of any uncertain matching concerning certain matching. Under the "missing" semantics, the probability of $c_j(y)\Re c_j(x)$ equals to "1" iff y are certainly suited to x on c_j, so that the total probability of all the certain suited attributes equals to "1" and is denoted by $P^\equiv$, otherwise, it equals to "0". When $c_j(y) = * \wedge c_j(x) \neq *$, from Definition 1, we assert that $P(c_j(y)\Re c_j(x))$ is a joint probability on $P^\vDash$ and $P^\equiv$, this equation comes into existence when $c_j(x) = * \wedge c_j(y) \neq *$ due to the symmetry of the tolerance relation. Furthermore, $c_j(y) = c_j(x) = *$ has a bilateral effect on the total probability of two objects. From all the above, the probability of two objects with $x\tau y$ held depends on the $P^\vDash$ exponentially, and the power is the arisen times of $*$. The similarity relation holds Proposition 2 except for the range of the percentage and the power due to its unilateralism.

The threshold λ is used to control the power of the total probability. Therefore, the neighborhood of a given object can be controlled, and accordingly, the probability of all objects in the neighborhood of the given objects is not less than $(1 - \lambda)^{|C| \times \lambda}$.

4.   Probabilistic Approximations Regions

The classical rough set theory is extended by variable precision rough set method (VPRS) in [7, 9, 10, 11], partial classification is taken into account by introducing an error probability threshold $\beta \in [0, 0.5)$, and it identifies all the condition classes with any decision class if the error ratio is not higher than this threshold. Given the approximation space (U, IND), an *absolute certainty gain (gabs)* is proposed to qualify the degree of the dependency from determinative class to conditional class:

DEFINITION 3 *If Y is definable in (U, IND), then the absolute certainty gain between sets X and Y is given by:*

$$gabs(X|Y) = \frac{\left|\sum_{E \subseteq Y} P(E)P(X|E) - P(X)\sum_{E \subseteq Y} P(E)\right|}{\sum_{E \subseteq Y} P(E)}, \tag{6}$$

where $P(E)$ and $P(X)$ are the probabilities of conditional class E and determinative class X, and $P(X|E)$ is the conditional probability of X. All these probabilities are estimated by the ratios of cardinalities of the sample data. The probability of the rule $s \to t$ is depicted by $gabs(r_{X|Y}) = gabs(X|Y)$, while X and Y are the corresponding classes of s and t. With the symmetric limits proposed, a precision control parameter denoted with β is utilized to define the positive and negative regions of X. All the rules with approximation threshold β satisfied can guarantee the corresponding associated level of classification quality of the both approximation regions, and the domination of the approximation regions can be elucidated with $POS_\beta(X, \neg X) = \cup\{E : gabs(X|E) \geq \beta - P(X)\}$. Let $X, Y \subseteq U$ be a non empty set of objects, the error ratio of X pertinent to Y denoted by $c(X, Y)$ is defined as:

$$c(X, Y) = \begin{cases} 1 - |X \cap Y|/|X|, & |X| > 0, \\ 0, & |X| = 0. \end{cases} \tag{7}$$

The operator $||$ denotes the cardinality in short. For given $\beta \in [0, 0.5)$, therefore, the $B - lower$ and $B - upper$ approximations of X with threshold β derived from $B \subseteq A$ are $R_B^\beta(X) = \{x \in U | c([x]_B, X) \leq \beta\}$; $R_\beta^B(X) = \{x \in U | c([x]_B, X) < 1 - \beta\}$ respectively. Here, $[x]_B$ denotes the equivalence class including $x \in U$ with respect to B and it can be expressed as: $[x]_B = \{E \in U/B | x \in E\}$.

From Proposition 2, the associate level of quality of the neighborhood can be dominated by a granulation threshold λ with predefined covering certainty satisfied, and it can be denoted with $I_\tau(x) = \cup\{y : P(x \tau y) \geq (1 - \lambda)^{|B| \times \lambda}\}$. For a given threshold pair (λ, β), the neighborhood system (U, IC) like equation (2) can be generated so that each $I(x)$ includes any object y with no less matching probability than $(1 - \lambda)^{|B| \times \lambda}$. Therefore, the absolute certainty gain between any sets X and the universe U can be depicted by $P(X) P(X | I_\tau(x))$ and $P(I_\tau(x))$ similarly with equation (6), and the graduation threshold β can be utilized to guarantee the associated level of quality of neighborhood of the approximation regions. To depict the elements of all three cases in Proposition 2, let $\overset{*}{E}(x, y) = \{c_j \in C | c_j(x) = c_j(y) = *\}$ denotes the attributes subset where x and y are unavailable, $E^*(x, y) = \{c_j \in C | c_j(x) = * \wedge c_j(y) \neq *\}$ and $E_*(x, y) = \{c_j \in C | c_j(x) \neq * \wedge c_j(y) = *\}$ denote the similar meaning. Because similarity relation has a unilateral effect on both $P^\models$ and the joint power compared with tolerance relation as shown in Proposition 2, the two-layer domination has different forms for both the "missing value" and "absent value" semantics.

For the "missing value" semantics, the unavailable value is just lost. Following the discussion in Proposition 2, the error ratio is

$$c_T(x, y) = 1 - \frac{|\overset{*}{E}(x, y)| + |E^*(x, y)| + |E_*(x, y)|}{2|C|}. \tag{8}$$

Let T_B be tolerance relation, then $T_B^\lambda(x)$ denotes the tolerance class of x according to the threshold of the credible granulation $\lambda \in (0.5, 1]$, and it can be denoted with $T_B^\lambda(x) = \{y \in U | T_B(x, y) \wedge c_T(x, y) > \lambda\}$. For the tolerance relation with the granulation and graduation credible threshold pair (λ, β), the two-layer approximation regions can be induced with the predefined associated level of quality of both the granulation and graduation certainty satisfied.

DEFINITION 4 *The two-layer lower and upper approximations of $X \subseteq U$ are*

$$X_{BT}^{\lambda\beta} = \left\{ x \in U \left| \frac{|T_B^\lambda(x) \cap |X|}{|T_B^\lambda(x)|} \geq \beta \right. \right\}; \quad X_{\lambda\beta}^{BT} = \left\{ x \in U \left| \frac{|T_B^\lambda(x) \cap |X|}{|T_B^\lambda(x)|} > 1 - \beta \right. \right\}.$$

For the "absent value" semantics, the unavailable value is not to be considered. $\overset{*}{E}$ does not affect the granulation credibility as discussed in Proposition 2, the error ratio is

$$c_S(x, y) = 1 - \frac{|E^*(x, y)| + |E_*(x, y)|}{2|C|}. \tag{9}$$

Let S_B be non-symmetric similarity relation, then $R_B^\lambda(x)$ denotes the similarity class and $R_\lambda^B(x)$ denotes converse similarity class of x with the granulation credibility threshold $\lambda \in (0.5, 1]$ satisfied are $R_B^\lambda(x) = \{y \in U | S_B(y, x) \wedge c_S(x, y) > \lambda$ and

$R_\lambda^B(x) = \{y \in U | S_B(x, y) \wedge c_S(x, y) > \lambda\}$ respectively. For the non-symmetric similarity relation and the credibility threshold pair (λ, β), the two-layer approximation regions can be induced as:

DEFINITION 5 *The two-layer lower and upper approximations of $X \subseteq U$ are*

$$X_{BS}^{\lambda\beta} = \left\{ x \in U \,\middle|\, \frac{|R_\lambda^B(x)| \cap |X|}{|R_\lambda^B(x)|} \geq \beta \right\}; \quad X_{\lambda\beta}^{BS} = \left\{ x \in U \,\middle|\, \frac{|R_B^\lambda(x)| \cap |X|}{|R_B^\lambda(x)|} > 1 - \beta \right\}$$

We suppose any decision class D_w in $U/\{d\} = \{D_1, D_2...D_r\}$ according to $D_w = \{x \in U | d(x) = w\}$ where $w = \{1, 2...r\}$, then the universal form of decision class can be derived from this form through a simple transformation, so a decision rule can be presented in the following form where $D_{wB}^{\lambda\beta}$ denotes the positive region of D_w under relation τ.

PROPOSITION 6 *For the approximation space based on a neighborhood relation τ, each $x \in D_{wB}^{\lambda\beta}$ can induce a decision rule as:*

$$\bigwedge_{c_j \in B} (c_j, c_j(x)) \xrightarrow[\lambda]{\beta} d(x) = w. \tag{10}$$

5.   Comparisons and Experiments

Compare the model in Definition 4-5 with their counterparts in Chapter 3. Our approximation model will provide some advantages. Let $BN_B^T(X) = X_T^B \backslash X_B^T$, $BN_B^S(X) = X_S^B \backslash X_B^S$, $BN_{BT}^{\lambda\beta}(X) = X_{\lambda\beta}^{BT} \backslash X_{BT}^{\lambda\beta}$ and $BN_{ST}^{\lambda\beta}(X) = X_{\lambda\beta}^{ST} \backslash X_{ST}^{\lambda\beta}$, we give the most important properties as follows:

(1) $X_{BT}^{0,1} = X_B^T$; $X_{0,1}^{BT} = X_T^B$; $X_{BS}^{0,1} = X_B^S$; $X_{0,1}^{BS} = X_S^B$

(2) $X_B^T \subseteq X_{BT}^{\lambda\beta} \subseteq X_{BS}^{\lambda\beta} \subseteq X \subseteq X_{\lambda\beta}^{BS} \subseteq X_{\lambda\beta}^{BT} \subseteq X_T^B$

(3) $X_B^S \subseteq X_{BS}^{\lambda\beta} \subseteq X \subseteq X_{\lambda\beta}^{BS} \subseteq X_S^B$

(4) $BN_{BT}^{\lambda\beta}(X) \leq BN_B^T(X)$; $BN_{BS}^{\lambda\beta}(X) \leq BN_B^S(X)$

From the definition of the two-layer probabilistic model in the former two sections, property (1) is obvious.

For property (2), the partial order of the lower approximation based on tolerance between the two-layer and classic method(denoted by $X_B^T \subseteq X_{BT}^{\lambda\beta}$) can be considered into the two threshold respectively. Because $\lambda \in [0.5, 1)$, some objects which partially match x are in $I_B(x)$ while not in $T_B^\lambda(x)$. All objects in $I_B(x)$ must belong to $T_B^\lambda(x)$ because of the complete inclusion of the objects in tolerance relation class, and it results in $T_B^\lambda(x) \subseteq I_B(x)$. For each $x \in U$, suppose $I_B(x) \subseteq X$, then $T_B^\lambda(x) \subseteq X$ and the reverse does not exist because the objects in $T_B^\lambda(x) \backslash I_B(x)$ do not definitely belong to X. From the analysis above, supposing $X_{BT}^\lambda = \{x \in U | T_B^\lambda(x) \subseteq X\}$, we assert $X_B^T \subseteq X_{BT}^\lambda$. Given the neighborhood noted by $T_B^\lambda(x)$ of any object in the universe, $X_{BT}^{\lambda\beta}$ includes all the objects according to $|T_B^\lambda(x) \cap X|/|T_B^\lambda(x)| \geq \beta$

but X_{BT}^{λ} only includes the objects whose neighborhood outright belong to X, so the existence of the objects supports $1 > |T_B^{\lambda}(x) \cap X|/|T_B^{\lambda}(x)| \geq \beta$, and it results in $X_{BT}^{\lambda} \subseteq X_{BT}^{\lambda\beta}$. From all the above, we assert $X_B^T \subseteq X_{BT}^{\lambda\beta} \subseteq X$. The proof of $X_{BT}^{\lambda\beta} \subseteq X_{BS}^{\lambda\beta}$ is similar with $X_B^T \subseteq X_B^S$ in [6], so we assert $X_B^T \subseteq X_{BT}^{\lambda\beta} \subseteq X_{BS}^{\lambda\beta} \subseteq X$; also because the upper approximation is symmetric to the lower approximation, property (2) is proven.

Similar with the above proof, the partial order relation between $R_{\lambda}^B(x)$ and $I_B(x)$ can induce property (3).

We can deduce property (4) from property (2) and (3).

Example in Table 1 is introduced to compare the tolerance, similarity and probabilistic approximation model. The probabilistic approximations based on similarity are a refinement of those obtained under the tolerance relation as shown in property (4), so the following analyzes the probabilistic method only based on tolerance relation and the results of the former is better.

Table 1. An given incomplete table

C	a_1	a_2	a_3	a_4	a_5	a_6	a_7	a_8	a_9	a_{10}	a_{11}	a_{12}
c_1	3	2	2	*	*	2	3	*	3	1	*	3
c_2	2	3	3	2	2	3	*	0	2	*	2	2
c_3	1	2	2	*	*	2	*	0	1	*	*	1
c_4	0	0	0	1	1	1	3	*	3	*	*	*
d	Φ	Φ	Ψ	Φ	Ψ	Ψ	Φ	Ψ	Ψ	Φ	Ψ	Φ

For the above system $DS = \{U, B; \{d\}, V, f\}$, the results of two-layer tolerance neighborhood and approximation regions with the threshold pair $(0.6, 0.6)$ are:

$T_B^{\lambda}(a_1) : (a_1, a_{11}, a_{12}),\quad T_B^{\lambda}(a_2) : (a_2, a_3),\quad T_B^{\lambda}(a_3) : (a_2, a_3),$

$T_B^{\lambda}(a_4) : (a_4, a_{12}),\quad T_B^{\lambda}(a_5) : (a_5, a_{12}),\quad T_B^{\lambda}(a_6) : (a_6),$

$T_B^{\lambda}(a_7) : (a_7, a_9, a_{12}),\quad T_B^{\lambda}(a_8) : (a_8),\quad T_B^{\lambda}(a_9) : (a_7, a_9, a_{11}, a_{12}),$

$T_B^{\lambda}(a_{10}) : (a_{10}),\quad T_B^{\lambda}(a_{11}) : (a_1, a_9, a_{11}),\quad T_B^{\lambda}(a_{12}) : (a_1, a_4, a_5, a_7, a_9, a_{12});$

$\Phi_{BT}^{\lambda\beta} = (a_1, a_4, a_7, a_{10}, a_{12});\quad \Phi_{\lambda\beta}^{BT} = (a_1, a_2, a_3, a_4, a_5, a_7, a_9, a_{10}, a_{12});$

$\Psi_{BT}^{\lambda\beta} = (a_6, a_8, a_{11});\quad \Psi_{\lambda\beta}^{BT}|(0.6, 0.6) = (a_2, a_3, a_5, a_6, a_8, a_9, a_{11}).$

Table 2. The cardinality of approximation result

App	T_B	S_B	Probabilistic method with pair(λ, β)			
			(0.6,0.6)	(0.6,0.7)	(0.7,0.6)	(0.7,0.7)
$|L(\Phi)|$	0	2	5	3	5	3
$|H(\Phi)|$	11	9	9	10	8	8
$|L(\Psi)|$	1	3	3	2	4	4
$|H(\Psi)|$	12	10	7	10	7	9

Given different threshold pairs, the cardinalities of the lower and upper approximations through two-layer method are listed in Table 2 for comparison, where T_B and S_B are classical methods. Except for the properties mentioned above, relative to the existent methods, the probabilistic method has another two advantages to control the boundary concerning the precision thresholds quantitatively. The probability based two-layer method can increase the positive region and decrease the boundary through the threshold pair (λ, β); the quality of the two-layer method decreases while λ rises and the quality rises while β rises.

6.   Conclusion

This paper begins with the functions of approximation sets in the view of decision reducing, and then it expands the boundary approximation with a probabilistic method though two layers. The major contribution of this paper is to control the cardinality of the rough set of decision class under both the granulation credibility threshold and the graduation credibility threshold. More topics such as reducing algorithm development and the experimental analysis of parameters on large real-life dataset will be done in further research.

References

1. Pawlak Z. (1991) Rough Sets: Theoretical Aspects of Reasoning about Data. Kluwer Academic Publishers, Dordrecht, Vol. 9.
2. Stenfanowski J., A. Tsoukias, (2001) Incomplete information tables and rough classification. *Computational Intelligence*, 17:454-466.
3. Skowron A., Slowinski R., Synak P. (2005) Approximation spaces and information granulation. *T. Rough Sets.* pages 175-189
4. Kryszkiewicz M. (1998) Rough set approach to incomplete information system. *Information Sciences.* 112:39-49.
5. Slowinski R., Vanderpooten D. (2000) A generalized definition of rough approximation based on similarity. *IEEE Transactions on Data and Knowledge Engineering.*
6. Stefanowski J., Tsoukias A. (1999) On the extension of rough sets under incomplete information. In: *N. Zhong, A. Skowron, S. Ohsuga, (ads.), New Directions in Rough Sets, Data Mining and Granular Soft Computing.* LNAI 1711:73-81.
7. Ziarko W. (2005) Probabilistic Rough Sets. *RSFDGrC.* 1:283-293.
8. Wang G. Y. (2002) Extension of Rough Set Under Incomplete Information Systems. *Journal of Computer Research and Development.* 39(10):1238-1243.
9. Gong Z. T., Sun B. Z., Shao Y. B., Chen D. G., He Q. (2004) Variable Precision Rough Set Model Based on General Relation. *Proceedings of the Third International Conference on Machine Learning and Cybernetics, Shanghai.* pages 26-29.
10. Wang J. Y., Zhou G. C. (2005) Variable Precision Rough Set model in Incomplete Information System. *Proceeding of the Fourth International Conference on Machine Learning and Cybernetics, Guangzhou,* pages 1883-1887.
11. Mi J. S., Wu W. Z., Zhang W. X. (2004) Approaches to knowledge reduction based on variable precision rough set model. *Information Sciences.* 159:255-272.
12. Lenarcik A., Piasta Z. (1887) Probabilistic rough classifiers with mixture of discrete and continuous attributes. In *Lin T.Y., Cerone N.(ed.), Rough sets and Data Mining, Kluwer Academic Publisher.* pages 373-390.

DDL: EMBRACING ACTIONS INTO SEMANTIC WEB

He Huang
Key Laboratory of Intelligent Information Processing, Institute of Computing Technology, Chinese Academy of Sciences, P.O. Box 2704-28, Beijing 100080 China
Graduate School of the Chinese Academy of Sciences, Beijing, China
huangh@ics.ict.ac.cn

Zhongzhi Shi
Key Laboratory of Intelligent Information Processing, Institute of Computing Technology, Chinese Academy of Sciences, P.O. Box 2704-28, Beijing 100080 China
shizz@ics.ict.ac.cn

Jianwu Wang
Institute of Computing Technology, Chinese Academy of Sciences, P.O.Box 2704-28, Beijing 100080 China
Graduate School of the Chinese Academy of Sciences, Beijing, China
wjw@software.ict.ac.cn

Rui Huang
Key Laboratory of Intelligent Information Processing, Institute of Computing Technology, Chinese Academy of Sciences, P.O. Box 2704-28, Beijing 100080 China
Graduate School of the Chinese Academy of Sciences, Beijing, China
huangr@ics.ict.ac.cn

Abstract   Service description usually presumes a representation of the world model. The Description Logic (DL) is an efficient way for representing the world model, esp. on Semantic Web, because of its framework, decidable reasoning, and popularity. DL can bring structure to services, but only DL itself is inadequate for modelling dynamic aspect of Web services. In this paper, Dynamic Description Logic (DDL) is proposed to combine DLs with action formalisms. The interaction between actions and the DL-based world model is embodied in two aspects. On one hand, DL knowledge base provides knowledge and information for the reasoning on actions; on the other hand, the information stored in DL knowledge base is changed by the execution of actions. In DDL, two basic reasoning tasks

Please use the following format when citing this chapter:

Huang, H., Shi, Z., Wang, J., Huang, R., 2006, in IFIP International Federation for Information Processing, Volume 228, Intelligent Information Processing III, eds. Z. Shi, Shimohara K., Feng D., (Boston: Springer), pp. 81–90.

are defined to check precondition and effects of actions. Based on the relationship between DDL and a transition system, a reasoning support for DDL is also given by translating actions into logic programs. By the combination of DLs and actions, DDL brings a better view of how services impact the world, facilitates interoperation between services, and enables the reuse of already available algorithms and engines for service reasoning. Thus, it can provide a logical way for embracing actions into Semantic Web.

Keywords: Dynamic Description Logic, action formalism, Semantic Web, Web Services

1.   Introduction

Now we are witnessing the proliferation of service offers accumulated on the Web. As the next generation of the Web, the Semantic Web [Berners-Lee et al., 2001] should support reasoning on not only semantic content but also services. Description Logics (DLs) [Baader et al., 2002] are a family of logic-based knowledge representation languages. Several DL-based ontology languages (e.g., OWL [Patel-Schneider et al., 2004]) are used to develop ontologies of Web services, e.g. OWL-S [Coalition, 2004]. However, DL by itself is inadequate for service reasoning. DLs were originally designed for representing only static knowledge. Without notion of modelling changes, DLs are unable to model the dynamic aspect of services (i.e., what changes of the world they cause under certain conditions), and neither to support reasoning on a series of such changes.

Based on our previous work on Dynamic Description Logics (DDL)[Shi et al., 2005], we extends DDL to model the dynamic aspect of services and support reasoning on services. DDL is designed to combine DLs with action formalisms by taking consideration of the following two aspects. On one hand, Web services can be abstracted as actions with preconditions and effects in the sense that services impact the world by changing the state of the world [McIlraith et al., 2001]. Thus, theories about actions in AI communities can be applied to model dynamic feature of Web service. On the other hand, service description usually presumes a representation of the world model, where the preconditions and effects of services root in [Ponnekanti and Fox, 2002]. DLs are suitable for the world model description, esp. on the Semantic Web, in that DLs can describe structural knowledge in a formal and network-based way, and provide decidable reasoning, too.

In DDL, the structure of the world is captured in TBox and the current information (or facts) about the world is stored in ABox. A formal meaning is given to the interaction between actions and the DL-based world model. Preconditions and effects of an action are defined by using vocabulary defined in TBox. The execution of an action causes the changes of facts stored in ABox and the semantics of the action is interpreted as interpretation transformation that corresponds to the changes. A group of action constructors are defined for forming complex actions out of primitive ones. Two basic reasoning problems (i.e. executability and projection) are discussed. A reasoning support for DDL is also given by translating actions into logic programs. By the combination, DDL provides a logical way for embracing actions into Semantic Web. It also brings several advantages to Web services on Semantic Web, such as a better view of how services impact the world, interoperation between services, and the reuse of algorithms and engines available for service reasoning.

Due to space limitation, we do not introduce the DLs in this paper. Interested readers can refer to [Baader et al., 2002] for review. The rest of this paper is organized as follows. The DDL formalism is described in section 2. A reasoning support for DDL is given in section 3. Related works are discussed in section 4. A conclusion and future research are given in section 5.

2.   Dynamic Description Logic Formalism

Let $\mathcal{K} = (\mathcal{T}, \mathcal{A})$ be a DL knowledge base composed of an acyclic TBox $\mathcal{T}$ and an ABox $\mathcal{A}$. In this paper, we restrict ourselves on *acyclic* TBox. Based on it, we introduce the DDL formalism by defining the syntax and semantics of actions. Two reasoning tasks are described.

Syntax and Semantics of Actions

Actions without variables are called *ground actions*. Actions can be parameterized by introducing variables in place of object names. Ground actions can be viewed as actions where parameters have already been instantiated by object names, while parametric actions should be viewed as a compact representation of all its ground instances. For simplicity, we concentrate on *ground actions*. Actions can be nondeterministic, but in DDL we only consider deterministic actions.

DEFINITION 1 (ATOMIC ACTION[SHI ET AL., 2005]) *Given $\mathcal{K}$, an atomic action description based on $\mathcal{K}$ is in the form of $\mathbb{A} = (P_{\mathbb{A}}, E_{\mathbb{A}})$, where*

- $\mathbb{A}$ *is the action name;*

- *the pre-condition, $P_{\mathbb{A}}$, is a finite set of ABox assertions;*

- *the effects of the action, $E_{\mathbb{A}}$, is a finite set of pairs of the form b_i/h_i, where b_i is a finite set of ABox assertions, while h_i is a literal of an assertion, e.g., $C(a)$, $R(a,b)$, $\neg C(a)$, or $\neg R(a,b)$.*

An atom action is specified by first stating the preconditions under which the action is applicable. Secondly, one must specify how the action impacts the world with effects b_i/h_i. b_i/h_i describes under the condition b_i (called body) doing the action results in the addition of h_i (called head) if h_i is in the positive form, or the remove of $\neg h_i$ if h_i is in the negative form. According to the law of inertia, only those facts that are forced to change by the effects should be changed by the performance of the action [Reiter, 2001]. Given two different atomic actions, we say that they are similar if they differ only by the heads in their effects. This paper focuses only on those actions that are not similar.

Given a declarative specification of the atomic actions, a complex action can be specified in terms of atomic ones.

DEFINITION 2 (ACTIONS[SHI ET AL., 2005]) *Let N_A be a set of atomic action names, an action is in the form of:*

$$A, B \rightarrow A_S \,|\, A; B \,|\, A \cup B \,|\, A^* \,|\, \psi? \tag{1}$$

An action can be defined as either an atomic action A_S, or a complex action composed of these defined atomic actions by using constructors. Sequential composition of actions, $A; B$, means "Do A and then do B". Non-deterministic choice of actions, $A \cup B$, means "Do either A or B". Iteration of action, A^*, means "iteratively do A finitely many (including zero) times". Test of formula, $\psi?$, means the test of current truth value of ψ, i.e., $\psi? \equiv (\{\psi\}, \{\})$, where ψ is a DL formula.

The widely used conditional choice and loops can be defined in terms of these constructs:

$$\text{if } \psi \text{ then } A \text{ else } B \equiv (\psi?; A) \cup (\neg\psi?; B)$$
$$\text{while } \psi \text{ do } A \text{ endWhile} \equiv (\psi?; A)^*; \neg\psi?$$

In this paper, we focus on acyclic actions, which means an action can not be composed of itself or can not appear on the right side of its own definition. Given an acyclic action, an action can be always expanded into a sequence that is composed with only atomic actions.

Now, we define the semantic of the action by showing how it makes an interpretation transformed into another.

DEFINITION 3 (ORDERED INTERPRETATIONS[BAADER ET AL., 2005]) *Given $\mathcal{K}$ and an interpretation $\mathcal{I}$ that $\mathcal{I} \models \mathcal{K}$. The performance of A in $\mathcal{K}$ results in a new interpretation $\mathcal{I}'$. We say that $\mathcal{I}'$ is the A-induced ordered interpretation to $\mathcal{I}$, denoted $\mathcal{I} \preceq_A \mathcal{I}'$, if $\mathcal{I}'$ is obtained through following steps:*

- *if A is an atomic action and $A = (P_A, E_A)$,*

  - *for each primitive concept A in $\mathcal{T}$,*

$$A^{\mathcal{I}'} = A^{\mathcal{I}} \cup \{a^{\mathcal{I}} \,|\, \forall(\varphi/A(a)) \in E_A, \mathcal{I} \models \varphi\}$$
$$\setminus \{a^{\mathcal{I}} \,|\, \forall(\varphi/\neg A(a)) \in E_A, \mathcal{I} \models \varphi\} \tag{2}$$

– *for each role R in $\mathcal{T}$,*

$$R^{\mathcal{I}'} = R^{\mathcal{I}} \cup \{(a^{\mathcal{I}}, b^{\mathcal{I}}) \mid \forall(\varphi/R(a,b)) \in E_{\mathbb{A}}, \mathcal{I} \models \varphi\}$$
$$\setminus \{(a^{\mathcal{I}}, b^{\mathcal{I}}) \mid \forall(\varphi/\neg R(a,b)) \in E_{\mathbb{A}}, \mathcal{I} \models \varphi\} \quad (3)$$

– *for each defined concept C, it is expanded into C' which contains only primitive concepts. The interpretation of C is uniquely determined by the interpretation of the primitive concepts in C'.*

- *if $\mathbb{A} = \mathbb{B}\,;\mathbb{C}$, and $\exists \mathcal{I}'', \mathcal{I} \preceq_{\mathbb{B}} \mathcal{I}'' \wedge \mathcal{I}'' \preceq_{\mathbb{C}} \mathcal{I}';$*

- *if $\mathbb{A} = \mathbb{B} \cup \mathbb{C}$, and $\mathcal{I} \preceq_{\mathbb{B}} \mathcal{I}' \vee \mathcal{I} \preceq_{\mathbb{C}} \mathcal{I}';$*

- *if $\mathbb{A} = \mathbb{B}^*$, and $\forall n(\geq 0), \forall i(0 \leq i \leq n), \exists \mathcal{I}'', \mathcal{I} \preceq_{\mathbb{B}^i} \mathcal{I}'' \wedge \mathcal{I}'' \preceq_{\mathbb{B}^{n-i}} \mathcal{I}';$*

- *if $\mathbb{A} = \psi\,?$, and $\mathcal{I} \preceq_{\mathbb{A}} \mathcal{I}.$*

Clearly, $\mathcal{I}$ and $\mathcal{I}'$ share the same domain and individual name interpretation, and $\mathcal{I}'$ is determined by $\mathbb{A}$, $\mathcal{T}$ and $\mathcal{I}$.

Reasoning about Actions

Before trying to perform an action, it is needed to check whether it is executable in the current state[Baader et al., 2005], i.e., whether all necessary preconditions are satisfied.

DEFINITION 4 (EXECUTABILITY) *Given $\mathcal{K}$ and an interpretation $\mathcal{I}$ that $\mathcal{I} \models \mathcal{K}$, an action $\mathbb{A}$ is said to be executable in $\mathcal{I}$, denoted $poss(\mathbb{A}, \mathcal{I})$,*

- *if $\mathbb{A}$ is an atomic action, $\mathbb{A} = (P_{\mathbb{A}}, E_{\mathbb{A}})$, and $\mathcal{I} \models P_{\mathbb{A}};$*

- *if $\mathbb{A} = \mathbb{B}\,;\mathbb{C}$, and $poss(\mathbb{B}, \mathcal{I}) \wedge \mathcal{I} \preceq_{\mathbb{B}} \mathcal{I}' \wedge poss(\mathbb{C}, \mathcal{I}');$*

- *if $\mathbb{A} = \mathbb{B} \cup \mathbb{C}$, and $poss(\mathbb{B}, \mathcal{I}) \vee poss(\mathbb{C}, \mathcal{I});$*

- *if $\mathbb{A} = \mathbb{B}^*$, and $\forall n(\geq 0), \forall i(0 \leq i \leq n), poss(\mathbb{B}^i, \mathcal{I}) \wedge \mathcal{I} \preceq_{\mathbb{B}^i} \mathcal{I}' \wedge poss(\mathbb{B}^{n-i}, \mathcal{I}');$*

- *if $\mathbb{A} = \psi\,?$, and $\mathcal{I} \models \psi.$*

Since an action impacts the world, it is needed to check whether performing it can result in the desired effects, i.e., whether a formula that we want to make true really holds after the performance[Baader et al., 2005].

DEFINITION 5 (PROJECTION) *Given $\mathcal{K}$ and an interpretation $\mathcal{I}$ that $\mathcal{I} \models \mathcal{K}$, a DL formula φ is a consequence of performing $\mathbb{A}$ in $\mathcal{I}$, denoted $[\mathbb{A}]\varphi$, iff $\mathcal{I} \preceq_{\mathbb{A}} \mathcal{I}' \wedge \mathcal{I}' \models \varphi.$*

Actually, executability and projection can be reduced into each other [Baader et al., 2005]. Therefore, we only consider the reasoning task of executability in section 3.

3. Reasoning Support for DDL

In DDL, $\mathcal{T}$ brings structure to the world model of an action domain. Each interpretation that models $\mathcal{T}$ denotes a state of the world. A set of actions defined on the world model depicts the dynamic features of the action domain. The execution of an action causes the interpretation transformation. In this context, DDL can be viewed as a transition system consisting of:

1 a set $W = \{\mathcal{I}_1, ..., \mathcal{I}_n\}$, where $\forall i \, (1 \leq i \leq n), \mathcal{I}_i \models \mathcal{T}$, and $\mathcal{I}_i$ is called a *state*;

2 a function $V : F \times W \rightarrow \{$true,false$\}$, where F is the set of DL formulae and $V(\psi, \mathcal{I}_i)$ means whether $\mathcal{I}_i \models \psi$ is true or false;

3 a set $T \subseteq W \times S \times W$, where S is the set of actions, and $\langle \mathcal{I}_i, \mathbb{A}, \mathcal{I}_j \rangle \in T$ denotes that $\mathcal{I}_i \preceq_\mathbb{A} \mathcal{I}_j$.

Logic Program (see, e.g., [Baral and Gelfond, 1994] for review) is an efficient way for representing a transition system [Lifschitz and Turner, 1999]. In order to provide reasoning support for DDL, we translate actions into a logic program. Based on this translation, the action reasoning in DDL can be transformed into computing answer sets on a logic program.

Several symbols are needed for the translation. There is a distinguished binary function symbol $do : S \times W \rightarrow W$; $do(\mathbb{A}, \mathcal{I})$ denotes the successor state to $\mathcal{I}$ resulting from performing the action $\mathbb{A}$. The qualification problem for actions is denoted by a predicate symbol $poss : S \times W$; $poss(\mathbb{A}, \mathcal{I})$ means that $\mathbb{A}$ is executable in $\mathcal{I}$. And another function $holds(\psi, \mathcal{I})$ asserts that a certain fact "holds" in a certain state, i.e., $\mathcal{I} \models \psi$.

Now we are ready for defining the translation π from DDL to logic programming. We tailor the methods mentioned in [Gelfond and Lifschitz, 1993, Lifschitz and Turner, 1999] to do the translation.

Translating Atomic Actions

Let D be a domain description of DDL without similar actions. The program πD will consist of four rules which are motivated by the "commonsense law of inertia". These rules are used to specify that DL formulae normally remain the same after performing an action.

$$holds(\psi, do(\mathbb{A}, \mathcal{I})) \leftarrow holds(\psi, \mathcal{I}), not\ Noninertial(\psi, \mathbb{A}, \mathcal{I}) \qquad (4)$$
$$\neg holds(\psi, do(\mathbb{A}, \mathcal{I})) \leftarrow \neg holds(\psi, \mathcal{I}), not\ Noninertial(\psi, \mathbb{A}, \mathcal{I}) \qquad (5)$$
$$holds(\psi, \mathcal{I}) \leftarrow holds(\psi, do(\mathbb{A}, \mathcal{I})), not\ Noninertial(\psi, \mathbb{A}, \mathcal{I})$$
$$(6)$$
$$\neg holds(\psi, \mathcal{I}) \leftarrow \neg holds(\psi, do(\mathbb{A}, \mathcal{I})), not\ Noninertial(\psi, \mathbb{A}, \mathcal{I})$$
$$(7)$$

Rules (4) and (5) state that, when a formula is known to be true (or false) in the past, generally it remains true (or false) after performing an action. Rules (6) and (7) state that, when a formula is known to be true (or false) after performing an action, generally it was true (or false) before the performance. The auxiliary predicate $Noninertial$ is used to show the abnormal cases.

The translation of an primitive action $\mathbb{A} = (P_{\mathbb{A}}, E_{\mathbb{A}})$ is, for all formulae $\psi_1, ..., \psi_n \in P_{\mathbb{A}}$,

$$poss(\mathbb{A}, \mathcal{I}) \leftarrow holds(\psi_1, \mathcal{I}), ..., holds(\psi_n, \mathcal{I}) \qquad (8)$$

and for each condition $b_i/h_i(1 \leq i \leq m) \in E_{\mathbb{A}}$,

$$holds(h_i, do(\mathbb{A}, \mathcal{I})) \leftarrow poss(\mathbb{A}, \mathcal{I}), holds(b_i, \mathcal{I}) \qquad (9)$$
$$holds(b_i, \mathcal{I}) \leftarrow poss(\mathbb{A}, \mathcal{I}), \overline{holds(h_i, \mathcal{I})}, holds(h_i, do(\mathbb{A}, \mathcal{I}))$$
$$(10)$$
$$\overline{holds(b_i, \mathcal{I})} \leftarrow poss(\mathbb{A}, \mathcal{I}), \overline{holds(h_i, do(\mathbb{A}, \mathcal{I}))} \qquad (11)$$
$$Noninertial(|h_i|, \mathbb{A}, \mathcal{I}) \leftarrow poss(\mathbb{A}, \mathcal{I}), \overline{holds(h_i, \mathcal{I})}, holds(b_i, \mathcal{I}) \qquad (12)$$

where $\overline{holds(x, y)}$ is the literal complementary to $holds(x, y)$ and $|x|$ means the absolute value of x. These rules have following meanings:

- Rule (8) allows us to prove the action is executable, if the preconditions h_i $(1 \leq i \leq m)$ are satisfied.

- For each each condition $b_i/h_i(1 \leq i \leq m) \in E_{\mathbb{A}}$, when $\mathbb{A}$ is executable,

  - Rule (9) allow us to prove that h_i will hold after performing $\mathbb{A}$ under the condition of b_i;
  - Rule (10) justifies if the truth value of h_i has changed to true after performing $\mathbb{A}$, then we can conclude that b_i was satisfied when $\mathbb{A}$ was performed.
  - Rule (11) allows us to conclude that b_i was false from the fact that performing an action did not lead to h_i to be true after performing the action.

– Rule (12) states $|h_i|$ is affected by performing $\mathbb{A}$. $Noninertial(|h_i|, \mathbb{A}, \mathcal{I})$ means that $|h_i|$ does not conform to the law of inertial. It disables the inertial rules (4 – 7) in the cases when $|h_i|$ can be affected by $\mathbb{A}$.

Translating Complex Actions

The translation of a complex $\mathbb{A}$ is defined as:

- if $\mathbb{A} = \mathbb{B}; \mathbb{C}$, then

$$poss(\mathbb{A}, \mathcal{I}) \leftarrow poss(\mathbb{B}, \mathcal{I}), poss(\mathbb{C}, do(\mathbb{B}, \mathcal{I})) \tag{13}$$

- if $\mathbb{A} = \mathbb{B} \cup \mathbb{C}$, then

$$poss(\mathbb{A}, \mathcal{I}) \leftarrow poss(\mathbb{B}, \mathcal{I}) \tag{14}$$
$$poss(\mathbb{A}, \mathcal{I}) \leftarrow poss(\mathbb{C}, \mathcal{I}) \tag{15}$$

- if $\mathbb{A} = \mathbb{B}^*$, then $\forall n (n \geq 0)$

$$poss(\mathbb{A}, \mathcal{I}) \leftarrow poss(\mathbb{B}^1, \mathcal{I}), poss(\mathbb{B}^2, \mathcal{I}), ..., poss(\mathbb{B}^n, \mathcal{I}) \tag{16}$$

- if $\mathbb{A} = \psi?$, then

$$poss(\mathbb{A}, \mathcal{I}) \leftarrow poss(\psi, \mathcal{I}) \tag{17}$$

Through the translation π on actions, the reasoning on DLL is transformed into computing answer set of a logic program. Of course, to compute the answer set needs to use DL reasoning for the DL fragment of DDL. The combination of DL reasoning and answer set semantics of logic programs for DDL reasoning, as well as the complexity of this hybrid reasoning, will be discussed in other papers.

4. Related Work

Motivated by the expressive limitations of DLs in non-structural knowledge representation, several methods (e.g., [Levy and Rousset, 1996, Horrocks et al., 2003]) have been proposed to combine DLs with rules. In these combinations, the rules can be viewed as constraints that the domain should satisfy. The rule-extended DLs still describe domain knowledge in a static sense. Thus, the representation of actions' functionalities is beyond the scope of them.

DLs were originally designed for representing only static knowledge. To take into account changes in time or under certain actions, it is natural to extend it by dynamics-related formalisms (e.g. modal logic, action formalisms, and temporal logic). In [Wolter and Zakharyaschev, 2000], a dynamic dimension was introduced via extending the DL with propositional dynamic logic (PDL) for representing and processing knowledge in dynamic application domain. In this method, actions were treated as modal operators, but no action description mechanism was given. In [Huang et al., 2005], an interval-based knowledge model was presented to bring structure to time-varying information by providing temporal constructs for concepts, relationships and integrity constraints, but no explicit action description was given. In [Baader et al., 2005], an action formalism based on DLs was presented to model dynamic features of Web services. The complexity of reasoning task was also analyzed according to different choice of DLs. But no other action operator except for sequential composition was defined, which weakens the capability of the formalism.

5. Conclusion and Future Work

In this paper, DDL is designed to combine DLs with action formalisms. The interactions between actions and the DL-based world model are embodied in two aspects. On one hand, DL reasoning provides basis for interpreting action semantics and checking executability and projection. On the other hand, actions are defined in terms of preconditions and effects by using vocabulary defined in DL, and executions of actions impact the DL knowledge bases by changing facts stored in ABox. We have shown that the interaction can be viewed as a transition system. Based on the observation, reasoning tasks in DDL can be translated into answer set computing in logic programs.

DDL provides a logical way for embracing actions into Semantic Web. And it can bring several advantages to Web Service applications, esp. on the Semantic Web. First, the framework of DLs makes a clear distinction between intensional knowledge in TBox and extensional knowledge in ABox. Thus, DDL enables a better view of how services impact the world by using DL to represent the world model. Second, DDL facilitates interoperation between services. Based on DLs, modelling services can reuse terms of those already existing domain ontologies, and thus provide services with shared knowledge. Third, the reasoning support for DDL enables the reuse of those efficient and scalable algorithms and engines available for DL reasoning and logic programming, and combine them for Web service composition, which is also our future work.

Acknowledgements

This work has been funded by the National Basic Research Priorities Programme (No.2003CB317004) and the National Science Foundation of China (No.90604017).

References

[Baader et al., 2005] Baader, F., Lutz, C., Milicic, M., Sattler, U., and Wolter, F. (2005). A description logic based approach to reasoning about web services. In *Proceedings of the WWW 2005 Workshop on Web Service Semantics (WSS2005)*, Chiba City, Japan.

[Baader et al., 2002] Baader, Franz, Calvanese, Diego, McGuinness, Deborah, Nardi, Daniele, and Patel-Schneider, Perter F. (2002). *The Description Logic Handbook: Theory, Implementation and Applciations*. Cambridge University Press.

[Baral and Gelfond, 1994] Baral, Chitta and Gelfond, Michael (1994). Logic programming and knowledge representation. *Journal of Logic Programming*, (19/20):73–148.

[Berners-Lee et al., 2001] Berners-Lee, T., Hendler, J., and Lassila, O. (2001). The semantic web. *Scientific American*, 284(5):34–43.

[Coalition, 2004] Coalition, The OWL-S (2004). Owl-s 1.1 release. http://www.daml.org/services/owl-s/1.1/.

[Gelfond and Lifschitz, 1993] Gelfond, Michael and Lifschitz, Vladimir (1993). Representing action and change by logic programs. *Journal of Logic Programming*, 17(2,3,4):301–321.

[Horrocks et al., 2003] Horrocks, Ian, Patel-Schneider, Peter F., Boley, Harold, Tabet, Said, Grosof, Benjamin, and Dean, Mike (2003). Swrl: A semantic web rule language combining owl and ruleml. (Version 0.5).

[Huang et al., 2005] Huang, He, Shi, Zhongzhi, He, Xiaoxiao, and Qiu, Lirong (2005). An interval-based knowledge model and query language for temporal information. In *Proceedings of Eighth Pacific Rim International Workshop on Multi-Agents (PRIMA'05)*, pages 401–415.

[Levy and Rousset, 1996] Levy, Alon Y. and Rousset, Marie-Christine (1996). CARIN: A representation language combining horn rules and description logics. In *European Conference on Artificial Intelligence*, pages 323–327.

[Lifschitz and Turner, 1999] Lifschitz, Vladimir and Turner, Hudson (1999). Representing transition systems by logic programs. In *Logic Programming and Non-monotonic Reasoning (LPNMR'99)*, number 1730 in Lecture Notes in AI (LNAI), pages 92–106.

[McIlraith et al., 2001] McIlraith, S., Son, T.C., and Zeng, H. (2001). Semantic web services. *IEEE Intelligent Systems. Special Issue on the Semantic Web*, 16(2):46–53.

[Patel-Schneider et al., 2004] Patel-Schneider, Peter F., Hayes, Patrick, and Horrocks, Ian (2004). Owl web ontology language semantics and abstract syntax. *W3C Recommendation*.

[Ponnekanti and Fox, 2002] Ponnekanti, S.R. and Fox, A. (2002). Sword: A developer toolkit for web service composition. In *Proceedings of the 11th World Wide Web Conference*.

[Reiter, 2001] Reiter, R. (2001). *Knowledge in Action*. MIT Press.

[Shi et al., 2005] Shi, Zhongzhi, Dong, Mingkai, Jiang, Yuncheng, and Zhang, Haijun (2005). A logic foundation for the semantic web. *Science in China, Series F Information Sciences*, 48(2):161–178.

[Wolter and Zakharyaschev, 2000] Wolter, Frank and Zakharyaschev, Michael (2000). Dynamic description logics. In Segerberg, K., de Rijke, M., Wansing, H., and Zakharyaschev, M., editors, *Advances in Modal Logic*, volume 2. CSLI Publications.

ONE AXIOMATIC SYSTEM
FOR THE ONTOLOGY REVISION*

Yu Sun,[1,2] Yuefei Sui,[2] and Zhiping Li[3]

[1] *School of Computer Science and Information Technology*
Yunnan Normal University, Kunming 650092
sunyu_km@hotmail.com

[2] *Key Laboratory of Intelligent Information Processing*
Institute of Computing Technology
Chinese Academy of Sciences, Beijing 100080
yfsui@ict.ac.cn

[3] *Education Technology Center*
Yunnan Normal University, Kunming 650092
ynnulzp@sohu.com

Abstract   An ontology consists of concepts and the subsumption relation between these concepts, and is assumed to be a tree under the subsumption relation. In the process of building and maintaining ontologies, new statements which may contradict with exiting statements are added to the ontologies constantly. The ontology revision is necessary to accommodate new statements. In terms of the method of the axiomatization, one axiom system for the ontology revision, called the Z axiom system, is given, which is proved to satisfy the principles of the success, consistency and minimal change. Unlike the belief revision which is monotonic, the ontology revision may not be monotonic, and not only extracts some statements contradictory with a revising statement, extracts statements which are not contradictory with the revising statement, but also adds new statements to keep the tree structure of the revised ontology and satisfy the minimal change. One concrete ontology revision operator is proposed, which is proved to satisfy the Z axiom system.

Keywords: Ontologies, Belief revision, Subsumption relation, Default inheritance

*This work is supported by the NSF (grant no. 60273019, 60496326, 60573063, and 60573064), the National 973 Programme (grants no. 2003CB317008 and G1999032701) and the Foundation of Yunnan Province (grants no. 04F00062, 2004YX42, 2004F0017Q, 03Y312D and 2005F0022Q).

Please use the following format when citing this chapter:

Sun, Y., Sui, Y., Li, Z., 2006, in IFIP International Federation for Information Processing, Volume 228, Intelligent Information Processing III, eds. Z. Shi, Shimohara K., Feng D., (Boston: Springer), pp. 91–100.

1.   Introduction

A general approach for studying belief revision is to provide a set of postulates for belief revision functions. These postulates constrain what revision
functions should satisfy in the process of revision, but say little about how to
implement these functions. The AGM approach [2,3] perhaps provides the
best-known set of such postulates and an extended discussion on the postulates
was given in [4,5]. The AGM axiom system is not very appropriate for the
iterated belief revision [1]. Hence, Darwiche and Pearl [1] put forward a well-
known proposal which extends the AGM axiom system with four additional
postulates for the iterated belief revision [6,7].

The belief revision has three basic principles [8,9]: the principles of the success, the consistency and the minimal change. Furthermore, the belief revision
is monotonic. That is, given two knowledge base K and K', if $K \vdash K'$, then
$K \circ \alpha \vdash K' \circ \alpha$, where $K \circ \alpha$ is the knowledge base resulted from revising
K by α. For a knowledge base K and a revising statement α, a belief revision
is not to revise statements in K, but to extract some statements in K to make
$K' \cup \{\alpha\}$ consistent for the remaining subset K' of K.

McGuinness [10] proposed that a simple ontology should contain the following items:

(1) finite controlled (extensible) vocabulary;

(2) unambiguous interpretation of classes and term relationships;

(3) strict hierarchical subclass relationships between classes.

In [11], the authors classified the currently used ontology languages according to whether ontologies contain concepts, taxonomies, relations and functions, axioms and instances. For the simplicity of discussion, we assume that
an ontology consists of the following three kinds of statements and their nega-
tions:

• the subsumption relation between concepts: $C \sqsubseteq D$;

• a concept having a property: $C \Rightarrow \varphi$;

• a concept defaultly having a property: $C \Rightarrow_d \varphi$,

where C, D are concepts, φ, ψ are properties. We assume that O is a tree under
the subsumption relation between concepts.

The ontology revision is a process of changing ontologies to accommodate
statements that are possibly inconsistent with existing statements. For an ontology O and a revising statement θ, let $O \circ \theta$ be the ontology that results from
revising O by θ. The ontology revision has the following properties which the
belief revision does not have:

◇ The ontology revision is not monotonic. That is, for any ontologies O, O'
and a revising statement θ, if $O \vdash O'$ then it is possible that $O \circ \theta \nvdash O' \circ \theta$.

◇ To keep the tree structure of $O \circ \theta$, according to the structure of O, we
not only extract a set of statements S from O to ensure that $(O \cup \{\theta\}) - S$

is consistent, but extract another set of statements Δ other than S from O and add a set of new statements T other than $\{\theta\}$ to $O \circ \theta$.

By the axiomatization, an axiom system for the ontology revision, called the Z axiom system, will be proposed, and proved to satisfy the principles of success, consistency and minimal change. According to the inconsistency of θ with O, $Th(O)$ and O^{CWA}, a concrete ontology revision operator will be given and proved to satisfy the Z axiom system.

The paper is organized as follows: in section 2, the definition and presuppositions of ontologies are given, and the logical implications in ontologies are discussed; in section 3, we give the presuppositions for the ontology revision and according to the structure of ontologies, we propose an axiom system, called the Z axiom system, for the ontology revision satisfying the principles of success, consistency and minimal change. In section 4, a concrete ontology revision operator $\circ$ is given, which is proved to satisfy the Z axiom system. The last section concludes the paper.

2.   Ontologies

In this section, we firstly give the definition and presuppositions of ontologies, then discuss the logical implications in ontologies.

Definition 1. *An ontology O consists of*

- *a set of concepts and properties;*
- *four binary relations: the subsumption relation $\sqsubseteq$ between concepts; the inheritance relation $\Rightarrow$ between concepts and properties, the default inheritance relation $\Rightarrow_d$ between concepts and properties; and*
- *a set of positive statements of forms $C \sqsubseteq D | C \Rightarrow \varphi | C \Rightarrow_d \varphi$ and their negations of forms $C \not\sqsubseteq D | C \not\Rightarrow \varphi | C \not\Rightarrow_d \varphi$, where C, D are concepts and φ, ψ are properties.*

We use U to denote the set of concepts and properties in O. For any concept C, concept C^* is a $\sqsubseteq$-minimal super-concept of C such that there is no D such that $C \sqsubseteq D \in O$ and $D \sqsubseteq C^* \in O$.

For the simplicity, we assume that O is a tree under subsumption relation $\sqsubseteq$, i.e., for any concept C, C^* is unique. This guarantees that as a default theory, O under the implication rules has a unique extension.

Given an ontology O, concepts C, D and properties φ and ψ in U, O is a default theory with defaults. The reasoning in O is the reasoning of default theory (O, W), where W is the set of defaults and implication rules showed in the following:

the transitivity of $\sqsubseteq$ $\qquad$ $\dfrac{C \sqsubseteq D, D \sqsubseteq E}{C \sqsubseteq E}$;

the inheritance rule $\qquad$ $\dfrac{C \sqsubseteq D, D \Rightarrow \varphi}{C \Rightarrow \varphi}$;

the default inheritance rule $\qquad$ $\dfrac{C \sqsubseteq D, D \Rightarrow_d \varphi : C \Rightarrow_d \varphi}{C \Rightarrow_d \varphi}$.

By the presupposition that O is a tree under $\sqsubseteq$, as a default theory, O has a unique extension. Let $Th(O)$ be the unique extension of O. Define $\vdash$ to be the implication relation defined by $Th(O)$, i.e., for any statement δ,

$$O \vdash \delta \text{ iff } \delta \in Th(O).$$

The default theory of $Th(O)$ under the closed world assumption has a unique extension, denoted by O^{CWA}, and

$$O^{\text{CWA}} = \{\neg\delta : O \not\vdash \delta\} \cup Th(O),$$

where δ is a positive statement.

Definition 2. *An ontology O is inconsistent if there is a statement δ such that* $\delta, \neg\delta \in O^{\text{CWA}}$.

Remark. Similar to belief revision, there are two kinds of ontology revision: ontology-set revision and ontology-base revision. In this paper, an ontology O is an ontology base, and its ontology set is $Th(O)$.

3. The ontology revision

In this section, we shall give firstly an example of the ontology revision, and secondly the presuppositions, and then the axioms for the ontology revision.

3.1 One example

Let us take a look at the following example. Example 1 shows our intuition for the ontology revision.

Example 1. We believe that **sparrow** and **penguin** are two kinds of **bird** and **bird** can fly. Formally, the ontology can be represented by

$$O = \{\textbf{sparrow} \sqsubseteq \textbf{bird}, \textbf{penguin} \sqsubseteq \textbf{bird}, \textbf{bird} \Rightarrow flying\}.$$

Assume that later, we find that **penguin** actually cannot fly, that is,

$$\theta = \textbf{penguin} \not\Rightarrow flying.$$

Then we do not believe that **bird** can fly, since **penguin** is a **bird**. In this example, $O \cup \{\theta\}$ is inconsistent and $\neg\theta \in Th(O)$, since $\neg\theta = \textbf{penguin} \Rightarrow$

flying can be inferred from O by the inheritance. Formally,

$$O \circ \theta = \{\text{sparrow} \sqsubseteq \text{bird}, \text{penguin} \sqsubseteq \text{bird},$$
$$\text{penguin} \not\Rightarrow flying\}$$
$$S = \{\text{bird} \Rightarrow flying\};$$
$$\Delta = \emptyset;$$
$$T = \emptyset.$$

This example can be realized by case 2.4.2 in section 4. The following figure shows O and $O \circ \theta$.

Fig. 1. O and $O \circ \theta$

Remark. In example 1, intuitively, we shall still believe that **sparrow** can fly after revision, since **sparrow** and **penguin** are two different kinds of **bird**, and the change of property **penguin** being *flying* should not affect that of **sparrow**. In other words, although **sparrow** $\Rightarrow$ *flying* is not stated explicitly in O, it can be inferred from O by the inheritance and this kind of implicit statements is what O has inherently. For the simplicity, we do not consider the preservation of such implicit statements in the ontology revision.

3.2 The presuppositions for the ontology revision

For an ontology O to be revised and a revising statement θ, we have the following presuppositions:

1. O is consistent;
2. $O \circ \theta$ is an ontology;
3. θ is of forms: $C \sqsubseteq D, C \not\sqsubseteq D, C \Rightarrow \varphi$ and $C \not\Rightarrow \varphi$;
4. The ontology revision satisfies the principle of the success: $\theta \in O \circ \theta$; the principle of the consistency: $O \circ \theta$ is consistent if O is consistent; and the principle of the minimal change: the symmetric difference between the set of statements in O and in $O \circ \theta$, denoted by $sd(O, O \circ \theta)$, is minimal, that is, let $\Gamma(O)$ be the set of statements in O, then $|(\Gamma(O) - \Gamma(O \circ \theta)) \cup (\Gamma(O \circ \theta) - \Gamma(O))|$ is minimal.
5. For the iterated ontology revision, the revising statements are always consistent with each other. For example, if $O \circ \varphi$ is an ontology to be revised and ψ is a revising statement then φ is consistent with ψ.

6. In order to keep the tree structure of $O \circ \theta$, we may add to $O \circ \theta$ new statements which are consistent with $O \cup \{\theta\}$ after the extraction of the statement of the subsumption relation between two concepts C and D if $\theta = C \not\sqsubseteq D$ and $O \cup \{\theta\}$ is inconsistent; and a set of statements may be extracted from O if $\theta = C \sqsubseteq D$ and $O \cup \{\theta\}$ is inconsistent.

Let S be the smallest set of statements extracted from O to ensure $(O \cup \{\theta\}) - S$ is consistent; Δ the smallest set of statements extracted from O other than S; and T the smallest set of new statements $\notin O \cup \{\theta\}$ added to $O \circ \theta$. To keep the tree structure of the revised ontology, we assume that

$$O \circ \theta = ((O \cup \{\theta\}) - S - \Delta) \cup T,$$

where $S \cap \Delta = \emptyset$.

3.3   The axioms for the ontology revision

To give the axioms for the ontology revision, we firstly notice the difference between the ontology revision and belief revision. In the belief revision, to be revised is a knowledge base K and to revise is a formula α. Every statement is constructed from atomic formulas in terms of the logical connectives. In the ontology revision, to be revised is an ontology O and to revise is a statement θ which is *atomic*.

Based on the discussion in section 3.1 and 3.2, we propose the Z axiom system for the ontology revision:

Z0. $O \circ \theta$ is an ontology.

Z1. $O \circ \theta$ is consistent if θ is not contradictory.

Z2. $\theta \in O \circ \theta$.

Z3. If $O \cup \{\theta\}$ is consistent, then $O \circ \theta = (O \cup \{\theta\}) - \Delta$.

Z4. If $O \cup \{\theta\}$ is inconsistent, then $O \circ \theta = ((O \cup \{\theta\}) - S - \Delta) \cup T$.

Z5. If $O \circ \theta \vdash \delta$ then $(O \circ \delta) \circ \theta \equiv O \circ \theta$.

The Z axiom system is a combination of the AGM axiom and the DP axiom in some sense, except that if $K \cup \{\alpha\}$ is consistent then $K \circ \alpha \equiv K \cup \{\alpha\}$. By Z3, even though $O \cup \{\theta\}$ is consistent, something has to be extracted from O to make O satisfy the presuppositions on O. For the ontology revision, such a combination is appropriate, because of δ being atomic.

Theorem 1. *The Z axiom system satisfies the principles of success, consistency and minimal change.*

Proof. By Z2, the Z axiom system satisfies the principle of success. By Z0 and Z1, the Z axiom system satisfies the principle of consistency.

If $O \cup \{\theta\}$ is inconsistent, then by Z4, $O \circ \theta = ((O \cup \{\theta\}) - S - \Delta) \cup T$. By presupposition 4 and the definitions of Δ, S and T, $sd(O, O \circ \theta) = |S \cup \Delta \cup T|$ is minimal. Similarly, we can prove that $sd(O, O \circ \theta)$ is minimal when $O \cup \{\theta\}$ is consistent.

Hence, the Z axiom system satisfies the principle of minimal change.

Remark. Here, the principle of the minimal change is syntactical. The minimal change in the belief revision has three readings: syntactical, semantical (i.e., the minimal distance of models), and set-theoretic (taking knowledge bases as sets).

4. One concrete ontology revision ○

In this section, we define an ontology revision operator ○ which satisfies the Z axiom system.

Given an ontology O and a revising statement θ, assume that θ is not contradictory (otherwise, let $O \circ \theta = \emptyset$). By presupposition 3, θ is of one of the following forms:

$$C \sqsubseteq D;\ C \not\sqsubseteq D;\ C \Rightarrow \varphi;\ C \not\Rightarrow \varphi,$$

and $O \cup \{\theta\}$ may be consistent or not.

When $O \cup \{\theta\}$ is consistent, if θ is positive then $\theta \in O, \theta \in Th(O)$ or $\neg\theta \in O^{\text{CWA}}$; otherwise, $\theta \in O, \theta \in Th(O)$ or $\theta \in O^{\text{CWA}}$.

When $O \cup \{\theta\}$ is inconsistent, $\neg\theta \in O$ or $\neg\theta \in Th(O)$.

To discuss the consistence of $O \cup \{\theta\}$, the introduction of O^{CWA} is necessary. For example, if $O = \{C \sqsubseteq E, D \sqsubseteq E\}$ and $\theta = C \sqsubseteq D$, then $\theta \notin O, \theta \notin Th(O)$ and $\neg\theta \notin O, \neg\theta \notin Th(O)$, but $\neg\theta \in O^{\text{CWA}}$.

We give a concrete ontology revision operator ○, based on the consistence of $O \cup \{\theta\}$ and the forms of θ.

Case 1. $O \cup \{\theta\}$ is consistent.

    Case 1.1. $\theta = C \not\sqsubseteq D$ or $C \not\Rightarrow \varphi$.

        Case 1.1.1. $\theta \in O$.   Let $O \circ \theta = O$.

        Case 1.1.2. $\theta \in Th(O)$.   Let $O \circ \theta = O \cup \{\theta\}$.

        Case 1.1.3. $\theta \in O^{\text{CWA}}$.   Let $O \circ \theta = O \cup \{\theta\}$.

    Case 1.2. $\theta = C \sqsubseteq D$.

        Case 1.2.1. $\theta \in O$.   Let $O \circ \theta = O$.

        Case 1.2.2. $\theta \in Th(O)$.   Let $O \circ \theta = O \cup \{\theta\}$.

        Case 1.2.3. $\neg\theta \in O^{\text{CWA}} - Th(O)$.

        Let $\Delta = \{C \sqsubseteq E \in O : D \sqsubseteq E \notin Th(O)\}$.

        Then, $O \circ \theta = (O \cup \{\theta\}) - \Delta$.

    Case 1.3. $\theta = C \Rightarrow \varphi$.

        Case 1.3.1. $\theta \in O$.   Let $O \circ \theta = O$.

        Case 1.3.2. $\theta \in Th(O)$.   Let $O \circ \theta = O \cup \{\theta\}$.

        Case 1.3.3. $\neg\theta \in O^{\text{CWA}} - Th(O)$.   Let $O \circ \theta = O \cup \{\theta\}$.

Case 2. $O \cup \{\theta\}$ is inconsistent.

    Assume that $O \circ \theta = ((O \cup \{\theta\}) - S - \Delta) \cup T$.

Case 2.1. $\theta = C \not\sqsubseteq D$.

   Case 2.1.1. $C \sqsubseteq D \in O$.

   Let $S = \{C \sqsubseteq D\}$; $\Delta = \emptyset$; and $T = \{C \sqsubseteq D^*\}$.

   Case 2.1.2. $C \sqsubseteq D \in Th(O)$.

   Let

$$S = \{C \sqsubseteq E \in O : E \sqsubseteq D \in Th(O)\};$$
$$\Delta = \emptyset; \; T = \{C \sqsubseteq D^*\}.$$

Case 2.2. $\theta = C \sqsubseteq D$.

   Case 2.2.1. $C \not\sqsubseteq D \in O$.

   Let

$$S = \{C \not\sqsubseteq D\};$$
$$\Delta = \{C \sqsubseteq E \in O : D \sqsubseteq E \notin Th(O)\};$$
$$T = \emptyset.$$

   Case 2.2.2. $C \not\sqsubseteq D \in Th(O)$.

   Let

$$S = \{C \not\Rightarrow \varphi \in O : D \Rightarrow \varphi \in Th(O)\} \cup$$
$$\{C \not\sqsubseteq E \in O : D \sqsubseteq E \in Th(O)\};$$
$$\Delta = \{C \sqsubseteq E \in O : D \sqsubseteq E \notin Th(O)\};$$
$$T = \emptyset.$$

Case 2.3. $\theta = C \Rightarrow \varphi$.

   Case 2.3.1. $C \not\Rightarrow \varphi \in O$.

   Let $S = \{C \not\Rightarrow \varphi\}, \Delta = T = \emptyset$.

   Case 2.3.2. $C \not\Rightarrow \varphi \in Th(O)$.

   Let

$$S = \{E \not\Rightarrow \varphi \in O : E \sqsubseteq C \in Th(O)\};$$
$$\Delta = T = \emptyset.$$

Case 2.4. $\theta = C \not\Rightarrow \varphi$.

   Case 2.4.1. $C \Rightarrow \varphi \in O$.

   Let $S = \{C \Rightarrow \varphi\}, \Delta = T = \emptyset$.

   Case 2.4.2. $C \Rightarrow \varphi \in Th(O)$.

   Let

$$S = \{D \Rightarrow \varphi \in O : C \sqsubseteq D \in Th(O)\};$$
$$\Delta = T = \emptyset.$$

By the definition of $\circ$, we have the following theorem.

Theorem 2. $\circ$ *satisfies the Z axiom system.*

Proof. It is a routine to verify that $\circ$ satisfies the Z axiom system. We prove the theorem for case 2.1.1.

In case 2.1.1, $\theta = C \not\sqsubseteq D, C \sqsubseteq D \in O$ and $O \cup \{\theta\}$ is inconsistent. Let $S = \{C \sqsubseteq D\}$; $\Delta = \emptyset$; and $T = \{C \sqsubseteq D^*\}$, then

$$O \circ \theta = ((O \cup \{\theta\}) - S - \Delta) \cup T.$$

By the definitions of S, Δ, T and $O \circ \theta$, we can see that C has only one $\sqsubseteq$-least super-concept D^* in $O \circ \theta$; T is consistent with $(O \cup \{\theta\}) - S - \Delta$

and $O \circ \theta$ is consistent. Hence, Z0 and Z1 are satisfied. Z2 is satisfied since $\theta \notin S \cup \Delta$; Z3 is satisfied, since $\theta, \neg\theta \in O \cup \{\theta\}$ and $O \cup \{\theta\}$ is inconsistent.

By the definitions of $O \circ \theta, S, \Delta$ and T, it can be proved that S is the smallest set of statements extracted from O to ensure $(O \cup \{\theta\}) - S$ is consistent; and Δ is the smallest set of statements extracted from O and T is the smallest set of statements added to $O \circ \theta$ to do the reclassification of concepts and to keep the tree structure of $O \circ \theta$ as what has been discussed in section 3.2. Hence, Z4 is satisfied.

For Z5, we only consider the case that $\delta = C \sqsubseteq D^*$, and other cases are similar. By our assumption, $C \sqsubseteq D \in O$, then $O \cup \{\delta\}$ is consistent. By case 1.2.3, we have

$$O \circ \delta = (O \cup \{\delta\}) - \{C \sqsubseteq D\}.$$

Hence, $C \sqsubseteq D \notin O \circ \delta$ and $(O \circ \delta) \cup \{\theta\}$ is consistent. By case 1.1.3, we have

$$O \circ \delta \circ \theta = O \circ \delta \cup \{\theta\} = O \circ \theta.$$

5.   Conclusion and further works

In terms of the method of axiomatization, an axiom system, called the Z axiom system, for the ontology revision is given, which is proved to satisfy the principles of the success, consistency and minimal change. The ontology revision satisfying the Z axiom system has the following properties:

(1) if θ is consistent with O, then $O \circ \theta = (O \cup \{\theta\}) - \Delta$;

(2) otherwise, $O \circ \theta = ((O \cup \{\theta\}) - S - \Delta) \cup T$,

where S, Δ and T are sets of statements. The Z axiom system contains the axioms for the iterated revision:

(3) if $O \circ \theta \vdash \delta$ then $(O \circ \delta) \circ \theta \equiv O \circ \theta$.

A concrete ontology revision is given, which is based on the cases that $O \cup \{\theta\}$ is consistent or not.

(4) If θ is consistent with O, then $\theta \in O, \theta \in Th(O)$, $\theta \in O^{CWA}$ if θ is negative or $\neg\theta \in O^{CWA}$ if θ is positive.

(5) otherwise, $\neg\theta \in O$ or $\neg\theta \in Th(O)$.

Then, a concrete ontology revision function is given, which is proved to satisfy the Z axiom system.

In discussing the properties of natural kind concepts, the induction is necessary. For example, if every instance of **bird** we have found has feathers, then we conclude that **bird** has feathers by induction. Our next work will include the induction process in the ontology revision; and the logical properties between $C \Rightarrow \varphi$ and $C \Rightarrow_d \varphi$; the structure of concepts and properties; and the structure of statements in ontologies.

References

[1] A. Darwiche and J. Pearl. On the logic of iterated belief revision. *Artificial Intelligence*, 89(1-2):1-29, 1997.

[2] C. E. Alchourrón, P. Gärdenfors and D. Makinson. On the logic of theory change: partial meet contraction and revision functions. *Journal of Symbolic Logic*, 50:510-530, 1985.

[3] P. Gärdenfors. *Knowledge in Flux: Modelling the Dynamics of Epistemic States*. The MIT Press, Cambridge, MA, 1988.

[4] S. O. Hansson. *A Textbook of Belief Dynamics*. Applied Logic Series. Kluwer Academic Publishers, 1999.

[5] H. Rott. *Change, Choice and Inference - A Study of Belief Revision and Nonmonotonic Reasoning*. Oxford: Clarendon Press, 2001.

[6] C. Boutilier and M. Goldszmidt. Revision by conditional beliefs. In *Proceedings of the AAAI National Conference on Artificial Intelligence*, pages 649-654. Morgan Kaufmann, Washington, D.C., July 1993.

[7] O. Papini. Iterated revision operations stemming from the history of an agent's observations. In M.-A. Williams and H. Rott, editors, *Frontiers in Belief Revision*, 22:279-301, Kluwer Academic Publishers, 2001.

[8] D. Dubois and H. Prade. Introduction: Revising, Updating and Combining knowledge. In D. M. Gabbay (eds.), *Handbook of Defeasible Reasoning and Uncertainty Management Systems*, 3:1-16, 1998.

[9] S. O. Hansson. Revision of Belief Sets and Belief Bases. In D. M. Gabbay (eds.), *Handbook of Defeasible Reasoning and Uncertainty Management Systems*, 3:17-75, 1998.

[10] D. L. McGuinness. Ontologies come of age. In D. Fensel, J. Hendler, H. Lieberman and W. Wahlster, (eds.), *Spinning the Semantic Web: Bringing the World Wide Web to Its Full Potential*. MIT Press, 2002.

[11] A. Gómez-Pérez and O. Corcho. Ontology languages for the semantic web. *IEEE Intelligent Systems*, 54-60, 2002.

[12] Y. Sun and Y. Sui. The Ontology Revision. In *Proc. of International Joint Conference of Artificial Intelligence*, 1583-1584, 2005.

[13] C. B. Cross. Nonmonotonic inconsistency. *Artificial Intelligence*, 149(2):161-178, 2003.

[14] R. Reiter, A Logic for Default Reasoning. *Artificial Intelligence*, 13:81-132, 1980.

A SURVEY OF AUTONOMIC COMPUTING SYSTEMS

Mohammad Reza Nami [1], Mohsen Sharifi [2]

[1]*Faculty of Computer Science, Shahid Beheshti University, The Iran* , [2]*Faculty of Computer Enginering, Iran University of Science and Technology, The Iran*
Phone: +98-21-22403133,Fax: +98-21-22413139,

nami@iau-saveh.ac.ir

, mshar@iust.ac.ir

Abstract   The evolution of networks and the Internet, which have presented high scalable and available services have made environments more complex. The increasing complexity, cost, and heterogeny in distributed computing systems have motivated researchers to investigate a new idea to cope with the management of complexity in IT industry. For this, Autonomic Computing Systems (ACSs) have been introduced. In this paper, we present a complete survey of ACSs. It consists of characteristics, their effects on quality factors, architecture of ACS building blockes, and challenges.

Keywords: Agent, Multi-agent System, Autonomic Computing Systems, Self-managing Systems.

1.   Introduction

In centralized applications, data and programs were kept at one site and this was a bottleneck in performance and availability of remote information in desktop computers. Therefore, the concept of distributed systems was emerged. During the 1990s, distributed databases and client-server packages were used for information exchange between remote desktop computers. In these years, Distributed Computing Systems (DCSs) consist of different computers which were connected to each other and located at geographically remote sites. This was the starting point for emerging concepts such as Peer, Peer-to-Peer (P2P) computing [3], Agent [1], and Grid [2]. The evolution of networks and the Internet, which have presented high scalable and available services have made environments more complex. This complexity has increased the cost and errors of managing IT infrastructures. The skilled persons who manage these systems are expensive and can't manage them in configuration, healing, optimization, protection, and maintenance. Moreover, IT managers look for ways

Please use the following format when citing this chapter:

Nami, M.R., Sharifi, M., 2006, in IFIP International Federation for Information Processing, Volume 228, Intelligent Information Processing III, eds. Z. Shi, Shimohara K., Feng D., (Boston: Springer), pp. 101–110.

to improve the Return On Investment (ROI) by reducing Total Cost of Ownership (TCO), improving Quality of Services (QoSs), and reducing the cost for managing of IT complexity. A study shows that 25 to 50 percent of IT resources are spent on problem determination and almost half of the total budget is spent to prevent and recover system from crashes [4]. All these issues have motivated researchers to investigate a new idea to cope with the management of complexity in IT industry and self-management systems have been introduced. On March 8, 2001, Paul Horn presented importance of these systems with introducing ACSs to the National Academy of Engineering at Harvard University. IBM Vice President of Autonomic Computing Alan Ganek [5] has written a message and explained the importance of autonomic computing and the aim of introducing ACSs as "The goal of our autonomic computing initiative is to help customers build more automated IT infrastructures to reduce costs, improve up-time, and make the most efficient use of increasingly scarce support skills." Some benefits of autonomic computing include reduction of costs and errors, improvement of services, and reduction of complexity.

This paper is organized as follows. Related works are surveyed in section 2. In section 3, we present an overview of ACSs including definitions, benefits, and their characteristics. Section 4 describes Autonomic Elements (AEs) architecture as building blocks in ACSs. In section 5, some challenges such as robustness,learning, and relationships among AEs are discussed. Finally, we present conclusions and further researches.

2.   Related Works

On March 8, 2001, Paul Horn presented a link between pervasiveness and self-regulation in body 's autonomic nervous system and introduced ACSs to the National Academy of Engineering at Harvard University. With choosing the term *autonomic*, researchers attempted to make autonomic capabilities in computer systems with the aim of decreasing the cost of developing and managing them. S. White et al in [6], and R. Sterritt and D. Bustard in [7] have described some general architectures for ACSs and their necessary elements called autonomic elements. J. A. McCann and M. C. Huebscher in [?] have proposed some metrics to evaluate ACSs such as adaptability. Some performance factors such as security and availability have been discussed by others [9]. ACS properties have been discussed by many researchers. These properties include self-optimization [10], self-configuration [1], self-healing [11], and self-protection [7]. Grand challenges in engineering and scientific have been discussed in [12]. Different projects and products have been developed in both by the industry and the academic. M. Salehie and L. Tahvildari have outlined some of these products in [4]. From another view, we can categorize researches carried out in this field in two groups as the follows:

- **Group 1:** Researches which describe technologies related to autonomic computing.

- **Group 2:** Researches which attempt to develop autonomic computing as an unified project.

However, the lake of appropriate tools for managing the complexities in large scale distributed systems has encouraged researchers to designing and implementing ACSs features.

3.   Autonomic Computing: Definitions and characteristics

This section present an overview of autonomic computing systems. The autonomic concept is inspired by the human body 's autonomic nervous system. The human body has good mechanisms for repairing physical damages. It is able to effectively monitor, control, and regulate the human body without external intervention. An autonomic system provides these facilities for a large-scale complex heterogeneous system. An ACS is a system that manages itself. According to Paul Horn 's definition, an ACS is a self-management system with eight elements. Self-configuration means that An ACS must dynamically configure and reconfigure itself under changing the conditions. Self-healing means that An ACS must detect failed components, eliminate it, or replace it with another component without disrupting the system. On the other hand, it must predict problems and prevent failures. Self-optimization is the capability of maximizing resource allocation and utilization for satisfying user requests. Resource utilization and work load management are two significant issues in self-optimization. An ACS must identify and detect attacks and cover all aspects of system security at different levels such as the platform, operating system, applications, etc. It must also predict problems based on sensor reports and attempt to avoid them. It is called as Self-protection. An ACS needs to know itself. It must be aware of its components, current status, and available resources. It must also know which resources can be borrowed or lended by it and which resources can be shared. It is Self-awareness or Self-knowledge property. An ACS must be also aware of the execution environment to react to environmental changes such as new policies. It is called as context-awareness or environment-awareness. Openness means that An ACS must operate in a heterogeneous environment and must be portable across multiple platforms. Finally, An ACS can anticipate its optimal required resources while hiding its complexity from the end user view and attempts to satisfy user requests. We consider self-configuration, self-healing, self-optimization, and self-protection as major characteristics and the rest as minor characteristics. We are going to present a survey of current definitions of ACSs which have been derived from Horn 's definition. The aim of this survey is to identify all the possible definitions about ACSs. The common researchers in this field have been considered for this survey. They are first author in their publications. Table 1 shows the list of each researcher 's autonomic computing definition. The list of definitions in table 1 shows that there are differences in interpretation and definition of ACSs. Of course, with closer examination of the papers, it is found that these definitions are derivred from the eight elements proposed by Horn in 2001. For example, D. M. Chess et al have used the term 'self-configuration' similar to Horn 's definition and have presented 'self-assembly' property in Unity as an autonomic computing product. As mentioned, the aim of Autonomic Computing (AC) is to improve the system abilities. Therefore, autonomic computing characteristics affect various measurements of quality. Table 2 specifies the relationships between autonomic computig properties and quality factors.

4.   Toward Autonomic Element Architecture

The goal of an autonomic computing architecture is to reduce intervention and carry out administrative functions according to predefined policies. Moving from manual to autonomic systems is introduced in a step-by-step manner by Tivoli group in IBM. ACSs also can make decisions and manage themselves in three scopes: resource element scope, group of resource elements scope, and business scope. In resource element scope, individual components such as servers and databases manage themselves. In group of resource elements scope, a pool of grouped resources that work together perform self-management. For example, a pool of servers can adjust work load to achieve high performance. Finally, overall business context can be self-managing. It is clear that increasing the maturity levels of AC will affect on level of making decision. The path to AC consists of five levels: basic, managed, predictive, adaptive, and autonomic. They are explained in the following [17]:

- **Basic Level:** At this level, each system element is managed by IT professionals. Configuring, optimizing, healing, and protecting IT components are performed manually.

- **Managed Level:** At this level, system management technologies can be used to collect information from different systems. It helps administrator to collect and analyze information. Most analysis is done by IT professionals, but it is starting point of automation of IT tasks.

- **Predictive Level:** At this level, individual components monitor themselves, analyze changes, and offer advices. Therefore, Dependency on persons is reduced and decision making is improved.

- **Adaptive Level:** At this level, IT components can individually and group monitor, analyze operations, and offer advices with minimal human intervention.

Table 1.   List of Different Definitions for Autonomic Computing System.

First Author	Definition of Autonomic Computing
Kephart [12]	Major characteristics and Self-managing
Chess [13]	Major characteristics
IBM Tivoli Group [14]	Major and Minor characteristics
Sterritt [15]	Major and Minor characteristics except anticipatory
Tianfield [16]	Self-mechanism including major characteristics, Self-planning, Self-learning, Self-scheduling, Self-evolution
Parashar [2]	Major characteristics, Self-adapting
Murch [17]	Major and Minor characteristics
Tesauro [1]	goal-driven self-assembly, self-healing, real-time self-optimizing
De Wolf [10]	Major characteristics
White [6]	Major characteristics, Self-managing
Ganek [18]	Major characteristics, Self-managing

Table 2.   Relationships Between Autonomic Computig Properties and Quality factors.

Autonomic Properties	Quality Factors
Self-configuration	Maintainability, Usability, Functionality, Portability
Self-healing	Reliability, Maintainability
Self-optimization	Efficiency, Maintainability, Functionality
Self-protection	Reliability, Functionality
Self-awareness	Functionality
Openess	Portability
Context-awareness	Functionality
Anticipatory	Efficiency, Maintainability

- **Autonomic Level:** At this level, system operations are managed by business policies established by the administrator. In fact, business policy drives overall IT management, while at adaptive level, there is an interaction between human and system.

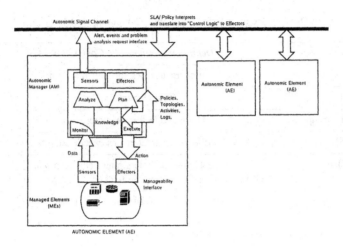

Figure 1.   Autonomic Element architecture

Autonomic Elements (AEs) are the basic building blocks of autonomic systems and their interactions produce self-managing behavior. We can consider
AEs as software agents and ACSs as multi-agent systems. Each AE has two
parts: Managed Element (ME) and Autonomic Manager (AM). In fact, ACSs
are established from Managed Elements (MEs) whose behaviors are controlled
by Autonomic Managers (AMs). AMs execute according to the administrator
policies and implement self-managing. An ME is a component from system. It
can be hardware, application software, or an entire system. Sensors retrieve information about the current state of the ME, then compare it with expectations
that are held in knowledge base by the AE. The required action is executed
by effectors. Therefore, sensors and effectors are linked together and create a
control loop.

Autonomic Managers (AMs) are the second part of an AE. An AM uses
a manageability interface to monitor and control the ME. It has four parts:
monitor, analyze, plan, and execute. The monitor part provides mechanisms
to collect information from a ME, monitor it, and manage it. Monitored data
is analyzed. It helps the AM to predict future states. Plan uses policy information and what is analyzed to achieve goals. Policies can be a set of administrator ideas and are stored as knowledge to guide AM. Plan assigns tasks
and resources based on the policies, adds, modifies, and deletes the policies [
6]. AMs can change resource allocation to optimize performance according
to the policies. Finally, the execute part controls the execution of a plan and
dispatches recommended actions into the ME. These four parts provide control
loop functionality. Communications between AMs provide self-managing and

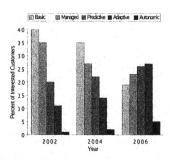

Figure 2.   Estimate of people trends toward autonomic products

context-awareness. External behavior of AEs is related to relationships among them. Figure 1 shows detailed architecture of AEs in an AC environment. AMs can be linked together via an autonomic signal channel.

Tivoli group has also presented an estimation of people trends to autonomic operations from 2002 to 2006. Figure 2 shows results of this estimate.

5.   Autonomic Computing Challenges

Since autonomic computing is a new concept in large-scale heterogeneous systems, there are different challenges and issues. Some of them have been explained in the following:

Issues in Relationships among AEs

Relationships among AEs have a key role in implementing self-management. This Relationships have a life cycle consists of specification, location, negotiation, provision, operation, and termination stages. Each stage has its own challenges [12]. Expressing set of output services that an AE can perform and set of input services that it requires in a standard form and establishing syntax and semantics of standard services for AEs can be a challenge in specification. As An AE must dynamically locate input services that it needs and other elements that need its output services must dynamically locate this element with looking it up, AE reliability can be a research area in location stage. AEs also need protocols and strategies to establish rules of negotiation and to manage the flow of messages among the negotiators. One of challenges is the designer to develop and analyze negotiation algorithms and protocols, then determine which negotiation algorithm can be effective. Autonomated provision can be also a research area for next stage. After agreement, The AMs of both AEs control the operation. If the agreement is violated, different solutions can be introduced. This can be a research area. Finally, after the both AEs agree to terminate the negotiated agreement, the procedure should be clarified.

Learning and Optimization Theory

A question raises this challenge: how can we transfer the management system knowledge from the human experts to ACSs? The master idea is that by observing that how several human experts solve a problem on different systems and by using traces of their activities, a robust learning procedure can be created. This procedure can automatically perform the same task on a new system. Of course, facilitating the knowledge acquisition from the human experts and producing systems that include this knowledge can be a challenge. One of reasons of the success of ACSs is their ability to manage themselves and react to changes. In short, in sophisticated autonomic systems, individual components that interact with each other, must adapt in a dynamic environment and learn to solve problems based on their past experiences. Optimization can be also a challenge, because in such systems, adaptation changes behavior of agents to reach optimization. The optimization is examined at AE level.

Robustness

There are many meanings for robustness. Robustness has been served in various sciences and systems such as ecology, engineering, and social systems. We can interpret it as stability, reliability, survivability, and fault-tolerance, although it does not mean all of these. Robustness is the ability of a system to maintain its functions in an active state and persistence, when changes occur in internal structure of the system or external environment. The persons often mistake it with stability. Although both stability and robustness focus on persistance, but robustness is broader than stability. It is possible that components of a system are not themselves robust, but interconnections among them make robustness at the system level. A robust system can perform multiple functionalities for resistancing without change in the structure. With design of instructions that permit system to preserve its identity even when it is disrupted, the robustness in systems can be increased. Robustness is one of grand scientific challenges which can be also examined in programming.

6.   Conclusions and Future works

In a Distributed Computing System, users and multiple computers are interconnected in an open, transparent, and geographical large-scalable system. Therefore, development and management of these systems are master problems for IT professionals. IBM proposed Autonomic Computing Systems as a solution. ACSs manage themelves. Four major characteristics of such systems include self-configuration, self-optimization, self-protection, and self-healing.

To achieve them, ACSs have four minor characteristics as self-awareness, context-awareness, openness, and anticipatory. Autonomic Elements (AEs) provide self-managing behavior in ACSs. They are the building blocks of ACSs and their interactions produce self-managing behavior. The various parts of AEs have been automated with evolution of AC levels. Engineering and scientific challenges have discussed in this field such as robustness, learning, and relationships among AEs.

In this paper, a survey of autonomic computing systems and their importance are presented. As future researches, the following topics can be proposed in autonomic distributed computing domain:

1 Performance evaluation of applying the autonomic behavior in a DCS model.

2 Designing an autonomic manager in multi-layer P2P form, so that autonomic behavior and management information as a knowledge base are stored in separated layers.

3 Studying languages which develop autonomic management behavior in a distributed computing environment.

4 Implementing a self-healing system in a virtual organization while one of partners failed.

Acknowledgement

Mohammad Reza Nami is a faculty member and researcher in the Islamic Azad University and Shahid Beheshti University from Iran. He has been ranked as number 1 in computer science examination in Iran in October 2002. For this, he has a scholarship from the Ministry of Science, Research, and Technology (MSRT) of Iran. He can be reached at nami@iau-saveh.ac.ir and nami1352@yahoo.com

References

1. Tesauro, G., and et al.:*A Multi-agent systems approach to autonomic computing*. IBM Press, (2004) 464-471.

2. Parashar, M., and et al.:*AutoMate: Enabling Autonomic Grid Applications*. Cluster Computing: The Journal of Networks, Software Tools, and Applications, Special Issue on Autonomic Computing, Kluwer Academic Publishers, Vol. 9, (2006).

3. Milojicic, D. S., and et al.:*Peer-to-Peer Computing*. In: Proceedings of the Second International Conference on Peer-to-Peer Computing, (2002) 1-51.

4. Salehie, M., Tahvildari, L.:*Autonomic Computing: emerging trends and open problems*. ACM SIGSOFT Software Engineering Notes, Vol. 30, (2005) 1-7.

5. Ganek, A.:*IBM Initiatives in autonomic computing and policy*.
http://www-03.ibm.com/autonomic/letter.shtml.

6. White, S., and et al.:*An architectural approach to autonomic computing*. In: Proceedings "International Conference on Autonomic Computing" (ICAC'04), NewYork, USA, (2004) 2-9.

7. Sterritt, R., and Bustard, D.:*Towards an autonomic computing environment*. In: 14th International Workshop on "Database and Expert Systems Applications" (DEXA '03), (2003) 694-698.

8. McCann, J. A., Huebscher, M. C.:*Evaluation issues in autonomic computing*. In: Proceedings of "Grid and Cooperative Computing" workshop (GCC-2004), Vol. 15, (2004) 597-608.

9. Chess, D. M., Palmer, C., and White, S. R.:*Security in an autonomic computing environment*. IBM System Journal, Vol. 42, (2003) 107-118.

10. De Wolf, T. and Holvoet, T.:*Evaluation and comparison of decentralised autonomic computing systems*. Department of Computer Science, K.U.Leuven, Report CW 437, Leuven, Belgium, (2006).

11. Hariri, S. and Parashar, M.:*Autonomic Computing: An overview*, Springer-Verlag Berlin Heidelberg, Vol. 3566, (2005) 247-259.

12. Kephart, J. O. and Chess, D. M.:*The vision of autonomic computing*. IEEE Computer, Vol. 36, (2003) 41-50.

13. Chess, D. M., Segal, A., Whalley, I., and White, S. R.:*Unity: experiences with a prototype autonomic computing system*. In: 1st "International Conference on Autonomic Computing" (ICAC 2004), New York, NY, USA, (2004) 140-147.

14. IBM Corporation Software Group:*The Tivoli software implementation of autonomic computing guidelines*. http://www-03.ibm.com/autonomic/pdfs/br-autonomic-guide.pdf.

15. Sterritt, R., Parashar, M., Tianfield, H., and Unland, R.:*A concise introduction to autonomic computing*. Advanced Engineering Informatics, Vo. 19, (2005) 181-187.

16. Tianfield, H.:*Multi-agent autonomic architecture and its application in e-medicine*. IEEE/WIC International Conference on "Intelligent Agent Technology" (IAT 2003), (2003) 601-604.

17. Murch, R.:*Autonomic Computing*. Prentice-Hall, (2004).

18. Ganek, A. G. and Corbi, T. A.:*The dawning of the autonomic computing era*. IBM System Journal, Vol. 42, (2003) 5-18.

TRUST CALCULATION

Semantic Agreement for Ontology Integration

Dennis Hooijmaijers

ACRC, University of SA, Australia

dennis.hooijmaijers@unisa.edu.au

Markus Stumptner

ACRC, University of SA, Australia

mst@cs.unisa.edu.au

Abstract   The Semantic Web is generally envisioned as a vast collection of document embedded knowledge that makes it highly improbable for agents traversing this space to know directly what entity, person, or organisation they are dealing with. In such an environment, the explicit representation of trust becomes an intrinsic part of calculating whether an agent can believe and use (or reuse) foreign sources. A key activity in this process is the step of integrating an agent's ontology with that of another document found on the Web. To assist in calculating trust values for this purpose, Riposte provides a set of trust models and trust manipulation algorithms to create a dynamic model of author trust based on work that is being provided to an agent. Riposte is an ontology integration tool that uses suggestions and bases trust on whether an object in the provided ontology confirms or refutes current beliefs. The author can be assigned an initial trust value and this value is recalculated after the integration process.

Keywords: Ontology, Bayesian Network, Trust

1.   INTRODUCTION

Authors can often refute or confirm claims of another author, and this can cause difficulties when merging ontologies, ensuring inconsistencies are not introduced and usability disrupted (Hooijmaijers and Bright, 2005). When considering an ontology for integration with one's existing conceptual setting, it is clearly desirable to ensure the reliability and credibility of the incoming ontology. A key consideration is the reliability and credibility of its author. Current integration solutions generally presume ontologies to be certain, error free, and take no consideration for the differences in bias. No other application scenario challenges this view more than the Semantic Web.

Please use the following format when citing this chapter:

Hooijmaijers, D., Stumptner, M., 2006, in IFIP International Federation for Information Processing, Volume 228, Intelligent Information Processing III, eds. Z. Shi, Shimohara K., Feng D., (Boston: Springer), pp. 111–121.

The Semantic Web will be a vast network that makes direct knowledge of authors unattainable (Ziegler and Lausen, 2004) and will often require an agent to outsource its requests for knowledge (Huang and Fox, 2005), resulting in knowledge being passed on from unknown agents, and being integrated with the requesting agent's ontology. In such cases it is necessary to ensure that such passed-on knowledge is credible and that the agent is reliable, and provisions for coherently integrating multiple, possibly mutually contradicting, sources, must exist. Any errors or inconsistencies provided by the new agent may cause the entire ontology to become unusable.

This paper introduces Riposte, an approach to ontology integration that takes into consideration the uncertainties, contained within the ontologies, and the trust and credibility of the author. Riposte attempts to minimise the harm caused by unknown authors by providing trust values for each component of the provided ontology, allowing for rating the providers based on the work they provide, thus creating a local trust metric (Ziegler and Lausen, 2004). Riposte provides an annotation model, a belief update model and reasoner for OWL ontologies. By providing annotation to existing ontologies that capture credibility at concept and property level, Riposte can provide a more realistic approach to decision making based on multiple sources. This paper defines appropriate models for capturing, updating, and propagating uncertainty in ontologies for integration purposes.

2.   TRUST AND ONTOLOGIES

Numerous trust models (Ziegler and Lausen, 2004; Golbeck et al., 2003; Bertino et al., 2004; Staab et al., 2005; Noy et al., 2005) have been proposed in recent years to rate or quantify belief in information provided by a person. A key distinction is between direct trust (local trust) and reputation (global trust) (Ziegler and Lausen, 2004). Direct trust is based on previous experience with the source of the information, while reputation requires a social network model to provide a similar measure. Some trust researchers (Bertino et al., 2004) also aim to provide a metric for authenticity. This 'security trust' aims to prevent document tampering (encryption) and ascertain authorship (digital signatures). These metrics often ignore the source's credibility and reliability (Golbeck et al., 2003). Credibility is the concept of trusting a source, in a domain, to provide information that is most likely to be correct (Ding et al., 2003; Golbeck et al., 2003), while reliability is the concept of ranking sources by their credibility ratings (Golbeck et al., 2003; Huang and Fox, 2005). This work focuses on the credibility of an ontology and author, and trust is considered a value that represents the belief that the author produces credible work.

In a Semantic Web environment it is unlikely that an agent will have previous experience with all agents it may need to interact with. To overcome this lack of previous experience a social model (Dumbill, 2002; Guha, 2003) is required. According to (Staab et al., 2005), communities will create their own ontologies for the Semantic Web where the social model of the community becomes an integral part of how the ontology is created. This results in the Semantic Web consisting of communities, their ontologies, and the content expressed through them. The social models generally provide a mechanism for assigning a rating value to each person that the agent had direct contact with. These models usually assign trust for a whole topic area.

The 'Web of Trust' approach (Guha et al., 2004) provides a technique to model trust between objects (ontologies or knowledge bases), users, reviews, ratings of reviews, and trust relations between users. The model allows for trust to be captured and rated between users. Also the model allows for each review to be ranked and to allow for the propagation of trust changes. When a user's trust rank is altered, their reviews of other users will gain additional value within the model to reflect their improved reputation. One problem is that the approach does not take into account the reliance between objects. If an ontology, ω_1, is built incorporating another ontology, ω_2, then the rating of ω_2 can not be higher than ω_1. Friend of a Friend (FOAF) (Dumbill, 2002) is an approach aiming to mark up trust relations between people in XML and RDF to enrich personal web pages. It provides a simple XML schema to allow an author to define people they know. This creates a directed graph with nodes representing people and edges representing direct trust. The FOAF approach has been extended to provide levels of trust, ranking from 1 'distrusts absolutely' to 9 'trusts absolutely' (Golbeck et al., 2003), and also allowing for the trust ratings to be related to specific topics. Trust can be calculated in three ways, via path capacity, path length and weighted averages. A similar approach is followed in (Ziegler and Lausen, 2004), but does not model distrust but rather 'lack of trust'.

2.1   Ontology Integration

Automated knowledge integration has been an active research area for some time (McGuinness et al., 2000; Noy and Musen, 1999), but so far has mostly concentrated on knowledge assumed to be stable, certain, and (for a particular problem or domain) complete. Automated advisors have been suggested to over come the 'knowledge acquisition bottleneck' (Gonzalez and Dankel, 1993) caused by reliance on human experts. Such systems, including PROMPT (Noy and Musen, 1999), OMEN (Noy et al., 2004) and Chimaera (McGuinness et al., 2000), use simple heuristics to assist users in making the best decisions. In real world situations, of course, knowledge is subjective and the creators of the knowledge are not always completely certain of the correct semantics between the concepts. The Chimaera ontology integration tool (McGuinness et al., 2000) uses a suggestion algorithm based on pattern matching on concept labels. It searches through the first model and then, using a set of reasoning rules, searches through the second model for a match. Chimaera mainly focuses on the subsumption hierarchies within ontologies. What Chimaera attempts to do is to integrate two hierarchies contained within multiple ontologies. This is achieved by determining if two similar concepts are the same or one is a subclass of the other.

PROMPT (Noy and Musen, 1999) was developed to semi-automatically merge ontologies, by guiding the user where it is unable to decide upon the correct results. Automated identification of likely concept mappings will reduce a domain expert's effort in searching through the ontologies. OMEN (Noy et al., 2004) is an extension of PROMPT that uses Bayesian networks to assign belief values to likely matches, thereby providing a finer graduation of candidate matchings. When a user selects a match, the beliefs are updated by propagating the new evidence through the network.

These systems assume that the ontologies to be matched are accurate and contain only definite concepts and semantics. Yet, since the reason to perform an ontology matching process is presumably the need incorporate from all sources involved, any long term usage scenario will find agents possessing and working with ontologies that have already undergone this matching process. Instead of going back to the "clean" source ontologies (which in any case may have long changed themselves, requiring multiple realignment processes), the most likely scenario will be to use the trust-annotated ontologies themselves as the source.

3.   RIPOSTE MODEL

The Riposte approach uses a trust model and integration model. The trust model deals with trust annotation and trust manipulation, while the integration model addresses ontology management, ontology integration and reasoning issues. In this paper we discuss the trust model and ontology integration section of the integration model.

3.1   Trust Annotation

The extension of ontology languages for uncertain knowledge has been a research topic for some time. In (Ding and Peng, 2004), the Web Ontology Language OWL was extended by an additional node type that expresses probabilistic information about concepts, to allow for "more accurate semantic integration" (Ding and Peng, 2004). This approach will work in uncertain domains where the concepts allow for uncertainty in regards to data membership, but does not allow assigning probabilities to semantic relationships; uncertainty nodes can be linked only to concepts (Hooijmaijers and Bright, 2005). The approach permits the use of Bayesian Network frameworks to perform the necessary actions, like propagating and updating beliefs in the network. Earlier work by (Jaeger, 1994) also provided a mechanism for capturing probability within Terminological Logics, annotating concepts and objects with probabilities. For semantic matching and integration purposes, these capabilities need to be extended (Hooijmaijers and Bright, 2005).

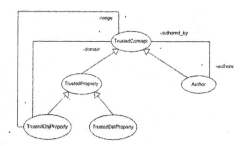

Figure 1.   Necessary Concepts for Trust Annotation

Figure 1 shows the necessary concepts required for the trusted integration approached discussed later in this paper. The annotation process adds these concepts to an ontology and adds all subclasses of "owl:Thing" as subclasses of "TrustedConcept". The superclass "owl:Thing" is then removed from each of these classes. All data and object properties in the ontology are added as instances of the appropriate "TrustedProperty". Finally the author is added in as an instance of Author. Once this annotation process is complete, the ontology is ready for the integration process. The "trustvalue" is then calculated from the authors that contribute the object to the ontology.

3.2   The Web of Trust Model

For ontology integration it is necessary to trust that an author has every component of their ontology correct. To do, we calculate a trust value for that author for each component in their ontology, following the "Web of Trust" (Guha et al., 2004) model. This approach provides an ability to apply trust to each individual object provided by an agent, thus providing a finer grained approach to ontology trust than just evaluating topics as a whole, as proposed by (Golbeck et al., 2003). The 'Web of Trust' model consists of:

1 A Set of objects, O:$\{O_1, O_2, \ldots\}$, in this case classes, $C \subset O$, object properties, that make up the set of objects.

2 A set of agents, A:$\{A_1, A_2, \ldots\}$, who are authors that in this case contribute a class or property, by using it in their ontology.

3 A set of possible values, P(O):$\{P(O_1), P(O_2), \ldots\}$, for rating the objects in this case values between -1 and 1, where -1 is complete distrust, 0 is unknown, and 1 is complete trust.

4 A set of values, P(A) :$\{ P(A_1), P(A_2), \ldots\}$, for rating the authors.

5 A partial function R: A x O $\rightarrow$ P(O) that corresponds to agent ratings for various objects

6 A partial function W: A x A $\rightarrow$ P(A) That corresponds to agent ratings for various agents.

W becomes a directed graph similar to FOAF (Dumbill, 2002). The graph W
is referred to as the 'Web of Trust'.

Revisable Web of Trust. Riposte extends the 'Web of Trust' to provide the ability to capture relationships between objects. The aim is to provide
a mechanism that allows for trust updating on an object to effect all other objects that are related. The objects in Riposte represent the components of the
ontologies as well as the authors who provide these components, enabling us to
capture the relationships and functions for updating trust for individual objects
and related objects.

A *revisable Web of Trust* is defined by the model above, with these additions:

1 an ontology ω comprised of the set of objects, O

2 A partial function L: O x O $\rightarrow$ $\{(O_a, O_l),(O_b, O_m),\dots\}$ that corresponds to a
   set of reliance measurements between objects. For example, an object property
   would rely on all domain and range classes existing for it to exist. The necessity
   of this reliance between objects in ontologies creates the necessity to include
   trust manipulation.

3 A function τ_O: Providing trust revision on an Object O.

3.3   Trust Manipulation

A number of propagation methods have been suggested as models for trust
calculation (Golbeck et al., 2003; Guha et al., 2004; Ziegler and Lausen, 2004),
generally trying to capture the structure of social networks that spread and
communicate trust values. Specific techniques, such as FOAF, attempt to calculate the "degrees of separation" and assign values based on closeness measures (Golbeck et al., 2003). Golbeck also introduces 9 categories of trust to
help differentiate between authors. The trust levels are also applied to individual topics. Other techniques use probability (Hooijmaijers and Bright, 2005)
to represent trust as a level of uncertainty in the work provided by the author.
Each technique has advantages; humans often find it easier to select a natural
language level over numerical values, while numerical values offer a greater
level of precision for use in belief revision.

Trust Update: Our trust update model is based on earlier work (Hooijmaijers and Bright, 2005) that used the Stanford certainty factor algebra (SCF)
(Luger, 2002) for belief revision. The beliefs can be strengthened or weak-
ened. In Riposte the trust model provides a similar belief concept, in that it is
stored in the ontology in a similar way and requires belief updating. The SCF
is not usable for object belief values in Riposte, as there are dependencies between the objects. This is true in particular for object properties being reliant
on the classes in the domain and range of the property. Bayes Theorem is used
for updating trust for each object within the integration process. In initial work
the calculation of initial author trust, P(A), is assumed to be independent. This

allows for the combination of author trusts:

$$P(A_1, A_2, \ldots, A_n) = P(A_1) \cdot P(A_2) \ldots P(A_n) \tag{1}$$

If an author is correct then all objects provided by that author are true $P(O|A) = 1$. If an object property, O_k is true this then increases the likelihood of all classes in the range $R : \{O_1, O_2, \ldots\}$, and domain, $D : \{O'_1, O'_2, \ldots\}$ adding the links from O_k to each $O \in R$ and $O \in D$ to the Bayesian network. Then for the purpose of calculating (3), O_k is treated as a contributing Author. This is due to the fact that both O_k and the contributing authors are treated as evidence for the purpose of calculating P(A—O). When calculating Author trust P(A) using (4), O_k is not considered as a contributing author.

$$P(O) = \sum_{i=0}^{n} P(O) + P(A_i) - P(O) \cdot P(A_i) \tag{2}$$

As authors confirm a given object, the trust that the object is correct is increased. If an author disagrees with the object O_n, as discussed in the Riposte algorithm it is necessary to weaken the trust in that object, $P(O_n)$. This is equivalent to strengthening $P(\neg O_n)$ using (2). Using (1) to calculate P(O) for multiple contributing authors Bayes Theorem gives:

$$P(O|A_1 \& A_2 \& \ldots A_n) = \frac{P(O) \cdot P(A_1 \& A_2 \& \ldots A_n|O)}{P(A_1 \& A_2 \& A_n)}$$

Assume at least one author is correct then $P(A_1 \& A_2 \& \ldots A_n|O)$ simplifies to 1 and this gives:

$$P(A_1 \& A_2 \& \ldots A_n|O) = \frac{P(O)}{P(A_1 \& A_2 \& \ldots A_n)} \tag{3}$$

3.4   Author Trust

Author trust can be calculated in multiple ways. In this work the trust of an author is based on the trust ratings of each object provided by that author. Similar to (Ziegler and Lausen, 2004) this is a local trust metric and is a trust according to the agent that has integrated objects supplied by the author. The author trust is calculated by calculating the trust using Jeffrey's conditioning:

$$Q(A_k) = \sum_{j=0}^{M} P(O_j) \cdot P_{O_j}(A_k) + (1 - P(O_j) \cdot P_{\neg O_j} P(A_k)) \tag{4}$$

3.5   Integration using PROMPT

The PROMPT algorithm, described in (Noy and Musen, 1999), is a suggestion based algorithm forintegration. PROMPT uses a recursive algorithm to
highlight likely mappings between the ontologies. It goes through the ontologies and finds initial suggestions. Once the user selects an operation, PROMPT
updates the resultant ontology and searches for conflicts. If conflicts are found
the user must resolve the conflict. Finally PROMPT checks for new possible mappings based on the operation and present the user with a new set of
suggestions. Riposte extends PROMPT to provide mechanisms to annotate,
manipulate, and calculate trust values. Riposte requires two ontologies ω_1 and
ω_2 each containing a set of objects, O, comprised of:

1 Set of Object Properties P_o $\{P_{o1}, P_{o2}, \dots\}$

2 Set of Data Properties P_d $\{P_{d1}, P_{d2}, \dots\}$

3 Set of concepts C $\{C_1, C_2, \dots\}$

We assume that there exist at least 2 pairs of C in both ω_1 and ω_2. The ontologies are assumed to have the concept 'owl:Thing' in common. (Clearly, if
there is no common node in ω_1 and ω_2 there is no reference for integration;
also owl:Thing is the root of OWL based modeling.)

3.6   Integration Algorithm

The items in the following algorithm emphasised in italics are modified from
the PROMPT algorithm as described in (Noy and Musen, 1999).

1 **If** necessary **then** annotate. This involves inserting the concepts and creating
   individuals as discussed in the Trust Annotation section previously. Initially
   all trust values of the 'TrustedConcepts' are set to the initial author trust value,
   using (2).

2 *Load two ontologies, ω_1 and ω_2 and select a preferred ontology. In Riposte the
   preferred ontology is usually that belonging to the agent performing the merge.*

3 *Generate the initial list of suggestions, $S:\{S_1, S_2, \dots\}$.*

4 **Begin Integration loop**

5 *The user selects an operation to perform. The set of possible basic operations
   is defined in (Noy and Musen, 1999) on an object, O_n.*

6 Ensure O_n has a trust value, P(O), assigned and a set of Authors, A_O, that
   contributed to that trust value.

7 Check ω_1 for author, $A_n \in A$. Often a user may have previous experience with
   an author. In this situation P(O) $\in \omega_2$ is calculated using (2). Otherwise, P(O)
   $\in \omega_2$ is set to 0.

   (a) **If** operation is a merge, **then**, once an object, O_n has been merged the
        object authors, $A_{O\omega_2}$ are added to the list of authors of object, O_n: $A_{\omega 1}$.

(b) *Create new suggestions S_2. Add any conflict γ_i to the set of conflicts, γ:* $\{\gamma_1, \gamma_2, \dots\}$.

(c) Check for refutation, χ: $\{\chi_1, \chi_2, \dots\}$, and confirmation, ψ: $\{\psi_1, \psi_2, \dots\}$, created by operation on ω_1 and O_n refutations and confirmations are populated using the following rules:

    i if O_n is a property, differences in Range will add to ψ. $O_n \in \omega_1$ has a range of C $O_n \in \omega_2$ has range of C' where $\forall C \in C \cap C'$ are added to ψ while $\forall C \in \overline{C \cap C'}$ are added to χ.

    ii if O_n is a property difference in restrictions can add to refutation. If a restriction, R, on $O_n \in \omega_1$ contradicts, R' on $O_n \in \omega_2$ then add O_n to ψ.

(d) **For each** $O \in \chi$ update the trust in O, P(O) using (2).

(e) **For each** $O \in \psi$ trust in O, P($\neg$O) using (2).

(f) **If** operation is a copy **then** O does not exist in ω_1; copy all contributing authors for O to ω_1 and calculate P(O) using (2).

8 *Perform automatic updates as described in (Noy and Musen, 1999).*

9 ***Repeat from 'Begin Integration loop' until*** *the ontologies are fully merged. Once fully merged there should be no conflicts, γ:* $\{\emptyset\}$.

10 Calculate Author Trust. Use (4) for all trust values, P(O) of $O \in \omega_1$ that has author as a contributing author $A_i \in A$. assign result to $P(A)_i$

4.   EVALUATION

We have compared Riposte to the PROMPT integration algorithm to check the resultant ontology, and to FOAF to compare the trust values of authors.

4.1   PROMPT Comparison

Riposte uses the same suggestion algorithm as PROMPT. To compare the results the PROMPT tutorial ontologies, an airline reservation ontology and a car rental ontology, were integrated using both Riposte and PROMPT. The steps to perform the merge were followed from the PROMPT tutorial. Once the resultant ontology was created it was necessary to remove the Riposte annotations. This is achieved by firstly changing all subclasses of 'TrustedConcept' to subclasses of 'owl:Thing'. Secondly removing 'TrustedConcept', 'Author', 'Property', 'ObjectProperty', and 'DataProperty'. Finally all individuals of these classes are also removed. The initial merging of the additional Riposte concepts annotated on the ontologies is performed automatically without the user being given the suggestions. This ensures that the Riposte suggestion list matches those given by PROMPT. By following the same order of operations, there was no visible difference between the suggestions. The resulting ontology in Riposte included all of the Riposte annotation classes. By removing the the Riposte annotations, the resultant ontologies had no were identical to the PROMPT ontologies. This result shows that Riposte has the ability to perform the same merges as PROMPT on OWL ontologies.

4.2   Trust Comparison

For comparison against the FOAF trust model each of the 9 levels of Golbeck's trust were assigned numerical equivalents ($1to1$). Two path length values were chosen for initial comparisons, firstly path length 1, a friend A_1, and secondly path length 2, a friend of a friend, A_2. To compare the Riposte trust value of A_2, $P(A_2)$, it is necessary for ω_1 to exclude the individual A_2, while ω_2 must contain the individual A_2 and some object A_2 has contributed to. The initial FOAF values for P(A_1) was 0.75, while P(A_2) was assigned 0.5. Once the ontologies were set up for Riposte, two different comparisons were performed. Firstly the initial trust value of the authors contained in ω_2 were set to the FOAF values for those authors. Secondly the initial trust values of those authors were set to 0. This allowed for the comparison of Riposte to update author trusts and also to provide an initial trust value given that the authors are completely unknown. The results provided an accurate model of author trust. For two ontologies with A_1 providing objects that confirmed and refuted in the following ratios, confirmation of 0.5, refutation of 0.15 and 0.35 new objects the value calculated increased by ~ 0.05. This displays an increased trust in the author, as they provided a greater percentile of confirmations. A similar result was achieved for achieved for A_2 where the overall trust went down ~ 0.01 due to higher refutations. The advantage over FOAF is that the ability to see exactly where the refutation appeared allows for a pinpointing of trust and distrust to a specific area of the ontology.

5.   CONCLUSION

We have extended PROMPT ontology integration algorithm to introduce trust calculations for all concepts and properties within two ontologies being merged. To achieve this it was necessary to annotate ontologies with a set of Riposte specific classes and to propagate individuals. This has allowed for the calculation of author trust values from the knowledge sources provided for integration. In initial tests, we have found that for moderate sized ontologies the trust value of an author is almost independent of any initial values. This allows for the calculation of trust based almost entirely on the ontology provided. Our next steps for the Riposte framework are to expand the belief propagation mechanisms, to propagate belief across related objects in an ontology, and to expand the integration mechanism to incorporate prior trust values for the objects in the source ontologies. This will permit the use of uncertain sources (that may have differing trust levels associated with their parts) as part of the merging process, enabling long-term knowledge use and reuse rather than starting from scratch.

References

Bertino, E., Ferrari, E., and Squicciarini, A. (2004). Trust negotiations: concepts, systems, and languages. *Computing in Science and Engineering*, 06(4):27–34.

Ding, L., Zhou, L., and Finin, T. (2003). Trust based knowledge outsourcing for Semantic Web agents. In *Proc. IEEE/WIC*, pages 379–387.

Ding, Zhongli and Peng, Yun (2004). A probabilistic extension to ontology language OWL. In *Proc. of the Hawaii International Conference on System Sciences.*, pages 1775–1784.

Dou, Dejing, McDermott, Drew, and Qi, Peishen. (2003). Ontology translation on the Semantic Web. In *Proc. ODBASE'03*, pages 952–969.

Dumbill, Ed (2002). XML watch: Finding friends with XML and RDF. *IBM's XML Watch.*

Golbeck, Jennifer, Parsia, Bijan, and Hendler, James (2003). Trust networks on the Semantic Web. In *7th International Workshop, CIA 2003*, LNAI 2782, pages 238–249.

Gonzalez, Avelino J. and Dankel, Douglas D. (1993). *The engineering of knowledge-based systems : theory and practice*. Prentice Hall.

Guha, R. V. (2003). Open rating systems. Technical report, Stanford Knowledge System Laboratory.

Guha, R. V., Kumar, R., Raghavan, P., and Tomkins, A. (2004). Propagation of trust and distrust. In *Proc. WWW*.

Hooijmaijers, Dennis and Bright, Damien (2005). Uncertain knowledge gathering: an evolutionary approach. In *Proc. ISMIS 05*, Saratoga Springs NY. Springer-Verlag.

Huang, Jingwei and Fox, M.S. (2005). Trust judgment in knowledge provenance. In *Proc. DEXA, 2005*, pages 524–528.

Jaeger, Manfred (1994). Probabilistic reasoning in Terminological Logics. In *Proc. KR Conf.*.

Luger, G. F. (2002). *Artificial Intelligence Structures and Strategies for Complex Problem Solving*. Addison Wesley, 4th edition.

McGuinness, D.L., Fikes, R., Rice, J., and Wilder, S. (2000). The Chimaera ontology environment. In *Proc. AAAI*.

Noy, N. F., Guha, R. V., and Musen, M. A. (2005). User ratings of ontologies: Who will rate the raters? In *Proc. AAAI*.

Noy, N. F., Mitra, P., and Jaiswal, A. R. (2004). OMEN: A probabilistic ontology mapping tool. In *Proc. ISWC '04*.

Noy, N. F. and Musen, M. A. (1999). An algorithm for merging and aligning ontologies: Automation and tool support. In *Proc. AAAI*.

Pearl, Judea (1988). *Probabilistic Reasoning in Intelligent Systems: Networks of Plausible Inference*. Morgan Kaufmann.

Staab, S., Domingos, P., Mike, P., Golbeck, J., Ding, Li, Finin, T., Joshi, A., Nowak, A., and Vallacher, R.R. (2005). Social networks applied. *IEEE Intelligent Systems*, 20(1):80–93.

Ziegler, Cai-Nicolas and Lausen, Georg (2004). Spreading activation models for trust propagation. In *Proc. EEE 2004*.

QA SYSTEM METIS BASED ON WEB SEARCHING AND SEMANTIC GRAPH MATCHING

Dongli HAN*, Yuhei KATO**, Kazuaki TAKEHARA**, Tetsuya YAMAMOTO**, Kazunori SUGIMURA**, and Minoru HARADA**
*Department of Computer Science and System Analysis, NIHON University
**Department of Integrated Information Technology, Aoyama Gakuin University

Abstract: We have developed a question-answering system Metis with natural-language interface. Metis generates the answer to a question by comparing the semantic graph of the question sentence with sentences discovered on the Internet as knowledge source. Specifically, we first get a set of semantic frames for the question sentence, as the output from a semantic analysis system, SAGE. Then we extract several keywords from all semantic frames using SVM. After that we search the Web to find knowledge sentences based on the keywords and input each knowledge sentence into SAGE in order to get its semantic graphs similarly. Finally, the similarities between the semantic graph of the question sentence and that of each knowledge sentence are calculated to determine the most reliable knowledge sentence, in which a constituent is chosen as the answer to the question. An experiment to examine the effectiveness of our method showed that 65% of the questions for which suitable knowledge sentences had been found were replied correctly.

Key words: Natural Language Processing, Question Answering System, Semantic Analysis, EDR-Dictionary

1. INTRODUCTION

QA systems with natural-language-interface have been popular recently. Here are some study cases. Endo etc. made efforts in trying to handle wider question type by employing classified type of named entity [1]. Kurata etc.

Please use the following format when citing this chapter:

Han, D., Kato, Y., Takehara, K., Yamamoto, T., Sugimura, K., Harada, M., 2006, in IFIP International Federation for Information Processing, Volume 228, Intelligent Information Processing III, eds. Z. Shi, Shimohara K., Feng D., (Boston: Springer), pp. 123–133.

adopted a measure of distance between nodes in the graph structure of the knowledge sentence to determine the answer among all candidates [2]. Sasaki etc. regarded the two components of a QA system, question analysis and answer extraction, as 2-class classification problems, then used SVM to determine the question type of a given question, and to select answer candidates that match the question type [3]. In another study, Murata etc. parsed syntactically both the question sentence and the knowledge one extracted from a database, and then extract the answer from the latter by comparing and matching their dependency structures [4].

As shown above, all studies are common in the point attempting to find the answer to the question by surface information only, without considering any semantic factors which might be quite important in this process. We believe this is the principal cause for the high ratio of wrong answers in most systems. In this study, we try to pick out a clause, or simply a word, from the knowledge sentence as the answer to the question by comparing the semantic graphs of the question sentence and the knowledge sentence. We believe the delicate comparison at the semantic level could reduce the mistakes occurred in the process.

Specifically, we first get a set of semantic frames for the question sentence, as the output from a semantic analysis system, SAGE. Then we extract several keywords from all semantic frames using a Support Vector Machine. After that we search the Web to find knowledge sentences based on the keywords and input each knowledge sentence into SAGE in order to get its semantic graphs similarly. Finally, the similarities between the semantic graph of the question sentence and that of each knowledge sentence are calculated and compared to determine the most reliable knowledge sentence, from which a constituent is chosen as the answer to the question.

2.   SEMANTIC ANALYSIS

The main difference between our method and the previous ones is we attempt to find the answer to a question based on not the raw text, but the tagged ones, i.e. the semantically analyzed texts. SAGE, the semantic analysis system built by Maezawa etc. does this for us [5][6][7]. It determines the word meanings and the semantic relations among words according to the definition and statistical information registered in the EDR Dictionary[1]. Each case-frame in the analytical results corresponds to a clause in the sentence. And as shown in Figure 1, a case-frame contains tow parts:

---

[1] http://www.iijnet.or.jp/edr/index.html

an "f" for the clause itself, and several "s" for morphemes included in the clause.

```
f: 1,今日は,は,ME,2,,[],[],[],,[]
   s: 2,今日,キョウ,,3c5a5b,JSM,JN4,,
   s: 3,は,ハ,,,FJJ,JJO,,
f: 4,休日にも関わらず、,,@renyou,DO,8,,[],[],[],,[否定]
   s: 5,休日,キュウジツ,,,FTM,JN1,,
   s: 6,に,ニ,,,KKJ,JJO,,
   s: 7,も,モ,,,FJJ,JJO,,
   s: 8,関わら,カカワラ,関わる,3c338d,DOS,JVE,子音動詞ラ行,未然形
   s: 9,ず,ズ,ぬ,,JOD,JJD,助動詞ぬ型,基本連用形
   s: 10,、,,,,TOT,JSY,,
f: 11,彼が,が,ME,12,,[],[],[ag4],,[]
   s: 12,彼,カレ,,2dc304,FTM,JN1,,
   s: 13,が,ガ,,,KKJ,JJO,,
f: 14,出勤している。,,DO,15,16,[ti1,cd4,ag11],[],[],,[非完結相]
   s: 15,出勤,シュッキン,,0f58cd,SAM,JSA,,
   s: 16,して,シテ,する,3d06c7,DOS,JVE,サ変動詞,タ系連用テ形
   s: 17,いる,イル,,,DOB,JJD,母音動詞,基本形
   s: 18,。,,,,KUT,JSY,,
e: 19,null,null,[mn14]
```

Figure 1. Case-frames for the sentence

「今日は休日にも関わらず、彼が出勤している。」

(He is working although it is not working day.)

Figure 2 is the graph generated based on the analytical results in Figure 1, and what we want for this study. Here, we expand Sowa's concept structure [8] to produce our semantic graphs.

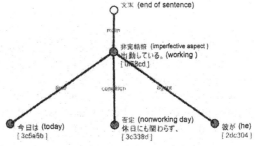

Figure 2. Semantic graph for the sentence

「今日は休日にも関わらず、彼が出勤している。」

(He is working although it is not working day.)

3.   PREPARATION FOR GRAPH MATCHING

We take the following steps to prepare for matching graphs between the question sentence and the knowledge sentence.

3.1   Question type identification

Taking the case-frames of a question sentence as the input, the first thing we have to do is to identify its question type. Here in this study, we classify questions into five categories: "what", "who", "where", "when", and "other". We determine the question type according to the EDR concept ID of the interrogative clause as shown in Table 1.

Table 1. Question types

question type	concept ID of the interrogative clause	category concept
what	0e451a, 3cf234	3aa966(concept)
who	3cfe2c, 101bab4	30f6b0(human)
where	101260	30f751(location), 30f746(organization)
	0e44fb	444d86(thing)
when	0e4d47	30f776(time), 30f7e4(event)
other	1014db, 101438, 101f65, 1012f8, 101439, etc.	3aa966(concept)

For instance, if the concept ID of the interrogative clause appears as "101bab" in its case-frame, we say the question is a "who" question, and assign a category concept "human" to the interrogative clause for the sake of similarity calculation between nodes in graphs later.

3.2   Keyword extraction by SVM

We extract keywords for later web searching using SVM[2]. SVM (Support Vector Machine) is an effective machine learning mechanism, and usually used to classify some data points into two classes. Here, we follow two steps to establish our SVM models. First we select 255 question sentences containing 1657 clauses from internet or books on quiz program as the training data, and divide all clauses into two classes: valuable keywords, and non-valuable keywords by handcraft. Then, we settle four characteristic measures for the calculation of SVM: POS, deep case, distance between the interrogative clause and the keyword itself, and the length of the keyword.

---

[2] http://www.chasen.org/~taku/software/TinySVM/

3.3 Web searching for knowledge

Using the extracted keywords, we conduct web searching for knowledge sentences. We use Google[3] as the search engine, and restrict the number of keywords within 4 empirically. In case the number of extracted keywords exceeds 4, combinations of every 4 keywords are tried for web searching. If no page hits with all combinations of 4-keyword, we reduce one keyword a time till hitting page appears or the number of used keywords becomes 0. Along this line, sentences in the hitting pages containing all keywords used for web searching are extracted as knowledge sentence candidates.

3.4 Paraphrase of the question sentence

According to our algorithm, we take the main predicate as the root of the graph and start graph matching from it. Thus graph matching intends to become harder if the interrogative word appears as the main predicate in the question sentence.

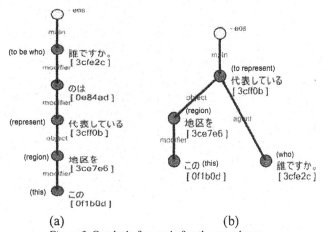

(a)   (b)

Figure 3. Graphs before and after the paraphrase

For instance, (a) in Figure 3 shows the semantic graph of "この地区を代表しているのは誰ですか" (who is the person representing this region) where the main predicate is the interrogative word. While in most cases, a knowledge sentence will probably appear as something like "鈴木一郎がこの地区を代表している" (Suzuki Ichiro represents this region) as shown in Figure 4. Obviously, a paraphrase as shown in Figure 3 from (a) to (b) will

---

[3] http://www.google.com/

enhance the matching performance as (b) in Figure 3 is much more similar to Figure 4.

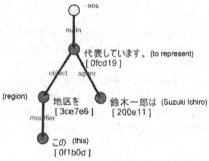

Figure 4. Semantic graph for the sentence
「鈴木一郎はこの地区を代表している。」
(Suzuki Ichiro represents this region.)

4. GRAPH MATCHING

As mentioned in Section 3.4, we start the matching process at the moment we succeed in locating the main predicate node in the graph of knowledge sentence. Then we visit the first adjacent node from the main predicate in the question sentence in a manner of depth-first search. Similarly, we also try to find the adjacent node of the main predicate in the knowledge sentence with the satisfaction that it matches the lately visited node in the question sentence. Repeat the above until all nodes in the question sentence have been visited, indicating the end of the matching process. In this section, we describe the matching procedure in detail.

4.1 Node matching

A node in the knowledge sentence must satisfy the following conditions to match a node in the question sentence.

Table 2. Matching rules for interrogative node

	node in question graph	node in knowledge graph
concept similarity	>= 0.5	
property	the same negation property	
POS	-	not verb
relation	relation similarity + concept similarity >= 1.5	

Table 3. Matching rules for general node

	node in question graph	node in knowledge graph
concept similarity	>= 0.27	
referent	general concept	-
	proper concept	the same referent
property	the same negation property	
relation	relation similarity + concept similarity >= 1.27	

Table 2 describes the case when the node in the question sentence is the interrogative node, and Table 3 is for the case of other nodes. Here, a concept similarity (denoted as CS below) is calculated by the following equation.

$$CS = \frac{2 \times dc(c_1, c_2)}{d(c_1) + d(c_2)}$$

In this equation, d(x) means the depth of the concept x in EDR's thesaurus, and dc(x, y) is the depth of the parent concept of x and y. Figure 5 is an example.

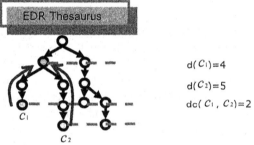

$d(C_1)=4$

$d(C_2)=5$

$dc(C_1, C_2)=2$

Figure 5. Depth of concepts in EDR thesaurus

In this way, the concept similarity between c_1 and c_2 is 0.44.

The concept of the interrogative node is replaced by the category concept as shown in Table 1 in section 3.1.

Another significant matching rule described in Table 2 and 3 is for the relation similarity. The relation similarity indicates the similarity between two relations: one in the question sentence and another in the knowledge sentence. A relation here means the semantic relation in the semantic graph from a parent node to its child node. In other words, besides the similarity of node pairs themselves, the relations they hold with their own children are also considered. It is easy to understand that the similarity will be 1 if the semantic relation between a pair of nodes in the question sentence is the same with the one in the knowledge sentence. How about the relations that are not the same? Table 4 shows the criteria for assigning similarities to relation pairs in this case.

Table 4. Similarities for relation pairs

relation similarity	deep case group
0.8	time,time-from,time-to
0.8	object,a-object,modifier
0.8	agent,object
0.8	a-object,modifier,possessor
0.6	goal,beneficiary,purpose
0.6	place,goal,from-to
0.4	place,goal,scene,a-object,modifier,from-to
0.4	cause,reason,logical
0.4	time,time-from,time-to,sequence,timing
0.4	manner,possessor,a-object,modifier

For instance, if the semantic relation is "agent" between a pair of nodes in the question graph, and "object" between the node pair being examined in the knowledge graph, we will assign the relation pairs with a similarity 0.8.

4.2   Node skipping

During the process described in section 4.1, not always could we go smoothly. Sometimes we are not able to continue our work due to the lack of matching nodes. The reason is variable including one that we might have just encountered some modification that is unconcerned, while the modified part following it is the node we are looking for. Here arises the necessity to skip one or more nodes in order to continue the matching work.

Node skipping takes place in both the question sentence and the knowledge sentence. Taking N_p as the visited node, N_c as the being examined node, i.e., the node to be skipped, and N_g as one of the children N_c holds, the algorithm will be as below.

foreach N_g {

generate a relation $N_p \rightarrow N_g$;

$N_p \rightarrow N_g = (N_p \rightarrow N_c, N_c \rightarrow N_g)$;

DeepCase($N_p \rightarrow N_g$)= (DeepCase($N_p \rightarrow N_c$), DeepCase($N_c \rightarrow N_g$));

delete $N_p \rightarrow N_c$ and $N_c \rightarrow N_g$;

}

The new relation $N_p \rightarrow N_g$ is a list, and will bring a problem when matching another relation with it as described in the posterior half of section 4.1. In fact, we assign 1 to $N_p \rightarrow N_g$, if the deep case of $N_p \rightarrow N_c$ or N_c

$\rightarrow N_g$ exists for the other relation, and the similarity defined in Table 4 to $N_p \rightarrow N_g$, if $N_p \rightarrow N_c$ or $N_c \rightarrow N_g$ of another relation belongs to the same group in Table 4. Here are two examples showing the node skipping respectively in the question sentence and the knowledge sentence.

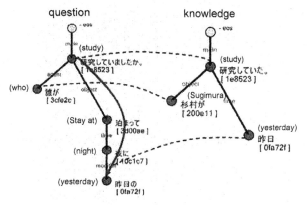

Figure 6. Node skipping in question sentence

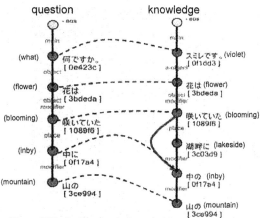

Figure 7. Node skipping in knowledge sentence

4.3 Calculation of graph similarities and answer extraction

Finally, after the above pcocedures, the node in the knowledge sentence matching the interrogative word in the question sentence is extracted as an answer candidate.

In case more than one answer candidate is available, similarities between the question graph and each knowledge graph are calculated as S_g and used to rank the answer candidates.

$$S_g = \frac{(S_n + S_a)}{2}$$

$$S_n = \frac{\sum N_{qk}}{N_q} \times 100$$

$$S_a = \frac{\sum A_{qk}}{A_q} \times 100$$

Here, N_{qk} represents the concept similarity of a pair of nodes, and N_q is the total number of nodes in the question sentence. Likewise, A_{qk} and A_q are for the Arcs, i.e., the relations..

5.   EXPERIMENTAL RESULTS

We conducted an experiment to examine the effectiveness our method. Table 5 shows the results. Here we randomly extract 100 sets of question and answer from a TV quiz program [9] as the experimental data.

Table 5. Experimental results

		correct answer	wrong answer	no answer
suitable knowledge found (55%)	top 1	65%(36)	13%(7)	22%(12)
	till top 3	71%(39)	7%(4)	22%(12)
unsuitable knowledge found (45%)		0	16%(7)	84%(38)

Here the percentages in the correct answer column indicate the ratio of questions with correct answers found among all the 100 sets. Top 1 represents the ratio of questions for which the correct answers have been found by the topmost answer candidates, and Top 3 by one of the top 3 answers in the answer candidate lists.

We know from the table that suitable knowledge have been found for only 55% of the questions. This could probably be caused by the method we extract knowledge: although knowledge may exist across several sentences sometimes, we extract only an individual sentence.

Among the questions with suitable knowledge found, the success rate is 65%, and the failure rate 13%. The figures are not perfect, but prove the reliability of our method, especially for the low failure rate. We believe the delicate matching algorithm at the semantic level has reduced the wrong answers. And this could probably be the reason why 84% of the questions with no suitable knowledge found refused to provide answers.

6.   CONCLUSION

The QA system we developed is effective in finding answers from Internet for given questions. We believe that we will get better performance with our system if we expand our method of extracting individual knowledge sentence to multiple ones. Also, it may be necessary to paraphrase the knowledge sentences, rather than the question sentences only as we do at present.

REFERENCES

1. Endo, T., and Fukumoto, J. : QA System using Classified Type of Named Entity. IPSJ SIG Notes. NL-159, pp.25-30 (2004).
2. Kurata, G., Okazaki, Naoki., and Ishizuka, Mitsuru. : Question Answering System with Graph Structure from Dependency Analysis. IPSJ SIG Notes. NL-158, pp.69-74 (2003).
3. Sasaki, Y., Isozaki, H., Suzuki, J., Kokuryou, K., Hirao, T., Kazawa, H., and Maeda, E. : SAIQA-II: A Trainable Japanese QA System with SVM (Natural Language Processing), Transactions of Information Processing Society of Japan. Vol.45, No. 2, pp.635-646 (2004).
4. Murata, M., Utiyama, M., and Isahara, H. : Question Answering System Using Similarity-Guided Reasoning. IPSJ SIG Notes. NL-135, pp181-188 (2000).
5. Maezawa, T., Menrai, M., Ueno, M., Han D., and Harada., M. : Improvement of the Precision of the Semantic Analysis System SAGE, and Generation of Conceptual Graph. Proceedings of the 66th National Convention of IPSJ, 2-6U-05, pp.177-178(2004).
6. Harada, M., Tabuchi, K., Oono, H. : Improvement of Speed and Accuracy of Japanese Semantic Analysis System SAGE and Its Accuracy Evaluation by Comparison with EDR Corpus. Transactions of Information Processing Society of Japan. Vol.43, No. 9, pp.2894-2902 (2002).
7. Harada, M., MIZUNO, T. : Japanese Semantic Analysis System SAGE using EDR. Transactions of the Japanese Society for Artificial Intelligence. Vol.16, No.1, pp.85-93 (2001).
8. Sowa, J. : Conceptual Structures, Information Processing in Mind and Machine, Addison-Wesley, Reading, MA (1984).
9. Quiz Millionaire, Fuji Television. (2002).

EXTENDED SEMANTIC NETWORK FOR KNOWLEDGE REPRESENTATION
An Hybrid Approach

Reena T. N. Shetty, Pierre-Michel Riccio, Joël Quinqueton
Doctorate-EMA Paris, Assistant-professor-LGI2P Nimes,Professor- LIRMM Montpellier

Abstract: The proposition Extended Semantic Network is an innovative tool for
               Knowledge Representation and Ontology construction, which not only
               infers meanings but looks for sets of associations between nodes as
               opposed to the present method of keyword association. The objective here
               is to achieve semi-supervised knowledge representation technique with
               good accuracy and minimum human intervention. This is realized by
               obtaining a technical co-operation between mathematical and mind
               models to harvest their collective intelligence.

Key words: Extended Semantic Network, Artificial Intelligence, Collective
              Intelligence, Proximal Network, Semantic Network, User Modeling,
              Knowledge, Knowledge Representation & Management, Information
              Retrieval .

1. INTRODUCTION

The past few years has witnessed tremendous upsurge in data availability in the electronic form, attributed to the ever mounting use of the World Wide Web (WWW). For many people, the World Wide Web has become an essential means of providing and searching for information leading to large amount of data accumulation. Searching web in its present form is however an infuriating experience since the data available is surplus and in diverse forms. Web users end up finding huge number of answers to their simple queries, consequentially investing more time in analyzing the output results due to its immenseness. Yet many results here turn out to be irrelevant and one can find some of the more interesting links left out from the result set.

One of the principal explanations for such unsatisfactory condition is the reason that majority of the existing data resources in its present form are designed for human comprehension. When using these data with

Please use the following format when citing this chapter:

Shetty, R.T.N., Riccio, P.-M., Quinqueton, J., 2006, in IFIP International Federation for Information Processing, Volume 228, Intelligent Information Processing III, eds. Z. Shi, Shimohara K., Feng D., (Boston: Springer), pp. 135–144.

machines, it becomes highly infeasible to obtain good results without human interventions at regular levels. So, one of the major challenges faced by the users as providers and consumers of web era is to imagine intelligent tools and theories in   knowledge representation and processing for making the present data, machine understandable.

Several researches has been carried out in this direction and some of the most interesting solutions proposed are the semantic web based ontology to incorporate data understanding by machines. The objective here is to intelligently represent data, enabling machines to better understand and enhance capture of existing information. Here the main emphasis is given to the thought for constructing meaning related concept networks [17] for knowledge representation. Eventually the idea is to direct machines in providing output results of high quality with minimum or no human intervention.

In recent years the development of ontology [2, 8] is gaining attention from various research groups across the globe. There are several definitions of ontology purely contingent on the application or task it is intended for. Ontology is one of the well established knowledge representation methods; on a formal ground ontology defines the common vocabulary for scientists who need to share information on a field or domain. One has seen in the past years that various research groups have been devotedly experimenting semantic related [17] ontology aimed at making web languages machine understandable.

2.   RELATED WORK

One of the most basic reasons for ontology construction [1] is to facilitate sharing of common knowledge about the structural information of data among humans or electronic agents. This property of ontology in turn enables reuse and sharing of information over the web by various agents for different purposes. Ontology [17, 25] can also be seen as one of the main means of knowledge representation through its ability to represent data with respect to semantic relation it shares with the other existing data.

There are several developed tools for ontology construction and representation like protégé-2000 [5], a graphical tool for ontology editing and knowledge acquisition that can be adapted to enable conceptual modeling with new and evolving Semantic web languages. Protégé-2000 has been used for many years now in the field of medicine and manufacturing. This is a highly customisable tool as an ontology editor credited to its significant features like an extensible knowledge model, a customisable file format for a text representation in any formal language, a customisable user interface and an extensible architecture that enables integration with other applications which makes it easily custom-tailored with several web languages. Even if it permits easier ontology construction, the downside is its requirement of human intervention at regular levels for structuring the concepts of its ontology.

The WWW Consortium (W3C) has developed a language for encoding knowledge on web to make it machine understandable, called the Resource Description Framework (RDF) [3]. Here it helps electronic media gather information on the data and makes it machine understandable. But however RDF itself does not define any primitives for developing ontologies. In conjunction with the W3C the Defence Advanced Research Projects Agency (DARPA), has developed DARPA Agent Markup Language (DAML) [4] by extending RDF with more expressive constructs aimed at facilitating agent interaction on the web. This is heavily inspired by research in description logics (DL) and allows several types of concept definitions in ontologies.

There are several other applications like the semantic search engine called the SHOE Search. The Unified Medical Language System is used in the medical domain to develop large semantic network. In the following section we introduce our approach to this problem of knowledge representation, management and information retrieval [19] and eventually discuss the possible solutions.

3.   HYBRID APPROACH- EXTENDED SEMANTIC NETWORK(ESN)

3.1   General View

Extended Semantic Network is data representing network resulting from the collaboration involving two networks, one automatically constructed proximal network and the second manually constructed semantic network. Here, the primary idea is to develop a modern approach combining the features of man and machine theory of concept [9], which can be of enormous use in the latest knowledge representation, classification, pattern matching and ontology development fields. We propose to visualize a novel method for knowledge representation [6] partly based on mind modeling and partly on the mathematical method.

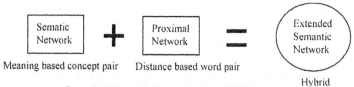

Figure1. Schematic Representation of ENS

In ESN we endeavor to develop a network of concepts based on human constructed semantic network projected as the main central part of the network which is later subjected to elaboration utilizing the statistical data obtained by our mathematical models based on the data clustering and mining algorithms. This generates a new approach for knowledge representation which can later be used for optimising, information search and classification procedures, and enabling easy and fast information retrieval. The ESN forms a hybrid structure [22] by inheriting the features of both the source networks; computed differently and independently, making it a robust and an optimal approach.

Our proposal is to construct a network of concepts similar to ontology but using a method where minimal human intervention is required. We call this a semi supervised network of concepts representing certain qualities of an ontology which later is expatiated by adding the information obtained from the mathematically elaborated proximal network. Our assumption here is that this method will produce the same output as any traditional ontology but will greatly decrease the construction time, attributed to its mathematical modeled extension. Some of the major points we hope to achieve through this method of knowledge representation network are:

- To make construction of semantic based concept networks cost effective by campaigning minimum human intervention
- To minimise time invested in construction by introducing mathematical models without loosing on quality.
- To identify a good balance between mind and mathematical models to develop better knowledge representing networks with good precision and high recall.

3.1.1 Semantic network

Semantic Network [8] is basically a labelled, directed graph permitting the use of generic rules, inheritance, and object-oriented programming [9]. It is often used as a form of knowledge representation. It is a directed graph consisting of vertices, which represent concepts and edges, representing semantic relations between the concepts. The most recent language to express semantic networks is KL-ONE [10].

There can exist labeled nodes and a single labeled edge relationship between Semantic nodes. Further, there can be more than one relationship between a single pair of connected words: for instance the relationship is not necessarily symmetrical and there can exist relationship between the nodes through other indirect paths. Below is a fragment of a conventional semantic net, showing 4 labelled nodes and three labelled edges between them.

Technically a semantic network is a node- and edge-labelled directed graph, and it is frequently depicted that way. The scope of the semantic network is broad, allowing for the semantic categorization of a wide range of terminology in multiple domains. Major groupings of semantic types include organisms, anatomical structures, biologic function, chemicals, events, physical objects, and concepts or ideas. The links between the semantic types provide the structure for the network and represent important relationships.

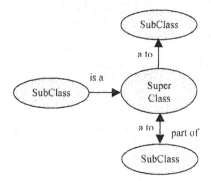

Figure 2. Multi-labeled Semantic Relation

In our semantic network prototype all concept relations are built based on the meaning each concept pair share, with a possibility of more than one relationship between a single pair of connected nodes. All the links used in connecting the node is based on the UML [11] links, consisting of four different types of associative lines as shown below.

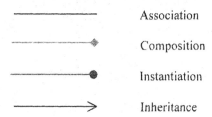

Figure 3. Links used in Semantic Network

They have been currently chosen on an experimental basis [12], after considering and analysing the requirements of our approach. We start with our domain name representing the super class in our approach. The super class is connected to its subclasses based on the category of the relation they share, which can be chosen from the four links we provide. The four links represent the simple UML links of association, composition, instantiation and inheritance.

3.1.2 Proximal network

Proximity is the ability of a person or thing to tell when it is near an object, or when something is near it. This sense keeps us from running into things and also can be used to measure the distance from one object to another object. The simplest proximity calculations can be used to calculate distance between entities thus avoiding a person from things he can hit. Proximity between entities is often believed to favour interactive learning, knowledge creation and innovation. The basic theory of proximity is concerned with the arrangement or categorisation of entities that relate to one another. When a number of entities are close in proximity a relationship is implied and if entities are logically positioned; they connect to form a structural hierarchy.

This concept is largely used in medical fields to describe human anatomy with respect to positioning of organs. The Proximal Network Prototype model is built based on this structural hierarchy, of word proximity in documents [13]. Here proximity is calculated purely considering the physical distance of its occurrence at a given instance. We use UML link of association to connect words or nodes proximally closer.

Results obtained from the semantic network are considered as the centre of our network on which the ESN network will be constructed. We extend the results of semantic network by adding on the results obtained by the proximal network thus making it an Extended Semantic Network. The demonstrable prototype of ESN has been developed based on the data of ToxNuc-E project [14].

3.2   Application on environmental nuclear toxicology

The Extended Semantic Network prototype has been developed in collaboration with the ToxNuc-E project funded by CEA (Commissariat à l'Energie Atomique). ToxNuc-E[14], is a project devoted to all the research activities carried out in Biological, Chemical and Nuclear domains in several research centres linked with CEA. It is a platform where researchers from different domains like biology, chemical, physics and nuclear working for a common purpose, meet and exchange their views on various nuclear toxicology related on-going research activities.

The ToxNuc-E [14] presently has around 660 researchers registered with their profile, background and area of research interest. The objective of our research is to assist these researchers to achieve better knowledge representation and to support for easy information retrieval from the vast data base of information. Currently we are experimenting on the 15 topics or domain chosen by the researchers as the domain of major research activities. All the data and the documents used in our experimental prototype of ESN are obtained from the ToxNuc-E platform.

3.2.1   Semantic network prototype

Our semantic network prototype is developed grounded on the view of a set of specialist representing each of the chosen domains from the project ToxNuc-E. To begin with, we choose a set of 50 concepts pertaining to the preferred domain of research. We then consult people who are either specialists or people possessing good level of knowledge in each of these areas of study.

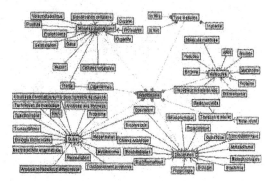

Figure 4. An Extract of Semantic representation of Concepts for arabidopsis using Graph Editor

These people are provided with the concept list on which they are requested to develop a semantic network depending on their individual view point. The network thus developed is then analyzed and merged to obtain one single semantic network for that domain. This process was repeated on different lists of concepts concerning to various domains to obtain one network for each domain. The semantic network is then stored into the MySql database and visualized using graph editor - a java application developed by us and used for facilitating construction of networks and also for editing purpose.

3.2.2   Proximal network prototype

The documents relating to the numerous research activities being carried out in the chosen 15 field of nuclear toxicology in plants and animals forms our data. These documents are subjected to a pre-treatment process to obtain a matrix of words and documents as rows and columns respectively. Here java is used as the programming language and all the data used are stored in the MySql database.

This program is primarily concerned with the physical distance that separates words in a given space. Currently, we have successfully processed around 3423 words to calculate the physical distance between them, using various mathematical algorithms. The result obtained here is then fed into the graph editor for graphical visualisation. This helps in displaying the results from the program along with a value calculated for every word pair – in this case 50,000 word pair, forming the proximal

Network. These results are then stored into the database which is later used to combine with the results of the semantic network.

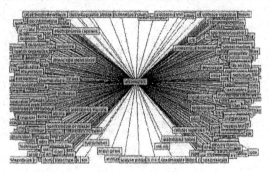

Figure5. An Extract from Proximal Network

At present, the 2 different results are combined with simple extension methods. Simultaneously, several other optimising algorithms are being considered to be utilised in merging the networks to build the Extended Semantic Network. We are exploring the possibilities of using the genetic algorithms and features of neural networks to obtain an optimal result.

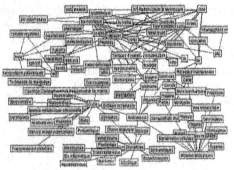

Figure6. An Extract of Extended Semantic Network

Our preliminary results have been verified by experts in comparison with human developed ontology and concept networks and have been validated for providing satisfactory results. We are now working on live data from ToxNuc-E to develop an ESN network to be later compared with classical ontology and rated by domain experts for attaining our benchmark.

3.3   Advantages and future work

The results of our algorithm have been subjected to testing, by human experts and have been judged to provide results very close to human constructed concept networks. It has also proved to take much less time for construction and very cost effective. We are also on the conclusion that the results are exceedingly customisable depending on the user's domain of interest. Our next step will be to include natural language processing techniques like stemming and lemmatises to our pre-treatment process. Our objective is to develop an application for document classification and indexation based on the results of Extended Semantic Network. This application library is intended to be used for classification purpose in the project ToxNuc-E for better data management on the platform.

We also plan to include user modelling [15] features by monitoring the behaviour; interests and research works carried out by the members of ToxNuc-E and then build a model unique to each user. This model consecutively builds a profile for each user and sequentially stores the details obtained into a database. These details can be utilized to better understand the user requirements thus helping the user in efficient data search, retrieval, management, and sharing.

4.   CONCLUSION

The question on knowledge representation, management, sharing and retrieval are both fascinating and complex, essentially with the co-emergence between man and machine. This research paper presents a novel collaborative working method, specifically in the context of knowledge representation and retrieval. The proposal attempts to present an hybrid knowledge representation approach accurate as ontologies but faster and easy to construct. The advantages of our methodology with respect to the previous work, is our innovative approach of combining machine calculations with human reasoning abilities.

We use the precise, non estimated results provided by human expertise in case of semantic network and then merge it with the machine calculated knowledge from proximal results. The fact that we try to combine results from two different aspects forms one of the most interesting features of our current research. We view our result as structured by mind and calculated by machines. One of the major drawbacks of this approach is finding the right balance for combining the concept networks of semantic network with the word network obtained from the proximal network. Our future work would be to identify this accurate combination between the two vast methods and setting up a benchmark to measure our prototype efficiency.

ACKNOWLEDGEMENTS

We would like to use this opportunity to thank all the researchers of ToxNuc-E for providing us with their data and expertise. We would also like to thank the reviewers of this paper for their useful comments.

REFERENCES

[1] Natalya F. Noy and Deborah L.McGuinness, Ontology Development 101: A Guide to Creating Your First Ontology, Stanford University, Stanford, CA.

[2] T.R. Gruber, "Toward Principle for the design of ontologies used for Knowledge Sharing", in Proc. Of International Workshop on Formal Ontology, March 1993.

[3] Brickley, D. and Guha, R.V. Resource Description Framework (RDF) Schema Specification. Proposed Recommendation: World Wide Web Consortium, 1999.

[4] Helder, J. and McGuinness, D.L., The DARPA Agent Markup Language. IEEE Intelligent Systems, 2000.

[5] Natalya F. Noy, Michel Sintek, Stefan Decker, onica Crubézy. Ray W. Fergerson and Mark A. Musen, Creating Semantic web Contents With protégé 2000, Stanford University, IEEE Intelligent Systems, 2001.

[6] J.F Sowa , Knowledge Representation: Logical, Philosophical, and Computational Foundations, Brooks Cole Publishing Co., Pacific Grove, CA, 2000.

[7] J Voss, P Danowski, B Chapter - citebase.eprints.org, 2005.

[8] M.R Quillian,, Semantic memory. M Minsky, Ed, Semantic Information Processing. pp.216-270. Cambridge, Massachusetts: MIT Press, 1968.

[9] J.F Sowa, Conceptual structures: information processing in mind and machine, Addison-Wesley Longman Publishing Co., Inc. Boston, MA. 1984.

[10] J Brachman, L Deborah, McGuinness, F Patel-Schneider, A Resnick Living with CLASSIC: When and How to Use a KL-ONE-Like Language, 1991.

[11] Rational Corporation: UML Notation Guide 2, 2000.

[12] M.E Winston, R Chaffin and D Hernnann, A taxonomy of part – Whole Relations Cognitive Science 11, 1987.

[13] S.A. Mahé, P.M. Riccio et S. Vailliès: des elements pour un modèle: la lutte des classes! Revue Génie Logiciel, n°58, Paris, septembre 2001.

[14] M Ménager, Programme Toxicologie Nucléaire Environnementale : Comment fédérer et créer une communauté scientifique autour d'un enjeu de société , Intelligence Collective Partage et Redistribution des Savoirs, Nimes, France, septembre, 2004.

[15] J Aberg & N Shahmehri, User Modelling an Aid for Human Web Assistants, User Modeling 2001: 8th International Conference, UM 2001, Southaven, Germany, July 13-17, 2001.

[16] E Reingold, J Nightingale, "Artificial Intelligence".

[17] Alexander maedche & Steffen Staab. "Ontology Learning for the Semantic Web".

[18] J Link-Pezet., P Glize, C Régis,, A cognitive approach to intelligent databases. On line, London: Learned Information, 1992.

[19] N.J Belkin, W.B Croft, Information Filtering and Information Retrieval: Two Sides of the Same Coin?, Communications of the ACM Vol. 35 n°12, 1992

[20] R Davis, B.G Buchanann, Meta-Level knowledge: Overview and applications, IJCAI, ACM SIGIR, n° 5, Cambridge, 1984.

[21] A Maedche, S Staab, Representation & Learning, IEEE Intelligent Systems, 2001.

[22] E Rosch and B. Mervis, Family Resemblances: Studies in the Internal Structure of Categories, University of California. Berkeley, 1989

[23] E Rosch Cognitive Representation of Semantic Categories, University of California, Berkeley, 1978

[24] E Rosch "Cognitive Reference Points", University of California, Berkeley, 1978.

[25] N. Cuarino, C. Masolo, and G. Vetere, "Ontoseek: Content-based Access to the Web," IEEE Intelligent Systems, Volume 14, no. 3, pp. 70-80, 1999

EDUCATION FOR RURAL SECTOR USING KNOWLEDGE NETWORK

B.G. Sangameshwara, U.M. Mallikarjuna Swamy[*]
Principal, S.J. College of Engg., Mysore – 570 006, Karnataka, India.
bgsangam@yahoo.com

[*] Lecturer, Dept. of Information Science & Engg., Mysore – 570 006, Karnataka, India.
mallisjce@yahoo.com

Abstract: Rural development in the Indian / III world context is still dominated by rural
              way of life up to now and likely to be for quite some time in the future. By
              simple statistics, up to 80% of the population lives in villages, or semi urban
              environment. Thus rural development / III world development has much more
              to do with attitudes, perceptions and sensitivities, and less with technology-
              per-se. The education for rural people using information technology (IT) in
              rural areas is very much required for the present scenario. If the people in the
              rural areas are educated, we can expect tremendous economy growth in the
              developing countries like India, China etc. and the African Continent. The
              main aim is to give IT based training and education for the rural peoples in the
              various part of Karnataka state, India using Knowledge Network.

Key words: IT, Education, Knowledge Network.

1.   INTRODUCTION

Ever since its inception Information Technology (IT) has expanded its
influence over all domains. IT has now become an integral part of all facets
of business, education, research etc. Unfortunately, IT has not made much
penetration into the rural sector. Hence, the developmental activities in the
rural arena especially in Asia and Africa have not witnessed much of

Please use the following format when citing this chapter:

Sangameshwara, B.G., Swamy, U.M.M., 2006, in IFIP International Federation for Information Processing, Volume
228, Intelligent Information Processing III, eds. Z. Shi, Shimohara K., Feng D., (Boston: Springer), pp. 145–150.

acceleration in its growth. Information Technology is the essential tool for economic development and material well-being in our age; it conditions power knowledge and creativity; it is for the time being, unevenly distributed within countries and between countries; and it requires, for the full realization of its development value, an inter-related system of flexible organizations and information-oriented institutions [1,2].

Our work proposes a novel approach to overcome the short comings in the rural development. IT is a key factor to alleviate the rural sector and can be leveraged to impart information, knowledge and education to the rural populace. It envisages a collaborative role to be played between Urban Nodes that can be any information-oriented intuition or any organization and Rural Nodes that is the recipient of services.

In computing, a Content Management System (CMS) is a system used to organize and facilitate collaborative creation of documents and other content. A CMS is frequently a web application used for managing websites and web content, though in many cases, Content Management Systems requires special client software for editing and constructing articles [3]. Plone is a content management framework that works hand-in-hand and sits on top of 'Z' Object Publishing Environment (Zope), a widely-used Open Source web application server and development system [4]. Plone powered websites offer dynamically updating the data and authorizes many users to update information based on their membership. This ensures a large dissemination of updated information.

2.   LEVERAGING IT FOR RURAL EDUCATION

Unlike the urban students, the rural students have to mostly compromise with the quality of instructors. Thus they are bereft of the experience of being taught by domain experts or at least by those who are acquainted with the domain. Our work envisages a modest infrastructure in the education centers in the rural areas like availability of computers and internet facilities to solve this issue.

Our work involves a close collaboration between centers of excellence in education, knowledge institutes, industry that we hence forth address as Knowledge Centers situated in the urban areas and the rural education centers. Thus, knowledge can be imparted from any of the collaborative partners and the rural education center being the ultimate consumer of service. Students in the rural education center can extensively use the internet to acquire domain specific information. Since, the information on the internet is unevenly spread across and cannot be uploaded from a single mount point we propose to develop a web portals that can be collaborative in nature. Such collaboration is possible by employing CMS.

The Knowledge Centers can upload the information beneficial to the students from their place dynamically and this information can range from simple text file to advanced multi-media files. Since, we envisage a single mount point the students can procure knowledge at a single place on the web as well as post their queries onto the same point.

We christen such an arrangement as 'Knowledge Network'. Our work focuses on three major traits of the Knowledge Network.

- *Flexibility:* This feature emphasizes the need for the uploading/downloading of the information dynamically from any part of the world without pushing the onus of document publication on the webmaster. This would ensure the speedy dissemination of information and would ensure closer interaction between the students and the domain experts.

- *Reliability:* This feature emphasizes the fact that the whole arrangement must be reliable such that all the actors of the Knowledge Network can perform their task without any hindrance such as server crash, network failure etc. Hence, the Knowledge Network must be equipped with features to cope up with crisis like server crash and also the safe storage of all the data.

- *Security:* Since the information can be uploaded from different points by different set of people the authenticity of the information and the credibility of the information providers is an important issue. Hence the CMS must contain a secure work flow and membership feature to enable only authentic persons to have the authority to manage critical access and privilege.

3.   DESIGN OF KNOWLEDGE NETWORK

The proposed Knowledge Network is defined to ensure the larger dissemination of information among the rural populace and this flow of information must be in such a manner that the system must extend flexibility and reliability. In order to offer flexibility a Content Management System like Plone is considered in the Knowledge Network. This will ensure the dynamic update of data online and this update can be performed from any where in the World Wide Web (WWW). The reliability of the network and the data fetching is ensured by employing the Cluster on Demand Architecture (Coda) and setting up replicated servers using Coda.

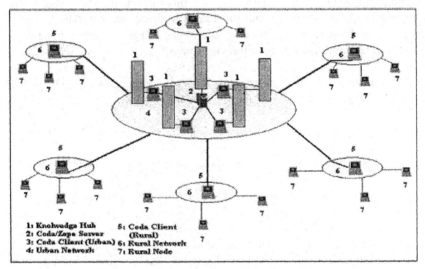

Figure 1. Design of the proposed Knowledge Network

The Knowledge Network consists of seven major components.

(1) *Knowledge Institutes:* The Knowledge Institutes have a crucial role in the Knowledge Network. The Knowledge Institutes host the Coda Server/Clients and the Zope Application Server. The Knowledge Institutes consist of domain experts who can share knowledge about IT and other creative issues with the rural populace leveraging the technology and the high speed networks. Since, Plone CMS is implemented the domain experts/knowledge leaders can feed information on the website which can viewed through the Rural Node over the Rural Network. There can be many such Knowledge Institutes than can play a collaborative role by dynamically authoring the WebPages.

(2) *Coda/Zope Server:* Coda is a state-of-the-art experimental file system [5]. The Coda Server contains one-to-one partitions for its clients. This partition on the server is visible to its clients in a virtualized manner. In the above case the Coda Server is integrated with Zope Web Application Server and the Zope Object Database (ZODB). Any changes made in the website or any updates are recorded in the ZODB. There can be any number of Coda

Servers and each of them undergo perfect replication of data and in the above case each server may have a copy of ZODB and any updates are reflected on the ZODB copy of each server.

(3) *Coda Client*: The Coda Client in the above case serves as the web replication server. The Coda Client is connected to the Coda Server and each client owns an individual partition on the Coda Server. The data in the partition on the server is visible to the client, though it is not stored on the client. The Coda Client has caching and disconnected operation features which enable it to store the important files in its local disk cache. This provision enables the client to store the ZODB available on the server partition into its local cache. Thus, in case if the connection between the client and the server fails due to some network failure the client will be still containing the important data and in this case the updated copy of ZODB

(4) *Urban Network:* The Urban Network is the supplier of knowledge and services to the Rural Network. The Urban Network must consist of high speed network lines and can be heterogeneous in nature. The Urban Network hosts the Coda Server, Coda Clients (Replication Servers), Knowledge Institutes.

(5) *Coda Client (Rural):* This Coda Client will also contain a copy of the ZODB and hence serve as Replication Server. Each rural network can contain a Coda Client. This will ensure a quick access to the server. The Coda Client can be maintained by a nodal center in each rural network. These nodal centers can serve as the knowledge acquisition points where rural people can provide useful information legible to be uploaded on the website.

(6) *Rural Network:* The Rural Network is the recipient of knowledge and services from the Urban Network. The Rural Network can be connected to the Urban Network through Optical Backplane Engineering techniques which would ensure a reliable and fast data transfer. The rural network consists of nodes which can systems in educational places like schools or composite colleges etc. The Rural Network can also consist of Coda Client (Replication Servers).

(7) *Rural Node:* The Rural Node is basically an end system which is a part of the rural network. The Rural Node is the end recipient of knowledge and services. The Rural Node is connected to the Coda Server/Replication Server through high speed network lines. Information flow is presented to the user

through Plone CMS which runs on the Coda Server/Replication Server. Since Plone CMS allows the dynamic updating of data on the website, the user can make data update from the rural node also. In an interactive learning session there can exist feedbacks to the instructor from the students. Since, a CMS is considered such feedbacks can be posted through a single login.

4.   CONCLUSION AND FUTURE WORK

The Knowledge Network is developed with the objective of providing quality distance education to the rural students and upgrading them to a degree of knowledge comparable to their urban peers. The penetration of IT into the rural world will result in the accelerated growth of the villages and will establish a balance between the rural populace and their urban peers. The rural traders will benefit from the knowledge network as they can procure the up-to-date prices of the commodities and can bid for fair prices. The agriculturists will be exposed to a knowledge arena and will introduce them to the urban markets and will result in exponential profits due to the absence of middle men in the dealings.

The Knowledge Network proposed relies heavily on Plone CMS and Coda. Plone is an open source project. Since, this network is envisaged for developing countries the Plone Community must direct sincere efforts towards internationalization. This will result in the Plone web pages being developed in different languages. There exists a project within the Plone Community called 'i18n' which aims at delivering Plone CMS in various languages. This feature will be beneficial for developing worlds like Asia and Africa where IT has not made much of penetration in the rural sector. Projects like 'i18n' will foster imparting education in the regional languages leveraging IT.

REFERENCES

1. Maneul Castells, Information Technolgy, Globalization and Social Development (UNRISD Discussion paper No. 114, September 1999).
2. B.G. Sangameshwara, Ph.D. Thesis "Information Technology for Rural Development : A System's Approach", University of Mysore, India.
3. Wikipedia, http://en.wikipedia.org/wiki/Content_management_system
4. Andy Mckay, The Definitive Guide to Plone (2004).
5. Peter J. Braam, Linux Journal (June 1998).

EXTRACTION OF LEADER-PAGES IN WWW
An Improved Approach based on Artificial Link Based Similarity and Higher-Order Link Based Cyclic Relationships

Ravi Shankar D, Pradeep Beerla
Tata Consultancy Services, Hyderabad, India

Abstract: WWW is the most popular and interactive medium to disseminate information. It creates many new challenges. Several initiatives have been taken to extract different kinds of knowledge from web. In our paper "Leader-page Resources in the World Wide Web" we defined a new method to rank the web pages entirely using the hyperlink information. The notion of "Leader-Page" is extended from the concept of leader from the leadership theory and the social networks. In a community, a leader is a person who interacts the most with other members of the community and whose characteristics are most similar to the characteristics of other members of the community. We have extended these properties of leader to identify leader-pages in WWW. In this paper we propose an improved approach to measure the "leadership score" of a web page based on artificial link based similarity and higher-order link based cyclic relationships it establishes with other web pages of the cyber community.

Key words: Search, Leadership, Artificial Links, Higher Order Cyclic links.

INTRODUCTION

The WWW is the single largest global repository of information and human knowledge. It continues to grow at a remarkable pace with contributions from allover the world. The knowledge discovered through navigation of this complex heterogeneous collection of text (content) and hyperlinks (that lend it a structure) is enormously benefiting the mankind. However owing to the hugeness and diversity of the web users are drowning in information and are facing information overload. It is very difficult to index all the information available on the web. Creating new knowledge out

Please use the following format when citing this chapter:

Shankar D, R., Beerla, P., 2006, in IFIP International Federation for Information Processing, Volume 228, Intelligent Information Processing III, eds. Z. Shi, Shimohara K., Feng D., (Boston: Springer), pp. 151–160.

of information available on the web is another problem. So, the ranking of searched results is very important. One can observe that the web is growing as a socializing medium to connect a group of like-minded people independent of their geographical location and time. Web has turned into one of the most important distribution channels for private, scientific and business information. With the time, web started to behave like a complex society. The social network theory, leadership theory and Mauss's gift exchange theory gave us insights for the concept of leader in the context of WWW. These concepts help in understanding the thought process of the sociology of web and other related issues. We earlier extended these concepts of leadership to World Wide Web [1] and proposed a new approach to rank the results of a search query. We defined a leader-page based on the cyclic and similarity relationships a web page establishes with other web pages of the cyber community. We considered only the hyperlink information to rank the web pages. Now we propose an improved approach to measure the "leadership score" by including the impact of content similarity and higher-order link based cyclic relationships in addition to the existing formulations. The central issue we would address within our framework is the application of this artificial links (content based similarity) and higher-order link based cyclic relationships to modify the "Leader-page algorithm" and rank the web pages accordingly.

The paper is organized as follows. In section 2, we discuss the related work. Here we explain the leadership theory, social network theory and Mauss's gift exchange theory. In section 3, we explain how we extended the concept of leader to define a "leader-page" in the context of WWW and the "leader-page" algorithm. In section 4, we define the "artificial links", "higher-order link based cyclic relationships" and present the modifications in the "leader-page" algorithm. In the last section, we present the summary and conclusions.

1.   RELATED WORK

Search engines perform both link and text based analysis to improve the quality of search results. We have used the concepts from several other theories to propose and improve the leader-page approach. Here we present the background for the social network theory, Mauss's gift exchange theory and leadership theory. We also discuss how leaders evolve in a community.

Social network theory [9] views actors and its relationships in a society as nodes and edges. A social network is a map of all of the relationships between the nodes. This relationship indicates the existence of information exchange among nodes.

Hierarchy in social networks is stated strictly in terms of position of a given node relative to other nodes, without assuming any content to position. The content is given by the nature of exchange and connection. Information exchange happens through the acquaintances in the zones to other nodes. So, a node can be connected to many other nodes by virtue of its own actions or preferences. In social networks, one's immediate zone of neighbors is connected to the immediate zone of those neighbors and so on, which allow a node to reach other nodes in very few steps. Thus nodes draw information, which it would not otherwise know. Thus information is not directly an attribute of individuals, but rather their ability to draw up to their position in a network. Another form of effect of networks is the concept of "threshold point". This idea refers to the extent to which a given phenomenon is allowed to spread through the network. Once a certain level has been reached, all the nodes join in the phenomenon. The probability of any individual node acting is a function of the number of other nodes in the network that have acted in a given way.

Mauss's Theory of gift exchange [10] says that when people give a gift, they are expecting a return gift and when they receive a gift they have a duty to give something in return. The gift embodies some kind of relation of economic reciprocity. So in a network of interactions, when someone gives a reference they expect to be referred by. Elaborating on these observations, given a phenomenon, it will flow through the network because of the interactions being reciprocated among the nodes. The more the nodes interact, the more they will like each other. And the more the nodes like each other, the more they interact (link based cyclic relationship). The more the nodes interact, the more their characteristics become similar (similarity based relationships). Once each node attains a certain level of information (i.e. greater than the threshold) the nodes join in the behavior of the phenomenon. So after some optimum level they start behaving similarly. The nodes, which are similar, form a community.

In any community, the phenomenon of leadership has a great prominence. A leader is interpreted as a person who sets direction in an effort and influences other members of the community to follow that direction. The leaders have strong mutual relationships with other members of the community. A community can be analyzed by studying the leadership phenomenon in the community. A scan of various theories of leadership can help to comprehend the leadership phenomenon. The phenomenon of leadership has been studied since Aristotle. Trait theory is one of the earliest theories on leadership. This theory of leadership focuses on the traits of the leader that make him a leader. The focus has shifted towards the behavior of the leader. Studies have led to the notion of "Charismatic leadership". A charismatic leader continually assesses the environment. He/she communicates with other people, and builds trust and commitment. Finally he/she is the role model of the whole community. Finally, we draw upon the work done by George C Homans [11] in the area of social exchange theory. According to Homan, the leader is a person who interact the most with other members of the group, both initiates and receives the communication, has more social contacts within the group and whose actions and sentiments are most similar to the group's own sentiments and actions. So, interactions (exchanges) among the members of a community help in increasing the similarity among its members finally leading to the evolution of leaders.

2.   LEADER IN WWW & LEADER-PAGE ALGORITHM

We have seen the evolution of leader with the foundations of social networks and gift exchange theories. We can see the analogy with information as flow in the context of WWW. In this section we see how we extend the concept of leader to the World Wide Web.

Creators of web pages exchange hyperlinks to other pages to express some relationship. When the creator of a web page Pi places a hyperlink to a page Pj while there is no hyperlink from Pj to Pi, we say that the creator of P has established an association with the creator of Q. At a later stage, a hyperlink placed from Pj to Pi will create a cyclic relationship between them. Our hypothesis is that the quality and credibility of the content of each of the two web pages of different creators is of higher value if the creators place hyperlinks to each other's web pages than in the case where only one of them places a link to other's pages. This relationship is the basis for the flow of information (exchange of hyperlinks) among the pages. The flow of information spreads a phenomenon among the pages of the web. The web pages that cross the threshold limit for the phenomenon (pages which are similar and have noticeable characteristics) start behaving similarly. This behavior of the information flow of the web pages leads to the development of a cyber Community [8]. There exist some web pages which interact the most with other web pages of the cyber community, both initiates and receives links, has more hyperlinks within the cyber community and whose characteristics are the most similar to the cyber community's own characteristics. Such web pages are called the leader-pages of the cyber community. There can be any number of such leader-pages for a cyber community.

In our paper on leader-page resources in WWW, we have identified the relationship between pages that contribute to the evolution of leader-pages entirely based on the hyperlink analysis. For a web page Pi, the leadership score L[Pi], is determined based on the direct link-based cyclic relationship, indirect link-based cyclic relationship, cocitation based similarity relationship and coupling based similarity relationship with other pages of the web. L[Pi] is the weighted sum of leadership scores of all the other pages which participate in preceding relationships with Pi. Leadership score of a page Pi is defined as **L[Pi]=k_{dl}(DL(Pi))+k_{indl}(INDL(Pi))+k_{coct}(COCT(Pi)) +k_{coup}(COUP(Pi))**, where **DL(Pi)**= sum of leadership scores of all pages in Direct Link based Cyclic relationship with Pi. **INDL(Pi)**= sum of leadership scores of all pages having Indirect Link based Cyclic relationship with Pi. **COCT(Pi)**=sum of leadership scores of all pages having Cocitation based similarity relationship with Pi. **COUP(Pi)**=sum of leadership scores of all pages having Coupling based similarity relationship with Pi. Here, k_{dl}, k_{indl}, k_{coct} and k_{coup} are the parameters that determine the weights of corresponding relationships in the measure of leadership score.

Given search query, the leader-page extraction algorithm first builds the focused sub-graph. The search query is given as input to a search engine. It takes a reasonable number of top pages in the output list and forms corresponding root-set. For each web page in the root-set, corresponding parents and children are extracted. A base-set is formed with the root set, its parents and children of pages in root set. Pre-processing techniques are applied on the base-set.

For each web page Pi in focused sub graph S, the leadership score of page L[Pi] is calculated in the following way

If Pi forms a Direct Link based cyclic relationship with Pj in S, then **L[Pi]=L[Pi]+k_{dl}(L[Pj])**, If Pi forms an Indirect Link based cyclic relationship with Pj&Pk in S, then **L[Pj]=L[Pi]+k_{indl}(L[Pj]+L[Pk])**, If Pi forms a Cocitation based similarity relationship with another Pj in S, then **L[Pi]=L[Pi]+k_{coct}(L[Pj])** and If Pi forms a Coupling based similarity relationship with Pj, then **L[Pi]=L[Pi]+k_{coup}(L[Pj])**. After updating the leadership scores of all web pages, we normalize the leadership scores. The web pages are sorted based on corresponding leadership scores. The values for parameters k_{dl}, k_{indl}, k_{coct} and k_{coup} should be selected based on the corresponding influence on the leadership score. The web pages with high leadership score are identified as the leader-pages. The results have proved that leader-page approach is a potential approach to rank the web pages as compared to hubs-authorities and google's page rank [3,4].

3.   IMPROVED LEADER-PAGE APPROACH

The Leader-page algorithm essentially concentrated on the importance of hyperlinks to calculate the leadership score of a web page. Using the analogy between the web community and a social community it identified the essential properties of leader-page to be the cyclic and similarity relationships it can establish with other web pages. The leader-page algorithm considered only the direct link-based cyclic relationship and indirect link-based relationship. But we can define higher-order link based cyclic relationships of order N. Also we can define artificial links based on content similarity between web pages and calculate the leadership score.

3.1   Higher-order link based cyclic relationships

Pair of web pages P0 & P1 participates in a direct link based cyclic relation ship if P0 establishes a link to P1 and P1 establishes a link to P0. This can be referred as 1st order link based cyclic relationship. Similarly web pages P0, P1 & P2 participate in an indirect link based cyclic relationship if P0 establishes a link to P1, P1 establishes a link to P2 and P2 establishes a link to Po. This can be referred as 2nd order link based cyclic relationship. We can generalize this kind of cyclic relationships. A set of pages P0, P1, P2...Pn participate in a kind of relationship such that P0 establishes a link to P1, P1 establishes a link to P2, ... Pi establishes link to Pi+1...Pn-1 establishes a link to Pn and finally Pn establishes a link to P0. Existence of such a relationship can be called as n^{th} order link based cyclic relationship. In general we can define any number of higher-order link based cyclic relationship of order N. As we use more levels the leadership score become more accurate. So while applying the leader page-algorithm, we can calculate the leadership scores using higher-order link based cyclic relationships till some order. Now for a web page Pi,   If Pi participates in a higher-order cyclic relationship of order N P0, P1, P2...Pn then $L[Pi]=L[Pi]+$ k_{cycN} (L[P0]+L[P1]+L[P2]+...L[Pn]) where k_{cycN} is the parameter that determines the impact of higher-order link based cyclic relationship of order N. A web page participating in many such relationships increases its potential to become a better leader-page.

3.2   Artificial Link based similarity relationship

Artificial links are links introduced between web pages based on content similarity irrespective of the presence of actual hyperlink between them. The objectives are to embed artificial links [5,6,7] among web pages based on text analysis methodologies and extract the required values based on these artificial links. For two web pages Pi and Pj, in this process all the hyperlinks and stop words present in the web pages are removed. Stop words are trivial words with no significance. A dictionary is used to exhaust them. All the words are stemmed and sorted alphabetically. A vector representation of the page with words and frequencies is made assuming all the dimensions are orthogonal. For each page in the data set, which is in vector format, a cluster can be formed with the page having a cosine similarity greater than the specified threshold value of other pages in the data set. A group is formed out of these pages. For each group, artificial links are incorporated among the constituents of the group. In each group, for each of the pages the cosine similarity with other pages is computed. The sum of cosine similarities for each page is computed. This total sum of cosine similarities for each page in a group is called the weight of the page. A sorted set of pages based on the weights is formed. Then artificial hyperlinks are incorporated between all pages in the group with the first page in the group (Lenient strategy). Originally there will not be any link between the web pages Pi and Pj, but with the introduction of an artificial link based on the above-mentioned process, we calculate the leadership score. As the artificial link is given after analysis of the content it is more powerful than a normal link and it has more weight. We give more weight to the artificial link.

So while applying the leader page-algorithm, we can calculate the leadership scores using artificial link based similarity relationships. Now for a web page Pi, If Pi participates in a artificial link based similarity relationship with Pj then $L[Pi]=L[Pi]+ k_{artl} (L[Pj])$ where k_{artl} is the parameter that determines the impact of artificial link based similarity relationship. A web page participating in many such relationships increases its potential to become a better leader-page.

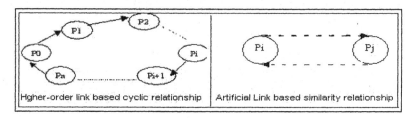

Figure 1. The improved Approach

3.3   Modification in the Leadership score formula

The leadership score formula is impacted by the higher-order link based cyclic relationship and artificial link based similarity relationship modified in the following way $L[Pi]=k_{cyc1}(CYC1(Pi))+k_{cyc2}(CYC2(Pi))+...+$ $k_{cycm}(CYCm(Pi))+....k_{cycn}(CYCn(Pi))+k_{coct}(COCT(Pi))+k_{coup}(COUP(Pi))$ $+k_{artl}(ARTL(Pi))$,Where CYC1(Pi)=sum of leadership scores of all pages having Direct link based cyclic relationship with Pi (order 1). CYC2(Pi)=

sum of leadership scores of all pages having higher order link based Cyclic relationship of order 2 with Pi (order 2). CYCm(Pi)= sum of leadership scores of all pages having higher order link based Cyclic relationship of order M Pi (order M). CYCn(Pi)= sum of leadership scores of all pages having higher order link based Cyclic relationship of order N with Pi (order N). COCT(Pi)=sum of leadership scores of all pages having Cocitation based similarity relationship with Pi. COUP(Pi)=sum of leadership scores of all pages having Coupling based similarity relationship with Pi. ARTL(Pi)=sum of leadership scores of all pages having artificial link based similarity relationship with Pi.

Here k_{cyc1}, k_{cyc2}, k_{cyc3}... k_{cycM}... k_{cycN}, k_{coct}, k_{coup} and k_{artl} are the parameters that determine the weights of corresponding of higher order link based cyclic relationships of order 1, 2, 3, …, N, Cocitation based similarity relationship, Coupling based similarity relationships and artificial link based similarity relationship.

3.4   Modification in the Leader-page algorithm

Given search query, the Leader-page algorithm extracts the corresponding "leader-pages" from WWW. The process of extraction of leader-pages is similar to the extraction of Hub and Authority web pages in HITS [2]. For the specific search query, we build a focused sub-graph. Next, we apply the leader-page extraction algorithm to calculate leadership scores to all the pages in the focused sub-graph. The pages with high leadership score are considered as leaders for the search query. The phases involved in the implementation are as follows.

Building the focused sub graph is build by giving the search query to a search engine. By taking a reasonable number of top pages in the output list corresponding root-set is formed. For each web page in the root-set, corresponding parents and Children are extracted. The parents and children of all the pages and pages of root set form a base-set. Pre-processing techniques are applied on the base-set. This is the focused sub-graph of WWW corresponding to search query.

The algorithm to calculate the leadership scores for the web pages in S is given below. L[Pi] denotes the leadership score of the page Pi and L denotes the leadership score vector for all the pages in S. The leadership scores of all the pages in S are initialized to one. For each web page Pi in S, we use the modified Leadership score formula. If Pi participates in a cyclic relationship of order M with P0, P1, P2...Pm then L[Pi]=L[Pi]+ k_{cycM} (L[P0]+L[P1]+L[P2]+...L[Pm])   where k_{cycM} is the parameter that determines the impact of link based cyclic relationship of order M (M can be any integer >= 1). If Pi forms a Artificial link based similarity relationship with Pj, then L[Pi]=L[Pi]+k_{artl}(L[Pj]) where k_{artl} is the parameter that determines the impact of artificial link based similarity relationship. If Pi forms a Cocitation based similarity relationship with Pj, then L[Pi]=L[Pi]+k_{coci}(L[Pj]) where k_{coci} is the parameter that determines the impact of cocitation based similarity relationship. If Pi forms a Coupling based similarity relationship with Pj, then L[Pi]=L[Pi]+k_{coup}(L[Pj]) where k_{coup} is the parameter that determines the impact of coupling based similarity relationship. After updating L[Pi], the leadership score vector is normalized. The leader-page extraction algorithm repeatedly updates and normalizes the leadership scores. This process is continued till we observe not many variations among the values of leadership scores for the pages in the focused sub graph. Thus the modified leader-page algorithm calculates the leadership scores of all the pages. We filter out top c leader pages for the specific broad topic query and declare them as the results.

4.   SUMMARY AND CONCLUSIONS

In this paper we brought in the concept of higher-order cyclic relationship and generalized the level of cyclic relationships that determine the leadership score of a web page. We also used the content-based similarity to define artificial links among web pages to contribute to the leadership score. We modified the leader-page algorithm. We presented a simple and efficient method to determine these leader pages using the modified leader-page algorithm. These leaders are web pages that we feel are more specific to be the results of a search query.

In our paper on "Leader-page resources in WWW", we have shown that the leader-page algorithm is an efficient measure of ranking the pages as compared to the hubs-authorities and Google's page rank. In this paper we have improved the algorithm by taking into consideration more information through higher-order cyclic relationships and content-based similarity (artificial links) along with the already defined formulations. So, this improved approaches promises better results.

As part of future work we plan to implement the improvements in the leader-page algorithm. The algorithm is still in its preliminary stages and it can be extended using various other algorithms. It can be used with already existing efficient measures to improve the results for a broad topic search query and the rankling methodology

In the improved approach, we plan to use the search results from the yahoo search engine for a search query by making a base set from it. Then we use our improved leader-page algorithm to identify the leaders. We have link based cyclic relationships and similarity based relationships. We will take a relative approach based on the normal links to give the values to the parameters (k_{cycM}, k_{arll}, k_{coct}, k_{coup}), which decide the impact of a relationship on the measure of leadership score. The leadership score for a web page in the focused sub graph is the cumulative weight of all kinds of link based cyclic relationships and similarity based relationships. The web pages with the high leadership score can be identified as the leaders. The various formulations should be instrumental to efficiently identify the leaders in World Wide Web for a specific search query. This whole process involves lot of computations. These computations need to be done offline due to the extensive time input that is needed to calculate the leadership scores.

The optimal value allocation for the parameters (k_{cycM}, k_{arll}, k_{coct}, k_{coup}) is yet to be decided. These parameter values determine the net leadership score of a web page. So it is crucial to identify the optimal values for the parameters in terms of the normal link between the pages.

Finally, using the leader-page approach we can observe the evolution of web leaders in the web communities, the way in which the cyber communities react with the leader pages and also the trends and changes in the community with respect to the leader pages in the World Wide Web. The leadership score acts an efficient ordering metric to develop web directories and web groups.

REFERENCES

[1] D.Ravi Shankar, Pradeep Beerla, P.Krishna Reddy Leader-page Resources in World Wide Web, 12th COMAD 2005b [link]

[2] Jon M. Kleinberg. Authoritative sources in a hyperlinked environment. 9th ACM-SIAM Symposium on Discrete Algorithms, 1998.

[3] L. Page, S. Brin, R. Motwani, and T. Winograd. PageRank Citation Ranking: Bringing order to Web. Stanford Digital Library Technologies Project, 1998.

[4] Sergey Brin and Lawrence Page. The Anatomy of a Large-Scale Hypertextual Web Search Engine. 7th WWW Conference, 1998.

[5] K.Bharat and M. Henzinger, "Improved algorithms for Topic Distillation in Hyperlinked environments", Proc 21st SIGR Conference, (1998).

[6] Soumen Chakrabarti, Byron Dom, Rakesh Agrawal, Prabhakar Raghavan, "Scalable feature selection, Classification and signature generation for organizing large text databases into hierarchical topic taxonomies", VLDB Journal, 1998.

[7] Sergey Brin, "Extracting patterns and relations from the world wide web", 6th EDBT, 1998.

[8] D. Gibson, J. Kleinberg, P. Raghavan, "Inferring Web Communities from Link Topology", 9th ACM Conf on Hypertext and Hypermedia, 1998.

[9] Charles Kadushin, "Intro to Social Network Theory", Brandeis University, 2004.

[10] Mauss,"The Gift Forms and functions of exchange in archaic societies", 1954.

[11] George C Homans. The Human Group. New York Harcourt, Brace & World, 1950.

[12] Northouse, P.G. Leadership theory and practice. Thousand Oaks, CA: Sage Publications, 2001.

SAFE USE OF PROTECTED WEB RESOURCES

Sylvia Encheva
Stord/Haugesund University College
Bjornsonsg. 45, 5528 Haugesund, Norway
sbe@hsh.no

Sharil Tumin
University of Bergen
IT-Dept., P. O. Box 7800, 5020 Bergen, Norway
edpst@it.uib.no

Abstract   This paper focuses on a framework that ensures the safe use of protected Web resources among independent organizations in collaboration. User membership and group membership in each organization are managed independently of other organizations. User authentication and user authorization for a protected resource in one organization is determined by user group membership in other organizations. Furthermore, users never discloses their user-identifiers and passwords in a foreign domain. Every set of related roles in a single organization is defined as an antichain and every set of related roles in the collaborating organizations is defined as a complete lattice. The ranking order of roles for a resource depends on operations. One can add or remove users from roles by managing their membership in corresponding groups.

Keywords: E-services

Introduction

One of the most difficult problems in managing large networked systems is information security. Computer-based access control can prescribe not only who or what process may have access to a specific system resource, but also the type of access that is permitted. In Role-Based Access Control (RBAC), access decisions are based on an individual's roles and responsibilities within the organization or user base [10].

The majority information and communication technology (ICT) based systems are constructed in such a way that user authentication and authorization data have to reside locally in their user database. As a consequence, any orga-

Please use the following format when citing this chapter:

Encheva, S., Tumin, S., 2006, in IFIP International Federation for Information Processing, Volume 228, Intelligent Information Processing III, eds. Z. Shi, Shimohara K., Feng D., (Boston: Springer), pp. 161–170.

nization using such a system is forced to export its users' data to that system. Such a requirement implies a complicated data synchronization mechanism.

User management in a large networked system is simplified by creating a group for each role where addition or removal of users from roles is done by managing their membership in corresponding groups. The problem of a person affiliated with many organizations at the same time is difficult to solve and may not be a major issue if a conflict of interests can be resolved in a role-group relationship. As a possible solution we suggest defining every set of related roles in a single organization as an antichain and every set of related roles in the system of collaborating organizations as a complete lattice.

Lattices have been used to describe secure information flow in [7] and [17]. However, to the best of our knowledge the problem of groups and roles has not been considered in relation to formal concept analysis, concept lattices and complete lattices.

The rest of the paper is organized as follows. Related work is listed in Section 1. Basic terms and concepts are presented in Section 2. A collaboration among independent organizations and a conflict of roles are discussed in Section 3. The paper ends with a conclusion.

1.   Related Work

Formal concept analysis [23] started as an attempt of promoting better communication between lattice theorists and users of lattice theory. Since 1980's formal concept analysis has been growing as a research field with a broad spectrum of applications. Various applications of formal concept analysis are presented in [11].

Methods for computing proper implications are presented in [4] and [22].

A formal model of RBAC is presented in [9]. Permissions in RBAC are associated with roles, and users are made members of appropriate roles, thereby acquiring the roles' permissions. The RBAC model defines three kinds of separation of duties - static, dynamic, and operational. Separation of duties was discussed in [2], [9] and [20]. The use of administrative roles for decentralization of administration of RBAC in large-scale systems is considered in [18]. Assigning roles to users in systems that cross organizational boundaries is discussed in [13] and [14]. A framework for modeling the delegation of roles from one user to another is proposed in [1]. A multiple-leveled RBAC model is presented in [5]. The design and implementation of an integrated approach to engineering and enforcing context constraints in RBAC environments is described in [21].

While RBAC provides a formal implementation model, Shibboleth [19] defines standards for implementation, based on OASIS Security Assertion Markup Language (SAML) [16]. Shibboleth defines a standard set of instructions between an identity provider (Origin site) and a service provider (Target site) to facilitate browser single sign-on and attribute exchange. Our work differs from Shibboleth in modeling implementation and user/group/role management. Shibboleth invests heavily on Java and SAML standards. Our model is more open-ended based on SOAP written in Python [12]. The Origin site manages user and group memberships of users while the Target site manages permissions and role memberships of groups. The Origin site provides procedures callable using SOAP from Target sites to facilitate authorization on a protected resource. Additional needed procedures come to being by mutual agreement between sites.

2. Users, Groups, Roles and Permissions

In this paper a *user* φ is defined as a valid net identity at a particular organization Γ. A valid net identity can be a human being, a machine or an intelligent autonomous agent.

A *group* Ω is a set of users $\{\varphi_j\}_1^s$, i.e. $\Omega = \{\varphi_j | \varphi_j \in \Gamma\}$. A group is used to help the administration of users. The security settings defined for a group are applied to all members of that group.

A *role* Φ contains a set of groups $\{\Omega_i\}_1^l$ associated with similar duty and authority. User administration is simplified by creating a group for each role. One can add or remove users from roles by managing their membership in corresponding groups.

A *resource* Υ defines a set of protected Web objects $\upsilon_j, j = 1, ..., m$.

An *action* Ψ, where

$$\Psi = \begin{pmatrix} (\varsigma_1, \upsilon_1) & \cdots & (\varsigma_1, \upsilon_l) & \cdots & (\varsigma_1, \upsilon_m) \\ \cdots & \cdots & \cdots & \cdots & \cdots \\ (\varsigma_i, \upsilon_1) & \cdots & (\varsigma_i, \upsilon_l) & \cdots & (\varsigma_i, \upsilon_m) \\ \cdots & \cdots & \cdots & \cdots & \cdots \\ (\varsigma_n, \upsilon_1) & \cdots & (\varsigma_n, \upsilon_l) & \cdots & (\varsigma_n, \upsilon_m) \end{pmatrix}$$

is a matrix of operations $\varsigma_i, i = 1, ..., n$ on objects $\upsilon_j \in \Upsilon, j = 1, ..., m$.

EXAMPLE 1 *If operations are read ρ, write ξ, delete τ, copy ϑ, and move μ on the objects $(\upsilon_1, \upsilon_2, \upsilon_3, \upsilon_4. \upsilon_5)$, then the action is*

$$\Psi = \begin{pmatrix} (\rho, \upsilon_1) & (\rho, \upsilon_2) & (\rho, \upsilon_3) & (\rho, \upsilon_4) & (\rho, \upsilon_5) \\ (\xi, \upsilon_1) & (\xi, \upsilon_2) & (\xi, \upsilon_3) & (\xi, \upsilon_4) & (\xi, \upsilon_5) \\ (\tau, \upsilon_1) & (\tau, \upsilon_2) & (\tau, \upsilon_3) & (\tau, \upsilon_4) & (\tau, \upsilon_5) \\ (\vartheta, \upsilon_1) & (\vartheta, \upsilon_2) & (\vartheta, \upsilon_3) & (\vartheta, \upsilon_4) & (\vartheta, \upsilon_5) \\ (\mu, \upsilon_1) & (\mu, \upsilon_2) & (\mu, \upsilon_3) & (\mu, \upsilon_4) & (\mu, \upsilon_5) \end{pmatrix}$$

A *permission* Λ defines a right of a role Φ to perform an action Ψ_Φ on a resource Υ. A user φ has a role Φ_Ω when $\varphi \in \Omega$ and Ω has a role Φ.

A user has a permission only if the user is a member of a group with authorized actions associated with a role. A user φ automatically inherits all permissions associated with the groups to which φ belongs. An authorization gives a set of permissions to a user to execute a set of operations (e.g. read, write, update, copy) on a specific set of resources (e.g. files, directories, programs). An authorization also controls which actions an authenticated user can perform within a Web-based system. A non zero element of the matrix Ψ_ϕ defines a permission. All non zero elements of the matrix Ψ_ϕ^o (see Example 2) define the permissions of a role within a system.

EXAMPLE 2 *If operations are read ρ, write ξ, delete τ, copy ϑ, and move μ on objects $(v_1, v_2, v_3, v_4, v_5)$, then*

$$
\Psi_{\phi^o} = \begin{pmatrix}
(\rho, v_1) & 0 & (\rho, v_3) & (\rho, v_4) & (\rho, v_5) \\
(\xi, v_1) & (\xi, v_2) & 0 & (\xi, v_4) & (\xi, v_5) \\
0 & (\tau, v_2) & (\tau, v_3) & 0 & (\tau, v_5) \\
(\vartheta, v_1) & (\vartheta, v_2) & 0 & (\vartheta, v_4) & (\vartheta, v_5) \\
(\mu, v_1) & (\mu, v_2) & (\mu, v_3) & (\mu, v_4) & 0
\end{pmatrix}
$$

By Ψ_{ϕ^o} we denote the matrix Ψ where at least one of its elements is equal to 0.

An authenticated user, who belongs to a group Ω in an organization Γ_i, will have permissions to perform actions at another organization Γ_j if Ω defined at Γ_i is a member of a role in Γ_j.

DEFINITION 3 *A set P is an* ordered *set if $x \leq y$ only if $x = y$ for all $x, y \in P$.*

Let P be a set. An order *(or partial order) on P is a binary relation $\leq$ on P such that, for all $x, y, z \in P$,*
i) $x \leq x$,
ii) $x \leq y$ and $y \leq x$ imply $x = y$,
iii) $x \leq y$ and $y \leq z$ imply $x \leq z$.

A set P equipped with an order relation $\leq$ is said to be an *ordered set*. An ordered set $\mathcal{P}$ is an *antichain* if $x \leq y$ in $\mathcal{P}$ only if $x = y$. For $x, y \in \mathcal{P}$, we say x is *covered* by y, if $x < y$ and $x \leq x < y$ implies $z = x$.

Let $S \supseteq P$. An element $x \in P$ is an upper bound of S if $s \leq x$ for all $s \in S$. A lower bound is defined dually. The least element in the set of all upper bounds of S is called the *supremum* of S and is denoted by $supS$. The greatest lower bound of S is called the *infimum* of S and is denoted by $infS$.

DEFINITION 4 *Let P be a non-empty ordered set.*
i) If $sup\{x,y\}$ and $inf\{x,y\}$ exist for all $x,y \in P$, then P is called a lattice.
ii) If supS and infS exist for all $S \subseteq P$, then P is called a complete lattice.

A *context* is a triple (G, M, I) where G and M are sets and $I \subset G \times M$. The elements of G and M are called *objects* and *attributes* respectively [6]. The set of all concepts of the context (G, M, I) is a complete lattice and it is known as the *concept lattice* of the context (G, M, I).

For $A \subseteq G$ and $B \subseteq M$, define

$$A' = \{m \in M \mid (\forall g \in A)\ gIm\}, \quad B' = \{g \in G \mid (\forall m \in B)\ gIm\}$$

so A' is the set of attributes common to all the objects in A and B' is the set of objects possessing the attributes in B. Then a *concept* of the context (G, M, I) is defined to be a pair (A, B) where $A \subseteq G$, $B \subseteq M$, $A' = B$ and $B' = A$. The *extent* of the concept (A, B) is A while its intent is B.

3.   Collaborative Management Model

Suppose an organization provides services and defines which domains can share its resources by giving a specific role membership to a group from another domain. A security administrator, working at this organization, needs a model for enforcing a policy of static separation of duties and dynamic separation of duty.

We propose an SOAP communication mechanism for determining a domain user authentication and authorization where a role with less permissions has lower rank than a role with more permissions, and every set of related roles in each organization is an *antichain* [6].

An alternative way is to only allow the minimum permission if a domain user has conflicting roles on the same resource. This is possible only if every set of related roles is a *complete lattice*. What is actually needed is that every set of related roles is a lattice, since a set of related roles in collaborating organizations is a finite set and any finite lattice is a complete lattice [6].

Roles can be ranked in such a way that a higher ranked role also contains all the rights of all lower ranked roles. Thus both roles and permissions are ordered sets with a *covering relation*. The ranking order of roles on a resource depends on operations. Role managers define a ranking order of roles on a resource.

EXAMPLE 5 *Suppose a user has two roles Φ_1 and Φ_2 effectively activated at the same session. Φ_1 and Φ_2 are defined in Table 1 and Table 2 respectively. The resulting role is role Φ^* that the system will provide under conditions defined in Table 3.*

Table 1.   Context for role Φ_1

	read (r)	copy (c)	write (w)	delete (d)	move (m)
file 1 (f1)	×				
file 2 (f2)	×	×			
file 3 (f3)		×	×		×
file 6 (f6)	×	×		×	×

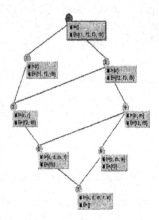

Figure 1.   Context lattice for the role Φ_1

Table 2.   Context for role Φ_2

	read (r)	copy (c)	write (w)	delete (d)	move (m)
file 1 (f1)		×			
file 2 (f2)		×	×		
file 4 (f3)	×		×	×	
file 5 (f5)	×	×			×
file 7 (f7)	×		×	×	×

Table 3.   Context for role Φ^*

	read (r)	copy (c)	write (w)	delete (d)	move (m)
file 1 (f1)	×				
file 2 (f2)	×	×			
file 3 (f3)		×	×		×
file 4 (f4)	×		×	×	
file 5 (f5)	×	×			×
file 6 (f6)	×	×		×	×
file 7 (f7)	×		×	×	×

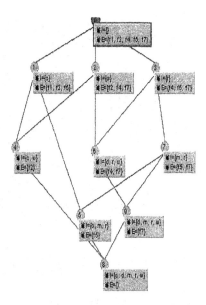

Figure 2. Context lattice for the role Φ_2

A role is given to a user after authentication, defines authorization on a resource, defines operational rights and responsibilities of a user on a resource, and is a dynamic attribute of a user operating on a resource. Roles conflicts appear when a user simultaneously has both a higher ranked role and lower ranked roles on a resource. In such a case, the use will get the role with the least rank, and, therefore receives minimum permission on that resource. Role data in a service provider organization contains references to external group data from client organizations.

EXAMPLE 6 *Let* $\Phi_{org2}^{(m)} = \{\Omega_{org4}^{(m)}, \Omega_{org3}^{(m)}, \Omega_{org2}^{(m)}, \Omega_{org1}^{(m)}\}$ *be a defined role at* (org2) *and a user* $\varphi \in \Omega_{org1}^{(m)}$ *also belongs to* $\Phi_{org2}^{(m)}$. *Then the administration for each group in* $\{\Omega_{org4}^{(m)}, \Omega_{org3}^{(m)}, \Omega_{org2}^{(m)}, \Omega_{org1}^{(m)}\}$ *is done locally at the corresponding organizations* (org4, org3, org2, org1), *while the administration for* $\Phi_{org2}^{(m)}$ *is done by the resource owner* (org2). *A permission* $\Lambda_{org2}^{(m)}$ *defines a right of the role* $\Phi_{org2}^{(m)}$ *on a resource* $\Upsilon_{org2}^{(m)}$.

A number of caveats exist that should be considered under implementation. Some of the more important are that:

- a Web-browser must support cookies,

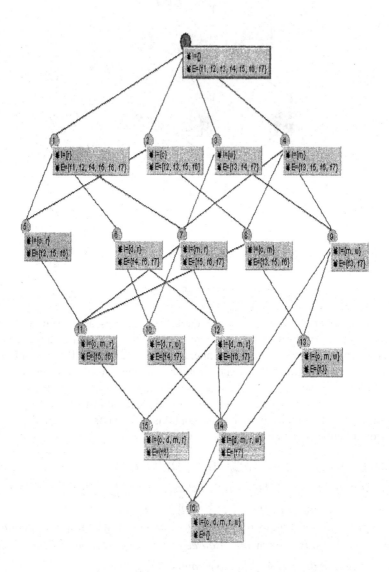

Figure 3.   Context lattice for the role Φ^*

- a Web-browser must not change its IP address, i.e., behind an Internet service provider that rotates client IP addresses,

- an XML-RPC port must be allowed to pass through a firewall, and

- a Web-browser must be able to do redirection.

4.   Conclusion

In this paper we propose a model that simplifies user management in co-operating educational organizations by creating a group for each role. Organizations share their user and group data with each other through a common communication mechanism using SOAP.

Arranging users into groups and roles makes it easier to grant or deny permissions to many users at once. We argue that our model may be used across organizations, based on the group structure and independent collaborative administration; and in the future, because it provides a high level of flexibility and usability.

References

[1] E. Barka and R. Sandhu. Role-based delegation model/ hierarchical roles. *20th Annual Computer Security Applications Conference*, Tucson, Arizona, 2004.

[2] E. Bertino E., P.A. Bonatti and E. Ferrari. TRBAC: A temporal Role-Based Access Control model. *ACM Transactions on information and system security* 3(3):191-223, 2001.

[3] R. Bhatti, E. Bertino, A. Ghafoor and J.B.D. Joshi. XML-based specification for Web services document security. *IEEE Computer* 37(4), 2004.

[4] C. Carpineto and G. Romano. *Concept Data Analysis: Theory and Applications.* John Wiley and Sons, Ltd., 2004.

[5] S-C. Chou. L^nRBAC: A multiple-levelled Role-Based Access Control model for protecting privacy in object-oriented systems. *Journal of Object Technology* 3(3):91-120, 2004.

[6] B.A. Davey and H.A. Priestley. *Introduction to lattices and order.* Cambridge University Press, 2005.

[7] D. Denning. A lattice model of secure information flow. *Communications of the ACM* 19(5) 1976.

[8] J. Dowling and V. Cahill. Self-managed decentralized systems using K-components and collaborative reinforcement learning. *Proceedings of the Workshop on Self-Managed Systems*, 41-49, 2004.

[9] D. Ferraiolo, R. Sandhu, S. Gavrila, R.D. Kuhn and R. Chandramouli. Proposed NIST standard for Role-Based Access Control. *ACM Transactions on Information and System Security.* 4(3):224-274, 2001.

[10] D. Ferraiolo, and R.D. Kuhn and R. Chandramouli. Role-Based Access Control. *Computer Security Series.* Artech House, 2003.

[11] B. Ganter, G. Stumme and R. Wille. *Formal Concept Analysis - Foundations and Applications.* Springer LNCS 114, Berlin, 3626, 2005.

[12] A. Martelli and D. Ascher. *Python Cookbook*. O'Reilly, UK, 2002.

[13] T. Hildmann and J. Barholdt. Managing trust between collaborating companies using outsourced role based control. *4rd ACM Workshop on RBAC*, 105-111, 1999.

[14] A. Herzberg, Y. Mass, J. Mihaeli, D. Naor and Y. Ravid. Access control meets public key infrastructure, Or: Assigning roles to strangers. *IEEE Symposium on security and privacy*, 2000.

[15] B. Kropp and M. Gallaher. Role-based access control systems can save organizations time and money. *Information Security Magazine*, 2005.

[16] http://www.oasis-open.org

[17] R. Sandhu. Lattice-Based access control models. *IEEE Computer*, 26(11), 1993.

[18] R. Sandhu. Role activation hierarchies. *3rd ACM Workshop on RBAC*, 33-40, 1998.

[19] http://shibboleth.internet2.edu/shib-intro.html

[20] R. Simon and M. Zurko. Separation of duty in role-based environments. *Proceedings of 10th IEEE Computer Security Foundations Workshop*. Rockport, Mass., 183–194, 1997.

[21] M. Strembeck and G. Neumann. An integrated approach to engineer and enforce context constraints in RBAC environments. *ACM Transactions on Information and System Security*, 7(3):392-427, 2004.

[22] R. Taouil and Y. Bastide. Computing proper implications. *Proceedings of the ICCS-2001 International Workshop on Concept Lattice-Based Theory, methods and Tools for Knowledge Discovery in Databases*, Palo Alto, CA, USA, 49–61 2001.

[23] R. Wille. Concept lattices and conceptual knowledge systems. *Computers Math. Applic.* 23(6-9):493–515, 1992.

APPLYING QUANTUM SEARCH TO A KNOWN-PLAINTEXT ATTACK ON TWO-KEY TRIPLE ENCRYPTION

Phaneendra H.D. , Vidya Raj C. , Dr. M.S. Shivakumar
Assistant Professor, Department of Computer Science and Engineering, The National Institute of Engineering, Mysore, Karnataka, India

Assistant Professor, Department of Computer Science and Engineering, The National Institute of Engineering, Mysore, Karnataka, India

Principal, The National Institute of Engineering, Mysore, Karnataka, India

Abstract: The process of disguising a plaintext into ciphertext is called encryption and back into plaintext is called decryption. A cryptographic algorithm, is also called a cipher, is the mathematical function used for encryption and decryption. Many algorithms are available for this purpose. Triple DES is such an algorithm. Encryption using triple DES is possible in two different ways; they are triple DES with two keys and triple DES with three different keys. Cryptanalysis can be used to recover the plaintext of a message from the ciphertext without access to or knowing the key. Exhaustive key search remains the most practical and efficient attack on Triple DES with two keys. The principles of quantum mechanics can be used to build and analyze a quantum computer and its algorithms. Quantum searching is one such algorithm. The key search in Triple DES with two keys is possible using quantum search algorithm, which is more efficient compare to any other methods. In this paper we are presenting how quantum search can be used to crack Triple DES with two keys searching for a key.

Keywords: Quantum mechanics, Quantum algorithm, qubits, Quantum search, 3DES, exhaustive search

Please use the following format when citing this chapter:

Phaneendra, H.D., Vidya, R.C., Shivakumar, M.S., 2006, in IFIP International Federation for Information Processing, Volume 228, Intelligent Information Processing III, eds. Z. Shi, Shimohara K., Feng D., (Boston: Springer), pp. 171–178.

1.   INTRODUCTION

1.1   Quantum computation

Quantum Computation is the field of study, which focused on developing computer technology based on the principles of quantum theory. The aim of this paragraph is to make computer scientists to go through the barriers that separate quantum computing from conventional computing. We have introduced the basic principles of quantum computing and tried to implement it in applications like key searching for cracking cryptographic algorithms like DES, Double DES and 3DES. It is important for the computer science community to understand these new developments since they may radically change the way we think about computation, programming, and complexity [1]. The basic variable used in quantum computing is a qubit, represented as a vector in a two dimensional complex Hilbert space where $|$ 0> and $|$ 1> form a basis in the space. The difference between qubits and bits is that a qubit can be in a state other than $|$ 0> or $|$ 1> whereas a bit has only one state, either 0 or 1. It is also possible to form linear combination of states, often called superposition. The state of a qubit can be described by

$$| \psi> = \alpha | 0> + \beta | 1> \tag{1}$$

The numbers α and β are complex numbers. The special states $|$ 0> and $|$ 1> are known as computational basis states. We can examine a bit to determine whether it is in the state 0 or 1 but we cannot directly examine a qubit to determine its quantum state, that is values of α and β. When we measure a qubit we get either the result 0, with probability $| \alpha |^2$ or the result 1, with probability $| \beta |^2$, where $| \alpha |^2 + | \beta |^2 = 1$, since the probabilities must sum to one. Consider the case of two qubits. In two classical bits there would be four possible states, 00, 01, 10 and 11. Correspondingly, a two qubit system has four computational basis states denoted $|$ 00>, $|$ 01>, $|$ 10> and $|$ 11>. A pair of qubits can also exist in a superposition of these four states, so the quantum state of two qubits involves associating a complex coefficient, sometimes called amplitude, with each computational basis state, which is given as

$$| \psi> = \alpha_{00} | 00> + \alpha_{01} | 01> + \alpha_{10} | 10> + \alpha_{11} | 11> \tag{2}$$

The logic that can be implemented with qubits is quite distinct from Boolean logic, and this is what has made quantum computing exciting by opening new possibilities [8].

1.2   Quantum algorithms

Quantum algorithms are based on the principles of quantum mechanics. They are different from classical computing in two specific features: superposition and entanglement. Superposition can transfer the complexity of the problem from a large number of sequential steps to a large number of coherently superposed quantum states. Entanglement is used to create complicated correlation's that permit the desired interference.

A typical quantum algorithm starts with a highly superposed state, builds up entanglement, and then eliminates the undesired components providing compact results. In classical systems, the time taken to do certain computations can be decreased by using parallel processors. To achieve an exponential decrease in time, it requires an exponential increase in the number of processors, and hence an exponential increase in the amount of physical space. However, in quantum systems the amount of parallelism increases exponentially with the size of the system. Thus, an exponential increase in parallelism requires only a linear increase in the amount of physical space. This property is called quantum parallelism [8][2][5].

Suppose we are given a map containing many cities, and wish to determine the shortest route passing through all the cities on the map. A simple algorithm to find this route is to search all possible routes through the cities, keeping a running record of which route has the shortest length. On a classical computer, if there are N possible routes, it takes $O(N)$ operations to determine the shortest route using this method. But quantum search algorithm enables this search method to be sped up substantially, requiring only $O(\sqrt{N})$ operations.

The quantum search algorithm is general in the sense that it can be applied far beyond the route finding example just described to speed up many (though not all) classical algorithms that use search heuristics. Thus given a search space of size N, and no prior knowledge about the structure of information in it, if we want to find an element in search space satisfying a known property, then this problem requires approximately N operations, but the quantum search algorithm allows it to be solved using approximately $\sqrt{N}$ operations[8][5].

2.   TRIPLE DES

The Data Encryption Standard (DES) is a widely-used algorithm for encrypting data. It was developed by IBM under the name Lucifer. DES is a product block encryption algorithm (a cipher) in which 16 iterations, or rounds, of the substitution and transposition (permutation) process are cascaded. The block size is 64 bits, so that a 64-bit block of data (plaintext) can be encrypted into a 64-bit ciphertext. The key, which controls the transformation, also consists of 64 bits. Only 56 bits of these, however, are at the user's disposal; the remaining eight bits are used for checking parity. The actual key length used for encryption is therefore 56 bits. The same key is used for decryption [12]. DES is vulnerable to brute force attack, where key space can be searched for possible key to decrypt the message. Alternative is double DES. This scheme apparently involves a key length of 56 x 2 = 112 bits, resulting in a dramatic increase in cryptographic strength. Brute-force requires an exhaustive search of 2^{112} keys [12]. But this can be attacked by means of an algorithm known as meet-in-the middle attack.

The key which is used for encryption of the plaintext in DES and Double DES can also be found by means of using quantum search algorithm, sometimes called Grover's search algorithm. The algorithm enables search method to be sped up substantially requiring only O ($\sqrt{(N)}$) operations.

An obvious counter to these attacks is to use three stages of encryption with three different keys. This raises the cost of brute-force attack to 2^{168} keys, because it requires a key length of 56 x 3 = 168 bits. This also raises the known plain-text attack to 2^{112} keys.

Encryption using triple DES is possible in two different ways; they are triple DES with two keys and triple DES with three different keys.

2.1   Triple DES with two Keys

This method was proposed by Tuchman that uses only two keys. The method follows an encrypt-decrypt-encrypt (EDE) sequence as shown in the following figure 1. [3].

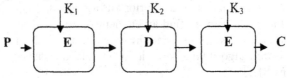

Figure 1. Triple DES with two Keys

The method operates on a block three times with two keys, with the first key, then with the second key, and finally with the first key again. That means the sender first encrypt with the first key, then decrypt with the second key, and finally encrypt with the first key. The receiver decrypts with the first key, then encrypts with the second key, and finally decrypts with the first key.

$$C = E_{K1}(D_{K2}(E_{K1}(P)))$$
$$P = D_{K1}(E_{K2}(D_{K1}(C)))$$

The triple encryption with two keys is susceptible to chosen-plaintext attack and known-plaintext attack.

The chosen-plaintext attack requires an enormous amount of chosen-plaintext to mount. It requires 2^n time and memory (where n is the length of the key), and 2^m chosen- plaintexts. It is not very practical, but it becomes a weakness.

The known-plaintext attack, requires p known plaintexts, and assumes encryption is made using EDE (encrypt-decrypt-encrypt) mode. The algorithm for this is given by   P.C. Van Oorschot and M.J. Wiener [3] [9].

3.   THE PROPOSED METHOD USING QUANTUM SEARCH

The keys that are used for encryption of the plaintext in triple encryption with two keys can be found by means of using quantum search algorithm, sometimes called Grover's search algorithm. The algorithm enables search method to be sped up substantially requiring only O ($\sqrt{N}$) operations. The algorithm for this is as follows.

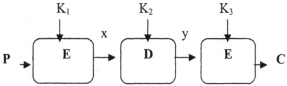

Figure 2. EDE mode.

1. We need to guess the first intermediate value, x (figure 2)
2.   Then store, for each of the 256 possible K1, the second intermediate value, y, when the first intermediate value is x, using known plaintext:

$$y = D_{K1}(C)$$

Where C is the resulting ciphertext from a known plaintext.

(Resulting values need not be sorted, because quantum search works onto nonordered values)

Table 1. Table of intermediate values and key

y	K₁
.	.
.	.
.	.
.	.

3.   Quantum search the table 1, for each of the 256 possible K2, elements with a matching second intermediate value, y:

$$y = E_{K2}(x)$$

If there is a match, then the corresponding key K_1 from table and the current value of K_2 are candidate values for the unknown keys (K_1, K_2).

(Search is possible with O $(\sqrt{(2^{K_1})})$ for each K_2)

4.   The probability of success is p/m, where p is the number of known plaintexts and m is the block size. If there is no match, try another x and start again from step 1.

This algorithm reduces the number of searches required for the keys.

The keys can be found with only $\sqrt{(2^{K_1})}$ searches with the best case, and $2^{K2} * \sqrt{(2^{K_1})}$ with the worst case. On an average $2^{K2}/2 * \sqrt{(2^{K_1})}$ searches are required for finding the keys K_1 and K_2.

4.   THE TIME AND SPACE ANALYSIS

In this section, we briefly summarize the running time and amount of memory required considering the algorithm given by   P.C. Van Oorschot and M.J. Wiener [9] and our proposed algorithm.

There are three different cases arises for time and space analysis.

Case 1: The resulting values produced in step 2 will be stored onto a table, and the table need not be sorted. If this table is searched in step 3, the time required for a match is the order of 2^{56} at the worst case.

Case 2:   The resulting values produced in step 2 will be stored onto a table, and the table is sorted. If this table is searched in step 3, the time required for a match is the order of O $(\log_2 2^{56})$. Here we have to consider the time required for sorting the table.

Case 3: The resulting values produced in step 2 will be stored onto a table, and the table need not be sorted. If this table is searched in step 3, the time required for a match is the order of O $(\sqrt{(2^{56})})$ (quantum search works onto nonordered values).

The space required to store resulting values in case 1 and case 2 are of the order of 2^{56} i.e., $O(2^{56})$.

The space required to store the resulting values in case 3 is difficult to specify, because quantum search works on quantum computers and it uses concept of superposition and quantum parallelism.

5.   PERFORMANCE ANALYSIS BY SIMULATION.

Table 2. Comparison between Linear and Quantum search

No of Keys	Linear search (Non ordered values)	Quantum search (Non ordered values)
256	128	16
512	256	22
1024	512	32
2048	1024	45
4096	2048	64
8192	4096	90
16384	8192	128
32768	16384	181
65536	32768	256
131072	65536	362
262144	131072	512
524288	262144	724
1048576	524288	1024

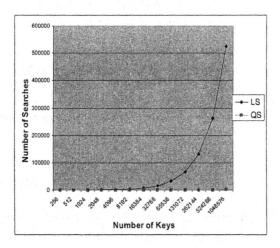

Graph1. Comparison between Linear and Quantum search

Here the table 2 gives the comparison between use linear search and quantum search for key searching. We are not comparing binary search since it needs values are to be sorted before searching, and sorting takes considerable amount of time. The graph shows how quantum search out performs the linear search.

6.   CONCLUSION

In this paper, we studied and analyzed quantum search algorithm based on quantum mechanics, by applying to a known-plaintext attack on two-key triple encryption. This algorithm works on unsorted list (step 2 of the algorithm), and provides a quadratic speed-up and the desired item is located with $O (\sqrt{(2^{K1})})$ queries (step 3 of the algorithm) with the best case. Theoretically it can be concluded that quantum search algorithm provide fast results by taking the help of quantum mechanics concepts like quantum parallelism and superposition. Quantum computing is a field in its infancy. When quantum computing was first systematically investigated, the main fear was that the natural world would not be able to realize any accuracy. These early concerns are now being overshadowed by the greater accomplishments in quantum computing. The consensus is that triple encryption with two keys, when used properly, is still secure. But a known-plaintext attack becomes easy looking at the research in quantum computation.

REFERENCES

1. Amardeep Singh and Sarbjeet Singh,(2003), Applying quantum search to automated test pattern generation for VLSI circuits, International Journal of Quantum Information,Vol.1 No. 1, 79-91.
2. Apoorva Patel, Quantum Database Search can do without Sorting, quant-ph/0012149.
3. Bruce Schneier,(2002), Applied Cryptography, Wiley International Pvt Ltd, New Delhi.
4. Grover L.K, (1996), A Fast Quantum mechanical Algorithm for Database Search, In proceedings of the 28th Annual ACM Symposium on the Theory of Computing,pp.212-219,quant-ph/9605043.
5. Grover L.K. (2002), Tradeoffs in the Quantum Search Algorithm, quant-ph/0201152.
6. Nielsen M and Chaung, I (2000), Quantum Computation and Quantum Information, Cambridge University press, Cambridge, United Kingdom.
7. P.C. Van Oorschot and M.J. Wiener A Known-Plaintext Attack on Two-Key Triple Encryption.Advances in Cryptology – EUROCRYPT 90 Proceedings.
8. Terry Rudolph and Dr. Lov Grover,(2002), Quantum Searching a classical database, quant-ph/0206066.
9. William Stallings, (2003), Cryptography and Network Security, Principles and Practices. Pearson Education, New Delhi.

QUANTUM SEARCH: REDUCES THE TIME AND COST FOR SEARCHING FOR OBJECTS IN MULTIPLE-SERVER PEER-TO-PEER NETWORKS

Phaneendra H.D. , Dr. M.S. Shivakumar

Assistant Professor, Department of Computer Science and Engineering, The National Institute of Engineering, Mysore, Karnataka, India

Principal, The National Institute of Engineering, Mysore, Karnataka, India

Abstract: In number of Internet applications we need to search for objects to down load them. This includes peer-to-peer (P2P) file sharing, grid computing and content distribution networks. Here the single object will be searched for in multiple servers. There are many searching algorithms existing today for this purpose and uses the concept of classical physics and classical algorithms. The principles of quantum mechanics can be used to build and analyze a quantum computer and its algorithms. Quantum searching is one such algorithm. In this paper we are proposing a search method based on quantum physics and quantum algorithms.

Keywords: Quantum mechanics, Quantum algorithm, qubits, Quantum search, linear search, object.

1.   INTRODUCTION

1.1   Quantum computation

Quantum Computation is the field of study, which focused on developing computer technology based on the principles of quantum theory. The aim of this paragraph is to make computer scientists to go through the barriers that

Please use the following format when citing this chapter:

Phaneendra, H.D., Shivakumar, M.S., 2006, in IFIP International Federation for Information Processing, Volume 228, Intelligent Information Processing III, eds. Z. Shi, Shimohara K., Feng D., (Boston: Springer), pp. 179–186.

separate quantum computing from conventional computing. We have introduced the basic principles of quantum computing. It is important for the computer science community to understand these new developments since they may radically change the way we think about computation, programming, and complexity [1]. The basic variable used in quantum computing is a qubit, represented as a vector in a two dimensional complex Hilbert space where $|0>$ and $|1>$ form a basis in the space. The difference between qubits and bits is that a qubit can be in a state other than $|0>$ or $|1>$ whereas a bit has only one state, either 0 or 1. It is also possible to form linear combination of states, often called superposition. The state of a qubit can be described by

$$|\psi> = \alpha|0> + \beta|1> \tag{1}$$

The numbers α and β are complex numbers. The special states $|0>$ and $|1>$ are known as computational basis states. We can examine a bit to determine whether it is in the state 0 or 1 but we cannot directly examine a qubit to determine its quantum state, that is values of α and β. When we measure a qubit we get either the result 0, with probability $|\alpha|^2$ or the result 1, with probability $|\beta|^2$, where $|\alpha|^2 + |\beta|^2 = 1$, since the probabilities must sum to one. Consider the case of two qubits. In two classical bits there would be four possible states, 00, 01, 10 and 11. Correspondingly, a two qubit system has four computational basis states denoted $|00>$, $|01>$, $|10>$ and $|11>$. A pair of qubits can also exist in a superposition of these four states, which is given as

$$|\psi> = \alpha_{00}|00> + \alpha_{01}|01> + \alpha_{10}|10> + \alpha_{11}|11> \tag{2}$$

The logic that can be implemented with qubits [6].

1.2   Quantum algorithms

Quantum algorithms are based on the principles of quantum mechanics. They are different from classical computing in two specific features: superposition and entanglement. Superposition can transfer the complexity of the problem from a large number of sequential steps to a large number of coherently superposed quantum states. Entanglement is used to create complicated correlation's that permit the desired interference.

A typical quantum algorithm starts with a highly superposed state, builds up entanglement, and then eliminates the undesired components providing compact results. In classical systems, the time taken to do certain computations can be decreased by using parallel processors. To achieve an exponential decrease in time, it requires an exponential increase in the number of processors, and hence an exponential increase in the amount of physical space. However, in quantum systems the amount of parallelism increases exponentially with the size of the system. Thus, an exponential increase in parallelism requires only a linear increase in the amount of physical space. This property is called quantum parallelism [6][2][5].

For example Traveling salesman problem can be solved with O ($\sqrt{N}$) operations using quantum algorithm, which requires O(N) operations in classical algorithm.

The quantum search algorithm is general in the sense that it can be applied far beyond the route finding example just described to speed up many (though not all) classical algorithms that use search heuristics. Thus given a search space of size N, and no prior knowledge about the structure of information in it, if we want to find an element in search space satisfying a known property, then this problem requires approximately N operations, but the quantum search algorithm allows it to be solved using approximately $\sqrt{N}$ operations [5][6].

2.   PEER-TO-PEER NETWORKS

Efficiently looking for a single object in multiple servers is fundamental to many emerging applications on the Internet. For example, in peer-to-peer (P2P) file sharing a single file is searched for in multiple "servent" nodes that act as servers. A servent is a node in a P2P network having both server and client capabilities. An efficient search for the object returns with the location of the searched object quickly and with a low cost. Cost can be measured as the total server utilization per search [4].

One of the methods for an efficient search is to maintain a centralized directory of all objects. A centralized directory is the approach Napster [4] used for P2P file sharing in the Internet. However, for reasons of robustness distributed solutions are also typically sought.

Another and simple approach is a fully distributed search based on a broadcast search. Here the search query is broadcasted to all servers. Gnutella uses this broadcast approach in an overlay network on the Internet. The time to find an object is small, however the cost is significant – all Gnutella servents are queried independently of the likelihood of (the servent) having the searched object. It has been shown that broadcast based search does not scale well for systems with many servers [8]. As the number of servers, N, in a system increases linearly, the load on each server increases exponentially. Currently, at least 25% of the traffic in the Internet is P2P file query related [4]. Thus, to reduce load on P2P nodes and reduce traffic in the Internet new ideas in searching in P2P networks are needed [4].

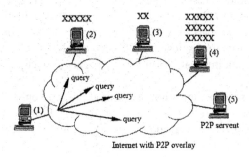

Figure 1. P2P network with stored objects

Here X means shared object. Node (1) is for sending queries. Node (4) has the most objects stored. Nodes (2) and (3) are also stored with some objects. Nodes (1) and (5) are free riders

Characterization of P2P networks has shown that connectivity of servents to other servents follows a power law where very few servents are high degree and the majority of servents are low degree [9]. File sharing also follows a power-law where few servents contain the majority of files shared (and many servents may share no files at all and are so called "free riders") [4]. These Characterizations clearly show that connectivity and file distribution between servents are not uniformly distributed. Hence exploiting these characteristics can result in greater search efficiency.

3.   THE QUANTUM SEARCH METHOD

In this section we show that how quantum search is possible looking for a single object. We develop a quantum search method for finding objects. The quantum search method exploits superposition and quantum parallelism and a non-ordered distribution of objects in nodes to achieve an efficient search in terms of search time and cost. Figure. 1 shows a P2P network with multiple servents that stores the objects.

The object required can be obtained in three different methods. They are
1. Centralized directory of all objects
2. Centralized directory of all objects along with server names.
3. The directory of objects in various servers.

In the first method the server contains a directory of all objects. This directory is searched for required object, if found can be downloaded. The query for this purpose directly searches this directory. The object names stored in this directory could be an unordered list. The quantum search works onto an unordered list efficiently, by searching for the object in the order of $\sqrt{N}$, where N is the number of objects in the server.

Here linear search on the directory is possible, because the directory with object names is an unordered list (other searching methods requires object names to be stored in some order, for example binary search requires list must be sorted in ascending order). The linear search takes O (N) steps to search for an object at the worst case and $O(N/2)$ in an average . Therefore quantum search is better than the linear search, and object can be added the server and object names can be added to the directory without sorting.

The objects can be searched with only $\sqrt{N}$ steps rather than $O(N/2)$ steps with a single query.

This method suffers with scalability, where it requires more space to store objects and the number of entries to the directory increases with more number of objects.

The second method, again the server contains a directory of all objects, but the difference is each entry in the directory contains two columns with entries (object name, server name). The first query is made to the server with object name required, if found, will give the server name, where exactly the object is available. Now another query can be sent directly to the server, where the object is present, quantum search for it, and can be downloaded.

The required object can be searched with two queries with $\sqrt{N}$ steps in each query, rather than O(N) steps.

This method also overcomes the problem of scalability, where objects can be added to the servers in the second level, along with an entry to the directory in the server which maintains the centralized directory of all objects. The cost here is it requires two queries to search for an object.

In the last method the directory of objects along with objects are maintained in various servers. The query with desired object is broadcasted to all servers. Quantum search of each directory in each server is carried out independently and simultaneously. The server which contains the desired object responds after quantum searching its directory.

The required object can be searched with only one query with O ($\sqrt{N}$) steps, rather than O (N) steps.

This method further overcomes the problem of scalability, where more servers can be added to the network. When an object is added to the server, the entry for this object should be made only in the directory of the respective server

4.   ALGORITHMS FOR THESE METHODS

The algorithms for searching for an object using the above three methods are as follows.

Method 1:

*Figure 2.*Directory with object names

Step 1: Send a query to the server, which maintains the centralized directory of all objects (Figure 2).

Step 2: Quantum search the directory

Step 3: If the object is found in the server then download the object.

Method 2:

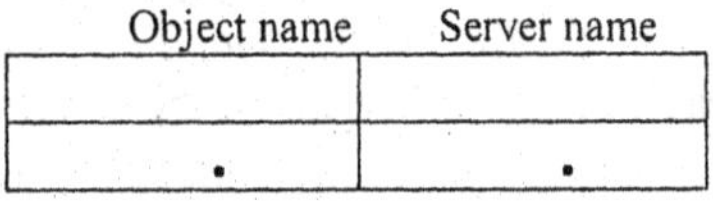

Object name	Server name
•	•

Figure 3. Directory with object and server names

Step 1: Send a query to the server, in the first level, which maintains the centralized directory of all objects (Figure 3).

Step 2: Quantum search the directory

Step 3: If object is found, obtain the server name where it is available

Step 4: Send query again to the server name obtained in step 3

Step 4: If the object is found in the server then download the object.

Method 3:

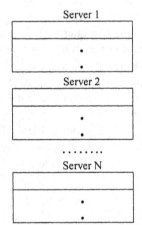

Figure 4. Directory with object names in each of the N servers

Step 1: Broadcast a query to all N servers.

Step 2: Quantum search the directory in each server independently and simultaneously (Figure 4).

Step 3: If the object is found, then download the object from the respective server.

5 PERFORMANCE EVALUATION OF QUANTUM SEARCH

Table 1. Comparison between Linear and Quantum Search

Number of Objects(N)	Linear Search (Unordered list)	Quantum Search (Unordered list)
8	4	3
16	8	4
32	16	6
64	32	8
128	64	11
256	128	16
512	256	22
1024	512	32

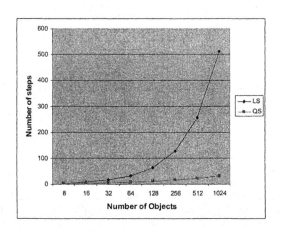

Graph 1

Here the table 1 gives the comparison between use of linear search and quantum search for searching the objects. The graph shows how quantum search out performs the linear search, searching in an unordered list of objects.

Method 1 requires single query with $\sqrt{N}$ steps, to find an object.

Method 2 requires two queries with $\sqrt{N}$ steps for each query, to find an object

Method 3 requires a broadcasted query with $\sqrt{N}$ steps to find an object

6.   CONCLUSION

In this paper, we studied and analyzed quantum search algorithm based on quantum mechanics, by applying to multiple-server peer-to-peer networks searching for an object. This algorithm works on unsorted list of objects, and provides a quadratic speed-up and the desired object is located with $O(\sqrt{N})$ steps with the best case. Theoretically it can be concluded that quantum search algorithm provide fast results by taking the help of quantum mechanics concepts like quantum parallelism and superposition. The consensus is that looking at the research in quantum computation and quantum information, quantum search could supplement the classical search problems.

REFERENCES

1. Apoorva Patel, Quantum Database Search can do without Sorting,   quant-ph/0012149.
2. Graciela perera, Ken Christensen and Allen Roginsky, Targeted search: Reducing the Time and Cost for Searching for Objects in Multiple-Server Networks, IEEE transaction, 2005,   pp 143-149.
3. Grover L.K, (1996), A Fast Quantum mechanical Algorithm for Database Search, In proceedings of the 28th Annual ACM Symposium on the Theory of Computing,pp.212-219,quant-ph/9605043.
4. Nielsen M and Chaung, I (2000), Quantum Computation and Quantum Information, Cambridge University press, Cambridge, United Kingdom.
5. S. Saroiu, P. Gummadi, and S. Gribble, A measurement Study of Peer-to-Peer File Sharing Systems, Proceedings of SPIE, pp. 156-170, 2001.
6. R. Schollmeier and G. Schollmeier, Why Peer-to-Peer (P2P) Does Scale: An Analysis of P2P Traffic Patterns, Proceedings of the 2nd International Conference on Peer-to-Peer Computing, pp. 112-119, 2002.
7. B. Yang, P. Cao, and H. Molina, Efficient Search in Peer-to-Peer Networks, Proceedings of the International Conference on Distributed Computing Systems, pp. 5-14,2002.
8. Terry Rudolph and Dr. Lov Grover,(2002), Quantum Searching a classical database, quant-ph/0206066.

EFFICIENT KNOWLEDGE ASSESSMENT BASED ON CONVEX GEOMETRIES

Sylvia Encheva
Stord/Haugesund University College
Bjornsonsg. 45, 5528 Haugesund, Norway
sbe@hsh.no

Sharil Tumin
University of Bergen
IT-Dept., P. O. Box 7800, 5020 Bergen, Norway
edpst@it.uib.no

Abstract

The goal of this paper is to develop a theoretical framework for efficient assessment of learners' understanding of carefully chosen terms and concepts. The model is based on the theory of knowledge spaces and lattices of convex geometries. The structure of the latter is used to select only knowledge states that imply understanding of key ideas and minimize the effect of lucky guesses while determining learner's knowledge.

Keywords: Knowledge, lattices

Introduction

Assessing the initial knowledge of a student and updating this assessment as the student progresses through a course is an important part of an intelligent tutoring system. A framework for representing and measuring students' knowledge is developed in [7]. The key concepts in the theory of knowledge spaces are the *knowledge state* - a subset of problems that an individual is capable of solving correctly, and the *knowledge structure* - a distinguished collection of knowledge states [10].

Establishing the knowledge state of a student in a subject may be require a long sequence of questions. Therefore it might not be very effective for providing immediate help to the student while he/she is working on a particular part of the curriculum. In this paper we propose a model for automated assessment

Please use the following format when citing this chapter:

Encheva, S., Tumin, S., 2006, in IFIP International Federation for Information Processing, Volume 228, Intelligent Information Processing III, eds. Z. Shi, Shimohara K., Feng D., (Boston: Springer), pp. 187–196.

of learner's understanding of comparatively small units that are considered to be fundamental in a subject. The model is based on knowledge spaces and lattices of convex geometries.

Systems like 'Assessment and LEarning in Knowledge Spaces' (ALEKS) [16] and Relational Adaptive Tutoring Hypertext (RATH) [17] aim at establishing the knowledge state of each student in a certain knowledge domain and then provide further guidance and personalized help.

This model differs from existing systems in the following:

- it is based on multiple choice tests,

- can assess high level thinking,

- rewards partial knowledge,

- does not apply coefficients for guessing correction, and

- knowledge states are arranged in meet-distributive lattices and student's understanding of an atom is found satisfactory if his/her response belongs to a sublattice of a lattice of the convex geometries on the set of related atoms.

Tests are designed to assess critical thinking applying Bloom's Taxonomy [2]. Such tests contain stems asking students to identify the correct outcome of a given circumstance, map the relationship between two items into a different context, respond to what is missing or needs to be changed within a provided scenario, and evaluate the proposed solution based upon criteria provided.

The rest of the paper is organized as follows. Related work is listed in Section 1. Selected theory used for the model development is presented in Section 2. The model description can be found in Section 3. The paper ends with a conclusion placed in Section 4.

1.   Related Work

A model for student knowledge diagnosis through adaptive testing is presented in [13]. Permutational multiple choice question tests have been used for assessing high-level thinking [11]. Students' conceptual thinking can be assessed by presenting them with tests where all the correct answers should be chosen and/or answers require integration of several components or approaches [3] and [11].

The use of formula in a spreadsheet to convert the raw assessment marks into marks or grades corrected for guessing or additionally allowing for the maximum expected mark is demonstrated in [14].

An excellent introduction to ordered sets and lattices and to their contemporary applications can be found in [5].

Subsets of relevent examination questions and certain skills from a branch of knowledge are listed as examples of knowledge states in [8]. They are followed by an important remark that not all possible subsets of such items turn out to be knowledge states.

ALEKS [16] is based on mathematical cognitive science and involves computer algorithms while constructing specific knowledge structures. Markovian procedures are further employed for analyzing of a particular student's knowledge.

RATH [17] combines mathematical hypertext model and knowledge space theory and is focused on teaching.

2.   Preliminaries

Let Q be a finite set. A family $\mathcal{K}$ of subsets of Q is a *knowledge space* on Q [7] if
i) the empty set and the total set Q are members of the family $\mathcal{K}$, and
ii) the family $\mathcal{K}$ is closed under union.

An atom at item q in knowledge space theory is a minimal knowledge state containing q. A state is called an atom if it is an atom at q for some item q.

A *base* for a knowledge structure $(Q, \mathcal{K})$ is a minimal family $\mathcal{A}$ of states spanning $\mathcal{K}$ ('minimal' with respect to set inclusion, i.e. if $\mathcal{F} \subseteq \mathcal{A}$ is any family of states spanning $\mathcal{K}$, then $\mathcal{F} = \mathcal{A}$).

A closure system on a finite set M is a set $\mathcal{F}$ of subsets of M such that
1) $M \in \mathcal{F}$ and
2) $C, C^1 \in \mathcal{F} \Rightarrow C \cap C^1 \in \mathcal{F}$

A knowledge space is a closure system [7]. A closure system on set M is convex geometry if it satisfies the following properties:

- the empty set is closed

- for every closed set $M_1 \neq M$ there exists $m \notin M_1$ such that $M_1 + m$ is a closed set.

A lattice is a partially ordered set, closed under least upper and greatest lower bounds. The least upper bound of x and y is called the join of x and y, and is sometimes written as $x + y$; the greatest lower bound is called the meet and is sometimes written as $x\dot{y}$.

X is a sublattice of Y if Y is a lattice, X is a subset of Y and X is a lattice with the same join and meet operations as Y. A lattice L is meet-distributive if for each $y \in L$, if $x \in L$ is the meet of (all the) elements covered by y, then the interval $[x; y]$ is a boolean algebra.

Convex geometries are closure systems which satisfy anti-exchange property, and they are known as dual of antimatroids. The set of closed sets of a

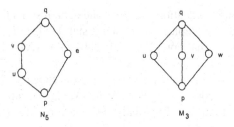

Figure 1.   The two lattices N_5 and M_3

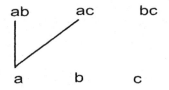

Figure 2.   Rule 1 - one basic question from B and two related questions from R

convex geometry, form a lattice when ordered by set inclusion. Such lattices are precisely the meet- distributive lattices.

THEOREM 1 *[5] Let L be a lattice.*
i)   L is non-modular if and only if L has a sublattice isomorphic to N_5.
ii) L is non-distributive if and only if L has a sublattice isomorphic to N_5 or M_3.

3.   A Unit Followed by Six Questions

After going through a larger unit in a subject, a student is suggested to take a test with six questions. Three of the questions consider understanding of new terms or applying new skills, and are denoted by $\{a, b, c\} = B$. The other three are denoted by $\{ab, ac, bc\} = R$ and indicate student's ability to apply both a and b at the same time (denoted ab), both a and c at the same time (denoted ac) and both b and c at the same time (denoted bc). For the sake of presentation simplicity we do not involve more questions. Further more we assume that a student has sufficient knowledge and understanding of a question if he/she gives correct answers to:

- one basic question from the set B, say c and the two related to c questions from the set R, i.e. ac, bc (see Fig. 2), or

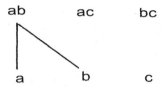

Figure 3.   Rule 2 - two basic questions from $\mathcal{B}$ and the related question from $\mathcal{R}$

Table 1.   Correct answer combinations leading to a reduced test in a consecutive trial in the case of six questions

Correctly answered questions in a current test						Questions to be excluded in a consecutive trial
a	b	c	ab	ac	bc	
●			●	●		a
	●		●		●	b
		●		●	●	c
●	●		●			ab
●		●			●	ac
		●	●		●	bc
●	●		●	●		a, ab
●	●	●		●		b, ab
●		●	●		●	a, ac
	●	●	●		●	b, bc
	●	●		●	●	c, bc
●		●		●	●	c, ac
●	●	●	●	●		a, ab, ac
●	●	●	●		●	b, ab, bc
●	●	●		●	●	c, ac, bc

- two basic question from the set $\mathcal{B}$, say a, b and the related to a and b question from the set $\mathcal{R}$, i.e. ab (see Fig. 3).

In other words we want to filter out all answer combinations that do not contain basic questions and the related to them questions, f. ex. a, b, ac in Fig. 4. The lattice in Fig. 4 is a M_3 lattice from Theorem 1.

Insted of applying one of the numerous ways of penalizing students for guessing we apply the rules illustrated in Fig. 2 and Fig. 3. The outcome is listed in Table 1 and has a graphical representation shown by Fig. 5.

Case 1:
If a student can answer correctly to less than three questions or to exactly three questions from either $\mathcal{B}$ or $\mathcal{R}$, the system will present him/her with selected

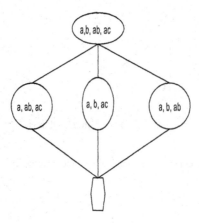

Figure 4.   A modular lattice which is not distributive

learning materials (theory and examples). Next time the student takes the same
test he/she will be presented with six similar questions but developed by another course builder.

Case 2:
Suppose a student answers correctly to questions c, ac, bc, (see Fig. 6). This
answer combination indicates mastering question c and makes no assumptions
about other questions. The student will then be advised to work with selected
learning materials (theory and examples) concerning questions a and b. Next
time the student takes the same test he/she will be presented with five questions a, c, ab, ac, bc again developed by another course builder. If the student
answers correctly to all of them, the process of questioning is terminated. If the
students fails to give correct answers to some of the questions a, b, ab, ac, bc
then procedures similar to the following cases will be applied.

Case 3:
Suppose a student answers correctly to questions b, c, bc (see Fig. 7). This answer combination indicates mastering question bc and makes no assumptions
about other questions. The student will then be advised to work with selected
learning materials (theory and examples) concerning questions a, b and c. Next
time the student takes the same test he/she will be presented with five questions
a, b, c, ab, ac again developed by another course builder. If the student answers
correctly to all of them the process of questioning is terminated. If the students
fails to give correct answers to some of the questions a, b, c, ab, ac then procedures similar to the following cases will be applied.

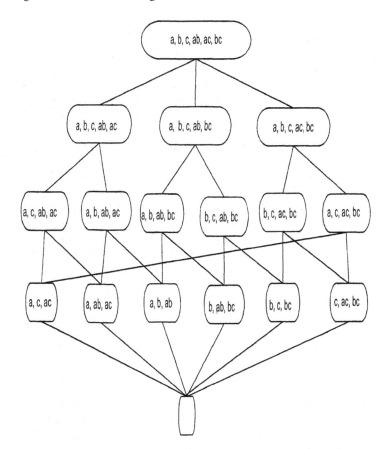

Figure 5.   The sublattice of the convex geometries on the basic set of questions a, b, c

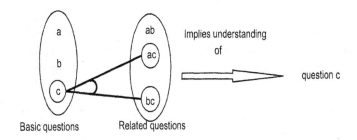

Figure 6.   Correct answers to questions c, ac, bc

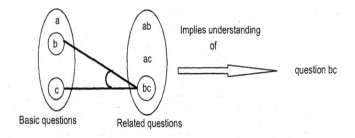

Figure 7.   Correct answers to questions b, c, bc

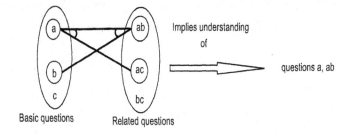

Figure 8.   Correct answers to questions a, b, ab, ac

Case 4:

Suppose a student answers correctly to questions a, b, ab, ac (see Fig. 8). This answer combination indicates mastering questions a and ab and makes no assumptions about other questions. The student will then be advised to work with selected learning materials (theory and examples) concerning questions b and c. In this case we still repeat question b since by not answering correctly to question bc the student might have a problem applying knowledge from question b to other domains. Next time the student takes the same test he/she will be presented with four questions b, c, ac, bc again developed by another course builder. If the student answers correctly to all of them the process of questioning is terminated. If the students fails to give correct answers to some of the questions b, c, ac, bc then procedures similar to the following case will be applied.

Case 5:

Suppose a student answers correctly to questions a, b, c, ab, bc (see Fig. 9). This answer combination indicates mastering questions b, ab and bc and makes no assumptions about other domains. The student will then be advised to work with selected learning materials (theory and examples) concerning questions a and c. In this case we still repeat questions a, c since by not answering cor-

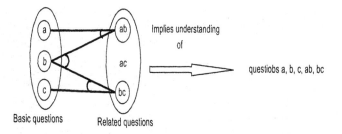

Basic questions   Related questions

Figure 9.   Correct answers to questions a, b, c, ab, bc

rectly to question ac the student might have a problem applying knowledge from questions a, c to other arias. Next time the student takes the same test he/she will be presented with three questions a, c, ac again developed by another course builder. If the student answers correctly to all of them the process of questioning is terminated. If the students fails to give correct answers to some of the questions a, c, ac then a similar procedure will be applied.

4.   Conclusion

A theoretical framework for efficient assessment of learners' understanding of carefully chosen terms and concepts is presented. The model is based on the theory of knowledge spaces and lattices of convex geometries.

References

[1]   D. Albert and J. Lukas (eds.). *Knowledge Spaces.* Lawrence Erlbaum Associates, 1999.

[2]   B. Bloom. The 2 sigma problem: The search for methods of group instruction as effective as one-to- one tutoring. *Educational Researcher*, 13(6):4-16, 1984.

[3]   M. Bush. A multiple choice test that rewards partial knowledge. *Journal of Further and Higher Education*, 25(2):157–163, 2001.

[4]   C. Carpineto and G. Romano. *Concept Data Analysis: Theory and Applications.* John Wiley and Sons, Ltd., 2004.

[5]   B. A. Davey and H. A. Priestley. *Introduction to lattices and order.* Cambridge University Press, Cambridge, 2005.

[6]   J.-P. Doignon and J.-C. Falmagne. Well graded families of relations. *Discrete Mathematics*, 173(1-3):35–44, 1997.

[7]   J.-P. Doignon and J.-C. Falmagne. *Knowledge Spaces.* Springer-Verlag, 1999.

[8]   C.E. Dowling. On the irredundant generation of knowledge spaces. *Journal of Mathematical Psychology*, 37, 49-62, 1993.

[9]   P.H. Edelman and R.E. Jamison. The theory of convex geometries. *Geom. Dedicata*, 19, 247–270, 1985.

[10] J.-C. Falmagne, M. Koppen, M. Villand, L. Johannesen. Introduction to knowledge spaces: How to build test and search them. *Psychological Review*, 97, 201-224, 1990.

[11] D.W. Farthing. Permutational multiple choice questions: An objective and efficient alternative to essay-type examination questions. *Proceedings of the 3rd Annual Conference on Integrating Technology into Computer Science Education* (ITiCSE'98), 1998.

[12] P. Gruber and J. Wills. *Handbook of Convex Geometry*. North Holland, 1993.

[13] E. Guzman and R. Conejo. A model for student knowledge diagnosis through adaptive testing. *Springer-Verlag*, LNCS 3220, 12–2,1 Berlin Heidelberg New Jork, 2004.

[14] R. Harper. Correcting computer-based assessments for guessing. *Journal of Computer Assisted Learning*, 19(1):2–8, 2003.

[15] M. Koppen. Extracting human expertise for constructing knowledge spaces: an algorithm. *Journal of mathematical psychology*, 37, 1–20, 1993.

[16] http://www.aleks.com

[17] http://wundt.uni-graz.at/projects/rath

A NEW CLUSTER MERGING ALGORITHM OF SUFFIX TREE CLUSTERING

Jianhua Wang, Ruixu Li

Computer Science Department, Yantai University, Yantai, Shandong, China

Abstract: Document clustering methods can be used to structure large sets of text or hypertext documents. Suffix Tree Clustering has been proved to be a good approach for documents clustering. However, the cluster merging algorithm of Suffix Tree Clustering is based on the overlap of their document sets, which totally ignore the similarity between the non-overlap parts of different clusters. In this paper, we introduce a novel cluster merging approach which will combines the cosine similarity and overlap percentage. Using this method, we can get a better clustering result and a comparative small number of clusters.

Key words: suffix tree clustering, cluster merging algorithm

1.   INTRODUCTION

Document clustering has been studied intensively recently because of its wide applicability in areas such as web mining, search engines, information retrieval, and topological analysis. Clustering documents into groups can organize large bodies of text for efficient browsing and searching. A lot of different text clustering algorithms have been proposed in the literature, including Agglomerative Hierarchical Clustering (AHC) [5], Scatter/Gather [2] and K-Means [4].

Zamir and Etzioni presented a Suffix Tree Clustering(STC) algorithm on document clustering in[3]. STC is a linear time clustering algorithm that is based on a suffix tree which efficiently identifies sets of documents that share common phrases. STC treats a document as a string, making use of proximity information between words, at the same time, it is incremental and has an $O(n)$ time complexity.

In Zamir and Etzioni's Suffix Tree Clustering algorithm, after the suffix tree construction, the overlap of the different clusters is calculated, and the clusters are merged if they have more than 50% overlap. This merging method is fast, however, it is too simple to yield the best merging result because it totally neglects the similarity between the non-overlap parts. Considering such situation: two different clusters have much related and similar documents, but none of the documents are contained in both clusters, that is, no overlap between the two clusters. According to Zamir and Etzioni's merging algorithm, the two clusters have no chance be merged. This obvious is not a good choice because we actually hope the two clusters can be merged due to their much related documents. Another problem is this simple merging algorithm can result in too many clusters, usually hundreds even thousands of clusters, with only a small amount of documents in each of it. This really frustrates the browsers to locate the desired information.

In this paper, we present a novel approach which introduces the well-known cosine similarity algorithm into the cluster merging process. In our algorithm, the similarity of the two clusters is not only decided by the overlap of their documents, but also by the similarity of the non-overlap parts. This is quite natural, because the related and similar documents she▓ also contribute to the similarity between two clusters. The following experiments show that this algorithm has more accuracy that the original one. The new algorithm also has another advantage: with adjusting to some parameters, we can control the number of final clusters we get. This is very useful in some cases.

The rest of this paper is organized as follows. Section 2 briefly introduces Suffix Tree Clustering and its cluster merging algorithm. In section 3, we introduce our novel cluster

Please use the following format when citing this chapter:

Wang, J., Li, R., 2006, in IFIP International Federation for Information Processing, Volume 228, Intelligent Information Processing III, eds. Z. Shi, Shimohara K., Feng D., (Boston: Springer), pp. 197–203.

merging algorithm which combines the overlap percentage and cosine similarity. An experimental evaluation was conducted, and section 4 reports its major results. A summarization of the paper is presented in section 5.

2.   RELATED WORKS

As a data structure, suffix tree has been studied a lot in information retrieval field [3], [13],[15]. A suffix tree is a trie data structure built over all the suffixes of the text. Each node of the suffix tree represents a group of documents and a phrase that is common to all of them. The label of the node represents the common phrase.   In Zamir and Etzioni's paper[3], they found that using suffix tree to cluster web search results yielded better results than other clustering methods. STC algorithm has several steps:
(1) Document Preprocessing, including stemming, html tags and stopwords filtering out.
(2) Suffix Tree Construction. Construct a suffix tree for the document collections.
(3) Cluster Merging. Merge similar clusters according to their similarity measure.
(4) Clusters Ranking. Rank the cluster according to their relevance to the query.
In the cluster merging step, Zamir and Etzioni defined a similarity measure between clusters based on the overlap of their document sets. The two clusters are merged only when they have enough overlap. Despite its simplicity and fastness, this method is not accurate enough to merge all related clusters. In this paper, we propose a new similarity measure algorithm which takes more factors into account.

3.   A NEW DOCUMENT CLUSTERING ALGORITHM

Before constructing the suffix tree and getting the documents clusters for merging, a preprocessing step must be done. First, any non-textual information such as HTML-tags and punctuation is removed from the documents. Stopwords such as "I", "am", "and" are also removed. Second, All capitals in the documents are converted to lowercase. Then, the remaining words are stemmed by removing prefixes/suffixes and reducing plural to singular. Through the above preprocessing, we get rid of all noise and produce a cleaned document for further processing.

The construction of a suffix tree can be viewed as the creation of an inverted index of phrases for the document collections. This process can be done in linear time with the size of the document set, and can be done incrementally as the documents are being read. At each node, after construction, we get a list of documents that correspond exactly to that particular node, as well as an index that allows us to locate phrases in the document.

After construction of the suffix tree, we should merge the related clusters based on its similarity. In [3], Zamir and Etzioni defined a similarity measure between clusters based on the document overlap.   Given the two base clusters B_m and B_n, with sizes $|B_m|$ and $|B_n|$ respectively, and $|B_m \cap B_n|$ representing the number of documents common to both clusters. The two clusters are merged only when:

$$\frac{|B_m \cap B_n|}{|B_m|} > 0.5 \quad and \quad \frac{|B_m \cap B_n|}{|B_n|} > 0.5 \tag{1}$$

There are two disadvantage of Equation 1:
First, it is not suitable for two clusters when $|B_m|/|B_n|$ is too big or too small. Here is an example: B_m contains 100 documents and Bn contains 10 documents, all of which are totally overlapped by the documents in B_m. That is, B_n is a subset of B_m. Obviously we should merge

B_n into B_m. But if we follow Equation 2, $| B_m \cap Bn|/| B_m | = 0.1 < 0.5$, we cannot merge them together.

Here, we employ a better equation to calculate the overlap of two different clusters.

$$Overlap(B_m, B_n) = \frac{| B_m | \cap | B_n |}{Min(| B_m |,| B_n |)} \qquad (2)$$

Second, it neglects the similarity between the non-overlapped parts. Consider the flowing situation: There are several different but very similar and related documents located in two clusters, and no overlap between the two clusters.

Due to all the documents in the two clusters are similar and related, we should merge them together. However, using the equation 1, they will never be merged because there is no overlap between them. That is, in Zamir and Etzioni's merging algorithm, only the same documents located in different clusters can contribute to the similarity measure. Similar but different documents cannot contribute anything to the merging decision. This is obvious inappropriate.

To solve this problem, we introduce the well-known cosine similarity to the merging algorithm and employ the cosine similarity to evaluate the similarity between different clusters. Given $B_m' = B_m - | B_m \cap B_n |$, $B_n' = B_n - | B_m \cap B_n |$, the similarity between B_m' and B_n' is:

$$Sim(B_m', B_n') = \frac{\overrightarrow{B_m'} \bullet \overrightarrow{B_n'}}{| \overrightarrow{B_m'} | \times | \overrightarrow{B_n'} |} = \frac{\sum_{i=1}^{t}(w_{i,m} \times w_{i,n})}{\sqrt{\sum_{i=1}^{t} w_{i,m}^2} \times \sqrt{\sum_{i=1}^{t} w_{i,n}^2}} \qquad (3)$$

Where $B_j = (w_{1,j}, w_{2,j} \ldots w_{t,j})$ is the term frequency vector representation of cluster B_j and t is the total number of index term in the system. w_{ij} is the weight of term k_i in cluster j. We calculate w_{ij} using the *TFIDF algorithm*.

$$w_{ij} = f_{ij} \times idf_i = \frac{freq_{i,j}}{max\ freq_j} \times \log \frac{N}{n_i} \qquad (4)$$

Where N is the total number of clusters and n_i is the number of clusters in which the index term k_i appears. $freq_{i,j}$ is the number of times the term k_i appears in the text of the cluster B_j. Max $freq_j$ is maximum frequency of all terms which are mentioned in the text of the cluster B_j.

Using this representation, we can calculate the similarity between the non-overlap parts of the two clusters based on the similarity of their term vectors.

After we get the overlap of the two clusters from Equation 2 and the similarity of the non-overlap parts from Equation 3, we can calculate the overall normalized similarity of the two clusters:

$$S_{m,n} = a*Overlap(B_m, B_n) + (1-\alpha)* Sim(B_m', B_n') \qquad (5)$$

And merge them only if:

$$S_{m,n} > k \qquad (6)$$

B_m' and B_n' is the non-overlap parts of the Cluster B_m and Cluster B_n, that is, $B_m' = B_m - |B_m \cap B_n|$, $B_n' = B_n - |B_m \cap B_n|$. In our experiments, we assigned $\alpha=0.6$. Changing the value of k in Equaion 6 can adjust the number of merged clusters we get. A smaller k means the merging condition is easy to satisfy and can result in less merged clusters. While a bigger k set a more restrictive condition and can result in more merged clusters. So, we can adjust the parameter k to make the merging algorithm suitable to different fields.

The whole merging process is not a single step, but an iterative process described as follow:

1. We compute the pairwise similarity among all clusters according to Equation 5.
2. We select the maximum $S_{m,n}$ ($S_{m,n} > k$) and merge the cluster B_m and cluster B_n.
3. Step 1 and step 2 is iteratively executed until maximum $S_{m,n} \le k$.

The initial time complexity of the cluster merging process is $O(n^2)$. To keep the cost of this process constant, we don't calculate the similarity of all base clusters, but only calculate the n top ranking base clusters. We found that $n=500$ was sufficient to ensure good performance. The ranking score of clusters is determined by the number of documents and their ranking position.

$$rs(B) = \sum_{i=1}^{p} \frac{1}{\log(R_i + e)} \tag{7}$$

Here p is the number of the documents contained in the cluster, and e is a positive parameter to adjust the ranking position in relation to the score. A bigger e can weaken the effect of the ranking position, while a smaller e can strengthen the ranking position's effect. We considered $e=2$ to be a good choice.

R_i is the position of the document in the documents list returned and ranked by the search engine. In Equation 7, the highly ranked documents in the ranking list always contribute more to the score than the lower ranked ones. We take the document ranking into account because we think the number of the documents contained in the cluster cannot reflect the importance of the cluster very well only by itself. For example, one cluster might contain the top 15 documents returned by the search engine, while another cluster contains the 1001th to 1020th documents in the ranking list. If we only consider the number of the documents, we can easily conclude that the second cluster is more important than the first one, which, in this example, is obviously wrong.

The cost of "cleaning" the documents is obviously linear with the collection size. The cost of organizing documents into the suffix tree is also linear with the collection size. And due to only a fix number of clusters is merged, the overall time complexity of this whole process is linear with regard to the collection size.

4.   EXPERIMENTS

We conduct several experiments to validate the effectiveness of the new algorithm.

4.1   The number of merged clusters with different α and k

In this experiment, we submitted 10 different queries to Google[11] search engine and get 10 different searching results, each of which has 2000 document snippets in it. Then, for each result, we preprocessed it and constructed the suffix trees. After that, we merged the suffix tree clusters using the algorithm described in this paper. First, we chose 0.5 as the value of k in Equation 6 and   merged the base clusters with different value of α. When the 10 cluster merging processes were finished, we calculated the average number of final merged clusters. The results are shown in Figure 1.

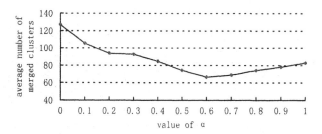

Figure 1.   The average number of final merged clusters for different α

From Figure 1, we can see that we get the least number of merged clusters when the value of α is 0.6.   In our experiments, 0.6 is a good value for α due to its effectiveness on merging similar clusters together.

We also calculated the average number of merged clusters for different *k* in Equation 6. The results are shown in Figure 2.

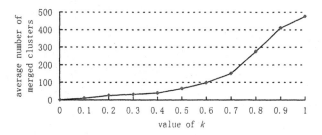

Figure 2. The average number of final merged clusters for different k

From Figure 2, we can see that the value of *k* can dramatically affect the number of the merged clusters. A smaller *k* can result in a small number of the merged clusters, but the similarity between the documents in the merged cluster is not strong. With a bigger *k* we can get very similar documents in the same merged cluster, however, the number of the merged clusters is usually large. Here, we think *k*=0.5 is a good choice.

4.2   Precision Evaluation

There are many approaches to precision evaluation. To compare with the traditional STC algorithm, we adopted the same evaluation process described in [3].

The process was as follows: "We first defined 10 queries by specifying their topics(e.g., "black bear attacks") and their descriptions(e.g. "we are interested in accounts of black bear attacks on humans or information about how to prevent such attacks"). The words appearing in each query's topic field were used as keywords for a web search using Google search engine. We generated 10 collections of 200 documents from the results of these queries. We manually assigned a relevance judgment (relevant or not) to each document in these collections based on the query's descriptions.

In our experiment we applied the various clustering algorithm to the document collection and compared their effectiveness for information retrieval."[3]

We used the results of the clustering algorithms to reorder the list of documents returned by the search engine. We ordered the clusters according to which labels seemed most relevant to the information needed. In this step we looked only at the cluster labels, ignoring the contents of each cluster. We then defined the ordering of the results as the ordering of the documents in the highest rank cluster, followed by the documents in the next ranked cluster, and so on through the lowest ranked cluster. Documents appearing in multiple clusters were removed from all but the highest ranked cluster in which they appeared, so as to avoid duplicates.

After reordering the documents with clusters, we considered only the top 20 documents in the reordered list and used them to calculate the percentage of relevant documents.

As seen in Figure 3, the STC algorithm with the cluster merging method described in this paper is more precise than all the others. The top 20 documents cover more than 40% relevant documents. The reason for this is mostly because we used a more accurate merging algorithm in this paper.

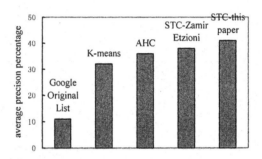

Figure 3. The average precision of the clustering algorithms and of the original ranked list returned by Google.

5.   CONCLUSION

We reformed the Suffix Tree Cluster merging algorithm by combining the overlap percentage of two clusters and the similarity between the non-overlap parts of two clusters. First, we revise the overlap percentage calculation method to better reflect the overlap between two clusters. Then, we employ the cosine similarity to calculate the similarity between the non-overlap parts. Our preliminary results are encouraging and show a better result in helping the user to locate the desired documents more easily.

ACKNOWLEDGEMENTS

We thank Prof. Song Yibin and Bi Yuanwei for their advice about this paper.   We also appreciate all the experiments done by Wang Zhaoguan, Yu Wei and Wang Bo. Without the help for all of them, this paper can hardly be done.

REFERENCES

1. Liu B., Chin C. W., and Ng, H. T.   Mining Topic-Specific Concepts and Definitions on the Web. In *Proceedings of the Twelfth International World Wide Web Conference (WWW'03)*, Budapest, Hungary, 2003.

2. Cutting D.R., Karger D.R., Pedersen J.O., Tukey J.W. Scatter / Gather: A Cluster-based Approach to Browsing Large Document Collection, *Proc. ACM SIGIR 92*, 1992

3. Zamir O., Etzioni O. Web Document Clustering: A Feasibility Demonstration, In *Proceedings of the 19th International ACM SIGIR Conference on Research and Development of Information Retrieval (SIGIR'98)*, 1998.

4 J. J. Rocchio, Document retrieval systems – optimization and evaluation, Ph.D. Thesis, Harvard University, 1966.

5   P. Willet.   Recent trends in hierarchical document clustering: a critical review. *Information Processing and Management*, 24:577-97, 1988.

6. Leuski A. and Allan J. Improving Interactive Retrieval by Combining Ranked List and Clustering. *Proceedings of RIAO, College de France*, pp. 665-681, 2000.

7. Smith, D.A.   Detecting and Browsing Events in Unstructured Text. In *Proceedings of ACM/SIGIR'2002*.

8. Sergey Brin, and Larry Page. The anatomy of a large scale hypertextual web search engine. In *Proceedings of WWW7*, Brisbane,Australia, April 1998.

9. Hua-Jun Zeng Qi-Cai He Zheng Chen Wei-Ying Ma Jinwen Ma   Learning to cluster web search results *SIGIR*'04, July 25 29, Sheffield, South Yorkshire, UK , 2004

10. X. Shen, B. Tan, and C. Zhai. Intelligent search using implicit user model. Technical report, Department of Computer Science, University of Illinois at Urbana-Champaign, 2005.

11. Google search engine,   http://www.google.com.

12. Yahoo search engine,   http://www.yahoo.com

13. Ricardo Baeza-Yates. Berthier Ribeiro-Neto, *Modern Information Retrieval* , Addison Wesley Press, 1999

14. Ian.H.Written, Alistair Moffat, Timothy.C. Bell. *Managing Gigabyte*, Morgan Kaufmann publishing, 1999

15. P. Weiner. Linear pattern matching algorithms. In Proceedings of the 14th Annual Symposium on Foundations of Computer Science (FOCS), pages 1-11, 1973.

FUZZY LINGUISTIC VARIABLE MATRIX AND PARABOLA-BASED FUZZY NORMAL DISTRIBUTION
A Method for Designing Fuzzy Linguistic terms

K.K.F. Yuen, H.C.W. Lau

Department of Industrial and Systems Engineering ,Hong Kong Polytechnic University, Hung Hom,Kowloon, Hong Kong, China,
Email:{ise.kevinyuen, mfhenry}@polyu.edu.hk
Tel:(852)-60112169,27666628

Abstract: This paper attempts to present the new approach to design sufficient number of systematic fuzzy linguistics in matrix form and map the Fuzzy Linguistic Variable Matrix, which contains linguistic terms, into numeric domain using Fuzzy Normal Distribution based on the Parabola-based Membership Function. Existing fuzzy set theory is difficult to design the systematic and sufficient fuzzy linguistics. Due to this reason, in most practice, giving insufficient fuzzy linguistics induces inaccurate calculation whilst giving excessive fuzzy linguistics induces the parameter design problems and calculation performance. This paper presents Fuzzy Linguistic Variable Matrix and Parabola-based Fuzzy Normal Distribution (FND) as preferred framework to address the problem.

Keywords: Fuzzy Set, Fuzzy Logic, Fuzzy Linguistics Variable Matrix, Parabola-based Membership Function, Fuzzy Normal Distribution, Directional Hedge Linguistics

1.   INTRODUCTION

It is well known that most people use Gaussian normal distribution for the statistic model and probability model, which is widely used in many applications. However, fundamental assumption of Gaussian normal distribution is entailed by the axiom of additively where all probabilities that satisfy specific properties must add to 1. This forces the conclusion that

Please use the following format when citing this chapter:

Yuen, K.K.F., Lau, H.C.W., 2006, in IFIP International Federation for Information Processing, Volume 228, Intelligent Information Processing III, eds. Z. Shi, Shimohara K., Feng D., (Boston: Springer), pp. 205–215.

probability of an event necessarily entails knowledge of remaining events. This articulates the challenge of modeling any uncertainty associated with an expert judgment.

For The fuzzy set theory, axiom of additives of where all probabilities (memberships) equal to 1 is not applied due to the fact that fuzzy set is the study of possibility instead of probability (D. Dubois and H. Prade, 1988). In addition, the motivation for selecting fuzzy set theory and fuzzy logic can be characterized by the following reasons:
1. when the measurement of the event is not given(J. C., Helton, 1997);
2. when that information is nonspecific, ambiguous, or conflicting(J. C. Helton, 1997);
3. when the information can be described by human using adverb or adjective;

For above reasons, it seems that there is a lack of models to handle the uncertainty on the basis of the classical probability. With consideration of the capability dealing with uncertainty and ambiguity for above reasons, fuzzy set theory and fuzzy logic are the preferred choices of the models. As the age of the fuzzy set theory is still young (L.A Zadeh, 1965), it has great potential to improve its theory. This project introduces the concept of Fuzzy Linguistic Variable Matrix (FLVM) and Parabola-based Fuzzy Normal Distribution (FND) for dealing with uncertainty and ambiguity.

Firstly the fundamental concept of fuzzy set theory in explained in section 2. Then the definition of FLVM and Parabola-based Membership Function (PbMF) are depicted in section 3 and section 4 respectively. The concept of FND with Fuzzy Density Function (FDF) is depicted in section 5. Finally the conclusion as well as the identification of future study is depicted in section 6.

2.   FUNDAMENTAL CONCEPT

Fuzzy sets were introduced by Zadeh (1965) was specifically designed to mathematically represent uncertainty and vagueness and to provide formalized tools for dealing with the imprecision intrinsic to many problems. To illustrate the idea how this paper innovatively modifies the existing fuzzy set theory, it is necessary to review the fundamental concept of fuzzy set theory and fuzzy logic.

Definition 2.1: Let X be a nonempty set, A fuzzy set α in X is characterized by its membership function: $\mu_\alpha : X \rightarrow [0,1]$, and $\mu_\alpha(x)$ is interpreted as the degree of membership of element x in Set α for each $x \in X$ (L.A Zadeh, 1965).

Definition 2.2: A linguistic variable is characterized by a quintuple in which x is the name of variable; T(x) is the term set of x, that is, the set of names of linguistic values of x with each value being a fuzzy number defined on U; G is a syntactic rule for generating the names of values of x; and M is a semantic rule for associating with each value its meaning. (L.A Zadeh, 1978)

Most application researches apply triangular membership function. Other membership functions widely used include Cauchy, Gaussian, sigmoidal, and trapezoidal membership functions. However, the designs or/and the calculations of the membership functions are relatively complex or inefficient. To simplify them, this paper proposes FLVM and PbMF as the preferred alternatives for the fuzzy applications.

3.   FUZZY LINGUISTIC VARIABLE MATRIX

This section introduces the approach to design fuzzy linguistic terms using FLVM. The human intelligence possesses the superior capability of fuzzy classification, fuzzy judgment, and fuzzy reasoning. If there is suitable linguistic schema, there will be the framework making the classification, judgment and reasoning more objective.

Definition 3.1 (Fuzzy syntactic representation): The syntactic pattern of a fuzzy linguistic variable set,α, consists of three syntactic components: a direction linguistic variable set, a hedge linguistic variable set, and an atomic linguistic variable set, denoted as V_d, V_h, V_a respectively. In syntactic terms, the expression is $\alpha = (V_h + V_d) + V_a$, where ($V_h + V_d$) forms syntactic terms set as a directional hedge linguistic set denoted as V_{hd}.

Let X be the universal set, V_{hd} gives the column vector, V_a gives the row vector, and α_{ij} is the fuzzy linguistic variable (set) which its linguistic syntactic representation is determined by its row and column position.

$$X = \begin{bmatrix} \alpha_{ij} \end{bmatrix} = \begin{bmatrix} & [V_a]_1 & \cdots & [V_a]_n \\ \hline [V_{hd}]_1 & \alpha_{11} & \cdots & \alpha_{1n} \\ \vdots & \vdots & \ddots & \vdots \\ [V_{hd}]_m & \alpha_{m1} & \cdots & \alpha_{mn} \end{bmatrix}$$

Definition 3.2 (Fuzzy semantic constraint): In the universal set X_{mn},

$\underset{\substack{j=n \\ 1 \le i \le (m-1)/2}}{\forall} \alpha_{ij} = \Phi$ and $\underset{\substack{j=1 \\ (m+1)/2 \le i \le m}}{\forall} \alpha_{ij} = \Phi$ where Φ is null set and is

regarded as 0.

Example 1

Provided that

$$V_d = \{above, below\}$$
$$V_h = \{much, quite, little, absolutely\}$$
$$V_a = \{poor, average, excellent\}$$

V_h and V_d are used together as V_{hd} to modify the V_a. Therefore,

$$V_{hd} = \begin{Bmatrix} much \ above, \ quite \ above, \ little \ above, \ absolutely, \\ little \ below, \ quite \ below, \ much \ below \end{Bmatrix}$$

Assign V_{hd} as row matrix and V_a as column matrix, then get table 1.

Table 1: Matrix of Fuzzy Linguistic terms for a variable

	Poor	Average	Excellent
Much Above	much above poor	much above average	-
Quite Above	quite above poor	quite above average	-
Little Above	little above poor	little above average	-
Absolutely	absolutely poor	absolutely average	absolutely excellent
Little Below	-	little below average	little below excellent
Quite Below	-	quite below average	quite below excellent
Much Below	-	much below average	much below excellent

Let X be the universal set, its fuzzy subsets are represented in a matrix form on the basis of table 1 such that

$$X = \begin{vmatrix} \alpha_{11} & \alpha_{12} & \alpha_{13} \\ \alpha_{21} & \alpha_{22} & \alpha_{23} \\ \alpha_{31} & \alpha_{32} & \alpha_{33} \\ \alpha_{41} & \alpha_{42} & \alpha_{43} \\ \alpha_{51} & \alpha_{52} & \alpha_{53} \\ \alpha_{61} & \alpha_{62} & \alpha_{63} \\ \alpha_{71} & \alpha_{72} & \alpha_{73} \end{vmatrix} = \begin{vmatrix} MA-P & MA-A & 0 \\ QA-P & QA-A & 0 \\ LA-P & LA-A & 0 \\ A-P & A-A & A-E \\ 0 & LB-A & LB-E \\ 0 & QB-A & QB-E \\ 0 & MB-A & MB-E \end{vmatrix}$$

4.   PARABOLA-BASED MEMBERSHIP FUNCTION

"A correct and good membership function is determined by the user based on his scientific knowledge, working experience, and actual need for the particular application in question. This selection is more or less subjective, but the situation is just like in the classical probability theory and statistics where if one says 'we assume that the noise is Gaussian and while,' what he uses to start with all the rigorous mathematics is a subjective hypothesis that may not be very true, simply because the noise in question may not be exactly Gaussian and may not be perfectly white." (Chen Guanrong and Trung Tat Pham, 2001). This paper assumes the membership function shape is parabolic, and the parabolic shape can be modified with g-level method.

Definition 4.1 (symmetric fuzzy set, γ_{α_n} and d_{α_n}): A symmetric fuzzy set is determined by its membership function where there is only one element (or singleton), γ_{α_n}, with membership = 1 and the two end points with equal distance, d_{α_n}, to γ_{α_n}.

Definition 4.2 (PMF): Let X be the universal set, and x is any element in the set X. α is the fuzzy subset. There are n subsets of α, which is a nonempty set. For each subset α_n, $\alpha_n \subseteq X$ where finite n = {1, 2, 3...i}. In other words, α_n is the subset with index n. Therefore, the Parabolic Membership Function (PMF) of α_n, $y_{\alpha_n} : \alpha_n \to [0,1]$, is defined as:

$$y_{\alpha_n}(x) = a_{\alpha_n} x^2 + b_{\alpha_n} x + c_{\alpha_n}, \text{ where } x \in \alpha_n \tag{1}$$

Theorem 1 (PMF): On the basis of the definition 4.1 and 4.2, the parabolic membership function can be expressed as

$$y_{\alpha_n}(d_{\alpha_n}, \gamma_{\alpha_n}, x) = \frac{-1}{d_{\alpha_n}^2} x^2 + \frac{2\gamma_{\alpha_n}}{d_{\alpha_n}^2} x + \frac{d_{\alpha_n}^2 - \gamma_{\alpha_n}^2}{d_{\alpha_n}^2} \tag{2}$$

The membership function is used for the atomic linguistic variable.

Theorem 2 (fuzzy set overlap): The fuzzy set overlap, δ, is defined as the cross point at a degree of the membership of two adjacent sets

$(0 \le \delta < 1)$. To obtain the cross point in the parabolic membership function, d_{α_n} is defined as:

$$d_{\alpha_n} = \frac{\gamma_{\alpha_{n+1}} - \gamma_{\alpha_n}}{2\sqrt{1-\delta}} \qquad (3)$$

Definition 4.3 (g-level, PbMF): The shape of the PMF can be tuned as PbMF by giving the power of g_{α_n}, where $4 \ge g > 0$ suggested. The assignment of g_{α_n} is called g-level. The new membership function of PbMF, $\mu_{\alpha_n}(x)$, is defined as:

$$\mu_{\alpha_n}(x) = \left[y_{\alpha_n}(x) \right]^{g_{\alpha_n}} \qquad (4)$$

The PbMF is used for the atomic linguistic set.

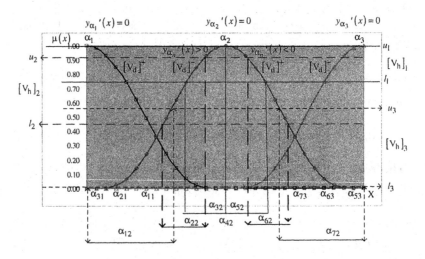

Figure 1: Fuzzy Normal Distribution

5.   FUZZY NORMAL DISTRIBUTION

Fuzzy Normal Distribution (FND) is characterized by PbMF. The objective of FND is to find a suitable fuzzy number represented for a linguistic term. Figure 1 exhibits the graphical overview of FND on the basis of the PbMF, membership fuzziness, fuzzy interval, and V-partition, which are further defined as follows.

Definition 5.1 ($[V_a]_j$, extension of definition 3.1): an atomic set $[V_a]_j$ where $1 \le j \le n$, is the super fuzzy set that contains any linguistic terms (subsets) with semantic meaning and syntactic symbol of the atomic variable itself. For all j, $\forall \alpha_{ij} \in [V_a]_j = \alpha_j$, i.e. $\alpha_n = \{\alpha_{1n} \quad \cdots \quad \alpha_{mn}\}$.
$$1 \le i \le m$$

Definition 5.2 (L, U): the lower boundary (L) and upper boundary (U) are designed by the distribution (ratio) of hedge linguistics, which is characterized by a distance function (which is used to find the crisp boundary, L` and U`) and the membership overlap factor ($0 < \lambda < 1$) (which is used for make the crisp boundary fuzzy). The distance function is defined by

$$dis\left([V_h]_j\right) = \frac{M\left([V_h]_j\right)}{\sum M\left([V_h]\right)} \quad \text{where } j \in \{1, 2, \cdots, \eta\}, \quad \eta \text{ is the maximum}$$

number of V_h, and M() is the measure function determined by the expert judgment.

Definition 5.3 (membership fuzziness): The membership [0, 1] can be fuzzified by directional hedge linguistic set V_{dh}. The fuzzy interval of the membership is determined by L and U. Adding the membership overlap factor (**MOF**), λ, makes boundary in fuzziness. Therefore, we have

$$Inv(V_{dh}) = \begin{bmatrix} \underline{\quad\quad L\quad\quad} & \underline{\quad\quad U\quad\quad} \\ (1-\lambda)\sum_{i=2}^{\eta} dis\left([V_h]_i\right) & 1 \\ (1-\lambda)\sum_{i=3}^{\eta} dis\left([V_h]_i\right) & min\left((1+\lambda)\sum_{i=2}^{\eta} dis\left([V_h]_i\right), 1\right) \\ \vdots & \vdots \\ (1-\lambda) dis\left([V_h]_\eta\right) & min\left((1+\lambda)\sum_{i=\eta-1}^{\eta} dis\left([V_h]_i\right), 1\right) \\ 0 & min\left((1+\lambda) dis\left([V_h]_\eta\right), 1\right) \end{bmatrix} \quad (5)$$

Example 2:

From   example   1,   we   get $V_h = \{$much,quite,little,absolutely$\}$,
"absolutely" can be ignored as it makes the atomic variable into a singleton
after   combination.   Therefore, $V_h = \{$little,quite,much$\}$.   For   the
measurement of V_h , we assume we have M(little) =1, M(quite)=2,
M(much)=3, then

$$\mathrm{dis}(V_h) = \left[\mathrm{dis}(\text{little})\ \mathrm{dis}(\text{quite})\ \mathrm{dis}(\text{much})\right] = \begin{bmatrix} \dfrac{1}{6} & \dfrac{1}{3} & \dfrac{1}{2} \end{bmatrix},$$

The crisp boundary is:

$$\begin{bmatrix} [V_h]_1 \\ [V_h]_2 \\ [V_h]_3 \end{bmatrix} \xrightarrow{\ Inv'(V_h)\ } \begin{bmatrix} l' & u' \\ 0.8333 & 1 \\ 0.5 & 0.8333 \\ 0 & 0.5 \end{bmatrix}$$

For overlap factor $(\lambda) = 0.1$, we have the membership fuzziness interval:

$$\begin{bmatrix} L' & U' \\ 0.8333 & 1 \\ 0.5 & 0.8333 \\ 0 & 0.5 \end{bmatrix} \xrightarrow[U=\mathbf{min}(U'(1+\lambda),1)]{L=L'(1-\lambda)} \begin{bmatrix} L & U \\ 0.75 & 1 \\ 0.45 & 0.9167 \\ 0 & 0.55 \end{bmatrix}$$

Definition 5.4 (V_d, Directional Hedge): Iff $y_{\alpha_n}{}'(x) > 0$, then V_d is
negatively directional in semantic meaning. Iff $y_{\alpha_n}{}'(x) = 0$, V_d is static.
Iff $y_{\alpha_n}{}'(x) < 0$, V_d is positively directional.

Definition 5.5 (L and U in V_{dh}): Elements of L and U in the positive
direction ($V_d{}^+$) of V_h, denoted as $V_h{}^+$, are **"self-inverse-reflect"** to ones
in negative direction ($V_d{}^-$) of V_h, denoted as $V_h{}^-$.

Theorem 3 (V-Partition by membership fuzziness): If V_d is negatively
directional in semantic meaning, then the corresponding fuzzy number x in

the fuzzy boundary (L, U) is $x = \gamma_{\alpha_n} - d\sqrt{1 - (\mu_{\alpha_n})^{1/g_{\alpha_n}}}$; If V_d is

positively directional, then $x = \gamma_{\alpha_n} + d\sqrt{1 - (\mu_{\alpha_n})^{1/g_{\alpha_n}}}$. If V_d is static, then $x = \gamma_{\alpha_n}$. The fuzzy set is vertically partitioned (V-Partition) by the fuzzy boundaries, which is illustrated by example 3.

From theorem 3, the fuzzy interval is assigned for each linguistic variable on the basis of membership fuzziness in the atomic fuzzy set. Definition 5.6 is to find the crisp value or fuzzy number to represent each linguistic variable.

Definition 5.6 (cen(α_{ij})): The crisp value, ζ_{ij}, of a linguistic variable α_{ij} is obtained by the center function.

$$\zeta_{ij} = cen(\alpha_{ij}) = \frac{max(\alpha_{ij}) + min(\alpha_{ij})}{2} \qquad (6)$$

Example 3:
Continue to Example 2, we get Inv(little)=[0.75 1]; Inv(quite)=[0.45 0.9167];Inv(Much)=[0 0.55].Assume the continuous universal set is X=[1,15], the fuzzy set "average" is determined by a PMF with γ_{α_n} =8, d=7. Find the V-partitions of PMF.

By applying theorem 3, we have:
negative direction (with the linguistic word "below"):

$$\begin{array}{c} \\ LB-A \\ QB-A \\ MB-A \end{array}\begin{bmatrix} L & U \\ 0.75 & 1 \\ 0.45 & 0.9167 \\ 0 & 0.55 \end{bmatrix}^{-} \xrightarrow{\begin{array}{c} x_l = \gamma_{\alpha_2} - d\sqrt{1-y_{\alpha_2}}(l) \\ x_u = \gamma_{\alpha_2} - d\sqrt{1-y_{\alpha_n}}(u) \end{array}} \begin{bmatrix} X_L & X_U \\ 4.50 & 8.00 \\ 2.81 & 5.98 \\ 1.00 & 3.30 \end{bmatrix}$$

static: As A-A is the static point or singleton, A= 8

positive direction (with the linguistic word "above"):

$$\begin{array}{c} \\ LA-A \\ QA-A \\ MA-A \end{array}\begin{bmatrix} L & U \\ 1 & 0.75 \\ 0.9167 & 0.45 \\ 0.55 & 0 \end{bmatrix}^{+} \xrightarrow{\begin{array}{c} x_l = \gamma_{\alpha_2} + d\sqrt{1-y_{\alpha_2}}(l) \\ x_u = \gamma_{\alpha_2} + d\sqrt{1-y_{\alpha_2}}(u) \end{array}} \begin{bmatrix} X_L & X_U \\ 8.00 & 11.50 \\ 10.02 & 13.19 \\ 12.70 & 15.00 \end{bmatrix}$$

$$\text{Therefore, } V_{dh} = \begin{bmatrix} V_h^+ \\ V_h^0 \\ V_h^- \end{bmatrix} = \begin{bmatrix} \begin{bmatrix} 12.70 & 15.00 \\ 10.02 & 13.19 \\ 8.00 & 11.50 \end{bmatrix}^+ \\ \begin{bmatrix} 8.00 & 8.00 \end{bmatrix}' \\ \begin{bmatrix} 4.50 & 8.00 \\ 2.81 & 5.98 \\ 1.00 & 3.30 \end{bmatrix}^- \end{bmatrix}$$

Find the fuzzy number to represent each linguistic term using cen() method, then we have table 2.

Table 2: Fuzzy numbers for the linguistic terms

		L=min	U=max	cen()
much above average	MA-A	12.70	15.00	13.85
quite above average	QB-A	10.02	13.19	11.61
little above average	LA-A	8.00	11.50	9.75
absolutely average	A-A	8.00	8.00	8.00
little below average	LB-A	4.50	8.00	6.25
quite below average	QB-A	2.81	5.98	4.40
much below average	MB-A	1.00	3.30	2.15

6.   DISCUSSION AND CONCLUSION

This paper introduces the new concept of fuzzy mathematical models describing Fuzzy Linguistic Variable Matrix (FLVM) which is mapped into numeric domain by Fuzzy Normal Distribution (FND) characterized by the Parabola-based Membership Functions (PbMF) and V-partition method of membership fuzziness. Fuzzy Normal Distribution applies the fundamental assumption of the fuzzy set theory on the basis of the possibility. Similar to the assumption of Gaussian distribution, this study assumes the fuzzy distribution of atomic linguistic variable is on the basis of Parabola-based Membership Function (PbMF), which is the Parabolic Membership Function (PMF) with g-level tuning.

This model can be the preferred framework for modeling human subjective judgment which can be applied in the domain of qualitative evaluation, especially transformation the solution of the linguistics evaluation problem into the solution of an arithmetic problem.

Limitation of this approach is that the tuning method is not well defined. The future of the study will discuss the method of "fuzzy tuning for FND" using numerical analysis, which means the best practices to find out the suitable FLVM, overlap, and g-level to model the input FLVM.

Another limitation is that the new method does not merge the existing well known fuzzy logic systems. The further study discusses the fusion of the new method and existing fuzzy set theory. The main reasons include the definitions of FLVM and FND are not comparable with existing definitions of fuzzy linguistic variable, atomic variable and linguistic hedge variable.

ACKNOWLEDGEMENT

Research was supported in part through a grant of an Innovation Technology Fund (UIT/74) from the Innovation and Technology Commission HKSAR.

REFERENCE

1. Chen Guanrong, and Trung Tat Pham, "Introduction to fuzzy sets, fuzzy logic, and fuzzy control systems", page 6, CRC Press, 2001
2. D. Dubois and H. Prade, "Possibility Theory", Plenum Press, New York, 1988
3. J. C Helton, "Uncertainty and Sensitivity Analysis in the Presence of Stochastic and Subjective Uncertainty." Journal of Statistical Computation and Simulation 57: 3-76 1997.
4. L.A. Zadeh, "Fuzzy Sets", Information and Control 8(3): 338-353 1965
5. L.A. Zadeh, "The concept of a linguistic variable and its application to approximate reasoning – I". Inf. Sci. 8(3): 199-249 1975

A NEW METHOD FOR MODELING PRINCIPAL CURVE

Hao JiSheng[1,2] He Qing[2] Shi Zhongzhi[2]

¹College of Computer Science, Yanan University, Shanxi Yanan, 716000,China

²Key Laboratory of Intelligence Information Processing, Institute of Computing Technology, Chinese Academy of Science, Beijing 100080,China.Email:haojs@ics.ict.ac.cn

Abstract: Principal curve pass through the middle of a multidimensional data set, to express the distributing shape of the points in the data set, we model principal curve for it. The new method of modeling the complex principal curve, based on B-spline network, is proposed. This method combines the polygonal line algorithm of learning principal curve with B-spline network. At one time, the algorithm finding a bifurcate point of the complex principal curve is presented. Our experimental results on simulate data demonstrate that it is feasible and effective.

Key words: Principal Curve, The Polygonal Line Algorithm, B-spline Network, Bifurcate Point

1.   INTRODUCTION

Principal curves were firstly introduced by Hastie and Stuetzle [1], and have been defined as satisfying the self-consistency property. Because complicated mathematics idea was used in describing its elements, then it wasn't noticed in computer science domain. At present, although there are a good many of problems on mathematics in the study of principal curve, yet principal curve approaches has attracted attention owning to its advantages and there are many reports on principal curve application. Actual applications involve the domain of visualization of image, speech recognition, time data analysis, pattern classification, recognition of handwritten digits, pattern clustering, process monitoring and so on[6]-[9]. Principal Curves are the nonlinear generalization of first principal components, and have been defined as smooth one-dimensional curves,

Please use the following format when citing this chapter:

Hao, J., He, Q., Shi, Z., 2006, in IFIP International Federation for Information Processing, Volume 228, Intelligent Information Processing III, eds. Z. Shi, Shimohara K., Feng D., (Boston: Springer), pp. 217–226.

which pass through the middle of a multidimensional data set. At present, there are a good many of the principal curve algorithm proposed and these algorithms merely gained discrete points on principal curve without modeling principal curve. By modeling principal curve, its model can express the nonlinear relation among variables in a data set.

B-spline network is the association memory network composed of three-layer structure [3][5], its structure is illustrated in **Fig.1.** B-spline function in latent layer is used as the basic function. For a random input, in latent layer a few B-spline basic function is active and the network output is a linear combination of these active basic function. Since the support set of the basic function is finite region, the network has the following features: a) the knowledge in the network is locally stored without whole and distributed, learning is local. Therefore the learning from a part in input space isn't influence the learning results in other part .b) the learning algorithm converges quickly. The network is convenient for real time application online. Thereby this kind network draws attention and is applied to the field of controlling, modeling, pattern recognition etc [5].

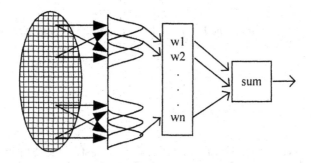

Fig.1. B-spline network structure

In this paper, the method of modeling principal curve is proposed. The kind of principal curve with branches is mainly considered, its form is illustrated in **Fig.3,** at a bifurcate point, the principal curve is partitioned into two branches. In modeling this kind principal curve, a key problem is how a bifurcate point of principal curve is found from a given data set. Thus the problem of modeling principal curve with branches is converted into one of modeling principal curve without branch, therefore, we propose a iterative algorithm for finding a bifurcate point of principal curves (its detail is given in section 3). In the algorithm proposed by us, firstly, the iterative algorithm for finding a bifurcate point of principal curve is used for searching a bifurcate point and the principal curve with branch is partitioned into three branches. Secondly, the polygonal lines algorithm of learning principal curve [3] is respectively applied to three branch and three polygonal lines are found. Finally, the vertex set of three polygonal lines is regarded as the set of B-spline network training sample and the network is trained. Since B-spline network has the features of a short training time and a fast convergence speed, therefore the approach may quickly create the model of principal curve. To compare with the existent principal curve algorithm, our method may create the model of a smooth principal curve since the basic function of B-spline network is the continuous function.

In the following of this paper, we firstly introduce the definitions of principal curve and the polygonal lines algorithm of learning principal curve in section 2. Then in section 3, we propose the algorithm for searching bifurcate point of principal curve. The new method of modeling principal curves is proposed in section 4. In section 5 our experimental results on simulate data sets are given. Conclusions are provided in the last section.

2.   THE DEFINITIONS OF PRINCIPAL CURVES AND THE POLYGONAL LINES ALGORITHM OF LEARNING PRINCIPAL CURVES

In this section, we introduce the definitions of principal curves [1][2][4] and the polygonal lines algorithm of learning principal curves [4].

2. 1   Definitions of principal curves

Definition1. The principal curve f of data distributing $D \subset R^d$ with continuous probability density $h(x)$ is a member in manifold M satisfying the self-consistency property. A curve $f \in M$ is the self-consistency if $E(X|\lambda_f(X) = \lambda) = f(\lambda)$, $\forall \lambda \in I$, where I is close interval on real number axis, $M = \{M_f: f \subset F\}$, $M_f = f(D) = \{f(X): X \in D\}$, F is a function set, to each $f \in F$, $f: D \to R^d$.

Definition2. The smooth curve $f(\lambda)$ is a principal curve if the following hold:

a) $f(\lambda)$ does not intersect itself.

b) $f(\lambda)$ has finite length inside any bounded subset of R^d and.

c) $f(\lambda)$ is self-consistent, i.e. $f(\lambda) = E(X|\lambda_f(X) = \lambda)$

Definition3. A curve f^* is called a principal curve of length L for X if f^* minimizes $\Delta(f)$ over all curves of length less than or equal to L. Where $\Delta(f) = E[\Delta(X, f)] = E[\inf\|X - f(\lambda)\|^2] = E[\|X - f(\lambda_f(X))\|^2]$.

According to definition of principal curve, principal curve is a smooth curve of satisfying the self-consistency property. It is essentially low-dimensional manifold embedded in the high-dimensional space. Any point on the curve is the conditional mean of data set over those points of the space which project to this point, it can factually reflect distributing form of data set

2.2   The polygonal line algorithm of learning principal curve

The polygonal lines algorithm of learning principal curve was proposed by Kégl B [4] , the algorithm is composed of the following steps.
  Algorithm1: The Polygonal Line Algorithm;
1.   Initialization:
  Given a set of data points $X_n = \{(x_1, y_1), (x_2, y_2), ..., (x_n, y_n)\} \subset R^2$, the algorithm starts with a straight line segment, the shortest segment of the first principal component line which contains all of the projected data points.

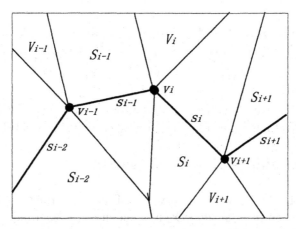

Fig. 2. A nearest-neighbor partition of R^2 induced by the vertices and segments of the polygonal line..

2.   The Projection Step:
   In the step the data points are partitioned into "nearest neighbor regions" according to which segment or vertex they project and it is illustrated in **Fig.2**. The nearest point of f to any point in the set V_i is the vertex v_i . The nearest point of f to any point in the set S_i is a point of the line segment s_i .
3.   The Vertex Optimization Step:
   In the step the new position of each vertex v_i is determined in a line search to minimize an objective function that consists an average squared distance term and a curvature penalty. While all other vertices are kept fixed.
4.   Adding a New Vertex:
   The inner loop consists of a projection step and an optimization step, these two steps are iterated so that the optimization step is applied to each vertex

v_i, $i = 1,2,...,k+1$, in a cyclic fashion (so that after v_{k+1}, the procedure starts again with v_1) until convergence is achieved and $f_{k,n}$ is produced. Then, a new vertex is added.

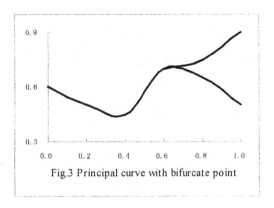

0. 9

0. 6

0. 3

0. 0   0. 2   0. 4   0. 6   0. 8   1. 0

Fig.3 Principal curve with bifurcate point

The algorithm stops when the number k of vertices exceeds a threshold $c(n,\Delta)$. This stopping criterion is based on a heuristic complexity measure, determined by the number of segments k, the number of data points n, and the average squared distance $\Delta_n(f_{k,n})$.

3. THE ALGORITHM FOR FINDING A BIFURCATE POINT OF PRINCIPAL CURVES

In this section, we propose a algorithm of searching a bifurcate point of principal curves.

Consider a set of data points $X_n = \{(x_i, y_i)\} \subset R^2$, where $i \in N = \{1,2,\cdots,n\}$. Let $x_{min} = \min_{i \in N}\{x_i\}$, $x_{max} = \max_{i \in N}\{x_i\}$, $I^{(0)} = [x_{min}, x_{max}]$, $\left|I^{(0)}\right|$ denotes the length of interval $I^{(0)}$, (x,y) denotes a bifurcate point for a set of data points X_n.

A algorithm for finding a bifurcate point is given below.

Algorithm2: Algorithm searching bifurcate point;

Input : a set of data points $X_n = \{(x_i, y_i)\} \subset R^2$ $i \in N = \{1,2,\cdots,n\}$

Output: a bifurcate point (x,y) for a set of data points X_n

Process:

{   Let $t = 0$;

Do { the Interval $I^{(t)}$ is parted into m parts, where m is the positive
integer.

m small intervals are produced, denoted by I_i, $i = 1,2,\cdots,m$.

Let $J_i = \{y_j | \forall (x_j, y_j) \in X_n, x_j \in I_i\}$. $i = 1,2,\cdots,m$;

$y_i = \dfrac{1}{n_i} \sum_{y_j \in J_i} y_j$, $i = 1,2,\cdots,m$;

$$\sigma_i = \frac{1}{n_i} \sum (y_j - \overline{y}_i)^2, \quad i = 1, 2, \cdots, m ;$$

n_i denotes the number of the data points in I_i .

Where $n_1 + n_2 + \cdots + n_k = n$.

Compute $\{\sigma_{i+1} - \sigma_i\}$, $i = 1, 2, \cdots, m-1$;

$\exists i, \ni (\sigma_{j+1} - \sigma_j) \in \{\sigma_{j+1} - \sigma_j\}$ $j = i, i+1, \cdots, k-1$;

$\sigma_{j+1} - \sigma_j \geq 0$, and is increase rigorously;

The abscissa of a bifurcate point $(\overline{x}, \overline{y})$ for X_n is in I_{i+1};

If $(|I_{i+1}| > \varepsilon)$ Then

$\quad \{ \ t = t+1 ; \quad I^{(t)} = I_{i+1} ; \ \}$

$\qquad$ Where ε is the small positive number given

$\quad\}$

While $(|I_{i+1}| > \varepsilon)$

$\qquad$ Let $\overline{x} = \frac{1}{n_{i+1}} \sum_{x_j \in I_{i+1}} x_j$, $\overline{y} = \frac{1}{n_{i+1}} \sum_{y_j \in I_{i+1}} y_j$. $(\overline{x}, \overline{y})$ is a bifurcate point

$\}$ The algorithm end.!

Since $\left| I^{(0)} \right| = x_{max} - x_{min}$, $\left| I^{(1)} \right| = \frac{1}{2} \left| I^{(0)} \right|$, $\left| I^{(t)} \right| = \frac{1}{m^t} \left| I^{(0)} \right|$, $\lim_{t \to +\infty} \left| I^{(t)} \right| = 0$, thus the algorithm is convergence. While m is bigger it converges quickly.

4.   A NEW METHOD OF MODELING PRINCIPAL CURVES

In this section, we propose a new method of modeling principal curves, based on the algorithm2 in section 3 for searching a bifurcate point of principal curves and the polygonal line algorithm1 in section 2.2 and B-spline network.

Given a set of data points $X_n = \{(x_1, y_1), (x_2, y_2), \ldots, (x_n, y_n)\} \subset R^2$.

The basic idea of the algorithm is: **Firstly**, the algorithm2 in section 3 is used for finding the bifurcate point and the bifurcate point $(\overline{x}, \overline{y})$ is found.

Let $\quad X^{(1)} = \{(x_i, y_i) | i \in N, (x_i, y_i) \in X_n, x_i < \overline{x}\}$

$\quad X^{(21)} = \{(x_i, y_i) | i \in N, (x_i, y_i) \in X_n, x_i \geq \overline{x}, y_i \geq \overline{y}\}$

$\quad X^{(22)} = \{(x_i, y_i) | i \in N, (x_i, y_i) \in X_n, x_i \geq \overline{x}, y_i < \overline{y}\}$

$\quad X^{(2)} = X^{(21)} \cup X^{(22)}$.

Distinctly X_n is partitioned into $X^{(1)}$ and $X^{(2)}$ making use of the abscissa $\overline{x}$ for bifurcate point $(\overline{x}, \overline{y})$, where $X_n = X^{(1)} \cup X^{(2)}$, $X^{(1)} \cap X^{(2)} = \phi$; $X^{(2)}$ is partitioned into $X^{(21)}$ and $X^{(22)}$ making use of the ordinate $\overline{y}$ for bifurcate point $(\overline{x}, \overline{y})$. thus X_n is partitioned into $X^{(1)}$, $X^{(21)}$ and $X^{(22)}$,where $X_n = X^{(1)} \cup X^{(21)} \cup X^{(22)}$, $X^{(1)} \cap X^{(21)} \cap X^{(22)} = \phi$. $X^{(1)}$, $X^{(21)}$ and $X^{(22)}$ respectively correspond to the three braches of the principal curves for X_n.

Secondly, by using the polygonal line algorithm1 in section 2.2 three polygonal line is found corresponding to three subset of X_n: $X^{(1)}$, $X^{(21)}$ and $X^{(22)}$. For each subset, a polygonal $f_{k,n}$ line with k line segments and $k+1$ vertices are gained, different subset has different k value.

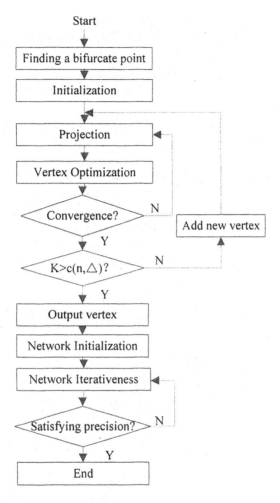

Fig.4.The flow chart of the approach

Finally, $k+1$ vertices of every polygonal line are regarded as the training sample for B-spline network and it is trained. The principal curve for a set of data points $X_n = \{(x_1, y_1), (x_2, y_2), ..., (x_n, y_n)\} \subset R^2$ is created. While B-spline network is trained, the points in $X^{(21)}$ and $X^{(22)}$ are respectively trained and the training results are respectively stored.

The flow chart of the approach, proposed by us, is given in **Fig.4**.

5.   THE EXPERIMENT RESULTS ON SIMULATE DATA SET

To test the algorithm presented above, we conducted experiments on simulate data sets. Our experiment results on simulate data set are given in **Fig.5** and **Fig.6.** We can see that the principal curves constructed with the proposed algorithm have approximated to the origin continuous functions.

In the **Fig.5** consider the $y = \sin x, 0 \le x \le 2\pi$, randomly select 400 points, and add independent Gaussian noise $\varepsilon_i \sim N_1(0,0.1)$.

In the **Fig.6** consider the $y = \sin x, 0 \le x \le \frac{3}{2}\pi$ and the $y = -\sin x, \pi \le x \le \frac{3}{2}\pi$, randomly select 300 points and 100 points, and add independent Gaussian noise $\varepsilon_i \sim N(0,0.1)$.

Based on above experiment results, we can see the approach of modeling principal curve, combining B-spline network with the polygonal line learning algorithm, may construct a smooth curve model and is a feasible and effective method. The presented learning principal curve algorithm merely gained discrete points on approximate principal curve without modeling principal curve.

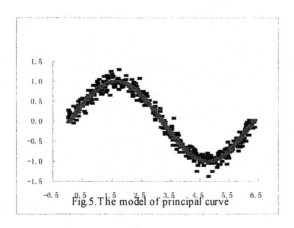

Fig.5.The model of principal curve

6. CONCLUSION

For the data points set given, the proposed approach in the paper, based on B-spline network, can model a smooth principal curve of it. To compare with the presented algorithm of principal curve, **firstly,** our method may construct the model of principal curve for a data points set and this is a improvement and perfection on the presented algorithm of principal curve in some sense; **Secondly,** since the basic function of B-spline network is continuous function the principal curve constructed using our proposed method is a smooth curve. **Finally,** because the knowledge in B-spline network is locally stored and the network has the features of a short training time and a fast convergence speed, therefore the approach may quickly create the model of principal curve.

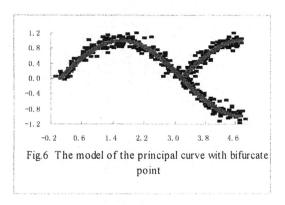

Fig.6 The model of the principal curve with bifurcate point

Our experiment results on simulate data sets demonstrate that the proposed method, based on B-spline network and the polygonal line algorithm of learning principal curve is feasible and effective for modeling principal curve of the data points set given. This method is applied to the fields of modeling and the process controlling and so on.

ACKNOWLEDGEMENTS

This work is supported by the National Natural Science Foundation of China (No.60435010, 90604017), the 973 Project (No.2003CB17004), the Natural Science Foundation of Beijing (No. 4052025).

REFERENCES

1. Hastie T. Principal Curves and surfaces. Laboratory for Computational Statistics, Stanford University, Department of Statistics : Technical Report 11, 1984.
2. Hastie T and Stuetzle W. Principal Curves. Journal of the American Statistical Association. 1989,84: 502-516.
3. Moody J. Fastlearning in multi-resolution hierarchies. Advances in Neural information Processing System, vol.1, 1989 : 29-39.
4. Kégl B, Krzyzak A, Linder T and Zeger K. Learning and design of principal curves. IEEE Trans. On Pattern Analysis and Machine Intelligence. 2000, 22 (3): 281-297.
5. Martin Brown, Chris Harris. Neurofuzzy adaptive modeling and control. Prentice Hall International (UK) Limited, 1994: 89-100.
6. Stanford D. and Raftery A.E. Finding Curvilinear Features in Spatial Point Patterns: Principal Curve Clustering with Noise. IEEE Trans. on Pattern Analysis and Machine Intelligence. 2000,22(6): 601-609.

7. Kegl B and Krzyzak A. Piecewise linear skeletonization using principal curves. IEEE
    Trans on Pattern Analysis and Machine Intelligence 2002,24(1): 59-74.
8. Hemann T, Meinicke P, and Ritter H. Principal curve sonification. International
    Conference on Auditory Display 2000: 81-86,
9. Einbeck J, Tutz G, and Evers L. Exploring Multivariate Data Structures with Local
    Principal Curves". In: C. Weihs and W. Gaul (Eds.): Classification - The Ubiquitous
    Challenge, Springer, Heidelberg2005: 256-263.

Solving Cluster Ensemble Problems by Correlation's matrix & GA

Dr. Morteza analoui   analoui@iust.ir

Niloufar sadighian   todaybox@yahoo.ca ,
n_sadighian@iust.ir

Abstract

Clustering ensembles have emerged as a powerful method for improving both the robustness and the stability of unsupervised classification solutions. However, finding a consensus clustering from multiple partitions is a difficult problem that can be approached from graph-based, combinatorial or statistical perspectives. We offer a probabilistic model of consensus using a finite mixture of multinomial distributions in a space of clustering. A combined partition is found as a solution to the corresponding maximum likelihood problem using the GA algorithm. The excellent scalability of this algorithm and comprehensible underlying model are particularly important for clustering of large datasets. This study includes two sections, at the first, calculate correlation matrix .this matrix show correlation between samples and we found the best samples that can be in the center of clusters. In the other section a genetic algorithm is employed to produce the most stable partitions from an evolving ensemble (population) of clustering algorithms along with a special objective function. The objective function evaluates multiple partitions according to changes caused by data perturbations and prefers those clustering that are least susceptible to those perturbations.

Introduction

Clustering for unsupervised data exploration and analysis has been investigated for decades in the statistics, data mining, and machine learning communities. A recent advance of clustering techniques is the development of cluster ensemble or consensus clustering techniques (Strehl & Ghosh, $\Upsilon \cdot \cdot \Upsilon$; Fern & Brodley, $\Upsilon \cdot \cdot \Upsilon$; Monti et al., $\Upsilon \cdot \cdot \Upsilon$; Topchy et al., $\Upsilon \cdot \cdot \Upsilon$), which seek to improve clustering performance by first generating multiple partitions of a given data set and then combining them to form a final (presumably superior) clustering solution. Such techniques have been shown to provide a generic tool for improving the performance of basic clustering algorithms. At the most clustering techniques use similarity attributes between samples for separate samples that can be such as Euclidean distance or   .

There are too much manner for clustering information, for example they are Ants,Isodata, K_means ,Forgy,

A critical problem in this clustering manner is how to adjust initial parameters, for example in Forgy's algorithm there are two parameters that should adjust:

$\backslash$- cluster's number.

Υ- seed point samples .

In this paper we approach this problem by create correlation's matrix [section $\backslash$] and GA's algorithm [section Υ].

$\backslash$ .correlation matrix

Algorithm :

this algorithm is execute in Υ steps :

  $\backslash$- *repeat one of the clustering methods like (Ants , ISODATA, K_mean ,Forgy clustering) and create correlation matrix*

  Υ- *divided correlation matrix into some cluster*

  Υ- *apply changed Forgy loop*

$\backslash$-$\backslash$ repeat one of the clustering methods and create correlation matrix

In this step a clustering algorithm such as (Ants , ISODATA, K_mean , Forgy clustering) execute for some iterations . Suppose we know cluster's number, then we can use Fforgy's algorithm .

Forgy's algorithm :

$\backslash$. *Initialize the cluster centroids to the seed points.*

Υ. *For each sample, find the cluster centroid nearest it. Put the sample in the cluster identified with this nearest cluster centroid.*

Υ. *If no samples changed clusters in step Υ, stop.*

Υ. *Compute the centroids of the resulting clusters and go to step Υ.*

There are Υ way for iteration's time:

  (1) *Iteration=samples/clusters*

Please use the following format when citing this chapter:

analoui, M., sadighian, N., 2006, in IFIP International Federation for Information Processing, Volume 228, Intelligent Information Processing III, eds. Z. Shi, Shimohara K., Feng D., (Boston: Springer), pp. 227–231.

$$(\mathbf{1}) \quad Iteration = \begin{pmatrix} Samples \\ \\ Clusters \end{pmatrix}$$

Correlation's matrix is n*n matrix .
n is sample's number.
The value of C[I,j] shows how many time sample I
and sample J   are   at one   cluster. This matrix is
symmetric and the manner of update this matrix shows
flow:
For I= • to samples- 1
 For J= • to samples- 1
  If samplecluster[I]=samplecluster[J]   then
        Correlation[I,J]=correlation[I,J]+ 1
  End if
 Next J
Next I

1-Г Dividing correlation's matrix into some clusters

There is one correlation's matrix that shows relevant
between samples . We should divide these samples
into k clusters .First of all we choose k samples as
seed points . We could choose these k samples from
the correlation's matrix that have minimum relevant
and correlation to each others. May be according to
this we got some noisy seed points values . I suggest
new solution for this problem :   choose a sample as
seed point , that p samples in all of points have
correlation with it at least Ѵ•٪ of iterations .

$$p = (\frac{samples}{\mathbf{Y} * clusters})$$

There are (*samples/clusters*)   Sample   in each
cluster. Algorithm for choose seed points is written
follow:

1-Limit = 1
Г-find < samples I,J > where Correlation
                [I][J] < Limit

Г-for all samples if number of samples that
Correlation[I][samples] >(Ѵ•٪ Iteration)
                is greater than p
                seedpoints ← I
If (seed<clusters)   then
        For all samples if number of samples
        that Correlation[J][samples] > Ѵ•٪
                        Iteration
                is greater than p
                seedpoints ← J
    If (seed<clusters)   then

                Limit++ and go to step Г
Else
End the Algorithm

After we found seed points, we choose $(\dfrac{samples}{clusters})$
points for each cluster that have most Correlation with
them.

Г. Clustering by genetic algorithm

In this section we present a scheme driven by
evolutionary computation to overcome the problem of
comparing clustering results. The clustering results are
achieved   by   qualitatively   different   clustering
algorithms, which produce different partitioning. Our
scheme helps us to overcome these problems of
algorithms by generating clustering ones and selecting
the best evaluated to evolve in another generation until
the whole procedure reaches a robust result.
The proposed scheme generates clustering-bitstrings
by clustering the *l* modifications with all clustering
algorithm in use. Then these clustering-bitstrings are
evaluated, compared through a fitness function. The
best ones continue their evolution to the next
generation.
The final clustering bitstrings have evolved towards
the stable schemata, which provide us a robust
partition of the data points in the set.

Г-1 Search of Schemata
Evolutionary algorithms are a family of
computer models based on the mechanics of
natural selection and natural genetics. Among
them are genetic algorithms (GA) [ΥΥ] and
genetic programming (GP) [ΥҒ]. Genetic algorithms
were introduced and investigated by John Holland
[ΥΥ]. Later, they became popular by the book of
David Goldberg [Υ۵].

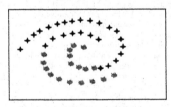

Figure ۱: Intertwined spirals clustered by the
average linkage algorithm.

Also, consider the GA tutorial of David Whitley [ΥҒ]
as a very good introduction to the field. GAs and GPs
are typically used for optimization problems. An
optimization problem is given by a mapping $F : X → Y$

The task is to find an element $x \in X$ for which $y = f(x)$; $y \in Y$ is optimal in some sense. Genetic algorithms encodes a potential solution on its simple chromosome-like data structure, and apply genetic operators such as crossover or mutation to these structures. Then, the potential solution is decoded to the value x in the search space X, and $y = f(x)$ is computed.

The obtained value y is considered as a quality measure, i.e. the fitness for this data structure. Some genetic operators, such as the mating selection, are under control of these fitness values, some other, like the mutation, are not related to fitness at all. An implementation of a GA begins with a population of "chromosomes" (generation ١). For standard GA, each chromosome (also referred to as individual) is represented as a bitstring of a fixed length (e.g. 0101101 as a bitstring of length ٧). Then, the genetic operators are applied onto all bitstrings iteratively in a fixed order, going from one generation to the next until a given goal (e.g. fitness value exceeds a given threshold or a predefined number of generations was completed) is met. Finally, the individual (or chromosome) with the best fitness value in the final generation is taken as the evolved solution of the optimization problem .At first, ٢m bitstrings are selected out of the k individuals of generation n for mating. Usually, this is done by fitness-proportionate selection , i.e., the relative probability for an individual to be selected is proportional to its fitness value. The better the fitness, the better is the chance to spread out its "genetic material" (i.e., some of its bits) over the next generation .Once the ٢m individuals are chosen, they are paired. In the two bitstrings of each pair, a common splitting point is randomly selected, and a new bitstring is constructed by combining a half of the first bitstring with the other half of the other bitstring. Then, the new individuals are mutated, i.e. some of its bits are reversed with a given (usually small) probability. This gives the so-called m children of parent generation n. Now, the fitness values of the children are evaluated by decoding them into x values and computing the $f(x)$.

Some of the children might have a better fitness than its parents. From the k individuals of generation n and the m children, the best k individuals constitute the next generation $(n+١)$. While randomized, GAs are no simple random walks. For the standard GA, John Holland has derived the well-known Schemata Theorem, which models a GA by means of the so-called schematas (or similarity templates). A schema is an incomplete bitstring in the sense that it contains unspecified bits. An example for a schema is 10*110, which leaves position ٣ unspecified. 101110 is a realization of this schema. Generation n contains each possible schema to some extent. It can be said, that such a schema is tested by the GA, or that trials are allocated to it by the GA. Now, one measure for a schema is the average fitness of all of its realizations. A second measure is the ratio of this average to the "average average" of all schemata present in the generation n, i.e. its above-averageness . The Schemata Theorem relates the rate of a schema within

a population with this measure. It says, that the rate of a schema within a population grows exponentially with its above averageness. The most important point here is that all schematas are tested in parallel.

Strongly related to the application of a GA is the encoding problem. In general, GAs are applied to highly non-linear, complex problems, where it is hard to find a model which provides an approach to the solution. In these applications, they are the most simple approach. However, a GA is not guaranteed to find the global optimum of a problem. It only ensures, by the Schemata Theorem, to find better solutions than the random initialized ones. GAs find evolved solutions.

٢-٢ Fitness Function

The fitness function $y = f(x)$; $x \in X$ in search, has to keep track of the difference of the tested indiviual compared to all other (original) individuals. Because all individuals are given as bitstrings, the Hamming distance, which keeps track of inverted bitstrings will be the right measure.

So we define the fitness function $y(b)$ as follows:

$$y(b) = \frac{1}{m} \sum_{i=1}^{m} \min \left[\sum_{j=1}^{n} |x_{ij} - b_j|, \sum_{j=1}^{n} |(1 - x_{ij}) - b_j| \right]$$

where:
n = length of the Bitstring
m = number of orginals (clusterstrings)
$x_g \in X$
so that:
x_{gv} is the vth bit of gth original clustering-string
The alternating measure of the fitness function reflects the issue that different clustering approaches may decide differently for assigning class ١ or ٢. Hence, the more suitable schema should be more similar to either the cluster string or its inverted form.

٣. Experimental Results

We started our experiment so that ٢٨ original clustering strings with a length of ١٠٠ bit were computed. As parameterization of the Genetic Algorithm we decided to chose :
- as the stop criteria ٣٠٠ generations
- ٣٠ parents in each generation
- ٧٠ children in each generation
- uniform crossover with p.= ٠,٥
- mutation:
  - probability = ٠,٧٥
  - mutation methods: swap mutation
- selection metode : Tournament selection with Tournament size=٢

The highest fitness $1/y(b)$ we achieved was $1/y(b_{best}) = ٠;٠٢١٥٥٦$. This bit string b_{best} was not equal to any original clustering-string, but had a very low distance (Hamming distance) to the first of the originals.

That's why we decided to name the clustering bit string with The minimal Hamming distance compared with the individual reaching the highest fitness (b_{hevt}) where $y(b_{hevt}) = \min(y(b)) \wedge b \wedge X$) the result of the procedure. The first original clustering-string, which represents, according to our results, the most appropriate clustering, is the one shown in figure ١, which shows obviously the correct partitioning of the intertwined spirals problem. After some more trials we got even more results leading again to the first original clustering bit string with even higher fitnesses , i.e. $١/y(b_{best}) = ٠.٠۴.٠.٩۶$ with only four different bits inside the compared strings.

۴. Conclusions

In this paper we have presented a scheme driven by evolutionary computation to overcome the problem of comparing results achieved by qualitatively different clustering algorithms. We have produced a couple of noisy copies of a given two-class clustering problem. Because it was a two-class problems, which means that we were clustering all data into two clusters, the clustering results could be represented as binary bit strings , so they were compatible to the format genetic algorithms work on. Taking the whole lot of clustering results as input to the genetic algorithm we assumed to let it find the scheme of the right clustering for the presented problem.

At the end we achieved reproducible result, for many runs of the genetic algorithm were leading to the same original clustering-bit string which of course points to the most appropriate clustering algorithm. It is, according to our results, possible to find the appropriate clustering for a given problem, but it is also possible to identify the most suitable clustering algorithm for an unknown dataset. Last but not least it seems to be feasible, to classify clustering problems in comparison to their appropriate clustering algorithm.

References

[١] Peng-Yeng Yin and Ling-Hwei Chen. A new non iterative approach for clustering. *Pattern Recognition Letters*, ١۵:١٢۵–١٣٣, ١٩٩۴.

[٢] D. Chaudhuri, B. B. Chaudhuri, and C. A.Murthy. A new split-and-merge clustering technique. *Pattern Recognition Letters*, ١٣:٣٩٩–۴٠٩, ١٩٩٢.

[٣] Torbjorn Eltoft and Rui J. P. DeFigueiredo. A new neural network for cluster-detection-and labeling. *IEEE Transactions on Neural Networks*, ٩(۵):١٠٢١–١٠٣۴, September ١٩٩٨.

[۴] C. L. Begovich and V. E. Kane. Estimating the number of groups and group membership using simulation cluster analysis. *Pattern Recognition*, ١۵(۴):٣٣۵–٣۴٢, ١٩٨٢.

[۵] Donald E. Brown, Christopher L. Huntley, and Paul J. Garvey. Clustering of homogeneous subsets. *Pattern Recognition Letters*, ١٢:۴٠١–۴٠٨, ١٩٩١.

[۶] Lei Xu, Adam Krzyzak, and Erkki Oja. Rival penalized competitive learning for clustering analysis, rbf net, and curve detection. *IEEE Transactions on Neural Networks*, ۴(۴):۶٣۶–۶۴٩, ١٩٩٣.

[٧] Lei Xu. Bayesian ying-yang machine, clustering and number of clusters. *Pattern Recognition Letters*, ١٨:١١۶٧–١١٧٨, ١٩٩٧.

[٨] G. Celeux and G. Soromenho. An entropy criterion for assessing the number of clusters in amixture model. *Journal of Classification*, ١٣:١٩۵–٢١٢, ١٩٩۶.

[٩] Christophe Biernacki, Gilles Celeux, and Gerard Govaert. Assessing a mixture model for clustering with the integrated classification likelihood. Rapport de recherche ٣۵٢١, Theme ۴, Unite de recherche INRIA Lorraine, http://www.inria.fr, ١٩٩٧.

[١٠] Richard S. Wallace and Takeo Kanade. Finding natural clusters having minimum description length. In *Proceedings of the ١٠th International Conference on Pattern Recognition*, volume ١, pages ۴٣٨–۴۴٢, Los Alamitos, CA, USA, ١٩٩٠. IEEE Comput. S. Press.

[١١] A. Marazzi, P. Gamba, A. Mecocci, and A. Semboloni. Automatic selection of the number of clusters in multidimensional data problems. In *Proceedings of the International Conference on Image Processing*, volume ٣, pages ۶٣١–۶٣۴, NY, USA, ١٩٩۶. IEEE.

[١٢] Shri Kant, T. L. Rao, and P. N. Sundaram. An automatic and stable clustering algorithm. *Pattern Recognotion Letters*, ١۵:۵۴٣–۵۴٩, ١٩٩۴.

[١٣] G. H. Ball and D. J. Hall. Isodata, a novel method of data analysis and pattern classification. Technical report, Stanford Research Institute, Menlo Park, ١٩۶۵.

[١۴] G. Carpenter and S. Grossberg. Adaptive resonance theory: Stable selforganization of neural recognition codes in response to arbitrary lists of input patterns. In *Proc. ٨th Annu. Conf. Cognitive Sci. Soc.*, pages ۴۵–۶٢, ١٩٨۶.

[١٥] R. J. P. DeFigueiredo. The oi, os, omni and osman networks as best approximations of nonlinear systems under training data constraints. In *Proc. IEEE Int. Symp. Circuits Syst.*, Seattle, WA, ١٩٩۶.

[١۶] Yoseph Linde, Andrs Buzo, and Robert M. Gray. An algorithm for vector quantizer design. COM- ٢٨(١):٨۴–٩۵, January ١٩٨٠.

[١٧] Thomas M. Martinetz, Stanislav G.Berkovich, and Klaus J. Schulten. "Neural-Gas" network for vector quantization and its application to timeseries prediction. ۴(۴):۵۵٨–۵۶٩, July ١٩٩٣.

[١٨] A. Weingessel E. Dimitriadou and K. Hornik. A voting-merging clustering algorithm. In Fuzzy-Neuro Systems '٩٩, editor, *SFB "Adaptive Information Systems and Modeling in Economics and Management Science*, number Working Paper ٣١،١٩٩٩.

[١٩] A. Weingessel E. Dimitriadou and K. Hornik. Fuzzy voting in clustering. In Fuzzy-Neuro Systems '٩٩, editor, *G. Brewka, R. Der S. Gottwald and A. Schierwagen*, pages ۶٣–٧۴, ١٩٩٩.

[٢٠] Wolfgang von der Gablentz and Mario K"oppen. agglomerative single-linkage clustering and its capability for solving the interwtined spirals problem, a technical report. experimental results, Fraunhofer IPK, http://www.ipk.fhg.de, ٢٠٠٠.

[٢١] Marvin L. Minsky and Seymour A. Papert. *Perceptrons – Expanded Edition*. MIT Press, ١٩٨٨.

[٢٢] Cran. http://cran.at.r-projects.org.

[٢٣] J. A. Holland. *Adaptation in natural and artificial systems*. MIT Press, Cambridge,MA, ١٩٧۵.

[٢۴] J. Koza. *Genetic programming — On the programming of computers by means of natural selection*. MIT Press, Cambridge, MA, ١٩٩٢.

[٢۵] D. E. Goldberg. *Genetic algorithms in search, optimization & machine learning*. Addison- Wesley,Reading, MA, ١٩٨٩.

[٢۶] D.Whitley. A genetic algorithmtutorial. In *Statistics and Computing*, ۴, pages ۶۵–٨۵, ١٩٩۴.

[٢٧] R. G. Reynolds. An introduction tu cultural algorithm. In *In Proceedings of Evolutionary Programming*, EP-٩۴. San Diego. CA, ١٩٩۴.

STUDY ON COMPOUND GENETIC AND BACK PROPAGATION ALGORITHM FOR PREDICTION OF COAL AND GAS OUTBURST RISK

Yaqin Wu [1], Kai Wang [2], Maoguang Wang [1,3]

[1] School of Computer Science & Technology, China University of Mining and Technology, Xuzhou 221008, Jiangsu, China

[2] School of Mining & Safety Engineering, China University of Mining and Technology, Xuzhou 221008, Jiangsu, China

[3] Institute of Computing Technology, Chinese Academy of Sciences, Beijing 100080, China

Abstract: Coal and gas outburst is a very complex phenomenon of dynamic disaster in coal mine. There exists a complex non-linear mapping relationship which could not be described with functions between outburst risk and its influential factors. Due to the originality and superiority of artificial neural network (ANN) for modeling and imitating non-linear problems, an ANN model for prediction of outburst risk is set up. Then through practical application, the performance of commonly applied Back Propagation (BP) network for outburst risk prediction is analyzed. Aimed at the weakness of BP algorithm and based on the overall searching characteristic of Genetic Algorithm (GA), an improved compound GA-BP algorithm is used to optimize the model, then both the performance of the network and the predicting reliability of the model are improved.

Key words: outburst risk prediction, artificial neural network, compound GA-BP algorithm

Please use the following format when citing this chapter:

Wu, Y., Wang, K., Wang, M., 2006, in IFIP International Federation for Information Processing, Volume 228, Intelligent Information Processing III, eds. Z. Shi, Shimohara K., Feng D., (Boston: Springer), pp. 233–241.

1.   INTRODUCTION

Coal and gas outburst (briefly named "outburst") is one of the biggest natural disasters which are seriously imperiling safe productivity of coal mine. Further studies of reliable outburst prediction methods are essential to effective prevention of outburst. It is known through numerous researches that the occurrence of outburst is a catastrophic behavior of a complex non-linear dynamic system during its evolution in time and space, and there exists a complex non-linear mapping relationship which could not be described with functions between outburst risk and its influential factors[1]. Artificial neural network (ANN) possesses originality and superiority of modeling and imitating for dealing with such non-linear problems. Recently, the model of ANN has been tried to apply in outburst prediction and its effect has also been validated through applications.However ANN itself has some weakness. In this paper, through analyzing the performance of commonly applied Back Propagation (BP) neural network for outburst risk prediction, it is indicated that there exists some weakness of BP algorithm such as easily falling into local extremum, slow speed of convergence and vibrating effect, especially the result of BP algorithm is closely related to the initial status of the network. Consequently, in order to improve the performence of BP neural network, based on the overall searching characteristic of Genetic Algorithm (GA), an improved compound genetic and back propagation (GA-BP) algorithm is adopted to optimize the ANN model.

2.   DESCRIPTION OF THE PROBLEM

Based on the synthetical hypothesis of outburst mechanism and statistical data from the spot, it can be drawn that the factors which control the occurrence and intensity of outburst mainly include: gas pressure (gas content), ground stress, coal mass strength and the thickness of soft coal seam. Moreover, the factors such as geological structure and pitch angle of coal seam, passage tunnel for outburst and the action of mining and drivage also influence the occurrence and intensity of outburst. Through simulating tests in laboratory of CUMT, the above first four factors are analyzed and their influence upon the possibility of outburst occurrence is investigated systematically [1, 2].

During the simulating tests, there occurred two typical dynamic phenomena which can be classified as: (I) non outburst risk, (II) outburst. Respectively using P0, Pg, Hm, Sc to represent ground stress, gas pressure, thickness of soft coal body and sieving modulus of coal mass, the concrete experimental conditions and results of the tests are listed in Table 1, where the strength of coal mass is expressed as sieving modulus. The larger sieving modulus is, the smaller coal mass strength is.

In this paper, the method of ANN will be adopted to set up the mapping relationship between outburst risk and P_0, P_g, H_m, S_c, so as to realize precise prediction of outburst risk.

Table 1. Experiment data and results of outburst simulating tests

No.	Site for Sampling	P_0/MPa	P_g/MPa	H_m/mm	S_c	Outburst Risk
1	Luling 82	14.37	0.18	109.0	8.1	I
2	Luling 83	14.37	0.21	38.0	6.2	I
3	Kongzhuang 8#	16.61	0.22	37.0	11.1	I
4	Jiahe 2#	13.09	0.13	163.5	7.8	I
5	Jiahe 9#	17.24	0.21	85.5	14.7	I
6	Majiagou 9#	14.69	0.23	30.5	15.1	I
7	Jiulishan Y	13.73	0.14	76.0	7.7	I
8	Jinggezhuang	18.52	0.27	33.0	13.2	I
9	Panji No.1 Mine	11.50	0.20	96.5	7.6	I
10	Panji No.3 Mine	16.61	0.10	142.5	7.1	I
11	Jiaoxi Hard Coal	14.05	0.32	105.0	4.9	II
12	Luling 83	14.37	0.72	85.5	6.2	II
13	Luling 9#	15.01	0.44	79.0	11.2	II
14	Luling 9#	15.01	0.36	62.0	11.2	II
15	Luling 10#	13.09	0.35	60.0	7.3	II
16	Kongzhuang 8#	16.61	0.35	127.0	11.1	II
17	Jiahe 7#	12.77	0.43	125.0	8.8	II
18	Majiagou 9#	14.69	0.48	68.0	15.1	II
19	Majiagou 12	11.50	0.52	33.5	12.1	II
20	Majiagou 12	11.50	0.55	67.0	12.1	II
21	Baishanping 6#	13.73	0.22	34.5	6.8	II
22	Baishanping 6#	13.73	0.41	34.5	6.8	II
23	Jiulishan Y	13.73	0.36	75.5	7.7	II
24	Xinzhuangzi	14.37	0.48	75.5	8.7	II
25	Jinggezhuang	18.52	0.25	118.5	13.2	II
26	Panji No.1 Mine	11.50	0.44	97.5	7.6	II
27	Panji No.2 Mine	13.41	0.49	73.0	12.5	II
28	Panji No.2 Mine	13.41	0.39	56.5	12.5	II
29	Panji No.3 Mine	16.61	0.48	142.5	7.1	II
30	Jiaoxi Hard Coal	14.05	0.74	105.0	4.9	II
31	Jiaoxi Soft Coal	12.77	0.30	191.5	11.8	II
32	Jiaoxi Soft Coal	12.77	0.75	74.5	11.8	II
33	Luling 82	14.37	0.65	110.0	8.1	II
34	Luling 10#	13.10	0.85	172.0	7.3	II
35	Kongzhuang 7#	17.24	0.82	118.0	5.9	II
36	Jiahe 2#	13.36	0.82	162.5	7.8	II
37	Jiahe 7#	12.77	1.0	37.0	8.8	II
38	Majiagou 9#	14.69	1.16	30.5	15.1	II

39	Mixed Coal 1#	11.82	0.91	161.0	7.6	II
40	Mixed Coal 2#	19.48	0.61	107.5	6.6	II
41	Xinzhuangzi	14.37	0.93	154.5	8.7	II

3. ANALYSIS ON THE ABILITY OF BP ALGORITHM FOR OUTBURST RISK PREDICTION

3.1 Back Propagation Neural Network

In current applications of ANN, BP network model and its varied forms are usually mainly adopted because they represent the essence of ANN. BP network is a multi-layer forward network with unidirectional propagation, its construction is shown in Fig.1 [3,4]. BP network can be regarded as a highly non-linear mapping relationship between the input and output which can approximate complex function through compounding the simple non-linear functions time after time. It has been proved through theoretical research that BP network could realize any successive function at any due precision.

The learning process of BP network is a typically tutorial one realized by BP Algorithm which is the most popular training and learning method of ANN. The advantages of standard BP Algorithm based on gradient descending method and other improved forms lie in the accurate optimality searching and the ability of self-learning.

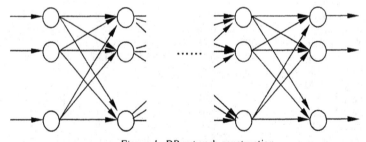

Figure 1. BP network construction

3.2 Establishment of the ANN Model

In this paper, a three-layer BP neural network is set up. And there are four units in input layer which respectively represent the four influence factors of outburst. According to the test calculation results, it is determined that the network consists of two hidden layers of which the first one includes four units and the second one includes three units. The output layer includes one unit which represents outburst risk. The logarithmic tangent function is selected as the transferring function of the network between the input layer and the first hidden layer, the first hidden layer and the second hidden layer. The linear function is selected as the transferring function of the network between the second hidden layer and output layer. The calculating process of the network is programmed by MATLAB software. The function "trainlm" is selected as the training function and "learngdm" as the learning function. The sum-squared error function "sse" is selected as the training performance function of the network.

Firstly normalize the data of 41 samples in Table 1 through transforming all sample data into the number of which the average value is 0 and the standard error is 1. Then analyze their main composition to get rid of the data whose variation is lower than 0.01. The handled samples are divided into two groups among which 80% (33) samples are taken as the training samples and 20% (8) samples are taken as the predicting samples. The requirements for dividing groups are that both of the groups should include the two classifications of outburst risk, and the training samples should exclude predicting samples and contain the features of all samples. The training objective is $0.01^2 \times 33 = 0.0033$.

3.3   Analysis of the Training and Prediction Results

According to the estabilished BP neural network model, the training and predicting process for outburst risk prediction has been conducted for many times. It is shown through analyzing every training and prediction results that there exist the following limitations of BP algorithm:

(1) The failure probability of network training is higher. The main reason is as follows. The goal of the network is trying to get the overall extremum of the complex non-linear function, however there usually exist several local extrema of such function, therefore as an optimizing method through local searching BP Algorithm is prone to fall into local extremum, converge slowly and even vibrate, so as to fail in training the network.

(2) The prediction result of the network is not so satisfied. There are two main reasons. Firstly, there exists contradictory between prediction ability and training ability of the network. Generally, the prediction ability of network will increase as its training ability improves, but there is an extreme limit of this trend beyond which the prediction ability of network will decrease as its training ability improves on the contrary. This is so-called

"Over Fitness". Secondly, for all of the training processes, there is not only one final combination of weights and threshold values which satisfy the due training precision, so different combinations of weights (and threshold values) will lead to distinct prediction results.

4.   ANALYSIS OF COMPOUND GA-BP ALGORITHM AND ITS PREDICTION RESULT

4.1   Genetic Algorithm

Genetic algorithm (GA) is basically based on natural biological evolution. A GA functions by generating an initial population from a random selection of possible solutions (which are analagous to chromosomes) to a given problem. It then evaluates each of those solutions, and a value for fitness is assigned to each solution (chromosome) depending on how close it actually is to solving the problem (thus arriving to the answer of the desired problem). Those chromosomes with a higher fitness value are more likely selected to reproduce new solutions (offspring, which can mutate after reproduction). The offspring is a product of the father and mother, whose composition consists of a combination of genes from them (this process is known as "crossing over"). If the new generation contains a solution that produces an output that is close enough or equal to the desired answer then the problem has been solved. If this is not the case, then the new generation will go through the same process as their parents did. This will continue until some condition (for example number of populations or improvement of the best solution) is satisfied [4, 5].

Compared with BP algorithm, Genetic algorithm (GA) possesses the following characteristics:

(1) The outstanding advantages of GA lie in that the gradient information of error function is unnecessary, and it is also unnecessarily considered whether the error function is differential or not. If it is easy to obtain the gradient information during the training process, perhaps BP algorithm will be superior to Genetic evolution algorithm in the speed of convergence.

(2) Both of the results of two algorithms are sensitive to their calculating parameters. Especially the result of BP algorithm is closely related to the initial status of the network.

(3) As the optimizing process of objective function is concerned, GA is good at overall searching, on the contrary BP algorithm is more effective in local searching.

(4) Limited by encoding precision, sometimes GA is hard to reach higher training precision.

4.2   Compound GA-BP Algorithm

It can be known through the above analysis that both GA and BP algorithms have their own advantages and disadvantages. If combining their advantages, the better training results will be obtained. Because GA possesses very strong ability of overall searching for optimization of the objective function, and can get the overall optimal solution in higher probability, so that the weakness of BP algorithm can be overcome by using GA to search during the earlier stage. It is shown by some related researches that the training efficiency and effect of compound GA-BP algorithm are significantly improved compared with GA or BP algorithm alone.

In this paper, the compound GA-BP algorithm is used to realize the learning and predicting ability of the network, so that the training process of the network can be divided into two steps: firstly, optimizing the initial weights (and threshold values) of BP network by GA and then obtaining the overall optimal solution in a certain range; then using BP algorithm to correct the network weights (and threshold values) and acquire precise solution.

The concrete method for realizing compound GA-BP algorithm is as follows:

(1) Select the network construction and the learning rule, set up the network parameters.

(2) Estimate the solution space of the network weights (and threshold values) by the designed BP network, and preliminarily design the range of the solution space of the network weights (and threshold values).

(3) Compile the calculating program of fitness function. In this paper, the fitness function is determined as e^{-E}, among which E is average square error.

(4) Select the parameters of GA. In this paper, the population size is 70, the gene encoding pattern is float code, the number of genetic generations is 500, the crossover rate is 0.6 and the mutation rate is 0.05.

(5) Use the operators of crossover, mutation and selection to complete the optimization of the network weights (and threshold values) until reaching the genetic objective.

(6) Take the optimized weights (and threshold values) by GA as the initial weights (and threshold values) of the BP network, then use BP algorithm to conduct precise training.

(7) Training process will end if the due training precision can be satisfied after the sixth step, whereas go back to the fifth step until reaching the training objective.

4.3   Analysis of the Training and Prediction Results

The topologic network structure of the model is also 4- 4- 3- 1. During the training process, the advantage of the compound GA-BP algorithm in the speed of convergence has been validated. In addition, it is shown from the training results of many times of calculations that the final combinations number and varying range of the network weights and threshold values trained by compound GA-BP algorithm are both less than those traned by BP algorithm, consequently the reliability of prediction result can be improved.

After the training process finished while the due training precision is satisfied, the weights between the input layer and the hidden layer, the hidden layer and the output layer, and the threshold values of every units are listed in Table 2. The prediction results are shown in Table 3.

Table 2. The final network weights and threshold values trained by compound GA-BP algorithm

	Weights				Threshold values
From input layer to the first hidden layer	-2.3002	1.5414	-0.62597	-0.57284	-2.3972
	-0.49192	2.338	2.3407	-2.4808	2.9269
	0.22918	-2.721	0.95017	1.2658	-0.80139
	3.0541	-2.6617	-1.1212	-1.8284	3.1951
From the first hidden layer to the second one	-2.027	-2.9971	1.1971	1.0783	0.46792
	2.3091	1.2167	2.1645	1.9621	1.3673
	2.2576	2.1872	-2.123	2.3071	1.1887
From hidden layer to output layer	-0.67477	0.34548	-0.057811		0.46792
Running time /s	6.5				
Training steps	10				

Table 3. The prediction results

No.	Site for Sampling	Prediction Output	Due Output	Outburst risk Prediction	Test
1	Luling 82	0.025694	0	I	I
3	Kongzhuang 8#	0.022138	0	I	I
12	Luling 83	1	1	II	II

18	Majiagou 9#	0.99974	1	II	II
24	Xinzhuangzi	0.99972	1	II	II
27	Panji No.2 Mine	0.9997	1	II	II
33	Luling 82	1.0001	1	II	II
38	Majiagou 9#	0.99984	1	II	II

5. CONCLUSIONS

Through analyzing the ability of BP algorithm and compound GA-BP algorithm for the ANN model of outburst risk prediction, it is indicated that the running efficiency and predicting effect of compound GA-BP algorithm are obviously improved compared with BP algorithm. By adopting GA-BP compound algorithm, the performance of the network is improved, then the predicting accuracy and reliability of the model is also increased.

ACKNOLEDGEMENT

This work is supported by National Natural Science Foundation of China (No.50404016, 50534090), Fok Ying Tung Education Foundation (No.101050) and Youth Research Programme of CUMT (No. 0D4789)

REFERENCES

1. Wang Kai, Yu Qixiang. Non-linear Characteristics and Prediction Model of Coal and Gas Outburst. Xuzhou: China University of Mining and Technology Press, 2005.3 (In Chinese)
2. Wang Kai, Yu Qixiang, Jiang Chenglin, Wu Yaqin. Experimental Study on the Intensity of Coal and Gas Outburst. New Development on Rock Mechanics and Engineering: Proceedings of 2nd International Conference on Rock Mechanics and Engineering. Rinton Press, USA, 2002. 227-230
3. The research center of Feisi technology product. MATLAB 6.5 Assistant Analysis and Design of Neural Network. Beijing: Electronics Industry Press, 2003.1 (In Chinese)
4. Yang Xingjun, Zheng Junli. The Artificial Neural Network and Blind Signal Handling. Beijing: TsingHua University Press, 2003.1 (In Chinese)
5. Yuan Ximin, Li Hongyan. Application of Neural Network and Genetic Algorithm in Hydraulic Science. Beijing: China Hydraulic Power Press, 2002.8 (In Chinese)

DEVELOPMENT OF AN OLAP- FUZZY BASED PROCESS MINING SYSTEM FOR QUALITY IMPROVEMENT

G.T.S Ho, H.C.W Lau

Department of Industrial & Systems Engineering, mfhenry@inet.polyu.edu.hk

Abstract: Currently, companies active in the development of high-tech products has become more and more complex in the age of mass customization. Not only do they have to focus on improving product quality, but rather on gaining experience to modify the current processes in order to streamline the integrated workflow. A real-time process mining system (R-PMS) is developed to analyze the proposed XML based process data for discovering the hid-den relationship between processes. The new feature of this system is the in-corporation of the process mining engine, which is characterized by the combined capabilities of the Online Analytical Processing (OLAP) and fuzzy logic (FL), to form a robust framework for highlighting the undesirable process set-ting and parameters for further improvement in a real-time manner. The simulation results indicate that the OLAP based fuzzy approach is generally superior to those of conventional methods which offer higher flexibility on production process management with decision support ability. In this paper, the de-tailed architecture and a case study are included to demonstrate the feasibility of the proposed system.

Key words: Online Analytical Processing, Fuzzy Logic, Extensible Markup Language

1. INTRODUCTION

As organizations become more conscious, management of processes and process data with temporal context is gaining increased attention [5]. Process mining can be seen to contribute to this. It aims at extracting information

Please use the following format when citing this chapter:

Ho, G.T.S., Lau, H.C.W., 2006, in IFIP International Federation for Information Processing, Volume 228, Intelligent Information Processing III, eds. Z. Shi, Shimohara K., Feng D., (Boston: Springer), pp. 243–258.

from event logs to capture the business process as it is being executed [15]. Process management is primarily concerned with the integration of task and context knowledge in application. Processes vary from place to place and from organization to organization. Future management systems are expected to incorporate process management that enable the operations staff to shift its focus from managing equipment to managing processes. Management will become a distributed, co-operative problem-solving activity [9]. Many enterprise work very hard to produce goods and services to a high standard. In order to do so, every process must be effective and efficient, i.e., do the right things and do the things right. As a result, knowledge and information sharing within the enterprise become a must in a fast changing market environment. The utilization of information technology (IT) is taking up momentum to meet this challenge. In particular, data mining (DM), artificial intelligence (AI) and distributed object technology have achieved significant attention for achieving agility of manufacturing system, which has played an important role in transforming quality to new generation.

The objective of this research is to develop the real time process mining system for continual quality enhancement. This paper is divided into three main sections. Section one describes the framework of proposed process mining engine- OLAP based Fuzzy approach. Section two examines the process mining engine on how to improve the finished quality in any process continuously. Section three describes the procedures of system development and its findings of implemented system. Section four concludes the paper and discusses further improvement of R-PMS.

2.   RELATED STUDIES

In order to attract and retain customers as well as business partners, organizations need to provide their services (i.e., execute their processes) with a high consistent, and predictable quality [4]. Many companies work very hard to produce goods and services to a high standard. In order to do so, every process must be effective and efficient, i.e., do the right things and do the things right. Poor process decisions from any individual may lead to poor customer satisfaction and the ultimate goal is to achieve better collaboration for making right decision anytime in any enterprise member. A process is a series of steps or sequence of business activities the outcome of which to achieve customer satisfaction by providing the customer with what they need, when they require it and in the manner which they expect [12].

In fact, the recent trend of global manufacturing is to implement system infrastructure that allows analysis being performed on vastly distributed data according to the corporate objectives in order to make decisions on elements of business strategies. In the area of information-based management, the key of success is to recognize the company's competitive advantages and weaknesses with the support of information technologies for decision support. For the business intelligence of an enterprise, there are only about 20 %information can be extracted from formatted data stored in relational database. The remaining 80 % information is hidden in unstructured or semi-structured documents. Recently, data mining technology, which aims at the conversion of clusters of complex data into useful information, has been under active research [1] [7] [8] [10]. In this project, the On-Line Analytical Processing (OLAP), which is based on data mining technologies, would be deployed as the tool for knowledge discovery to ensure efficient process interactions in the production workflow.

Recent years have seen a number of publications related process improvement and process mining. An intelligent system, which is able to improve an organization's current performance by mining and understanding the historical process data, is still an area that requires more in depth study and investigation. The issue is addressed in this paper with the incorporation of various computational intelligence techniques including Extensible Markup Language, Online Analytical Processing and Fuzzy reasoning. This paper describes the development of a Real time Process Mining System (R-PMS) architecture that enable process engineers to drill down and monitor the quality of finished products in different levels. The advantages of this system over conventional production expert system can be characterized as follows: (a) In-depth and fast analysis can be performed on distributed process data; and (b) Real- time decision support is provided for eliminating the number of failure products.

3 INFRASTRUCTURE OF A REAL-TIME PROCESS MINING SYSTEM

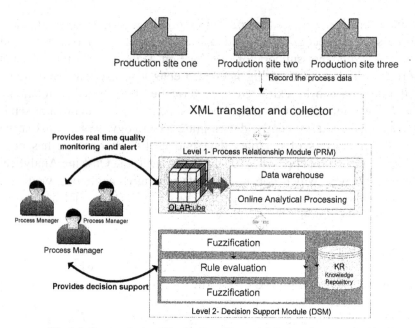

Fig 1 Infrastructure of Real- time Process Mining System (R-PMS)

The infrastructure of the proposed R-PMS is shown in Fig.1. R-PMS consists of two levels: level 1- Process Relationship Module (PRM) and level 2- Decision Support Module (DSM). It is designed for capturing the process quality data from different departments and converting into knowledge to support real- time quality control and continual improvement. In fact, it allows process and quality engineers within the production line to access the process mining engine to retrieve the updated current inspection status and suggested corrective action in terms of optimized control parameters. The system also allows collaboration and data sharing and provides engineers with the ability to generate the defect reports through the common interface. The proposed system can be divided into server and client sides with the server side as the centralized process mining engine and client side referring to different process engineers along the production sites. To support and realize the total quality management for the production of high- quality goods, every process engineers must keep monitoring the process quality. The system will also provide some corrective actions provided that the existing process is out of control in order to ensure "Do it right at the first time" in each process. It is developed for mastering the continual quality enhancement for high- quality products based on the proposed OLAP based Fuzzy approach.

3.1   LEVEL ONE- PROCESS RELATIONSHIP
            MODULE (PRM)

The distributed process data within the enterprise is interchanged through the Inter-net and the purpose of the XML translator is to integrate the enterprises' existing data models and stored in a centralized data warehouse.

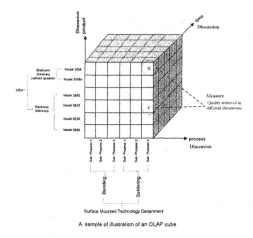

Fig 2. A sample of illustration of an OLAP cube

Whilst the process data is stored in the data warehouse, the further step is to conduct data analysis and reporting in order to alert or assist quality or process engineers in solving quality problems. The technique of Online Analytical Processing (OLAP) is suggested in this module. It facilitates timely access and manipulation of the process data and the application to drill down into data to obtain further information. The OLAP acts as a multidimensional data model which organizes process data into a hierarchy that represents levels of details on the data. It allows engineers to analyze, create and performs process quality reports online. This powerful query engine assists engineers to find and retrieve the defected statistics or performance measurement with the dimensions of time, process, operator and project which can keep monitoring the performance of production line in a real time manner.

The essential characteristic of OLAP is that it performs a numerical and statistical analysis of data and the data is organized in multi-dimension. In OLAP data model, it consists of descriptive data (dimensions) and quantitative value (measures) which builds up the OLAP data cube (Fig 2).

In the OLAP data cube, it builds up with two elements: fact table and dimension. In the fact table, the measures are defined for data analysis and used the defined measures to create user-defined measures (calculated members) which are used on data analysis, e.g. a control chart for keeping a continuing record of a particular quality characteristic in a 'real-time' manner. In the dimension table, different dimension levels are defined to use on different views of OLAP data cube which allows engineers to browse the process quality or control charts based on time-to-time variation, process-to-process variation and within-product model variation

3.2   LEVEL TWO- DECISION SUPPORT MODULE (DSM)

After the quality problem is highlighted in PRM, Some modifications of operating process parameters will be suggested to minimize the defect during production. Most of the process parameters settings are decided by experienced process engineers and controllers and it is a hard task for them to select the optimal settings when different specifications and requirements are required by customers. Moreover, the parameters setting must be adjusted or fine-tuned due to the variation of quality achieved in previous process. The purpose of this module is to provide decision support in each sub-process by using fuzzy technique. In creating decision support functionality, a mechanism, which is able to combine and coordinate many sets of diversified data into a unified and consistent body of useful information, is required. In larger organizations, many different types of users with varied needs must utilize the same massive data warehouse to retrieve the right information for the right purpose. Whilst data warehouse is referred as a very large repository of historical data pertaining to an organization, data mining is more concerned with the collection, management and distribution of organized data in an effective way. The nature of a data warehouse includes integrated data, detailed and summarized data, historical data and metadata. Integrated data enable enterprise members to easily and quickly look across vistas of data. Detailed data is important when they wishes to examine data in its most detailed form while historical data is essential because important information are hidden in this type of data. The data flow between PRM and DSM has been depicted in Figure 3. It should be noted that when the abnormal trends of achieved quality are obtained, the OLAP will extract the crisp values and convert the data into recognized format for generating suggestions in DSM. OLAP can also act as a bridge between PRM and DSM by passing the right data for further analysis. After the process of fuzzy inference is conducted, the crisp output of suggested operating parameters will be packaged as an XML based document and distribute to related enterprise members for carrying adjustment of operating parameters. The query result can also be published on the web page in order to provide decision functionality required by organizations anywhere. Thus, the R-PMS assists the engineers or related staffs to make efficient data analysis on the proposed infrastructure and to assimilate the analysis results to different locations.

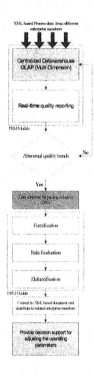

Fig 3. The process data flow between PRM and DSM

A number of factors or rules must be firstly identified by engineering experts in the organization that may affect the quality of finished products and stored in knowledge base. The knowledge base contains the knowledge related to the remedial actions when the quality problems and defects are found. The fuzzy rules are stored and defined as a conditional statement in IF-THEN form, e.g. IF rate of deposition is short THEN time of sputtering is adjusted to slightly long. This kind of linguistic variables include fuzzy sets, such as extremely low, low, medium and high which can greatly reduce a number of production rules.

The core of this module is fuzzy inference; it is the process of formulating the mapping from a given input to an output using fuzzy logic. The mapping then provides a basis from which decisions can be made, or patterns discerned (MathWorks 2002). Mamdani's fuzzy inference method is commonly used in engineering application and is performed four steps: fuzzification, rule evaluation, aggregation of the rule outputs and defuzzification. For the Decision Support Module (DSM) of R-PMS, the first step is to extract the crisp values obtained in PRM (the achieved quality is within the upper or lower limits), and uses pre-defined fuzzy sets to determine the relevant degree of these inputs. After all the inputs have been fuzzified, they will be applied to the antecedents of the fuzzy rules stored in the knowledge base. As the rules defined have multiple antecedents, the fuzzy operator is used to obtain the single truth value. The classical fuzzy operation union and intersection are used to evaluate the conjunction and disjunction of the rule antecedents and calculated as below.

OR fuzzy operation

$$\mu_{A \cup B}(x) = \max[\mu_A(x), \mu_B(x)]$$

AND fuzzy operation

$$\mu_{A \cap B}(x) = \min[\mu_A(x), \mu_B(x)]$$

where μA and μB represent two fuzzy sets A and B on universe X

The outputs of all rules will be unified in order to generate a single fuzzy set for defuzzification. Among several defuzzification methods, Centre of Gravity (COG) is adopted and its equation can be expressed as below.

$$COG = \frac{\sum_{x=a}^{b} \mu_A(x)x}{\sum_{x=a}^{b} \mu_A(x)}$$

This equation represents the centre of gravity of fuzzy set, A on the interval, ab can be calculated over a sample of points along x axis.

4 CASE STUDY

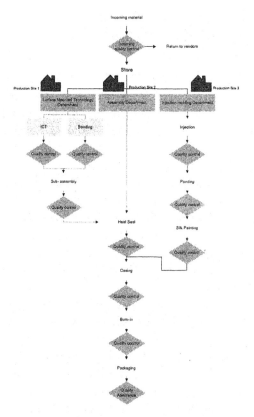

Fig4. The workflow of electronic dictionary manufacturer

In order to validate the proposed concept, structure and techniques, a rapid conceptual prototype of R-PMS was developed. The prototype was validated in electronic product manufacturer- GSL and shown to have more expressive power that renders its applicability in more realistic applications involving quality enhancement. GSL is proficient in designing and manufacturing a wide range of hand-held electronic products for consumers to acquire and to utilize information in a convenient and fast manner for education, entertainment, data storage and communication purposes. It designs and manufactures a wide range of products including electronic dictionaries, personal digital assistant (PDA), translators and electronic organizers. GSL currently employs over 3001-6000 people in China and Hong Kong. GSL founded in 1988 and launched of the first Instant-Dict electronic dictionary EC1000 in 1989. GSL established the brand as

"Instant-Dict" and start OBM early rather than transforming from OEM or ODM to OBM.

4.2   PROBLEM DESCRIPTION

The case study focuses on improving three production sites' current performance by reviewing the way its processes are organized and taking proactive actions in order to avoid the cost of rework and ensure the finished product that performs at or near perfection. The current process flow chart of electronic dictionary manufacturing is illustrated as Figure 4. There are three production sites which are responsible for manufacturing some parts of electronic dictionary. One failure or quality problems found in any production site should cause the finished product- electronic dictionary rework or wasted. In the traditional approach, all of the process quality data is captured in different production sites and stored in proprietary and fragmented discrete database systems. Check sheets, problem and work distribution logs are the tools for quantifying the number of incorrect area of activities which occur in the areas of blockage. However, this approach cannot provide quality engineers to identify the relevant process data in a real time manner and no decision support for workers when quality problems are addressed. In response to the demands of the marketplace, GSL has recognized the need to change the way they operate. Improving and reorganizing the processes by which a business achieves its customer satisfaction is a powerful mechanism for change. In order to conduct data analysis from vast amount of process data in a real time manner, it needs to organize the data into different levels with different views in order to discover the relationship between processes. In addition, documenting issues surrounding the process, GSL considers such problems as duplication of effort, unnecessary controls and poor communication. GSL supports the view that XML can be used as a universal data standard for replacing the flat files exchange between production sites. It helps to sort the process data into logical order and present them in a readable format, outing next steps to be taken as the review progresses. A Real time Process Mining System (R-PMS) is then proposed to obtain the quality work piece in each production site and achieve the continual quality enhancement of the integrated workflow. The major tasks of R-PMS are (i) to assist the setup of a corporate database; (ii) to help the extraction of useful information from the database; and (iii) discovering the trends and relationships in the data in order to take proactive actions using that information.

5   PROPOSED ROADMAP FOR IMPLEMENTATION OF R-PMS

In order to develop a useful generic process mining approach, the following phases were taken into consideration in designing the R-PMS.

Phase1: Infrastructural design of R-PMS

Based on the findings of this study, an approach is then formulated for the step-by-step development of the R-PMS. The hybrid Module (OLAP based Fuzzy approach) is an integral component of the R-PMS and can be considered as the most critical research element of this research. In particular, the inclusion of Fuzzy and OLAP will achieve a high performance of decision support functionality. The main development tools for the hybrid module includes the OLAP and Fuzzy packages plus other supporting programming and computational intelligence tools, which will be adopted by the research personnel to work out the design of the hybrid model. Computing tools related to object technology (Visual Basic) and Fuzzy (using a tool called MATLAB Fuzzy Toolbox) are already available as they have been in use over the past years by different investigators.

It is important that the hybrid model will integrate with the object technology to ensure the smooth running of the whole system. With the strengthening of the capability of the system realized by the augmentation of the OLAP based Fuzzy technology, the R-PMS can perform tasks which are normally seen to be difficult to achieve, such as fine tuning of process parameters based on varied finished quality. This can ensure that a more effective monitoring of the production workflow where early alertness of potential quality problems and the quick adaptation to improve are crucial.

Phase 2: Prototyping of R-PMS

With the availability of the framework of R-PMS, a prototype can be developed based on the infrastructural details and the design methodologies resulting from the Phase 1 research. Basically, there are primarily two modules within the R-PMS, namely the PRM and DSM. Building up a centralized relational data warehouse is the first step for the storage of distributed process data. It maintains the necessary information on PRM and building up a linkage between them.

Preparation for Process Relationship Module (PRM)

Before implementing OLAP approach on real- time process quality monitoring and reporting, the relationship of the fact tables must be defined in the OLAP server. In the data cube, the dimension, measures and calculated member is defined as follows.

Dimension

In "Project" dimension, the "Customer ID", "Project No" and "Product barcode" fields are used to trace the reasons of failed products based on the complains from specified customers.

In "Process" dimension, the "ProcessID" field is used to find the quality information of work piece based on the specified manufacturing process.

In "Time" dimension, the "RecordDate" and "Time" field are used to find the defect statistics or quality performance of specified process based on different period of time.

In "Operation" dimension, the "MachineID" and "OperatorID" fields are used to find the quality characteristics of work piece machined by different operators and machines.

Measures

The "Product Acceptance_level", "Frequency _of _rework" and "Frequency _of _scrap" fields are defined as measures that are used to provide the overview of quality records.

Calculated Member

The calculated member of OLAP is used to calculate the mean, standard deviation, accumulative defect statistics required for plotting the real-time two dimensional control charts.

Preparation for Decision Support Module (DSM)

The initial rule repository for this fuzzy module is given by the experience of expert. The behavior of the skilled operators is captured from the operation log book or interviews. Different membership function is determined by a single expert in the organization and must vary between 0 and 1. In general, there are several types of membership functions available, including Gaussian distribution function, the sigmoid curve, and quadratic and cubic polynomial curves. In this case study, trapezoid and triangular membership functions (Figure 5) are chosen to represent all process parameters as they provide an adequate representation of the expert knowledge. The expert knowledge related to the bonding, plating, painting and casing production line is then defined as "if- then" rules, which are easily implemented by fuzzy conditional in fuzzy logic.

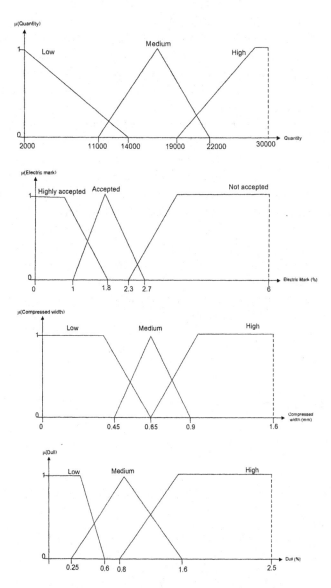

Fig 5. The fuzzy sets of the case example

Phase 3: Site-testing and monitoring the change process

The third phase is concerned with the overall site evaluation of the system. It is important that the R-PMS is able to be linked with other information systems and the integrated system is to be field-tested by the actual end-users in order to determine the possible problems when operating in a practical industrial environment. Basically, R-PMS is to be linked with other systems of the dispersed network such as user interface, system database and information update. Before this evaluation process, the application software programs have to be modified to suit the actual situation. The project team members will work closely with the potential end-users to ensure that the developed software can actually meet the practical requirements of the enterprise as well as other enterprises. A closely-monitored progress and continuous feedback and comments from the end-users will be proactively checked and followed. It is expected that a number of "bugs" will be found and subsequently, significant software refinement, updating and modifications of the original prototype programs and substantial site tests are all needed to cope with the possible flaws of the system. This is a continuous and arduous process until satisfactory results are obtained. It is also important to identify what further modification of the package is necessary be-fore finalizing the design of R-PMS. As this phase covers substantial analytical effort and huge amount of programming work related to modifications and additions of source code as well as the successful application to production systems, duration of one year is needed.

6   EVALUATION

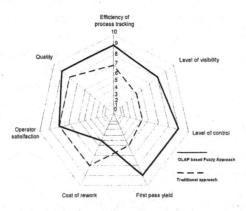

Fig 6. The radar chart for prototype for evaluation

There is a radar chart which illustrates the important categories of performance and makes visible concentrations of strengths and weakness compared with the traditional approach of electronic dictionary manufacturer implemented. Each spoke is subdivided into number of increments established in the rating scale. The scoring range is defined as 0 to 10 with 10 being full performance. The operators, process engineers and quality engineers were invited to participate in the prototype evaluation. The response rate was about one- fifth of the population. 136 responses are included in the summary statistics for the evaluation of R-PMS

For the radar chart (Figure 6) shown as above, those subjective attributes are re-served to the measurable dimensions which are (1) First pass yield (2) Level of control (3) Cost of rework (4) Level of visibility (5) Quality (6) Operator satisfaction (7) Efficiency process tracking. Referring to the radar chart, it is found that the first pass yield is enhanced. Operators found that R-PMS helps taking proactive actions to eliminate the quality problems in various areas which lead to poor customer satisfaction. Furthermore, it provides higher visibility of process because engineers can browse the quality trend in a real time manner.

In summary, the benefit of the system is concerned with improving quality of finished products in order to achieve cost-effectiveness and competitive advantages. However, there are other implications arising from the proposed model. The implementation of this system paves the way for a fundamental shift of enterprise strategy and sharpens the competitive edge of the company in the volatile and ever-changing industry.

7   CONCLUSION

This paper proposes an integrated system, R-PMS, which incorporates the concept of data mining and artificial intelligence, to form a robust approach for quality enhancement. It was pointed out that the OLAP based Fuzzy approach is feasible for discovering the hidden relationship and providing suggestions from vast amount of captured process data. The major contribution of the proposed system is to improve the way a discrete set of business activities is organized and managed. Further re-search on the structural configuration of the system is needed in order to further enhance its benefits. In general, this model paves the way for a novice approach to deal with the quality management by using process mining with proposed innovative information technologies. It is expected that this proposed system will support manufacturing of quality finished products as to fulfill the customer satisfaction.

ACKNOWLEDGEMENTS

The authors wish to thank the Research Office of the Hong Kong Polytechnic University for the support of this research project.

REFERENCES

[1] Berson, A. and Smith, S.J., (1997) Data Warehousing, Data Mining, & OLAP, McGraw-Hill, New York

[2] Dick, Kevin (2000). XML A Manager's Guide: Addison- Wesley.

[3] Erasala, Naveen., Yen, David C., and Rajkumar T.M. (2003), "Enterprise Application Inte-gration in the electronic commerce", Computers Standards & Interfaces, Vol 25, Issue 2, May 2003, Pages 69-82.

[4]Grigori, Daniela., Casati, Fabio., Castellanos, Malu., Dayal, Umeshwar., Sayal, Mehmet. and Shan, Ming- Chien., (2004), "Business Process Intelligence", Computers in Industry 53 (2004) 321-343.

[5] Hwang, San- Yih., Wei, Chih- Ping. and Yang, Wan- Shiou., (2004), "Discovery of temporal patterns from process instances", Computers in industry 53 (2004) 345-364.

[6] MathWorks (2002). Fuzzy Logic Toolbox User's Guide. The MathWorks. Inc

[7] Michael, L.G. and Bel, G.R., (1999), "Data mining - a powerful information creating tool", OCLC Systems & Services, Vol.15, No. 2

[8] Peterson, T. (2000) Microsoft OLAP unleashed, 2nd edition, Sams Pubishing, Indianapolis.

[9] Ray, Pradeep. (2000). Cooperative management of enterprise networks: Kluwer Academic/ Plenum Publishers, New York.

[10] Robert, S.C., Joseph A.V. and David B., (1999) Microsoft Data Warehousing, John Wiley & Sons.

[11] Salvato, G., Leontaritis, P., Zelm, M., Rivers- Moore and Salvato, D., "Presentation and exchange of business models with CIMOSA-XML". Computers in Industry, Vol 40, Issues 2-3, November 1999,125-139.

[12] Sarah, Cook. (1996). Process improvement: A Handbook for managers: Gower Publishing Limited, USA.

[14] Tseng, Frank S.C. (2004)., " Design of a multi- dimensional query expression for document warehouses". Information Sciences (available online).

[15] Van der Aalst W.M.P., Van Dongen B.F., Herbst J., Maruster L., Schimm G.. & Weijters A.J.M.M. (2003). Workflow mining: A survey of issues and approaches. Data & Knowl-edge Engineering 47 (2003) 237-267.

INNOVATION KNOWLEDGE ACQUISITION:
The Tacit Knowledge of Novices

Peter Busch, Debbie Richards
Computing Department,
Division of Information and Communication Sciences,
Macquarie University, Australia
{*busch,richards}@ics.mq.edu.au*}

Abstract: Innovation has become recognized as a key factor in the success and even sustainability of an organization but solutions to acquiring knowledge related to innovation are lacking. Strategies such as multidisciplinary teams, suggestion boxes and incentive schemes, flat organizational structures allowing the mail clerk access to the CEO are some of the techniques employed in industry. In this paper, we suggest a psychology-based technique using scenarios to measure innovation expertise. To date we have used our inventory on a novice population, but will soon administer it to an expert population. We present the findings to one of the scenarios and note that the results are contrary to what was actually done or suggested by the innovator.

Key words: Innovation, tacit knowledge, innovation knowledge, knowledge management

1. INTRODUCTION

For many organisations, innovation has become accepted as a vital part of sustainability. However, recognizing and managing innovation is not so well understood. Innovation is more than being new, different or first. "Innovation is… a significant and complex dimension of learning in work, involving a mix of rational, intuitive, emotional and social processes embedded in activities of a particular community of practice"[5 p.123]. Viewing innovation as a process is a key aspect of our approach. Thomas, Watts-Sussman and Henderson [16] state that these processes include making sense of our environment, particularly ambiguous new events, in a way which allows new connections to be made to familiar situations. However, innovation is not simply a process of trial-and-error rooted in experience.

Please use the following format when citing this chapter:

Richards, D., Busch, P., 2006, in IFIP International Federation for Information Processing, Volume 228, Intelligent Information Processing III, eds. Z. Shi, Shimohara K., Feng D., (Boston: Springer), pp. 259–268.

Innovation needs to produce timely and ongoing results "involving a complex mix of tacit knowledge, implicit learning processes and intuition" [6 p. 124].

Gloet and Terziovski [8] point out that innovation is often defined as the turning of knowledge into "new products, processes and services to improve competitive advantage and meet customers' changing needs" [p. 404)]. Also, since innovation is closely tied to an organizations culture [15] strategies for knowledge management will play a vital role within the organization to nurture creativity and innovation type knowledge [8].

There is clearly a connection between tacit knowledge and innovation knowledge [11]. Both have been recognized to support competitive advantage, are highly experience based and difficult to articulate. We have thus adapted our research using work-place scenarios to capture tacit knowledge to the capture of innovation knowledge which we consider to be a form of 'workplace smarts'.

Unlike approaches using techniques focused on identifying innovators, such as the Kirton Adaption-Innovation (KAI) [10] Inventory or the Myers-Briggs Type Indicator (MBTI) Creativity index [9], we focus on the behaviour (response to a situation) of individuals who have had results rather than on character or personality traits (such as self-confidence, independence or risk-taker). This is because, in keeping with the findings from the longitudinal Minnesota studies of Van de Ven, Angle and Pool [17], we consider innovation to be a process tending to involve a group rather than a number of "discrete acts of a single entrepreneur". Individuals will vary in their ability to "think out of the box" at different phases – sometimes coming up with a new problem to fit the solution invented, sometimes taking a risk and putting all the resources into quickly developing a better material for the product or sometimes being slow and methodical to ensure that the safety regulations are clearly met.

The approach that we propose captures knowledge-in-action via scenarios, which can be viewed as cases grounded in the real world and based on experience, thus spanning both codified (explicit) and practical (tacit) knowledge [12]. While this project focuses on innovation knowledge, the approach to be developed will be extensible to the capture of other types of knowledge and will further our understanding of expert behaviour, expertise and knowledge itself.

2.   THE APPROACH

The proposed work will carry on and extend the previous work of Busch and Richards [4, 3, 2] with a narrowing of focus on innovative and creative type knowledge and a change of direction into application of the approach to personnel recruitment and training. The focus will be on the patterns of behaviour which emerge, how they fit into the various phases of the innovation process and how these responses correspond to our current understanding of innovation including the various psychological models, instruments and approaches which exist [15, 19]. As in our previous work, the inventory will initially be based on case studies in the literature, interviews and a pilot study. In this study we will additionally allow experts to enter and maintain their own experiences via a supporting tool. Easy and self-managed maintenance is an important feature when dealing with knowledge which is by nature continually changing and evolving.

We have adopted the Novelty-Generation-Model (NGM) developed by Schweizer [14] a clinical psychologist in the Dept of Technology and Innovation, Erasmus University Rotterdam. The NGM is well-grounded in the theory and previous work on creativity and innovation and provides definitions and concepts which we apply to the development of an innovation knowledge inventory. The NGM is a bio-psycho-social approach. The approach recognises that at a genetic level some people are, for instance, more inclined to look for new problems and able to come up with novel solutions. In the model, the first step is novelty seeking followed by creativity which is broken into novelty-finding and novelty-production. To move beyond the novelty phases requires development of something that can be recognised by others and is highly dependent on two specific motivations that are part of motivation and achievement goal theory: (1) mastery goals which concerns the degree to which an individual personally wishes to become competent in something and (2) performance goals which concerns the degree to which the individual wishes to prove their competence to others [18]. These two motivations can be classified as intrinsic and extrinsic, respectively. The existence of extrinsic motivations highlights the importance of social factors when it comes to creativity and innovation. Schweizer's model will be used as a framework for structuring the capture and application of the innovation knowledge inventory. We will seek to capture scenarios that address each of the personality/cognitive traits and skills; individual behaviours, individual motivations and the behaviour of others.

In conjunction with content analysis of the related literature to clarify the concepts and phases, development of our inventory has begun with possible scenarios based on innovation stories recorded in the literature. Professor Gordon Bell's [1] book on "*High Tech Ventures: The Guide To Entrepreneurial Success*", see Figure 1 for an example, and Edward De Bono's 30+ books related to thinking, and 'lateral thinking' in particular, provide excellent starting points. Schoen's [13] landmark book "*The Reflective Practitioner*" provides valuable vocation specific guidance in the interpretation of the literature and interviews. Initial validation of our scenarios with innovation experts, such as Bell, is also underway. For example, the initial scenario in Figure 1 has been reviewed by Bell resulting in 8 answer options instead of the original six evaluated by novices in our study described in the next two sections.

Scenario 1

You've come up with an innovative new software product. You get a lot of money to start making this product. You start working on developing the software. However it seems that development isn't going as quickly and smoothly as you would wish. Your technology and product development departments are understaffed compared to your marketing and sales departments and you find that while you are making great progress marketing and sales-wise, your product development leaves a lot to be desired. You begin to fear that the product may never actually be completed.

Do you:

a)   Cease operations and return any remaining funds to the investors because the technology is inadequate to support the product. **(what Bell suggested)**

b)   Reduce the company to a minimal marketing effort until a product can be built.

c)   Do nothing and hope the problem resolves itself. **(what Bell suggested)**

d)   Hire more technology and product development people.

e)   Give the product up for dead and instead concentrate on marketing and sales and spend more money with the hope of generating indeterminate future revenues. **(what Bell actually did (bad))**

f)   Grab the money and escape to the Bahamas.

Figure 1: Scenario 1 developed from Bell and McNamara [1] pp. 273 – 276
Ovation: The case of the missing product

3.   THE APPROACH

Similar to our previous work in developing an IT Tacit Knowledge inventory, we have established an inventory with twelve 'innovation' scenarios. A screenshot including a scenario based on Figure 1. We want our two sample populations to

1. rate via a Likert scale the good(ness) or bad(ness) of given answers to relevant innovation scenarios
2. consider extending the inventory/questionnaire by adding innovative scenarios and answer options of their own, if the participants can think of any

In other words we would like not only to capture data with regard to how people answer our scenarios, we would also like to extend our questionnaire for future use.

Each individual (innovator or novice) will work with no more than about 4-5 scenarios. We feel from prior research that respondents are likely to concentrate more if given less to do. We value the quality of their feedback. The time taken would be roughly 30 minutes.

We will be using our two sample populations to:

1. obtain 'expert' innovative feedback from our innovators.
2. obtain 'novice' feedback who will be acting as a 'control' group

We hope to find differences in the responses to our questionnaire/inventory based on the sample populations. Through incorporating biographical information we may find differences in the answering of the scenarios on the basis of gender, or employment seniority, language other than English and so on. As Information and Communication Technology (ICT) is·our field of expertise, we will initially focus on this discipline.

As our novice population we have chosen the MPCE360 (Maths, Physics, Computing, Electronics) class. MPCE360 is a 'management' unit rather than a Maths, Physics, Computing or Electronics unit per se. The unit is concerned with innovation and how to come up with an idea, turn it into a product, how to build a business plan and market it. The unit is offered to all students at Macquarie University, although usually only (Division of) ICS (Information and Communication Sciences, i.e. Departments of Maths, Physics, Computing, Electronics) students tend to enroll in it. They require (at least) 41 credit points of subject completion and a GPA of at least 2.0 to be allowed to enroll in the subject. The MPCE360 class tends to vary from 20 (they are 3rd year students) to about 30 years of age.

For the innovators, we could expect recent (university) graduates and upwards to be involved in this study. Realistically though an innovator is likely to be somewhat older than an average fresh 'out of university' graduate. We would expect the age ranges to vary from roughly 30 to 80 years of age. These are however 'ballpark' figures. Of the 'innovator' cohort, we expect anywhere from 6 (pessimistically) to 12 (optimistically) 'innovators' to participate. To be 'recognised' as an innovator, as opposed to merely 'claiming' to be one, infers a process of public scrutiny. Therefore, we intend to contact recipients of innovation awards and other known innovators. The individuals we will be approaching will by definition generally fit within the category of people experienced at what they do.

4.   RESULTS AND FINDINGS

Seventy-three (73) MPCE360 students were introduced to the study in a practical session and invited to participate. Those who chose to participate (71) filled out the paper based version of the (anonymous) questionnaires with their biographical information and their responses to 4 randomly assigned scenarios.

We present only a small selection of our results here to illustrate our technique. These results concentrate on the findings of our novices, of whom 23 answered Scenario 1 (figure 1) with its associated options for dealing with the given scenario.

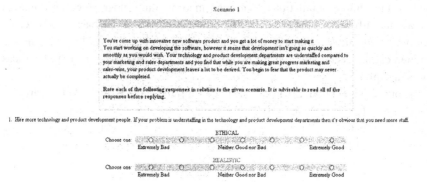

Innovation Knowledge Inventory for Information Systems

We realise that any of the following questionnaire scenarios may be tackled from an IDEAL (ethical) and a REALISTIC (perhaps unethical) point of view. We would like you to select BOTH an IDEAL AND REALISTIC value for each answer option.

Read each scenario and select what you consider to be the most appropriate scale for each answer option. Remember we would like you to select BOTH an IDEAL AND REALISTIC value for each answer option.

Scenario 1

You've come up with innovative new software product and you get a lot of money to start making it You start working on developing the software, however it seems that development isn't going as quickly and smoothly as you would wish. Your technology and product development departments are understaffed compared to your marketing and sales departments and you find that while you are making great progress marketing and sales-wise, your product development leaves a lot to be desired. You begin to fear that the product may never actually be completed.

Rate each of the following responses in relation to the given scenario. It is advisable to read all of the responses before replying.

1. Hire more technology and product development people. If your problem is understaffing in the technology and product development departments then it's obvious that you need more staff.

ETHICAL
Choose one: Extremely Bad   Neither Good nor Bad   Extremely Good

REALISTIC
Choose one: Extremely Bad   Neither Good nor Bad   Extremely Good

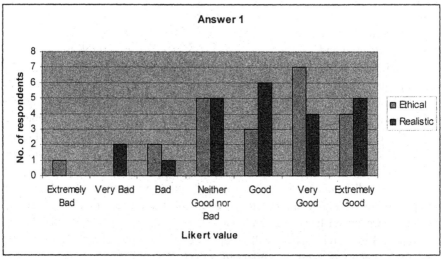

Figure 1. Scenario 1, answer 1 (n=23)

An examination of table 1 reveals our sample population is young (20 to 27 years of age, but heavily concentrated in their early 20s), mainly male (18 out of our 23 participants), overwhelmingly ethnic (where ethnic in the Australian context refers to non Anglo-Celtic) and more specifically concentrated in the Chinese and to a lesser extent, the sub-continental ethnic groups. Finally the novices were generally school leavers (highest qualification was typically the HSC) as one would expect.

Turning our attention to Answer 1 (figure 1) for Scenario 1 ("Hire more technology and development people. If your problem is understaffing in the technology and product development departments then it's obvious that you need more staff"), there is clearly a skew towards answering this question in the affirmative.

Table 1. Our sample population (MPCE360) who answered Scenario 1; n=23
Fields: gender; age; 1st language other than English; occupation now; highest qualification gained.

G.	Age	1st LOE	Occ. Now	Highest Qual.
M	24	Marathi	Student	Bachelor
M	23	Arabic	IT support	
F	27		Project Coordinator	
M	23	Chinese	Student	
M	24	Chinese	Student	HSC
M	23	Mandarin	Student	HSC
M	21	Hindi	Student	HSC
F	21	Farsi	Student	Certificate
F	20	Indonesian		Dipl. of Comp. Sci.
F	22	Indonesian	Student	HSC
M				Associate Diploma
M	22	Chinese	Assistant Accountant	B.Sc.
M	22	Chinese	Student	SIBT Diploma
M	26	Farsi	Student	B.Soft.Eng.
M	21	Italian	IT	Certificate
M	27	Mandarin	Student	HSC
M	21	Cantonese	Sales	
M	26	Tamil	Director/Manager (Telec Contr)	Diploma
M	23	German	Student	
F	21		Computer Developer	HSC
M	22	French	Retail Assistant	HSC
M	21	Italian	IT	HSC
M	23	Chinese	Student	HSC

Our novices on the whole (with the exception of a few ambivalent "Neither Good nor Bad") considered the hiring of more staff both ideally (ethically) and realistically a good idea.

In responding to Answer 2 ("Recommend to the board to cease operations and return any remaining funds to the investors"), our novices tended towards the negative. Again a grouping were ambivalent, expressing a neutral opinion, but the majority clearly felt this answer was not a good idea, surprisingly feeling more strongly about this answer from a realistic point of view.

Answer 3 ("Give the product up for dead and instead concentrate on marketing and sales and spend more money with the hope of generating indeterminate future revenues") was also greeted in the negative by the novice sample population. Very few thought this option a good idea. Again there were some 5 students who were undecided on this point.

With regard to Answer 4 ("Reduce the company to a minimal marketing effort until a product can be built. It'd be a shame to give up on something so promising") our novices were almost evenly divided in their opinions, although marginally more considered the reduction in marketing a generally good idea. Interestingly some 5 and 7 novices (ethical and realistic) respectively took a neutral stance on this answer. One can speculate this is so either because they genuinely felt the option to be neither a good nor bad idea, or alternatively because they could not be bothered concentrating on the problem at hand (a couple of novices appeared to select "Neither Good nor Bad" for all answers).

Turning our attention to Answer 5 ("Do nothing safe in the knowledge that the problem will most likely resolve itself") the novices were overwhelmingly opposed to this option. Again some 6 and 8 (ethical/realistic) out of 23 novices took an impartial stance. Only 2 novices felt this to be a good idea (ethically and realistically).

Not that surprisingly, Answer 6 ("Grab the money and escape to Switzerland") was also viewed overwhelmingly negatively by the novices (18 ethically, 13 realistically). A few novices (4 ethically, 8 realistically) felt running off with the money was actually not such a bad idea. Notably very few (1 ethically, 2 realistically) remained impartial on this issue (probably the novices who had chosen to remain neutral for all questions.

With regard to Answer 7 ("Call up someone you respect and ask them for help") our novices mostly thought of this as being a good idea (14 ethical; 16 realistic). Again a small proportion (5 ethical; 4 realistic) took an ambivalent stance, with some 4 novices (ethical) and 5 novices (realistic) considering asking for help from one more experienced to be a bad idea.

The results for Answer 8 ("Attempt to buy more time, confident that the vast funds you have will allow you this") are more evenly distributed, with a slightly higher proportion (11 ethical, 13 realistic) feeling this was a good idea. At the same time a proportion of novices (9 ethical, 9 realistic) felt stalling was a bad idea. Three novices (ethical and realistic) didn't care one way or the other.

Finally the last Answer option ("Find a scapegoat (someone who will take the blame)") was answered in the negative for the most part (14 ethical, 11 realistic). Five novices took a noncommittal stance, whilst 3 novices and 7 novices (ethical and realistic respectively) felt another to blame was actually a good idea, in fact of this last cohort, 4 novices thought this to be an extremely good idea.

The results are as one would expect, insofar as our novice population appears to have answered our questions sensibly. Certainly a small proportion choose to avoid thinking carefully about the responses preferring to simply choose the middle of the road approach, but we estimate this to be no more than 2-3 students (after examining questionnaires). Even from this small subset of the data we can see that our novices believed that the options a), c) and e) in Figure 1 (which is what Bell had suggested and/or done in his book) were bad options and preferred other options which Bell, the expert, had not thought were a good idea. It will certainly be interesting to compare the results of the expert sample population with those of the novices.

5.   CONCLUSION AND FUTURE WORK

Through comparison of similarities and differences between the novice and expert populations we will be able to find if any patterns of novice versus expert behaviour exist when it comes to innovation. As part of that analysis we intend to employ more elaborate data analysis techniques such as our use of Formal Concept Analysis [7] should provide more detailed results.

Once we have developed and validated our innovation inventory, we intend to adapt and extend the tool to allow the scenarios to be randomly assigned to potential and existing employees so that it can be used to identify individuals, and to what extent, they behave similarly to the identified innovators. We will need to devise various algorithms to determine acceptable ranges of behaviour and incorporate the use of weightings to allow some scenarios to be more or less important in generating a score. For personnel selection, the goal would be to provide an innovation index/score ranking applicants to assist with the selection process. The tool may be extended to allow other details regarding other selection criteria to be included to make the process more streamlined. For training purposes, algorithms will be developed which will provide scores indicating what knowledge is currently lacking in the individual and to propose a training programme for the individual. To achieve this goal we will need to refer to and incorporate other research in the psychology, training and recruitment literature.

We intend to compare our approach to the key psychometric approaches offered for innovation testing. We propose to administer techniques such as MBTI, KAI or other psychology-based techniques in order to correlate our findings with these other approaches and to validate the NGM. For instance, we will test whether certain personality traits and characteristics or motivations correspond to the phases in the NGM.

ACKNOWLEDGEMENTS

Our first thanks must go to Professor Gordon Bell [1] for providing feedback on our 'innovation inventory'. We would also like to take the opportunity to thank our MPCE360 class at Macquarie University for providing the 'novice' dataset necessary for our innovation research.

REFERENCES

1.   Bell, G., McNamara, J.F. (1991) *McHigh-Tech ventures : the guide for entrepreneurial success* Perseus Books Publishing L.L.C. New York U.S.A.

2. Busch, P., Richards, D., (2003) "Building and Utilising an IT Tacit Knowledge Inventory" *Proceedings 14th Australasian Conference on Information Systems* (ACIS2003) November 26-28 Perth Australia.
3. Busch, P. Richards, D. (2004) "Acquisition of articulable tacit knowledge" *Proceedings of the Pacific Knowledge Acquisition Workshop (PKAW'04)*, in conjunction with *The 8th Pac.Rim Int.l Conf. on AI*, Aug 9-13, 2004, Auckland, NZ, :87-101.
4. Busch, P., Richards, D., (2005) "An Approach to Understand, Capture and Nurture Creativity and Innovation Knowledge" *Proc. 15th Australasian Conference on Information Systems (ACIS2005)* Nov 30-Dec 2nd, Sydney, Australia.
5. Cottrill, K., (1998) "Reinventing innovation" *Journal of Business* Strategy Vol. 19(2) pp. 47-51.
6. Fenwick, (2003) Innovation: examining workplace learning in new enterprises *Journal of Workplace Learning 15(3):123-132.*
7. Ganter, R., Wille, R., (1999) *Formal concept analysis: Mathematical foundations* Springer-Verlag Berlin Germany.
8. Gloet, M. and Terziovski, M. (2004) Exploring the relationship between knowledge management practices and innovation Performance *Journal of Manufacturing Technology Management, 15 (5): 402-409.*
9. Gough, H. (1981) "Studies of the Myers-Briggs Type Indicator in a Personality Assessment Research Institute" *Fourth National Conference on the Myers-Briggs Type Indicator,* Stanford University, July 1981, CA.
10. Kirton, M. (2001) "Adaptors and Innovators: why new initiatives get blocked" J. Henry (ed.) *Creative Management* 2nd Edition, Cromwell Press Ltd, London, 169-180.
11. Leonard, D., Sensiper, S., (1998) "The role of tacit knowledge in group innovation" *California Management Review* Berkeley; Spring 40(3) (electronic).
12. Richards, D., Busch, P., (2002) "Knowledge in Action: Blurring the Distinction Between Explicit and Tacit Knowledge, G. Forgionne, J.N.D, Gupta and M. Mora (eds) Journal of Decision Systems Editions Hermes 11(2) pp. 149-164
13. Schoen, D.A. (1987) *Educating the Reflective Practitioner* Jossey-Bass, San Francisco, CA.
14. Schweizer, T.S. (2004) *An Individual Psychology of Novelty-Seeking, Creativity and Innovation* ERIM Ph.D. Series, 48.
15. Sternberg, R., Wagner, R., Williams, W., Horvath, J., (1995) "Testing common sense" *American psychologist* 50(11) :912-927.
16. Thomas, J., Watts-Sussman, S., Henderson, J., (2001) "Understanding strategic learning: Linking organizational learning, knowledge management and sensemaking" *Organization Science* 12(3) :331-345.
17. Van de Ven, A. H., Angle, H., Poole, M.S. (2000) *Research on the Management of Innovation: The Minnesota studies,* New York: Oxford University Press August (paperback) Originally printed 1989.
18. Van Yperen, N. W. (2003). "Task interest and actual performance: The moderating effects of assigned and adopted purpose goals" *Journal of Personality and Social Psychology, 85(6),* 1006-1015.
19. Wagner, R., Sternberg, R., (1991) *TKIM: The common sense manager: Tacit knowledge inventory for managers: Test Booklet* The Psychological Corporation Harcourt Brace Jovanovich San Antonio U.S.A.

EVOLVING HYPERPARAMETERS OF SUPPORT VECTOR MACHINES BASED ON MULTI-SCALE RBF KERNELS

Tanasanee Phienthrakul and Boonserm Kijsirikul

Department of Conputer Engineering, Chulalongkorn University, Thailand

Abstract: Kernel functions are used in support vector machines (SVMs) to compute dot product in a higher dimensional space. The performance of classification depends on the chosen kernel. Each kernel function is suitable for some tasks. In order to obtain a more flexible kernel function, a family of RBF kernels is proposed. Multi-scale RBF kernels are combined by including weights. These kernels allow better discrimination in the feature space, and are proved to be the Mercer's kernels. Then, the evolutionary strategies are applied for adjusting the hyperparameters of SVM. Subsets cross validation is used to be the objective function in evolutionary process. The experimental results show that the accuracy of the proposed method is better than the ordinary approach.

Key words: Support Vector Machines, Evolutionary Strategies, Kernel Methods, Radial Basis Function

1.   INTRODUCTION

Support Vector Machines (SVMs) are learning algorithms that have been widely used in many applications such as pattern recognitions and function approximations [1]. Basically, SVM operates a linear separation in an augmented space by means of some defined kernels satisfying Mercer's condition [1, 2, 3]. These kernels map the input vectors into a very high dimensional space, possibly of infinite dimension, where linear separation is more likely [3]. Then, a linear separating hyperplane is found by maximizing the margin between two classes in this space.

Hence, the complexity of the separating hyperplane depends on the nature and the properties of the used kernel [3]. There are many types of kernel functions such as linear kernel, polynomial kernel, sigmoid kernel, and RBF kernel. The RBF

Please use the following format when citing this chapter:

Phienthrakul, T., Kijsirikul, B., 2006, in IFIP International Federation for Information Processing, Volume 228, Intelligent Information Processing III, eds. Z. Shi, Shimohara K., Feng D., (Boston: Springer), pp. 269–278.

kernel is a most successful kernel in many problems, but it still has the restrictions in some complex problems.

Therefore, we propose to improve the efficiency of classification by using the combination of RBF kernels at different scales. These kernels are combined by including weights. These weights, the widths of the RBF kernels, and regularization parameter of SVM are called *hyperparameters*. In general, the hyperparameters are usually determined by grid search. These hyperparameters are varied with a fixed step-size in a range of values, which consume a lot of time. Hence, we propose to use the evolutionary strategies (ESs) for choosing these hyperparameters. Moreover, we propose to use subset cross validation for evaluating our kernel in evolutionary process.

A short description of support vector machines is presented in Section 2. In Section 3, we propose the multi-scale RBF kernel and apply evolutionary strategies to determine the hyperparameters of the kernel. The proposed kernels with the help of ES are tested in Section 4. Finally, the conclusions are described in Section 5.

2. SUPPORT VECTOR MACHINES

Support vector machine is a classifier which finds an optimal separating hyperplane. In the simple pattern recognitions, SVM uses a linear separating hyperplane to create a classifier with a maximum margin [4]. Consider the problem of binary classification. The training dataset are given as $(x_1, y_1), (x_2, y_2), \ldots, (x_l, y_l)$, where $x_i \in R^N$ and $y_i \in \{-1, 1\}$ for $i = 1, \ldots, l$ when x_i is a sample data and y_i is its label [5]. A linear decision surface is defined by the equation:

$$w \cdot x + b = 0 . \tag{1}$$

The goal of learning is to find $w \in R^N$ and the scalar b such that the margin between positive and negative examples is maximized. An example of the decision surface and the margin is shown in Figure 1.

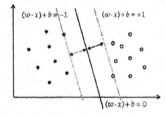

Figure 1. An example of decision surface and margin

This surface can be achieved by minimizing $\|w\|^2$, and the conditions for classification without training error are $y_i((w \cdot x_i) + b) \geq 1$ for $i = 1, \ldots, l$, that are a quadratic optimization problem [4]. This yields the decision function as

$$f(x) = sign\left(\sum_{i=1}^{l} \alpha_i \, y_i \, x_i \, x \, + \, b\right).$$ (2)

The data examples x_i which correspond to non-zero α_i values are called *support vectors*.

However, the quadratic programming solutions cannot be used in the case of overlapping because the constraints cannot be satisfied [4]. In such a situation, this algorithm must allow some data to be unclassified, or on the wrong side of a decision surface [4]. In practice, we allow a soft margin, and all data inside this margin are neglected. The width of soft margin can be controlled by a corresponding regularization parameter C that determines the trade-off the training error and the VC dimension of the model [4].

In most cases, seeking a suitable linearly hyperplane in an input space has the restrictions. There is an important technique that enables these machines to produce complex nonlinear boundaries inside the original space. This performs by mapping the input space into a higher dimensional feature space through a mapping function Φ and separating there [6]. This can be achieved by substitution $\Phi(x_i)$ for each training example x_i.

However, a good property of SVM is that it is not necessary to know the explicit form of Φ. Only the inner product in feature space, called kernel function $K(x, y) = \Phi(x) \cdot \Phi(y)$, must be defined. The decision function becomes the following equation:

$$f(x) = sign\left(\sum_{i=1}^{l} \alpha_i \, y_i \, K(x_i, x) \, + \, b\right).$$ (3)

where $\alpha_i \geq 0$ is the coefficient associated with a support vector x_i and b is an offset.

3.   EVOLVING MULTI-SCALE RBF KERNEL

The evolutionary strategies (ES) are the algorithms that imitate the natural processes (natural selection and survival of the fittest principle), which were developed by Rechenberg and Schwefel [7, 8, 9]. ES was developed for numerical optimization problems, and they are significantly faster than traditional genetic algorithms [10]. In this section, the multi-scale RBF kernel is proposed for SVM on classification problems. Then, the evolutionary strategies are applied to evolve hyperparameters of SVM.

3.1   Multi-scale RBF kernel

The Gaussian RBF kernel is widely used in many problems. It uses the Euclidean distance between two points in the original space to find the correlation in the augmented space [3]. Although, the RBF kernel yields good results on various applications, it has only one parameter for adjusting the width of RBF which is not powerful enough for some complex problems. In order to get a better kernel, the combination of RBF kernels at difference scale is proposed. The analytic expression of this kernel is following:

$$K(x,y) = \sum_{i=1}^{n} a_i K(x,y,\gamma_i).$$

(4)

where n is a positive integer, a_i for $i = 1,...,n$ are the arbitrary nonnegative weighting constants, and

$$K(x,y,\gamma_i) = \exp(-\gamma_i \|x-y\|^2).$$

(5)

is the RBF kernel at the width γ_i for $i = 1,...,n$.

The RBF is a well-known Mercer's kernel. Therefore, the non-negative linear combination of RBFs in equation 5 can be proved to be an admissible kernel by the Mercer's theorem [5] that is showed in Figure 2.

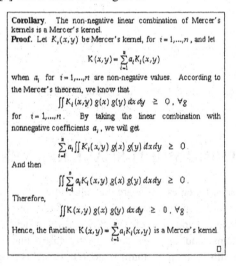

Figure 2. Proving of the proposed kernel

When the various RBF functions are combined, the results of classification are more flexible than using a single RBF function. The examples of classification with a simple RBF kernel and a combination of two RBF kernels are showed in Figure 3.

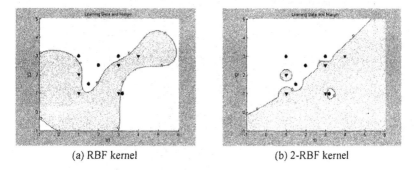

| (a) RBF kernel | (b) 2-RBF kernel |

Figure 3. The examples of classification

In these examples, the training data are non-linearly separable. The SVM with a single RBF and 2-RBF (the multi-scale RBF kernel with n =2) kernels can correctly classify the data. However, the 2-RBF kernel yields the result that is more flexible and easier to comprehend. Moreover, the margin of the 2-RBF kernel in this example is larger than the single RBF kernel. This means that the classification results of the 2-RBF kernel on unseen data are more plausible than those of the single RBF kernel.

3.2   Evolving hyperparameters of SVM

In this sub-section, the ES is applied to evolve the optimal hyperparameters of SVM. There are several different versions of the ES. Nevertheless, we prefer to use the ($\mu + \lambda$)-ES where μ parents produce λ offspring. Both parents and offspring compete equally for survival [11].

Form equation 4, there are $2n$ parameters when n terms of RBF kernels are used (n parameters for adjusting weights and n values of the widths of RBF). However, we notice that the number of parameters can be reduced to $2n-1$ by fixing a value of the first parameter to 1. The multi-scale RBF kernel that will be used in the rest of this paper is in the form:

$$K(x,y) = K(x,y,\gamma_0) + \sum_{i=1}^{n-1} a_i K(x,y,\gamma_i) . \tag{6}$$

Let $\bar{v}$ be the non-negative real value of the hyperparameter vector that has $2n+1$ dimensions. The vector $\bar{v}$ is represented in the form:

$$\bar{v} = (C, n, \gamma_0, a_1, \gamma_1, a_2, \gamma_2, \ldots, a_{n-1}, \gamma_{n-1}). \tag{7}$$

where C is the regularization parameter, n is the number of RBFs, γ_i are the widths of RBFs, and a_i are the weights of RBFs. Our goal is to find $\bar{v}$ that maximizes the objective function $f(\bar{v})$. The (5+10)-ES is applied to adjust these hyperparameters. The algorithm of (5+10)-ES is showed in Figure 4.

```
t = 0;
initialization(v̄₁,..., v̄₅, σ̄);
evaluation f(v̄₁),..., f(v̄₅);
while (t < 1000) do
    for i =1 to 10 do
        v̄ᵢ' = recombination(v̄₁,..., v̄₅);
        v̄ᵢ' = mutate(v̄ᵢ');
        evaluate f(v̄ᵢ');
    end
    (v̄₁,..., v̄₅) = select(v̄₁,..., v̄₅, v̄₁',..., v̄₁₀')
    σ̄ = mutate_σ(σ̄);
    t = t+1;
end
```

Figure 4. (5+10)-ES algorithm

This algorithm starts with the 0th generation (t=0) in which 5 solutions $\bar{v}_1, \ldots, \bar{v}_5$ and standard deviation $\bar{\sigma} \in R_+^{2n+1}$ are selected randomly. These initial solutions are evaluated. Then, the solutions are used to create 10 new solutions by the global intermediary recombination method. Ten pairs of solutions are selected from conventional 5 solutions. The average of each pair of vector solutions, element by element, is a new solution.

$$\bar{v}_1' = \frac{1}{2}(\bar{v}_1 + \bar{v}_2) \tag{8}$$

$$\bar{v}_2' = \frac{1}{2}(\bar{v}_1 + \bar{v}_3) \tag{9}$$

$$\vdots$$

$$\bar{v}_{10}' = \frac{1}{2}(\bar{v}_4 + \bar{v}_5) \tag{10}$$

After that, these solutions are mutated by the following function:

$$mutate(\bar{v}) = (C + z_1, n + z_1, \gamma_0 + z_2 \; a_1 + z_3, \gamma_1 + z_4, \ldots, a_{n-1} + z_{2n}, \gamma_{n-1} + z_{2n+1})\,(11)$$

$$z_i \sim N_i(0, \sigma_i^2). \tag{12}$$

The $\bar{v}_i'$ for $i = 1,..,10$ are mutated by adding $\bar{v}'$ with ($z_1, z_2, \ldots, z_{2n+1}$), and z_i is a random value from normal distribution with zero mean and σ_i^2 variation. In each generation, the standard deviation will be adjusted by the equation 13.

$$mutate_\sigma(\bar{\sigma}) = (\sigma_1 \cdot e^{z_1}, \sigma_2 \cdot e^{z_2}, \ldots, \sigma_{2n+1} \cdot e^{z_{2n+1}}) \tag{13}$$

$$z_i \sim N_i(0, \tau^2), \tag{14}$$

when τ is an arbitrary constant.

Only the 5 fittest solutions are selected from 5+10 solutions to be the parents in the next generation. These processes will be repeated until a fixed number of generations have been produced or the acceptance criterion is reached.

For evaluating the hyperparameters of SVM, there are many ways to define an objective function. Although, training rate will be the easiest objective function, it maybe over-fit with training data. In many time, our data has a lot of noise. If the decision functions over-fit to these noisy data, the target concept may be wrong. Therefore, we propose to train the decision function with subsets cross validation; a good set of parameters should perform well on all these subsets.

At the beginning, the training data are divided into five subsets, each of which has the same number of data. For each generation of ES, the classifier is trained and validated five times. In the i th iteration ($i = 1, 2, 3, 4, 5$), the classifier is trained on all subsets except the i th one. Then, the accuracy of classification is evaluated for the i th subset.

Only real training data sets are used to produce the classifiers by a set of parameters. Then, the validation set are used for calculating the accuracies of the classifiers. The average of these five accuracies is used to be the objective function $f(\bar{v})$. It is a rather good estimate of the generalization accuracy for adjusting the parameters. The testing data set is reserved for testing the final classifier with the best parameters found by the evolutionary strategy.

4.   EXPERIMENTAL RESULTS

In order to verify the performance of the proposed method, SVMs with the multi-scale RBF kernel are trained and tested on datasets from the UCI repository [12]. The evolutionary strategies are used to find the optimal hyperparameters of

SVM. The proposed method is evaluated by 5 folds cross-validation. The regularization parameter, the widths of RBFs (γ_i), and the weights of RBFs (a_i) are real numbers between 0.0 and 10.0. The number of RBF terms is a positive integer that is less than or equal to 10. These hyperparameters are inspected within 1000 generations of ES. Then, the best hyperparameters will be used to test on validation data. The value of τ in evaluation process of these experiments is 1.0. The experiments are divided into 2 parts as two-class problems and multi-class problems.

4.1   Two-class problems

Fifteen datasets from UCI are used for testing. Each of datasets contains two classes. The proposed method is compared with GridSearch and the ES that uses training rate as the objective function. GridSearch is applied on single RBF kernel, while ES with training rates is applied on multi-scale RBF kernel. The number of attributes, the sample size, and the average accuracies on 5 folds of each dataset are shown in Table 1.

Table 1. Results of two-class problems

Datasets	No. of attributes	No. of examples	Average accuracy		
			RBF GridSearch	Multi-scale RBF kernel + ES (obj: training rates)	Proposed method
Checkers	2	192	**83.32**	81.73	83.31
Spiral	2	582	**100.00**	100.00	100.00
LiverDisorders	6	345	61.74	63.19	66.38
IndiansDiabetes	8	768	64.97	65.10	76.16*
ThreeOfNine	9	512	53.51	53.51	100.00*
TicTacToe	9	958	65.34	65.34	99.48*
BreastCancer	10	699	86.41	88.41	95.99*
ParityBits	10	1024	48.05	48.54	57.71
SolarFlare	10	1066	**80.87**	80.87	80.87
ClevelandHeart	13	270	55.56	55.55	83.34*
Australian	14	690	55.51	55.51	56.38
German-org	24	1000	70.10	70.20	74.80
Ionosphere	34	351	66.10	66.38	95.15*
Tokyo	44	959	81.02	82.17	90.82*
Sonar	60	208	70.67	75.96	89.41*

* Statistical significance at level 0.01 for the difference between the proposed method and RBF GridSearch.

These results show the accuracies of the proposed method (using the multi-scale RBF kernel and ES with 5 subsets cross validation) that are significantly higher than GridSearch on almost all datasets. Although the training rates can be the objective function, their average accuracies is not higher than GridSearch for some datasets.

This is because it may over-fit training data when the kernel is more flexible. Hence, subsets cross validation is a good choice to avoid the over-fitting problem.

4.2 Multi-class problems

SVM is the binary classifier for two-class data. However, the multi-class classification problems can be solved by voting schema methods based on a combination of many binary classifiers [3]. One possible approach to solve k-class problem is to consider the problem as a collection of k binary classification problems. k-classifiers can be constructed, one for each class. The kth classifier constructs a hyperplane between class k and the k-1 other classes [3]. A new example will be classified according to a classifier that yields the maximum value of decision function. This schema is commonly called *one against the rest* and showed in Figure 5.

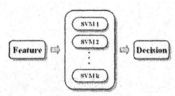

Figure 5. Multi-class problem

The proposed method has been tested on two multi-class problems from UCI. Both problems are composed of 3 classes. The experimental results are shown in Table 2. These results show that the accuracies of the proposed method are better than those of the RBF kernel using GridSearch on both problems.

Table 2. Results of multi-class problems

Datasets	No. of attributes	No. of examples	Average accuracies	
			RBF GridSearch	Proposed method
BalanceScale	4	625	85.92	**88.16**
Waveform	21	5000	33.92	**46.84**

5. CONCLUSIONS

The non-negative linear combination of multiple RBF kernels with including weights is proposed for support vector classification. The proposed kernel is proved to be the admissible kernels by Mercer's condition. Then, the evolutionary strategy is applied to adjust the hyperparameters of SVM. Subsets cross validation are considered to be the objective function in evolutionary process to escape from the over-fitting problem.

The experimental results show the abilities of the proposed method through their average accuracies on 5 folds cross validation. The multi-scale RBF kernel yields the better results. Furthermore, the experimental results also show the evolutionary strategy is effective in optimizing the hyperparameters, especially when the ranges of each parameter are large. Other methods for optimizing the parameters can also be used, such as gradient based methods. We decided to use (5+10)-ES because the ability to escape from local minima and the population size is not large so that it fast converges to an optimal solution. Therefore, this method is very suitable for the problems where we have no prior knowledge about parameters.

ACKNOWLEDGEMENTS

The authors acknowledge the financial support provided by the Thailand Research Fund and the Royal Golden Jubilee Ph.D. Program.

REFERENCES

1. V.N. Vapnik, *The Nature of Statistical Learning Theory*. Springer-Verlag, New York, USA, 1995.
2. B. Schölkopf, C. Burges, and A.J. Smola, *Advances in Kernel Methods: Support Vector Machines*. MIT Press, Cambridge, MA, 1998.
3. N.E. Ayat, M. Cheriet, L. Remaki, and C.Y. Suen, "KMOD-A New Support Vector Machine Kernel with Moderate Decreasing for Pattern Recognition," *Proceedings on Document Analysis and Recognition*, pp. 1215-1219, Seattle, USA, 10-13 Sept. 2001.
4. V. Kecman, *Learning and Soft Computing: Support Vector Machines, Neural Networks, and Fuzzy Logic Models*, MIT Press, London, 2001.
5. J. Shawe-Taylor and N. Cristianini, *Kernel Methods for Pattern Analysis*, Cambridge University Press, UK, 2004.
6. B. Schölkopf, and A.J. Smola, *Learning with Kernels: Support Vector Machines, Regularization, Optimization, and Beyond*, MIT Press, London, 2002.
7. I. Rechenberg, *Evolutionsstrategie: Optimierung technischer systeme nach prinzipien der biologischen evolution*, Frommann-Holzboog Verlag, Stuttgart, Germany, 1973.
8. H.-P. Schwefel, *Evolution and Optimum Seeking*, John Wiley and Sons, Inc., New York, 1995.
9. H.-G. Beyer and H.-P. Schwefel, "Evolution strategies: A comprehensive introduction," *Natural Computing*, Vol. 1, No. 1, pp. 3-52, 2002.
10. D.E. Goldberg, *Genetic Algorithms in Search, Optimization and Machine Learning*. Addison-Wesley, US, 1989.
11. E. deDoncker, A. Gupta, and G. Greenwood, "Adaptive Integration Using Evolutionary Strategies," *Proceedings of 3rd International Conference on High Performance Computing*, pp. 94-99, 19-22 December 1996.
12. C.L. Blake and C.J. Merz, "UCI Repository of machine learning databases [http://www.ics.uci.edu/~mlearn/MLRepository.html]," Irvine, CA: University of California, Department of Information and Computer Science, 1998.

An Iterative Heuristics Expert System for Enhancing Consolidation Shipment Process in Logistics Operations

HCW Lau, WT Tsui

The Hong Kong Polytechnic University

Abstract

Shipment consolidation is a laborious and, sometimes, tedious task for airfreight forwarders since there is enormous information to be considered and literally quite a number of practical constraints to be fulfilled. In Hong Kong, the unique forwarding operation and rapid cargo flow has further complicated the consolidating process in such a way that local forwarders are almost impossible to achieve the best selection of logistics workflow through the functions of human brain solely. However, none of the currently available intelligent logistics system is able to aid forwarders in making decisions on this crucial operation through the entire supply chain.

This paper presents an Iterative Heuristics Expert System (IHES) for solving shipment consolidation problem, adopting rule-based reasoning to provide expert advice for cargo allocation and subsequently applying container loading specific heuristics to support the cargo loading process. Afterwards, the iterative improvement mechanism of IHES undertakes all outcomes until the most optimal solution is found. A presentation of the concept of IHES and its development are included in this paper with a case study conducted in Oriented Delivery Limited (a Hong Kong-based company) to validate its feasibility.

Keywords: Airfreight forwarding; rule-based reasoning; heuristics; iterative, consolidation shipment process; logistics.

1. Introduction

Airfreight forwarders are typically third party logistics. They are responsible for supervising the movement of cargoes from receiving shippers' cargo to dedicated consignees. They are also responsible for suggesting and offering variety of professional services which is able to fulfil the customers' needs. In general, consolidation of shipments is the primary means to lower costs among shipments by achieving better utilization of resources.

The current consolidating shipment process is done manually and based on the personal experiences of a few experts. As a result, it is uncertain that this approach can achieve the most optimized decision in terms of profit maximization, high efficiency and delivery accuracy. Therefore, a systematic and reliable approach is strongly desired for obtaining the most optimal decision that is able to deal with all related activities within the chain of shipment consolidation.

This article presents the development of an expert system which can be easily deployed by airfreight forwarders. This system aims at enhancing the problem-solving capabilities which normally rely on human experts. An Iterative Heuristics Expert System (IHES), which comprises rule-based

Please use the following format when citing this chapter:

Lau, H.C.W., Tsui, W.T., 2006, in IFIP International Federation for Information Processing, Volume 228, Intelligent Information Processing III, eds. Z. Shi, Shimohara K., Feng D., (Boston: Springer), pp. 279–289.

inference, container loading specific heuristics and iterative algorithm, is constructed and embedded in the system for enhancing decision capability of shipment consolidation. IHES is developed for optimizing the essential activities within the chain of shipment consolidation, including the flight selection, ULD identification and load plan generation, taking into account the profit, cost and other practical constraints.

In this research, shipment consolidation has a number of operations which includes cargo allocation and cargo loading domain. By means of a computer model of expert inferencing mechanism, the IHES not only deals with cargo allocation problem more quickly but also gets solutions as good as experts (Liebowitz, 1998; Building, 1996). After that, the cargo loading problem is solved by container loading specific heuristics so that optimal load plan can be generated. In particular, the quality of generated solutions can be enhanced through the iterative continuous improvement process in a cost-effective manner. By doing do, the forwarders could make decision based on the level of optimization.

2. Traditional approach of shipment consolidation in Hong Kong

Figure 1 shows the traditional approach of shipment consolidation in Hong Kong. The shipment consolidation includes two domains, i.e. cargo allocation and cargo loading. These two domains are completely different but highly interrelated. However, due to the fact that these two domains are performed separately by two groups of specialists, forwarders have no idea about the way to link up these two domains, thus hindering the optimization of related activities within the chain of shipment consolidation. Hence, an expert system approach, which should be able to leverage and exploit the interaction between cargo allocation and cargo loading domains, is necessary to be in place to aid forwarders in enhancing their quality of shipment consolidation decision as well as operational efficiency.

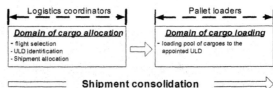

Figure 1. Domain knowledge involved in shipment consolidation

3. Literature Review

Expert systems have been a subject of considerable research in wide-range applications in recent years. This section briefly describes several previous works of expert systems. After that, the rule-based inference technique and container loading specific heuristics are presented respectively.

3.1. Expert system

The advantage of applying expert systems to assist problem solving is that the confidence of correct decision can be greatly increased (Giarratano and Riley 1994). Such approach has been widely used in various industries. It has the potential to provide solution of shipment consolidation which is usually worked out by limited and unconstructive experience of human experts.

3.2. Rule-based reasoning

The efficiency of expert systems depends largely on the design of inference mechanism. A number of contemporary publications in this area are available (Krishnamoorthy and Rajeev 1996; Lee and Kwon, 1995; Hartle and Jambunathan, 1996; Kamel, 1995; Ragothaman et al., 1995). All of them state that the inference processes operate by selecting knowledge rules then matching the symbols of facts.   In this research, the inference mechanism employs a "data-driven" technique. The design and inference process of this technique is described in Figure 2.

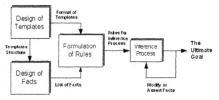

Figure 2. "Data-driven" inference mechanism

3.3. Container loading problem and Heuristics

For dealing with container loading problem in varies shape rather than rectangular solely, Pisinger (2002) suggests a doable approach which is based on the design of wall-building method (George and Robinson, 1980). This approach is a new heuristics method focusing on arranging the given cargo into a number of vertical layers which again are spilt into a number of strips. This is done through a tree search algorithm with a backtracking technology to improve solution quality. The packing of a strip may be formulated and solved optimally as knapsack problem with capacity equal to width or height of the container. However, imagining that the cargo loading process starts at building a single vertical layers into the pallet, the wall must fall down since it the wall lacks of support from its' neighbors. Therefore, the approach needs to be modified so that layers are built horizontally and initialized from the bottom of the ULDs. The proposed method is shown in Figure 3. The advantages of doing this are that all different shapes of ULDs, such as trapezoid, could be catered, and the solution becomes practical to be implemented in the real situation.

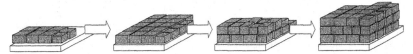

Take in Figure 3. Modified wall building approach for ULDs

In summary, review of contemporary publications indicates that whilst many researches are done on expert systems, rule-based forward chaining and container loading heuristics, the research related to the seamless integration between them and the application for consolidating shipment process have not received the attention it deserves. These issues are addressed in this paper with the introduction of an expert system incorporated with an innovative technology which will be fully described in the following section.

4. Iterative Heuristics Expert Technology (IHET)

IHET is the embedded technology of the proposed expert system (IHES) in this research. The aim of IHES is to support optimization of shipment consolidation by utilizing two problem domains, namely, cargo allocation and cargo loading. The information flow of IHES is shown in Figure 4.

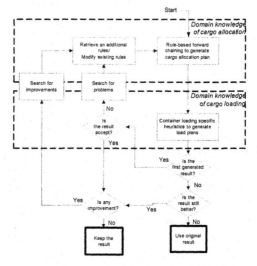

Figure 4. Information Flow of IHES

The IHES starts with adopting computational intelligence technologies such as rule-based forward chaining to utilize cargo allocation knowledge for supporting the generation of cargo allocation plans. Afterwards, container loading specific heuristics is applied to support the generation of load plans through the use of cargo loading knowledge. In order to guarantee the solution quality, it is necessary that the acquisition of useful expert knowledge is in place to assist in identifying flaws and improvements. Therefore, based on the result performance, problems and correspondent improvements will be searched automatically in order to enhance the solution quality in terms of practicability and feasibility. If problems and possible improvements are identified, appropriate knowledge rules will be retrieved and inserted into the inference engine for conducting the inference operation again. Generally, it will provide a more competitive cargo allocation advice and consequently form a more favorable load plan through the operation of specific container loading heuristics. This iterative process will operate continuously until the most optimal solution is found.

Generally speaking, the innovative technology (IHET) covers the all related activities in the chain of shipment consolidation by the adoption of rule-based forwarding chaining and container loading specific heuristics. Moreover, the quality of a particular consolidating decision can be further enhanced through continuous improvement mechanism. Thus, the IHET not only rectifies the existing problems but also provides a more optimal and reliable solution that cannot be easily conducted by human experts. The implementation of IHES is described in the next section.

5. System design

The proposed system in this research is used for local airfreight forwarders to master its core competence by means of shipment consolidation. The structure of the IHES is shown in Figure 5.

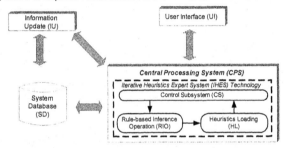

Figure 5. Structure of IHES

IHES consists of four components, i.e. the User Interface (UI), System Database (SD), Information Update (IU) and Central Processing System (CPS). The UI is the communication "outlet" between the users and the system. The SD is the central data storage system and the IU enables system administrators to update the information in the repository which store various groups of data for different processes. The CPS is the "brain" of the whole system, responsible for running IHES technology and monitoring the operations carried out within the system. The CPS consists of three main components, i.e. the Control Subsystem (CS), Rule-based Inference Operation (RIO) and Heuristics Loading (HL).

After the completion of knowledge acquisition stage and system design, the knowledge representation had been started. This section will focus on the components in the CPS.

Rule-based Inference Operation (RIO) – RIO consists of knowledge rules that are given by the expert in the field. The RIO draws the conclusion based on the information (facts) supplied by users and knowledge rules. RIO starts at retracting inappropriate flight schedule for stowing one or more customers' shipments. Some critical criteria of searching process includes Port of Load (POL), Port of Discharge (POD), Loading time, Arrival time, Accepted cost, Number of via and Quotation. After the completion of inference process, RIO returns a list of cargo allocation plans, in which contain one or more possible combinations among customers' shipments and suggested ULDs. However, such plans are formed according to preliminary considerations, such as total size of cargoes and ULD size. These plans may be impossible to be implemented because the spaces occupied by cargoes in a load plan actually exceed the size limit of container. Therefore, Heuristics Loading(HL) is necessary in place to evaluate such plans through the process of load plan generation.

Heuristics Loading (HL) – According to the work of Pisinger (2002), a tree-search algorithm, which is based on the wall-building approach presented by George and Robinson (1980), is developed. This is an improved algorithm that incorporates a backtracking step to improve the solution quality. This type of heuristic is relevant to apply in load plan generation process. In this part, the mechanism of Heuristics Formulation (HF) is built based on the work of Pisinger, but some of those are simplified and redesigned.

For each cargo allocation plan, frequency functions, which are labeled by f^1, f^2 and f^3, are applied to analyze the cargoes' physical features for arranging the priority of cargo loading sequences. Before going on, some information must be given:

(1) Let α and β be the smallest and largest dimensions of the cargoes
      respectively.

(2) k is a given value

(3) The width, height and depth of a cargo is represented by w_i, h_i and d_i.

The first frequency function f^1 returns the number of occurrences of this dimension among the cargos, considering all dimensions w_i; h_i; d_i of the cargoes:

$$f^1_k = \sum_{i=1}^{n} 1_{(w_i=k \vee h_i=k \vee d_i=k)} \quad \text{for } k = x_1,\ldots,x_n.$$

The second frequency function f^2 returns the number of occurrences of dimension k among the remaining cargoes, considering only the largest dimension of each cargo:

$$f^2_k = \sum_{i=1}^{n} 1_{(\max\{w_i,h_i,d_i\}=k)} \quad \text{for } k = x_1,\ldots,x_n.$$

The third frequency function f^3 returns the number of occurrences of dimension k among the remaining cargoes, considering only the smallest dimension of each cargo:

$$f^3_k = \sum_{i=1}^{n} 1_{(\min\{w_i,h_i,d_i\}=k)} \quad \text{for } k = x_1,\ldots,x_n.$$

After three statistics results are provided by correspondent frequency function. A ranking rule is then applied to those results to choose the most frequency occurrence of dimension in order to obtain a strip. The ranking rule is defined as: the dimension with larger frequency is chosen first. Then, the dimension with decreasing frequency is chose. If two different dimensions have the same frequency, the dimension, which is near to the previous chosen dimension, will have the priority to be used first. After ranking all dimensions, heuristic formulation will set the ranked dimensions as the depth of boxes. The strip is filled by the box that is defined as the first of priority after ranking result. Then, the strip is filled by the remaining box in order. During the strip filling process, box needs to be rotated such that, height is minimized and $W_{box} <= W_{strip}$. By following the same way, the strip will be generated until no space can be filled.

For each load plan, the total weight of each horizontal layer is calculated and then ranked in order. The heaviest layer is placed at the bottom of the container while the lightest layer is placed at the top of the container. The planned wall is generated after the completion of the process.

Control Subsystem (CS) – The CS has two functions. The first is to work as a system coordinator, ensuring smooth and efficient exchange of information within the CPS as well as between UI and CPS. Besides, it also manipulates the input and output data, and therefore deciding whether running the iterative process to modify the solution.

6. Case study

In order to demonstrate the feasibility of adopting IHES in the logistics community, five reference sites were selected as the pilot users for evaluating the system prototype and for system performance tooling. In this section, the case study of IHES is conducted in Oriented Delivery (HK) Limited is discussed.

Oriented Delivery is a local freight forwarder, offering transportation service by sea and by air. IHES is applied in the areas of simplifying the company's operational workflow and providing decision support for optimal shipment consolidation.

The first step of using IHES is to enter customers' order. From the Input Shipment Screen shown in Figure 6, the explicit information such as customer name, schedule, cargo and necessary remarks, is required to enter into the interface thoroughly.

Figure 7 shows the Flight Schedule screen. Each load device is specified by an individual Pallet ID. According to the expertise' experiences, there are a number of pallets with given flights to be adopted frequently, because the allotment have been made with particular airline company. Therefore, the storage of frequent used pallets will make users more convenient when using the program. The specific pallet information will be displayed by highlighting the particular pallet in the list of Pallet ID on the right hand side of the screen. Some essential information like the given flight number, carrier, type, quantity and cost charged are shown.

Figure 6. Shipment Input Screen

Figure 7. Flight Schedule Screen

Figure 8. Rule Selection Screen

Rule Selection screen aims at assisting users in determining the specific settings of the proposed system. As seen from Figure 8, the Rule Selection screen includes three main elements, namely, Space Utilization, Exit Criteria and Heuristics Settings. After inputting all information, IHES applies IHET for identifying appropriate load device and then determines the optimal solution of shipment consolidation. The output data will be ranked in descending order according to their competence.

In figure 9, the option '0' got the highest utilization rate, 82.81%. The details of option '0' are shown at the left hand side when highlighting it in Option Summary. Under this option, the pallet "160-96270636" is adopted. The details of this pallet are shown in the left hand side. The cargoes stowed in this pallet are listed in the frame of cargo loaded. The 3D load plan of pallet 160-96270636 is shown in Figure 10.

 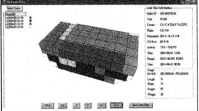

Figure 9. The list of cargo allocation arrangement   Figure 10. The 3D load Plan

7. System evaluation and benefits

In order to demonstrate the practicality of the IHES, Oriented Delivery conducted experiment to evaluate the system performance in respect to level of optimization and computational time. To perform the experiment, 24 sets of historical shipment projects have been obtained. Each set contains ten different data which have the same number of combination among cargoes and load devices. As shown in Figure 11(a) and 11(b), the results conducted by both experience-based approach and expert system approach have been obtained.

After implementing IHES for the shipment consolidation in various logistics projects, the performance was compared with those using experience-based approach. The performance criteria are the company satisfaction rate, degree of delay in delivery, service quality and the customer claims. As shown in Table 1, there is significant improvement using IHES in the process of shipment consolidation, which is shown by the increase in the percentage of service quality. Also, the significant decrease in the percentage of delay in delivery and customer claims indicates that expert system contributes to the improvement of performance of logistics operations. Moreover, the total saving based on the IHES model is about 1% comparing with the traditional approach, contributing to additional saving cost of about HK$ 70,000.

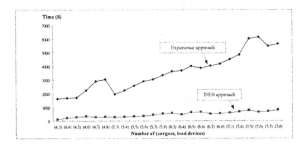

Figure 11(a). The computational time between IHES and experience approach

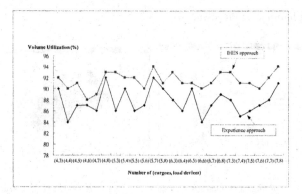

Figure 11(b). The volume utilization between IHES and experience approach

	By human (%)	By IHES (%)	The company expected(%)
Delay in delivery	20	12	10
Service quality	75	85	90
Customer claims	23	18	15

Table 1. The performance indication by human and IHES.

8. Conclusion

This paper provides an insight related to the problems of logistics shipment issues and the approaches to deal with them, suggesting the design and implementation of an expert system embedded with a new technology which is based on a combined artificial intelligence and heuristics techniques. This system is primarily designed for the use in airfreight forwarding environment, however, the same principle can be applied to other forwarding support systems, e.g. those used in the loading of railway, truck as well as ship. The case study of this paper demonstrates that it can be used in an actual freight forwarding environment, resulting in the enhancement of competitiveness and efficiency of local forwarders in the marketplace. In conclusion, this system is favorable to the progressive introduction of captured knowledge into the operation and is expected to influence the design of the next generation of logistics supporting systems particularly in airfreight forwarding business.

Reference:

1. Building, D.M. (1996). *Expert system in Prolog*. Berlin: Springer.

2. George, J.A., & Robinson, D.F. (1980). A heuristics for packing boxes into a container. *Computers and Operational Research*, 7(1980), 147-156.

3. Giarratano, J., & Riley, G.. (1994). Expert System: Principles and Programming. PWS Publishing Company 20 Park Plaza, Boston, MA 02116

4.   Hartle, S.L., & Jambunathan, K. (1996). Knowledge representation and inferencing techniques developed for a knowledge-based front end. *Engineering Applications of Artificial Intelligent*, Vol. 9, No. 3, pp. 245-259.

5.   Krishnamoorthy, C. S. & Rajeev, S. (1996). *Artificial Intelligence and Expert system for Engineers*. CRC Press

6.   Lee J. K., & Kwon S. B. (1995). ES: An expert system development planner using a constraint and rule-based approach. *Expert systems with Applications*, 9 (1), 3-14.

7.   Liebowitz, J. (1998). *Introduction to expert system.* Watsonville, CA: Mitchell Publishing/McGraw Hill

8.   Pistinger, D. (2002). Heuristics for the container loading problem. *European Journal of Operational Research,* 141(2002), 382-392.

9.   Ragothaman, S., Carpenter, J., & Buttars T. (1995). Using rule induction for knowledge acquisition; an expert systems approach to evaluating material errors and irregularities. Expert systems with Applications, 9(4) 483-490.

A Fast JPDA-IMM-PF based DFS Algorithm for Tracking Highly Maneuvering Targets

Mohand Saïd DJOUADI

Laboratoire robotique & productique,
Ecole militaire polytechnique, Bp : 17
Bordj El Bahri 16111 Alger, Algérie.
Email: msdjouadi@yahoo.fr

Yacine Morsly

Laboratoire robotique & productique,
Ecole militaire polytechnique, Bp : 17
Bordj El Bahri 16111 Alger, Algérie.
Email: ymorsly@yahoo.fr

Daoud BERKANI

Electrical & Computer Engineering,
Ecole Nationale Polytechnique, 10, Avenue
Hassen Badi, BP.182, 16200 El Harrach
Alger, Algérie.
Email: dberkani@hotmail.com

Abstract— **In this paper, we present an interesting filtering algorithm to perform accurate estimation in jump Markov nonlinear systems, in case of multi-target tracking. With this paper, we aim to contribute in solving the problem of model-based body motion estimation by using data coming from visual sensors. The Interacting Multiple Model (IMM) algorithm is specially designed to track accurately targets whose state and/or measurement (assumed to be linear) models changes during motion transition. However, when these models are nonlinear, the IMM algorithm must be modified in order to guarantee an accurate track. In order to deal with this problem, the IMM algorithm was combined with the Unscented Kalman Filter (UKF) [6]. Even if the later algorithm proved its efficacy in nonlinear model case; it presents a serious drawback in case of non Gaussian noise. To deal with this problem we propose to substitute the UKF with the Particle Filter (PF). To overcome the problem of data association, we propose the use of an accelerated JPDA approach based on the depth first search (DFS) technique [12]. The derived algorithm from the combination of the IMM-PF algorithm and the DFS-JPDA approach is noted DFS-JPDA-IMM-PF.**

Index Terms— **Estimation, Kalman filtering, Particle filtering JPDA, Multi-Target Tracking, Visual servoing, data association.**

I. INTRODUCTION

This paper hope to be a contribution within the field of visual-based control of robots, especially in visual-based tracking [3]; tracking maneuvring targets, which may themselves be robots, is a complex problem, to ensure a good track when the target switches abruptly from a motion model to another is not evident. Because of the complexity and difficulty of the problem, a simple case is considered. The study is restricted to 2-D motions of a point, whose position is given at sampling instants in terms of its Cartesian coordinates. This point may be the center of gravity of the projection of an object into a camera plane, or the result of the localisation of a mobile robot moving on a planar ground.

Several of maneuvering target tracking algorithms are developed. Among them, the interacting multiple model (IMM) method based on the optimal Kalman filter, yields good performance with efficient computation especially when the measurement and state models are linear with Gaussian noise. However, if the later are nonlinear and/or non Gaussian

noise, the standard Kalman filter should be substituted, in our study we choose the Particle Filter (PF). The algorithm derived from this combination is called IMM-PF. The other problem treated in this paper, is about the data association. Effectively, at each sample time, the sensor (camera) present, several measures and observations, coming from different targets; the problem is how to affect each measure to the correct target, to deal with this problem we choose an accelerated version of the JPDA algorithm based on the depth first search (DFS). The algorithm derived from the combination of DFS-JPDA and the non linear IMM algorithms is noted DFS- JPDA-IMM-PF.

The paper is organized as follows. In section II the mathematical formulation of 2-D motion is presented. In section III we describe the IMM algorithm PF based. In section IV we present the DFS algorithm and than in section V we present DFS-JPDA-IMM-PF algorithm. In section VI we present and discuss the results of simulations. Finally in section VII we draw the conclusion.

II. MATHEMATICAL FORMULATION OF 2-D MOTION

The mathematical formulation of 2-D motion used is mainly inspired from Danes, Djouadi, and al in [4]. They make the hypothesis that the measurements are only the 2-D Cartesian coordinates of the moving point.

Let s(.) denote the curvilinear abscissa of M over time onto its trajectory, the origin of curvilinear abscissae is set arbitrarily. Functions x(.) and y(.), represent the Cartesian coordinates of M. The measurement equation may be written as:

$$\begin{pmatrix} x(t) \\ y(t) \end{pmatrix} = \underline{h}\left(\underline{s}(t), \underline{p}(t)\right) \qquad (1)$$

Where $\underline{p}(.)$ is a parameter vector function of minimal size.

We can see that equation (1) is independent of the type of the motion of M onto its trajectory.

The state equation could be written as:

$$\underline{\dot{X}}(t) = A\underline{X}(t) \qquad (2)$$

Please use the following format when citing this chapter:

Djouadi, M.S., Morsly, Y., Berkani, D., 2006, in IFIP International Federation for Information Processing, Volume 228, Intelligent Information Processing III, eds. Z. Shi, Shimohara K., Feng D., (Boston: Springer), pp. 291–296.

with $\underline{X}(t) = \begin{pmatrix} \underline{s}(t) \\ \underline{p}(t) \end{pmatrix}$

A equals $\begin{pmatrix} A_s & 0 \\ 0 & 0 \end{pmatrix}$, with A_s the $n \times n$ zero matrix with ones added on its first upper diagonal, and 0 the matrices of convenient sizes. The continuous time state equation (2) is linear time invariant and independent of M's trajectory, except on the sizes of $\underline{s}(.)$ and $\underline{p}(.)$. Moreover, it may be shown that the fundamental matrix F involved its exact discretization at the period T takes the form

$$F \stackrel{\Delta}{=} \exp(AT) = \sum_{i=0}^{n-1} \frac{(AT)^i}{i!}.$$

The dynamic and measurement noises are supposed to be stationary, white and Gaussian, non inter-correlated with known covariances.

A. Canonical motion equations

The point M is supposed to move on straight or circular trajectories at constant or uniformly time-varying speed (constant speed or constant acceleration). Those motions belong to the set of the possible behaviours of a non-holonomic robot whose wheels are driven at constant velocities or accelerations.

1) Output equations: One minimal description of a straight line is defined by the vector $\underline{p} = (\alpha, d)^T$ shown in figure 1(a), which is related to Plucker coordinates. Concerning a circular trajectory one minimal description is defined by the vector $\underline{p} = (R0, x_0, y_0)^T$ shown in figure 1(b). The origin of curvilinear abscissa is uniquely defined from those parameterizations.

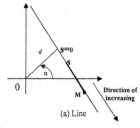

(a) Line

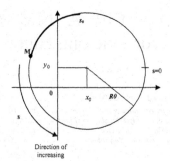

(b) Circle
Fig.1. Trajectory Parameterization

The output equations are as follows (trajectory parameter are considered time-invariant):

Straight Line: $z(k) \stackrel{\Delta}{=} \begin{pmatrix} x(k) \\ y(k) \end{pmatrix} = \begin{pmatrix} d\cos\alpha + s(k)\sin\alpha \\ d\sin\alpha - s(k)\cos\alpha \end{pmatrix} + v(k)$ (3)

Circle: $z(k) \stackrel{\Delta}{=} \begin{pmatrix} x(k) \\ y(k) \end{pmatrix} = \begin{pmatrix} x_0 + R0\cos\dfrac{s(k)}{R0} \\ y_0 + R0\sin\dfrac{s(k)}{R0} \end{pmatrix} + v(k)$ (4)

with $s(k)$ distance covered by the target and $v(\cdot)$ measurement noise *with density* $d_{v(k)}(v)$.

2) State Equations

Constant velocity $\begin{cases} \underline{s}(k+1) = \begin{pmatrix} 1 & T \\ 0 & 1 \end{pmatrix} \underline{s}(k) + w_s(k) \\ \underline{p}(k+1) = \underline{p}(k) + w_p(k) \end{cases}$ (5)

Constant acceleration

$$\begin{cases} \underline{s}(k+1) = \begin{pmatrix} 1 & T & \dfrac{T^2}{2} \\ 0 & 1 & T \\ 0 & 0 & 1 \end{pmatrix} \underline{s}(k) + w_s(k) \\ \underline{p}(k+1) = \underline{p}(k) + w_p(k) \end{cases}$$ (6)

where the random vectors
$x(0) = \left(\underline{s}(0)^T, \underline{p}(0)^T \right)^T$, $w(\cdot) = \left(w_s(\cdot)^T, w_p(\cdot)^T \right)^T$

and $\underline{s}(k) = \begin{bmatrix} s(k) \\ \dot{s}(k) \\ \ddot{s}(k) \end{bmatrix}$ vector of the point M dynamics

$\underline{p}(k)$ Trajectory parameters vector

III. THE IMM-PARTICLE FILTER ALGORITHM

The basic idea is to combine the IMM approach [1], with a particle filter one. In the derivation of the standard IMM filter, a merging and filtering process are defined. We adopt a regularized particle filter for this filtering step, and perform the merging step on the probability densities, represented by a Gaussian mixture. One consequence of the discrete nature of the approximation of the a posteriori density is that it cannot directly be applied to an IMM framework as it is used in [1].

To obtain a good continuous approximation of the a posteriori density, we use a regularized version of the bootstrap filter as first reported in [8,9] for tracking targets in clutter. In this hybrid version of the bootstrap filter, the probability density function, that has been computed as a point mass probability density on a number of grid points in the state space, is fitted to a continuous probability density function that is a sum of a prefixed number of Gaussian density functions. Moreover, by using a hybrid type of sampling filter as an alternative for direct resampling, degeneracy in the effective number of particles is avoided [8,9]. The main advantages of the new method that we propose here are:

✓ the method is able to deal with nonlinearities and non-Gaussian noise in a mode;
✓ the method uses a fixed number of particles in each mode, independent of the mode probability.

Algorithm

Let a system be described by the equations:

$$x(k) = f[x(k-1), k-1, M(k)] + w[k-1, M(k)]$$
$$z(k) = h[x(k), k, M(k)] + v[k, M(k)] \tag{7}$$

The process noise and the measurement noise are possibly mode-dependent. Their densities are denoted by: $d_{w[k,M(k)]}(w)$ and $d_{v[k,M(k)]}(v)$.

Where $M(k)$ denotes the model at time k. It's a finite state Markov process tacking values in $\{M_i\}_{j=1}^r$, according to a Markov transition probability matrix p assumed to be known.

The probability density of the initial state is known, $x(0) \sim P_0(x)$. Define the information up to and including time step k as:

$$Z(k) = \{z(1),......, z(k)\}$$

The filtering problem that has to be solved is:
Given a realization of Z(k) associated with (7) compute p(x(k)|Z(k)); i.e. the conditional probability density of the state x(k) given the set of measurements Z(k).

A cycle of the IMM algorithm could be summarized in four steps:

✓ *Interaction stage*

Compute Mixing probabilities

$$\mu_{i/j}(k-1/k-1) = \frac{1}{c_j} p_{ij}\mu_i(k-1) \tag{8}$$

Compute Normalizing factors

$$c_j = \sum_{i\in M} p_{ij}\mu_i(k-1) \tag{9}$$

Compute A priori probability density in mode j

$$\hat{p}_0^{\,j}\big(x_{0j}(k-1)/Z(k-1)\big) =$$
$$\sum_{i\in M} \hat{p}^{\,i}\big(x_i(k-1/Z(k-1))\big) * \mu_{i/j}(k-1/k-1) \tag{10}$$

✓ *Filtering stage*

$\forall j \in M$ draw N samples $\bar{x}_i^j(k-1)$ according to $\hat{p}_0^{\,j}\big(x_{0j}(k-1)/Z(k-1)\big)$

The predicted samples are:

$$\hat{x}_j^i(k) = f\big(\bar{x}_j^i(k-1), k-1, j\big) + w^i(k-1, j) \tag{11}$$

Where $w^i(k-1, j)$ are samples obtained from $d_{w(k-1,j)}(w)$

The predicted output

$$z_j^i(k/k-1) = h\big(\hat{x}_j^i(k), k, j\big) \tag{12}$$

The probability weight

$$\bar{q}_j^i(k) = d_{v(k,j)}\big(z(k) - \hat{z}_j^i(k/k-1)\big) \tag{13}$$

Normalizing

$$\tilde{q}_j(k) = \sum_{l=1}^N \bar{q}_j^l(k) \tag{14}$$

Normalized probability masses

$$q_j^i = \frac{\bar{q}_j^i(k)}{\tilde{q}_j(k)} \tag{15}$$

Mean of the state over the sample set

$$\bar{x}_j(k) = \sum_{l=1}^N q_j^l \hat{x}_j^l(k) \tag{16}$$

Covariance of the state over the sample set

$$\hat{P}_j(k) = \sum_{l=1}^N q_j^l \big(\hat{x}_j^l(k) - \bar{x}_j(k)\big)\big(\hat{x}_j^l(k) - \bar{x}_j(k)\big)^T \tag{17}$$

From the conditional probability density function for the state in mode j based on a mixture of N Gaussian densities

$$\hat{P}_N^j\big(x_j(k)/Z(k)\big) = \sum_{l=1}^N q_j^l N\big(\hat{x}_j^l(k), v_j \hat{P}_j(k)\big) \tag{18}$$

Where $v_j = 0.5N^{-2/d_j}$, and d_j is the dimension of the state space.

We obtain the probability density function for the state in mode j after mixture reduction, i.e. based on a mixture of $N_r \leq N$ Gaussian densities.

$$\hat{p}^j\left(x_j(k)/Z(k)\right) = \sum_{l=1}^{N_r} q_j^{r,l} N\left(\hat{x}_j^{r,l}(k), v_j \hat{P}_j^r(k)\right) \qquad (19)$$

The mean of predicted output over the sample set

$$\bar{h}_j(k) = \sum_{l=1}^{N} h\left(\hat{x}_j^l(k), k, j\right) \qquad (20)$$

Residual covariance over the sample set

$$\hat{S}_j(k) = \sum_{l=1}^{N} q\left(h\left(\hat{x}_j^l(k), k, j\right) - \bar{h}_j(k)\right)\left(h\left(\hat{x}_j^l(k), k, j\right) - \bar{h}_j(k)\right)^T \qquad (21)$$

Innovations

$$\gamma_j^l(k) = z(k) - h\left(\hat{x}_j^l(k), k, j\right) \qquad (22)$$

Probability density function for the innovations

$$\hat{p}^j\left(\gamma_j(k)/Z(k)\right) = \sum_{l=1}^{N} q_j^l N\left(0, \hat{S}_j(k)\right) = N\left(0, \hat{S}_j(k)\right) \qquad (23)$$

Likelihoods

$$L_j^l(k) = N\left(\gamma_j^l(k); 0, \hat{S}_j(k)\right) \qquad (24)$$

Mode probabilities

$$\mu_j(k) = \frac{1}{c} L_j(k) c_j \qquad (25)$$

Where

$$c = \sum_{j \in M} L_j(k) c_j \qquad (26)$$

✓ **Combination stage**

The a posteriori conditional probability density function for the stae

$$\hat{p}(x(k)/Z(k)) = \sum_{j \in M} \hat{p}^j\left(x_j(k)/Z(k)\right) \mu_j(k) \qquad (27)$$

IV. DFS ALGORITHM

Let m and n be the numbers of measurements and targets, respectively, in a particular cluster. The computational cost of data association increases exponentially with m and n. The efficiency of the algorithm used in the generation of the data association hypothesis is particularly important when m and n are large. In order to develop an efficient algorithm to generate all data association hypotheses, a mathematical model is developed for data association. One of the most used models for a combinational problem is called *exhaustive search with constraints* [13].

In the context of tracking multitarget, data association can be modeled as an exhaustive search with a set of proper notations. Let $X_j (j = 1,2,...,m)$ denote measurement j. The value of X_j belongs to a set Z_j. The value of Xj identifies the target which is hypothesized to be associated with measurement j. For example, $X_j = 2$ implies that measurement j is hypothesized to be associated with target 2. There, the set Z_j is defined by:

$$Z_j = \{t | w_{jt} = 1\}, \quad j = 1,2,...,m \text{ and } t = 1,2,...,n.$$

Where w_{jt} takes two values, 1 if measurement j is associated to target t, 0 else.

Based on the validation matrix $\Omega(w_{jt})$, data association hypotheses [14] are generated subject to two restrictions: (1) each measurement can have only one origin, and (2) no more than one measurement originates from a target.

In a JPDA scenario, the above two constraints can be easily translated into the language of exhaustive search problem for data association. Usually, an m-tuple, $\left(X_1, X_2,..., X_p,..., X_q,..., X_m\right)$, is a solution the these two constraints are satisfied:
1. If $p \neq q$, $X_p \neq 0$, and $X_q \neq 0$, then $X_p \neq X_q$.
2. If $X_p = X_q$ and $p \neq q$, then $X_p = X_q = 0$.

All data association hypotheses can be generated by solving the exhaustive search problem considered above.

Here we use the specialized DFS algorithm proposed in [12] for the generation of data association hypotheses.
In general, in exhaustive search problem, no solutions are known in advance. However, in the problem of data association, a solution which is always known, is (0,0, ,0). The other solutions can be generated systematically from various valid combinations of non-zero values of the elements. For more precision see [12].

V. DFS-JPDA-IMM-PF ALGORITHM

The principle of the JPDA algorithm is the computation of probabilities association for each track and new measurement. These probabilities are then used as weighting coefficients in the formation of the averaged state estimate, which is used for updating each track. For a better description of the JPDA algorithm, see [2,5].

The combination of the JPDA and the IMM-PF algorithms done as follows. A single set of validated measurements for JPDA-IMM-PF is obtained by considering the intersection Z_k, of r sets of measurements corresponding to individual models:

$$Z_k = \bigcap_{j=1}^{r} Z_k^j$$

Where Z_k^j represents the set of validated measurements under the assumption that model j is effective. The combined likelihood functions for the r modes of the IMM-PF algorithm are computed as in [6].

The prior mixed state estimates for model j and the validation regions for individual models are also computed as in [2,6]. The new mode probabilities, output state estimates, and corresponding error covariances are obtained as in [2,6].

VI. SIMULATIONS AND RESULTS

In this section, we perform some simulations to evaluate our algorithm (DFS-JPDA-IMM-PF).

The motion models considered are: - constant velocity on straight line (M_1), -constant acceleration on straight line (M_2), - constant velocity on circle (M_3), - constant acceleration on circle (M_4).

To explore the capability of our JPDA-IMM-UKF algorithm to track maneuvring targets, various scenarios are considered; among of them we select the typical case of three highly maneuvring targets with crossing trajectories.

We assume that the target is in a 2-D space and its position is sampled every T=1s. we run the DFS-JPDA-IMM-PF with 1000 samples in each mode.

- The probability transition matrix of four models is

$$p = \begin{bmatrix} 0.97 & 0.01 & 0.01 & 0.01 \\ 0.01 & 0.97 & 0.01 & 0.01 \\ 0.01 & 0.01 & 0.97 & 0.01 \\ 0.01 & 0.01 & 0.01 & 0.97 \end{bmatrix}$$

- The initial probability of selecting a model is 0.25, that's to say, at the start all models have the same chance to be selected.
- The curvilinear abscissa s (.) remains continuous even if a trajectory jump occurs.

A. Considered scenario

We consider that we have to track simultaneously three maneuvring targets. In order to complicate the scenario, we suppose that the targets follow during there movements, crossing trajectories.

a) Target 1(black):

The target starts moving according to model M_1 until the 50th sample when an abrupt trajectory change occur and still moving according to this during 50 samples (switching from model M_1 to M_3).

b) Target 2 (blue):

The target starts moving according to model M_3 until the 50th sample when an abrupt acceleration about 0.2 m/s^2 occur and still moving according to this during 50 samples (switching from model M_3 to M_4).

c) Target 3 (green):

The target starts moving according to model M_1 until the 50th sample when an abrupt acceleration about 0.2 m/s^2 occur and still moving according to this during 50 samples (switching from model M_1 to M_2).

d) Target 4 (red):

As the target 3 ,the target 4 starts moving according to model M_1 until the 50th sample when an abrupt acceleration about 0.2 m/s^2 occur and still moving according to this during 50 samples (switching from model M_1 to M_2).

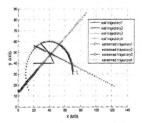

Fig.2. Real and Esteemed Trajectories

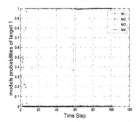

Fig.3. Models Probabilities for target 1

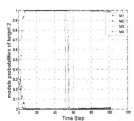

Fig.4. Models Probabilities 2

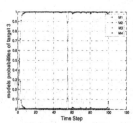

Fig.5. Models Probabilities 3

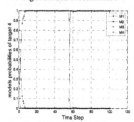

Fig.6. Models Probabilities 4

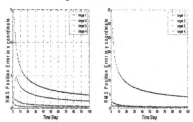

Fig.7. RMS x and y position error

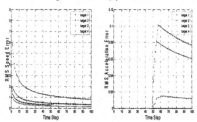

Fig.8. RMS Acceleration and Speed Error

B. Results interpretation:

Figure 2 shows that the esteemed and the real trajectory for the three targets are superposable and almost identical even if an abrupt change occurs on the tracked target dynamic. This result is confirmed by the figures (3,4,5,6,7,8), from this we can say that the tracker based IMM-PF algorithm is a pertinent solution to the problem of visual-based tracking highly maneuvering targets. In the Other hand figure 2 shows also that the data association ´is correctly done even if the trajectories cross each other. This should permit us to say that the JPDA algorithm computes perfectly and its combination with the IMM-PF algorithm (DFS-JPDA-IMM-PF) would be an efficient solution to the problem of highly maneuvering multi-target visual-based tracking.

VII. CONCLUSION

The model-based body motion estimation by using data coming from visual sensors still an open problem on which we try to provide a contribution. In this paper we presented a nonlinear algorithm which attempts to track efficiently a highly maneuvering target whose trajectory and/or dynamic could change abruptly, and the noise distribution is not necessary Gaussian; the algorithm proposed is noted IMM-PF. To extend this algorithm to multi-target case, we combined the later with a fast version of the JPDA algorithm noted DFS-JPDA to ensure good data association.
Simulations show that the DFS-JPDA-IMM-PF is a good investment while we are asked to track a highly maneuvrable targets whose measurement and/or state models present a strong nonlinearities, and the noises are not Gaussian and when there different trajectories cross each other.

REFERENCES

[1]   Y.Bar-Shalom and T.E.Fortman, "Tracking and Data Association," *Mathematics in Science and Engineering*, volume 179, Academic Press, 1988.
[2]   Y.Bar-Shalom and X. R. Li, "Estimation and Tracking, *Principles, Techniques and Software*," *Artech House*, Boston, MA (USA), 1993.
[3]   B.Espiau, F.Chaumette, and P.Rives, " A new approach to visual servoing in robotics,"*IEEE Transactions on Robotics and Automation*, 8(3):313-326, June 1992.
[4]   P.Danes, M.S.Djouadi, D.Bellot, "A 2-D Point-Wise Motion Estimation Scheme for Visual-Based Robotic Tasks," *7th International Symposium on Intelligent Robotic Systems (SIRS'99)*, Coimbra (Portugal), 20-23 July 1999, pp.119-128
[5]   Y.Bar-Shalom and X. R. Li, "Multi-target Multi-sensor Tracking: Principles and Techniques," *Storrs, CT* , YBS Publishing, 1995.
[6]   M.S.Djouadi, A.Sebbagh, D.Berkani, "IMM-UKF and IMM-EKF Algorithms for Tracking Highly Maneuvring Target," *Archive of Control Sciences*, Vol: 1, issue: 1, 2005.
[7]   M. Hadzagic, H. Mchalska, A. Jouan, " IMM-JVC and IMM-JPDA for closely maneuvering targets," IEEE, 2001.
[8]   Y. Boers, JN. Driessen, " Interacting multiple model particle filter", *IEE Proc- Radar Sonar Navig, Vol.150, No. 5,* October 2003.
[9]   S. McGinnity, G.W. Irwin, "Multiple model bootstrap filter for maneuvering target tracking," *IEEE Trans. Aerosp. Electron. Syst.,2000, 36, (3), pp. 1006 1012.*
[10] S. McGinnity, G.W. Irwin, "Manoeuvering target tracking using a multiple-model bootstrap filter," in Doucet, A., de Freitas, N. and Gordon, N. (Eds.): 'Sequential Monte Carlo methods in practice' (Springer, New York, 2001), pp. 247 271
[11] N.J. Gordon,"A hybrid bootstrap filter for target tracking in clutter," IEEE Trans. Aerosp. Electron Syst., 1997, 33, (1), pp. 353 358
[12] B.Zhou, N.K. Bose, " Multitarget tracking in clutter: Fast Algorithm for Data Association," *IEEE trans. Aero. Elect.* Vol.29, Nº.2 April 1993.
[13] E.M. Reingold, J. Neivergelt, N. Deo, " Combinational Algorithms, Theory and Practice," *Prentice-Hall*, 1977.
[14] T.E. Fortmann, Y. Bar-Shalom, M. Scheffe, "Sonar tracking of multiple targets using joint probabilistic data association," *IEEE Journal of Oceanic Engineering*, OE-8 , July 1983.

AN IMPROVED PARTICLE FILTER ALGORITHM BASED ON NEURAL NETWORK FOR TARGET TRACKING

Qin Wen, Peng Qicong

140 Lab, Institution of Communication and Information Engineering, University of Electronic Science and Technology of China, Chengdu, China

Abstract: To the shortcoming of general particle filter, an improved algorithm based on neural network is proposed and is shown to be more efficient than the general algorithm in the same sample size. The improved algorithm has mainly optimized the choice of importance density. After receiving the samples drawn from prior density, and then adjust the samples with general regression neural network (GRNN), make them approximate the importance density. Apply the new method to target tracking problem, has made the result more precise than the general particle filter.

Key words: particle filter, target tracking, general regression neural network

1.   INTRODUCTION

In practice of target tracking, the dynamic system usually is non-linear and non Gaussian. The general method (e.g. Kalman filter) is unable to reach the optimal estimate of target. However, particle filter algorithm based on Bayesian rule uniformly made very good result in state estimate of non-linear and non-Gaussian system. So, it will be a good choice to apply particle filter to the target tracking system.

But, the shortcoming of particle filter can not be ignored either. Because the importance density function is difficult to realize in project practice, so usually adopt prior density and substitute it. This kind of method will reduce

Please use the following format when citing this chapter:

Wen, Q., Qicong, P., 2006, in IFIP International Federation for Information Processing, Volume 228, Intelligent Information Processing III, eds. Z. Shi, Shimohara K., Feng D., (Boston: Springer), pp. 297–305.

the precision of state estimate. So, people are always studying a better method to approximate the importance density. This paper explores the possibility of using neural network to get optimal result. The below will describe this kind of method and analyze the performance improvement brought by it.

2.   PARTICLE FILTER

2.1   Bayesian Rule

The problem of tracking is a process of the state sequence estimated. The dynamics of single state vector at time k is described by a stochastic difference equation

$$x_k = f(x_{k-1}, w_{k-1}) \tag{1}$$

where w_{k-1} is an i.i.d. process noise vector with a known distribution and f is a possibly nonlinear function of the state x_{k-1}. At each discrete time point an observation z_k is obtained, related to the state vector by

$$z_k = h(x_k, v_k) \tag{2}$$

where v_k is an i.i.d. measure noise vector and h is called the measurement function.

Then the state prediction equation

$$p(x_k \mid z_{1:k-1}) = \int p(x_k \mid x_{k-1}) p(x_{k-1} \mid z_{1:k-1}) dx_{k-1} \tag{3}$$

The state update equation

$$p(x_k \mid z_{1:k}) = \frac{p(z_k \mid x_k) p(x_k \mid z_{1:k-1})}{p(z_k \mid z_{1:k-1})} \tag{4}$$

where the normalizing constant

$$p(z_k \mid z_{1:k-1}) = \int p(z_k \mid x_k) p(x_k \mid z_{1:k-1}) dx_k \tag{5}$$

The above describes the Bayesian estimate rule. Generally, the analytic solution in (3) does exist in some dynamic system. But, it cannot be determined analytically in nonlinear and non-Gaussian system. Therefore, particle filter is a good choice to approximate optimal Bayesian solution.

2.2   Particle Filtering Method

Particle filter is a technique for implementing a recursive Bayesian filter by Monte Carlo simulations. The key idea is to represent the required posterior density function by a set of random samples with associated weights and to compute estimates based on these samples and weights. As the number of samples becomes very large, this MC characterization becomes an equivalent representation to the usual functional description of posterior probability density function, and the SIS (Sequential Importance Sampling) filter approaches the optimal Bayesian estimate [1].

Let $\left\{x_k^i, w_k^i\right\}_{i=1}^{N_x}$ denote a random measure that characterizes the posterior density function $p(x_k \mid z_{1:k})$, where $\left\{x_k^i, i = 0, \cdots, N_s\right\}$ is a set of support points with associated weight $\left\{w_k^i, i = 1, \cdots, N_s\right\}$. Then, as $N_x \to \infty$, the posterior density at k can be approximated as

$$p(x_k \mid z_{1:k}) \approx \sum_{i=1}^{N_x} w_k^i \delta(x_k - x_k^i) \qquad (6)$$

In the SIS algorithm, the samples x_k^i are drawn from an importance density $q(x_k \mid x_{k-1}^i, z_{1:k})$, then the weights in (6) update equation can be shown as

$$w_k^i \propto w_{k-1}^i \frac{p(z_k \mid x_k^i) p(x_k^i \mid x_{k-1}^i)}{q(x_k^i \mid x_{k-1}^i, z_k)} \qquad (7)$$

In the paper [2], the optimal importance density function that minimizes the variance of the true weights w_k^i conditioned on x_{k-1}^i and z_k has been shown

$$q(x_k \mid x_{k-1}^i, z_k) = p(x_k \mid x_{k-1}^i, z_k) \qquad (8)$$

The SIS algorithm consists of recursive propagation of the weights and support points as each measurement is received sequentially. A pseudo-code description of this algorithm is give by Algorithm 1.

Algorithm 1 . SIS Particle Filter

·for $i = 1 : N_s$

— draw $x_k^i \sim q(x_k \mid x_{k-1}^i, z_k)$

— assign the particle a weight, w_k^i according to (7)

·end for

·normalize the weight $w_k^i = w_k^i / \mathrm{sum}[\{w_k^i\}_{i=1}^{N_s}]$

·resample the sample w_k^{i*}

3. CHOICE OF IMPORTANCE DENSITY BASED ON NEURAL NETWORK

3.1 Shortcoming of SIS

In practice, it is often convenient to choose the importance density to be the prior

$$q(x_k \mid x_{k-1}^i, z_k) = p(x_k \mid x_{k-1}^i) \tag{9}$$

Then, substitution of (9) into (7)

$$w_k^i \propto w_{k-1}^i p(z_k \mid x_k^i) \tag{10}$$

In a situation that the observe precision is low, this method can make better result, but the precision of estimate is not high. Because the current measure value z_k is not considered in importance density function, the samples drawn from importance density and from the real posterior density have greater deviations. Especially when likelihood function is at the end of system state transfer probability density function or measure model has very high precision, the kinds of deviation are more obvious. This can see from Figure1.

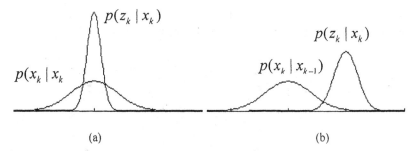

Figure 1. The prior density and likelihood function. (a) The likelihood function is peak. (b) The likelihood function is at the end of prior density function.

To the shortcoming of SIS algorithm, A.Doucet proposes to construct suboptimal importance density to the optimal importance density by using local linearization techniques [2]. R van der Merwe, A.Doucet, etc. propose to estimate a Gaussian approximation to importance density using the unscented transform [3]. Yuan Zejian and Zheng Nanning, etc. propose using Gauss-Hermite filter to sample and reconstruct the importance density in [4]. Peter Torma, etc. propose a local search method to adjust samples, make it more approximate importance density function [5].

This paper applies artificial neural network to the choice of importance density. Using general regression neural network (GRNN) to adjust samples after prediction step can get good result, make samples accord with the posterior density further.

3.2   GRNN

GRNN is a novel neural network proposed by Donald F.Specht in 1991[6]. The basic theory is nonlinear regression analysis. GRNN is different with the BP network. The traditional BP neural network is one kind of typical universal approximation network. One or more weights are influence to each output in network. It causes study speed to be slower; moreover, the weight determined is stochastic, which causes the relationship between input and output after each step of training unstable and the forecast result deviation. The GRNN only needs a simple smooth parameter, does not need to carry on the training process circularly, and does not adjust weight between the neurons in the training process. The network is steady and the computation speed is quick. Therefore, in the real-time target tracking application, GRNN has the superiority compared to BP.

What show in Figure 2 is a feed forward network that can be used to estimate a vector Y from a measurement vector X.

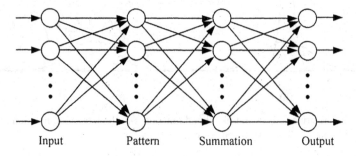

| Input | Pattern | Summation | Output |

Figure2. GRNN block diagram

Let X be a particular measured value of random variable x, and X^i is sample value of x.

Defining the scalar function

$$D_i^2 = (X - X^i)^T (X - X^i)$$ (11)

and performing the indicated integrations yields the following

$$\hat{Y}(X) = \frac{\sum_{i=1}^{n} Y^i \exp(-\frac{D_i^2}{2\sigma^2})}{\sum_{i=1}^{n} \exp(-\frac{D_i^2}{2\sigma^2})}$$ (12)

where Y^i is sample value of Y. σ is the width of sample probability for each sample X^i and Y^i.

GRNN can be used to adjust samples in particle filter algorithm according to measurement value z_k.

Because when in a concrete target tracking scene, the profile of likelihood function is fixed at any time of k, but its mathematic expression is not clear, only can be obtained by some separate observed values through image processing methods. So we may train the network according to the observed value and make it approach the likelihood function, and then utilizes this network to any samples to carry on the adjustment.

Firstly, the input vector and object vector should be structured to train the network. A group of samples are obtained by sampling equal-space likelihood function. n neighborhood samples and their likelihood function values constitute the input vector and object vector respectively. The dimension of input vector n and the number of study sample m determine the network configuration: $n \times m \times (n+1) \times n$.

After the network is trained, the samples in particle filter algorithm should be adjusted in form of input vector, and then it can be apply to the network. Firstly, construct a n dimension vector $X_k^i = [x_k^i, x_k^i \pm j\Delta]$, $j\Delta < L$, ($j= 1,\cdots,n/2$). The parameter L defines the adjustment range. Then, transform $X_k^i \rightarrow h(X_k^i) - z_k$ as the input vector of GRNN trained.

Finally, through the indication of output vector of network, the sample x_k^i is substituted by optimal point $x_k^i \pm j\Delta$. A series of samples adjusted are more optimally approximate the importance density.

4.   SIMULATION

Let X_k represent the state variable at time k, corresponding to the position of the target in the state space

$$X_k = \begin{bmatrix} x_k & y_k \end{bmatrix}^T$$

The two-dimensional target dynamics is given by [5]

$$\hat{X}_{k+1} = X_k + S_{k+1}\Delta_k + W_k$$
$$S_{k+1} = (2B_{k+1} - 1)S_k$$
$$U_{k+1} = \chi(|\hat{X}_{k+1}| \le K)$$
$$X_{k+1} = U_{k+1}\hat{X}_{k+1} + (1 - U_{k+1})X_k$$
$$\Delta_{k+1} = U_{k+1}(X_{k+1} - X_k) + (1 - U_{k+1})(X_{k+1} - \hat{X}_{k+1})$$

where $W_k \sim N(0, \sigma^2)$ are i.i.d. Gaussian random variables, and B_k is a Bernoulli variable.

The measure model is $Z_k = X_k + V_k$, where $V_k \sim N(0, \delta^2)$ i.i.d. The dynamics is highly nonlinear.

We test the general SIS algorithm and the improved algorithm based on GRNN to this dynamics model respectively. Figure 3 shows a typical sequence of tracking a ball. The number of particles was chosen to be as 100 in two kinds of algorithms. The dimension of input vector in GRNN is 7. Obviously, the two algorithms all find the position of ball precisely along with the movement of target. However, the improved algorithm has higher accuracy than general one. Figure 4 shows the tracking precision as a function of the time. The improved algorithm has the obvious superiority compared to the general particle filter algorithm at the average deviation pixels.

(a)

(b)

Figure 3. The result of simulation. (a) The result of tracking with the general SIS algorithm. (b) The result of tracking with the improved algorithm based on GRNN adjustment

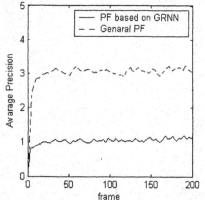

Figure 4. Tracking precision as a function of time

5.   CONCLUSION

In this article, an improved particle filter algorithm based on GRNN is proposed to solve the problem of importance density function choosing. The new method is shown to improve the performance of samples and to increase robustness as compared with the previous method proposed, whilst the novel algorithm minimizes the expected distortion in the configuration space.

One weakness of the approach is that the GRNN will spend more time than general particle filter algorithm. However, the price of time is worth. Moreover, it is in the range that the system can bear.

In conclusion, we believe that it is a significative exploration to adopt neural network to solve the optimal importance density. It will be a valuable step towards the implementation of highly efficient tracking.

REFERENCES

1. M.Sanjeev Arulampalam, Simon Maskell, Neil Gordon. A Tutorial on Particle Filters for Online Nonlinear/Non-Gaussian Bayesian Tracking. IEEE Transactions on Signal Processing, 2002,50(2):174~188
2. A.Doucet. On sequential Monte Carlo methods for Bayesian filtering. Dept. Eng., Univ. Cambridge, UK, Tech. Rep., 1998.
3. R.van der Merwe, A.Doucet, N.de Freitas, E.Wan. The Unscented Particle Filter. Adv. Neural Inform. Process. Syst., Dec.2000
4. Yuan Zejian, Zheng Nanning, Jia Xinchun. The Gauss-Hermite Particle Filter. Dian Zi Xue Bao, 2003,31(7):970~973
5. Peter Torma, Csaba Szepesvari. LS-N-IPS:an improvement of particle filters by means of local search. In Proc. Non-Linear Control Systems (NOLCOS'01),2001
6. Specht D F. A General Regression Neural Network. IEEE Transactions on Neural Networks, 1991, 2 (6):568~576

A MIMETIC ALGORITHM FOR REFINEMENT OF LOWER BOUND OF NUMBER OF TRACKS IN CHANNEL ROUTING PROBLEM

Debasri Saha[1], Rajat K. Pal[2] and Samar Sen Sarma[3]
[123]DEPARTMENT OF COMPUTER SCIENCE, UNIVERSITY OF CALCUTTA

Abstract: Study of algorithms and its design can be progressed in various dimensions. In this paper, we have a definite refinement of lower bound on the number of tracks required to route a channel. The attack is from a complementary viewpoint. Our algorithm succeeds to avoid all kind of approximation. The approach performs exact mapping of the problem into graphical presentation and analyzes the graph taking help of mimetic algorithm, which uses combination of sequential and GA based vertex coloring. Performance of the algorithm depends on how effectively mimetic approach can applied selecting appropriate values for the parameters to evaluate the graphical presentation of the problem. This viewpoint has immense contribution against sticking at local minima for this optimization problem. The finer result clearly exemplifies instances, which give better or at least the same lower bound in VLSI channel routing problem.

Key words: Manhattan Routing model, Channel routing problem, Constraint graphs, Maximum Independent set, Mimetic algorithm

1. INTRODUCTION

1.1 Channel routing problem

Channel routing problem(CRP) is NP hard in nature [10]. Extensive effort and attention has been attempted to tackle it. With the advancement of VLSI technology, as millions of gates have been accommodated in a tiny chip area, wiring the terminals of logic blocks altogether using minimum possible area has become a tedious task. If electrically equivalent pins are wired using rectangular routing region with terminals only on opposite sides, this strategy is termed as channel routing.

Please use the following format when citing this chapter:

Saha, D., Pal, R.K., Sarma, S.S., 2006, in IFIP International Federation for Information Processing, Volume 228, Intelligent Information Processing III, eds. Z. Shi, Shimohara K., Feng D., (Boston: Springer), pp. 307–316.

CRP is constrained form of optimization problem, where horizontal span of nets are assigned in horizontal tracks, avoiding conflicts so that track requirement is minimized. As CRP is NP hard [1,2,3], to design an algorithm with much lower complexity, we have taken heuristic support. As practical lower bound deviates much from the trivial one, our algorithm focuses on the computation of nontrivial lower bound on the number of tracks. The evolutionary techniques of mimetic algorithm, which efficiently handles hybrid optimization problems, are effectively incorporated here to find a better non-trivial solution. It generates near-optimal results for a number of well-known benchmark channels in reasonable time.

Here we consider grid based reserved layer Manhattan routing model, which is rectilinear in nature and each layer is restricted to accommodate a certain type (horizontal or vertical) of wire.

1.2   Constraints of CRP and their significance

Routing of wires should satisfy both kind of constraints- Horizontal constraints and Vertical constraints. Two nets n_i and n_j are said to have horizontal constraints, if their horizontal spans have at least one column common. Two nets n_i and n_j are said to have vertical constraints, if there exists a column such that the terminal on the top of the column belongs to net n_i and the terminal on the bottom of the column belongs to net n_j or vice versa.

These constraints can be well visualized by two constraint graphs – HCG(Horizontal Constraint Graph) and VCG(Vertical Constraint Graph)[4].

HCG G=(V,E) is an undirected graph where each vertex $v_i \in V$ represents a net n_i and each edge $(v_i,v_j) \in E$ represents horizontal constraint between net n_i and net n_j. It signifies that if there is an edge between vertices v_i and v_j, then nets n_i and n_j cannot be placed in the same track.

Horizontal constraint can have a complementary representation through HNCG(Horizontal Non-Constraint Graph). HNCG G=(V,E) is an undirected graph where each vertex $v_i \in V$ represents a net n_i and each edge $(v_i,v_j) \in E$ indicates that net n_i and net n_j are horizontal constraint-free i.e. horizontal span of net n_i and n_j have no common column. It implies that if there is an edge between vertices v_i and v_j, then net n_i and n_j can be placed in the same track if only horizontal constraint is taken into account.

VCG   G=(V,E) is a directed graph where each vertex $v_i \in V$ represents a net n_i and each directed edge $<v_i,v_j> \in E$ represents vertical constraint between net n_i and net n_j such that there exists a column for which the top terminal belongs to net n_i and the bottom terminal belongs to net n_j. Interpretation of VCG is that if there is a directed edge from vertices v_i to v_j, then net n_i must be placed in a track above the track where net n_j is placed. That means it emphasize the ordering of net assignments in the channel.

The maximum number of nets, which crosses a column gives the knowledge of Channel Density (d_{max}). If we neglect vertical constraint, minimum number of track requirement is equal to d_{max} . This information is extracted either from HCG or from HNCG. In case of HCG, computation of Clique Number generates the value of channel density where as if HNCG is considered, we have to calculate Independence Number. Here we introduce the definition of clique number and independence number of a graph.

Definition 1 :Clique Number of a graph is the size of maximal complete sub-graph of the graph.

Definition 2:A set of vertices in a graph is said to be an independent set of vertices or simply independent set if no two vertices in the set are adjacent.
Definition 3:A maximal independent set is an independent set to which no other vertex can be added without destroying its independent property.
Definition 4:The number of vertices in the largest independent set of a graph is called the independence number.

On the other hand, VCG contributes the value of v_{max} , which is nothing but the length of longest chain in VCG. It indicates that, if we consider only vertical constraints, at least v_{max} number of track is required.

The rest of the paper is organized as follows. Section2 discusses the motivation of the work. Section3 discusses the proposed algorithm and section4 throws light on the time complexity of the algorithm. Section5 illustrates the execution of the algorithm by an example. Section6 focuses on the definite refinement on minimum number of tracks to route a channel and discusses the empirical observations on some randomly generated instances. Section7 extends our proposed algorithm for two-layer restricted doglegging model. Section8 concludes the paper & discusses scope for future work.

2.   MOTIVATION AND CONTRIBUTION

Our work is motivated as we have analyzed a lots of practical instances of channel, which cannot be routed using either d_{max} or v_{max} number of tracks. Apparently max (d_{max}, v_{max}) is formulated as an estimate of *trivial lower bound*. But simultaneous consideration of both the constraints generates a practical situation where a greater number of tracks are necessary to route a channel. It encourages us to combine the information from two constraint graphs into a single one, so that the resulted composite constraint graph can conjointly helps us to find the *non-trivial lower bound*.

HCG is an interval graph, whereas it's complement graph is a comparability graph [5]. The common feature of them is that they are both perfect in nature. A graph is said to be perfect, if it has no induced sub-graph with odd cycle of length greater than or equal to five.

But VCG can be any directed acyclic graph (if we take only cycle free VCG). If we proceed by extracting constraint based information from VCG and incorporating those into HNCG, it results into a modified HNCG, which may not still remain perfect in nature. Although Clique number or Independence number of perfect graph is polynomial-time computable, the possibility for modified HNCG of being non-perfect restricts us guaranteeing a deterministic polynomial time algorithm for independence number computation.

Success of mimetic algorithm in handling NP hard optimization problems inspired us to introduce it in our problem solving [6,9]. In our paper, mimetic algorithm tries to optimally color the vertices of the composite graph. The result is equivalent to finding maximal independent set of maximum cardinality.

In our previous paper[7], we deliberately kept composite constraint graph(Modified HCG) chordal as clique number of chordal graph is polynomially computable. But to do so, some vertical constraint based information is lost, which is treated as approximation. Hence there the Modified HCG reflects only approximated lower bound, not the exact one. Here we preserve all constraint related information in modified HNCG and this information is processed using GA operators to produce practical lower bound.

3.   CONTRIBUTION OF THE ALGORITHM

3.1   Construction of composite graph

We propose a hybrid GA based heuristic algorithm to determine the non-trivial lower bound on the number of tracks required to route a channel in polynomial time. An edge between vertices v_i and v_j in HNCG signifies that, net n_i and n_j have no horizontal overlapping. That doesn't mean those can be placed in the same track, as vertical constraint may impose ordering on their tracks. In VCG, if directed edges $<i, j>$ and $<j, k>$ are present, that indicates net n_i has to be placed above net n_j and net n_j above net n_k. Hence net n_i has to be placed above net n_k. This transitive closure property is strictly followed by vertical constraints. So net n_i cannot be accommodated with net n_k, even if those are horizontal constraint free. . It is focused that none of the constraint graph can alone cover all constraint information So we extract this vertical constraint based information from VCG and incorporate those into HNCG to highlight all constraint information through a single graph.

We find out all possible directed paths between each pair of source (indegree zero) and sink (Outdegree zero) vertices in VCG, then apply transitive closure property (if a-> b and b-> c, then a-> c) to construct an edge list E, which contains edges between all pair of vertices having a directed path between them in VCG, but without any directed edge between them. The directed edges already present in VCG reflects direct vertical constraint, hence those are automatically covered by horizontal constraint consideration. Hence E contains only those edges, which reflect indirect or derived vertical constraints.

Each edge (v_i, v_j) of edge list E, if present in HNCG, indicates that the corresponding nets n_i and n_j are not horizontally constrained but only vertically. Our strategy is to delete all such edges from HNCG. The Modified HNCG, thus obtained, is termed as Composite graph as it focuses combined effect of all constraints.

Definition 5: For composite graph $G = (V, E)$, each vertex $v_i \in V$ represents a net n_i and each edge $(v_i, v_j) \in E$ implies corresponding nets n_i and n_j are constraint-free and can be placed in same track.

Conversely we can say, two disconnected vertices v_i and v_j reflects the fact that corresponding nets n_i and n_j are mutually constrained, hence occupy separate tracks. Independence number I, i.e. the maximum number of mutually unconnected vertices of the Composite graph gives an estimate of lower bound (Lbound) of tracks.

3.2   Computation of Independence Number using Mimetic Algorithm

The problem of finding Independence number I of Composite graph is mapped into the problem of proper coloring of vertices, where connected vertices are colored with distinct colors. Our algorithm proceeds with proper coloring of Composite graph satisfying the objective that as many vertices as possible are colored by each color applied. That means, if each color is assigned to as many vertices as possible obeying proper coloring, the maximum number of vertices colored with identical color specifies Independence Number I.

In this context, the order of sequential coloring of vertices is of great significance. The vertices of composite graph are arranged in increasing order of their degree and considered for proper coloring in this sequence. We stack for use as many colors as the number of vertices in Composite graph. Each color is encoded as an integer. GA works by evolving a population of strings over generations. We use random selection of a color, consider vertices in minimum degree sequence, continue assigning the color till the violation of proper coloring, followed by selection of another color. Fitness value of a string is evaluated as the maximum occurrences of a single color (integer) in the string. GA attempts to optimize this fitness function through effective application of GA parameters Reproduction, Crossover and Mutation [8] with appropriate probability. Reproduction emphasizes survival of highly fit strings. Crossover provides encouraging results against sticking to local optima. Random selection of mutation location also helps to reach global minima.

3.3   Detection of obstruction condition

Let us consider the following two channel specifications:

TOP: 3   1   2   0   2   0   TOP: 1   1   4   0   2   0
BOTTOM: 0   3   0   1   4   4   BOTTOM: 0   3   0   3   4   2

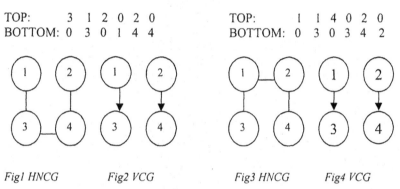

Fig1 HNCG   *Fig2 VCG*   *Fig3 HNCG*   *Fig4 VCG*

In both cases, Composite graph is same as HNCG. Independence number I is 2 but track requirement is 3, as net 1 and net 2 can't be placed in same track for fig1 and net 3 and net 4 can't be placed in same track for fig3. So at least three tracks are required to route the channel.

Lemma1: For a pair of directed paths (chain) from source to sink vertices, with length difference <=1 and at least one with length v_{max}, then if source vertices, or sink vertices, or both pairs are disconnected in HNCG, at least one extra track is the essentially required.

Our proposed algorithm searches for the presence of obstruction condition, if found, at least one extra track is needed. Hence minimum increment in number of track requirement, INCR is 1.

3.4   Algorithms

Algorithm MIMETIC_LBOUND

Input: Channel specification
Output: Lbound, Non-trivial lower bound on the number of tracks.
Step1: Construct HNCG and VCG from channel specification.
Step2:   Using the transitive closure property, compute the list of edges, E between all possible pair of vertices having shortest directed path length>=2 between them in VCG.
Step 3: If E is empty, consider HNCG as Composite graph (Modified HNCG).

Go to Step 5.

Step 4: Delete each edge e of the list E from HNCG, if present in HNCG.

Finally resulted graph is denoted as Composite graph (Modified HNCG).

Step 5: If the Composite graph is a null graph (having   only isolated vertices), then

Lbound = No of vertices in Composite graph,

Else compute independence number, I, of the Composite graph using mimetic algorithm.

Step 6: Check for the presence of *obstruction* condition

If present, compute increment in lower bound, INCR due to that,

Else INCR = 0.

Finally, Lbound = I + INCR.

Following are the steps of mimetic algorithm to compute the independence number of a graph

Mimetic Algorithm I_number

Input: Composite graph, size of initial population, No of iteration n,   Crossover probability pcross,Mutation probability pmutate.

Output: I, Independence number of Composite graph.

Step1:Generate initial population containing valid and unique strings of colors using sequentialvertex coloring.

Step2: Compute maximum fitness value, max_fitness, of strings in current population.

Repeat up to step6 for n times

Step3: Select strings of high fitness value to generate mating pool. (Reproduction)

Repeat step4 for ncross* times

Step4:Select parents and crossover site; Perform crossover.

Check validity of new strings; if valid, replace previous one by it.

Repeat step5 for nmutate* times

Step5: Select string for mutation, site and replacing color; perform mutation.

Check validity of new strings; if valid, replace previous one by it.

Step6:Compute maximum fitness value, new_max_fitness, of the new generation population.

If new_max_fitness > max_fitness, max_fitness← new_max_fitness;

Replace current population with new generation population

Step7: I ← max_fitness

*(Compute ncross(number of crossover) from pcross and nmutate(number of mutation) from pmutate.)

4.   COMPLEXITY ANALYSIS OF MIMETIC_LBOUND

Complexity calculation in Mimetic algorithm based design is not straightforward. This paper emphasizes on finding a better non-trivial lower bound than our earlier deterministic algorithm [7]. Let us try to give some highlights of time complexity of our algorithm, Sequential vertex coloring requires $O(n^2)$, where n is the number of nets. The initial population of Genetic algorithm is thus obtained in $O(n^2)$ time complexity.

For mimetic algorithm based heuristic search, we know that it is suitable for MIMD parallel computing and distributed computing environment as these are composed by network of workstations. However we have seen that CPU time required for executing our algorithm using single Pentium4 processor is reasonable for all practical purposes.

5.   ILLUSTRATION WITH EXAMPLE

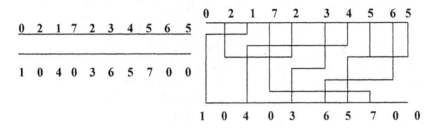

Fig5: Channel Instance and its routing

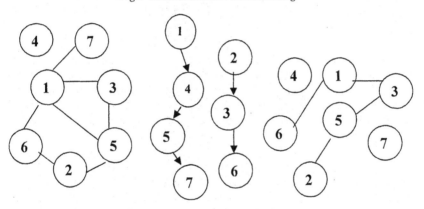

Fig6: HNCG   Fig7: VCG   Fig8: Composite graph

Using transitive closure property, the final edge list E is constructed. E={(1,5),(1,7),(4,7),(2,6)} Edges in these list indicates derived or indirect vertical constraints between corresponding nets. Among these edges, (1,5), (1,7) and (2,6) are present in HNCG and those have to be eliminated from HNCG. Deletion of those edges generates Composite graph. The Maximum Independent Set is {2,3,4,6,7}.Independence number I=5. Analyzing VCG, it is revealed that there are 2 directed paths from source to sink vertices with lengths 4(v_{max}) and 3. Those are (1->4->5->7) and (2->3->6). The source vertices 1 and 2 are horizontally constrained and the edge (1,2) is absent in HNCG. Thus *obstruction* condition is satisfied for this channel instance. So INCR=1. Hence minimum number of track requirement by our algorithm MIMETIC_LBOUND is 5+1 or 6. Practical solution shows that, the minimum number of tracks requirement is 6, Hence the result obtained by MIMETIC_LBOUND tallies with practical solution.

6.   REFINEMENT OF LOWR BOUND OF NUMBER OF TRACK REQUIREMENT THROUGH OUR ALGORITHM

Theorem: MIMETIC_LBOUND computes exact lower bound on the number of track requirement to route a channel without any approximation, and result is better or at least equal to that found in LOWER_BOUND algorithm.

We demonstrate the refinement in results achieved by MIMETIC_LBOUND in comparison to other algorithms in tabular form.

*Table 1:*Lower bound using MIMETIC_LBOUND and comparison with other algorithms

Channel Instance	d_{max}	v_{max}	Max(d_{max}, v_{max})	Lbound by our algo	CPU time	Best solution known
CH1	4	4	4	6	.002s	5
CH2	3	5	5	6	.0023s	5
CH3	4	4	4	6	.0025s	5
CH4	4	4	4	6	.0024s	5
CH5	5	5	5	7	.0034s	6
RKPC1	3	3	3	4	.002s	4
RKPC6	4	5	5	7	.11s	7
RKPC8	5	5	5	7	.06s	7
RKPC9	6	6	6	10	.16s	10
DDE	19	23	23	28	1min 54.16s	28

The result is achieved implementing MIMETIC_LBOUND in matlab using Pentium4   machine with clock frequency 1.5 GHz. CH1 through CH5 [mentioned in appendix], clearly demonstrate refinement in results. For next four channel instances [10], MIMETIC_LBOUND results tally with previous results. MIMETIC_LBOUND also provide result as good as other conventional algorithm for Deutsch's difficult example (DDE).

Table 2: Suitable values of GA parameters to obtain optimum solution for some channel instances using MIMETIC_LBOUND

Channel instance	GA related parameters for optimum Lbound			
	Initial Population	No of iteration	Crossover Probability	Mutation Probability
CH1	10	2	.4	.001
CH2	10	2	.4	.001
CH3	10	2	.4	.001
CH4	10	2	.4	.001
CH5	20	6	.8	.001
RKPC1	16	6	.8	.001
RKPC6	14	4	.6	.001
RKPC8	12	2	.4	.001
RKPC9	30	4	.8	.001
DDE	140	12	.8	.001

Regarding track minimization problem of CRP, our proposed algorithm is able to overcome approximation included in our previous paper and ascertains better results for a number of channel instances. With the help of algorithm LOWER_BOUND of previous paper [7] minimum number of tracks required to route the channel (described in section 5) is 5. This result varies from practical solution as it is an approximated result. But MIMETIC_LBOUND concludes nontrivial lower bound is 6, which tallies with the practical solution. As our approach preserves all constraint-based information in composite graph, it enhances the accuracy in result.

7.   TWO LAYER RESTRICTED DOGLEG ROUTING

For channels with multi-terminal nets, restricted doglegging often remove cycles from VCG and can route such channels. It sometimes produces better routing solution. Our algorithm can invariantly be applied for multi-terminal nets, if horizontal wire segment of such net is splitted into set of two terminal subnets and HCG (or HNCG) and VCG are constructed as follows.

For both HCG $G_H' = (V', E_1')$ and VCG $G_V' = (V', E_2')$, V' is the set of vertices corresponding to two terminal subnets of nets. If e_{1i} and e_{1j} are two subnets of net n_i and n_j respectively, then $(e_{1i}, e_{1j}) \in E_1'$ when e_{1i} and e_{1j} overlaps. HNCG G_{HN}' is obtained by complementing the edges of G_H'. For constructing edges of VCG, if net n_i and n_j both cross through some column c, where l_i and r_i are subnets of net n_i and l_j and r_j are subnets of net n_j to the right and left of column c, then directed edges $<l_i,l_j>$, $<l_i,r_j>$, $<r_i,l_j>$ and $<r_i,r_j>$ have to be introduced in VCG. Construction of HNCG and VCG and hence lower bound on number of tracks for channels with multi-terminal nets can be demonstrated by an example.

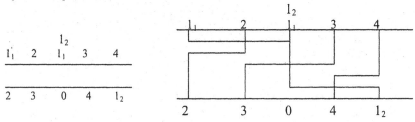

Fig9: Channel instance and its routing

VCG of this channel forms a cycle, so doglegging is applied. l_1 and l_2 are two subnets of net 1.

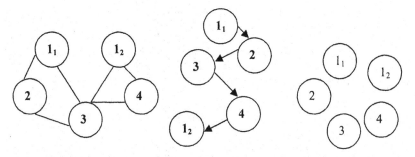

Fig10: HNCG G_{HN}'   *Fig11:VCG G_V'*   *Fig12:Composite Graph*

Composite graph is null graph. Hence Independence Number I=5 and lower bound on number of tracks requirement is also 5, which tallies with the practical solution for routing the nets, as shown.

8.   CONCLUSION

Heuristic algorithm in general, outperforms Approximation algorithm. In this paper, we tried to solve non-trivial lower bound in the restricted two layer (VH) channel routing problem. The algorithm presented is non-deterministic in nature and specifically NP hard. The deterministic version that was presented in the paper [7], approximates the problem and solved it deterministically in $O(n^4)$ time. However the solution is ratio-bound to lower bound solution. We have taken here the exact problem and solved the problem by a mimetic algorithm that gives near-optimal solution. The result is encouraging as it shows a better lower bound on number of tracks in many instances.

The extension of the work in multi-layer environment is our next projected extension of the work.

APPENDIX

```
CH1:   TOP:      0   2   1   7   2   3   4   5   6   5
       BOTTOM:1  0   4   0   3   6   5   7   0   0
CH2:   TOP:      9   8   7   5   6   1   0   0   2   4   3
       BOTTOM: 0 0   9   8   7   6   2   1   4   3   5
CH3:   TOP:      0   2   1   9   2   4   0   3   5   6   7   0
       BOTTOM:1  0   3   0   4   6   9   5   7   8   0   8
CH4:   TOP:      0   4   1   4   2   0   3   5   9   6   7   0
       BOTTOM: 1 0   3   2   6   9   5   7   0   8   0   8
CH5:   TOP:      0   4   1   11  4   2   3   5   6   7   8   0   9   0
       BOTTOM:1  0   3   0   2   6   5   7   8   9   10  11  0   10
```

REFERENCES

[1] A.S. LaPaugh, Algorithm for integrated circuit layout: An analytic approach, Ph.D.dissertation,MIT Laboratory for Computer Science, Nov. 1980.

[2] R.K Pal, S.P. Pal, A. Pal, On the Computational complexity of multiplayer channel routing, Technical Report: TR/IIT/CSE/92/02, Department of Computer Science and Engineering, Indian Institute of Technology, Kharagpur 721 302, India,1992

[3] R.K Pal, S.P. Pal, A.K. Datta, A. Pal, NP- completeness of multi-layer no-dogleg channel routing and an efficient heuristic, Proc. 6th Int. Conf. On VLSI Design, 1993, pp.80-83.

[4] G.A. Scaper, Multi-layer channel routing, Ph.D. dissertation, Computer Science Department, University of Central Florida, Orlando, Fla., Aug. 1989.

[5] M.C. Golumbic, Algorithmic Graph Theory and Perfect Graphs, Academic Press, New York, 1980

[6] Ricardo Blanco-vega, Jose Hemandez Orallo, Analyzing the Trade-off between comprehensibility & accuracy in Mimetic Models, Dept of System Informatics & Computation

[7] Integration, the VLSI journal 25(1998) pp. 71-84.

[8] Optimization for Engineering Design, Kalyanmoy Deb.

[9] Pinaki Mazumder, Elizabeth M. Rudnick, Genetic Algorithms for VLSI Design, Layout & Test automation.

[10] R.K. Pal, Multi-layer Channel Routing. Narosa Publishing House, India.

TRAINING RBF NETWORKS WITH AN EXTENDED KALMAN FILTER OPTIMIZED USING FUZZY LOGIC

Jun Wang, Li Zhu, Zhihua Cai, Wenyin Gong , Xinwei Lu
School of Computer, China University of Geosciences, Wuhan 43007, P. R. China
junwang8151@163.com

Abstract   In this paper we propose a novel training algorithm for RBF networks that is based on extended kalman filter and fuzzy logic. After the user choose how many prototypes to include in the network. the extended kalman filter simultancously solves for the prototype vectors and the weight matrix. The fuzzy logic is used to cope with the devergence problem caused by the insufficiently known a priori filter statistics. Results are presented on RBF networks as applied to the Iris classification problem. It is shown that the use of the extended Kalman filter and fuzzy logic results in faster learning and better results than conventional RBF networks.

Keywords: kalman filter, fuzzy logic, RBF networks

Please use the following format when citing this chapter:

Wang, J., Zhu, L., Cai, Z., Gong, W., Lu, X., 2006, in IFIP International Federation for Information Processing, Volume 228, Intelligent Information Processing III, eds. Z. Shi, Shimohara K., Feng D., (Boston: Springer), pp. 317–326.

1.   Introduction

Radial Basis Functions emerged as a variant of artificial neural network in late 1980's. Their excellent approximation capabilities have been studied in [1,2]. RBF networks have been successfully applied to a large diversity of applications including interpolation [6], system identification, control engineering [7], data fusion [8], etc.

Training a neural network is, in general, a challenging nonlinear optimization problem. Various derivative-based methods have been used to train neural networks, including gradient descent [3], Kalman filtering [4, 5], and back-propagation [9], etc. Gradient descent training of RBF networks has proven to be much more effective than more conventional methods [3].However; gradient descent training can be computationally expensive. Another method based on Kalman filtering proves to be quicker than gradient descent training [10]. However, a significant difficulty in designing a KF (refers to both LKF and EKF) can often be traced to incomplete a priori knowledge of the process noise covariance matrix Q and measurement noise covariance matrix R. It has been shown that insufficiently known a priori filter statistics can on the one hand reduce the precision of the estimated filter states or introduces biases to their estimates. In addition, incorrect a priori information can lead to practical divergence of the filter.

This paper extends the results of [10] and formulates a training method for RBFs based on extended kalman filter and fuzzy logic. The fuzzy logic techniques are used to adjust the R matrix of the extended kalman filter so that the method can be self-tuning and adaptive. This idea comes from [11, 12].We refer this method as FKF which means fuzzy adaptive kalman filter. There have been studies and applications on extended kalman filter and fuzzy logic. However, this paper is the first known use of these techniques to train the RBF network. We demonstrate the proformance of the method on the Iris classification problem and compare it with RBF optimization using gradient descent and extend kalman filter. It is shown that the new method converges more quickly than gradient descent and finds a better solution than extend kalman filter.

2.   RBF Network

A radial basis function (RBF) neural network is trained to perform a mapping from an m-dimensional input space to an n-dimensional output space. Suppose there are c neurons in the hidden layer. Each of the c neurons in the hidden layer applies an activation function which is a function of the Euclidean distance between the input and an m-dimensional prototype vector. Each hidden neuron contains its own prototype vector as a parameter. The output of each hidden neuron is then weighted and passed to the output layer. The outputs of the network consist of sums of the weighted hidden layer neurons.

In this paper, the RBF network is used in supervised applications. we set the hidden layer functions of the form of Eq.(1)

$$g(\| x - v \|^2) = (\| x - v \|^2 + 1)^{-\frac{1}{3}} \tag{1}$$

Where x is the input matrix and v is the prototype matrix, and $\| \cdot \|^2$ is the sum of the squares of the elements of the matrix.Our task is to minimize the training error, we can define the error function:

$$E = \frac{1}{2} \| Y - \hat{Y} \|_F^2 \tag{2}$$

Where Y is the matrix of the target (desired) value for the RBF output, $\hat{Y}$ is the matrix of the actual value of the RBF output, and $\| \cdot \|_F^2$ is the square of the Froebinius norm of a matrix, which is equal to the sum of the squares of the elements of the matrix.

3.   Fuzzy adaptive kalman filter

3.1   Extended kalman filter

The extended kalman filter is a widely used estimation algorithm.In this section we briefly outline the algorithm and give the extended kalman recursion.More details of the extended kalman filter are widely available in the literature[14]. Consider a nonlinear finite dimensional discrete time system of the form:

$$\begin{aligned} \theta_{k+1} &= f(\theta_k) + \omega_k \\ y_k &= h(\theta_{k-1}) + \nu_k \end{aligned} \tag{3}$$

Where the vector θ_k is the state of the system at time k, ω_k is the process noise, y_k is the observation vector, ν_k is the observation noise, and $f(\cdot)$ and $h(\cdot)$ are nonlinear vector functions of the state. Assume that the initial state θ_0 and the noise sequences $\{\nu_k\}$ and $\{\omega_k\}$ are Gaussian and independent from each other with $AE(\theta_0) = \bar{\theta}_0, AE[(\theta_0 - \bar{\theta}_0)(\theta_0 - \bar{\theta}_0)^T] = p_0, AE(\omega_k) = 0, AE(\omega_k\omega_t^T) = Q\delta_{kt}, AE(\nu_k) = 0, AE(\nu_k\nu_t^T) = R\nu_{kt}$, where $AE(\cdot)$ is the expectation operator and δ_{kt} is the Kronecker delta. The problem addressed by the extended Kalman filter is to find an estimated $\hat{\theta}_{n+1}$ of θ_{k+1} given y_j $(j = 0, \ldots, k)$ by the recursion

$$\begin{aligned} \hat{\theta}_k &= f(\hat{\theta}_k) + K_k[y_k - h(\hat{\theta}_{k-1})] \\ K_k &= P_k H_k (R + H_k^T P_k H_k)^{-1} \\ P_{k+1} &= F_k(P_k - K_k H_k^T P_k)F_k^T + Q \end{aligned} \tag{4}$$

where F_k and H_k^T can be obtained by

$$\begin{aligned} F_k &= \frac{\partial f(\theta)}{\partial \theta}|_{\theta=\hat{\theta}_k} \\ H_k^T &= \frac{\partial h(\theta)}{\partial \theta}|_{\theta=\hat{\theta}_k} \end{aligned} \tag{5}$$

K_k is known as the kalman gain,Q is the process noise covariance matrix and R is the measurement noise covariance matrix.

3.2   Fuzzy adaptive Kalman Filter

The optimality of the estimation algorithm in the KF setting is closely connected to the quality of a priori information about the process and measurement noise. If a priori filter statistics is insufficiently known, the precision of the estimated filter states can be reduced and biases to the estimates may be introduced. In addition, incorrect a priori information can lead to practical divergence of the filter. From the aforementioned it may be argued that the conventional KF with fixed R and/or Q should be replaced by an adaptive estimation formulation. In this paper an innovation adaptive estimation (IAE) approach coupled with fuzzy logic techniques is used to adjust the R matrix of the KF. Here the innovation Inn_k at sample time k in the KF algorithm is the difference between the real measurement y_k, received by the filter and its estimated (predicted) $\hat{y}_k$, and is computed as follows:

$$Inn_k = y_k - \hat{y}_k \tag{6}$$

The predicted measurement is the projection of the filter predicted states $\hat{\theta}_{k-1}$ onto the measurement space,

$$y_k = h(\hat{\theta}_{k-1}) \tag{7}$$

The actual covariance is defined as an approximation of the Inn_k sample covariance through averaging inside a moving estimation window of size N which takes the following form:

$$\hat{C}_{r_i} = \frac{1}{M} \sum_{i=i_0}^{N} (Inn_k Inn_k^T) \tag{8}$$

Where $i_0 = k - M + 1$ is the first sample inside the estimation window. An empirical experiment is conducted to choose the window size M. From experimentation it was found that a good size for the moving window in Eq.(8) is 15.

The theoretical covariance of the innovation sequence is defined as

$$S_k = H_k P_k^- H_k^T + R_k \tag{9}$$

The logic of the adaptation algorithm using covariance matching technique can be qualitatively described as follows. If the actual covariance value $\hat{C}_{r_i}$ is observed, whose value is within the range predicted by theory S_k and the difference is very near to zero, this indicates that both covariances match almost perfectly and only a small change is needed to be made on the value of R. If the actual covariance is greater than its theoretical value, the value of R should be decreased. On the contrary, if $\hat{C}_{r_i}$ is less than S_k, the value of R should be increased. This adjustment mechanism lends itself very well to being dealt with using a fuzzy-logic approach based on rules of the kind:

$$\text{IF} < antecedent > \text{THEN} < consequent > \tag{10}$$

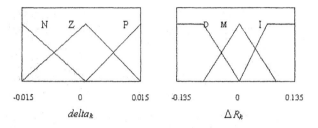

Figure 1.   Membership function of $delta_k$ and $\triangle R_k$.

Where antecedent and consequent are of the form $x \in M_i$, $y \in N_i$, $i = 1, 2, \ldots$ respectively, where x and y are the input and output variables respectively, and M_i and N_i are the fuzzy sets.

To implement the above covariance matching technique using the fuzzy logic approach, a new variable called delta, is defined to detect the discrepancy between $\hat{C}_{r_i}$ and S_k. The following three fuzzy rules of the kind (10) are used :

IF $< delta_k \cong 0 >$ THEN $< R_k$ is unchanged $>$
IF $< delta_k > 0 >$ THEN $< R_k$ is unchanged $>$
IF $< delta_k < 0 >$ THEN $< R_k$ is unchanged $>$

Thus R is adjusted according to $R_k = R_{k-1} + \triangle R_k$, where $\triangle R_k$ is added or subtracted from R at each instant of time. Here $delta_k$ is the input to the fuzzy inference system (FIS) and $\triangle R_k$ is the output.

On the basis of the above adaptation hypothesis, the FIS can be implemented using three fuzzy sets for $delta_k$; $N = Negative, Z = Zero$ and $P = Positive$. For $\triangle R_k$ the fuzzy sets are specified as $I = Increase, M = Maintain$ and $D = decrease$. The membership functions of these fuzzy sets are shown in Fig.1.

By excuting the FIS, we obtain the adjusting value $\triangle R$ of R.Thus,the extended kalman filter recursion of Eq.(4) can be modified as follows:

$$\begin{aligned}
\hat{\theta}_k &= f(\hat{\theta}_k) + K_k[y_k - h(\hat{\theta}_{k-1})] \\
K_k &= P_k H_k (R_k + H_k^T P_k H_k)^{-1} \\
R_k &= R_{k-1} + \triangle R_k \\
P_{k+1} &= F_k (P_k - K_k H_k^T P_k) F_k^T + Q
\end{aligned} \qquad (11)$$

4.   Training RBF networks with the fuzzy adaptive kalman filter

In this section we apply the fuzzy adaptive Kalman filter to the training of RBF networks. In general, we can view the optimization of the weight matrix W and the prototypes v_j as a weighted least-squares minimization problem, where the error vector is the difference between the RBF outputs and the target values for those outputs. Consider the RBF network with m inputs, c prototypes, and n outputs. We use y to denote the target vector for the RBF outputs,and $h(\hat{\theta}_k)$ to denote the actual outputs at the kth iteration of the optimization algorithm.

$$
\begin{aligned}
y &= [y_{11} \dots y_{1M} \dots y_{n1} \dots y_{nM}]^T \\
h(\hat{\theta}_k) &= [\hat{y}_{11} \dots \hat{y}_{1M} \dots \hat{y}_{n1} \dots \hat{y}_{nM}]_k^T
\end{aligned}
\tag{12}
$$

Note that the y and $\hat{y}$ vectors each consist of nM elements, where n is the dimension of the RBF output and M is the number of training samples. In order to cast the optimization problem in a form suitable for fuzzy adaptive kalman filter, we let the elements of the weight matrix W and the elements of the prototypes v_j constitute the state of a nonlinear system, and we let the output of the RBF network constitute the output of the nonlinear system to which the fuzzy adaptive kalman filter is applied. The state of the nonlinear system can then be represented as $\theta = [w_1^T \dots w_n^T v_1^T \dots v_c^T]^T$,the vector θ thus consists of all$(n(c+1)+mc)$ of the RBF parameters arranged in a linear array. The nonlinear system model to which the fuzzy adaptive kalman filter can be applied as

$$
\begin{aligned}
\theta_{k+1} &= \theta_k + \omega_k \\
y_k &= h(\theta_k) + \nu_k
\end{aligned}
\tag{13}
$$

where $h(\theta_k)$ is the RBF network's nonlinear mapping between its parameters and its output, ω_k and ν_k are artificial process noise and measurement noise added to the system model. Now we can apply the fuzzy adaptive kalman filter recursion of Eq.(11).$f(\cdot)$is the identity mapping and y_k the target output of the RBF network.(Note that although y_k written as a function of the Kalman iteration number k, it is actually a constant.) $h(\theta_k)$ is the actual output of the RBF network given the RBF parameters at the kth iteration of the fuzzy Kalman recursion. H_k is the partial derivative of the RBF output with respect to the RBF network parameters at the kth iteration of the fuzzy Kalman recursion. F_k is the identity matrix(a constant even though it is written as a function of k). The Q and R matrices are tuning parameters which can be considered as covariance matrices of the artificial noise processes and , respectively. The partial derivative of the RBF output with respect to the RBF network parameters is given by

$$
H_k = \begin{bmatrix} H_v \\ H_w \end{bmatrix}
\tag{14}
$$

where H_v is given by

$$H_v = \begin{bmatrix} -w_{11}g'_{11}2(x_1 - v_1) & \cdots & -w_{11}g'_{m1}2(x_m - v_1) & \cdots \\ \vdots & \vdots & \vdots & \vdots \\ -w_{11}g'_{11}2(x_1 - v_1) & \cdots & -w_{11}g'_{m1}2(x_m - v_1) & \cdots \end{bmatrix}$$
$$\begin{bmatrix} -w_{n1}g'_{11}2(x_1 - v_1) & \cdots & -w_{n1}g'_{m1}2(x_m - v_1) \\ \vdots & \vdots & \vdots \\ -w_{nc}g'_{1c}2(x_1 - v_c) & \cdots & -w_{nc}g'_{mc}2(x_m - v_c) \end{bmatrix} \quad (15)$$

where w_{ij} is the element in the ith row and jth column of the W weight matrix, $g'_{ij} = g'(\|x_i - v_j\|^2) = -\frac{1}{3}(\|x_i - v_j\|^2 + 1)^{-\frac{4}{3}}$ (where $g(\cdot)$ is the activation function at the hidden layer), x_i is the ith input vector, and v_j is the jth prototype vector. H_v in Eq.(15) is an $mc \times nM$ matrix. H_w is given by

$$H_w = \begin{bmatrix} H & 0 & \cdots & 0 \\ 0 & H & \cdots & 0 \\ \vdots & \vdots & \vdots & \vdots \\ 0 & \cdots & 0 & H \end{bmatrix} \quad (16)$$

Where H is given by

$$H = [h_1 \ldots h_M] = \begin{bmatrix} h_{01} & \cdots & h_{0M} \\ h_{11} & \cdots & h_{1M} \\ \vdots & \vdots & \vdots \\ h_{c1} & \cdots & h_{cM} \end{bmatrix} \quad (17)$$

Where $h_{0k} = 1(k = 1,, M), h_{jk} = g(\|x_k - v_j\|^2)(k = 1,, M), (j = 1,, c)$. H_w in Eq.(16) is an $n(c + 1) \times nM$ matrix. And H_k in Eq.(14) is an $[n(c + 1) + mc] \times nM$ Matrix. Now that we have the H_k matrix, we can execute the recursion of Eq.(11), thus using the fuzzy adaptive kalman filter in order to determine the weight matrix W and the prototypes v_j.

5. Simulations

In this section we describe and illustrate the use of fuzzy adaptive kalman filter training for the parameters of an RBF network. We tested the algorithms on the classical Iris classification problem [13]. The networks were trained to respond with the target value $y_{ik} = 1$, and $y_{jk} = 0 \ \forall j \neq i$, when presented with an input vector x_k from the ith category. The reformulated RBF networks were trained using the hidden layer function of Eq.(1). The training algorithms were initialized with prototype vectors randomly selected from the input data, and with the weight W set to 0. In order to test the performance of the algorithm, we compare the results with gradient descend and extended kalman filter from the following aspects: percent of correctly classified (Fig.1), average number of iterations required for learning convergence (Fig. 2) and average CPU time

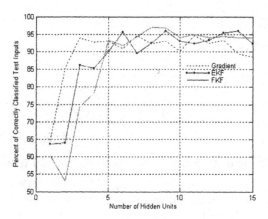

Figure 2.   Average percent of correctly classified.

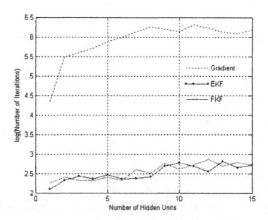

Figure 3.   Average number of iterations required for learning convergence.

required for learning convergence (Fig. 3). The gradient descent optimization algorithm was terminated when the error function of Eq.(2) decreased by less than 0.1%. The extend kalman filter parameters of Eq.(9) were initialized with $P_0 = 40I$, $Q = 40I$, and $R = 40I$, where I is the identity matrix of appropriate dimensions. The extended kalman filter recursion was terminated when the error function of Eq.(2) decreased by less than 0.1%. The fuzzy adaptive kalman filter parameters of Eq.(15) were initialized with $P_0 = 40I$, $Q = 40I$, and $R_0 = 40I$, and where I is the identity matrix of appropriate dimensions. The number of hidden units in the RBF network was varied between 1 and 15.

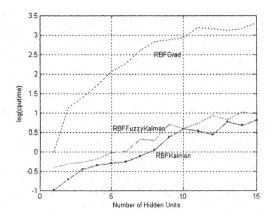

Figure 4.   Average CPU time required for learning convergence.

Fig.1. depicts the performance of the RBF network on the test data when the network was trained with gradient descent, extended kalman filter and fuzzy adaptive kalman filter. It can be seen from the figure that, at first, gradient descent training resulted in a better performing network than extended kalman filter and fuzzy adaptive kalman filter. But as the number of hidden units increases, the fuzzy adaptive kalman filter training resulted in better performance than gradient descent training and extended kalman filter training gradually. The RBF network reaches a peak performance of about 97% by the fuzzy adaptive kalman filter training while the best performance by extended kalman filter training and gradient descent training is about 96% and 95% respectively. Fig.2 shows the number of iterations required for convergence for gradient descent training, extended kalman filter training, and fuzzy adaptive kalman filter training. Fig. 3 compares the CPU time required for convergence for the three training methods. (The CPU time is measured in seconds on a Pentium(R) 4 2.93GHz CPU running MATLAB.) With just one or two hidden units, the CPU time is comparable for each of the three methods. But as the number of hidden units increases above one or two, the CPU time is required by gradient descent reaches a fully order of magnitude greater than that required by the extended kalman filter and the fuzzy adaptive kalman filter. The fuzzy adaptive kalman filter requires a little more amount of CPU time than required by the extended kalman filter. This is because that the fuzzy adaptive kalman filter requires a fraction of the computational effort to compute the fuzzy control system.

6.   Conclusion and Future Work

This paper demonstrates that how to train RBF network kalman filter. The problem with incomplete a priori knowledge of Q and R matrices is considered. An adaptive Kalman filter approach, based on the filter innovation sequence coupled with fuzzy logic techniques is discussed. A performance comparison is made among gradient descent, extended kalman filter and fuzzy adaptive kalman filter. Simulation results show that fuzzy adaptive kalman filter training converges more quickly than gradient descent training and finds a better solution than extended kalman filter training.

Further research could focus on the application of fuzzy adaptive kalman filter to other type networks. Additional efforts could be focused on applying the technique to large problems.

References

[1]Park,J., Sandberg,J.W., (1991) "Universal approximation using radial basis functions network," Neural Computation, Vol.3, 246-257.

[2]Poggio,T., Girosi , F., (1990) "Networks for approximation and learning,"Proc IEEE vol.78, no.9, 1481-1497.

[3]N. Kraryiannis, (1999) "Reformulated radial basis neural networks trained by gradient descent," IEEE Trans. Neural Networks, 3, 657-671.

[4]J. sum, C. Leung, G. Young, W. Kan, (1999) "On the Kalman Filtering method in Neural network training and pruning," IEEE Trans. Neural Networks 10, 161-166.

[5]Y. Zhang, X. Li, (1999) "A fast U-D factorization-based learning algorithm with applications to nonlinear system modeling and identification," IEEE Trans. Neural Networks 10, 930-938.

[6]Broomhead, D.S., Lowe,D. (1988) "Multivarialble functional interpolation and adaptive networks," Complex Systems, vol. 2, 321-355.

[7]Sanner, R. M., Slotine, J. J. E., (1994) "Gaussian networks for direct adaptive control," IEEE Trans. on Neural Networks, vol. 3, no. 6, 837-863.

[8]Chatzis, V., Bors, A. G., Pitas, I., (1999) "Multimodal decision-level fusion for person authentification," IEEE Trans. on Systems. Man. and Cybernetics, part A: Systems and Humans,vol.29, no.6, 674-680.

[9]R. Duro, J. Reyes, (1999) "Discrete-time backprogagation for training synaptic delay-based artificial neural networks," IEEE Trans. Nerual Networks 10, 779-789.

[10]Dan Simon, (2002) "Training radial basis neural networks with the extended Kalman filter," Neurocomputing. Vol.48, 455-475.

[11]Loebis D., Sutton R. and Chudley J. (2004) "A Fuzzy Kalman Filter Optimized Using a Multiobjective Algorithm for an Enhanced Navigation System of an Autonomous Underwater Vehicle," Proceedings of the Institution of Mechanical Engineers Part M, 218 (M1), 53-69.

[12]Loebis D., Sutton R., Chudley J. and Naeem W. "Adaptive Tuning of a Kalman Filter via Fuzzy Logic for an Intelligent AUV Navigation," System Control Engineering Practice, 12(12), November, 1531-1539.

[13]J.Bezdek, J.Kelle, R.Krishnapuram, L.Kuncheva, H.Pal, (1999) "Will the real Iris data please stand up," IEEE Trans. Fuzzy Systems 7368-369.

[14]B.Anderson,J.Moore,Optimal Filtering,Prentice-Hall,Englewood Cliffs,NJ,1979.

MRBF: A METHOD FOR PREDICTING HIV-1 DRUG RESISTANCE

Anantaporn Srisawat and Boonserm Kijsirikul
Computer Engineering Department, Chulalongkorn University, Thailand

Abstract: This paper presents the MRBF network, a new algorithm adapted from the RBF network, to construct the classifiers for predicting phenotypic resistance on 6 protease inhibitors. The performance of the prediction was measured by 10-fold cross-validation. The results show that MRBF gives the lowest average mean square error (MSE) when compared with the traditional RBF network and multiple linear regression analysis (REG). Moreover, it provides the best average predictive accuracy when compared with HIVdb, REG, and Support Vector Machines (SVM).

Key words: RBF Network, RReliefF, predicting HIV-1 drug resistance

1. INTRODUCTION

Nowadays, there are seventeen approved antiretroviral agents: seven drugs for Nucleoside Reverse Transcriptase Inhibitor (NRTI), three drugs for Non-Nucleoside Reverse Transcriptase Inhibitor (NNRTI), and seven drugs for Protease Inhibitor (PI), but HIV-1 therapies are still not very successful. The limit of treatment success is the decrease of the viral sensitivity to the drug called drug resistance. The cause of drug resistance is the mutations in the reverse transcriptase (RT) and protease enzymes of HIV-1. In addition, it has been estimated that every possible single point mutation occurs between 10^4 and 10^5 times per day in an untreated HIV-1 infected individual and that double mutants also occur commonly [1]. Thus resistance testing is an important role in management of HIV infections.

Currently there are two methodologies for resistance testing: genotyping and phenotyping [2]. For genotyping, resistance testing can be performed by scanning the viral genome for resistance-associated mutations, where phenotyping can be performed by measuring viral activity in the presence and absence of drug. The

Please use the following format when citing this chapter:

Srisawat, A., Kijsirikul, B., 2006, in IFIP International Federation for Information Processing, Volume 228, Intelligent Information Processing III, eds. Z. Shi, Shimohara K., Feng D., (Boston: Springer), pp. 327–336.

advantages of genotyping are faster and cheaper than phenotyping. On the other hand, phenotypic results are easier to interpret than genotypic results because the phenotypic results are represented by a single number for each drug called fold change.

The fold change refers to the fraction between 50% inhibitory drug concentration value (IC_{50}) of the patient's virus to the IC_{50} value of the standardized wild type virus ($IC_{50(patient)}/IC_{50(reference)}$). If the fold change is above a certain value called cutoff the virus is resistant to that drug.

To overcome the drawbacks of genotyping and phenotyping methods, the advantage of genotyping and phenotyping are combined by using genotypic data to predict phenotypic results. This paper proposes a new method, called Multi-RBF (MRBF) network. This method applied the Radial Basis Function (RBF) network for predicting the fold change of 6 protease inhibitors (PI): saquinavir (SQV), indinavir (IDV), ritonavir (RTV), nelfinavir (NFV), amprenavir (APV), and lopinavir(LPV).

Since the number of amino acid positions of HIV-1 protease gene is quite large (99 positions), we also used the RReliefF algorithm [3], a feature subset selection technique, to select the amino acid positions that are considered to be relevant to the drug susceptibility and eliminate irrelevant amino acid positions.

2.   RELATED WORKS

A variety of techniques have been applied to predict phenotype from genotype such as rule-based, statistical analysis, and machine learning techniques. The phenotypic results from these techniques are classified into two or more classes of drug susceptibility depending on the certain cutoff values.

Rule-based algorithms such as HIVdb [4], ANRS [5], Rega [6], and VGI [7] contain the rules encoding information from the medical literature as the knowledge base. The HIVdb system used the mutation scoring tables to calculate a score from each sequence and interpreted drug susceptibility into one of five classes ranging from susceptible to high-level resistant.

For statistical analysis, multiple linear regression analysis (REG) was applied to construct a separate regression model for each drug [8]. In the model, the dependent variable is the logarithm of the IC50 fold change, while the independent variables are dummy variables corresponding to mutations. In addition, this technique used the stepwise regression method to optimize the parameters for each independent variable.

Besides rule-based and statistical analysis, machine learning is the most popular approach applied to predict phenotype from genotype. Many supervised learning algorithms have been used to deal with this problem such as decision trees [9, 10], support vector machines (SVMs) [9, 11], and artificial neural networks (ANNs) [12]. These algorithms classify drug susceptibility into one of two classes:

susceptible or resistant. Furthermore, the self-organizing map (SOM), an unsupervised learning algorithm, was used to classify drug susceptibility into one of three classes: high, medium, or low resistant [13].

3. RADIAL BASIS FUNCTION (RBF) NETWORK

The RBF network is an approach for function approximation that is closely related to distance-weighted regression and also to artificial neural networks [14, 15, 16]. The construction of the traditional RBF network involves three layers with entirely different roles as illustrated in Figure 1.

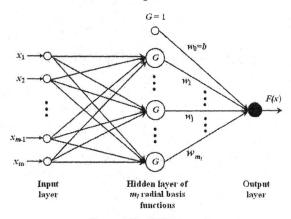

Figure 1. The RBF Network

As shown in Figure 1, the RBF network consists of three layers [17]. The first layer is composed of input nodes whose number is equal to the dimension of the input vector. The second layer is a hidden layer. This layer consists of nonlinear units that are connected directly to all of the nodes in the input layer. The activation functions of the individual hidden units are defined by a Gaussian function. The output layer consists of a single linear combination unit, being fully connected to the hidden layer. In this approach, the value of the output unit is a function given in (1).

$$F(x) = w_0 + \sum_{i=1}^{m_1} w_i G(\|x - t_i\|)$$ (1)

where m_1 is the number of centers, vector t represents the center points, vector w is the weights in the output layer, and G is the Gaussian function (see Figure 1).

In training step, the weight vector w in the output layer of the network will be calculated by matrix computation as shown in (2).

$$w = G^+ d$$ (2)

Where G^+ is the pseudo inverse of matrix G defined in (3) and d is the desired response vector in the training set.

$$G^+ = (G^T G)^{-1} G^T \tag{3}$$

where
$$G = \{g_{ji}\} \tag{4}$$

$$g_{ji} = \exp\left(-\frac{\|x_j - t_i\|^2}{2\sigma_i^2}\right) \tag{5}$$

where $i=j=1,2,\ldots,m_1$, x_j is the j th input vector of the training sample and t_i is the i th vector of the center and σ denotes the width of the Gaussian function.

4.   MULTI RBF (MRBF) NETWORK

To improve the performance of the RBF network in estimating the IC50 fold change (FC) for predicting HIV-1 drug resistance, we present a new approach called Multi RBF (MRBF) network. The idea of MRBF is to separately construct the RBF networks class by class to increase the ability of estimating the output value. This method consists of three RBF networks: RBF-all, RBF-S, and RBF-R for estimating the IC50 fold change. The construction of an MRBF network is shown in Figure 2.

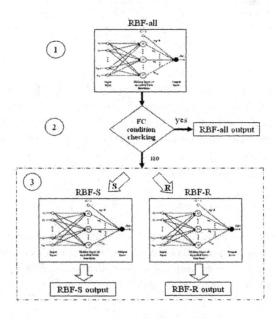

*Figure 2.*The MRBF Network

In the MRBF learning step, the calculation of vector w of each network of the MRBF is the same as the RBF network described in section 3. The center vectors in a hidden layer of 3 networks have to be determined in a different way. The centers of the RBF-all network are whole training examples whereas the RBF-S uses only the training examples belonging to the susceptible class and vice versa for the RBF-R network.

There are three parts in the testing process of the MRBF network. First, an RBF-all network (see Figure 2) roughly estimates the FC of an instance x , then it uses the logarithm of the cutoff value to classify the FC of the instance x into one of two classes: susceptible or resistance.

The second part is called FC condition checking. This step checks the output of the instance x from the RBF-all network with two criteria. The criteria are following.
1. FC falls in the boundary zone.
2. The class labels between RBF-all and kNN algorithm are different.

If the FC satisfies both criteria, the final FC of the instance x is the output from the RBF-all network, and the testing process is terminated. If any of them is not satisfied, the instance x will be fed into the RBF-S or RBF-R network.

The boundary zone in the first criterion has the value between cutoff-*bound* and cutoff+*bound*, where *bound* is calculated by (6).

$$bound = \sqrt{\frac{\sum_{i=1}^{n}(FC_i - cutoff)^2}{n}} \qquad (6)$$

where n is total training instances, FC_i is target value of the training instance i.

For the second criterion, kNN classification is used to measure the confidence of the prediction from the RBF-all network. In another word, if the output of RBF-all is the same as that of kNN, it is probable that RBF-all gives the correct classification result, and thus the instance x is fed to the third part to estimate more precise FC. On the other hand, if the output of RBF-all and kNN are not the same, the testing process is terminated since RBF-all may misclassify. This condition prevents feeding the instance x into the wrong network in the third step. As the distance between the training instances are already computed in the learning process of RBF-all, kNN is a suitable technique for checking the confidence of the RBF-all network.

In the third part, the instance x is fed again into another RBF network: RBF-S or RBF-R depending on its class label. If the FC from RBF-all of the instance x is labeled as susceptible, the instance x will be an input of the RBF-S network. On the other hand, it will be fed into the RBF-R, if its output is labeled as resistant. Finally, the final FC of instance x is the output from the corresponding network.

5.   FEATURE SELECTION PROCESS

Since the total amino acid positions of HIV-1 protease gene are 99 and some of them are irrelevant or redundant, these attributes may decrease the performance of the learning algorithm. To solve this problem, we used feature selection techniques to select important attributes in the preprocessing step.

Moreover, the time complexity of learning the RBF network is depended on the number of dimension of the input. It takes $O(mn^2)$ for calculating Gaussian functions of the hidden layer, where m is the number of input nodes and n is the number of training instances. When an amino acid position is transformed to a vector of the input node of the RBF network, each amino acid position provides 20 binary input nodes (there are 20 variables of amino acids which may occur in any position). As there are 99 positions in the sequence of an HIV-1 protease gene, the number of input node is 1980. Thus, it takes a lot of time in the MRBF learning step. For that reason, if we use feature selection techniques to select some important amino acid positions (or attributes) to construct the MRBF model instate of using all positions, the number of the input nodes will be reduced significantly. Subsequently the learning time is decreased.

In this paper, three different approaches of feature selection techniques are used in the preprocessing process: Allmutant, Rule-based, and RReliefF. In Allmutant approach, the attribute with only one value on the total transactions of each drug was eliminated. For Rule-based, we selected the important attributes, recommenced by Stanford HIV Drug Resistance Database and [18]. For RReliefF, we ran RReliefF, a classical feature estimation algorithm, to select important attributes for each drug. The main idea of RReliefF is to estimate the weight of each attribute according to how well its value distinguishes between instances that are near to each other [3]. Using RReliefF, we selected the attributes, which have the weight higher than or equal to θ, where θ was set to 0.01. Table 1 shows the number of input attributes selected by each feature selection approach.

Table 1. The number of input attributes for each feature selection approaches

Feature selection approach	Number of input attributes for each drug					
	LPV	APV	NFV	IDV	SQV	RTV
Allmutant	72	77	78	78	78	78
Rule-based	19	19	18	20	16	19
RReliefF	33	27	22	27	28	26

6.   EXPERIMENTS

6.1   Data source

In the experiments, genotype-phenotype data for 6 protease inhibitors were downloaded from Stanford HIV RT and Protease Sequence Database (http://hivdb.stanford.Edu/cgi-bin/PR_Phenotype.cgi) with the ViroLogic Susceptibility test method. The total cases and the cutoff value for each PI drug are shown in Table 2. The phenotypic results were assigned into one of two classes: susceptible or resistant according to the cutoff value of each PI. Each case of genotype-phenotype data was compared with HIV reference strain NL4-3 to create the full strain of HIV-1 protease gene as the input of the MRBF network.

Table 2. Total case and cutoff value for each PI drug

PI drug	LPV	APV	NFV	IDV	SQV	RTV
Number of cases	319	541	626	595	606	573
Cutoff value	10.0	2.0	2.5	2.1	1.7	2.5

6.2   Prediction by RBF and MRBF

For constructing the classifiers using the RBF network, each training example was represented as a center in the hidden layer and σ for each center was set to the same value. Thus the number of hidden nodes is equal to the number of total training examples. The target value is the logarithm of the IC50 fold change. We used the logarithm of IC50 fold change because the distributions of IC50 fold change are usually highly range because of a few highly resistant variants.

For constructing the classifiers using the MRBF network, we also set the value of σ as same as in the RBF network. In the preprocessing process of the MRBF network, we selected one of three feature selection approaches which has the highest predictive accuracy of the RBF network. Since the outputs of the MRBF network are real values representing the fold change, to evaluate the performance of the MRBF network and other algorithms, the outputs are classified into two classes: susceptible and resistant according to the logarithm of the cutoff values described in section 6.1 and used 10-fold cross-validation to assess the predictive accuracy.

6.3   Prediction by other algorithms

The predictive accuracy of the MRBF network was compared with the HIVdb system, REG, SVM, and the original RBF network. The phenotypic prediction by HIVdb was done through the HIVdb version 4.1.2 online system (http://hivdb6.stanford.edu/asi/deployed/HIVdb.html). For REG, the prediction of this technique was done through the statistics software SPSS version 12. For SVM classification, a linear kernel function was used to construct the classifier. In addition, RReliefF was used for selecting the relevant attributes in the preprocessing step of SVM. The performance of the prediction of REG, SVM, and the conventional RBF were measured by 10-fold cross-validation on the same datasets as those of the MRBF network.

7.   RESULTS

In the learning step, the classifiers of the three models with different input attributes depending on each feature selection approach in Table 1 were constructed by the conventional RBF network. The predictive accuracy of each model is shown in Table 3.

Table 3. The predictive accuracy for three feature selection approaches

Drug	Allmutant	Rule-based	RReliefF
LPV	**88.70**	87.16	88.06
APV	**89.82**	89.82	88.34
NFV	92.97	**93.29**	**93.29**
IDV	91.58	92.60	**93.93**
SQV	88.93	89.25	**90.91**
RTV	92.32	93.89	**94.94**
Average	90.72	91.00	**91.58**

The result in Table 3 shows that most of the drugs, using RReliefF in the preprocessing step, have the highest accuracy, compared with the other feature selection approaches. In addition, RReliefF also has the highest average accuracy of 6 drugs. From this result, it confirmed that RReliefF efficiently selected attributes important to data classification. Thus, in the following experiments, we used the important attributes that were selected by RReliefF for the MRBF network and SVM.

Table 4. The comparison of MSE with various algorithms

Drug	REG	RBF+RReliefF	MRBF+RReliefF
LPV	0.148	0.189	**0.121**
APV	0.163	0.157	**0.116**
NFV	0.180	**0.110**	0.113
IDV	0.135	**0.092**	0.094
SQV	0.184	0.154	**0.144**
RTV	0.118	0.114	**0.105**
Average	0.155	0.136	**0.115**

The result in Table 4 shows that most of the drugs of MRBF have the smaller mean square error (MSE) than the RBF network. It indicates that MRBF improved the performance of the traditional RBF network in estimating the fold change values. Furthermore, MRBF provided the lower MSE than REG for all drugs.

Table 5. The comparison of the accuracy for various algorithms

Drug	HIVdb	REG	SVM+RReliefF	MRBF+RReliefF
LPV	73.98	83.35	88.09	**89.01**
APV	85.58	85.01	87.79	**88.16**
NFV	**94.25**	92.82	93.30	93.93
IDV	92.10	90.74	92.43	**93.77**
SQV	86.80	88.44	88.94	**90.75**
RTV	94.24	93.54	94.41	**95.46**
Average	87.83	88.98	90.83	**91.85**

As shown in Table 5, MRBF with RReliefF has the highest average accuracy when compared with HIVdb, REG, and SVM. Furthermore the predictive accuracy of MRBF also outperforms the others in 5 drugs expect for NFV.

8.   CONCLUSION

This paper presents MRBF network, a new method adapted from the RBF network, to predict HIV-1 phenotypic resistance from genotypic data. The main idea of MRBF is to separately construct the RBF networks class by class to increase the ability of estimating the phenotypic value (FC). The MRBF network consists of three RBF networks: RBF-all, RBF-S, and RBF-R. In the first step of testing MRBF, an RBF-all network roughly estimates the FC. Then, FC from the RBF-all network is checked with two criteria. Finally, if any of the criteria is not satisfied, the RBF-S or RBF-R network is used to estimate more precise FC.

To enhance the performance of the classifier, we also used three different feature selection approaches for selecting the relevant attributes in the preprocessing step. Experimental results on the RBF network show that RReliefF gives the highest average accuracy for 6 drugs compared with other feature selection techniques. Then we used RReliefF in the preprocessing step of MRBF and SVM.

The results indicate that MRBF improves the ability of RBF in estimating the fold change values. In conclusion, MRBF has high ability in predicting HIV-1 drug resistance since it provides the highest predictive accuracy for 5 drugs except for NFV when compared with other techniques such as HIVdb, REG, and SVM.

ACKNOWLEDGEMENTS

This work was supported by National Center for Genetic Engineering and Biotechnology (BIOTEC), Thailand.

REFERENCES

1. J.M. Coffin, "HIV population dynamics in vivo: implications for genetic variation, pathogenesis, and therapy", *Science*, vol. 267, 1995, pp. 483-489.
2. L. Demeter, R. Haubrich, "Phenotypic and genotypic resistance assays: methodology, reliability, and interpretations", *Journal of Acquired Immune Deficiency Syndromes*, vol. 26, 2001, pp. S3-S9.
3. M. Robnik Sikonja and I. Kononenko, "An adaptation of relief for attribute estimation in regression", *Machine Learning: Proceedings of the Fourteenth International Conference (ICML '97)*, 1997, pp. 296-304.
4. R.W. Shafer, D.R. Jung, B.J. Betts, "Human immunodeficiency virus type 1 reverse transcriptase and protease mutation search engine for queries", *NAT Med*, vol. 6, 2000, pp. 1290-1292.
5. JL. Meynard, M. Vray, L. Morand-Joubert, et al, "Phenotypic or genotypic resistance testing for choosing antiretroviral therapy after treatment failure: a randomized trial", *AIDS*, vol. 16, 2002, pp. 727-736.
6. K. Van Laethem, A. Ke Luca, A, Antinori, et al. "A genotypic drug resistance interpretation algorithm that significantly predicts therapy response in HIV-1 infected patients", *Antiviral Ther*, vol. 7, 2002, pp. 123-129.
7. C. Reid, R. Bassett, S. Day, et al, "A dynamic rules-based interpretation system derived by an expert panel is predictive of virological failure", *Antiviral Ther*, vol. 7, 2002, pp. s91.
8. K. Wang,, E. Jenwitheesuk, , R. Samudrala, J.E. Mitter, "Simple linear model provides highly accurate genotypic predictions of HIV-1 drug resistance", *Antivir. Ther*, vol. 9, 2004, pp. 343-352.
9. N. Beerenwinkel, B. Schmidt, H. Walter, R. Kaiser, T. Lengauer, D. Hoffmann,K. Korn, and J. Selbig, "Geno2pheno: interpreting genotypic HIV drug resistance test", *IEEE Intellig. Syst*, vol. 16, 2001, pp. 35-41.
10. N. Beerenwinkel, B. Schmidt, H. Walter, R. Kaiser, T. Lengauer, D. Hoffmann, K. Korn, and J. Selbig, "Diversity and complexity of HIV-1 drug resistance: a bioinformatics approach to prediction phenotype from genotype", *Proceedings of Natl Acad. Sc*, USA, 2002, pp. 8271-8276.
11. N. Beerenwinkel, M. Daumer, M. Oette, K. Korn, D. Hoffmann, R. Kaiser, T. Lengauer, J. Selbig, and H. Walter, "Geno2Pheno: estimating phenotypic drug resistance from HIV-1 genotypes", *Nucleic Acids Research*, vol. 31, 2003, pp. 3850-3855.
12. D. Wang and B. Larder, "Enhanced prediction of lopinavir resistance from genotype by use of artificial neural networks", *Infectious Disease*, vol. 188, 2003, pp. 653-660.
13. S. Draghici and B. Potter, "Predicting HIV drug resistance with neural networks", *Bioinformatics*, vol. 19, 2003, pp. 98-107.
14. M. Powell, "Radial basis function for multivariable interpolation: A review", *Algorithms for approximation*, 1987, pp. 143-167.
15. D. S. Broomhead and D. Lowe, "Mutivariable functional interpolation and adaptive networks", *Complex System 2*, 1988, pp. 321-355.
16. J. Moody and C. J. Darken, "Fast learning in networks of locally-tuned processing units", *Neural Computation*, 1(2), 1989, pp. 281-294.
17. S. Haykin, *Neural Networks: A comprehensive foundation*, Prentice Hall, New Jersey, 1999, pp. 256-312.
18. S. W. Robert, "Genotypic Testing for Human Immunodeficiency Virus Type 1 Drug Resistance", *Clinical Microbiology Regviews*, vol. 15, 2002, pp. 247-277.

THE PGNN FOR THE DIFFERENTIATION OF SYNDROMES OF THE KIDNEY

Yun Wu[1] Changle Zhou[2] Zhifeng Zhang[3]

[1] Institute of Artificial Intelligence, XiaMen University, FuJian XiaMen 361005, China
{E-mail: yininwu@126.com}
[2] Institute of Artificial Intelligence, XiaMen University, FuJian XiaMen 361005, China
{E-mail: dozero@xmu.edu.cn}
[3] Shanghai University of Traditional Chinese Medicine, ShangHai 201203, China
{E-mail: rchbt@163.com}

Abstract: The research into the impersonality and information of the Traditional Chinese-medicine Diagnosis (TCMD) is recognized to be a crucial work, especially for the Traditional Chinese-medicine (TCM) medicine examination system. However the tongue is like a mirror of the Viscera, and the pathological changes of them can reflect on the tongue. So according the information of the Sizhen for the syndromes of the Kidney, we design the initial structure of the PGNN(Probabilistic Genetic Neural Network), and its connection weight and the structure of the PGNN automatically will be optimized by the GA and others optimal way. It is certain that the groping research will be use for the modernization of the TCM.

Keywords: TCMD (Traditional Chinese Medical Diagnosis); Differentiation of Syndromes of the Viscera; Syndromes of the Kidney; PGNN; Genetic Algorithm (GA).

1. INTRODUCTION

Sizhen is the crucial way to collect information for the TCM diagnosis, specially the inspection of the tongue, which is the symptom information. Because in the clinic it has been proved that the symptom of the tongue changed rapidly and brilliantly during the developing of the diseases. It is like a mirror of the Viscera, and the pathological changes can reflect on the tongue, namely the symptom information of the tongue is changed. So it

Please use the following format when citing this chapter:

Wu, Y., Zhou, C., Zhang, Z., 2006, in IFIP International Federation for Information Processing, Volume 228, Intelligent Information Processing III, eds. Z. Shi, Shimohara K., Feng D., (Boston: Springer), pp. 337–345.

becomes the important evidence for the TCMD. But in fact, only using the symptom information of the tongue to diagnose the Syndromes of the Viscera is not enough, so some others common manifestations are also used auxiliarily.

Many successful medicine systems are based on the theory of the western medicine, which uses the symbol processing method to express the medicine information. It is mostly because the computer can process the formalized information of the western medicine. But this way does not suit the TCMD, which information is fuzzy, incomplete and unclear. If we also use the symbol processing method to express the information of the TCMD, it will easily lose much important information, and lots of information can not be processed, which makes the system has low validity.

So the TCM medical examination system which we design integrates some AI technologies, such as logic, ANN (Artificial Neural Network), GA, and others soft computing. The main theories are: First according the characteristics of the manifestation, and get the logical rule. Second construct the ANN for every kind of the TCMD diagnosis. The common ANN has very weak automaticity, which can not satisfy the variety of the TCM clinic, so using the Probabilistic GNN to construct the TCMD NN database. In the practices, the TCM medical examination system will select ANN form TCMD ANN database to compute the diagnosis result. So the computing capability of the TCMD ANN is the most important knowledge database to the TCM medical examination system.

This paper is organized as follows. In section 2, we mainly present the PGNN, which base on the symptoms of tongue and others common information for the differentiation of syndromes of the Kidney. In section 3, we introduce the improved GA to optimize the PGNN, which forms are presented in section 2. In section 4, the test results are discussed. The conclusions and the future work are disused in section 5.

2.   THE PGNN FOR THE DIFFERENTIATION OF SYNDROMES OF THE KIDNEY

2.1   The structure of the PGNN for the Differentiation of Syndromes of the Kidney

The initial PGNN is a forward NN, which consists of three layers. The first layer is the input layer (the $x_i \in [0,1]$), generally consisting of sixty neural cells determined by the symptom manifestations. The second layer is the hidden layer, which is determined initially by our experience, but finally is determined by input training set. The last layer is the output layer, which has generally the same size as the syndromes which need to be diagnosed by the PGNN. The initial structure is shown in figure1.

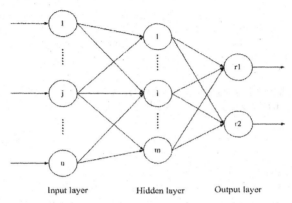

Input layer   Hidden layer   Output layer

Figure 1. the three-layer PGNN's structure

2.2 The region division of the tongue

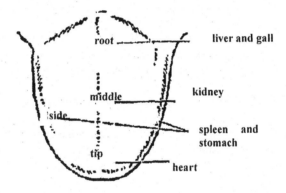

Figure 2. the division of the tongue body

During clinical practice, human discover the pathological changes of the bowels can reflect to the change of the tongue features. So it has been formed the dissertation that the pathological changes of the viscera will be reflected on the tongue, and the pathological changes of the different viscera organs will reflect on different subareas of the tongue. Usually the tongue would be divided five subareas[1], as show in picture 2, according to the symptoms on the different subareas, the diagnosis system will select different ANN from the diagnosis ANN database. The sides of the tongue reflect the pathological changes of the liver and gall. The tip of the tongue reflects the pathological changes of the heart. The middle of the tongue reflects the pathological changes of the spleen and stomach. The root of the tongue reflects the pathological changes of the kidney. So if some viscera organs have pathological changes, some symptoms will appear on the subareas of the tongue. So if the kidney has some disease, the root of the tongue will have some unusual symptom manifestations.

2.3   The symptoms information of the Differentiation of Syndromes of the Kidney

The symptom manifestations of the tongue are sorted to thirty-one, such as:
The color of the tongue body: light white; light red; crimson; bluish purple.
The shape quality of the tongue body: tender; old; fat; thin; fissured; prickled; emaciated; petechia; canker; Teeth-printed.
The state of the tongue: wry; tremulous; stiff; shortened; flaccid.
The color of the coating: white; yellow; gray-black.
The color of the tongue vessel: light color; deep color.
The proper of the coating: thin; thick; moist; dry; greasy; crude; exfoliative;
These informations of the tongue are very important to diagnose the syndrome. For example, if the color of the root of the tongue body is yellow, the kidney maybe has the hot syndrome. So each symptom like that is an input neural cell in the Probabilistic GNN. This information is summed up form the clinic case of the Shanghai University of Traditional Chinese Medicine and the Hospital of Taicang, which are our cooperators.

2.4   Others manifestation of symptoms

In order to improve the validity of the diagnosis, some others common symptom manifestations are added, which are auxiliary informations to differentiate the Syndrome of the Kidney Disease. Such as, Interrogation informations: fearing cold; fearing heat; the pain (such as head; chest; coerce; stomach; abdomen; waist; extremity, est.); the state of the head and the body (such as swirling; swimming; thin; fat, est.).
For the sake of confirming the correction of the diagnosis, those informations are also necessary.

2.5   The PGNN

According the symptoms manifestations of the patient, the Probabilistic NN differentiates the syndrome can be simply abstract to this formula:

$$f(R \times C \times D) \rightarrow p(x_1) \times p(x_2) \times \cdots \times p(x_n)$$

The R means the set of the subareas of the tongue body; the C means the set of all the unusual symptom manifestations of the tongue; the D means the set of all the others unusual symptom manifestations. f is a value function that is used to compute the strong-wreak degree of the syndrome's appearing. The $x_1, x_2, \ldots, x_n$ means there are n syndromes is needed to diagnose, the $0 \le p(x_i) \le 1$ is the appearing probability of the x_i syndrome. So in here, the probability of the symptom manifestations in the sets of the R, C and D is the input value of the Probabilistic NN, the $p(x_i)$ is the output value of the Probabilistic GNN, the f is just the Probabilistic NN. According the experience of the TCM expert, there is a threshold α is needed, which compare with the $p(x_i)$. If $\alpha \le p(x_i)$, the x_i syndrome maybe appear, else it maybe not. At the same time, in order to make the Probabilistic NN is the best for the CTMD, the structure and the link-value of the Probabilistic NN is optimized by the Genetic Algorithm, which is the Probabilistic GNN (PGNN).

3.   THE OPTIMIZING ALGORITHM

The main steps of the GA for optimizing the PGNN are:

(1). Hybrid encoding. The neural network (PGNN) is written to one real-valued two-matrix and one binary-valued two-matrix. The real-valued matrix shows the link-weights of the network. The other matrix shows the validity of the link between neurons and the link-weights, which is propitious to adjust the construction of the PGNN.

(2). Initialization. Randomly generate an initial population of the PGNN, which has the characters talked above. Before next step, each network is partially trained, which can avoid overstraining. At the same time, given the error value $\delta > 0$.

(3). Fitness function. The stylebook data are divided into two sets, namely training set (T) and validation set (V), which will be adjusted properly during the computing process. After partially trained, calculate the fitness of each PGNN. The fitness function is:

$$f(x) = \alpha \times E(T) + \beta \times D(N) + \gamma \times L(N)$$

$$E(T) = \frac{1}{MSE(x)}$$

The $D(N)$ is the number of the hidden neural cells. The $L(N)$ is the number of the links. It means that the PGNN whose size is small is better than whose size is big, even if they have the same $E(T)$. The α, β and γ are fixed parameter.

(4). Genetic operation. In order to keep the good genes, K individuals whose fitness is good are directly copied to next generation. The others offspring comes from these operators.

① Selection: According the fitness, the ith individual is selected with such probabilistic of

$$p_i = \frac{f(x_i)}{\sum_{i=1}^{m} f(x_i)}$$

If the $\eta < p_i$, the individual is selected. The η is a random number.

② Crossover. In order to avoid the permutation, this is a difficult resolved problem in the structure adjustment. It means that after the crossover operation, the structure of the PGNN maybe became invaluable. So in this algorithm, the crossover operation has been canceled.

③ Mutation. Select individuals and conduct mutations according to the current mutation rate p_m. Considering the method of the case learning which are always applied in the TCM expert systems, so the mutation uses the thought of PSO[4], namely according the fitness of the best individual and the worst individual, randomly select two individuals, such as i and j, then mutation is implemented as follows:

$$x'_{i,j} = x_{i,j} + \phi_1 \times (f(p_g(t)) - f(x_{i,j})) + \phi_2 \times (f(p_d(t)) - f(x_{i,j}))$$

the $p_g(t)$ is the best evolutionary PGNN of the all generation, $p_d(t)$ is the best evolutionary PGNN of this generation, $\phi_1, \phi_2 \in [-1,1]$ are random number. This method simulates the thought of TCM case learning, and is propitious to the convergence of the GA.

(5). Structure adjustment. If those operations can not prove the calculating capability of the PGNN, then adjust its structure. They include four operators. The first one is deleting one link between two hidden neural cells. The second is deleting on hidden neural cell, so the links between the deleted cell and others hidden cell are also delete. The third is adding one link between two hidden cells. And at last it is adding one hidden neural cell. As usually, the deleting operation is preceded the add operation, which is benefit for keeping the structure of the PGNN is small. In one time, as long as one operation works, the others operators do not be used and return to make a new computing.

(6). Ending condition. If the maximal evolutionary epoch is reached or the error value is less than the α, the optimizing process is over.

4.   DISCUSSION

The test data come from the Shanghai University of Traditional Chinese Medicine and the Hospital of Taicang. So in the test-data, there are hundred data come from the reference book[1], fifty clinical data(the Deficiency of the Kidney-yang or the Deficiency of the kidney-yin) comes form the Shanghai University of Traditional Chinese Medicine and the Hospital of Taicang. In next works, we will increase the clinical data to test it.
In the optimizing process, the error value is shown as Figure 3.

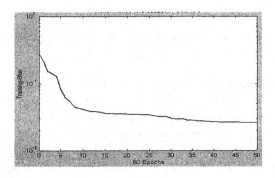

Figure 3. the training graph.

After learning the clinical data, the diagnosis result of the PGNN could be consist with the clinic cases, which in the T set, but to the clinic cases in the S set, the correct ratio is about 70%. But not stable. however the PGNN exhibits the capability to distinguish the Deficiency of the Kidney-yang and the Deficiency of the kidney-yin, if the patient has the clinical manifestations of the Deficiency of the Kidney-yang or the Deficiency of the kidney-yin, such as lassitude in the loins and knees, cold limbs, feeling listless and inert; swollen tongue with white fur. If the probability of these clinical manifestations is more than 60% and there are not any other conflict information, the PGNN can diagnosis the patient who has the Deficiency of the Kidney-yang. So if the PGNN can learn more useful information form the clinical cases, it will be more stabile. But the computing time will be up.

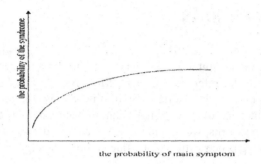

Figure 4. the approximate relationship between of the syndrome and the single main symptom.

As shown in figure 4, a disease will appear some symptom with high probability. And the probability of the symptom is higher, the ratio of the syndrome is higher. But following the probability of the symptom up, the ratio of the syndrome stop going up (it is concluded form the experiment result, which adjust the probabilistic of one main symptom and only a trend line). For example the white tongue coating is the main symptom of the Deficiency of the Yang on tongue. If we increase the input probabilistic value, the probability of the Deficiency of the Yang will be up. But if we continue to increase the value, the value of the output will be stop to up. So in some degree, it makes us sure that if we can correctly conclude the main symptom of the syndrome, the PGNN can resolve some TCMD computing problems, which maybe still has some subjectivity.

On the other side, the PGNN also can better process some problems than the traditional symbol technique, such as indeterminable information; low-efficiency learning capability, and the difficulty to manage the information DB, which is decided by the characteristic of the PGNN. And it also can automatically learn information from the training data to adjust itself, which lowers these demerits, such as the TCM expert's knowledge is deficient. And can prove the automaticity, reliability, validity and the intelligence of the TCM medicine examination system.

5.   CONCLUSION

This paper discusses the PGNN, which is used to TCMD——the Differentiation Syndromes of the Kidney based on the Sizhen information, especially the symptom of the tongue. And after optimizing the weight value and the structure of the PGNN by the GA, the PGNN has better performance than common NN. In some degreed, it can diagnose the viscera syndromes correctly, but in some clinic data, it difficultly differentiate the syndromes, specially the clinic manifestations is not evidence, even if there are some conflict or faintness symptoms manifestations appear on the patient. So it need to add others technique to solve these information—Fuzzy technique, and some others optimized ways, which is our next research works.

REFERENCES

1. Wenfeng Zhu，Traditional Chinese Medicine Diagnostics [M]Beijing：Chinese Medicaments Press，2004
2. Nenggan Zhang，TCM-SIRD:An Intergrated Aided System for Traditional Chinese Medicine Sizheng[J]，2004 IEEE International Conference on System, Man and Cybernetics，2004，(3864-3868)
3. Xuezhong Zhou，TCMMDB:A Distributed MultiDatabase Query System and It's Key Technique Implement，2004，IEEE(1095-1098)
4. Chia-Feng Juang，On The Hybrid of Genetic Algorithm and Particle Swarm Optimization For Evolving Recurrent Neural Network，2004，IEEE (2285-2288)
5. Z.-H Tan，Hybrid evolutionary approach for designing neural networks for classification，ELECTRONICS LETTERS 22nd July 2004 Vol. 40 No. 15
6. Xu Ning, Neural Network Based Expert System for Palmprint Diagnosis, Compute Application and Research, 2001. Vol.4-6.
7. Yun Wu, Genetic Neural Network for Traditional Chinese Medicine, 2005 international Conference on Neural Networks and Brain, 2005,Vol.339-342

DEVIATION ANALYSIS AND FAILURE DIAGNOSIS OF DIESEL ENGINE

[1]Yihuai Hu, [2]B. Gangadhara Prusty, [1]Yijian Liu
[1]*Shanghai Maritime University*, [2]*University of New South Wales*

Abstract: A computer-based filling and emptying diesel engine simulation model has been developed, which can simulate the operational behavior of diesel engine under different performance failures and different running conditions. This paper firstly describes the simulation models and simulated results of a four-stroke, turbo-charged diesel engine. The calculated results in terms of relative deviation are analyzed which reveal the relations between thermodynamic variables, performance failures, running conditions and ship operation conditions. Further, it provides more complete understanding of failures' behaviors under different running conditions and help to detect the failures amongst complex symptoms. Relative deviation of thermodynamic variables under different running conditions exhibits strong similarity, which induces a new information source for failure detection. Compared to experiments on board ship, this simulative modeling possesses advantages of shorter studying period, less research investment, lower risk in failure simulation and more symptomatic information. Finally an example is introduced to verify the feasibility of relative deviation analysis in the use of diesel engine failure diagnosis with artificial neural network method.

Key words: deviation analysis, failure diagnosis, diesel engine simulation

1. INTRODUCTION

Condition monitoring and failure diagnosis techniques are considered of major importance to higher reliability of machinery and can be of great benefits in reducing manning levels, especially for big and critical systems such as gas turbines, aircraft, nuclear power stations and marine engines. With several unique properties of little disturbance from outside, high

Please use the following format when citing this chapter:

Hu, Y., Prusty, B.G., Liu, Y., 2006, in IFIP International Federation for Information Processing, Volume 228, Intelligent Information Processing III, eds. Z. Shi, Shimohara K., Feng D., (Boston: Springer), pp. 347–356.

quality of information, wide range for diagnosis and strong availability in application, thermodynamic variables of marine diesel engine are usually regarded as the most abundant symptomatic source for failure diagnosis. But large bore marine diesel engine is a complex system composted of mechanical, electronic, thermal and hydraulic subsystems. This kind of system always has lots of failure motivating sources and confusing symptoms. So far, most of knowledge about relations between performance failures and thermodynamic variables is mainly from experiments, which is very difficult to be carried out onboard ship. Experimental modeling of big, complex diesel engine for failure diagnosis has been the "bottleneck" in intelligent failure diagnosis of marine diesel engine.

Deviation analysis based on simulation model, proposed in this paper, will give us a more complete understanding of failures' behaviors under different running conditions, help us to detect the failures amongst complex symptoms and, if accurate enough, provide modeling specimen for artificial neural network in failure diagnosis of marine diesel engine.

2.   SIMULATION MODEL

The engine model referred to in this paper is based on a general purpose engine thermodynamic simulation code[1]. This model treats a multi-cylinder engine as a series of thermodynamic control volumes interconnected through valves and ports. Several modifications have been made to meet the demand for failure simulation and performance prediction at different running, which are described in this article.

To take into account the influence of performance failures to combustion procedure, a term called combustion efficiency was introduced into the Wiebe's combustion function[2]. The term is defined as the ratio of completely burned fuel and injected fuel, which is the function of excess air factor α defined as [2]

$$\eta_u = \begin{cases} 3\alpha/5 & (\alpha < 1.25) \\ (\alpha+1)/3 & (1.25 \le \alpha \le 2) \\ 1 & (\alpha > 2) \end{cases}$$

(1)

Then the rate of heat release can be defined as

$$\frac{dQ_f}{d\varphi} = 6.908 \frac{\eta_u g_f H_u}{\Delta\varphi}(m+1)(\frac{\varphi-\varphi_{VB}}{\Delta\varphi})^m e^{-6.908(\frac{\varphi-\varphi_{VB}}{\Delta\varphi})^{m+1}}$$

(2)

where the ignition advance angle is

$$\varphi_{VB} = \theta_g + \Delta\theta_1 + \Delta\theta_2$$

(3)

the heat release duration angle is

$$\Delta\varphi = \Delta\varphi_0 (\frac{\alpha_0}{\alpha})^{0.6} (\frac{n}{n_0})^{0.5}$$

(4)

the heat release shape factor is

$$m = m_0 (\frac{\Delta\theta_{20}}{\Delta\theta_2})^{0.5} (\frac{p_a}{p_{a0}} \frac{T_{a0}}{T_a})(\frac{n_0}{n})^{0.8}$$

(5)

where Q_f :released heat of combussted fueloil;

   φ : crankshaft rotating angle of diesel engine;

   θ_g : fuel injection angle;

   $\Delta\theta_1$: injection lag angle;

   $\Delta\theta_2$: ignition lag angle;

   $\Delta\varphi_0$: heat release duration angle at rated condition with no performance
       failure;

   α_0 : excess air factor at rated condition with no performance failure;

   α : excess air factor at calculated condition;

   n_0 : running speed at rated condition;

   n : running speed at calculated condition;

   m_0 : heat release shape factor at rated condition with no performance
       failure;

   $\Delta\varphi_{20}$: ignition lag angle at rated condition;

   $\Delta\varphi_2$: ignition lag angle at calculated condition;

   p_{a0} : chamber pressure at compression stroke's beginning at rated
       condition;

   p_a : chamber pressure at compression stroke's beginning at calculated
       condition;

   T_{a0} : chamber temperature at compression stroke's beginning at rated
       condition;

   T_a : chamber temperature at compression stroke's beginning at the
       calculated condition;

The variables $\Delta\varphi_1$ and $\Delta\varphi_2$ in equation (3) are defined as:

$$\Delta\theta_1 = \Delta\theta_{10} \frac{n}{n_0}$$

(6)

$$\Delta\theta_2 = 6n\tau_i \times 10^{-3}$$

(7)

$$\tau_i = 0.1 + 2.627e^{\frac{1967}{T}} p^{-0.87}$$

(8)

where $\Delta\varphi_{10}$:   ignition lag angle at rated condition ;

τ_i :   ignition delay duration;

T :   chamber temperature at compression stroke end;

p: chamber pressure at compression stroke end.

To simulate the scavenging process a three-zone scavenging mode, with fresh air, exhaust gas and mixing zones, was utilized. Turbocharger compressor and turbine experimental performance maps were included in digitized form and the code can interpolate within the data to find the operating point.

Example: A large, medium speed, four-stroke, six-cylinder fish-boat main diesel engine, adapted with a VTR-201 type turbocharger, was chosen to be simulated. Previous publication had formed good agreement of the model prediction with available experimental data[2]. By carefully adjustment of the appropriate input data and model coefficients, 14 typical performance failures and 4 ship operation conditions were simulated. The selected input data and model coefficients of simulated failures refereed to the normal condition are presented in Table 1.

Table 1. Input data and model coefficients

Failure	Performance Failure	Input Data and Model Coefficients		
Index	Operation Condition	Normal Data	Abnormal Data	Data Descriptions
a	Blocked turbocharger exhaust casing	p_{OT}=0.1033(MPa)	p_{OT}=0.1074(MPa)	turbine outlet Back-pressure
b	Low ambient temperature	T_0=27(°C)	T_0=−20(°C)	Air inlet temperature of compressor
c	High ambient temperature	T_0=27(°C)	T_0=40(°C)	Air inlet temperature of compressor
d	Blocked air filter of turbocharger	P_0=0.1033(MPa)	P_0=0.095(MPa)	Air inlet pressure of compressor
e	Poorly cooled cylinder liner	TW=200(°C)	TW=500(°C)	Average temperature on liner surface
f	Poorly cooled piston cap	TWI=300(°C)	TWI=600(°C)	Average temperature on piston head
g	High inlet cooling water temperature of intercooler	CMX0=45(°C)	CMX0=70(°C)	Cooling water inlet temperature of intercooler
h	Low inlet cooling water temperature of intercooler	CMXO=45(°C)	CMX0=10(°C)	Cooling water inlet temperature of intercooler
i	Deposited air intake manifold	USM=0.45	USM=0.15	Air flow coefficient at inlet port
j	Deposited gas exhaust manifold	UEM=0.50	UEM=0.20	Air flow coefficient at output port
k	Fouled intercooler on air side	CMXN=0.8 CM=14.8	CMXN=0.35 CM=8.0	Cooling efficiency and resistance efficient
l	Deposited turbine nozzle	FC=0.0054(m²)	FC=0.0044(m²)	Geometric flow area of turbine nozzle
m	Worn turbocharger bearing	NTM=0.98	NTM=0.95	Mechanical efficiency of turbocharger bearing
n	Air-blocked inside cylinder jacket	CJ=1.0	CJ=0.25	Heat transfer correcting coefficient of burning gas to liner wall
o	Retarded injection timing	AZ1=-6(CA)	AZ1=13(CA)	Ignition angle
p	Worn fuel pump plunger	DAZ=80(CA) M=1.0	DAZ=104(CA) M=1.3	Heat release duration and shape factor

q	25° rudder angle adjusted	Pe=73.55(kW)	Pe=91.94(kW)	Effective power of single cylinder
r	4 class wind encountered	Pe=73.55(kW)	Pe=110.33(kW)	Effective power of single cylinder

3.   SIMULATED RESULTS

As thermodynamic variables usually vary within very wide range, the simulated results are normalized in terms of relative deviations ξ in order to indicate the relations between different thermodynamic variables and performance failures. The term ξ is defined as

$$\xi = \frac{x-x_0}{x_0} \tag{9}$$

The parameters x_0 and x refer to the thermodynamic variables at normal and abnormal conditions respectively. The calculated relative deviations at rated condition with 450 r/min engine speed and 441.3kW effective power, and at a partial condition with 315 r/min engine speed and 308.9 kW effective power are shown in Figure 1 and Figure 2 respectively. From Figure 1 and Figure 2 it is easy to find the variable, which is most sensitive to failure. Several interesting phenomena can be found after further analysis as:

Blocked turbocharger exhaust casing (a) mainly makes decrease in temperature difference DT_k and pressure difference of intercooler air Dp_k and slight rise in exhaust manifold temperature T_{bt} due to higher backpressure of turbocharger. Blocked turbocharger filter (d) makes obvious decrease in pressures of compressor discharge air p_k, intake manifold air p_s, maximum combustion gas presure p_{zmax}, intercooler air pressure difference Dp_k and obvious rise in gas exhaust manifold temperature T_{bt} due to bigger resistance of air flow and less air/fuel ratio inside chamber.

Poorly cooled cylinder liner (e) and piston cap (f) due to failures from cooling water system have very similar symptoms of obvious rising in compressor discharge temperature T_k, air intake manifold pressure p_s, air temperature difference of intercooler DT_k, maximum combustion gas pressure $p_{z\max}$ and metal temperature of liner or piston cap. This is because poor cooling water takes away less heat and leaves more energy, but cylinder liner has a bigger influence due to its larger cooling surface. Air-blocked inside cylinder jacket (n) reduces its cooling efficiency and hence induces increase in pressure difference Dp_k and temperature difference DT_k of inter-cooler and decrease in fuel consumption ratio G_e. The symptoms of this failure are like that of poorly cooled cylinder liner due to the same reason.

High inlet cooling water temperature of intercooler (g) due to failures from cooling water system only induces obvious decrease in air temperature difference of intercooler DT_k and obvious increase in air intake manifold temperature T_s, and vice versa (h). Symptoms of fouled intercooler on airside (k) are similar to that of high inlet cooling water temperature failure except for the decrease in pressure difference of intercooler Dp_k. This is due to its less heat exchange efficiency and higher airs flow resistance.

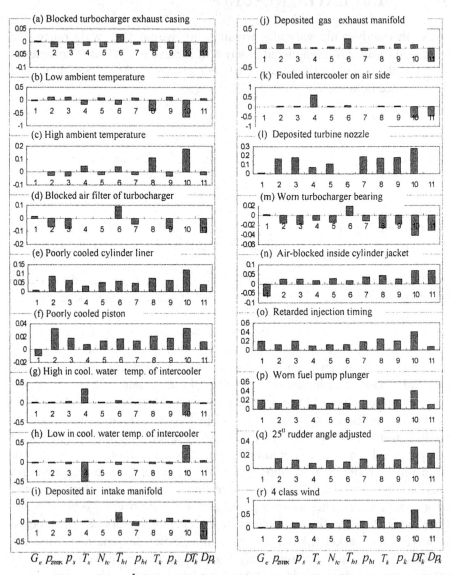

Figure 1 Relative deviation of failures at rated condition

Deposited turbine nozzle (l) increases gas exhaust manifold pressure p_{ht} and turbocharger running speed N_{tc}. This therefore makes the rise in compressor discharge air temperature T_k and pressure p_k, maximum gas combustion pressure $p_{z\,max}$ and temperature difference of intercooler DT_k due to the increase of circling airflow G_k. Worn-out turbocharger bearing (m) affects turbocharger's working efficiency and has just a opposite symptom due to the decrease of circling air flow G_k

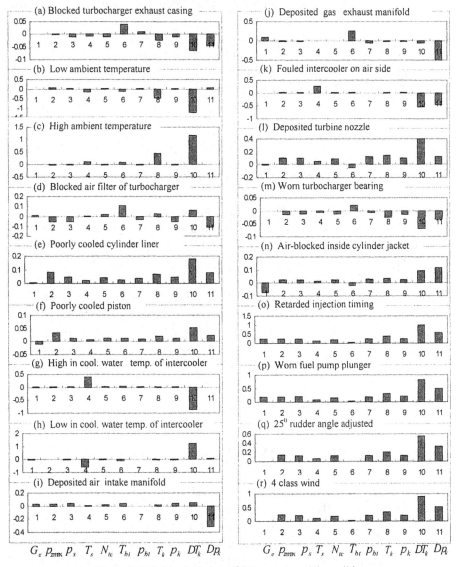

Figure 2 Relative deviation of failures at partial condition

Retarded injection timing (o) and worn-out fuel pump plunger (p) have very similar symptoms of the most obvious rise in temperature difference of intercooler and obvious increase in compressor discharge air temperature T_k, maximum gas combustion pressure $p_{z\,max}$, gas exhaust manifold temperature T_{bt} and pressure p_{bt}, turbocharger running speed N_{tc} and fuel consumption ratio G_e. This is mainly because the too late injection timing increases the diffusion combustion and worn pump plunger harms the fuel atomization which all worsen the combustion inside combustion chamber. To supply the same power under the same running speed diesel engine needed more fuel and more fresh air.

Ship rudder angle (q) and encountered strong wind (r) during navigation enlarge ship's resistance and need bigger engine power for the same running speed. This brings with the increase in most of variables similar to retarded injection timing and worn fuel pump plunger failures. Ambient temperature (b)(c) has some influence on engine performance. With lower ambient temperature the temperature difference of intercooler DT_k descends greatly and compressor discharge air temperature T_k drops obviously. So in practical failure diagnosis procedure ship navigation condition and weather condition have to be taken into account.

Comparing Figure 1 and Figure 2, it is found that relative deviations represent very similar trends at rated condition and partial condition. It is implied that relative deviations can be utilized as symptomatic parameters even diesel engine thermodynamic variables usually vary within very wide range at different running conditions. In this way different engine conditions can be taken into account and artificial neural network method can be used in diesel engine failure diagnosis without much modeling work and great difficulty.

Due to the inherent relations beyond diesel engine working principle some variables always have congruent behavior such as compressor discharge air pressure p_k and air intake manifold pressure p_s. It is necessary to make some cancellations of variables to simplify the modeling process in practical failure diagnosis.

4.   FAILURE DIAGNOSIS

With diesel engine simulation method reference values and symptomatic parameters under different performance failures can be obtained without much experimental modeling. With relative deviation analysis of thermodynamic variables one failure's modeling can be utilized at any probable running condition encountered during ship navigation. By this way artificial neural network can be used in failure diagnosis of marine diesel engine.

Assuming the network input vector, $X \in R^n$, the output vector, $Y \in R^n$, and the network conjunction weight set W_l (l=1,2,...,L) then the artificial neural network can be defined in equation (10) and shown in Figure 3 .

$$Y = f(W_L f(W_{L-1} \cdots f(W_1 X) \cdots)) \tag{10}$$

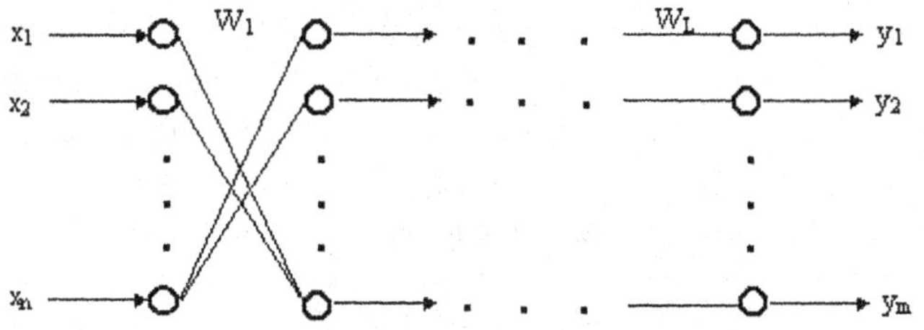

Figure 3 Sketch of the artificial neural network

Then the relative deviations under different failures at partial condition were used as input vector X together with the calculated W_l ($l=1,2,...,L$) as network conjunction weight set. The diagnosis results are shown in Table 2, where values in row i and column j indicate the confidence of relative deviation sample i to failure j. As can be seen from the diagnosed results (in black) in table 2 that only failure (q) was completely failed to be detected amongest the 18 failures and failures (j), (n), (o) were mistaken as other failures because of their similar symptoms. To get more accurate results, more parameters have to be taken into account such as fuel injection pressure, cylinder liner temperature and superficial vibration signals.

Table2. The diagnosed results with artificial neural network method

*	Specimen Record Code																	
	a	b	c	d	e	f	g	h	i	j	k	l	m	n	o	p	q	r
a	1.0	0	0	0	0	0	0	0	0	0	0	0	0	0	0	0	0	0
b	0	1.0	0	0	0	0	0.01	0	0	0	0	0	0	0	0	0	0	0
c	0	0	1.0	0	0	0	0	0	0	0	0	0	0	0	0	0	0	0
d	0	0	0	0.98	0	0	0	0	0	0	0	0	0	0	0	0	0	0
e	0	0	0	0	0.79	0	0	0	0	1	0	0.81	0	0	0.66	0.65	0.05	0.97
f	0	0.01	0	0	0.01	1.0	0.14	0	0	0	0	0	0	1	0	0	0	0
g	0	0	0	0	0	0	1.0	0	0	0	0	0	0	0	0	0	0	0
h	0	0	0	0	0	0	0	1.0	0	0	0	0	0	0	0	0	0	0
i	0	0	0	0	0	0	0	0	1.0	0	0	0.03	0	0	0	0	0	0
j	0	0	0	0	0	0	0	0.02	0	0.19	0	0	0	0	0	0	0	0
k	0	0	0	0	0	0	0	0	0.02	0	1.0	0	0	0	0	0	0	0
l	0	0	0	0	0	0	0	0	0.87	0	0	0.99	0	0	0	0	0	0
m	0	0	0.01	0	0	0	0.03	0	0	0	0	0	1.0	0	.15	0	0	0
n	0	0	0	0	0	0	0.01	0	0	0	0	0	0	0.0	0.02	0	0	0
o	0	0	0	0	0	0	0	0	0	0	0	0	0	0.99	0.0	0	0	0
p	0	0	0	0	0	0	0	0	0	0	0	0.02	0	0	0.94	0.94	0	0.06
q	0	0	0	0	0	0	0	0	0	0	0	0	0	0	0	0	0.0	0
r	0	0	0	0	0	0	0	0	0	0	0	0	0	0	0	0	0	0.96

* Failure Code

CONCLUSION

Relative deviation analysis, proposed in this article, is proved to be a good tool for failure analysis of diesel engine thermodynamic variables with different performance failures and under different running conditions. It is easier to find out which variable is the most sensitive to some a failure and which failures have similar symptoms under different running conditions. This will make the modelling quite easier for the large bore diesel engine failure diagnosis with artificial neural network method. Further research is needed to find the similar behaviors between different thermodynamic variables and between different performance failures in order to reduce modelling variables and make the failure diagnosis more practical.

ACKNOWLEDGEMENTS

This paper was founded by Shanghai Leading Academic Discipline Project (Code: T0603) and supported by Shanghai Education Committee.

REFERENCES

1. Gu Hongzhong, Marine diesel engine handbook (3), National defense industry press, 1979 (in Chinese)
2. Hu Yihuai, Wan Biyu, Zhan Yulong, Performance failures simulation and informational characters analysis for diesel engine, Transactions of Chinese society for internal combustion engines, Vol. 17, No. 4, 1999 (in Chinese)
3. Gao Xiaohong, Simulation techniques for internal combustion engine, National defense industry press, 1995 (in Chinese)
4. Tang Tianhao etc, A study of integrate intelligent marine monitoring system, Proceedings Of IMECE'97, Shanghai, P. R. China, May, 1997

UTILIZING STRUCTURAL CONTEXT FOR REGION CLASSIFICATION

Zhiyong Wang
School of Information Technologies
The University of Sydney, Australia
zhiyong@it.usyd.edu.au

David D. Feng
School of Information Technologies
The University of Sydney, Australia
and
Department of Electronic and Information Engineering
Hong Kong Polytechnic University
feng@it.usyd.edu.au

Abstract   In this paper, we propose to take structural context of image regions into account for region classification through a structural neural network. Firstly, a tree structure of each region is formed to characterize the relationship among the region and its neighbours. Such structures integrate both visual attributes of regions and their structural contexts. Then the structural representations are learned through a Back-propagation Through Structure (BPTS) training algorithm. Comprehensive experimental results demonstrate that our proposed approach has a great potential in region classification.

Keywords: Region Classification, Structural Context, Neural Networks

1.   Introduction

While an ever increasing number of digital images play a more and more important role in improving the quality of daily life, users are also confronted with the difficulties in accessing specific images. Content-based image retrieval (CBIR) has been proposed and investigated to allow users to access images in terms of their true content, due to the great demand posed by the drastic growth of digital visual content (Smeulders et al., 2000). However, it is also realized that the semantic gap between low level visual features (e.g. color, shape, and texture) and semantic contents (e.g. objects and events) is

Please use the following format when citing this chapter:

Wang, Z., Feng, D.D., 2006, in IFIP International Federation for Information Processing, Volume 228, Intelligent Information Processing III, eds. Z. Shi, Shimohara K., Feng D., (Boston: Springer), pp. 357–366.

the biggest obstacle of the successful applications of image access (e.g. retrieval, filtering, and summarization) in terms of semantic contents. Automatic or semi-automatic image content understanding is a key to build intelligent image management systems. Image regions, which are meaningful primitives of images, contribute to semantic content of images significantly. In addition, region semantics can be utilized to derive high level semantic concepts. Therefore, it will be ideal to classify individual region into one of the semantic classes.

Various Pattern recognition approaches have been widely employed for region classification. In general, there are two key issues, feature extraction and classifier, involved in region classification. For example, based on visual features (e.g. color, texture, shape, size, and centroid), Campbell *et al.* proposed to classify image regions into semantic classes (e.g. sky, vegetation, and road) by using a three-layer neural network (Campbell et al., 1997). However, the performance of traditional region classification has been seriously limited due to segmentation noise and ambiguity of visual features (e.g. cloud vs. snow). On the other hand, contextual information of regions can be utilized to further improve the performance of region classification, since it is certain that the presence of some concepts or contents can provide important information for identifying other concepts or contents.

There are generally two types of contexts, conceptual context (i.e. global context) and content context, in region classification. Conceptual context is useful for modeling semantics at image level and can be utilized to increase the confidence of assigning certain labels to certain regions as well as the confidence of excluding some labels in terms of a given image theme. For example, it is much less possible to assign *grass* to a green region if an image has been identified as *indoors*. Conceptual context is generally obtained through image classification. For example, Vailaya *et al.* proposed a Bayesian classification approach to classify vacation images hierarchically (e.g. City vs. Landscape, Mountain vs. Coast)(Vailaya et al., 2001). Recently, conceptual context can also be derived through a set of words, since more and more images are accompanied with abundant annotations (e.g. web images). Therefore, many approaches consider extracting conceptual context as a problem of associating *a bag of words* with images by exploiting the co-occurrence of two modalities, visual attributes and labels, of images. The co-occurrence of those two modalities was first investigated by Mori *et al.* (Mori et al., 1999). It is assumed that a region corresponds to a label if they co-occur in images frequently. In (Barnard et al., 2003a), a translation model is proposed to translate a vocabulary of blobs to a vocabulary of terms based on the joint probability of images and terms, and a probabilistic model was established to classify each region into one of the terms. However, such classification is only a by-product of

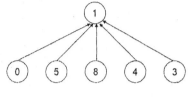

Figure 1.   An illustration of an adjacency structure of region 1.

the model, since not all the textual labels correspond to a particular region or object.

Content context, which represents the context of individual regions, can also be employed to enhance region classification and even identify objects. In (Singhal et al., 2003), content context was represented as the spatial relationship (e.g. above and below) between regions. However, structural context based on spatial adjacency, which is seldom investigated, is also important in region annotation. For example, a white region can be labelled as *cloud* with higher confidence if it is surrounded by *sky* regions. In this paper, we propose to characterize such structural context existing among regions by forming an adjacency graph. In such a graph, each node representing a region receive two inputs, its visual features and structural context (i.e. connections among its neighbours). Therefore, both attributes and context are integrated seamlessly. As shown in our previous study (Wang et al., 2002)(Wang et al., 2004), this graph representation is also effective and efficient in characterizing image content with only a small number of features.

Neural networks have been proposed to process structural data and the back-propagation through structure (BPTS) algorithm can be employed to learn the tree-structure representation(Frasconi et al., 1998). Such an algorithm has been successfully utilized for scene classification (Wang et al., 2004). Therefore, in this paper, we employ such learning algorithm to perform the task of region classification.

2.   Representation of Structural Context

It is noticed that human beings perceive the real world in a structure way so that both entities and their relationship can contribute to their content representation. For example, being told that a region is surrounded by "sea", we may think of "beach", island, and "ship". Therefore, the more structural context is available, the more accurate the classification will be. As a result, a formal representation needs to be formed to characterize such structural context for each region. As shown in Figure 1, the neighbour regions of Region 1 form its

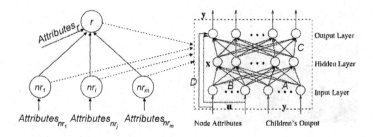

Figure 2.   An illustration of a tree-structure encoding network with a single hidden layer.

structural context through a graph. Such structure representation can be noted as a graph $G = \{V, E\}$, where V and E indicate the set of nodes (i.e. regions) and edges (i.e. structural context among regions), respectively.

To process the graph representation, we need to figure out what structure information is and how to model it for each region class. In general, any relationship among regions can be abstracted as structural information, such as spatial relationship and visual similarity. In (Chang et al., 2004), it was proposed to explicitly utilize graph matching methods based on the similarity assigned to each edge and graph isomorphism. As explained in the next section, we employ a structural neural network model to process such structural representation adaptively.

3.   Back-propagation Through Structure (BPTS)

Connectionist models have been successfully employed to solve learning tasks characterized by relatively poor representations in data structure such as static pattern or sequence. Most structured information presented in real world, however, can hardly be represented by simple sequences. Although many early approaches based on syntactic pattern recognition were developed to learn structured information, devising a proper grammar is often a very difficult task because domain knowledge is incomplete or insufficient. On the contrary, the graph representation varies in the size of input units and can organize data flexibly. An encoding process of a tree structure is shown in Figure 2. Each node represents a neural network on the right of Figure 2 and all the nodes share the same set of parameters. Neural networks for processing data structures have been proposed by Sperduti (Sperduti and Starita, 1997). It has been shown that they can be used to process data structures using an algorithm namely back-propagation through structure(BPTS). The algorithm extends the time unfolding carried out by back-propagation through time(BPTT) in the case of sequences. A general framework of adaptive processing of data structures was introduced by Tsoi (Tsoi, 1998) and Frasconi *et al.* (Frasconi et al., 1998). Considering a generalized formulation of graph encoding shown in Figure 2, we have

$$x = F_n(Aq^{-1}y + Bu) \tag{1}$$

$$y = F_p(Cx + Du) \tag{2}$$

where x, u and y are respectively the n dimensional output vector of the n hidden layer neurons, the m dimensional inputs to the neurons, and the p dimensional outputs of the neurons. q^{-1} is merely a notation to indicate that the input to the node is taken from its children. The A matrix is defined as follows:

$$A = [A^1 A^2 ... A^c] \tag{3}$$

where c is the maximal out degree of the graph. $A^i, i = 1, 2, ..., c$ is an $n \times p$ matrix, and is formed from the vector a_j^i, $j = 1, 2, ..., n$. A is a $c \times (n \times p)$ matrix. And B, C, and D are respectively matrices of dimensions $n \times m, p \times n$ and $p \times m$. $F_n(.)$ is an n dimensional vector given as follows:

$$F_n(\alpha) = [f(\alpha)\ f(\alpha)\ ...\ f(\alpha)]^T \tag{4}$$

where $f(.)$ is the nonlinear function such as a Sigmoidal function.

Note that we have assumed only one hidden layer in the formulation, because a single hidden layer with sufficient number of neurons is a universal approximator (Scarselli and Tsoi, 1998).

The training process is to estimate the parameters A, B, C and D from a set of input/output samples by minimizing the cost criterion:

$$J = \frac{1}{2}\sum_{i=1} N_T ||d_i - y_i||^2 \tag{5}$$

where y_i denotes the output of the root of the i-th sample, d_i denotes the desired output of the i-th sample, and N_T is the number of the samples. The derivation of the training algorithm minimizing the cost criterion (5) will follow a fashion similar to gradient learning by computing the partial derivation of the cost J with respect to A, B, C and D.

4.   Experiments and Discussions

The image database used in our experiments has 304 images taken by ourselves, half of which is used for training, the other half for testing. A sample of each category is shown in Figure 3. All the images are segmented by using EdgeFlow technique (Ma and Manjunath, 2000) since the segmentation can be finely tuned by specifying different scales σ of Gaussian functions. By setting σ to 4, 3064 training regions and 2091 test regions are obtained. These regions are manually labelled with a set of terms. The region classes with less than 20

Figure 3.   Samples of the image database.

instances have been removed. Finally, we identified 13 region classes, *auditorium, building, field, flower, grass, ground, people, sand, sky, stone, tree, wall, water*. Each region is characterized with 7-dimension features including the number of colors, percentage of the three most dominant color, average pixel values, standard deviation of pixel values, and region size.

Neighbour regions are not equally important in modeling spatial context, which should be taken into account for structure context. For example, sky region is more informative than building region in classifying a region as mountain. Furthermore, due to the error-prone segmentation, some neighbors are not true neighbors. In order to select important and representative neighbor regions, the length of the boundary between a neighbor region and the target region is considered to investigate the impact of different neighbor regions. In our experiments, the top $M, M = 0, ...5$ regions with the longest boundary length other than the biggest region size will be studied. While M is set to 0, the experiment is the baseline.

Three experimental tasks have been conducted to evaluate the performance of our proposed approach. At first, our approach is benchmarked with neural network methods by using multi-layer perceptrons. Then, the impacts of different segmentation and different visual features are investigated.

Performance Against Multi-layer Perceptron

We compare the proposed approach with the classical pattern classification approach, multi-layer peceptron (MLP). In order to make the comparison fair, we also consider neighbor information by concatenating feature vectors of neighbor regions into a higher dimension feature vector in the MLP method. That is, the feature vector is in $(N + 1) \times d$-dimension, if N neighbor regions are taken into account and each region is represented with a d-dimension feature vector. In this evaluation, regions are segmented by setting σ to 4 and represented with 7-dimension features, and neighbor regions are selected in the descending order of the length of the boundary adjacent to the target re-

Table 1. Comparison between the proposed approach and the MLP method on the test set

| | MLP Approach | | Proposed Approach | |
	Accuracy (%)	#Hidden neurons	Accuracy (%)	#Hidden neurons
0-neighbor	54.15	15	N/A	N/A
1-neighbor	54.53	20	62.36	20
2-neighbor	60.46	20	61.08	10
3-neighbor	61.65	10	60.46	10
4-neighbor	63.25	10	56.08	10
5-neighbor	55.46	15	57.50	15

gion. An MLP with single hidden layer is adopted in this evaluation, since it can be a universal approximator provided with a sufficient number of hidden neurons (Scarselli and Tsoi, 1998). In order to tune the performance of the MLP method, we vary the number of hidden neurons from 5 to 20 and choose the best performance in each case.

As shown in Table 1, our proposed approach clearly outperforms the MLP method while not many neighbour regions (e.g. 1 or 2 neighbour regions) are utilized. In particular, the performance increases 14% while one neighbour region is utilized. It is also noticed that utilizing more neighbor regions is not always helpful, because the performance of both our proposed approach and the MLP method decreases while 5 neighbour regions have been utilized. For example, the performance of 5-neighbor (55.46%) is not as good as that of 2-neighbor (60.46%) for the MLP method. Such experimental results coincide with our assumption that not all the neighbour regions equally contribute to the classification task. More neighbour regions may add noise into the training session and demands higher learning capacity from classifiers. It is noticed that the most significant performance improvement happens while only one neighbor is taken into account. Therefore, it is essential to identify the most informative neighbor regions more effectively, other than simply using the boundary length, to further improve the performance.

Table 1 also shows that MLP methods achieve higher accuracy exceptionally while 4 neighbors are considered. The reason may be that our current database favors the MLP method for such a particular case. For our proposed approach, the classifier learns both structural information and region attributes, which requires more representative training data. Further research on this issue will be conducted.

Impact of Different Segmentation

Segmentation under different conditions generally introduces variations in region extraction and spatial context. As shown in Figure 4, images will be over-segmented at small scales and less over-segmented at great scales. In or-

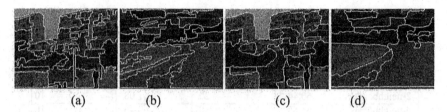

| | (a) | (b) | (c) | (d) |

Figure 4.   Segmentation samples at different scales. (a) and (b) σ = 4; (c) and (d) σ=12;

Table 2.   The number of regions of images segmented at different scales

	Training Set	Test Set	# of Region Classes
σ=4	3064	2901	13
σ=12	1972	1807	13

Table 3.   Classification accuracy (%) of different segmentation

	1-neighbor	2-neighbor	3-neighbor	4-neighbor	5-neighbor
σ=4	62.36	61.08	60.46	56.08	57.50
σ=12	61.21	61.10	60.43	60.10	58.99

der to evaluate the impact of different segmentation, images are segmented by setting σ to 4 and 12 since these settings can generate a reasonable number of homogeneous regions for our image set. The number of training regions, test regions, and the number of region classes are listed in Table 2 for different segmentation scales, respectively. Obviously, segmentation at scale 4 generates more regions than at scale 12. As shown in Table 3, both segmentations can achieve similar performance. There are also two differences between them. First, performance of a larger scale (i.e. σ=12) decreases slightly. It may be that over-segmentation is reduced while segmentation scale increases. Hence, each segmented region is less homogeneous, which demands efficient content representation through visual feature extraction. As a result, we also investigated the impact of using different visual features. Second, the proposed approach is more robust at a larger scale. As can bee seen in Table 3, the classification accuracy of the segmentation at scale 12 is more around 60%. It may be that less over-segmentation introduces less variation for neighbor structures and makes learning slightly easier. Hence, additional experiments will be conducted to explore these discoveries.

Impact of Different Features

Besides the 7-dimension features, five more features including averages of R, G, B components and region centroid (x, y) are used to evaluate the impact

Table 4.   Impact of different feature sets at segmentation scale 4

Dimension	1-neighbor	2-neighbor	3-neighbor	4-neighbor	5-neighbor
7	62.36	61.08	60.46	56.08	57.50
12	75.11	75.35	71.49	73.22	70.15

Table 5.   Impact of different feature sets at segmentation scale 12

Dimension	1-neighbor	2-neighbor	3-neighbor	4-neighbor	5-neighbor
7	61.21	61.10	60.43	60.10	58.99
12	73.82	73.60	72.16	71.94	69.29

of different feature sets. As shown in Tables 4 and 5 where the best performance of each case is listed, much better performance has been achieved while the new 12-dimension features are adopted. Compared with the 7-dimension features, the 12-dimension features present more helpful information (e.g. region centroid) and benefit region classification, although both of them are quite simple. It can be expected that more representative feature sets will further improve the performance of our proposed approach. As indicated in (Barnard et al., 2003b), color and texture are the most representative features for scenery images, we need to include more texture features such as oriented energy coefficients in our future study.

5.   Conclusion and Future Work

A novel region classification approach is present in this paper. Such an approach integrates structural context of image regions and the unique and powerful learning capacity of the BPTS learning algorithm. Comprehensive experiments have been conducted to evaluate our proposed approach. Experimental results demonstrate that our proposed approach can gain significant improvement even when only one neighbour region is utilized. In addition, our proposed approach is robust to the selection of neighbour regions, if suitable segmentation can be obtained.

It is also observed that segmentation and visual features do affect the performance of the proposed approach. For example, more neighbour regions do not always contribute to better classification accuracy, since structural variation also increases the requirement of learning capacity. Therefore, it is worthwhile to investigate how to identify more salient neighbour regions more efficiently based on large scale image databases. Since segmentation, salient regions, and visual features are closely related and interact with each other, it is also essential to balance them to achieve optimal classification performance. Another extension to our current work is to discover the second order structure rather than the adjacency structure exploited here.

Acknowledgement

This research is supported by the ARC and UGC grants.

References

Barnard, K., Duygulu, P., de Freitas, N., Forsyth, D., Blei, D., and Jordan, M. (2003a). Matching words and pictures. *Journal of Machine Learning Research*, 3:1107–1135.

Barnard, K., Duygulu, P., Guru, R., Gabbur, P., and Forsyth, D. (2003b). The effects of segmentation and feature choice in a translation model of object recognition. In *The IEEE International Conference on Computer Vision and Pattern Recognition*, volume 2, pages 675–682. Wisconsin, USA.

Campbell, N. W., Mackeown, W. P. J., Thomas, B. T., and Troscianko, T. (1997). Interpreting image databases by region classification. *Pattern Recognition*, 30(4):555–563.

Chang, R.-F., Chen, C.-J., and Liao, C.-H. (2004). Region-based image retrieval using edge-flow segmentation and regioin adjacency graph. In *The IEEE International Conference on Multimedia and Expo (ICME2004)*, volume 1, pages 1883–1886. Taiwan.

Frasconi, P., Gori, M., and Sperduir, A. (1998). A general framework for adaptive processing of data structures. *IEEE Trans. on Neural Networks*, 9(5):768 – 786.

Ma, W.-Y. and Manjunath, B. S. (2000). EdgeFlow: a technique for boundary detection and image segmentation. *IEEE Trans. on Image Processing*, 9(8):1375–1388.

Mori, Y., Takahashi, H., and Oka, R. (1999). Image-to-word transformation based on dividing and vector quantizing images with words. In *The First International Workshop on Multimedia Intelligent Storage and Retrieval Management (MISRM99)*. Florida, USA.

Scarselli, F. and Tsoi, A. C. (1998). Universal approximation using feedforward neural networks: a survey of some existing methods, and some new results. *Neural Networks*, 11(1):15–38.

Singhal, A., Luo, J., and Zhang, W. (2003). Probabilistic spatial context models for scene content understanding. In *The IEEE International Conference on Computer Vision and Pattern Recognition*, volume 1, pages 235–241. Wisconsin, USA.

Smeulders, A. W. M., Worring, M., Santini, S., Gupta, A., and Jain, R. (2000). Content-based image retrieval at the end of the early years. *IEEE Trans. on Pattern Analysis and Machine Intelligence*, 22(12):1349–1380.

Sperduti, A. and Starita, A. (1997). Supervised neural networks for the classification of structures. *IEEE Trans. on Neural Networks*, 8(3):714–735.

Tsoi, A. C. (1998). Adaptive processing of data structures:an expository overview and comments. Technique report, Faculty of Informatics, University of Wollongong, Australia.

Vailaya, A., Figueiredo, M. A. T., Jain, A. K., and jiang Zhang, H. (2001). Image classification for content-based indexing. *IEEE Trans. on Image Processing*, 10(1):117–130.

Wang, Z., Feng, D., and Chi, Z. (2004). Comparison of image partition methods for adaptive image categorization based on structural image representation. In *The 8th International Conference on Control, Automation, Robotics, and Vision*, pages 676–680. Kunming, China.

Wang, Z., Hargenbuchner, M., Tsoi, A. C., Cho, S. Y., and Chi, Z. (2002). Image classification with structured self-organizing map. In *IEEE International Joint Conference on Neural Networks (IJCNN2002)*. Hawaii, USA.

A Neuro-Fuzzy System for Automatic Multi-Level Image Segmentation using KFCM and Exponential Entropy

G. Raghotham Reddy[1], E. Suresh[2] , S.Uma Maheshwar[3] and M. Sampath Reddy[4]

[1,2,3] *Lecturer, Kakatiya Institute of Technology and Science, Warangal, A. P., India*
[4] *Lecturer, Ramappa Engineering College, Mahabubabad, A. P., India*
E-mail: grr_ece@ yahoo.com

Abstract

An auto adaptive neuro-fuzzy segmentation and edge detection architecture is presented. This system consists of a multilayer perceptron (MLP)-like network that performs image segmentation by adaptive thresholding of the input image using labels automatically pre-selected by kernel based fuzzy clustering technique. The proposed architecture is feed forward, but unlike the conventional MLP the learning is unsupervised. The output status of the network is described as a fuzzy set. Fuzzy entropy is used as a measure of the error of the segmentation system as well as a criterion for determining potential edge pixels. Exponential entropy was employed to overcome the drawbacks of using conventional logarithmic entropy. The proposed system is capable to perform automatic multilevel segmentation of images, based solely on information contained by the image itself. No a priory assumptions whatsoever are made about the image (type, features, contents, stochastic model, etc.). Such an "universal" algorithm is most useful for applications that are supposed to work with different (and possibly initially unknown) types of images. The proposed system can be readily employed, "as is," or as a basic building block by a more sophisticated and/or application-specific image segmentation algorithm. By monitoring the fuzzy entropy relaxation process, the system is able to detect edge pixels

Keywords: Image Segmentation, Adaptive Tresholding, Error backpropagation Neural Network System and Kernal Fuzzy C-means Clustering algorithm.

1.0 ADAPTIVE NEURO-FUZZY SYSTEM WITH KFCM

The Adaptive Neuro-Fuzzy system consists of a multilayer neural network that performs adaptive, multilevel thresholding of the image using labels automatically pre selected by a fuzzy clustering technique. The learning technique employed is self-supervised allowing, therefore, automatic adaptation of the NN. The output status of the network is described as a fuzzy partition. Fuzzy entropy is used as a measure of the error of the system as well as a criterion for determining potential edge pixels. Given an input image, the system is forced to evolve toward a minimum fuzzy entropy state in order to obtain image segmentation. Pixels most affected by the consecutive training iterations (due to the amount of their contribution to the fuzzy entropy of the system) are labeled as edge pixels.

1.1 Description of Adaptive Neuro-Fuzzy System

Block diagram of the system is shown in fig. 1. Labels are found by applying the KFCM algorithm to the image histogram. Then, the information about the labels is employed to build the network activation and error functions. The input to a neuron in the input layer is normalized between [0-1], proportionally to the gray value of the correspondent pixel. The image information is first propagated forward using (1) to get the output status of the network. The output value of each neuron lies in the interval [0-1]. Then, the output error is calculated and back propagated to update the weights [(4)]. Training continues either until a minimum error or until a maximum number of iterations reached. The output of the system at this stage constitutes the segmented image. Integrating (summing) the thresholded (binared) differences between the outputs at consecutive epochs yield the edge image.

Please use the following format when citing this chapter:

Reddy, G.R., Suresh, E., Maheshwar, S.U., Reddy, M.S., 2006, in IFIP International Federation for Information Processing, Volume 228, Intelligent Information Processing III, eds. Z. Shi, Shimohara K., Feng D., (Boston: Springer), pp. 367–372.

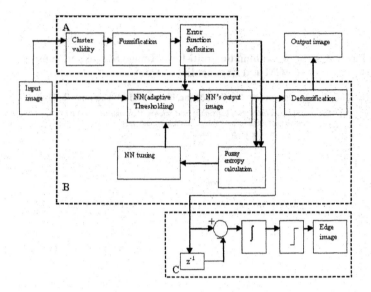

Fig. 1: Block Diagram of Neuro Fuzzy System

1.1.1 Error Function Definition Block

The purpose of this block is to provide the objective error function to be used by the adaptive thresholding block. First, the cluster validity block determines the number of objects in the input image, then the fuzzification block divides the input image into that number of fuzzy sets using KFCM as shown in Fig. 2(b), and then the error function definition block generates error function by determining the contribution of each gray level to the fuzzy entropy of the partition as shown in Fig. 2(c). The cluster validity block automatically determines the number of objects in the input image, for this it iterates the KFCM algorithm for a range of hypothesized number of clusters and chooses best option based on a cluster validity measure (e.g., the partition coefficient and the partition entropy).

1.1.2 Adaptive Thresholding Block

This contains the Neural Network (NN) block, the fuzzy entropy calculation block and NN tuning block. Its inputs are the input image and the error function determined by the block (A), and its output is the segmented image. **Neural Network:** The neural network block performs adaptive thresholding of the input image. The network architecture is shown in Fig. 3. It consists of an input layer, an output layer and at least one hidden layer. Each layer consists of $M \times N$ neurons, every neuron corresponding to an image pixel. Each neuron in the one layer is only connected to the corresponding neuron in the previous layer and the neurons in its d-th order neighborhood.

A neighborhood system over a $M \times N$ lattice L is defined as

$$n^d = \left\{ n_{ij}^d \subset L : (i, j) \in L \right\}$$

where n_{ij}^d, called the d-th order neighborhood of (i, j), is such that

- $(i, j) \notin n_{ij}^d$;

- $(k, l) \in n_{ij}^d$

There are no connections between neurons in the same layer. The NNs' weights cannot be randomly initialized or they will alter the input image. In this work, all weights were initialized to 1, but it is also possible to initialize the weights using some kind of weighting window within the neighborhood of each pixel.

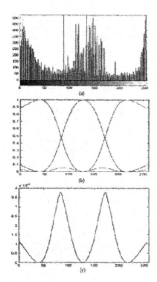

Fig. 2: (a) Histogram of the Panda image (b) Partion found by
KFCM (c) Error function

Activation function: A *multi-sigmoid* activation function
was used to allow more than two stable states of the neuron
output. The *multi-sigmoid* function is defined as (Fig.4).

$$f(x)=\sum_{k}\left(\frac{y_k-y_{k-1}}{1+e^{-(x-\theta_k)/\theta_0}}+y_{k-1}\right)\times\left[u(x-y_{k-1}*d^2)-u(x-y_k*d^2)\right] \quad (1)$$

where

u	step function;
θ_k	thresholds;
y_k	target level of each sigmoid, will constitute the systems' labels;
θ_0	steepness parameter;
d	size of the neighborhood, as defined in the previous section

The thresholds and the target values are obtained from the
error function, as the gray levels with the maximal and with
the minimal levels of fuzziness respectively. Because the

range of the neuron input levels depend on the number of
neurons in the previous layer to which it is connected (the
size of the neighborhood), the threshold values are adapted
to reflect this dependency (by multiplying them by d^2, the
number of input links).

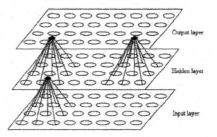

Fig. 3: Neural Network

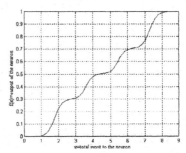

Fig. 4: Multi Sigmoid Activation function

Training: The back-propagation algorithm is employed for
training. As we apply input image the neurons in the first
layer receives the input, and will apply it to the Linear
Combiner and the Activation Function and produce the
output this output, will become the input for the neurons in
the next layer. So the next layer will feed forward the data,
to the next layer. And so on, until the last layer is reached
We compare the desired and actual output compute the
error as the difference between desired output and actual
output. Once we decided what adjustment we need to do to
the neurons in the output layer, we back propagate the
changes to the previous layers of the network. Indeed, as
soon as we have desired outputs for the output layer, we
make adjustment to reduce the error (the difference
between the output and the desired output). Adjustment will
change weights of the input nodes of the neurons in the
output layer. The weights are updated as follows:

$$\Delta w_{ji} = \begin{cases} \eta \left(-\dfrac{\partial E}{\partial o_j} \right) \dfrac{\partial o_j}{\partial I_j} o_i & \text{outputlaye} \\[3mm] \eta \left(\sum_k \left(-\dfrac{\partial E}{\partial o_k} \dfrac{\partial o_k}{\partial I_k} w_{kj} \right) \right) \dfrac{\partial o_j}{\partial I_j} o_i & \text{otherlayer} \end{cases} \quad (2)$$

where

I_i total input to the i th neuron;

w_{ji} weight of link from neuron i in one layer to

neuron j in the next layer;

o_i output of the i th neuron in the previous layer;

E error in the network's output (relative to the

desired target image);

η learning rate.

Note: *For simplicity 1-D indexes in the above equations are used, the extension to fit the 2-D NN is straightforward.*

For a *multi-sigmoid* as previously defined

$$\frac{\partial o_j}{\partial I_j} = o_j (y_n - y_{n-1} - o_j) \quad (3)$$

and the equations for Δw_{ji} become

$$\Delta w_{ji} = \begin{cases} \eta \left(-\dfrac{\partial E}{\partial o_j} \right) o_j \left(y_n - y_{n-1} - o_j \right) o_i \\[3mm] \eta \left(\sum_k -\dfrac{\partial E}{\partial o_k} \dfrac{\partial o_k}{\partial I_k} w_{kj} \right) o_j \left(y_n - y_{n-1} - o_j \right) o_i \end{cases} \quad (4)$$

for the output and the other layers respectively

Defuzzification: The output of the neural network is initially obtained in terms of the gray levels, which are then "fuzzyfied" in order to determine the error. In the idle case when the network converges with no error at all (E=0), the outputs have only values who's membership values are "1" or "0," defuzzification is not necessary. When the network does not converge completely (whether stopped intentionally or not), the fuzzification of the output image does not result in merely crisp membership values. The information about the membership values of the pixels might be useful for further processing, depending on the application at hand. If crisp labeling is required, a defuzzification stage must be added. For display purposes, the simplest defuzzification method is thresholding the fuzzy partition, so that each pixel is uniquely assigned to the class in which it has the highest membership value.

1.1.3 Edge Detection Block

This subsystem is based on the assumption that the edge pixels have the most ambiguous values in the image, i.e., they give the largest contribution to the fuzzy entropy of the output image at each iteration. Thus, these pixels are those that undergo the changes during the training/tuning of the system. Here, monitoring the changes that take place in the pixels' values between two consecutive iterations and integrating these changes over the whole training period obtain the edge image.

2.0 RESULTS

The Adaptive Neuro-Fuzzy system is implemented in MATLAB environment. The execution time of the Neural Network training epochs depends on the image size and the neighborhood size. Theoretically, the number of required epochs depends on the error and activation functions (which intern depend on the nature of the data), on the learning rate and on the required precision. Practically, the training may usually be stopped after about ten epochs. In terms of runtime memory requirements, these systems require four floating-point matrices of size $d^2 * M * N$ (neighborhood size multiplied by the size of the image) are needed for the two layers of weights and their corresponding updates, and three floating-point matrices of size $M * N$ (the image size) are needed to store the three layers of the network (input, hidden, and output).

2.1 Segmentaion Results

The output of the system is the segmented image enhancing the object over the background. As we can observe in the figures followed. The effect of using KFCM, Selecting thresholds by second derivative of the image histogram and considering exponential form of fuzzy entropy as error function can be seen very clearly. They give smoother image which is more robust to noise. Moreover by employing KFCM instead of FCM makes it applicable to wider range of images, i.e., for those having spherical and non spherical edges. Use of Kfcm made the Adaptive Neuro-Fuzzy system robust to some real life 'complication' like the addition of noise, and changing illumination conditions. Kfcm is also capable of handling uneven sized clusters.

(a)

(b)

Fig. 5: (a) Original Image (b) Segmented image

2.2 Convergence Analysis

The convergence of the adaptive threshold system of Adaptive Neuro-Fuzzy system is visualized in Fig.6. This figure shows the histogram of the output image after 2 and 50 and 100 training epochs (when applied to the Panda image), clearly indicating the convergence of the pixel values to the chosen labels.

2.3 Edge Detection Results

The edge detection subsystem of Neuro-fuzzy system was found to perform poorly compared to some of the better edge detected algorithms existing today, sometimes even worse than the classical, gradient type edge detector (Prewitt, Sobel, etc.). Fig.7 below shows the results of the edge detection subsystem of Neuro-Fuzzy system applied to the cameraman image, compared to the results of the Sebel operator.

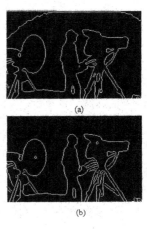

(a)

(b)

Fig. 7: (a) Edge image of Neuro-fuzzy System (b) Edge image using Sobel operators

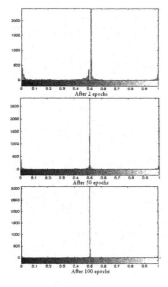

Fig. 6: Convergence Analysis

3.0 CONCLUSION

The proposed adaptive neuro fuzzy system has been proven to be efficient than many other existing methods of segmentation. It does not require any priori assumptions of the input. Employing KFCM made the system applicable wider range of images. As you can observe in the results it worked for spherical edges in panda and non spherical edges in cameraman image. Use of exponential entropy yielded smoother images at less number of iterations as compared to logarithmic form .It is also robust to noise. Increase of neighbourhood results in more loss of details. This system can also be extended for edge detection but this isn't as efficient as general canny or sobel operators

REFERENCE

[1] Victor Boskovitz and Hugo Guterman (2002), "An Adaptive Neuro-Fuzzy System for automatic Image Segmentation and Edge Detection", *IEEE Trans. On Fuzzy Systems*, Volume_10(No. 2), pp. 247-252.

[2] Rafael C. Gonzalez and Richard E. Woods, (2002), "Digital Image Processing", Pearson Education, New Delhi

COMPARISON OF IMAGE ANALYSIS FOR THAI HANDWRITTEN CHARACTER RECOGNITION

Olarik Surinta, Chatklaw Jareanpon
Department of Computer Science and Management Information System
Faculty of Informatics, Mahasarakham University
Mahasarakham City, Thailand
e-mail: olarik.s@msu.ac.th, Chatklaw.j@msu.ac.th
Telephone: +6643754322 ext 2497
Fax: +6643754359

Abstract: This paper is proposing the method for Thai handwritten character recognition. The methods are Robust C-Prototype and Back-Propagation Neural Network. The objective of experimental is recognition on Thai handwritten character. This is the result of both methods to be appearing accuracy more than 85%.

Keywords: Robust C-Prototype, Back-Propagation Neural Network, Thai Handwritten Character Recognition

1. INTRODUCTION

Pattern recognition scheme has numerously become a suffice tool utilized in character recognition. Generally, computer will be programmed to provide the functionality in order to classify each of character's property separately, defined as input character. These inputs will be determined for matching with the provided character patterns consequently. This paper proposes the offline processing, which the input data, gray scale of 256 levels. The processing is based on Thai characters on which preprocessing have been conducted. There are 44 Thai characters:

Please use the following format when citing this chapter:

Surinta, O., Jareanpon, C., 2006, in IFIP International Federation for Information Processing, Volume 228, Intelligent Information Processing III, eds. Z. Shi, Shimohara K., Feng D., (Boston: Springer), pp. 373–382.

ก ข ฃ ค ต ฆ ง   จ ฉ ช ซ ฌ ญ
ฎ ฏ ฐ ฑ ฒ ณ   ด ต ถ ท ธ น
บ ป ผ ฝ พ ฟ   ภ ม ย ร ล ว
ศ ษ ส ห ฬ อ ฮ

2.   DATA PREPROCESSING

Character-images are images of Thai handwritten characters written
down on a piece of paper. The outputs are stored as digital data by scanning.
One bitmap file with grey scale pattern (256 levels) specifies one character.

2.1   Edge Detection

Edge detection is an important step of the image processing phase.
Detecting edges in any object has two important conventions: the object
(image) must be a continuous image and the image must be scaled as black
and white tone. This paper uses a Chain code technique to detect the image's
edge. Simply put this technique move along the edge of the image and stops
at the beginning position in order to get the image's edge. [1]

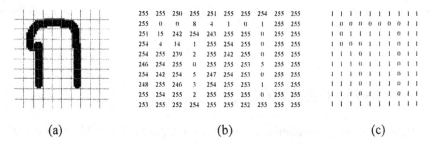

| (a) | (b) | (c) |

Figure 1. A diagram of extracting the object component from
the background component an the image.

2.2   Binarization

Binarization converts grey-level image to a black-white level image.
Basically, an image is separated into two components. The first component
is the object, while the other is background. The object in general is smaller
(in size) than the background. To extract the object component from the
background component, this scheme checks every point of pixel value with
one intermediate value (called the Thresholding value). The thresholding
value can be calculated from the following formula: [2]

$$g'(x,y) = \begin{cases} 0 & if \quad g(x,y) < T \\ 1 & if \quad g(x,y) \geq T \end{cases} \qquad (1)$$

In this paper, data (the image file of the Thai handwritten character) is stored in bitmap pattern. The individual bit carries one of two possible values:

1   refers to background and,
0   refers to object or content

2.3   The extraction of the outer edge from the object component

From the previous step, we have got the object and have got rid of its background in which all bits contain 1. This step is then used to detect the outer rims (laying on the object's edge) of the object and to separate them from the object in order to get the edge. There are several methodologies used on this particular case, e.g. chain code, morphology, etc. This paper uses a chain code convention. [2]

The resulting image (from binarization) is actually a structural character, comprising many points lying on the image. Therefore, detecting the direction of those points has been applied in order to simplify the processing. This implementation is based on a chain code technique to change the points to a numerical representation. Eventually, the direction is classified by 8 categories.

Once the edge of the image has discovered, the process needs to find the character line. The coordinate (x_k, y_k) is then represented by a complex number as the following formula:

$$u_k = x_k , i y_k \qquad (2)$$

2.4   Fourier Descriptors

Fourier Features are used to describe an edge of an object. They work by identifying coordinates (x_k, y_k); $k = 0,1,...,N-1$ where N is any other area in the image. All points (x_k, y_k) are represented as complex numbers, shown as: [3, 4, 5]

$$u_k = x_k + i y_k \qquad (3)$$

Where

$$i = \sqrt{-1}$$

Therefore, the DFT (Discrete Fourier Transform) (f_l) can be derived from:

$$f_l = \sum_{k=0}^{N-1} u_k \exp\left(-j\frac{2\pi}{N}lk\right) \tag{4}$$

Where

$$l = 0,1,...,N-1$$

From the above formula, a coefficient vector is automatically calculated. This vector fits as one dimension with the size of (1×10) or $(1 \times n)$

3.   FUZZY C-MEAN (FCM) ALGORITHM

The FCM algorithm minimizes the following objective function [6]

$$J_F(B,U;X) = \sum_{i=1}^{C}\sum_{j=1}^{N}(u_{ij})^m d_{ij}^2 \tag{5}$$

Where

$$u_{ij} \in [0,1] \text{ and } \sum_{i=1}^{C} u_{ij} = 1 \; \forall \; j$$

X = the set of feature vectors $\overline{x}_j$

$j = 1,2,...,N : N$ represents the image pixel

C = the group of images

$m \in [1,\alpha)$ = Fuzzifier

d_{ij}^2 = the distance from Feature Vector to the group of patterns

u_{ij} = member indicator of x_j in β_i

$B = (\beta_1,...,\beta_C)$ = C-tuple indicating C - Cluster

$U = \lfloor u_{ij} \rfloor$ = matrix, $C \times N$ in size, representing the condition

3.1   Object-Function Minimization in Robust C-Prototypes (RCP)

RCP can be determined in grouping phase in order to estimate C-Prototypes spontaneously, utilizing loss function (ρ) and square distance to reduce some noise. The definition can be expressed as: [6, 7]

$$J_F(B,U;X) = \sum_{i=1}^{C} \sum_{j=1}^{N} (u_{ij})^m \rho_i d_{ij}^2 \tag{6}$$

Where

$$u_{ij} \in [0,1] \text{ and } \sum_{i=1}^{C} u_{ij} = 1 \quad \forall j$$

The highest efficiency can be calculated as follow:

$$u_{ij} = \frac{1}{\sum_{k=1}^{C} \left[\frac{\rho_i (d_{ij}^2)}{\rho_i (d_{ik}^2)} \right]^{\left(\frac{1}{m-1}\right)}} \tag{7}$$

The best portion of weight function is that function with significant impact and efficiency in the RCP-Algorithm. This weight function used for general estimation, has been designed as symmetric distribution, whose center is the original point that differs from RCP-Algorithm used in this experiment. Therefore, the weight function must be rebuilt:

$$w : \Re^+ \to [0,1] \text{ Subject to}$$

$$\Im_1 : w(d^2) \text{ ; Monotonically function}$$

$$\Im_1 : w(d^2) = 0 \text{ for } d^2 > T + \alpha S$$

T and S are robust estimates of the average of the square of distance and standard deviation, while α is any constant.

$$p_1 : w(0) = 1, w(T) = 0.5, w'(0) = 0$$

T and S are truly important for constructing the weight function. Therefore, the process needs the efficiency estimation. Obviously, Med-Median and Median of Absolute Deviation have been identified to be used in estimation, which is:

$$T_i = \underset{x_i \in X_j}{Med}(d_{ij}^2) \text{ and} \tag{8}$$

$$S_i = 1.418 \times \underset{x_i \in X_j}{MAD}(d_{ij}^2) \tag{9}$$

Where

$$X_i = \left\{ x_j \mid d_{ij}^2 \le d_{kj}^2 \quad \forall k \ne i \right\}$$

The weight function $w : \Re^+ \to [0,1]$ is defined as $\Im_1 - \Im_3$, which is :

$$w_i(d^2) = \begin{cases} 1 - \dfrac{d^4}{2T_i^2} & \text{if } d^2 \in [0,T] \\[2ex] \dfrac{[d^2 - (T_i \alpha S_i)]^2}{2\alpha^2 S_i^2} & \text{if } d^2 \in [T_i, T_i + \alpha S_i] \\[2ex] 0 & \text{if } d^2 > T_i + \alpha S_i \end{cases} \tag{10}$$

The Loss function derived from the weight function can be calculated regarding to (10)

$$\rho_i(d^2) = \begin{cases} d^2 - \dfrac{d^6}{6T_i^2} & \text{if } d^2 \in [0,T] \\[2ex] \dfrac{[d^2 - (T_i + \alpha S_i)]^3}{6\alpha^2 S_i^2} + \dfrac{5T_i + \alpha S_i}{6} & \text{if } d^2 \in [T_i, T_i + \alpha S_i] \\[2ex] \dfrac{5T_i + \alpha S_i}{6} + K_i & \text{if } d^2 > T_i + \alpha S_i \end{cases} \tag{11}$$

K_i is a constant;

$$K_i = \max_{1 \le j \le c} \left\{ \frac{5T_j + \alpha S_j}{6} \right\} - \frac{5T_i + \alpha S_i}{6}$$

for $i = 1, \dots, C$

In (11), K_i must be added in order to impede any noise. This will force the total values of the loss function to be at least the average value of normal data, which every point of noise has the same member value.

3.2 Calculating the distance between groups of images and the relation among them

The required conditions to adjust the pattern characters for the Mahalanobis Distance is

$$d_{ij}^2 = (\bar{x}_j - \bar{c}_i)^T M (\bar{x}_j - \bar{c}_i) \tag{12}$$

$\bar{x}_j$; The feature vector of group of data

$\bar{c}_i$; Center vector of each cluster

M_i ; Symmetric vector, which is a positive definite matrix derived from

$$\bar{c}_i = \sum_{j=1}^{N} \left(u_{ij} \right)^m w_{ij} \bar{x}_j \Big/ \sum_{j=1}^{N} \left(u_{ij} \right)^m w_{ij} \qquad (13)$$

and

$$M_i = \left| R_i \right|^{1/n} R_i^{-1} \qquad (14)$$

Where

$$C_i = \sum_{j=1}^{N} \left(u_{ij} \right)^m w_{ij} \left(\bar{x}_j - \bar{c}_i \right) \left(\bar{x}_j - \bar{c}_i \right)^T \Big/ \sum_{J=1}^{N} \left(u_{ij} \right)^m w_{ij}$$

C_i is the "Robust Fuzzy Covariant Matrix"

4. ARTIFICIAL NEURAL NETWORKS

An Artificial Neural Network (ANN) is an information processing paradigm that is inspired by the way biological nervous systems, such as the brain, process information. It is composed of a large number of highly interconnected processing elements (neurons) working in unison to solve specific problems. An ANN is configured for a specific application, such as pattern recognition or data classification, through a learning process. Figure 2 shows the diagram of a neural network. [8]

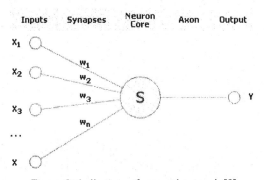

Figure 2. A diagram of a neural network [8]

Figure 2 shows that an artificial neuron consists of synapses connecting the neuron inputs with the nucleus, a neuron nucleus processing input signals and an axon connecting the neuron with those of the next layer. Every synapse has its own weight, which determines how the corresponding neuron input influences its condition. The neuron condition is calculated by the following formula:

$$S = \sum_{i=1}^{n} x_i w_i \qquad (15)$$

Where

n = number of neuron inputs

x_i = neuron input value

w_i = synapse weight

4.1   Back-Propagation Neural Network

Back-Propagation neural networks are tools for searching regularities, forecasting, and qualitative analysis. Back propagation neural network use a learning algorithm use in which an error moves from the output layer to the input one.

Back-Propagation neural networks consists of several neuron layers, each neuron of layer i being connected to each neuron of layer $i+1$.

The task of training neural network comes down to finding a functional dependence $y = f(x)$, where x is an input vector and y is an output one. In the general case this task with a limited set of input data has an infinite set of solutions. To limit the search space during the training, the task is allotted to minimize the efficiency function of the neural network error, which is found with the least squares estimator.

$$E(w) = \frac{1}{2} \sum_{j=1}^{p} (y_j - d_j)^2 \qquad (16)$$

Where

y_j = network output value

d_j = target value of output

p = number of neurons in the output layer

The neural network training is conducted by the gradient descent method, in each iteration the weight change is made according to the following formula:

$$\Delta w_{ij} = -\eta \cdot \frac{\partial E}{\partial w_{ij}} \qquad (17)$$

Where

$$\frac{\partial E}{\partial w_{ij}} = \frac{\partial E}{\partial y_j} \cdot \frac{dy_j}{dS_j} \cdot \frac{\partial S_j}{\partial w_{ij}}$$

Where

y_j = neuron output value,

S_j = weighted total of output signals determined by the formula (15).

With the multiplier

$$\frac{\partial S_j}{\partial w_{ij}} \equiv x_i \tag{18}$$

Where

x_i = the neuron input value

In the training phase, the correct class for each record is known (this is termed supervised training), and the output nodes can therefore be assigned "correct" values -- "1" for the node corresponding to the correct class, and "0" for the others. (In practice it has been found better to use values of 0.9 and 0.1, respectively.) It is thus possible to compare the network's calculated values for the output nodes to these "correct" values, and calculate an error term for each node (the "Delta" rule). These error terms are then used to adjust the weights in the hidden layers so that, hopefully, the next time around the output values will be closer to the "correct" values. [9]

5.   EXPERIMENTAL RESULT

The data in this experiment have 2 sets. The first set is "the learning set" containing 4,400 characters. The second set is the "test set" containing 440 characters. All data is Thai handwritten and generated by 100 persons.

The experiment is divided into two parts. The first part is "Robust C-Prototype". And the second part is "Back-Propagation neural network". The features of these structures are shown in table 1. The comparisons of both methods are shown in table 2.

Table 1. Back-Propagation Neural Network Structure

Training Algorithm	Back-Propagation
Performance Function	Mean-Square Error
Performance Goal	0.002
Minimum Gradient	le-9

Table 2. Comparison between Robust C-Prototype and Back-propagation neural network

Topic	Robust C-Prototype	Back-Propagation neural network
Time of learning	1.5 Hour	2.45 Hour
Accuracy test on "Test set"	91.5%	88%

6. CONCLUSION

This paper looks at Thai handwritten character recognition. We compared Robust C-Prototype and Back-Propagation neural networks. The Experimental results of both methods have accuracy more than 85%. This paper is concerned with the recognition of only a single character. Future work is to recognize entire handwritten words or signatures.

ACKNOWLEDGEMENTS

We are grateful for the support of the Faculty of Informatics at Mahasarakham University.

REFERENCES

1. Castleman, K. R. Digital Image Processing. Prentice Hall. NJ, n.p. , 1995.
2. Sergios Theodoridis, Konstantinos Koutroumbas. Pattern Recognition. Academic Press 24-28 Oval Road London: Department of Informatics. University of Athens; 1998.
3. Yerin Yoo. Tutorial on Fourier Theory. n.p. , 2001.
4. Yi Lu, Steven Schlosser, Michael Janeczko. Fourier Descriptors and Handwritten Digit Recognition. Machine Vision and Application. 1993.
5. B. Pinkowski. Fourier Descriptors for Characterizing Object Contour. Western Michigan University.
6. Hichem Frigui and Raghu Krishapuram. A Robust Algorithm for Automatic Extraction of an Unknown Number of Clusters from Noisy Data. Pattern Recognition Letters(17). 1223-1232, n.p. , 1996.
7. Olarik Surinta and Supot Nitsuwat. Handwritten Thai Character Recognition Using Fourier Descriptors and Robust C-Prototype. Proceeding of The National Conference on Computing and Information Technology (NCCIT2005). Bangkok, Thailand. 24-25 May 2005.
8. Alexey Starikov. Neural Networks. <http://www.basegroup.ru/neural/math.en.htm> 5 May 2006.
9. Chatklaw Jareanpon and Olarik Surinta. Handwritten Recognition with Neural Network. Proceeding of International Workshop on Advanced Image Technology (IWAIT2006). Okinawa, Japan. 9-10 January 2006.

2D CONDITIONAL RANDOM FIELDS FOR IMAGE CLASSIFICATION

Ming Wen, Hui Han, Lu Wang and Wenyuan Wang
Department of Automation, Tsinghua University
Beijing, 100084, P.R.China
{wenm03, hanh01, l-wang02}@mails.tsinghua.edu.cn, wwy-dau@tsinghua.edu.cn

Abstract   For grid-based image classification, an image is divided into blocks, and a feature vector is formed for each block. Conventional grid-based classification algorithms suffer from inability to take into account the two-dimensional neighborhood interactions of blocks. We present a classification method based on two-dimensional Conditional Random Fields which can avoid the limitation. As a discriminative approach, the proposed method offers several advantages over generative approaches, including the ability to relax the assumption of conditional independence of the observations.

Keywords: multimedia data mining, image classification, 2D conditional random fields, loopy belief propagation

1.   Introduction

Image classification is one of the most actively researched areas in multimedia data mining. Given a training set (x^k, y^k) for $k = 1, ..., K$, where x^k is the k'th image and y^k is the corresponding label, i.e. the category of the image, we would like to learn a model that maps images to labels. In general, current image classification algorithms can be divided into two groups according to the features used in classification: global approaches and component-based approaches [1]. The global approaches use global features which are usually computed with little cost. For example, Chapelle et al. [2] trained Support Vector Machines (SVMs) on color histograms to classify the images into the predefined categories. Vailaya et al. [11] extracted edge direction histograms and used Bayesian classifiers to discriminate between city and landscape images. However, global features are often unable to depict the internal structure and important details of an image. Therefore, a lot of component-based approaches have been proposed to exploit local and spatial information of the images. Fergus et al. [3] proposed a generative model to recognize object classes from unsegmented cluttered scenes. This classification system models

Please use the following format when citing this chapter:

Wen, M., Han, H., Wang, L., Wang, W., 2006, in IFIP International Federation for Information Processing, Volume 228, Intelligent Information Processing III, eds. Z. Shi, Shimohara K., Feng D., (Boston: Springer), pp. 383–390.

the appearance, shape, occlusion and relative scale of local parts extracted by an interest point detector. Smith and Li [9] proposed a method for classifying and querying images based on the spatial orderings of regions or objects using composite region templates. In the method introduced by Szummer and Picard [10], an image is partitioned into non-overlapping blocks; color and texture features are extracted for each block. The image is then classified as indoor or outdoor scenes by combining the classification results of these blocks.

Our work was intended to proceed along the same philosophical lines as Szummer and Picard's method [10] which is referred to as the grid-based method. For grid-based image classification, an image x is divided into M-by-N blocks $x = \{x_{0,0}, x_{0,1}, ..., x_{M-1,N-1}\}$, and a feature vector $\Phi(x_{i,j})$ is formed for each block $x_{i,j}$. Traditional grid-based methods don't take into account the two-dimensional neighborhood interactions of image blocks. Generative models such as Bayesian networks or Markov random fields can be used to address this problem. However, generative models have fundamental limitations. One limitation is that they require specification of the data generation process, i.e., how data can be sampled from the model [7]. In many cases, this process is unknown and not of interest for the classification task. A second limitation is that to make the model support tractable inference, one has to assume conditional independence of the observed data given the labels. Conditional random fields [5] (CRFs) are a probabilistic framework for labeling and segmenting sequential data. The conditional nature of CRFs means that no effort is wasted on specification of the data generation process and one don't need to make unwarranted independence assumptions about the observations.

In this paper, we present an image classification method based on two-dimensional conditional random fields (2D CRFs). We introduce a sequence of image block labels $h = \{h_{0,0}, h_{0,1}, ..., h_{M-1,N-1}\}$ and assume (x, h) is a CRF. Since the image blocks are two-dimensionally laid out, we specify the graphical structure of this CRF as a 2D grid, where the relative location of vertex $h_{i,j}$ is determined by the relative location of patch $x_{i,j}$ in an image x. Borrowing ideas from [8], we define a conditional probabilistic model $p(y, h|x)$ to combine the 2D CRF (x, h) and image labels y into a unified framework for image classification. Hence $p(y|x) = \sum_h p(y, h|x)$. In this model, inference and parameter estimation can be carried out using loopy belief propagation [6].

The rest of this paper is organized as follows. We introduce 2D CRFs in the next section. Section 3 describes the details of our model. In section 4, we present our experimental setup and results. Section 5 brings this paper to a conclusion. Finally, we give our acknowledgements.

2.   2D Conditional Random Fields

2.1   Standard CRFs

A conditional random field is an undirected graphical model that defines a single exponential distribution over label sequences given a particular observation sequence. Let X be a random variable over the observations to be labeled, and H be a random variable over corresponding labels. All components H_i of H are assumed to range over a finite label alphabet $\mathcal{H}$. In a discriminative framework, CRFs construct a conditional model $p(H|X)$ from paired observations and labels. Formally, we have the following definition of CRFs [5]:

DEFINITION 1 *Let $G = (V, E)$ be an undirected graph such that $H = \{H_v\}_{v \in V}$. Then (X, H) is a conditional random field if, when conditioned on X, the random variables H_v obey the Markov property with respect to the graph: $p(H_v|X, H_{V-\{v\}}) = p(H_v|X, H_{N_v})$, where $V - \{v\}$ is the set of nodes in the graph except the node v and N_v is the set of neighbors of the node v in graph G.*

Thus, a CRF is a random field globally conditioned on the observations X. In theory the structure of graph G can be arbitrary, provided it represents the conditional independencies in the models.

If the graph G is a tree (of which a chain is the simplest case), its cliques are the edges and vertices. According to the Hammersley-Clifford Theorem [4], the conditional distribution of the label sequences H given the observations X has the form:

$$p(h|x) = \frac{1}{Z(x)} \exp\{\psi(h, x; \theta)\}$$

$$Z(x) = \sum_h \exp\{\psi(h, x; \theta)\}$$

$$\psi(h, x; \theta) = \sum_{v \in V, l} \theta_l^1 f_l^1(v, h|_v, x) + \sum_{e \in E, l} \theta_l^2 f_l^2(e, h|_e, x)$$

where $Z(x)$ is a normalization factor known as the partition function; $h|_v$ and $h|_e$ are the components of h associated with vertex v and edge e respectively; f_l^1 and f_l^2 are feature functions and θ (including θ_l^1 and θ_l^2) are parameters to be estimated from the training data.

2.2   2D CRFs

2D CRFs are a particular case of CRFs. The graphical structure of 2D CRFs is a 2D grid (see Figure 1). Here X denotes the random variable over observations, and H denotes the random variable over the corresponding label sequences. $H_{i,j}$ is the component of H at the vertex (i, j). Apparently, the cliques of this graph are its edges and vertices, so the conditional distribution of 2D CRFs has the same form as tree-structured CRFs. 2D CRFs can also be viewed as a finite-state model [12]. Each variable $H_{i,j}$ has a finite set of states. Out labels are associated with the states. It is possible for several states to have the same label, but in this paper we assume a one-to-one correspondence.

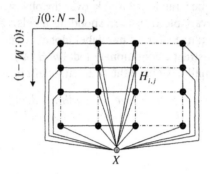

Figure 1.   The graphical structure of 2D CRFs

3.   Application to Image Classification

3.1   2D CRFs with Hidden Variables

Our task is to learn a model that maps images x to labels y. These labels belong to a finite image label alphabet $\mathcal{Y}$, e.g. $\mathcal{Y} = \{City, Landscape\}$.

We divide an image into M-by-N non-overlapping equal-sized blocks, and assume these image blocks can be classified into several categories, although these categories might not carry exact semantic meanings. Thus, we introduce a set of hidden variables $h_{0,0}, h_{0,1}, ..., h_{M-1,N-1}$, that correspond to block labels of an image x and form a label sequence h. Intuitively, (x, h) can be modeled with a 2D CRF. However, what we are concerned about is not block labels but image labels. Motivated by [8], we define a conditional probabilistic model:

$$p(y, h|x, \theta) = \frac{\exp\{\psi(y, h, x; \theta)\}}{\sum_{y',h} \exp\{\psi(y', h, x; \theta)\}}$$

$$\psi(y, h, x; \theta) = \sum_{v \in V, l} \theta_l^1 f_l^1(v, y, h_{i,j}, x) + \sum_{e \in E, l} \theta_l^2 f_l^2(e, y, h_{m,n}, h_{i,j}, x) \quad (1)$$

where (x, h) is a 2D CRF; $G = (V, E)$ is the graph of the 2D CRF; $h_{i,j}$ is the component of h associated with vertex v; $(h_{m,n}, h_{i,j})$ are the components of h associated with edge e; f_l^1 and f_l^2 are feature functions and θ (including θ_l^1

and θ_l^2) are the parameters of the model. It follows that

$$p(y|x, \theta) = \sum_h p(y, h|x, \theta) = \frac{\sum\limits_h \exp\{\psi(y, h, x; \theta)\}}{\sum\limits_{y', h} \exp\{\psi(y', h, x; \theta)\}}$$

Given the parameters θ^* estimated from the training data, a test image x will be labeled with

$$y = \arg\max_{y \in \mathcal{Y}} p(y|x, \theta^*)$$

We define ψ to take the following form as described in [8] :

$$\psi(y, h, x; \theta) = \sum_{v \in V} \phi(x_{i,j}) \cdot \theta(h_{i,j}) + \sum_{v \in V} \theta(h_{i,j}, y) + \sum_{e \in E} \theta(h_{i,j}, h_{m,n}, y) \quad (2)$$

Here $\theta(p) \in \mathbb{R}^d$ for $p \in \mathcal{H}$ is a parameter vector corresponding the p'th block state (block label). The inner-product $\phi(x_{i,j}) \cdot \theta(p)$ can be viewed as a measure of the compatibility between block $x_{i,j}$ and state p. $\theta(p, y) \in \mathbb{R}$ for $p \in \mathcal{H}, y \in \mathcal{Y}$ can be interpreted as a measure of the compatibility between state p and image label y. $\theta(p, q, y) \in \mathbb{R}$ for $p, q \in \mathcal{H}$ and $y \in \mathcal{Y}$ measures the compatibility between the label y and an edge with states p and q. Apparently, Eq. 2 can be written in the same form as Eq. 1.

3.2   Parameter Estimation

Given the training set (x^k, y^k) for $k = 1, ..., K$, we use the following objective function in training the parameters:

$$L(\theta) = \sum_k \log p(y^k|x^k, \theta) - \frac{1}{2\sigma^2} \|\theta\|^2 \quad (3)$$

where the first item is the log-likelihood of the training data, and the second item is the logarithm of a Gaussian prior with variance σ^2, i.e. $p(\theta) \sim \exp(\frac{1}{2\sigma^2} \|\theta\|^2)$. The parameter estimation problem is to find the parameters θ^* that maximize $L(\theta)$. It is worth noting that due to the use of hidden variables, $L(\theta)$ has multiple local extrema, i.e., this method is not guaranteed to reach the global optimal point [8]. During the course of optimization, it's very important to compute the gradient of $L(\theta)$. In the rest of this section, we discuss how the gradient can be calculated efficiently. Consider the likelihood term that is contributed by the k'th training data:

$$L^k(\theta) = \log p(y^k|x^k, \theta)$$

Taking the partial derivatives of $L^k(\theta)$ with respect to the parameters θ, we have the following equations:

$$\frac{\partial L^k(\theta)}{\partial \theta_l^1} = \sum_{v \in V, a} p(h_{i,j} = a | y^k, x^k, \theta) f_l^1(v, y^k, a, x^k)$$

$$- \sum_{y', v \in V, a} p(h_{i,j} = a, y' | x^k, \theta) f_l^1(v, y', a, x^k)$$

$$\frac{\partial L^k(\theta)}{\partial \theta_l^2} = \sum_{e \in E, a, b} p(h_{i,j} = a, h_{m,n} = b | y^k, x^k, \theta) f_l^2(e, y^k, a, b, x^k)$$

$$- \sum_{y', e \in E, a, b} p(h_{i,j} = a, h_{m,n} = b, y' | x^k, \theta) f_l^2(e, y', a, b, x^k)$$

It is obvious that $\partial L^k(\theta)/\partial \theta_l^1$ can be expressed in terms of components $p(h_{i,j} = a | y, x^k, \theta)$ and $p(y | x^k, \theta)$, which can be approximately calculated using loopy belief propagation, for 2D grid contains cycles. Similarly, $\partial L^k(\theta)/\partial \theta_l^2$ can also be expressed in terms of expressions which can be approximately calculated using loopy belief propagation.

4.   Experiments

4.1   Experimental Setup

We carried out three sets of experiments to distinguish car from background, city from landscape, and indoor scene from outdoor scene.

The image data set consists of 600 Corel images. All the images are in JPEG format of size 384×256 or 256×384. As a result of the tradeoff between cost and accuracy, every image is partitioned into 8-by-8 blocks, and a feature vector is formed for each block. The feature vector is made up of color histogram (CH), edge direction histogram (EDH), texture statistics based on Gabor filters and Discrete Cosine Transform (DCT) coefficients. CH is obtained by quantizing each component of the RGB color space into 16 bins. For the shape feature, EDH is selected. Sobel edge detector is applied to obtain the edge images. The computed EDH from the edge image of each block is quantized into 36 bins. To calculate the texture feature, we first apply a set of 2D Gabor filters to the blocks, and then calculate the means and standard deviations of the transformation coefficients. The filter bank is created with 5 orientations $(0°, 30°, 60°, 90°, 135°)$ and 6 frequencies $(0, 2, 4, 8, 16, 32)$. The DCT transform is performed on each block, and the 16 coefficients from the uppermost left 4-by-4 matrix are taken as features, representing the energy in the lower frequencies. Hence, a feature vector of 160 dimensions is formed for each block. Finally, Principal Components Analysis (PCA) is applied to reduce the feature vector of each block to 2 dimensions.

In our experiments, images within each category were randomly partitioned in half to form a training set and a test set, and five-state models were trained. We repeated each experiment for 5 random splits, and reported the average of the results obtained over 5 different test sets. The parameter σ^2 of the Gaussian prior in 2D CRFs was selected according to a two-fold cross-validation on the training set.

4.2   Experimental Results

To provide a more objective evaluation, we compared our method with a SVM based method. Different from the method in [2], the SVM based method we used in our experiments is a grid-based method. It packs the block feature vectors of an image into a single feature vector.

The average classification accuracies are presented in Table 1. From the results shown in Table 1, we can see that the proposed 2D CRFs based method performs better than the SVM based method. Though the SVM based method extracts local features and partially considers the spatial information of image blocks, it loses sight of the fact that the blocks are two-dimensionally laid out.

Table 1.   Comparison of the classification results for different methods

Experiment	2D CRFs	SVM
Car vs. Background	88.8%	87.0%
City vs. Landscape	89.0%	86.2%
Indoor scene vs. Outdoor scene	90.6%	86.4%

5.   Conclusions and Future Work

In this paper, we have presented a novel probabilistic model for grid-based image classification. Based on two-dimensional conditional random fields, the model not only takes into account the spatial information of image blocks, but also incorporates the two-dimensional neighborhood interactions of blocks. Experimental results show our method outperforms the SVM based classification method. In the future, we'll try to deduce the forward-backward vectors of this model for efficient inference.

Acknowledgments

We thank Chong Wang for many helpful discussions. We also thank Kevin Murphy very much for publishing the Conditional Random Field Toolbox for Matlab in the Web so that we can develop our experimental codes efficiently.

References

[1] Bi, J. and Chen, Y. (2005). A sparse support vector machine approach to region-based image categorization. In *Proc. of CVPR*.

[2] Chapelle, O., Haffner, P., and Vapnik, V. (1999). Support vector machines for histogram-based image classification. *IEEE Trans. on Neural Networks*, 10(5):1055–1064.

[3] Fergus, R., Perona, P., and Zisserman, A. (2003). Object class recognition by unsupervised scale-invariant learning. In *Proc. of CVPR*, volume 2, pages 264–271.

[4] Hammersley, J. and Clifford, P. (1971). Markov fields on finite graphs and lattices. Unpublished Manuscript.

[5] Lafferty, J., McCallum, A., and Pereira, F. (2001). Conditional random fields: Probabilistic models for segmenting and labeling sequence data. In *Proc. of ICML*.

[6] Murphy, K. P., Weiss, Y., and Jordan, M. I. (1999). Loopy belief propagation for approximate inference: An empirical study. In *Proc. of UAI*.

[7] Qi, Y., Szummer, M., and Minka, T. P. (2005). Bayesian conditional random fields. In *Proc. of the Tenth International Workshop on Artificial Intelligence and Statistics*.

[8] Quattoni, A., Collins, M., and Darrell, T. (2004). Conditional random fields for object recognition. In *Proc. of NIPS*.

[9] Smith, J. R. and Li, C.-S. (1999). Image classification and querying using composite region templates. *Journal of Computer Vision and Image Understanding*, 75(1/2):165–174.

[10] Szummer, M. and Picard, R. W. (1998). Indoor-outdoor image classification. In *Proc. of IEEE International Workshop on Content-Based Access of Image and Video Databases*, pages 42–51.

[11] Vailaya, A., Figueiredo, M. A. T., Jain, A. K., and Zhang, H.-J. (2001). Image classification for content-based indexing. *IEEE Trans. on Image Processing*, 10(1):117–130.

[12] Zhu, J., Nie, Z., Wen, J.-R., Zhang, B., and Ma, W.-Y. (2005). 2d conditional random fields for web information extraction. In *Proc. of ICML*.

IMAGE ENHANCEMENT USING NONSUBSAMPLED CONTOURLET TRANSFORM

Rafia Mumtaz[1], Raja Iqbal[2] and Dr.Shoab A.Khan[3]

[1,2]MCS, National Unioversity of Sciences and Technology, Rawalpindi, Pakistan;[3]EME, National University of Sciences nad Technology,Rawalpindi,Pakistan

Abstract: This paper presents a novel technique of image Enhancement which can be widely used in medical and biological imaging to improve the image quality. The principle objective of enhancement is to process an image so that the result is more suitable than the original image for a specific application. Image enhancement enhances weak edges or weak features in an image while keeping strong edges or features. All existing methods of image enhancement decompose images in a separable fashion, and thus cannot use the geometric information in the transform domain to distinguish weak edges from noises. Therefore, they either amplify noises or introduce visible artifacts, when they are applied to noisy images. The NonSubsampled Contourlet transform built upon NonSubsampled pyramids and NonSubsampled directional filter banks can provide a shift invariant directional multi resolution image representation. The geometric information is gathered pixel by pixel from the NonSubsampled Contourlet Transform coefficients. The proposed method achieved better enhancement results than the wavelet based methods of enhancement.

Key words: Enhancement, NonSubsampled, Contourlet Transform.

1.   INTRODUCTION

The aim of image enhancement is to improve the interpretability or perception of information in images for human viewers, or to provide `better' input for other automated image processing techniques. It enhances weak edges or weak features in an image while keeping strong edges or features. Traditional image enhancement methods such as unsharp masking, split an image into different frequency subbands

Please use the following format when citing this chapter:

Mumtaz, R., Iqbal, R., Khan, S.A., 2006, in IFIP International Federation for Information Processing, Volume 228, Intelligent Information Processing III, eds. Z. Shi, Shimohara K., Feng D., (Boston: Springer), pp. 391–400.

and amplify the high pass subbands. Although the wavelet transform has been proven to be powerful in many signal and image processing applications such as compression, noise removal, image edge enhancement, and feature extraction; wavelets are not optimal in capturing the two-dimensional singularities found in images. Several transforms have been proposed for image signals that have incorporated directionality and multiresolution and hence, could more efficiently capture edges in natural images [1]. Recently Do and Vetterli proposed an efficient directional multiresolution image representation called the Contourlet transform [2]. The Contourlet transform employs Laplacian pyramids to achieve multiresolution decomposition and directional filter banks to achieve directional de-composition. Due to downsampling and upsampling, the Contourlet transform is shift-variant. However, Shift sensitivity is an undesirable property because it implies that the transform coefficients fail to distinguish between input signal shifts [3]. Shift-invariance is desirable in image analysis applications such as edge detection, contour characterization, and image enhancement.

In this paper, the Nonsubsampled Contourlet transform (NSCT) is presented, which is a shift-invariant version of the Contourlet transform. The NSCT is built upon iterated nonsubsampled filter banks to obtain a shift-invariant directional multiresolution image representation. Based on the NSCT, a new method for image enhancement is introduced.

2.   CONSTRUCTION

2.1   NonSubsampled Contourlet Transform

The NSCT is a fully shift-invariant, multi-scale, and multidirectional expansion that has a fast implementation. Figure 1 (a) displays the overview of the proposed NSCT. The structure consists in a bank of filters that splits the 2-D frequency plane in the subbands illustrated in Figure 1(b). Our proposed transform can thus be divided into two shift-invariant parts which are as follow:
1. A nonsubsampled pyramid structure that ensures the multi-scale property and
2. A nonsubsampled DFB structure that gives directionality.

The contourlet transform employs Laplacian pyramids for multiscale decomposition, and directional filter banks (DFB) for directional decomposition. To achieve the shift-invariance, the *nonsubsampled* contourlet transform is built upon nonsubsampled pyramids and nonsubsampled DFB [4].

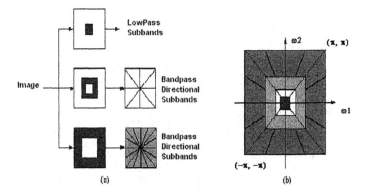

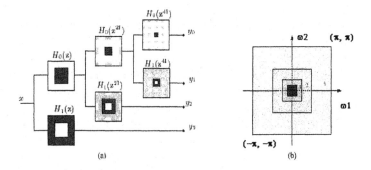

Figure 1. The NonSubsampled Contourlet Transform. (a) NonSubsampled filter bank structure that implements the NSCT. (b) The idealized frequency partitioning obtained with the proposed structure

Figure 2. The proposed NonSubsampled pyramid is a 2-D multi-resolution expansion similar to the 1-D NonSubsampled wavelet transform.

2.2   Nonsubsampled Pyramids

The multiscale property of the NSCT is obtained from a shift invariant filtering structure that achieves a subband decomposition similar to that of the Laplacian pyramid. This is achieved by using two-channel nonsubsampled 2-D filter banks [4].The nonsubsampled pyramid is completely different from the counterpart of the contourlet transform, the Laplacian pyramid. The building block of the nonsubsampled pyramid is a two-channel nonsubsampled filter bank as shown in Figure 2(a). A nonsubsampled filter bank has no downsampling or upsampling, and hence it is shift-invariant. The perfect reconstruction condition is obtained provided the filters satisfy the *Bezout identity*:

$$H_O(z)G_O(z) + H_1(z)G_1(z) = 1 \qquad\qquad\qquad (1)$$

This condition is much easier to satisfy than the perfect reconstruction condition for critically sampled filter banks, and thus allows better filters to be designed [5].

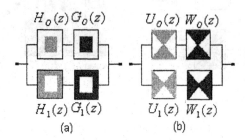

Figure 3. Ideal frequency response of the building block of: (a) NonSubsampled Pyramid; (b) NonSubsampled DFB

The ideal frequency response of the building block of the nonsubsampled pyramid is given in Figure 3(a). To achieve the multiscale decomposition, we construct nonsubsampled pyramids by iterated nonsubsampled filter banks. For the next level, we upsample all filters by 2 in both dimensions. Therefore, they also satisfy the perfect reconstruction condition. Note that filtering with the upsampled filter H(zM) has the same complexity as filtering with H(z) using the 'a trous' algorithm. The cascading of the analysis part is shown in Figure 4. These filters achieve multiresolution analysis as shown in Figure 5(a).

2.3   NonSubsampled Directional Filter Banks

The nonsubsampled DFB is a shift-invariant version of the critically sampled DFB in the contourlet transform. The building block of a nonsubsampled DFB is also a two-channel nonsubsampled filter bank. However, the ideal frequency response for a nonsubsampled DFB is different, as shown in Figure 3(b). The NSDFB is constructed by eliminating the downsamplers and upsamplers in the DFB. This is done by switching off the downsamplers/upsamplers in each two-channel filter bank in the DFB tree structure and upsampling the filters accordingly.

To obtain finer directional decomposition, we iterate nonsubsampled DFB's. For the next level, we upsample all filters by a quincunx matrix given by

$$Q = \begin{pmatrix} 1 & 1 \\ 1 & -1 \end{pmatrix} \qquad\qquad\qquad (2)$$

The frequency responses of two upsampled filters are given in Figure 6 and the cascading of the analysis part is shown in Figure 7. Then we obtain a four-direction frequency division as shown in Figure 5(b). The higher level decompositions follow the similar strategy, although they are more complex.

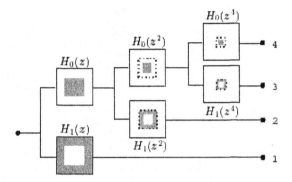

Figure 4. Iteration of two-channel nonsubsampled filter banks in the analysis part of a nonsubsampled pyramid. For upsampled filters, only effective pass bands within dotted boxes are shown.

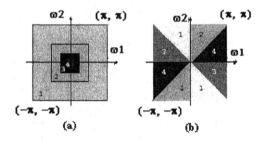

Figure 5. Frequency divisions of: (a) A NonSubsampled pyramid given in Figure 4. (b) A NonSubsampled DFB given in Figure.7

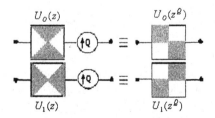

Figure 6. Upsampling filters by a Quincunx matrix Q

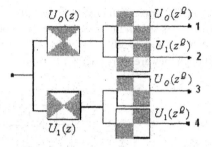

Figure 7. The analysis part of an iterated nonsubsampled directional filter bank.

2.4   NonSubsampled Contourlet Transform

The nonsubsampled contourlet transform combines nonsubsampled pyramids and nonsubsampled DFB's as shown in Figure 8. Nonsubsampled pyramids provide multiscale decomposition and nonsubsampled DFB's provide directional decomposition. This scheme can be iterated repeatedly on the low pass subband outputs of nonsubsampled pyramids. First, a nonsubsampled pyramid split the input into a low pass subband and a high pass subband. Then a nonsubsampled DFB decomposes the high pass subband into several directional subbands. The scheme is iterated repeatedly on the low pass subband [5].

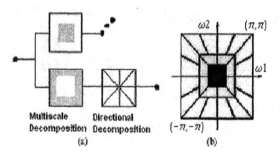

Figure 8. The NonSubsampled Contourlet Transform: (a) Block diagram. (b) Resulting frequency division, where the number of directions is increased with frequency.

In constructing the nonsubsampled contourlet transform, care must be taken when applying the directional filters to the coarser scales of the pyramid. Due to the tree-structure nature of the NSDFB, the directional response at the lower and upper frequencies suffers from aliasing which can be a problem in the upper stages of the pyramid. Its remedy is to judiciously upsample the NSDFB filters [4].

3. IMAGE ENHANCEMENT ALGORITHM

The nonsubsampled contourlet transform provides not only multiresolution analysis, but also geometric and directional representation. Since weak edges are geometric structures, while noises are not, we can use this geometric representation to distinguish them. The NSCT is shift-invariant such that each pixel of the transform subbands corresponds to that of the original image in the same location. Therefore, we gather the geometric information pixel by pixel from the NSCT coefficients. It has been observed that there are three classes of pixels: strong edges, weak edges, and noises. First, the strong edges correspond to those pixels with big-value coefficients in all subbands. Second, the weak edges correspond to those pixels with big-value coefficients in some directional subbands but small-value coefficients in other directional subbands within the same scale. Finally, the noises correspond to those pixels with small-value coefficients in all subbands. Based on this observation, pixels can be classified into three categories by analyzing the distribution of their coefficients in different subbands. One simple way is to compute the mean (denoted by mean) and the maximum (denoted by max) magnitude of the coefficients for each pixel, and then classify it by

$$
\begin{cases}
StrongEdge & if \quad mean \geq c\sigma \\
WeakEdge & if \quad mean < c\sigma, \max \geq c\sigma \\
Noise & if \quad mean < c\sigma, \max < c\sigma
\end{cases}
\tag{3}
$$

where c is a parameter ranging from 1 to 5, and   is the noise standard deviation of the subbands at a specific level. We first estimate the noise variance of the input image with the robust median operator and then compute the noise variance of each subband. The goal of image enhancement is to amplify weak edges and to suppress noises. To this end, we modify the NSCT coefficients according to the category of each pixel by a nonlinear mapping function.

$$
y(x) = \begin{cases}
x & StrongEdgePixels \\
\max((\frac{c\sigma}{|x|})^{p}, 1)x, & WeakEdgePixels \\
0 & NoisePixels
\end{cases}
\tag{4}
$$

where the input x is the original coefficient, and $0 < p < 1$ is the amplifying ratio. This function keeps the coefficients of strong edges, amplifies the coefficients of weak edges, and zeros the coefficients of noises. We summarize our enhancement method using the NSCT in the following algorithm:

1. Compute the NSCT of the input image for N levels.

2. For each level DFB,
   a) Estimate the noise variance.
   b) Compute the threshold and the amplifying ratio.
   c) At each pixel, compute the mean and the maximum magnitude of all directional subbands at this level, and classify it by (3) into strong edges, weak edges, or noises.
   d) For each directional subband, use the nonlinear mapping function given in (4) to modify the NSCT coefficients according to the classification.
3. Reconstruct the enhanced image from the modified NSCT coefficients.
4. Calculate the Detail and Background Variance.

4.   EXPERIMENTAL RESULTS

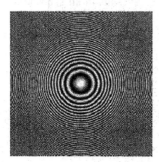 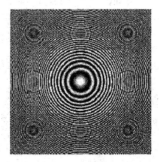

Figure 9. (a) Original Zoneplate image. (b) Enhanced by the NonSubsampled Contourlet Transform

Figure 10. (a) Original Lena image. (b) Enhanced by the NonSubsampled Contourlet Transform.

Figure 11. (a) Original Lena image. (b) Enhanced by the NonSubsampled Contourlet Transform

Figure 12. (a) Original Peppers image. (b) Enhanced by the NonSubsampled Contourlet Transform.

Table 1. Detail and Background Variance of different Images

Image	Original Image		Reconstructed Image	
	Detail Variance (DV)	Background Variance (BV)	Detail Variance (DV)	Background Variance (BV)
Zone plate	8186.665	114.383	69244.110	816.018
Lena	692.266	25.150	1061.337	38.227
Barbara	805.487	55.447	4379.570	113.118
Peppers	1142.621	32.987	2842.605	78.889

To evaluate the enhancement performance objectively, the *detailed variance* (DV) and *background variance* (BV) is calculated. The DV and BV values represent the variance of foreground and background pixels, respectively. Detail and background variance is calculated around every pixel by taking the variance of image intensities and classifying the pixel into foreground or background based on a threshold. The average of variance of foreground pixels gives Detail Variance (DV) and the average of variance of background pixels gives Background Variance (BV). A good enhancement method should increase the DV of the original image but not the BV. It has been observed that proposed algorithm offers better results in enhancing the weak edges in the textures.

5.   CONCLUSION

The proposed nonsubsampled Contourlet transform is constructed by iterated nonsubsampled filter banks. This transform provides shift-invariant directional multiresolution image representation. This new algorithm for image enhancement using the nonsubsampled Contourlet transform will show that better enhancement results can be obtained than the previous enhancement techniques.

6.   REFERENCES

1. Rumin Eslumi und Huyder Rudhu, "*Wavelet based Countourlet Transform and its application to Image Coding*", ECE Department, Michigan State University, East Lansing, MI 48824, USA.
2. Minh N. Do and Martin Vetterli, "The Countoulet Transform: An Efficient Directional Multiresolution Image Representaion", IEEE, Trans. Image Proc., 2005.
3. Panchamkumar D SHUKLA , Department of Electronic and Electrical Engineering, "Complex Wavelet Transform And Their Applications", University of Strathclyde, Glasgow G1 1XW, Scotland, United Kingdom.
4. L. Cunha, J. Zhou, and M. N. Do, "The nonsubsampled contourlet transform: theory, design and applications," *IEEE Trans. Image Proc.*, submitted, 2005.
5. L. Cunha, J. Zhou, and M. N. Do, "Nonsubsampled Contourlet Transform: Construction and Application in Enhancement," *IEEE Trans. Image Proc.*, submitted, 2005.

NONLINEAR SIMILARITY BASED IMAGE MATCHING

Muhammad Sirajul Islam
and Les Kitchen
Department of Computer Science and Software Engineering ,
The University of Melbourne, VIC 3010, Australia.
Email: $\{msislam, ljk+iip\}@csse.unimelb.edu.au$

Abstract   Image matching is an inarguably important operation for many practical sophisticated systems in machine vision and medical diagnosis. Many gray-level image matching applications use the sum-of-squared-difference *(SSD)* or sum-of-
absolute-differences *(SAD)*, which are very sensitive to noise. Almost all images
have some kind of noise, which causes the matching tasks significantly difficulty.
In this paper we explore a new, less noise sensitive image-matching technique.
It uses non linear similarity measure *min* or *median* on interest points to find
a match. The algorithm has been tested using a range of images with different gaussian noise. The result shows a significant improvement over traditional
Euclidean distance measure technique for image matching.

Keywords: Computer vision, Image processing, Interest points, Non maximum suppression,
Feature points.

1.   Introduction

Image matching is a common operation in many applications which include
object tracking, motion estimation of objects in two successive frames, medical diagnosis[1], etc. The greatest challenge in matching two images lies in
coping with the effects of noise. Noise may be caused by a wide variety of
effects, e.g., detector sensitivity variations, transmission or quantization error,
environmental variations, etc. Presence of noise in an image is very common
due to the nature of image capturing devices.

There are various techniques for image matching. They can be categorized
broadly into two classes: low-level (intensity level) image matching, and high-
level matching techniques. Depending on how the features for matching are
produced, the matching process can be divided into two types:

- Algorithms that deal with pixels directly for matching (low-level), for
  example cross-correlation techniques. In cross-correlation approaches
  two points are matched using some distance measure among the neigh-

---

Please use the following format when citing this chapter:

Islam, M.S., Kitchen, L., 2006, in IFIP International Federation for Information Processing, Volume 228, Intelligent
Information Processing III, eds. Z. Shi, Shimohara K., Feng D., (Boston: Springer), pp. 401–410.

bouring pixels of the two considered pixels. In an ideal situation this distance should be zero for a perfect match. This is not the case in the real world: as we mentioned earlier, the presence of noise is very common in digital images.

- The second category of matching uses description by extracted features, for example identifying edges and their relationships. Algorithms of this type highly depend on effective grouping of features and relationships among them.

The second type of matching relies on feature extraction and finding relationships among the extracted features. Finding relationships can be computationally expensive. One of the main disadvantages of cross-correlation or traditional Euclidean distance measures for image matching is that these techniques are significantly sensitive to noise and perturbations. Both of these two categories of matching algorithms may adopt some kind of probabilistic approach—like maximum likelihood image matching [2].

In this paper we describe a new technique for image matching which uses a nonlinear similarity based technique. Although our approach falls under the heading of low-level image matching technique, we try to improve the matching technique making it less sensitive to noise. Fuzzy logic has been an area of research in engineering since 1965. There are very few works, e.g., [3], using fuzzy information for image matching. Our algorithm has the flavour of fuzzy logic but does not strictly follow the steps of a fuzzy system, so we do not call it a complete fuzzy system based technique. A brief description of the steps is given in the next paragraph.

For matching two images it is very costly, in terms of time and memory, to match every point. Therefore, most of the matching techniques use a few hundred or so pixels, called *interest points (IP)*. We first extract IPs from two images and take the few hundred best points for pairing as matches. We use a 7×7 Moravec interest operator [4] for extracting IPs. The matching process treats the first image as a template which would be matched to the second. For similarity measures of an interest point the dot products of the normalized vectors, obtained by slicing a 3×3 neighborhood in the directions of NS, EW, NE, NW, are calculated. These four features are used to find the degree of similarity between interest points in two images. See Figure 1.

Our matching technique is based on the basic idea that the overall similarity of two points to be matched depends on the similarity of individual corresponding vectors. The experimental results show that our approach can detect 5 to 10% more correct matches than the traditional Euclidean distance transform measure.

Figure 1.   Vectors considered for feature extraction.

In Section 2 some related work is discussed. Section 3 describes our proposed technique; experimental results are shown in Section 4. Some final conclusions are drawn in Section 5.

2.   Related Work

Various approaches have been adopted for image matching (or finding a patch inside an image). One of the techniques uses the Hausdorff Distance [5] for matching. In this approach, edge extraction is usually done with one of the many edge detectors known in the image processing literature, like the Canny edge detector [6], Laplacian, Sobel, etc. After applying some algorithm that minimizes the Hausdorff Distance between two images, the best match is taken. This approach considers the shape of the objects in an image but does not consider the intensity value and it is feasible to find matches only for objects that exhibit sharp edges.

Another low-level feature-based image matching technique is RIMA [7] which is an extension to distance transform (*chamfer*) matching. In this technique, edge points are extracted from digital images, converted to binary images, which are distance transformed, and then the distance transform is used for image matching. The matching is estimated by superimposing the distance transform of the template on the distance transform of the source image. RIMA needs to keep a distance-transform image as well as the binary edge map. An advantage of our technique is that it does not use a binary image like RIMA, hence it requires less memory.

Matching algorithms based on fuzzy information are an interesting area of research and some work has been done on this. One piece of work based on fuzzy features is [8]. We claim our approach is somewhat fuzzy, but the significant difference between [8] and our work is that our algorithm does not strictly follow the steps of fuzzy systems. In [8], the matching task is done by coarse-to-fine matching; Fuzzy information is used for fine matching using steps of fuzzy systems like defining membership functions, creating fuzzy rules, etc. We do not use any membership function or fuzzy rules, although it can be a future work as discussed in Section 5.

(a) Left view.   (b) Right view.

Figure 2.   Different stereo views of corridor image.

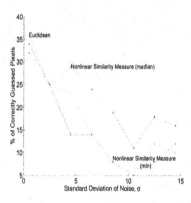

Figure 3.   Comparison for corridor image.

3.   Nonlinear Similarity based Matching

The general idea behind this approach is that two unit vectors are very similar if their dot product is very near to unity. This resembles to the fuzzy IF-THEN rule based formulation. In this section we describe our method of interest point extraction, how fuzzy features are extracted and what fuzzy operator is used and the reason behind that.

Interest Point Extraction

For extracting interest points we use a 7×7 Moravec operator [4], slightly modified to reduce directional bias, followed by 3×3 non-maximum suppression, with provision for resolving ties. We then choose the strongest few hundred points. However, to reduce the number of points that need to be solved, we first apply a conservative threshold to filter out the weaker interest points. For more details see [9].

Similarity Measure

In order to find a match we have to have some kind of similarity measure. To formulate such a measurement we consider the 3×3 neighborhood of the point of interest and extract four vectors as shown in Fig 1. Let a, b be two unit vectors and θ be the angle between them. So the dot product of these two vectors is $a \cdot b = \cos\theta$. As $\cos\theta$ approaches 1 the degree of similarity between these two vectors increases to the maximum. For a mathematical formulation of our algorithm let us consider two interest points i and j from the first and second images respectively. Let v^i_{rd}, v^i_{ld}, v^i_{hz}, v^i_{vt} be the normalized vectors along the NE (right diagonal), NW (left diagonal), EW (horizontal) and NS (vertical) directions, respectively, with respect to the center pixel i. Here, $v^i_{rd} \equiv [I(x+1, y-1), I(x,y), I(x-1, y+1)]$ and the definitions for the others are analogous. Now, four similarity measures S^{ij}_{rd}, S^{ij}_{ld}, S^{ij}_{hz}, and S^{ij}_{vt} are calculated taking the dot product of the pair of corresponding vectors of the two considered pixels i, j. For example, $S^{ij}_{rd} = v^i_{rd} \cdot v^j_{rd}$.

We are treating this similarity measure (zero to one) as a fuzzy grade of truth in the proposition that the corresponding vectors match. Using these values, we can take some decision about the degree of similarity of two considered pixels from the two noisy images. Because of noise, pixel values may change and hence the orientation in feature space of the four vectors will also change.

The Combination Operator

For estimating the similarity between two points from two images, we have to have some fuzzy operator. We can have fuzzy rules like:
$(S^{ij}_{rd} \ \varepsilon \ \text{High}) \wedge (S^{ij}_{ld} \ \varepsilon \ \text{High}) \wedge (S^{ij}_{hz} \ \varepsilon \ \text{High}) \wedge (S^{ij}_{vt} \ \varepsilon \ \text{High}) \Rightarrow$ (Pixels i and j are Highly Similar).

We know that traditionally the *minimum* operator is used for evaluating this AND connective (and *maximum* is used for OR). But the *minimum* and *maximum* operators are not good estimators. Zimmermann and Zysno (1980) revealed through experiments that the *minimum* operator does not work well as a model of the *and* connective, producing too conservative (low) results. Therefore they proposed some compensator operator. Let us consider a scenario from our experiment. Assume that the similarity measure along the right diagonal, S^{ij}_{rd}, is small because of some noise in that direction. On the other hand, the remaining three of the similarity measures are very high, because the two pixels are in fact really similar. Then it would be unjust to the three high values if we chose the minimum by using the *minimum* operator. Hence, we choose the *median* operator (we take the average of the middle two values), which as its very meaning explains that it is not biased towards any particular directional intensity change (caused by some random noise). Experimental results also conform with our view of choosing the *median* operator, as will be evident in Section 4.

(a) Cameraman image.   (b) Pepper image.

Figure 4.   Images used for experimental purpose.

4.   Experiments

Our experimental methodology is as follows: We have two images to be matched. We extract the best one hundred interest points from each image. For each interest point in the first image, we find the best match among the interest points in the second image. The best match is determined in three ways: The first way by finding the point with the maximum similarity according to our nonlinear similarity based approach, as laid out in Section 3, using the median to combine the similarities from the four neighborhood slices. The second way is similar, but uses the minimum of the four neighborhood-slice similarities instead of the median. And the third is by finding best match as the point with minimum Euclidean distance, treating the 3×3 neighborhood around each point as vector in a 9-dimensional Euclidean space.

For each way we compute the percentage of correct matches. A match is deemed to be *correct* if it lies within the neighborhood used for computing the interest points, that is, in our case, within three pixel positions of the exact-match position, for our 7×7 Moravec operator. Obviously, computing the percentage of correct matches requires knowing which matches are correct, that is, knowing the "ground truth" for the matching.

Figure 2 shows a pair of synthetically generated images (a stereo pair), taken from [10], for which the true matches are known. Figure 3 shows the percentage of correct matches for each of the three measures, for different levels of added Gaussian noise.

It is difficult and time-consuming to determine the ground truth for many pairs of images. Therefore, as an expedient for obtaining more data for comparisons, we adopt a tactic of matching an image to itself. In this case the ground truth is known trivially: a point should match to itself. Of course, for two identical images, the matching task is far too easy to be a fair basis for evaluation of matching techniques. However, we can make the matching task sufficiently difficult by adding two *different* sequences of noise respectively to two copies of the same image. This approximates reasonably well two frames from a motion sequence for which the motion just happens to be zero. Since the matching algorithm searches for the best match according to the measure that it is using, and does not "know" the ground truth, this does represent a reasonable task for evaluating matching techniques.

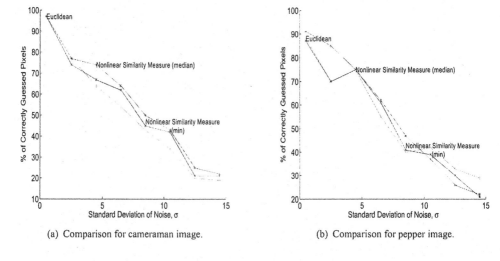

(a) Comparison for cameraman image.   (b) Comparison for pepper image.

Figure 5.   Comparison results.

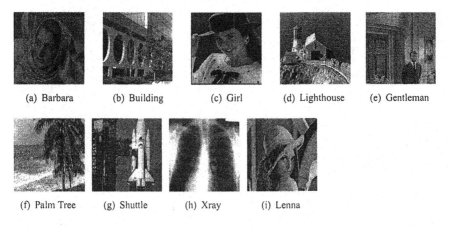

(a) Barbara   (b) Building   (c) Girl   (d) Lighthouse   (e) Gentleman

(f) Palm Tree   (g) Shuttle   (h) Xray   (i) Lenna

Figure 6.   Images used in experimentation.

Figures 5(a) to 5(b) (among a number of experimental results) show the matching performance for the different measures for different levels of noise on the task of self matching for the images shown in Figure 4. It is re-assuring that the results are reasonably similar to those obtained for the stereo pair of images in Figure 2, giving support to the idea that self-matching under noise does provide a reasonable way of evaluating matching techniques.

Some more experimental results for the images in Figure 6 are shown in Figures 7 and 8. While there is some variation across the images, and all methods

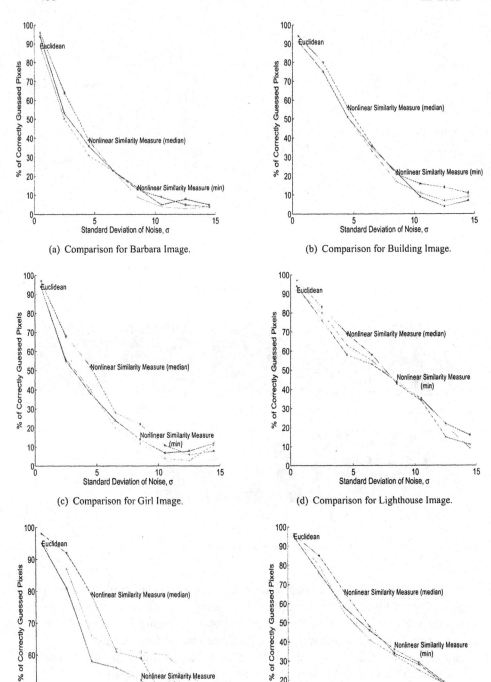

(a) Comparison for Barbara Image.

(b) Comparison for Building Image.

(c) Comparison for Girl Image.

(d) Comparison for Lighthouse Image.

(e) Comparison for Gentleman Image.

(f) Comparison for Palm Tree Image.

Figure 7. Comparison for images used in experimentation.

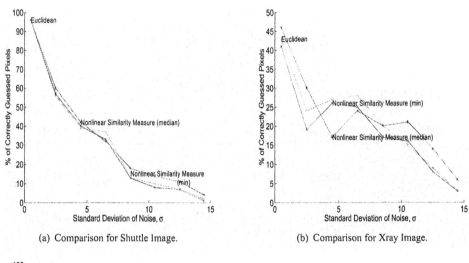

(a) Comparison for Shuttle Image.

(b) Comparison for Xray Image.

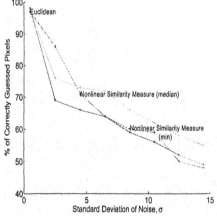

(c) Comparison for Lenna Image.

Figure 8.   Comparison for images used in experimentation(Continued).

perform worse as noise increases, in most cases the proposed technique with median performs noticeably better, in terms of percentage of correct matches, than either of the other matching techniques (the proposed technique with minimum and conventional Euclidean distance). In only a few cases does our matching approach with median perform equally with, or slightly worse than one of the other techniques.

5.   Conclusions

The proposed method is novel. Although it is a little more computationally expensive than matching using a Euclidean distance measure, its matching performance is in most cases appreciably greater. The experimental results show that our approach is less sensitive to noise, which is a common phenomenon in images. For future work, it would be very interesting to investigate in more detail why this method does perform better than euclidean distance measure, and whether the matching performance can be increased using steps of a fuzzy system model. It may be possible to make it more tolerant to noise by following fuzzy steps as done in the noise reduction in images by fuzzy filtering [8].

References

[1] Steven M. Vajdic, Jeremy Graham, and Shaun Voigt. An application of image matching/fusion in medicine. *1996 IEEE*, 1:42–47, 1996.

[2] Clark F. Olson. Maximum-likelihood image matching. *IEEE Transactions on Pattern Analysis and Machine Intelligence*, 24:853–857, 2002.

[3] Tian Jinwen, Huan Jianzhong, Liu Jian, and Li Dchua. Image matching based on fuzzy information. *3rd International Conference on Signal Processing*, 2:946–949, 1996.

[4] Moravec H.P. Towards automatic visual obstacle avoidance. *Proceedings of the 5th International Joint Conference on Artificial Intelligence*, page 584, 1977.

[5] Zhang Zhijia, Huang Shabai, and Shi Zelin. A fast strategy for image matching using Hausdorff distance. *2003 IEEE International Conference on Robotics, Intelligent Systems and Signal Processing*, 2:915–919, 2003.

[6] Canny J. A computational approach to edge detection. *PAMI*, 8:679–698, 1986.

[7] Abdul Ghafoor, Rao Naveed Iqbal, and Shoab Khan. Robust image matching algorithm. 4th *EURASIP Conference focused on Video/Image Processing and Multimedia Communications*, 1(7):155–160, January 2003.

[8] Dimitri Van De Ville, Mike Nachtegael, Dietrich Van der Weken, Wilfried Philips, and Ignace Lemahieu. Noise reduction by fuzzy image filtering. *IEEE Transactions on Fuzzy Systems*, 11:429–436, 2003.

[9] Muhammad Sirajul Islam and Les Kitchen. Image mathching using combo fuzzy measure. *http://www.cs.mu.oz.au/~msislam/cfm.pdf*.

[10] Volker Gerdes. Stereo images with ground truth disparity and occlusion. *http://www-dbv.cs.uni-bonn.de/stereo_data*.

[11] Christian Heipke. Overview of image matching techniques. *http://phot.epfl.ch/workshop/wks96/art_3_1.html*, 1996.

A FUZZY APPROACH FOR PERSIAN TEXT SEGMENTATION BASED ON SEMANTIC SIMILARITY OF SENTENCES

Amir Shahab Shahabi , Dr. Mohammad Reza Kangavari

Islamic Azad University South Tehran Branch,shahabi_amir@azad.ac.ir , Science & Industry of Iran University

Abstract: Multi-Document summarization strictly needs distinguishing the similarity between sentences & paragraphs of texts because repeated sentences shouldn't exist in final summary so in order to applying this anti-redundancy we need a mechanism that can determining semantic similarities between sentences and expressions and paragraphs and finally between texts. In this paper it's used a fuzzy approach to determining this semantic similarity. We use fuzzy similarity and fuzzy approximation relation for gaining this goal. At first , lemma of Persian words and verbs obtained and then synonyms create a fuzzy similarity relation and via that relation the sentences with near meaning calculated with help of fuzzy proximity relation. So we can produce an anti-redundant final summary that have more valuable information.

Key words: Multi-Document Summarizer , Fuzzy Similarity Relation , Fuzzy Proximity Relation , Lemma , Fuzzy Relations Composition , Anti-Redundancy , Syntax Parser , Meta Variable , Meta Rule , Paradigmatic , Tokenizer , Lemmatizer.

1.   INTRODUCTION

In a Multi-Document Summarizer opposite of a single document summarizer there exist a great need to distinguish of similar sentences &

Please use the following format when citing this chapter:

Shahabi, A.S., Kangavari, M.R., 2006, in IFIP International Federation for Information Processing, Volume 228, Intelligent Information Processing III, eds. Z. Shi, Shimohara K., Feng D., (Boston: Springer), pp. 411–420.

texts in order to achieving the anti-redundancy factor that one of the most important factors in Multi-Document Summarization [Goldstein J. , et al . (2000)]. For obtaining this goal many different efforts has been done that one of them is discussed in this paper. At this discussion a fuzzy approach used in order to distinguishing similarity of two sentences via their concept. This effort is done for Persian language and is based on concept and meaning of words, expressions, noun phrases and verb phrases in Persian language [Natel Khanlari , P. (1991)] , [Aboumahboob , A. (1996)]. For this job we should distinguish word and noun and verb phrases from a Persian text that is done by a grammar, tokenizer and parser [Shahabi , A. Sh. (1997)]. After finding words and nouns and verb phrases by tokenizer and syntactic parser the lemma of words and verbs is created by lemmatizer [Natel Khanlari , P. (1991)] , [Siemens R. G. (1996)] , [Dichy J. , et al. (2001)] , [Bateni , M. R. , (1992)]. Then for determining the meaning of the words we need to a special knowledge base. This knowledge base is created by a fuzzy relation. All words that can be substituted with their synonyms based on a paradigmatic relation, create a fuzzy similarity relation [Zimmermann H. J. (1996)], [Wang L. X. (1997)] and this relation creates our knowledge base. Then creating a fuzzy relation for any sentence in the text makes system capable of determining similarity between sentences via fuzzy relations composition. With compositing a relation of a sentence by our knowledge base we can conclude a new relation that tell us in a sentence which words from knowledgebase exist and which words can be substituted with their synonyms. We do this job for all sentences in the text and obtain a fuzzy relation for each sentence then select a pair of these relations and create a fuzzy proximity relation for them and then we can determine the similarity between those [Dubois D. et al.(1980)] , [Fujimato T. et al.(1997)]. Repeating this job for all pairs of sentence relations results clustering sentences based on their meanings. Clustering sentences is done by $\alpha - cut$ rule [Marcu D. et al. (2001)].

2.   TEXT TOKENIZING AND SYNTAX PARSING

For obtaining words as a noun , verb , noun phrase or verb phrase that can extract it's meaning from corpus we need first distinguish it's part of speech via a tokenizer and a syntactic parser based on Persian language grammar. For reaching this goal we need a suitable grammar. As we know a natural language grammar is unrestricted and this matter makes trouble for parsing because of ambiguity and making several parse tree for a sentence. For avoiding this problem a method is selected that converts a natural language grammar to a context free grammar that is not ambiguous, named *two level grammar* that contains some meta variables with initializing them we can obtain a context free grammar based on the value of those meta variables and then this grammar can be parsed much more easier [Krulee G. K. (1991)]. Of course for this job we need a bulk of rules that initialize the value of these meta-variables and this restriction makes us unable to cover wide area of a language.

3.   LEMMATIZING

Lemmatization is a function that eliminates the overhead of any word and extracts root or lemma of it. If the root of a word is obtained then finding the meaning of that word becomes much more convenient [Siemens R. G. (1996)]. Persian's and Arabic's words have four overhead types that includes [Dichy J., et al. (2001)]:

1. Enclitics – objective connected pronouns like BICHAREAM that the lemma is BICHARE (means poor) [Natel Khanlari P. (1991)].
2. Suffixes – plural sign or relative adjective signs like BARG HA that BARG is the lemma of it or IRANI that its lemma is IRAN.
3. Proclitics – like AL in Arabic words.
4. Prefixes – that can be noun, adjective or pronouns like HAMANDISHI that its lemma is ANDISHE.

4.   KNOWLEDGE BASE CREATION FOR SYNONYM WORDS

As we said before the knowledge base for the synonym words is a fuzzy relation. Our universal set is W that is set of all words in the text. These words can be noun , adjective , verb or any phrasal expression those are used in our Persian text. Now we want to obtain words that can be substituted with each other in sentences [Aboumahboob , A. (1996)] and for reaching this we need a fuzzy relation between set W and itself [Zimmermann H. J. (1996)]. We name this relation $\tilde{P}$ the first letter of the word *Paradigmatic*.

$$\tilde{P} = \{((w_1, w_2), \mu_{\tilde{p}}(w_1, w_2)) \mid (w_1, w_2) \in W \times W\}$$

w_1, w_2 are the words in Persian language and W is their set. $\tilde{P}$ is the paradigmatic relation between these words that is also a fuzzy relation. Its membership function is as below:

$$\mu_{\tilde{P}}(w_1, w_2)$$

the value of this function is between zero to one based on how much the words w_1 and w_2 are near to each other. Let's make an example. Assume that we have three sentences with their words as below and each of these words are related with each other via a membership function and this value express semantic similarity between them and should be determined by a literature specialist. Based on these sentences and above assumption we can define our knowledgebase. First of all we state the sentences in English:
- S1. Students go to school at educational year.
- S2. Students present in class at fall.
- S3. Lessons stated by instructors should have been learned by students.

At these sentences there exists similarity relation in meaning that we intend to find it via this method. Now we should create a knowledgebase of words and synonyms of these sentences. The word and phrase set of our example is as below:

$$W = \{student, togo, school, educationalyear, topresent, class, fall, lesson,$$
$$tostate, instructor, tolearn\}$$

and the fuzzy relation that specifies our knowledgebase is as follows:

Table 1. Fuzzy Relation $\tilde{P}$ for W

	student	To go	school	Educational year	To present	class	Fall	lesson	To state	instructor	To Learn
Student	1	0	0	0	0	0	0	0	0	0	0
To go	0	1	0	0	0.7	0	0	0	0	0	0
School	0	0	1	0	0	0.8	0	0	0	0	0
Educational Year	0	0	0	1	0	0	0.9	0	0	0	0
To present	0	0.7	0	0	1	0	0	0	0	0	0
Class	0	0	0.8	0	0	1	0	0	0	0	0
Fall	0	0	0	0.9	0	0	1	0	0	0	0
Lesson	0	0	0	0	0	0	0	1	0	0	0
To state	0	0	0	0	0	0	0	0	1	0	0
Instructor	0	0	0	0	0	0	0	0	0	1	0
To learn	0	0	0	0	0	0	0	0	0	0	1

5. DISTINGUISHING OF SENTENCES SIMILARITY RELATION

At first a fuzzy relation for any sentence should be created. This relation likes a vector that have n components and $n = |W|$. It means this fuzzy relation relates a sentence with all the words in our knowledgebase. If a word exists in a sentence its membership function value is 1 and if it doesn't exist the value is 0. For our example the fuzzy relations for each sentence are as follows:

Table 2. Fuzzy Relation of each sentence

		student	To go	School	Educational year	To present	class	fall	lesson	To State	instructor	To Learn
$\tilde{R}_1$	S1	1	1	1	1	0	0	0	0	0	0	0
$\tilde{R}_2$	S2	1	0	0	0	1	1	1	0	0	0	0
$\tilde{R}_3$	S3	1	0	0	0	0	0	0	1	1	1	1

Now we should determine which words in the knowledgebase can be substituted with the word in a sentence. For reaching this goal we can compose this sentence relation with the relation that shows our knowledgebase, so any words that could be substituted with its synonym in the sentence its membership value is between zero to one. This composition

is a fuzzy max-min composition between the sentence relations $\tilde{R}_1, \tilde{R}_2, \tilde{R}_3$

and the knowledgebase relation named $\tilde{P}$ described in previous section. At this point we have a fuzzy relation for any sentence that shows which words or their synonyms exist in it. For our example the results of their compositions are as follows:

Table 3. Fuzzy Max-Min Composition between sentences & knowledgebase

		student	To go	school	Educational year	To present	class	fall	lesson	To state	instructor	To Learn
$\tilde{R}_1 \circ \tilde{P}$	S1	1	1	1	1	0.7	0.8	0.9	0	0	0	0
$\tilde{R}_2 \circ \tilde{P}$	S2	1	0.7	0.8	0.9	1	1	1	0	0	0	0
$\tilde{R}_3 \circ \tilde{P}$	S3	1	0	0	0	0	0	0	1	1	1	1

Now for determining the similarity between these sentences we use a fuzzy proximity relation between the fuzzy relations of the sentences. The name of this relation is fuzzy tolerance relation [Dubios D. et al. (1998)]. This relation must be reflexive and symmetric and if transitive property adds to it, it will be a similarity relation. We define this relation as follows [Fujimato T. et al. (1997)]:

If we have a relation between two sets $X = \{x_1, x_2, ...\}, Y = \{y_1, y_2, ...\}$ and fuzzy relation R_{y_i} is a set or subset of X s that relates with y_i and R_{y_j} is a set or subset of Y s that relates with y_j then the similarity between R_{y_i} and R_{y_j} is defined as below:

$$S = \frac{|R_{y_i} \cap R_{y_j}|}{\min\{|R_{y_i}|, |R_{y_j}|\}}$$

as you see if $\tilde{A}$ is a fuzzy set then according to definition , $|\tilde{A}|$ is cardinality of fuzzy set $\tilde{A}$ and it's value is obtaining as follows [Wang L. X. (1997)][Zimmermann H. J. (1996)]:

$$|\tilde{A}| = \sum_{i=1}^{n} \mu_{\tilde{A}}(x_i)$$

and here S is the cardinality of intersection of R_{y_i} and R_{y_j} divide by minimum of cardinality of one of R_{y_i} or R_{y_j}. The S relation defined above is a proximity relation because it is reflexive and symmetric so we can use it for distinguishing the similarity of sentences. For our example the fuzzy proximity relation of the example's sentences are as follows:

$$S_{12} = \frac{5.8}{6.4} = 0.90625$$

$$S_{13} = \frac{1}{5} = 0.2$$

$$S_{23} = \frac{1}{5} = 0.2$$

So the similarity between the first and second sentences is so much but they differ from the third sentence.

We can use $\alpha - cut$ for clustering of sentences those are similar to each other. This is reached via a fuzzy similarity relation like $S \geq S_{\alpha}$ based on a suitable $\alpha - cut$ and this is a very good progress in a multi-document summarizing system.

6.   RESULTS

This system is tested by a text with 58 sentences that contains 15 clusters of the same meaning sentences based on distinguishing of a human specialist. Each cluster has some sentences that have the same meaning and number of these sentences and their normal weights mentions in the table below.

System initializes $S_\alpha = 0.7$ and after running on this sample makes 22 clusters of the same meaning sentences based on the knowledgebase that contains 946 words and synonyms. The error rate of the system shows in the table below:

Table 4. Results of performing system run on a text with 58 sentences

Text clusters Based on Human specialist Detection	Number of Sentences Per Cluster	Normal Weight Of a Cluster	Number of Sentences per Cluster made By system	Error rate Per Cluster
C1	9	0.9*1/15	7	22.2%
C2	6	0.6*1/15	6	0%
C3	10	1.0*1/15	5	50%
C4	4	0.4*1/15	4	0%
C5	3	0.3*1/15	2	33.3%
C6	8	0.8*1/15	8	0%
C7	9	0.9*1/15	7	22.2%
C8	1	0.1*1/15	2	50%
C9	1	0.1*1/15	1	0%
C10	1	0.1*1/15	1	0%
C11	2	0.2*1/15	2	0%
C12	1	0.1*1/15	2	50%
C13	1	0.1*1/15	2	50%
C14	1	0.1*1/15	1	0%
C15	1	0.1*1/15	1	0%

So if we calculate the average of error rate based on cluster weights as below:
1/15*[22.2*0.9+50*1+33.3*0.3+22.2*0.9+50*0.1+50*0.1+50*0.1] = 7.66
We will reach to 7.66% error. This means that system works at rate of 92.34% correctly on this sample.

7.   DISCUSSION

In this approach we found that text can be segmented via a fuzzy proximity relation. The point that is obtained from this research is if the α value in S_α is increased and get near to one then the system error will decrease. But we set S_α to 0.7 because in creating knowledgebase we had error in determining fuzzy membership between words and phrases that increase the error so with setting $S_\alpha = 0.7$ we are trying to delete the effect of that error.

8.   CONCLUSION

This manner prepares a solution for detecting the same meaning sentences based on paradigmatic relation. It means that if a word substitutes with it's synonym in a sentence, this manner can help distinguishing the similarity and preparing the ability of selecting one of them for inserting in summary in order to avoiding redundancy in it.

ACKNOWLEDGEMENTS

The authors wish to thank Dr. Mostafa Assi.

REFRENCES

1. Aboumahboob A. 1996. Farsi Language Structure. Mitra Pub.
2. Bateni M. R. 1992. Language Grammar a New Look. Agah Pub.
3. Dichy J., Krauwer S., Yaseen M., "On Lemmatization in Arabic, A formal Definition of Arabic Entries of Multilingual Lexical Databases," Proc. of the workshop on Arabic language Processing: Status and Prospects, PP. 20-30, July 6th , 2001. Association for Computational Linguistics 39th Annual Meeting and 10th Conference of European Chapter , Toulouse.
4. Dubois D., Prade H. 1980. Fuzzy sets and systems Theory and Applications. Academic press Inc.
5. Fujimato T., Sugano M., 1997. "Clustering verb, Adjective, Adjectival verb concepts using Proximity Relation," IEEE.
6. Goldstein J., Mittal V. Carbonell J., Callan J. ,"Creating and Evaluating Multi-Document Sentence Extract Summaries," Proc. of the 2000 CIKM International Conference of Information and Knowledge Management. Mclean VA, USA, PP. 165-172. 2000 November.
7. Krulee G. K. 1991. Computer Processing of Natural Language , Printice Hall Inc.
8. Marcu D. , Gerber L., "An Inquiry in to the Nature of Multi-Document Abstract , Extracts and their Evaluation," Proc. of Automatic Summarization Workshop, 2001.

9. Natel Khanlari P. 1991. Farsi Language Grammar. Toos Pub.

10. Shahabi A. Sh. 1997. Farsi Text Understanding. MS Dissertation.

11. Siemens R. G., "Lemmatization and Parsing with TACT Preprocessing Programs," Department of English University of British Columbia, 1996.

12. Wang L. X. 1997. A Course on Fuzzy Systems and Control. Printice Hall Inc.

13. Zimmermann H. J. 1996. Fuzzy Set Theory and its Application, Third Edition. Kluwer Academic Pub.

AN INTELLIGENT SYSTEM FOR SOLO TAXONOMY

John Vrettaros (1,2), George Vouros (2), Athanasios Drigas (1)
1) National Centre of Scientific Research "Demokritos"- Institute of Informatics and Telecommunications - Net Media Lab, Agia Paraskevi, Athens, Greece
2) University of Aegean, Information and Communication Systems Engineering, Karlovassi Samos, Greece

{jvr, dr}@imm.demokritos.gr
http://imm.demokritos.gr/

Abstract: The modeling of diagnostic systems of taxonomies using fuzzy logic is presented in this paper. Specifically the taxonomies system solo is studied, which that can be applied in a wide range of fields of diagnostic science. The intelligent system that is developed based on the presented modeling can make easier the use of diagnostic systems in education since the test correction is extremely hard and demands experts that are not always available. Additionally, the rate of the extraction of results is a reason for using and distributing such tools (diagnostic systems) in the educational process. It is very useful for e-learning systems [1], [2], and distance diagnostics systems.

Key words: fuzzy system, solo, taxonomy, diagnostics system, distance education, e-learning system

1.   INTRODUCTION

An intelligent system is based on an extended quantity of knowledge relevant to an area of problems. This knowledge is organized under the form of a set of rules, which allow inferencing of the system from the available data. This "knowledge-based" methodology that have been used for solving problems and generally designing systems, has constituted an evolutionary change in Artificial Intelligence, since it substituted the traditional form of a

Please use the following format when citing this chapter:

Vrettaros, J., Vouros, G., Drigas, A., 2006, in IFIP International Federation for Information Processing, Volume 228, Intelligent Information Processing III, eds. Z. Shi, Shimohara K., Feng D., (Boston: Springer), pp. 421–430.

program (data + algorithm = program) with a new architecture. This new architecture has as its core a knowledge base and an inference engine and is of the form:

Knowledge + Inferencing = System   (1)

The specific problem that has to be solved is the construction of an intelligent system, which will be able to evaluate and categorize students in different levels of knowledge based on some information that will be extracted from their answers. The results are based on a research that was made on some High School students and was about the broader field of Mathematics. The problems of categorizing student into different levels of knowledge, the study of transition in between knowledge levels, as well as the study of the semantic change, as it is mentioned, that takes place when students stop using an naïve (erroneous) model and start using a scientific (correct) model, are three of the most important problems in Cognitive Science. Many researchers have proposed methodologies for knowledge acquisition into different fields of science (Mathematics, physics, etc.) under the aid of computational systems and Artificial Intelligence models. The methods of computational intelligence present great interest from theoretical point of view, since they cope with complexity and uncertainty which are two of the most important problems of system theory that are strongly related to reality.[3]In the specific application the analysis begins with the processing of the answers from correctly formed and selected questionnaires, which are filled up by students. By this analysis some information is extracted that leads the categorization into levels in five different theme sections. Each section consists of four questions, and each question corresponds to one of the following knowledge levels: Single-Structural (S), Multi-Structural (M), Correlative (C), and Abstractive (A). [4], [5].

Table 1. Different fields of science

	(M)	(C)	(A)
ARITHMETIC	Quest. 1	Quest. 2	Quest. 3
ALGEBRA	Quest. 4	Quest. 5	Quest. 6
SPACE PERCEPTION	Quest. 7	Quest. .8	Quest .9
APPLICATION	Quest. 10	Quest. 1	Quest. 12
PROBABILITIES	Quest. 13	Quest. 14	Quest. 15

At this point it should be mentioned that the question that corresponds to the abstractive level couldn't be answered by students of this age. Consequently, it can be said that each theme section has three questions. In addition, if none of the three questions of a theme section is answered by a student, the student is categorized to the pro - structural (P) level. The questionnaire analysis is illustrated in the following figure (fig.1).

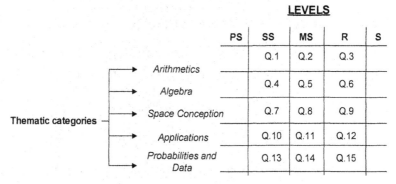

LEVELS

	PS	SS	MS	R	S
Arithmetics		Q.1	Q.2	Q.3	
Algebra		Q.4	Q.5	Q.6	
Space Conception		Q.7	Q.8	Q.9	
Applications		Q.10	Q.11	Q.12	
Probabilities and Data		Q.13	Q.14	Q.15	

Thematic categories

Figure 1. Questionnaire Analysis.

2.   SYSTEMS OF STUDENT LAYER SPECIFICATION TO THEME SECTION: CONTROVERSIAL ANSWERS

For the evaluation of these answers the following factors (that correspond to the factors that the teachers consider when they evaluate such controversial cases): 1) Difficulty of the specific theme that obviously affects its grading. 2) The number of the blank answers, meaning the number of unanswered questions for each student. This factor is considered since it affects the student's evaluation. For instance, let us consider the case where we want to grade a controversial answer (e.g. Answer 4 → WRONG, Answer 5 → CORRECT, Answer 6 → CORRECT,) and the student has a great number of unanswered questions. This means that the student probably doesn't answer randomly, but he/she answers after serious consideration of the question. We conclude that is most probable that the incorrect answer at question 4 is a careless mistake, since the correct answers at questions five and six (which are obviously more difficult than question 4) are not given by chance. Consequently the student can be categorized to the Correlative level for the corresponding theme section 3) The level of the student, meaning the general presentation of the student [6].

In general, it can be said that the selection of the layer for the controversial cases differs from one student to another. It is affected from the student's answers, the number of the questions that he/she left unanswered, and the level of the question. For the modelling of the controversial cases there have been designed and developed two fuzzy systems, which are analyzed in the following section. [7],[8].

2.1   Rigidity grading specification sub-system

The systems consist of three inputs and one output. The inputs are the factors that affect the grading of each controversial answer: the number of the unanswered questions, the level of the question and the level of the student. The output is just one: the rigidity (fig.2):

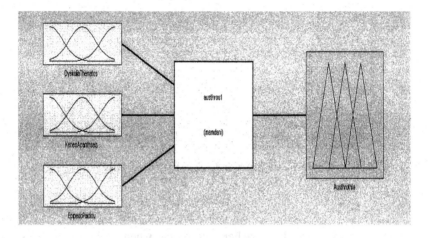

Figure 2. Inputs and Outputs of the System.

In this specific case the grades of every input are between two rates. The Difficulty of the Subject and the Number of the Blank Answers takes rates between 0 and 100, and the Child's Level between 0 and 3. The Difficulty of the Subject is calculated from the answers of the rest of the students. The X axis is normalized and takes rates obviously from 0 to 100. We can set a taxonomy on the definition level of the Difficulty of the Subject, for example we can say that if a rate of Difficulty belongs to the aggregation (0,30) then it is large, if it belongs to (30,65) then it is medium and finally if it belongs to (65,100) then it is small. This specific way of classic taxonomy inputs in principle a big uncertainty in some sections, e.g. close to 30, 65 and 100. That is if the rate of Difficulty is equal to 29 then the Difficulty consider small but if it is equal to 30 then it is considered medium. To avoid this problem we define a fuzzy taxonomy (one per input) in the definition levels of every input A1, A2 and A3.

Every fuzzy taxonomy is class 3. A fuzzy taxonomy B, class 3, we define also in the output definition level, which as we mentioned is [9]. The fuzzy taxonomies A1, A2, A3 and B are linguistic images of the definitions levels therefore their elements are linguistic terms of the form "SMALL", "LARGE", "MEDIUM".

2.2 Student level relevant to theme section specification sub-system

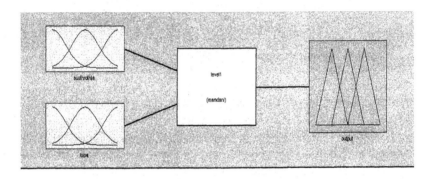

Figure 3. Inputs and outputs of the system

The second system specifies the level of the student at each theme section. The system has two inputs and one output. The first input is the rigidity and the second input is the three answers to that theme. The output is the number from 0 to 3 that corresponds to one of the four levels of knowledge (pro-structural, single-structural, multi-structural and correlative) for each theme section. The result for the controversial cases can be a decimal number. At fig. 3 the inputs and output of the system can be seen. [10]

The output takes rates from 0 to 3.   0-1 corresponds to single-structural, 1-2 in multi-structural and 2-3 in correlative.

The rules that join the inputs and output are the following:

1. If rigidity is "LARGE" then the Level is "SMALL".
2. If rigidity is "MEDIUM" then the Level is "MEDIUM".
3. If rigidity is "SMALL" then the Level is "LARGE".
4. If the Answers are "FEW" then the Level is "SMALL".
5. If the Answers are "ENOUGH" then the Level is "MEDIUM".

6. If the Answers are "PLENTY" then the Level is "LARGE".
An analytical representation of the rules sows in the Schematics. (fig 4)

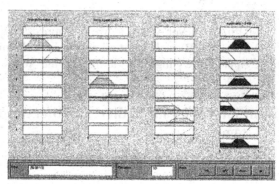

Figure 4.

3.   SPECIFICATION OF THE FINAL LEVEL

Up to this point there have been estimated the levels of knowledge for the students in five theme sections. Based on these levels the estimation of the final level will be implemented. The final level is a number from 0 to 3 that corresponds to one of the four levels of knowledge. At the previous sections we described the procedure of level estimation based on theme sections. The following procedure examines the students' answers based on the levels of knowledge and not the theme sections. This means that a grade of confidence should be estimated for each level. The grades of confidence will correspond to the percentage that each examined student belongs at each level. The grade of confidence is a number in the range from 0 to1.

The grades of confidence are three: one for the single-structural level, one for the multi-structural level, and one for the correlative level. For the pro-structural level no confidence number is estimated since its value is always set to 1, because there are no questions or answers and it is also the lowest level. Consequently the grade of confidence cannot be less than 1. Next, we estimate the final level by averaging the three available confidence grades. The averaging is done in accordance with the relevant level. Setting the confidence grade to 1 for the pro-structural level, 2 for the multi-structural level and 3 for the correlative level we then have:

$$\varepsilon = \frac{1C_1 + 2C_2 + 3C_3}{C_1 + C_2 + C_3} \qquad (2)$$

Where ε is the final level. ε can also be a decimal number.

4. CASE STUDY: THE SOLO PROGRAM

The SOLO program is the interface that contains a powerful Neural Network engine, which basically manages the data of the class and the students. It is very simple and easy to use, providing help support.

Below are stated some selections provided by the interface:

New Database:

This function provides to the user the possibility to create a new database. The window contains combo boxes and textboxes where the user inputs the variables. Using the add button the user inputs a new record to the database. With the delete button the user can delete the present record. By pressing the refresh button the user can refresh the database (for multi-user environment only). With the update button the user can post the database for the changes done, and with the exit button the user closes the window and returns to the main window of the application. By pressing the SaveDB the user saves the database to the hard-disk.

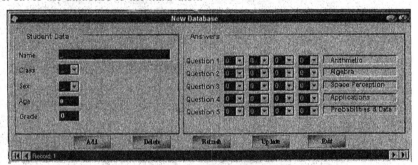

Figure 4.1. New Database Window

Open Database: This selection is used to load a database which is added to the main application's window, in the Combo box under the title Available Databases. By clicking there the user selects this database which is loaded in the form.

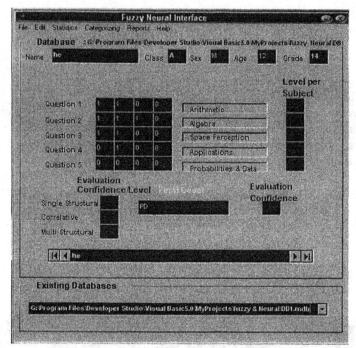

Figure 4.2. Open Database Window

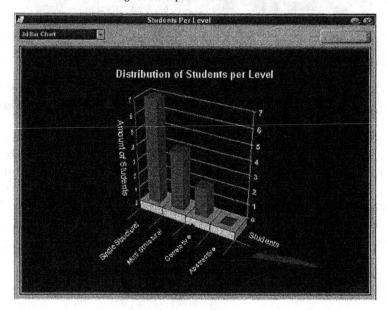

Figure 4.3. Students Per Level Graph

With this last selection above, the user is provided in 2D or 3D graph the distribution on the students depending on the level the students are.

5.   CONCLUSION

The developed system was applied on 100 high school and senior high school students, and it was tested on mathematics. The correction results obtained by the system were compared to the results obtained by the cognitive science expert. The system's results were found to be very close to the expert results, as it can be seen on the following table (fig. 5).[11]

Concluding, we can say that the diagnostic tools are trustworthy tools for the educators' cooperation and contribution.

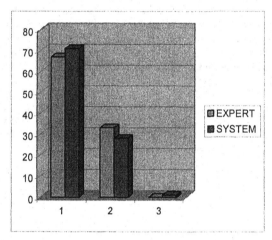

Figure 5. System - Expert Results Comparison. (blue color corresponds to the expert and red color corresponds to system).

REFERENCES

1.   A.S.Drigas, J.Vrettaros, D.Kouremenos, "Teleeducation and e-learning services for teaching English as a second language to Deaf People, whose first language is the Sign Language", WSEAS transactions on Information Science and Applications, Issue 3, Volume 1, September 2004.

2. A.S.Drigas, J.Vrettaros, L. Stavrou, D.Kouremenos, "E-learning Environment for Deaf people in the E-Commerce and New Technologies Sector", 6th WSEAS International Conference on E-Activities, Rethymno, October 20, 2004.

3. Maeda, S. and Murakami, S. (1993) The Use of a Fuzzy Decision-Making Method in a Large-Scale Computer System Choice Problem, Fuzzy Sets and Systems, 54, 235-249.

4. Biggs, J. B. and Collis, K. F. "Evaluating the Quality of Learning: the SOLO Taxonomy", New York: Academic Press, 1982.

5. Biggs, J. B. and Collis, K. F. Multimodal learning and the quality of intelligent behavior. In H. H. Rowe (Ed.) Intelligence: Reconceptualization and Measurement. Hillsdale, N. J.: Lawrence Erb.freemanm Associates and Hawthorn, Vic.: ACER, pp. 57-76, 1991.

6. Imrie, B.W. (1995) Assessment for Learning: Quality and Taxonomies, Assessment and Evaluation in Higher Education, 20, 2, 175-189.

7. J.Vrettaros, M.Grigoriadou, "Design of an hybrid architecture for fuzzy connectionist expert system and its application to approximate student model". CATE 96, The first international conference on computers and advanced technologies in education, Cairo, 1996.

8. Earl Cox, "The Fuzzy Systems Handbook: A Practitioner's Guide to Building, Using, & Maintaining Fuzzy Systems", 1999.

9. Gogus, O. and Boucher, T.O. (1997) A Consistency Test for Rational Weights in Multi-Criterion Decision Analysis with Fuzzy Pairwise Comparisons, Fuzzy Sets and Systems, 86, 129-138.

10. Zadeh, L.F. (1997) Toward a Theory of Fuzzy Information Granulation and its Centrality in Human Reasoning and Fuzzy Logic, Fuzzy Sets and Systems, 90, 111-127.

11. Drigas A, Kouremenos S, Vrettos S, Vrettaros J, Kouremenos D (Feb 2004), An expert system for job matching of the unemployed, Pergamon-Elsevier Science LTD, Oxford, IDS Number:763WW, ISSN: 0957-4174

EDUCATING *LIA*: THE DEVELOPMENT OF A LINGUISTICALLY ACCURATE MEMORY-BASED LEMMATISER FOR AFRIKAANS

Hendrik J. Groenewald
Centre for Text Technology,
North-West University,
2531 Potchefstroom, South Africa
eeihjg@puk.ac.za

Abstract

This paper describes the development of a memory-based lemmatiser for Afrikaans called *Lia*. The paper commences with a brief overview of Afrikaans lemmatisation and it is indicated that lemmatisation is seen as a simplified process of morphological analysis within the context of this paper. This overview is followed by an introduction to memory-based learning – the machine learning technique that is used in the development of the Afrikaans lemmatiser. The deployment of *Lia* is then discussed with specific emphasis on the format of the training and testing data that is used. The Afrikaans lemmatiser is then evaluated and it is indicated that *Lia* achieves a linguistic accuracy figure of over 90%. The paper concludes with some ideas on future work that can be done to improve the linguistic accuracy of the Afrikaans lemmatiser.

Keywords: Natural Language Processing, Machine Learning, Lemmatisation, Afrikaans, Memory-Based Learning

1.   Introduction

In 2003, a rule-based lemmatiser for Afrikaans (called *Ragel* – *"Reelgebaseerde Afrikaanse Grondwoord- en Lemma-identifiseerder"*) [Rule-Based Root and Lemma Identifier for Afrikaans] was developed at the North-West University and is currently included in a spelling checker for Afrikaans (Afrikaanse Speltoetser 3.0). *Ragel* was developed by using traditional methods for stemming/lemmatisation (i.e. affix stripping) (Porter, 1980; Kraaij and Pohlmann, 1994) and consists of language-specific rules for identifying word-forms in the lexicon of the spelling checker. However, *Ragel* cannot be considered either a "pure" lemmatiser or a "pure" stemmer in the true sense of the word,

Please use the following format when citing this chapter:

Groenewald, H.J., 2006, in IFIP International Federation for Information Processing, Volume 228, Intelligent Information Processing III, eds. Z. Shi, Shimohara K., Feng D., (Boston: Springer), pp. 431–440.

since it was developed specifically for purposes of spelling checking. In this sense, both derived and inflected word-forms that are not in the lexicon of the spelling checker are analysed by *Ragel*, only until a word in the lexicon is found, whether that word is a lemma or not (e.g. *"ontbossing"* 'deforestation' will be analysed as *"ontbos"* 'deforest' and not necessarily as *"bos"* 'forest'). Although no formal evaluation of *Ragel* was done, it obtained a disappointing linguistic accuracy figure of only 67% in an evaluation on a random 1,000 word dataset.

The purpose of this study is to develop a more "pure" lemmatiser for Afrikaans, using an alternative approach (i.e. memory-based learning). It is important that *Lia* [Lemma Identifier for Afrikaans] should achieve a better linguistic accuracy figure than *Ragel*, and the focus and objective are therefore to achieve a linguistic accuracy figure of at least 90%.

The following section presents background information on the problem of lemmatisation for Afrikaans and briefly discusses the inflectional morphemes used in this study. Memory-based learning and the Tilburg Memory-Based Learner (TiMBL) (Daelemans et al., 2004) are briefly introduced in Section 3, before discussing the actual development of *Lia* at length in Section 4. Here the focus will be explicitly on the architecture of the system, and the representation of the data for optimal linguistic accuracy. Section 5 describes the evaluation of *Lia*, with some general concluding remarks in Section 6.

2.   Lemmatisation for Afrikaans

Within the context of this study, lemmatisation is defined as a simplified process of morphological analysis (Daelemans and Strik, 2002) through which the inflected forms of a word are converted/normalised under the lemma or base-form (i.e. the simplest form of a word as it would appear as headword in a dictionary (Erjavec and Dzeroski, 2004; Hausser, 1999)) by removing inflectional affixes (Bussman, 1996). In this sense, lemmatisation should not be confused with stemming, which is the process whereby the stem of a word is retrieved by removing both inflectional and derivational morphemes from the word (Gearailt, 2005; Manning and Schutze, 1999). Also, it is usually expected of a lemmatiser to produce independent word forms, while a stemmer might also produce dependent forms, such as roots or stems (Plisson et al., 2004).

Given this general background, it would therefore be necessary to have a clear understanding of the inflectional affixes to be removed during the process of lemmatisation for a particular language. With regard to Afrikaans, there is still no general agreement among Afrikaans linguists on what the list of inflectional affixes should be. For instance, Combrink (1974) rejects the notion of inflection for Afrikaans altogether and describes it as a useless Latinism. On the other hand, linguists such as Du Toit (1982), Van Schoor (1983), and

Carstens (1992) have each defined their own lists of inflectional morphemes for Afrikaans. Although there is some degree of agreement between these lists, differences still exist. For the purpose of this study, we therefore simply accept all the inflectional categories presented by the previously-mentioned three authors. These inflectional categories are:

1. Plural (e.g. the *"-s"* in *"tafels"*, 'tables' and the *"e"* in *"mense"*, 'humans')

2. Degrees of comparison (e.g. the *"-er"* or *"-ste"* in *"kleiner"* 'smaller' and *"kleinste"* 'smallest')

3. Diminutive form (e.g. the *"-jie"* in *"hondjie"* 'puppy')

4. Past Tense (e.g. the *"ge-"* in *"geloop"* 'walked')

5. Past Participle form (e.g. the *"ge- -te"* in *"getrapte"* 'trampled')

6. Infinitive (e.g. the *"-e"* in *"drinke"* 'drink')

7. Attributive (e.g. the *"-e"* in *"pragtige"* 'exquisite')

8. Partitive Genitive (e.g. the *"-s"* in *"pragtigs"* 'exquisite')

Lia, or any lemmatiser for Afrikaans, should therefore be able to remove all affixes in these eight inflectional categories, yielding linguistically correct lemmas. Although it seems easy, Afrikaans lemmatisation proves to be no trivial task; it entails more than just removing the correct affix from the word to obtain the correct lemma. *Lia* has to deal with a number of further complexities, such as:

1. A rule-based lemmatiser will tend remove the suffix *-tjie* erroneously in the case of words like *"jobskraaltjie"* (a grass species) and *"suurpootjie"* (a tortoise specie), because *-tjie* normally indicates the diminutive form. The *-tjie* in these words however does not indicate the diminutive form, as it forms part of the lemma of the word.

2. Words that contain prefixes like *aange-* and *opge-* like in *"aangedryf"* 'drove' and *"opgelaai"* 'picked up' should be lemmatised by only removing the second prefix *-ge-* in the middle of the word.

3. Words that are in the past participle form like *"ingedraaide"* 'screwed in' should be lemmatised as *"indraai"* 'screw in'. This can be confusing, because it is differs from the lemmatisation method described under (2) above.

4. Words that are in the past participle form that start with *onge-* are not lemmatised according to the manner that other past participle form words are lemmatised. Only the suffixes *-de* or *-te* should be removed during lemmatisation. *"Ongenooide"* 'uninvited' must accordingly be lemmatised as *"ongenooi"*, instead of the invalid lemma *"*on-nooi"*.

5. Due to morphological processes, some words like *"paaie"* 'roads' are not lemmatised by just removing the *-e* that indicates the plural form; a *-d* should also be appended at the end of the word during the transformation to the lemma.

The next section describes the approach taken in this research to train *Lia* to produce grammatically correct lemmas for Afrikaans words.

3.   Memory-Based Learning

Previous experience with *Ragel* proved that it is quite difficult to define expert rules for accurate lemmatisation of Afrikaans word-forms. It was therefore decided to take an alternative computational approach in developing *Lia*, namely a machine-learning approach, using memory-based learning algorithms. Based on Mitchell's definition of machine learning (Mitchell, 1997), our basic assumption in this study can be formulated as follows:

> *Lia* is said to learn from a database of correctly lemmatised words (i.e. Experience), with respect to lemmatisation (i.e. Task) and the percentage of correctly lemmatised words (i.e. Performance Measure), if its performance at lemmatisation (**T**), as measured by the percentage of correctly lemmatised words (**P**), improves as the size of the database of correctly lemmatised words is increased (**E**).

This implies that *Lia* will improve (learn) with more and more experience (i.e. a larger and better database of correctly lemmatised words), so that predictions about new cases can be made based on the outcomes of similar cases in the past (Aloaydin, 1997). In order to foster such learning, we decided to follow a memory-based learning approach to train *Lia*.

Memory-based learning is based on the classic k-Nearest Neighbour (k-NN) algorithm, which is a powerful, yet basic classification algorithm. The assumption here is that all cases of a certain problem can be represented as points in an n-dimensional space, where the nearest-neighbour points can be computed using a distance formula $\Delta(X,Y)$. The class (category) of a new case is assigned by considering the classes that are most common with the nearest neighbours of the new case (Daelemans et al., 2004). It has been proven in the past that memory-based learning could be used with great success for natural language processing (NLP) tasks such as lemmatisation (Daelemans and Strik, 2002; Baldwin and Bond, 2003; Gustafson, 1999). A possible reason for this is that each instance is viewed as equally important during the classification process. (Daelemans et al., 1999).

The memory-based learning system on which *Lia* is based, is called TiMBL (Tilburg Memory-Based Learner). TiMBL was specifically developed with NLP tasks in mind, but it can be used successfully for classification tasks in other domains as well (Daelemans et al., 2004).

4.   *Lia*: Lemmatiser for Afrikaans

Architecture

The first step in the architecture of *Lia* consists of training the system with data. During this phase, the training data is examined and various statisti-

Figure 1.   The architecture of Lia

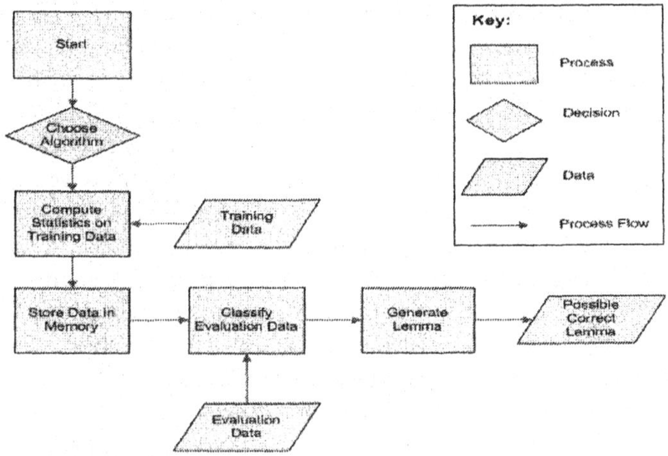

cal calculations are computed that aid the system during classification. This training data is then stored in memory as sets of data points. The evaluation instance(s) are then presented to the system and their class is computed by interpolation to the stored data points according to the selected algorithm and algorithm parameters. The last step in the process consists of generating the correct lemma(s) of the evaluation instance(s) according to the class that was awarded during the classification process.

Data

As was mentioned earlier, machine learning systems improve with experience. In the case of *Lia*, this *"experience"* is based on the amount of data used during training. The assumption here is that the more data *Lia* has access to during the training phase, the better the linguistic accuracy will be. The annotation of training data is, however, a labour-intensive, time-consuming process, especially for resource-scarce languages such as Afrikaans. The training data for this project was extracted from the lexicon of a spelling checker for Afrikaans that consists of 350,000 words (Afrikaanse Speltoetser 3.0). All the words that correspond in form to the inflectional forms defined for this project were extracted. For example, both the words *"geel"* 'yellow' and *"geslaap"* 'slept' were extracted during this process, because both words begin with the possible prefix *"ge-"*. The lemma of *"geslaap"* is *"slaap"* 'sleep', but the word *"geel"* 'yellow' is already a lemma. However, it is important to also train *Lia* with lemmas such as *"geel"* 'yellow', since *Lia* should not only learn how to lemmatise, but also when to lemmatise words and when not to. This extraction yielded 110,000 words, of which approximately 30% do not contain inflectional morphemes.

Defining the format of the classes was an important part of the data-con-struction phase. The logical way to go about the problem is to use grammati-cally motivated classes. For example, the class of the word *"hondjie"* 'puppy' should then have been *-jie*, implying that the suffix *-jie* should be removed from the word to lemmatise it. This approach turns out to be problematic in some cases, such as *"beeldskone"* 'beautiful' where the correct lemma is *"beeld-skoon"*. The linguistically correct class of *"beeldskone"* is *-e* (attributive), but simply removing an *-e* at the right-hand side of *"beeldskone"* will leave us with *"beeldskon"* which is not a valid lemma. This problem was overcome by using non-grammatically motivated classes as described in the next two paragraphs.

The extracted data is annotated manually by providing the lemma for each instance, after which the class of the instance is then automatically awarded on the basis of a comparison between the word and the correct lemma by means of a Perl script. The classes are derived by determining the character string (and the position thereof) to be removed and the possible replacement string during the transformation from word-form to lemma. The positions of the character string to be removed are annotated as L (left), R (right) and M (middle). If a word-form and its lemma are identical, the class awarded will be *"0"*, denoting the word should be left in the same form. This annotation scheme yields classes like in column three of Table 1.

Table 1.   Data preparation for *Lia*

Extracted Word-Form	Manually Identified Lemma	Automatically Derived Class
Geel 'yellow'	*Geel* 'yellow'	*0*
Geslaap 'slept'	*Slaap* 'sleep'	*Lge>*
Hondjie 'puppy'	*Hond* 'dog'	*Rjie>*
Bote 'ships'	*Boot* 'ship'	*Rte>ot*
Omgedraaide 'turned over'	*Omdraai* 'turn over'	*MgeRde>*

The class of *"geslaap"* 'slept' will be *Lge>*, where the L implies that the inflectional prefix *"ge-"* should be removed on the left-hand side of the word to lemmatise it. Accordingly, the class of the word *"bote"* 'boats' will be *Rte>ot*, denoting the *"te"* at the right-hand side of the word should be replaced by *"ot"*. Words in the past participle form, for instance *"omgedraaide"* 'turned over', will receive the class *MgeRde>*, meaning that the *"-ge-"* and the *"de"* should be removed respectively at the middle and at the right-hand side of the word.

This method of class assignment eliminates the generation of incorrect lem-mas like *"beeldskon"*, but in turn, it produces 311 different classes which also further complicates the lemmatisation process. An example of *Lia*'s training data is shown in Figure 2. The data is presented to TiMBL in C4.5 format (Quinlan, 1993), where each feature of each instance is separated by a comma.

The data is presented in a format that ensures equal amounts of features for each instance as this is required by TiMBL. To do this, it was assumed that the longest possible word to be analysed by *Lia* would consist of not more than 38 characters.[1] Accordingly, all instances were fitted to this format and underscores were added to words shorter than 38 characters, as can be seen in Figure 2. Further experiments will be done to determine the optimal amount of features, because too many or too few features have a negative influence on *Lia*'s accuracy. Too many features also increase the classification time.

Figure 2.   Training data in C4.5 format (right aligned without feature positioning)

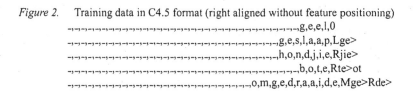

The training data was at first left-aligned, but this resulted in very low accuracy figures. We then realised that, since the majority of inflectional affixes are suffixes (only one inflectional prefix *"ge-"* occurs in Afrikaans, which can also be inserted between the preposition and stem in so-called particle verbs), the training data should be right-aligned. A remarkable increase in the accuracy figures was achieved by the right-alignment of the data. Right-alignment ensures that the suffix part of every word is always at the same feature position, which is not the case if the data is left-aligned.

A common mistake that *Lia* initially made was that the classes of words like *"geabsorbeerde"* 'absorbed' (class: *LgeRde*) was confused with the classes of words like *"verdofde"* 'dimmed' (class: *Rde>*). The reason for this is that the letters of the inflectional prefix *ge-* was at different feature positions for different instances when the data was right-aligned. The same confusion was experienced with words that were in the past participle form. The success achieved by right-alignment of the data lead us to define the concept of "feature-positioning", in order to reduce the amount of confusion experienced.

Figure 3.   Training data in C4.5 format (right aligned with feature positioning)

g,e,-,e,l,0
g,e,-,s,l,a,a,p,Lge>
-,h,o,n,d,j,i,e,Rjie>
-,b,o,t,e,Rte>ot
o,m,-,-,-,-,-,g,e,-,d,r,a,a,i,d,e,Mge>Rde>

Feature-positioning implies that all words containing the possible prefix *"ge-"*, is treated like *"geslaap"* 'slept' in Figure 3, or alternatively like *"omge-draaide"* 'turned-over' when *"-ge-"* is inserted in a participle verb. Feature-positioning ensures that similar features are always aligned at the same feature-positions and thereby eliminates any confusion that may arise. The accuracy gained by the use of feature-positioning is presented in the next section.

A dataset consisting of 56,000 words was randomly extracted from the original dataset of 110,000 words.[2] This dataset was annotated as described above, then manually checked by linguists, after which it was used to train *Lia* for evaluation purposes.

5.   Evaluation of *Lia*

Table 2.   Comparison of the results obtained with Right-Aligned data vs. Feature-Positioned Right-Aligned data

	Right-Aligned	Right-Aligned with feature-positioning	% Error Reduction
Dataset 1	88.9027	90.9285	18.2549
Dataset 2	89.3118	90.8945	14.8080
Dataset 3	89.2051	91.3036	19.4397
Dataset 4	88.4225	91.1242	23.3358
Dataset 5	89.4185	91.7823	22.3390
Dataset 6	88.6893	91.3925	23.8995
Dataset 7	88.8672	90.8929	18.1958
Dataset 8	88.3514	90.6261	19.5277
Dataset 9	89.2228	91.3569	19.8020
Dataset 10	88.6893	90.7862	18.5391
Average	**88.9081**	**91.1088**	**19.8141**

The IB1 algorithm was used in this section to verify if an accuracy figure of 90% is attainable. IB1 is the basic instance-based algorithm used in TiMBL and its operation is similar to the basic k-NN algorithm. The algorithm parameters used were determined through the use of the software package *Paramsearch 1.0* (van den Bosch, 2005). *Paramsearch* provides a (possibly optimal) set of algorithm parameters that are expected to do well on the task at hand. The parameters that *Paramsearch* yielded were:

Distance Metric: Modified Value Difference Metric
Feature Weighting: Information Gain
Nearest Neighbour Count: 11
Class voting weights: Inverse Linear

Table 2 shows a comparison of the linguistic accuracy figures for the cases where the data is right-aligned, compared to the cases where feature-positioning is used. The evaluation was done by means of ten-fold cross-validation. This means that the available data is split into ten equally sized parts. Each of the parts is then used as an evaluation set while the remaining nine sets are used as training data. The results for each set are displayed in Table 2, together with the resulting percentages of error reduction obtained when using feature-positioning. The error reduction is measured as the percentage of errors that was saved by using feature-positioning data.

As was stated in the introduction, one of the aims of this study is to develop a lemmatiser for Afrikaans, with an accuracy score of at least 90%. Table 2 shows that this objective is indeed achieved by the introduction of right-aligned, feature-positioned data, which results in an average accuracy figure of 91.1088%. Table 2 also indicates that the use of right-aligned, feature-positioned data results in an average error reduction of 19.8141%.

6.   Conclusion

The evaluation shows that an average linguistic accuracy of 88.9801% is obtained by training *Lia* with 56,000 words. A further improvement to 91.1088% is achieved by using feature-positioned data. The objective of this paper, namely obtaining an accuracy score of at least 90%, was successfully reached. Compared to the 67% accuracy figure for *Ragel*, this indicates that memory-based learning provides a suitable alternative to a rule-based approach considering the problem of lemmatisation for Afrikaans. This also confirms the conviction of Streiter and De Luca (2003) that example-based approaches (such as memory-based learning) offer an effective processing strategy for resource-scarce languages.

However, there is still much that can be done to improve the results obtained. Future work includes experimenting with different ways of data representation to see if further improvements in linguistic accuracy can be achieved. Memory-based learning algorithms are also very sensitive to changes in their parameter settings; experiments will therefore be done to determine the algorithm and optimal combinations of parameter settings to deliver the best performance for this particular task. We will also investigate why certain combinational settings deliver better results than other.

7.   Acknowledgements

I want to thank Proff. Gerhard B. van Huyssteen, Albertus S.J. Helberg and Antal van den Bosch for their useful comments, support and various opportunities granted. I also wish to thank the National Research Foundation (NRF) for their financial support of the project (NRF Project: Afrikaans Text Technology Modules GUN: FA_20040429000591).

Notes

1. Less than 0,1% of the words in the training set consist of more than 38 characters.

2. Section 5 indicates that 56,000 words are enough data for obtaining the desired linguistic accuracy.

References

Afrikaanse Speltoetser 3.0, Thesaurus 1.0 and Hyphenator, Potchefstroom: CTexT, North-West University, 2005.

E. Aloaydin. *Introduction to Machine Learning*. Cambridge: MIT Press, 2004.

T. Baldwin and F. Bond. *A Plethora of Methods for Learning English Countability*. Proceedings of the 2003 Conference on Empirical Methods in Natural Language Processing, 2003.

H. Bussman. *Routledge Dictionary of Language and Linguistics*. London: Routledge, 1996.

A. Carstens. *Basiskursus: Aspekte van die Afrikaanse Taalkunde 'Aspects of Afrikaans Linguistics'*. Bloemfontein: Patmos, 1992.

J. G. H. Combrinck. *Soek: Afrikaans se fleksie 'Wanted: The inflectional morphemes of Afrikaans'*. Taalkunde –'n Lewe 'Linguistics – a life'. Cape Town: Tafelberg, 1974.

W. Daelemans and H. Strik. *Het Nederlands in de taal- en spraaktechnologie: prioriteiten voor basisvoorzieningen*. 'Dutch in language and speech technology: priorities for basic provisions'. Dutch Language Union, 2002

W. Daelemans, A. van den Bosch and J. Zavrel. *Forgetting Exceptions is Harmful in Language Learning*. Machine Learning, 34(1):11–43, 1999.

W. Daelemans, A. Van den Bosch, J. Zavrel and K. Van der Sloot. *TiMBL: Tilburg Memory Based Learner, version 5.1, Reference Guide*. ILK Technical Report 04-02, 2004.

P. J. du Toit. *Taalleer vir Onderwyser en Student 'Language learning for Teacher and Student'*. Pretoria: Academica, 1982.

T. Erjavec and S. Dzeroski. *Machine Learning of Morphosyntactic Structure: Lemmatising Unknown Slovene Words*. Applied Artificial Intelligence 18(1):17–40, 2004.

D. N. Gearailt. *Dictionary characteristics in cross-language information retrieval*. Technical report UCAM-CL-TR-616. Cambridge: University of Cambridge Computer Laboratory, 2005.

J. Gustafson, N. Lindberg and M. Lundeberg. *The August Spoken Dialogue System*. Proceedings of Eurospeech, 1999.

R. Hausser. *Foundation of Computational Linguistics: man-machine communication in natural language*. Berlin: Springer, page 516, 1999.

W. Kraaij and R. Pohlmann. *Porter's Stemming Algorithm for Dutch*. in Informatiewetenschap 1994: Wetenschaplike bijdraen aan de derde STINFON Conferentie, pages 167-180, 1994.

C. D. Manning and H. Schutze. *Foundations of Statistical Natural Language Processing*. Cambridge: The MIT Press, 1999.

T. M. Mitchell. *Machine Learning*. Boston: McGraw-Hill, 1997.

J. Plisson, N. Lavrac and D. Mladenic. *A rule based approach to word lemmatisation*. Proceedings of the 7th International Multi-conference Information Society. Ljubljana: Institut Jozef Stefan, pages 83-86, 2004.

M. Porter. *An Algorithm for Suffix Stripping*. Program 14(3):1300-137, 1980.

J. R. Quinlan. *C4.5: Programs for Machine Learning* San Mateo: Morgan Kaufmann Publishers, 1993.

J. L. van Schoor. *Die Grammatika van Standaard-Afrikaans 'The Grammar of Standard Afrikaans'*. Cape Town: Lex Patria Publishers, 1983.

O. Streiter and E. W. de Luca. *Example-based NLP for Minority Languages: Tasks, Resources and Tools*. Proceedings of TALN 2003. Batz-sur-Mer, 11-14 June 2003.

A. van den Bosch. *Paramsearch 1.0 beta patch 24*. (2005).

ARABIC MORPHOLOGICAL GENERATION FROM INTERLINGUA
A Rule-based Approach

Khaled Shaalan[1&2], Azza Abdel Monem[3], Ahmed Rafea[4]

[1]Institute of Informatics,
  The British University in Dubai,
  P O Box 502216, Dubai,UAE
[2]Honorary Fellow, School of Informatics, University of Edinburgh
  khaled.shaalan@buid.ac.ae
[3]Central Lab. For Agricultural Expert Systems (CLAES),
  P O Box: 100 Dokki, Giza, Egypt,
  azza@mail.claes.sci.eg
[4]Computer Science Dept., Faculty of Computers and Information,
  Cairo Univ., 5 Ahmed Zewel St., Orman, Giza, Egypt,
  rafea@mail.claes.sci.eg

Abstract: Arabic is a Semitic language that is rich in its morphology. Arabic has very numerous and complex morphological rules. Arabic morphological analysis has gained the focus of Arabic natural language processing research for a long time in order to achieve the automated understanding of Arabic. With the recent technological advances, Arabic natural language generation has received attentions in order to allow for a room for wider applications such as machine translation. For machine translation systems that support a large number of languages, interlingua-based machine translation approaches are particularly attractive. In this paper, we report our attempt at developing a rule-based Arabic morphological generator for task-oriented interlingua-based spoken dialogues. Examples of morphological generation results from the Arabic morphological generator will be given and will illustrate how the system works. Nevertheless, we will discuss the issues related to the morphological generation of Arabic words from an interlingua representation, and present how we have handled them.

Key words: interlingua-based machine translation, Arabic morphological generation

Please use the following format when citing this chapter:

Shaalan, K., Monem, A.A., Rafea, A., 2006, in IFIP International Federation for Information Processing, Volume 228, Intelligent Information Processing III, eds. Z. Shi, Shimohara K., Feng D., (Boston: Springer), pp. 441–451.

1. Introduction

Arabic is morphologically rich language in which a single inflected word may correspond to a full sentence, (e.g. "كتبعمس"—I heard you). Arabic morphological analysis has gained the focus of Arabic natural language processing research for a long time in order to achieve the automated understanding of Arabic [8]. On the other hand, Arabic morphological generation has received little attention in spite of the fact that the types of generation problems can be as complex as those of the analysis [4].

The basic principle of morphological generation is to get inflected forms from a root and a set of features (lexical category and morphological properties). Generally, there are two categories of approaches to developing an Arabic morphological generator: approaches that use finite-state transducers (FSTs) and approaches that use rule-based transformations.

FSTs, such as the one described in [1], are limited to applications that are heavily dependent on morphological generation because the lexical and surface levels are very close. On the contrary, the rule-based transformation approach allows to morphologically generate an Arabic inflected word from the input which is usually a root with a specified feature list. This approach has been used by [3] [4]. The former is a prototype that is restricted in its coverage. The later follows the approach of [2] in that morphotactics and orthographic rules are built directly into the lexicon itself. Our approach is rule-based that uses general transformational rules to address the issue of generating inflected Arabic words in various prefix/suffix contexts. Unlike [4], we use general computational rules that interact to realize the output. The advantages of our approach are that it is easy to incorporate domain knowledge and heuristic rules.

In applications such as interlingua-based machine translation, Arabic morphological generation is an important issue for generating inflected Arabic word forms from semantic representation. This has led us to design and implement an Arabic morphological generator using Prolog. The Arabic word is represented as a feature structure (FS), a Prolog term, which is handled through unification during the morphological generation process. The morphological generator described here has also successfully been used in other natural language processing applications such as Arabic audio indexing [7] and intelligent computer assisted language learning for Arabic [6].

The Arabic generation approach described in this research is developed primarily within the framework of the NESPOLE! (NEgotiating through SPOken Language in E-commerce) multilingual speech-to-speech MT project. The goal of NESPOLE! is to provide speech-translation for common users engaged in real-world e-commerce applications for travel and tourism domain. There are six languages in NESPOLE, English, French, Italian, German, Japanese, and Korean. Arabic will be the seventh in this family. The Arabic morphological generator has been developed using the interlingua in Carnegie Mellon University (CMU) machine translation [1] and is compatible with the NESPOLE! interlingua specification[2].

The rest of the paper is organized as follows: description of the interlingua representation is summarized in section 2. This is followed by introducing the Arabic morphological generator in Section 3. Next, in Section 4, we discuss the set of important issues that we encountered during the design and implementation of the system. Finally, a conclusion and recommendations for further enhancements are given in section 5.

2. The Description of Interlingua

The NESPOLE! translation system [5] is designed to provide human-to-human speech-to-speech machine translation using an interlingua-based approach similar to that used in the JANUS system [9]. The domain addressed in NESPOLE! is the travel planning, a task-oriented domain. The NESPOLE machine translation project uses an interlingua representation called Interchange Format (IF), which is based on speaker intention rather than literal meaning. The IF defines a shallow semantic representation for task-oriented utterances that abstracts away from language-specific syntax and idiosyncrasies while capturing the meaning of the input. IF is based on a set of domain actions (DA) with parametric arguments. Each DA has up to four components: the *speech act*, the *concepts*, the *arguments*, and a *speaker tag*. Plus sign separate speech acts from the concepts and concepts from each other. In general, each DA has a speaker tag and at least one speech act optionally followed by string of concepts and optionally, a string of arguments. DAs can be roughly characterized as follows:

Speaker: speech act + concept* arguments*

1. a:on the twelfth we have a single and a double available.
   a: give-information+availability+room (provider=we,
   room-type= (operator=conjunct,[(single_room,
   quantity=plural),(double_room, quantity=plural)],
   time=(md=12))
2. a:and we+ll see you on February twelfth.
   a: greeting(conjunction= discourse, greeting=goodbye,
   to-whom=we, time=(month=2, md=12))

---

[1] See Carnegie Mellon University (CMU) web site for NESPOLE, http://www.is.cs.cmu.edu/nespole
[2] See interlingua specification for NESPOLE project,
   http://www.is.cs.cmu.edu/nespole/db/specification.html

3.   c:thank you very much
     c: thank

In example (1) the speech act is give-information, the concepts are
availability and room and the arguments are time and room-type. The
possible arguments of DA are determined by inheritance through a hierarchy of
speech acts and concepts. In this case time is an argument of availability and
room-type is an argument of room. Example (2) shows a DA which consists of
speech act with no concepts attached to it. The argument time is inherited from the
speech act greeting. Finally, Example (3) demonstrates a case of DA which
contains neither concepts nor arguments.

3. The Arabic Morphological Generator

Arabic morphological generation is an important issue for generating inflected
Arabic word forms from semantic representation.

3.1 The Lexicon

An Arabic lexicon was needed to successfully implement the morphological
generator. In our approach, we shall consider four basic morphological categories
for Arabic—noun, verb, and particle— each with a different set of features. The
Arabic word is represented as a FS. We differentiate among three lexical entries:
noun, verb, and particle.

The lexicon entry is implemented as a Prolog fact, i.e. lex/2. The first argument is
the Arabic stem and the second argument is the Arabic word FS written as a Prolog
list. The following describes the forms of the lexicon entry:
1.   **Nouns:** A noun has the following form:

 lex('Arabic-noun',[Stem,Category,Gender,Number,Sub_Cat,Case,

 Irrgular_plural]). Where:
   stem:'Arabic-noun'
   cat:noun
   gender:feminine/masculine/neuter
  • number:singular/dual/plural
   sub_cat:demonstrative/proper_noun/common_noun/
   adverb/adjective/question/...,
   definition:yes/no
   case:nomnative/accusative/genitive/...
  • irr_pl:'Broken_pl_form'
  Examples:
   • lex('أجازة',[stem:'أجازة',cat:noun,gender:feminine,number:sg,
    sub_cat:common_noun, definition:no,case:nom,irr_pl:[]]).

- lex('صيف',[stem:'صيف',cat:noun,gender:masculine,number:sg,
  sub_cat:common_noun, definition:no,case:nom,irr_pl:[]]).

.2 **Verbs:** A verb has the following form:

lex('Arabic-verb',[Stem,Category,Gender,Number,Tense,Case,Sub_Cat,Irregular_past]).
Where

> stem:'Arabic-verb'
> cat:verb
> gender: feminine/masculine
> number: singular/dual/plural

- tense:past/present/future
  case:nominative/accusative/...
  sub_cat:intrans/trans/sentence
- irr_past:'Past_Form'

Examples:

- lex('أخطط',[stem:'أخطط
  ',cat:verb,gender:masculine,number:sg,tense:present,case:
  nom,sub_cat:intrans, irr_past:[]]).
- lex('أرغب',[stem:'أرغب
  ',cat:verb,gender:masculine,number:sg,tense:present,case:n
  om,sub_cat:sentence, irr_past:[]]).

.3 **Particles:** A particle has the following form:

lex('Arabic-word',[Stem,Categor,Sub_Cat]). Where

> stem:'Arabicnoun'
> cat:particle

- sub_cat:conjunct/preposition...

Examples:

- lex('و',[stem:'و',cat:particle, sub_cat:conjunct]).
  lex('ل',[stem:'ل',cat:particle, sub_cat:preposition]).

3.2 Morphological Features in the Interlingua Representation

In the specification of IF, there are some argument-value pairs which encode the deep semantic of the intended inflected words in the target language. They are morphological features that can be used to generate inflected Arabic word forms from these features. These arguments include:

- object-spec=pronoun, In IF representation, this expression is used to indicate a third person pronoun (e.g. 'أحتاجه'—I need it). The generation of this pronoun depends on the gender and number of the Arabic stem.
- identifiability=yes/no, indicates the definiteness of a lexeme (e.g. 'الغرفة المزدوجة'—the double room). Other values include non-distant demonstrative (this— 'أسم الإشارة للقريب') and distant demonstrative (that— ' أسم الإشارة للبعيد').
- sex=male/female, indicates the gender of a lexeme (e.g. 'زوجة'—wife).
- whose=i/we/you/..., indicates a possessor (e.g. 'زوجتي'—my wife).
- quantity=all/entire/many/much/some/both, indicates quantity and quantifier (e.g. 'كل الغرف المزدوجة'—all double rooms).
- quantity=plural/integer, indicates quantity (e.g. 'ليلتان'—two nights).

- object-ref=any, indicates quantifier (e.g. 'أية مطاعم'—any restaurants).
- e-time=following/previous, indicates tense and in some cases it indicates verb "to be" (e.g. 'سنصل'—we will arrive).
- to-whom=i/we indicates first person pronoun such as "yeh el Khetab" (e.g. 'أخبرني'—tell me).

3.3 Morphological Generation Rules

A morphological generation rule takes a morphological feature-value pair to be applied and an Arabic word FS, retrieved from the lexicon, as input. Then it applies the required morphological generation action to update the current inflected Arabic word FS being constructed to reflect this change. Morphological generation rules can be classified into rules that are responsible for: synthesis of inflected noun, synthesis of inflected verb, and Synthesis of inflected particle.

Rules for synthesis of inflected noun. Rules for synthesis of inflected Arabic nouns are provided to define noun, feminize noun, pluralize noun, dualize noun, and conjugate a pronoun. Figure 1 shows an example of a noun synthesis rule that defines an Arabic noun. This rule ensures that the noun is not a proper noun, applies the addition of the prefix definition article to the noun, (possibly, a compound noun), then updates the Arabic word FS with then new value of the stem and the definition features.

```
rule: synthesize defined noun
input: Noun or adjective
output: defined noun or adjective
Example: الغرفة المزدوجة ـ الفنادق – الجيدة

If noun.sub_cat = proper_noun
Then return
else add_prefix(noun.stem,"ال")
```

Figure 1. An example of morphological generation rule for defining a noun

Rules for synthesis of inflected verb. Rules for synthesis of inflected Arabic verbs are provided to conjugate the verb form with regard to tense, number, and affix pronoun. Figure 2 shows an example of a rule for synthesizing a plural form of a verb. This rule conjugates with regard to the tense the number for the verb that may follow the first person pronoun 'we' ('نحن'), or similar expressions, e.g. (' أنا و 'زوجتي').

---

rule: synthesize plural verb

input: verb

output: pluralized verb

Eample: سنحتاج - نستطيع - لاحظنا

If verb.tense = future
then replace_prefix("سن","سا")
else if verb.tense = present
    then replace_prefix(verb.stem,"ن","أ")
    else add_suffix(verb.stem,"نا")

Figure 2. An example of morphological generation rule for synthesizing a plural form of a verb

Rules for synthesis of inflected particle. Rules for synthesis of inflected Arabic particle are provided to conjugate a particle with suffix pronoun. Figure 3 shows an example of a rule for synthesizing a particle suffix form. This rule conjugates the first person suffix pronoun 'ي' 'yeh' to the particle that connects two verbs.

---

rule: synthesize suffixed pronoun

input: pronoun

output: noun suffixed with connected pronoun

Example: اننا - أنني
          اظن أنني ساصل ...

If Pronoun.number = sg AND
   Pronoun.person = first
then add_suffix(particle.stem,"ني")
else Pronoun.number = pl AND
    Pronoun.person = first
    then add_suffix(particle.stem,"نا")

Figure 3. An example of morphological generation rule for synthesizing a suffix pronoun form of a particle

3.4 Morphological Generation Examples

Table 1 shows some examples of the Arabic morphological generation results that are produced form running the morphological generator on the input FSs to get the target inflected Arabic words. These examples illustrate how the inflectional morphology can make use of morphological features.

Table 1. Examples of generating inflected Arabic words from a stem and its morphological features.

Input	Inflected word Output
[...[...'زوج'...],'sex=',female, 'whose=', [... 'أنا'...] ...]	[...[...'زوجتي'...]...]
[...[...'غرفة'...],'whose=',[... 'أنت'...] ...]	[...[...'غرفتك'...]...]
[...[...'أحتاج'...], 'e-time=', following, 'object-spec=',pronoun ...]	[...[...'ساحتاجها'...]...]
[...[...'رؤية'...],'object-spec=', pronoun ...]	[...[...'رؤيتها'...]...]
[...['e-time=',following] ...]	[...[...'ساكون'...]...]
[...[...'أحجز'...],['e-time=', previous]...]	[...[...'حجز'...]...]
[...[...'أعطي'...],'to-whom=',[... 'أنا'...] ...]	[...[...'أعطني'...]...]
[...[...'أسمع'...],'to-whom=',[... 'أنت'...] ...]	[...[...'أسمعك'...]...]
[...['operator=[... 'و'],[[[...'أسرة'...], 'whose=',[... أنا '...]],[... 'أنا'...]]]...]	[...[...'أنا'...],[...'و'...] [...'أسرتي '...]...]
[...[...'أن'...],'whose=', [... 'أنا'...] ...]	[...[...'أنني'...]...]
[...[...'برامج شتوية'...],'whose=', [... 'نحن'...] ...]	[...[...'برامجنا الشتوية'...]...]

4. Issues and Problems

In this section, we will discuss issues related to the generation of Arabic text from an interlingua representation, and present how we have handled them. These issues have arisen when we were integrating the Arabic morphological generator with the Arabic generator module of the machine translation system.

4.1 Issues Related to Definite Nouns

The argument identifiability= has two values that can be used as morphological features (yes to indicate definite noun and no to indicate indefinite noun). Another value is non-distant that is used to indicate a demonstrative noun. They are mutually exclusive such that we cannot get a case where a noun is modified by a demonstrative and is also definite (i.e. substitution form). We found the substitution form is always the case with demonstratives. We solved this problem by assuming that the noun that the demonstrative modifies is definite with the article.

Numbers that are values of the argument quantity= indicates a number associated with a counted name—a value of the parent argument. Although we generate definite numbers in Arabic we cannot have this form because the IF specification of the argument quantity= does not have identifiability=

as a subargument. This problem is so specific to Arabic that we cannot generate definite numbers.

4.2 Issues Related to Numbers and Counted Nouns

Number-counted noun expression is governed by a set of complex rules for determining the gender, definiteness, and case markings. The markings of numbers depend on the occurrence of the number within the sentence.

- The number 'one', agreement is as expected, but there may be a reversal of word order (e.g. 'شخص واحد' *(one person)* and 'ليلة واحدة' *(one night))*.
- The number 'two' is expressed by the dual of the noun (e.g. 'شخصان—شخصين' *(two person)* and 'ليلتان—ليلتين' *(two nights))*.
- Numbers 'three' through 'ten' require the counted noun to be plural and the gender of the number to be the opposite of the gender of the singular noun. For example: خمس (five, masculine) سنوات (plural of سنة 'year', feminine) but خمسة (five, feminine) متاحف (plural of متحف 'museum', masculine).
- Compound numbers 'eleven' and 'twelve' require a singular counted noun in the indefinite accusative and agrees in the gender with the counted noun.
- Compound numbers 'thirteen' through 'nineteen' require a singular counted noun in the indefinite accusative. They also require the gender of the first part of the number to be the opposite of the gender of the counted noun and gender of the second part agrees with counted noun.
- Decades (Numbers '20' through '90', and hundred, thousand, etc.) require a singular counted noun in the indefinite accusative and the number to be sound masculine plural.
  Conjunction of numbers (units, tens, hundreds, thousands, etc.) follows the above rules and the individual numbers are separated by the conjunction particle waw 'و'.

Agreement decisions are made in the generator to synthesis the correct form of the numbers and their counted nouns.

Another issue is the mapping of ordinal numbers (first, second, etc.) and cardinal numbers (one, two, etc.). These depend on argument-value mapping. For example, the value of the argument hours= is mapped to a cardinal number and the value of the argument md= is mapped to an ordinal number.

```
your room will be available at eleven o'clock
a:give-information+feature+room (e-time=following, room-
spec=(room, whose=you), feature=(modifier=available),
time=(start-time=clock=(hours=2))))
```
        غرفتك ستكون متاحة الساعة الحادية عشر

```
I and my wife will be arriving February eleventh
```

```
c:give-information+arrival (who=(operator=conjunct,[i,(spouse,
sex=female,whose=I)]), e-time=following, time=(month=2,md=11))
```

أنـا وزوجـي سـنصل في الحـادي عشر مـن فـبرايـر

4.3 Issues Related to Arabic script

During inflectional morphology some letters of Arabic changes into other forms for example:

- The Alef letter ('ا') of the definite article 'ال' is dropped when used with preposition 'ل'. For example, using 'ل' with 'الطفل' produces 'للطفل'.
- The Hamza letter is changed to other forms during the morphological generation of the inflected word. For example, the use of Yeh ('ي') El-Khetab pronoun with the broken plural 'زملاء' should produce 'زملائي' instead of 'زملاءي'
- The feminine Teh ('ة') is change into ('ت') when a suffix is attached to it. For example, the dual of 'غرفة' is 'غرفتان-غرفتين'.

5. Conclusions and Future Work

In this paper, we described the development of a novel Arabic morphological generator. The morphological generator is implemented in SICStus Prolog and takes the advantage of Prolog's built-in term-unification. The morphological generator follows the rule-based approach. The advantages of this approach are that it is easy to incorporate domain knowledge and heuristic rules into the linguistic knowledge which provide highly accurate generations that represents a speaker's intention for each semantic segment. We have separately evaluated our Arabic morphological generator and the results were satisfactory. We have discussed the problems encountered in the generation of inflected Arabic words from the interlingua representation used in NESPOLE!. For these problems we have described how we handled them. Our morphological generator has also successfully been used in other natural language processing applications such as Arabic audio indexing and intelligent computer-assisted language learning for Arabic.

Future work will include extending the Arabic morphological generator to colloquial dialects of Arabic. Another interesting challenge would be to introduce diacritics into the lexicon. Text in Arabic is generally written without the diacritics (or vowels) and these are sometimes essential for the disambiguation of words.

References

1. Beesley, K. Arabic finite-state morphological analysis and generation. In Proceedings of the 16th International Conference on Computational Linguistics (COLING-96), Copenhagen, Denmark, (1996) (1): 89–94.
2. Buckwalter, T. Buckwalter Arabic Morphological Analyzer Version 1.0. Linguistic Data Consortium, University of Pennsylvania, 2002. LDC Catalog No.: LDC2002L49, 2002.
3. Cavalli-Sforza V., Soudi, A., Mitamura, T. Arabic morphology generation using a concatenative strategy. In Proceedings of the 6th Applied Natural Language Processing Conference (ANLP 2000), Seattle, Washington, USA, (2000) 86–93,.
4. Habash N. Large scale lexeme based Arabic morphological generation. In Proceedings of Traitement Automatique du Lan-gage Naturel (TALN-04). Fez, Morocco, 2004.
5. Lavie, A., Metze, F., Pianesi, F., Burger, S., Gates, D., Levin, L., Langley, C., Peterson, K., Schultz, T., Waibel, A., Wallace, D., McDonough, J., Soltau, H., Cattoni, R., Lazzari, G., Mana, N., Pianta, E., Costantini, E., Besacier, L., Blanchon, H., Vaufreydaz, D., Taddei, L., Enhancing the Usability and Performance of NESPOLE! - a Real-World Speech-to-Speech Translation System. In Proceedings of HLT-2002 Human Language Technology Conference, San Diego, CA, March (2002).
6. Shaalan K. An Intelligent Computer Assisted Language Learning System for Arabic Learners, Computer Assisted Language Learning: An International Journal, Taylor & Francis Group Ltd. (2005) 18(1 & 2): 81-108.
7. Shaalan, K., Talhami H., and Kamel I., A Morphological Generator for the Indexing of Arabic Audio, In the Proceedings of The IASTED International Conference on Artificial Intelligence and Soft Computing (ASC), September 12-14, Benidorm, Spain, (2005) 308-312.
8. Sughaiyer I., Al-Kharashi,I. Arabic Morphological Analysis Techniques: A Comprehensive Survey. Journal of The American Society for Information Science and Technology, (2004) 55(3):189-213.
9. Waibel, A., Jain, A., McNair, A., Tebelskis, J., Osterholtz, L., Saito, H., Schmidbauer, O., Sloboda, T., Woszczyna, M., JANUS: Speech-to-Speech Translation Using Connectionist and Non-Connectionist Techniques. Advances in Neural Information Processing Systems, (1992) (4).

DEVELOPMENT OF A MULTILINGUAL PARALLEL CORPUS AND A PART-OF-SPEECH TAGGER FOR AFRIKAANS

Julia Trushkina
Centre for Text Technology,
North-West University,
2531 Potchefstroom, South Africa
20215770@puk.ac.za

Abstract

This paper describes design and creation of a multilingual parallel corpus for South African languages. One of the applications of the corpus, namely, the induction of a part-of-speech tagger for Afrikaans from the data, is presented in the paper. Development of the Afrikaans part-of-speech tagger is based on a modified method for induction of linguistic tools from parallel corpora originally proposed by Yarowsky and Ngai (2001).

Keywords: Natural Language Processing, Parallel corpora, induction of linguistic tools, South African languages, Afrikaans, Part-of-Speech tagging.

1. Introduction

Multilingual annotated corpora, such as the Multext (Ide and Veronis, 1994) and the Multext-East (Dimitrova et al., 1998) corpora, are among the most valuable resources in current natural language processing. They underlie statistical research in multilingual tasks, such as machine translation, multilingual lexicography and word sense disambiguation, and can also be used in projects on monolingual studies.

For multilingual communities, such as the community of South Africa with eleven official languages, creation of a multilingual corpus has a special significance. It provides a basis for the development of multilingual language applications that can be used to facilitate or even avoid labor- and time-consuming processes of manual handling of multilingual information.

Additionally, such a corpus enables empowerment of minority languages of multilingual communities. With the use of a parallel corpus and the meth-

Please use the following format when citing this chapter:

Trushkina, J., 2006, in IFIP International Federation for Information Processing, Volume 228, Intelligent Information Processing III, eds. Z. Shi, Shimohara K., Feng D., (Boston: Springer), pp. 453–462.

ods which allow the transfer of linguistic annotations across languages, new resources and tools can be created for the minority languages.

The goal of the research project presented in this paper is the development of a multilingual corpus and basic tools and resources for South African languages. The current paper describes creation of such multilingual corpus and a development of a part-of-speech (POS) tagger for Afrikaans, one of the most prominent languages in South Africa. Although a member of the Indo-European family, Afrikaans is a language with very few resources. Several collections of unannotated Afrikaans texts exist, but the only corpus with incorporated linguistic information currently available for Afrikaans is a small corpus of approximately 20 000 tokens annotated with POS analyses (Pilon, 2006).

For the development of a POS tagger for Afrikaans, we apply a modified method of induction of linguistic tools from parallel data originally described in (Yarowsky and Ngai, 2001). project can be easily employed for additional development of tools for other South African languages.

2.   Potchefstroom Bible Corpus

Different sources of multilingual texts have been discussed in the literature. They include, among others, collections of law documents, such as the Canadian Hansard and the collection of European Parliamentary documents, translations of novels and other fiction, and multilingual versions of web pages (Resnik, 1999).

In the current project, the text of the Bible has been chosen as the basis for the multilingual corpus. The motivation of this choice is twofold. First, the Bible is available in many languages and is often accessible in electronic format, even for such rare languages as Maori and Swahili[1]. This makes the future expansion of corpus to other languages possible. The second reason for selecting the Bible as the content of the corpus is the close correspondence of the Bible translations in different languages.

At present, the corpus comprises the Bibles in five languages: Afrikaans, isiZulu, isiXhosa, English and Dutch. The first four languages are the most widely spoken languages in South Africa. An additional reason for the inclusion of the English data into the corpus is the high variety of freely available resources for English which can be used in annotation transfer. Dutch, the only language of the corpus which is not an official language of South Africa, has been included in the corpus since it is the closest relative of Afrikaans, which can make the transfer of linguistic analysis to Afrikaans more accurate.

The following Afrikaans, English and Dutch translations of the Bible have been chosen: the 1983 version of the Afrikaans translation, the World English Bible, and the Dutch Statenvertaling Bible. The choice of these versions has been motivated by two considerations: the modern language of the texts and the availability of the full text in machine-readable format. The size of the corpus ranges between 820 000 and 840 00 tokens for different languages.

The Afrikaans, English and Dutch parts of the corpus have been aligned on sentence and word level with freely available tools.[2] The Vanilla aligner (Danielsson and Ridings, 1997) has been used for sentence alignment, whereas word alignment has been performed with the GIZA software (Och and Ney, 2003).

Sentence Alignment

With the use of Vanilla aligner, optimal sentence alignments have been found for each pair of the Indo-European languages of the corpus. The results of the automatic alignment have been checked and corrected manually. Next, bilingual alignments have been combined into trilingual alignments. The principle of maximal span has been used for the combination: the span of the resulting trilingual aligned chunks of text corresponds to the span of the *"maximal"* pair of aligned sentences. Thus, for example, if Afrikaans-Dutch alignment is 2:1 (two Afrikaans sentences to one Dutch sentence) and corresponding Dutch-English alignment is 1:1, the resulting trilingual alignment is 2:1:1.

Word Alignment

For the word alignment of the corpus data, the GIZA software has been used. The software represents one of the open-source tools developed at the EGYPT project (Och et al., 1999) for machine translation. GIZA aligner relies on a statistical method based on co-occurrence of words of different languages in aligned sentences (Model 3 of the IBM statistical machine translation formalism (Brown et al., 1990).

GIZA produces only many-to-one alignments, i.e. any word of a source language can be aligned maximally with one word in a target language. The opposite situation, in which several words of a source language are linked to a single word in a target language, is possible. Since both many-to-one and one-to-many alignments occur in natural language, we have produced two alignments for each pair of the Indo-European languages of the corpus, assuming different translation directions in the experiments. The word alignment incorporated in the Potchefstroom Bible corpus is a combination of the six alignments obtained in this way. The combination has been performed in several steps.

First, the intersection of alignments for each language pair has been assumed to be a *"safe"*, or *"reliable"* alignment. Second, semi-automatic heuristics have been implemented to increase the number of reliable alignments. By semi-automatic nature of heuristics we mean the following: candidates for reliable alignments are proposed by a heuristic automatically, but a confirmation of a human is required for the inclusion of the candidate into the list of reliable alignments.

The following heuristics have been used:

- *Transitivity* heuristic:

  If reliable alignments exist between word W_a of language A and W_b of language B, as well as between word W_b and word W_c of language C, then a candidate reliable alignment between W_a and W_c is proposed, given that a link $W_a - W_c$ has been established in one of the six alignment experiments.

  $$W_a - W_b, \ W_b - W_c \longrightarrow W_a - W_c$$

- *Inter-span* heuristic:

  Let W^a_{n-1}, W^a_n and W^a_{n+1} be a sequence of words in language A, and W^b_{k-1}, W^b_k and W^b_{k+1} be a sequence of words in language B. If reliable alignments exist between W^a_{n-1} and W^b_{k-1}, as well as between W^a_{n+1} and W^b_{k+1}, then a candidate reliable alignment between W^a_n and W^b_k is proposed, given that GIZA established an alignment $W^a_n - W^b_k$ in one of the six experiments.

  $$W^a_{n-1} - W^b_{k-1}, \ W^a_{n+1} - W^b_{k+1} \longrightarrow W^a_n - W^b_k$$

  The heuristic has been very helpful in alignment of determiners. However, human inspection of the proposed links is necessary, since in many other cases the heuristic over-applies.

- *Correction* heuristic:

  A list of common alignment errors has been compiled for the three language pairs. The most common systematic errors have been corrected manually.

  For example, the Dutch version of the Bible includes a word *"En"* in the beginning of many sentences. The Afrikaans and the English parts of the Bible more often that not do not have a corresponding conjunction in the beginning of their sentences. In such cases, the statistical module of GIZA incorrectly and systematically aligns the word *"En"* with determiners *"Die"* (in Afrikaans sentences) and *"The"* (in English sentences), because they often co-occur in the sentence pairs with *"En"*. This error is easy to identify and to correct.

The share of reliable alignments compiled in the way described above is estimated to be 57.3% for the Afrikaans-Dutch language pair and 52.38% for the Afrikaans-English language pair. A manual inspection of a small portion of reliable alignments randomly chosen from the data demonstrated that the English-Afrikaans alignments are correct in 98.54% of cases, Dutch-Afrikaans alignments – in 98.11% of cases, and English-Dutch alignments – in 97.04% of cases.

Table 1 demonstrates an example of word-aligned data from the corpus. The first three lines represent aligned corpus sentences in Afrikaans, Dutch and English. A 6-column table under the sentences indicates alignment links for each word of the sentences.

Table 1. An example of word-aligned data from the Potchefstroom Bible corpus.

GEN 1:1 In die begin het God die hemel en die aarde geskep .
GEN 1:1 In den beginne schiep God den hemel en de aarde .
GEN 1:1 In the beginning God created the heavens and the earth

0	GEN	0	GEN	0	GEN
1	1:1	1	1:1	1	1:1
2	In	2	In	2	In
3	die	3	den	3	the
4	begin	4	beginne	4	beginning
5	het	5	schiep	6	created
6	God	6	God	5	God
7	die	7	den	7	the
8	hemel	8	hemel	8	heavens
9	en	9	en	9	and
10	die	10	de	10	the
11	aarde	11	aarde	11	earth
12	geskep	5	schiep	6	created
13	.	12	.		

3.   Corpus Annotation

Analysis of the English and the Dutch Parts of the Corpus

Analysis of the English part of the Potchefstroom Bible corpus has been performed with the Charniak's parser (Charniak, 2000) – an EM parser trained on the Penn Treebank corpus (Marcus et al., 1993). The choice of the parser has been motivated by its high performance: at present, the results reported for the parser performance are the highest results for English – 90.1%. Additionally, the annotation scheme of the Penn Treebank is the most cited and widely used scheme currently employed by computational linguists working on English. The parser performs full syntactic analysis together with POS tagging. It utilizes a POS tagset of 46 tags. The syntactic analysis is based on the annotation scheme of the Penn Treebank.

The Dutch part of the corpus has been analyzed with the Alpino parser (Bouma et al., 2001) developed for Dutch at the University of Groningen. The Alpino parser provides a full syntactic analysis of Dutch together with POS annotation. It is the best parser of Dutch currently available. The results reported in the literature by the parser developers reach an accuracy of 81.3% (Bouma et al., 2001). The syntactic analysis is based on the annotation scheme of the Alpino corpus of Dutch.

4.   Induction of Linguistic Analyses for Afrikaans

The annotation of the Afrikaans part of the corpus and the induction of a POS tagger for Afrikaans is based on the method proposed by Yarowsky and Ngai in (Yarowsky and Ngai, 2001).

The Method of Yarowsky and Ngai (2001)

The original model provides a high-quality annotation of a resource-poor language given a bilingual parallel corpus aligned on word level with annotation of one language part of the corpus. The method is based on an observation that linguistic analyses of translations of the same sentence in different languages often coincide.

Due to the differences in language structures and due to the often imperfect word alignments, the annotation resulting from a direct projection of analyses is of low quality. Yarowsky and Ngai (2001) report a performance of 69% for the direct projection of POS tags from English to French. The authors propose a method for robust learning from noisy POS projections by (a) downweighting or excluding poorly aligned sentences from consideration, (b) using a bigram model for learning, (c) training the lexical prior and tag sequence models separately using generalization techniques. (Yarowsky and Ngai, 2001) report an accuracy of 97% for French using the proposed model.

Modifications to the Original Method

We follow the main principles of the described model: at first, the part-of-speech tags are projected from the English data onto the Afrikaans tokens, and then an n-gram language model is trained on the POS tag projections.

However, we modified the original model in the following ways:

1 The Afrikaans language model is trained only on reliable alignments, excluding unsafe alignments completely.

   This modification is motivated by the low quality of the automatic word alignment in our experiments.

2 To compensate for the resulting data sparseness, not only reliably aligned sentences are taken into account, as proposed in (Yarowsky and Ngai, 2001), but all safe alignments identified by the heuristics described in Section 2.2. Such safe alignments may include subsequences of sentences and even separate words.

3 A trigram model is used instead of the originally proposed bigram model. This modification is introduced based on the generally higher performance of trigram models. Indeed, our experiments with a trigram and a bigram model have shown that the results are 1% lower for the bigram model.

4 The Afrikaans language model uses the full Penn Treebank set of 46 POS tags, unlike the originally described model which employs reduced tagsets of 14 and 9 core tags (representing main parts of speech, excluding punctuation).

5 No aggressive re-estimation of lexical probabilities in line with the original experiments is performed. Re-estimation of lexical probabilities has been advocated in (Yarowsky and Ngai, 2001) based on the low POS ambiguity of the data used in their experiments. However, a larger tagset leads to a higher POS ambiguity of tokens, which makes the aggressive re-estimation of lexical probabilities unfavourable.

The Trigram'n'Tags (TnT) tagger, an HMM trigram tagger developed and implemented by (Brants, 2000) has been used in our tagging experiments. The TnT tagger has been trained on the corpus of reliable projections of English POS tags onto Afrikaans data. Such training corpus has a rather different structure from the structure expected by TnT for training. First, the corpus is only partially annotated, since unreliable tag projections are not included. Second, a small part of the corpus is assigned multiple tags. These multiple tags are a result of one-to-many projections, such as projections produced in case of aligning a single Afrikaans token with an English phrase.

Since the TnT tagger has not been designed to train on partially annotated data with multiple tags, the Afrikaans language model provided to TnT has been created externally: the lexicon and the n-gram statistics files have been compiled in the way described below.

All tokens with reliable alignments have been used for the creation of the TnT lexicon file. For each token, a list of POS tags associated with the token in the corpus has been produced, together with the frequencies of the token and a tag/token pair.

If an Afrikaans word has been aligned with more than one English word, tags of each English translation are included in the lexical entry of the Afrikaans token. However, the entered frequency of such tags is reduced and represents a corresponding share of $1/n$, where n is a number of English words corresponding to the Afrikaans token.

In the creation of an n-gram statistics file, all sequences of reliably aligned text of corresponding length have been used. For example, each sequence of three words reliably aligned in the corpus has contributed to the compilation of trigrams statistics. For obtaining the statistics on unigrams, each Afrikaans word with a reliable alignment has been used.

Tagging Experiments

The TnT tagger provided with the language model compiled in the described way has been used for tagging the Afrikaans part of the corpus. The performance of the tagger has been evaluated against a manually annotated portion of the corpus. The size of the test set is 36 400 tokens. The evaluation demonstrated an accuracy of 83.98%.

When compared to the performance of the original tagger described in (Yarowsky and Ngai, 2001), the tagger induced from the Potchefstroom Bible corpus achieves a much lower accuracy. The main reason for this is a higher granularity of the tagset used in our experiments: 46 tags versus 9 tags in the original experiments.

An error analysis has demonstrated that the main sources of errors are confusion of verbal tags (32.31%), wrong tags for punctuation marks (18.06%), and mistakes that involve tag TO assigned in Penn Treebank to word *"to"* (15.28%). Mistakes in tagging of punctuation marks occur because punctuation often differs in English and Afrikaans. Table 2 presents the statistics on the occurrence of punctuation marks in the English and Afrikaans parts of the corpus. It shows a clear discrepancy in the usage of commas, full stops and semicolons. Such discrepancy leads to the projection of incorrect English tags onto Afrikaans punctuation marks.

Table 2. Statistics of the use of different punctuation marks in the Afrikaans and English parts of the corpus.

Punctuation mark	English	Afrikaans
period (.)	8 695	37 386
comma (,)	70 475	43 920
colon (:)	35 696	39 714
semicolon (;)	87 69	2 509

Errors in the use of verbal tags and the tag TO are due to the language differences of Afrikaans and English. The verbal system of Afrikaans is significantly simpler than that of English and therefore a set of nine verbal tags that distinguish between form, tense, number and person does not make sense for Afrikaans verbs and leads to a decrease in tagging performance. Quite similarly, the use of a single tag for all translations of the English word *"to"* obviously leads to tagging errors, since it results in assigning the same analysis to a diverse group of words.

To account for these phenomena, we have performed a second experiment with a modified tagset. In the modified tagset, a single tag for all punctuation marks except for parentheses and quotes has been introduced. Verbal tags have been restricted to tags VB for present tense verbs and VBD for past participles and past tense verbs. Tag TO has been collapsed with the tag for prepositions (IN). The resulting tagset contains 33 tags. These modifications to the tagset have lead to a significant improvement of the tagging performance and resulted in an accuracy of 92.45%.

Discussion and Future Work

The proposed model for the induction of a POS tagger from parallel data represents a modified version of the original algorithm described in (Yarowsky and Ngai, 2001). The model performs training on parts of aligned sentences, including small sections of text of one or more words which the heuristics described in Section 2.2 identified as reliably linked to their counterparts in the other language.

The induced POS tagger produces analyses of high granularity. Its performance has been compared to the performance of the only existing POS tagger for Afrikaans (Pilon, 2006) – a TnT tagger trained on the small corpus of manually annotated 20 000 tokens. Both taggers have been evaluated on the same test set.

The comparison of the two Afrikaans POS taggers demonstrated that the tagger induced from the Potchefstroom Bible corpus outperforms the tagger described in (Pilon, 2006) by 10%. However, the difference in the results is influenced by the difference in tagsets employed by the two taggers. The tagset of the smaller Afrikaans corpus comprises 119 tags.

Two main directions of research on the induction of linguistic tools for Afrikaans are intended for future. The first concerns expansion of the current model to trilingual data, including the Dutch part of the corpus into experiments. The second area for future research concerns induction of other tools from the corpus data, including a noun phrase bracketer, a chunker, a named entity recognizer and a parser.

5.   Conclusion

The paper described the development of a multilingual parallel corpus for South African languages, together with the experiments on the induction of a POS tagger for Afrikaans from this parallel corpus. The induction experiments have demonstrated promising results: the new POS tagger for Afrikaans outperforms a tagger trained on a small corpus of manually annotated Afrikaans corpus.

The project on the development of the corpus continues. Further development includes expansion of the corpus to other South African languages, deeper annotation of the Afrikaans part of the corpus, and alignment and linguistic analysis of the isiXhosa ans the isiZulu parts of the corpus.

Notes

1. See, for example, the Bible database website at http://www.bibledatabase.net/, which in April 2006 contained 51 versions of Bible translations in 30 languages.

2. Additional alignment of the isiZulu and the isiXhosa parts of the corpus is planned for immediate future.

References

G. Bouma, G. van Noord and R. Malouf. *Alpino: Wide-coverage Computational Analysis of Dutch*. Computational Linguistics in The Netherlands. 2001.

T. Brants. *TnT–A Statistical Part-of-Speech Tagger*. Proceedings of ANLP-2000. Seattle, 2000.

P. F. Brown, J. Cocke, S. Della Pietra, V. J. Della Pietra, F. Jelinek, J. D. Lafferty, R. L. Mercer and P. S. Roossin. *A Statistical Approach to Machine Translation*. Computational Linguistics 16(2):79–85, 1990.

E. Charniak. *A Maximum-Entropy-Inspired Parser*. Proceedings of ANLP/NAACL'2000. Seattle, 2000.

P. Danielsson and D. Ridings. *Practical presentation of a vanilla aligner*. Sprakbanken, Institutionen for svenska spraket, Goteborgs universitet, 1997.

L. Dimitrova, T. Erjavec, N. Ide, H.-J. Kaalep, V. Petkevic and D. Tufis. *Multext-East: Parallel and Comparable Corpora and Lexicons for Six Central and Eastern European Languages*. Proceedings of COLING'98. Montreal, 1998.

N. Ide and J. Vœronis. *Multext (multilingual tools and corpora)*. Proceedings of COLING'94, p. 90–96. Kyoto, 1994.

M. Marcus, B. Santorini and M. A. Marcinkiewicz. *Building a Large Annotated Corpus of English: The Penn Treebank*. Computational Linguistics 19(2): 313–330, 1993.

F. J. Och, C. Tillmann and H. Ney. *Improved alignment models for statistical machine translation*. Proceedins of the EMNLP/WVLC Conference. 1999.

F. J. Och and H. Ney. *A Systematic Comparison of Various Statistical Alignment Models*. Computational Linguistics 29(1):19–51, 2003.

S. Pilon. *Automatic part-of-speech tagging of Afrikaans*. MA thesis, North-West University, 2006.

F. Resnik. *Mining the Web for Bilingual Text*. Proceedings of ACL'99. Maryland, 1999.

D. Yarowsky and G. Ngai. *Inducing Multilingual POS Taggers and NP Bracketers via Robust Projection across Aligned Corpora*. Proceedings of NAACL 2001. Pittsburgh, 2001.

CONTENT-BASED FILTERING FOR MUSIC RECOMMENDATION BASED ON UBIQUITOUS COMPUTING

Jong-Hun Kim[1], Un-Gu, Kang[2] , and Jung-Hyun Lee[1]

[1] Department of Computer Science & Engineering Inha University
Yonghyun-dong, Nam-gu, Incheon, Korea
jhkim@hci.inha.ac.kr, jhlee@inha.ac.kr
[2] Department of Information Technology Gachon University of Medicine and Science
Yeonsu-dong, Yeonsu-ku, Incheon, Korea
ugkang@gachon.ac.kr

Abstract: In music search and recommendation methods used in the present time, a general filtering method that obtains a result by inquiring music information and recommends a music list using users' profiles is used. However, this filtering method presents a certain difficulty to obtain users' information according to their circumstances because it only considers users' static information, such as personal information. In order to solve this problem, this paper defines a type of context information used in music recommendations and develops a new filtering method based on statistics by applying it to a content-based filtering method. In addition, a recommendation system using a content-based filtering method that was implemented by a ubiquitous computing technology was used to support service mobility and distribution processes. Based on the results of the performance evaluation of the system used in this study, it significantly increases not only the satisfaction for the music selection, but also the quality of services.

Key words: Content-based Filtering, Ubiquitous Computing, OSGi

1.   INTRODUCTION

The amount of multimedia data that is processed by users has exponentially increased since the development and popularization of the

Please use the following format when citing this chapter:

Kim, J.-H., Kang, U.-G., Lee, J.-H., 2006, in IFIP International Federation for Information Processing, Volume 228, Intelligent Information Processing III, eds. Z. Shi, Shimohara K., Feng D., (Boston: Springer), pp. 463–472.

Internet. An increase in multimedia data presents difficulties in searching information within a user's desired time frame, which currently exceeds the limitation of data processing time for an individual user.

In order to solve these problems, a music search system that only provides the results of queries by rank using music information in a web environment has largely been used in the past and at the present time. Although a music search system has the advantage of being easily implemented, it may produce unwanted worthless information due to the exclusion of a user's interests and becomes a reason for a decrease in user satisfaction. In recent years, a recommendation system has been actively studied that predicts and recommends only information requested by a user. Various filtering methods are used in this recommendation system in order to estimate a user's preferences. For instance, a recommendation system using filtering methods have been used in some search engines such as Yahoo, Amazon online bookstore, and CDNow Internet shopping mall and have been well received by the user.

In this recommendation system, the similarity between the content of an item and user information was measured to recommend information desired by the user, and a content-based filtering method that based the rank on this measurement was also used. However, the recommendation of multimedia data is still limited [1] and is not highly reliable due to filtering only being based on static information. In particular, with a music recommendation system in the present web service environment, it is difficult to exactly recommend music that is desired by users because real-time context information like weather significantly affects a user's music selection.

Thus, this paper attempted to design a content-based music recommendation system (CBMRS) that is able to recommend music according to a user's interests and conditions by applying context information to a content-based filtering method. In order to apply context information to the CBMRS, data regarded as a factor in music selection was configured as context information and was based on ontology. In addition, data obtained using various sensors and an Radio Frequency Identification (RFID) Tag based on Open Service Gateway Initiative (OSGi) could be recognized as exact context information through an ontology database and inference engine. The recognized context information in this process could be used in a content-based filtering process based on statistics and also applied to provide a recommended list that was well received by the user. The system used in this study consisted of three large sections; a Context Manager section, Service Manager section, and Music Recommendation Manager section. The usefulness and results of this recommendation system satisfies a large number of persons in the results of the performance evaluation of the system used in this study.

2.   CONTENT-BASED FILTERING USING CONTEXT INFORMATION

This system defines contexts to recommend music by considering surrounding contexts and user information and configures a music list using a content-based filtering method. The content-based filtering used in a recommend process first configures a list by searching the music that corresponds to user preferences and user information from a Music Content Information Database (MCIDB) and builds an initial profile using this list.

The initial profile can be updated using the music title selected by users and the context information recognized in an OSGi environment in a music service. This profile is statistically analyzed and recommends a music list that corresponds to the context information from the MCIDB when a user inquires about a music service.

2.1   Configuration and Definition of Context Information

The definition of contexts created by Brown, defined information for a users' location or surroundings [2]. Brown's definition is an accurate method to develop application services, used to configure and determine proper context for a music recommendation service in this system.

This system determines the following factors which affect music selection: user sex, age, temperature, and weather before the configuration and determination of context.

The configuration of context information for the CBMRS consists of user information (sex, age, pulsation), weather, and outdoor temperature. In addition, user location information in the home is configured as context information. This allows a music recommendation service to employ certain applications regardless of the user's location in the home.

Table 1 presents the definition of context information as different spaces, such as class 2 for sex, class 5 for age, class 4 for pulsation, class 4 for temperature, class 7 for weather, and class 6 for location information. In particular, a pulsation below 40 or above 181 is defined as a dangerous condition to generate an event because the average pulsation of an adult is about 65~120. In addition, the service area is limited to homes, and the users' location is limited to the Balcony, Bathroom, Guestroom, Kitchen, and Living-room.

This system was implemented the ubiquitous network based on an OSGi framework in order to acquire automatic sensing datas. User information, temperature, and location information can be input from sensors based on OSGi framwork. User sex, age, and location information can be traced using an RFID Tag which is attached to a user's watch, and pulsation information can be obtained from a pulse sensor which is attached to a user's watch through real-time Zigbee communication. However, although weather information is predefined as ontology, its data can be established as a database retrieved from the Internet.

Table 1. Configuration and Definition of Context Information

Sex	Age		Pulsation		Weather	Temperature		Location
class	num.	class	num.	class	class	F°	class	class
MA-LE	0~7	Infant	0~40	Danger	Clear	-4~30.2	Cold	Balcony
	8~11	Child	41~65	Low	Sunny	32~68	Cool	Bathroom
	12~17	Young Adult	66~120	Normal	Cloudy	69.8~86	Warm	Bedroom
FEM-ALE	18~61	Adult	121~180	High	Shower	87.8~	Hot	Guestroom
	62~	Old Adult	181~	Danger	Rain			Kitchen
					Snow			Livingroom
					Storm			

The context of the CBMRS based on the context information used in this study is defined as Web Ontology Language (OWL) that is used on a Semantic Web in order to configure and express exact contexts and various relationships. Fig. 1 presents the hierarchy of OWL classes.

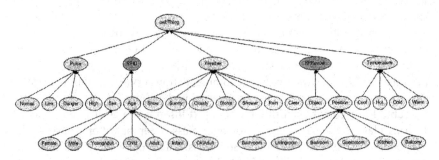

Fig.1. Ontology for Context in Content-based Music Recommendation System

2.2   Content-based Filtering Based on Statistical Method

At the present time, the filtering methods used in recommendation system are rule-based filtering, learning agent, content-based filtering, and collaborative filtering methods.

A rule-based filtering method identifies the preference of users and provides recommendations by connecting items to the characteristics of that item. The rule used in this method is predefined by experts. This method is effective with an item that has a high unit price and complicated characteristics. A content-based filtering method keeps the information related to items and recommends these items to the user who inputs a keyword, which is related to the property of the information. This method has been largely used in the field of information search [3]. A collaborative filtering method establishes a database according to the item preference of users and searches neighbors that have similar preferences when a new customer appears. In addition, the item that a neighbor is interested in is recommended to the customer under the assumption that the customer will be interested in the item [4].

This system remembers and creates a profile based on a selected item and context information when users are faced with specific context. In addition, when a user requires a recommended service, this system recommends a similar item to the user's former selection based on this profile. Thus, among previously mentioned filtering methods, a content-based filtering method can be used to configure a recommendation list.

To establish a Music Content Information Database (MCIDB), an automatic establishing method in web documents and user input methods were used. In an automatic establishing method, web documents can be extracted by a web robot agent. In addition, a database can be built using the analysis of morphology.

Table 2 shows the recorded value of the 'Winter Rain' in the MCIDB in which the key word was obtained by analyzing the song title using a morphological analysis.

Table 2. Example of a Music Content Information Database

Music Information	Extracted Nouns
Title	Winter Rain
Singer	Earl Klugh
Genre	Pop
Age	Young Adult
Weather	Rain
Temperature	Cold
Keyword	Winter, Rain

The earlier profile was configured as a title selected by the user according to the weather, temperature, and recommended ages from a music content information database. This means that context data, such as weather, temperature, and age profiles, could be obtained. Furthermore, a type of query profile is an additional profile configured using a music list which is selected from specific context. The query profile used in this profile becomes a selected music list according to the specific context of a user. For example, the profile can be automatically configured with the selected music list when context is presented as snow-cold-young_adult-normal. A profile can be produced according to a user's selected item for each context data set.

The recommendation method used in this system is as follows:

First, the frequency of words reappearing can be calculated using a morphological analysis method for a profile that corresponds to context information when a user requires a recommended service. For instance, if the context information is assumed to be snow-cold-young_adult-normal when a user requires a recommended service, the frequency of words reappearing can be calculated by analyzing the morphology of snow, cold, and young adult profiles. The frequency of a specific word reappearing can be expressed as $P(W_i)$ represented in Eq. (1).

$$P(W_i) = Freq_{max}(W_i) / \sum_{i=1}^{N} Freq_{max}(W_i) \times 100, \qquad 1 \le i \le N \qquad (1)$$

where W_i is the ith word in a specific profile, $Freq_{max}(W_i)$ is the total appearance number of W_i in the profile, and N is the total word in the profile except for the duplicated word.

Second, this method searches for the word that appears most frequently with each profile and song title, which coincides with the key word in the MCIDB and configures a list based on the results of these searches. Third, it combines these results into a single list excluding duplicate song titles. Fourth, it configures the priority of the list. In this process, the morphology of the query profile (snow-cold-young_adult-normal profile) that corresponds to the context information is analyzed and the word that appears with the highest frequency is extracted. In addition, a new list is configured according to the priority of the music, which coincides with the extracted key word from the query profile in the previously configured list. Moreover, music selected by users can be recorded in an inquiry profile, context data profiles and that be used as an accurate music list according to the repetition in selections.

3.   SYSTEM DESIGN AND IMPLEMENTATION

This chapter designed and implemented the CBMRS that was able to recommend proper music by estimating context information in a Java-based OSGi framework using the context definition and filtering method proposed in Chapter 2.

The system proposed in this study developed an OSGi gateway using the Knopflerfish 1.3.3, an open architecture source project which implemented a service framework. The OSGi is a type of industrial standard proposed by an OSGi organization in order to establish a standard connection method for

Internet devices, such as household information devices and security systems. It is JES-based gateway software, which is an open architecture Java embedded server able to provide high quality multimedia services with a high security level regardless of platform application software. In particular, it is an open architecture network technology that can support various network techniques, such as Bluetooth, Home Audio/Video Interoperability (HAVi), Home Phoneline Networking Alliance (PNA), Home Radio Frequency (RF), Universal Serial Bus (USB), Video Electronics Standards Association (VESA), and other networks [5].

Fig. 2 presents the diagram of the overall system. The CBMRS designed in this paper analyzed and suggested various data transferred from context recognition sensors and established it as information to recommend proper music through a filtering process for user profiles and MCIDB. In order to perform this process, the CBMRS consisted of a Context Manager, Service Manager, and Music Recommendation Manager.

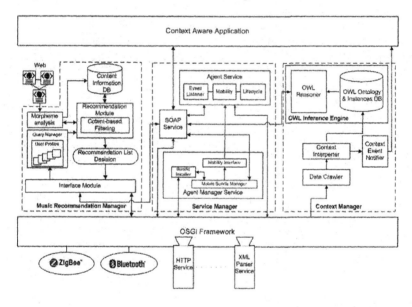

Fig. 2. Ontology for Context in Content-based Music Recommendation System

The Context Manager transfered data generated by events (sensing) to a context analyzer and that data was transfered to an OWL inference engine. The OWL inference engine transferred data received from the context manager to the Service Manager in which data was transformed as information using an OWL inferencer including OWL ontology object DB.

The Inference Engine in the Context Manager used an ontology inferencer Jena 2.0.

The Service Manager consisted of a Bundle Service that provided music recommendation service as a bundle in a Simple Object Access Protocol (SOAP) Service, OSGi framework installed device in order to transfer information received from the OWL inference engine to the music recommendation system, and an Application and Bundle Manager Service that supported the management of the mobility of bundles. Communication between the Context Manager, Music Recommendation Manager, and Music Service can be performed using the SOAP Service. This service makes possible a real-time process in music recommendation service using the context information between different systems. The Bundle Manager Service automatically manages Bundles and supports service mobility. Service mobility in a music recommendation system means that service is not interrupted by a different device that has an OSGi middleware even though a user's location has changed.

The Music Recommendation Manager played a role in the decision of an optimal music recommendation list in a recommendation module by applying the recommendation list that corresponded to certain context information received from the Service Manager with the user profile and MCIDB to a filtering process in a recommendation module. The Query Manager analyzed the context information received from the Service Manager, selected a proper profile according to user context information, and transferred it to the Recommendation Module. In addition, it performed an updating process for the music selected by users in the User Profile. The Recommendation Module performed the Morpheme analysis of the profile received from the Query Manager and configured a recommendation list by searching music from the MCIDB. The configured music list was ranked by the Recommendation List Decision and that was transferred as a new list to the Interface Module. The new list was then transferred to the Application through the SOAP Service.

4.   EXPERIMENT

This chapter tested whether user and context information is correctly recognized in an OSGi framework and whether a proper recommendation music list was provided by transferring this information to the Music Recommendation Manager in order to verify the CBMRS proposed in this study. The test environment consisted of the Context Manager and Service Manager as a bundle in an OSGi gateway on a home network in which the

Music Recommendation Manager was implemented on a desktop Personal Computer (PC). In addition, the MCIDB consisted of 300 pop songs.

Fig. 3 presents the output of context information produced by the Context Manager. The output was able to recognize the information as that of user Jong-Hun: age is Adult, sex is male, pulsation is normal, weather is snow, temperature is cold, and location is Guestroom. The transferred context information was used to make a proper music recommendation list for user context through the Music Recommendation Manager and was output to the PC in the Guestroom.

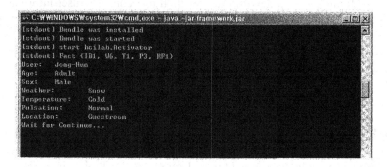

Fig. 3. An Execution View of Context Manager

In the paper, survey is used to evaluation of system. 50 users participated in system estimation. Users responded by value to 1 - 5 on question of table 3. Table 3 showed that user's satisfaction for system is high on the whole.

Table 3. Questionnaire and Results

Questionnaire	Result (average of users' value sum*20)
Does the weather influence in music selection?	79.2 %
Is music that recommend satisfied?	93.2 %
Do you think that CBMRS is useful?	94.4 %

5.   CONCLUSIONS AND FUTURE WORK

A music search and recommendation system that uses the conventional music search and recommendation method performs music search and recommendation by analyzing certain information that is passively received from users. This method presents a difficulty in a proper searching result for users' circumstances. Also, it has some problems that have to receive a lot of expressions from users in order to increase the satisfaction of users.

   This paper actively obtained and recognized user context information and designed a Content-based Music Recommendation System (CBMRS) that is appropriate to the user using the recommendation and inquiry of the content-based music recommendation system. The context introduced in this study was defined as ontology in order to use it as context information. In addition, a content-based filtering method, which was based on a statistical method, was developed. Also, this system was designed based on an OSGi framework in order to provide services without any interruptions wherever and whenever in a home network and that increased user satisfaction.

   As a future study, a new filtering method that considers user information to solve a specialization trend, which doesn't exceed the limited preferences of the CBMRS, is required. Finally, a middleware that is able to perform music recommendations and services without any interruptions to other services by considering a users various context information in a home network, is also necessary.

ACKNOWLEDGEMENT

This research was supported by the Brain Korea 21 Project in 2006.

REFERENCES

1. H. –C. Chen, and A. L. P. Chen, "A music recommendation system based on music data grouping and user interests," Proc. of the CIKM'01 (2001) 231-238
2. P. J. Brown, J. D. Bovey, and X. Chen, "Context-Aware Application: From the Laboratory to the Marketplace," IEEE Personal Communication (1997) 58-64
3. M. Balabanovic, and Y. Shoham, "Fab: Content-based, Collaborative Recommendation," Communication of the Association of Computing Machinery, Vol. 40, No. 3 (1997) 66-72
4. K. Y. Jung, and J. H. Lee, "User Preference Mining through Hybrid Collaborative Filtering and Content-based Filtering in Recommendation System," IEICE Transaction on Information and Systems, Vol. E87-D, No.12 (2004) 2781-2790
5. P. Dobrev, D. Famolari, C. Kurzke, and B. A. Miller, "Device and Service Discovery in Home Networks with OSGi," IEEE Communications Magazine, Vol. 40, Issue 8, August (2002) 86-92
6. C. Basu, H. Hirsh, and W. W. Cohen, "Recommendation as classification: Using social and content-based information in recommendation," In proceedings of the Fifteenth National Conference on Artificial Intelligence (1998) 714-720
7. K. Romer, T. Schoch, F. Mattern, and T. Dubendorfer, "Smart Identification Frameworks for Ubiquitous Computing Application," IEEE International Conference on Pervasive Computing and Communication (2003)
8. T. Gu, H. K. Pung, and D. Q. Zhang, "An Ontology-based Context Model in Intelligent Environments," Proceedings of Communication Networks and Distributed Systems Modeling and Simulation Conference (2004) 270-275

AN ITERATIVE APPROACH TO IMAGE SUPER-RESOLUTION

Vivek Bannore[1] and Leszek Swierkowski[2]

[1] *School of Electrical and Information Engineering, University of South Australia, Mawson Lakes SA 5095, Australia. Phone: +61-4-05149738, Vivek.Bannore@postgrads.unisa.edu.au*
[2] *Defence Science and Technology Organisation, Edinburgh SA 5111, Australia.*

Abstract: Undersampling and aliasing occurs frequently in many imaging systems leading to degradation of image quality. Super-resolution attempts to reconstruct a high-resolution image by fusing the incomplete scene information contained in the sequence of under-sampled images. This paper investigates iterative approaches to super-resolution. We propose algorithm that utilises a relatively small number of low-resolution images and is computationally inexpensive. Experimental results of reconstruction are presented.

Key words: Image processing, Super-Resolution, Iterative technique, Image Interpolation

Please use the following format when citing this chapter:

Bannore, V., Swierkowski, L., 2006, in IFIP International Federation for Information Processing, Volume 228, Intelligent Information Processing III, eds. Z. Shi, Shimohara K., Feng D., (Boston: Springer), pp. 473–482.

1.   INTRODUCTION

In many applications such as satellite imaging, remote sensing, forensic science and computer vision applications high-resolution imagery is essential. Despite the recent advances in sensor technology the requirements for high quality imagery very often exceed the capabilities of imaging systems. In such cases it is desirable to develop image processing techniques that enhance the resolution of images. A promising technique of super-resolution attempts to reconstruct a high-quality image from a number of undersampled images of the same scene.

The super-resolution technique takes advantage of the existence of relative motion between the sensor and the scene during the acquisition process. In the presence of such motion each low-resolution image frame acquired by the imaging system carries slightly different information about the scene. Super-resolution attempts to fuse this information during the image reconstruction process.

High-resolution image reconstruction techniques have been researched in both the frequency and the spatial domains. In general, the current techniques are unable to maintain a balance between improving spatial resolution and keeping the computational time low. Consequently, there is a challenge to develop new, more efficient techniques for super-resolution. Our aim is to address the shortcomings of algorithms proposed in literature and to explore the possibility of developing techniques that would be able to reconstruct high-resolution images without excessive computational cost.

In this paper we present a simple, iterative technique for super-resolution that is computationally inexpensive without sacrificing quality of the reconstructed image. The paper is organized as follows. In the next section a brief review of the existing super-resolution techniques is given. Section 3 describes image interpolation based super-resolution. The implementation of our algorithm is described in Section 4, and Section 5 describes iterative improvement technique. Finally, Section 6 presents our preliminary results of high-resolution image reconstruction.

2.   EXISTING SUPER-RESOLUTION TECHNIQUES

A variety of approaches can be found in the literature for the reconstruction of high-resolution image by fusing data from a series of low-resolution frames. For the purpose of this paper a brief description of existing techniques is presented in this section. More comprehensive overviews can be found in [1-3].

The super-resolution model [1,3-7] is based on a sequence of N low-resolution (LR) images $\underline{b}_K$ ($K=1...N$) of the same scene. The scene is represented by a single high-resolution (HR) image $\underline{X}$ that we wish to reconstruct. Each measured LR image is the result of sampling of the ideal high-resolution real scene and is subjected to camera and atmospheric blur, motion effects, geometrical warping and decimation. It is assumed that a linear operator A_K represents all these imaging factors and that the LR images are contaminated by an additive Gaussian noise E. Therefore, the super-resolution model is represented by the following equation:

$$\underline{b}_K = A_K \underline{X} + \underline{E},\tag{1}$$

where the images are represented as vectors (shown by an underscore), ordered column-wise lexicographically. The problem of super-resolution is then solved, in the least-squares sense, by minimization of the error τ between the actually measured and the predicted LR images:

$$\tau = \sum_{K=1}^{N} \left[\underline{b}_K - A_K \underline{X} \right]^2.\tag{2}$$

The estimation of the HR image from the equation (2) is known to be an ill-conditioned problem, in the sense that small perturbations of LR images can lead to large changes in the reconstructed image. As a result the reconstruction problem is intrinsically unstable. A commonly used procedure that alleviates this difficulty is adding a *Regularization* term to equation (2):

$$\tau = \sum_{K=1}^{N} \left[\underline{b}_K - A_K \underline{X} \right]^2 + \lambda \left[Q \underline{X} \right]^2.\tag{3}$$

Q represents here a stabilization matrix and $\lambda > 0$ is the regularization parameter. The regularization term can incorporate some *a priori* knowledge about the real high-resolution scene (smoothness, for example) and has to be chosen in such a way as to ensure that the reconstruction X is stable with respect to small variations in the image data.

Most published techniques attempt to solve equation (2) or its regularized version (3) for the case where image motion is characterized by a global translation or rotation [8, 9]. Hardie *et al* [8] used steepest descent and conjugate-gradient techniques for minimizing the cost function eq. (3) with a simple regularization term that enforced the smoothness of the solution. The iterative back-projection method was adopted in [9]. Tuinstra *et al* [10] proposed a method for treating non-global motion that used automated motion segmentation and registration.

The techniques based on optimization of the reconstructed image by minimization of the cost function (2) or (3) are usually applied in the spatial domain. In contrast, Tsai and Huang [11] were the first to propose the frequency domain approach for solving the super-resolution problem. This method directly addresses the removal of aliasing artifacts. The frequency domain approach is based on an assumption that the original high-resolution image is band-limited and exploits the translational property of the Fourier Transform. It makes use of the aliasing relationship between the Continuous Fourier Transform (CFT) of the original real scene and the Discrete Fourier Transform (DFT) of the observed low-resolution images.

In their paper, Tsai and Huang assumed the sequence of low-resolution frames to be free from distortions such as blur or noise. The computational cost of the method was found to be relatively low, but due to the limitation in geometric warping the approach did not gain much popularity.

In general, however, the problem of super-resolution is computationally expensive, ill-posed and underdetermined. In an attempt to alleviate the computational cost, Nguyen *et al.* [12, 13] introduced the concept of *Preconditioning* to the super-resolution problem. Preconditioning transforms the original system into one with the same solution but with better convergence properties. It therefore can be solved faster.

In this paper, we adopt a fast iterative approach for solving the problem of image super-resolution. In this method, a well-defined interpolation kernel is used to generate a first approximation to the reconstructed image. This approximation is then iteratively improved to produce the final high-resolution solution. The paper compares the most commonly-used interpolation kernels and evaluates the efficiency of the reconstruction as a function of the number of LR images.

3. IMAGE INTERPOLATION BASED SUPER-RESOLUTION

It is well known result that the reconstruction X in equation (3) tends to the generalized inverse solution as the regularization term vanishes ($\lambda \to 0$). This result is the starting point for the method adopted in this paper. Although the method can be derived explicitly from the equation (3), for the purpose of this short communication we adopt more intuitive description, deferring mathematically rigorous derivation to a future publication.

The method consists of several steps. At the initial stage the camera motion has to be taken into account. To accomplish this, a sequence of observed low-resolution images of the scene we want to super-resolve is registered precisely relative to the reference LR frame. Once this is achieved, a high-resolution image grid is populated with pixels from low-resolution images by placing them at the appropriate grid-points according to the registration information. Since the number of low-resolution images is limited, the whole composite grid template is not completely filled. It is worth mentioning at that point that under certain conditions this sparse image is related to the generalized inverse solution of equation (2).

The high-resolution image is finally estimated by interpolating the sparse grid to populate the empty pixels. This is an important step that has significant effect on the accuracy of the reconstruction. In an attempt to quantify the effect of interpolation on the reconstruction, the several image interpolation techniques were compared. Computer experiments were carried out using the following most commonly used interpolation methods:

a) Linear Interpolation
b) Nearest-Neighbor Interpolation
c) Truncated Sinc Interpolation
d) Lanczos2 Windowed Sinc Interpolation
e) Lanczos3 Windowed Sinc Interpolation
f) Cubic Spline Polynomial (Order 4 and 5)
g) Gaussian Interpolation (Order 2, 6 and 10)

4. IMPLEMENTATION

The algorithm described briefly in the previous section was coded in MATLAB, making use of the Image Processing Toolbox. A number of high-resolution images of sizes 512 by 512 and 1024 by 1024 were used for our testing purposes. In order to quantify the accuracy of the reconstruction a synthetic set of low-resolution images was generated for each HR image by applying random translations. The reconstruction procedure was then applied to the LR images and the reconstructed HR image was compared with the original. The interpolation methods listed above were implemented.

Two examples of the super-resolution reconstruction are presented here. Figure 1 shows LR images where only one image from each sequence is displayed. In these particular examples ten LR images were used for each reconstruction and the subsampling ratios were 16 and 12 for panels (a) and (b), respectively. The reconstructed HR images are shown in Figure 2. By inspecting the reconstructed images one can clearly see the deficiency of the reconstruction process. The periodic artifacts that are visible in the interpolated images are due to the high number of empty blocks in the composite high-resolution grid. These empty blocks appear in the HR grid as a result of irregular sampling of the scene caused by random movements between LR frames. The quality of the HR image increases significantly with the number of LR frames used in the reconstruction process. For practical reasons, however, it is important to keep the number of LR images as low as possible. Therefore, in the next section, we adopt an iterative approach to remove these visible artifacts and improve the estimated high-resolution solution.

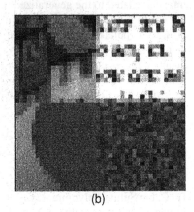

(a)   (b)

Figure 1. (a) One of the ten low-resolution images with sampling ratio of 16. Size - [64 x 64]. (b) One of the ten low-resolution images with sampling ratio of 12. Size - [42 x 42].

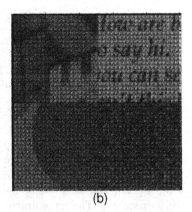

(a)   (b)

Figure 2. First Approximation interpolated images. (a) [1024 x 1024] (b) [504 x 504]

5. ITERATIVE IMPROVEMENT TECHNIQUE

A solution of the least-square problem eq. (3) can be sought by solving the equivalent normal equation, which involves the inversion of a linear operator. Suppose that only an approximate inverse is known, the solution can then be improved by an iterative approach described in [14].

In the context of super-resolution reconstruction, the approximate inverse operation is given by our interpolation-based reconstruction, as described in the previous sections. The interpolated HR image is fed into the iteration scheme as the *first approximation image X_1*. This image is then exposed to the same imaging conditions as the original (unknown) scene and as represented by the imaging operator A_K in equation (1). The result is that the set of LR images $b_K^{(1)}$ is generated. Since the image X_1 is only an approximation of the real scene, these new LR images are different from the original LR images b_K. The difference between the two sets forms the error vector that should vanish when the reconstructed image converges to the real scene. The error vector is now reconstructed into HR error image, using the interpolation procedure from the previous section, and added to X_1. The resultant image forms the *second approximation X_2* of the real scene. The image X_2 is the input for the next iteration. A new set of LR images is generated and subtracted from the original set to form the new error vector, which is reconstructed and added to X_2. The resultant image is the *third approximation X_3*. The process is repeated until convergence is achieved.

6. RESULTS

In order to quantify the fidelity of reconstruction we have again used several known high-resolution images to artificially generate lower-resolution images. The reconstructed HR images were then compared with the original images. A modified version of Root Mean Square Error (RMSE) has been used as a similarity measure. The modification was to ensure that the local spatial contents of images were compared and not their global brightness. The value of RMSE was calculated between the iteratively reconstructed high-resolution image and the original high-resolution image to monitor the reconstruction process.

It is worth mentioning that although the main purpose of the iteration procedure is to minimize artifacts appearing in the interpolated images, the process contains also an implicit regularization features. Both the size of the interpolation kernel as well as the number of iteration strongly affects the smoothness of the reconstructed image and controls the stability of the process.

Figure 3 shows two examples of the iterative reconstruction of the images from figures 1 and 2. It is evident that the algorithm successfully removed the artifacts that were visible in the interpolated images, figure 1 and 2.

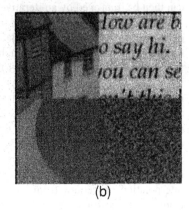

(a)   (b)

Figure 3. (a) and (b) - Iteratively Reconstructed High-Resolution Images

A number of different high-resolution test images have been used in the simulation to compare and analyze the performance of the interpolation techniques in generating high-resolution images. For all images the tendencies were similar. Although the RMSE numbers differed for each test image due to the different contents of the images, it has been observed that the most of the improvement occurred during the first few iterations. The further changes in the RMSE values were much smaller and eventually there was no discernible improvement. Typically, as many as 20 iterations were needed to achieve convergence.

The quality of the reconstruction procedure scaled with the number of LR images used in the process. The greater the number of LR images a more densely populated HR grid was generated, and hence the accuracy of the interpolation and reconstruction improved. Note that for larger magnification factors increasing numbers of LR images are necessary to maintain the same level of performance. In most cases, about 10 LR images were sufficient for magnification factors as large as 16.

7.   SUMMARY AND CONCLUSIONS

A hybrid reconstruction scheme has been proposed here for application to the problem of super-resolution restoration of high-resolution images from sequences of low-resolution images. The method makes use of interpolation techniques to produce the first approximation for the reconstructed image and then employs an iterative approach to generate the final solution. Preliminary results show that the algorithm is efficient and has a promise of being applicable for real time processing.

Computer experiments were conducted to validate the algorithm. The performance of the method was found to depend significantly on the interpolation method used in reconstruction. Several different interpolation techniques were implemented and tested. As expected, the higher degree interpolation methods were more accurate, leading to better reconstruction. The price for better accuracy, however, was longer computational time. Our results seemed to indicate that the cubic spline interpolation was the most promising in the tradeoff between the accuracy and the computational speed.

The approach presented in this paper requires a relatively small number of low-resolution images for efficient reconstruction. Good results were obtained with only 10 LR frames and for magnification factors as large as 16. This is important for practical applications, because if a large number of LR images were required the accumulation of errors would impede the reconstruction accuracy.

Although the algorithm has been applied to grayscale images only, its extension to RBG images should be straightforward. Further work is also required to test the robustness of the method to noise and registration errors. The extension of the algorithm to more general geometric warping is another future challenge. These issues are currently under investigation.

ACKNOWLEDGEMENTS

This work is partially supported by Defence Science & Technology Organisation. Vivek Bannore would like to thank Noel Martin and Lakhmi Jain for supporting this project. Leszek Swierkowski would like to acknowledge valuable discussions with Barnaby Smith.

REFERENCES

[1]   *Super-Resolution Imaging*, 1st ed: Kluwer Academic Publishers, 2001.

[2]   T. Komatsu, K. Aizawa, T. Igarashi, and T. Saito, "Signal-Processing Based
        Method For Acquiring Very High Resolution Images With Multiple Cameras And
        Its Theoretical Analysis," *Communications, Speech and Vision, IEE Proceedings I*,
        vol. 140(1), pp. 19-24, 1993 Feb.

[3]   S. C. Park, M. K. Park, and M. G. Kang, "Super-Resolution Image Reconstruction:
        A Technical Overview," *IEEE Signal Processing Magazine*, vol. 20, pp. 21-36,
        2003 May.

[4]   M. G. Kang and S. Chaudhuri, "Super-Resolution Image Reconstruction," *IEEE
        Signal Processing Magazine*, vol. 20, pp. 19-20, 2003 May.

[5]   M. Elad and A. Feuer, "Restoration of a Single SR Image from Several Blurred,
        Noisy, & Under-sampled Measured Images," *IEEE Trans. on Image Processing*,
        vol. 6, pp. 1646-1658, 1997 Dec.

[6]   W. Zhao and H. Sawhney, "Is Super-Resolution with Optical Flow Feasible?,"
        Proc. ECCV'2002, vol. 1, pp. 599-613, 2002.

[7]   M. Elad and A. Feuer, "Super-Resolution Restoration Of An Image Sequence:
        Adaptive Filtering Approach," *Image Processing, IEEE Transactions on*, vol. 8(3),
        pp. 387 - 395, 1999 March.

[8]   R. C. Hardie, J. G. Bognar, K. J. Barnard, and E. A. Watson, "High-Resolution
        Image Reconstruction from a Sequence of Rotated and Translated Frames and It's
        Application to an Infrared Imaging System," *Optical Engineering*, vol. 37, pp. 247-
        260, 1998 Jan.

[9]   M. Irani and S. Peleg, "Improving Resolution by Image Registration," *CVGIP:
        Graphic Models and Image Processing*, vol. 53, pp. 231-239, 1991 May.

[10]   T. R. Tuinstra and R. C. Hardie, "High-resolution image reconstruction from digital
        video by exploitation of non-global motion," *Optical Engineering*, vol. 38, pp. 806-
        814, 1999 May.

[11]   R. Y. Tsai and T. S. Huang, *Multiframe Image Restoration and Registration*, vol. 1.
        Greenwich: JAI Press Inc , pp. 317-339, 1984.

[12]   N. Nguyen, G. Golub, and P. Milanfar, "Preconditioners for Regularized Image
        Superresolution," *Acoustics, Speech, and Signal Processing, 1999. ICASSP '99.
        Proceedings., 1999 IEEE International Conference on*, vol. 6, pp. 3249 - 3252,
        1999 March.

[13]   N. Nguyen, P. Milanfar, and G. Golub, "A Computationally Efficient Super-
        Resolution Image Reconstruction Algorithm," *Image Processing, IEEE
        Transactions on*, vol. 10(4), pp. 573 - 583, 2001 April.

[14]   W. H. Press, B. P. Flannery, S. A. Teukolsky, and W. T. Vetterling, "Iterative
        Improvement of a Solution to Linear Equations," in *Numerical Recipes in C (2nd
        Edition)*: Cambridge University Press, 1992 Oct, pp. 1020.

INTERACTING WITH COMPUTER USING EARS AND TONGUE

Urmila Shrawankar[1] Anjali Mahajan[2]

[1]*Dept. of Information Technology, Government Polytechnic Institute, Nagpur– 440 001– INDIA*
urmilas@rediffmail.com Cell no. : +919422803996

[2]*Dept. of Computer Sci. & Engg G.H. Raisoni College of Engg., Nagpur– 440 016– INDIA*
armahajan@rediffmail.com

Abstract:
Human computer interaction is concerned in the way Users (humans) interact with the computers. Some users can interact with the computer using the traditional methods of a keyboard and mouse as the main input devices and the monitor as the main output device. Due to one or another reason, some users are enable to interact with machines using a mouse and keyboard device, hence there is need for special devices. If we use computer for more time it is really difficult to sit on the chair, keeping hands continuously on the keyboard or mouse and keep watching the monitor.

To relax our body and interact comfortably with computer, we need some special device or method, so that computer will understand and accept commands without keyboard or by clicking mouse.

Speech Recognition System helps users who are unable to use traditional Input and Output (I/O) devices. Since four decades, man has been dreaming for an "intelligent machine" which can master the natural speech. In its simplest form, this machine should consist of two subsystems, namely Automatic Speech Recognition (ASR) and Speech Understanding (SU). The goal of ASR is to transcribe natural speech while SU is to understand the meaning of the transcription. Recognising and understanding a spoken sentence is obviously a knowledge-intensive process, which must take into account all variable information about the speech communication process, from acoustics to semantics and pragmatics

Please use the following format when citing this chapter:

Shrawankar, U., Mahajan, A., 2006, in IFIP International Federation for Information Processing, Volume 228, Intelligent Information Processing III, eds. Z. Shi, Shimohara K., Feng D., (Boston: Springer), pp. 483–491.

Key words: Automatic Speech Recognition ,Text-To-Speech, Speech-To-Text, Interactive
Voice Response–Systems, Linear Prediction Coding, Hidden Markov Model

1.   INTRODUCTION

Speech is one of the oldest and most natural means of information exchange
between human beings. We, as humans speak and listen to each other in
human-human interface. The speech generation and production system is
described in following figure.

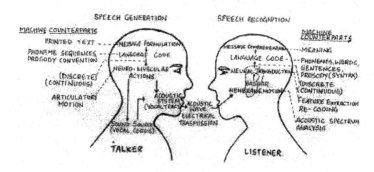

Fig.: Speech Generation and Production system.

Voice/speech recognition is a field of computer science that deals with
designing computer systems that recognize spoken words. It is a technology
that allows a computer to identify the words that a person speaks through a
microphone or telephone.

Speech recognition can be defined as the process of converting an acoustic
signal, captured by a microphone or a telephone to a set of words.

Automatic Speech Recognition (ASR) is one of the fastest developing fields
in the framework of speech science and engineering. In the new generation
of computing technology, it comes as the next major innovation in man-
machine interaction, after functionality of Text-To-Speech (TTS), supporting
Interactive Voice Response (IVR) systems.

Nowadays, the statistical techniques prevail over ASR applications.
Common speech recognition systems, these days can recognize thousands of
words. The evolution of ASR, has improved its scope of applications in
many aspects of daily life, for example, telephone applications, applications
for the physically handicapped and illiterates and many others in the area of

computer science. Speech recognition is considered as an input as well as an output during the Human Computer Interaction (HCI) design. HCI involves the design implementation and evaluation of interactive systems in the context of the users' task and work

2.   SPEECH RECOGNITION TECHNIQUES

Speech recognition techniques are as follows:

i. Template based approaches matching: Unknown speech is compared against a set of pre-recorded words (templates) in order to find the best match. This has the advantage of using perfectly accurate word models. But it also has the disadvantage that pre-recorded templates are fixed, so variations in speech can only be modeled by using many templates per word, which eventually becomes impractical. Dynamic time warping is such a typical approach.

In this approach, the templates usually consist of representative sequences of feature vectors for corresponding words. The basic idea here is to align the utterance to each of the template words and then select the word or word sequence that contains the best. For each utterance, the distance between the template and the observed feature vectors are computed using some distance measure and these local distances are accumulated along each possible alignment path. The lowest scoring path then identifies the optimal alignment for a word and the word template obtaining the lowest overall score depicts the recognised word or sequence of words.

ii. Knowledge based approaches: An expert knowledge about variations in speech is hand coded into a system. This has the advantage of explicit modeling variations in speech; but unfortunately such expert knowledge is difficult to obtain and use successfully.

Thus this approach was judged to be impractical and automatic learning procedure was sought instead.

iii. Statistical based approaches: In this variation, speech is modeled statistically using automatic, statistical learning procedure, typically the Hidden Markov Models (HMM). The approach represents the current state of the art. The main disadvantage of statistical models is that they must take priori-modeling assumptions, which are liable to be inaccurate, handicapping the system performance. In recent years, a new approach of challenging problems of conversational speech recognition has emerged, holding a promise to overcome some fundamental limitations of the conventional Hidden Markov Model (HMM) approach.

This new approach is a radical departure from the current HMM-based statistical modeling approaches. Rather than using a large number of unstructured Gaussian mixture components to account for the tremendous variations in the observable acoustic data of highly co-articulated spontaneous speech, the new speech model that have developed provides a rich structure for the partially observed (hidden) dynamics in the domain of vocal-tract resonance.

iv. Learning based approaches: To overcome the disadvantage of the HMMs, machine learning methods could be introduced such as neural networks and genetic algorithm / programming. In these machine-learning models, explicit rules or other domain expert knowledge need not be given. They can be learned automatically through emulations or evolutionary process.

v. The artificial intelligence approach attempts to mechanise the recognition procedure according to the way a person applies his intelligence in visualizing, analysing, and finally making a decision on the measured acoustic features. Expert system is used widely in this approach.

3.   MATCHING TECHNIQUES

Speech-recognition engines match a detected word to a known word using one of the following techniques.

i. Whole-word matching: The engine compares the incoming digital-audio signal against a pre-recorded template of the word. This technique takes much less processing than sub-word matching, but it requires the user (or someone) pre-record every word that will be recognized (sometimes several hundred thousand words). Whole-word templates also require large amounts of storage (between 50 and 512 bytes per word) and are practical only if the recognition vocabulary is known when the application is developed.

ii. Sub-word matching: The engine looks for sub-words, usually phonemes and then performs further pattern recognition. This technique takes more processing than whole-word matching, but it requires much less storage (between 5 and 20 bytes per word). In addition, the pronunciation of the word can be guessed from English text without requiring the user to speak the word beforehand. On discussing the research in the area of automatic speech recognition, it has been pursued for the last three decades, that only whole-word based speech recognition systems have found practical use and became commercial successful. Though whole-word models became successful but the researchers mentioned that, they still suffer from two major problems, i.e. co-articulation problems and requiring a lot of training to build a good recognizer.

4.   BUILDING AN APPLICATION BASED ON SPEECH INTERFACE

For building an application based on Speech Interface we need to follow following steps:

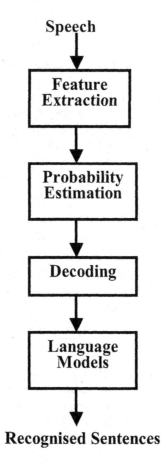

4.1 Input

Accept commands through Microphone.

4.2 Feature Extractions And Feature Matching

Feature extraction is the process that extracts a small amount of data from the voice that can later be used to represent each speech.
Feature matching involves the actual procedure to identify the unknown speech by comparing extracted features from his/her voice input.
All speech recognition systems have to serve two distinguished phases. The first one is referred to as enrollment sessions or training phase while the other is referred to as operation sessions or testing phase.

4.2.1 Speech Feature Extraction

The purpose of this module is to convert the speech waveform to some type of parametric representations for further analysis and processing. This is often referred to as the signal-processing front end.
A wide range of possibilities exists for parametrically representing the speech signal and the speech recognition task, such as Mel- Frequency Cepstrum Coefficients (MFCC), Linear Prediction Coding (LPC) and many more.

4.2.2 MFCC model :

MFCC's are based on the known variation of the human ear's critical bandwidths with frequency, filters spaced linearly at low frequencies and logarithmically at high frequencies have been used to capture the phonetically important characteristics of speech. This is expressed in the *mel-frequency* scale, that is linear frequency spacing below 1000 Hz and a logarithmic spacing above 1000 Hz.

4.2.3 LPC Model

Linear Predictive Coding (LPC) is one of the most powerful speech analysis techniques and is a useful method for encoding quality speech at a low bit rate. It provides accurate estimates of speech parameters and efficient for computations. It is a speaker and text independent, normalized speech model and therefore LPC is more suitable for this type of application.

4.3   Training and Matching

In this part, by providing the Artificial Intelligence to the machine it is trained to match new sample of data with the trained samples.

4.3.1 Artificial Neural Networks

Neural Networks are often used as a powerful discriminating classifier for tasks in automatic speech recognition. They have several advantages over parametric classifiers. However, there are disadvantages in terms of amount of training data required and length of training time. The FeedForward BackPropagation model is commonly used for automatic speech recognition process.

4.3.2 Hidden Markov Model:

In the context of statistical methods for speech recognition, Hidden Markov Models (HMM) have become a well known and widely used statistical approach to characterize the spectral properties of frames of speech. It is a probabilistic model. As a stochastic modeling tool, HMMs have an advantage of providing a natural and highly reliable way of recognizing speech for a wide variety of applications. Since the HMM also integrates well into systems incorporating information about both acoustics and syntax, it is currently the predominant approach for speech recognition.

4.4   Text-to-Speech (Speech Synthesis)

After getting the results finally text results are converted into speech and outputted through speakers.

5.   PROBLEMS IN DESIGNING SPEECH RECOGNITION SYSTEMS

ASR has been proved, that it is not an easy task. The main challenge in the implementation of ASR on desktops is the current existence of mature and efficient alternatives, the keyboard and mouse. In the past years, speech researchers have found several difficulties that contrast with the optimism of the first speech technology pioneers. According to Ray Reddy, in his review of speech recognition by machines says that the problems in designing ASR are due to the fact that it is related to so many other fields such as acoustics, signal processing, pattern recognition, phonetics, linguistics, psychology, neuroscience, and computer science. And all these problems can be described according to the tasks to be performed.

i. Number of speakers: With more than one speaker, an ASR system must cope-up with the difficult problem of speech variability from one speaker to another. This is usually achieved through the use of large speech database as training data.

ii. Nature of the utterance: Isolated word recognition imposes on the speaker the need to insert artificial pause between successive utterances. Continuous speech recognition systems are able to cope-up with natural speech utterances in which words may be tied together and may at times be strongly affected by co-articulation. Spontaneous speech recognition systems allow the possibility of pause and false starts in the utterance, the use of words not found in the lexicon etc.

iii. Vocabulary size: In general, increasing the size of the vocabulary decreases the recognition scores.

iv. Differences between speakers due to sex, age, accent and so on.

v. Language complexity: The task of continuous speech recognizers is simplified by limiting the number of possible utterances through the imposition of syntactic and semantic constraints.

vi. Environment conditions: The sites for real applications often present adverse conditions (such as noise, distorted signal, and transmission line variability) that can drastically degrade the system performance.

6. CONCLUSION

The dream of a true virtual reality, a complete human-computer interaction system will not come true unless we try to give some perception to machine and make it perceive the outside world as humans do. Machine perception comes before any intelligent system consideration.

Speech understanding by the machine and interacting with the human like human-to-human will be the real interface for human-to-machine interaction.

The Speech interface will be a boon for physically challenged people, aged people and people having computer operation phobia.

Such applications can be further developed in different languages.

REFERENCES:

1. Bridle, J., Deng, L., Picone, J., Richards, H., Ma, J., Kamm, T., Schuster, M., Pike, S., Reagan, R., 1998. An investigation of segmental hidden dynamic models of speech coarticulation for automatic speech recognition. Final Report for the 1998 Workshop on Language Engineering, Center for Language and Speech Processing at Johns Hopkins University, pp. 161.
2. Ma, J., Deng, L., 2004. Target-directed mixture linear dynamic models for spontaneous speech recognition. IEEE TRANSACTIONS ON SPEECH AND AUDIO ROCESSING, VOL. 12, NO. 1, JANUARY 2004.
3. Ma, J., Deng, L.,2004 A mixed-level switching dynamic system for continuous speech recognition. Elsevier Computer Speech and Language 18 (2004) 4965.
4. Mori R.D, Lam L., and Gilloux M. (1987). Learning and plan refinement in a knowledgebased system for automatic speech recognition. *IEEE Transaction on Pattern Analysis Machine Intelligence*, 9(2):289-305.
5. Picheny, M., (2002). Large vocabulary speech recognition, *IEEE Computer*, 35(4):42-50.
6. Rabiner, L., R., and Wilpon, J. G., (1979). Considerations in applying clustering techniques to speaker-independent word recognition.*Journal of Acoustic Society of America*.66(3):663-673.
7. Reddy D.R., (1976). Speech Recognition by Machine: a Review. *Proceeding of IEEE*,64(4):501-531
8. Rudnicky, A.I., Lee, K.F., and Hauptmann, A.G. (1992) Survey of current speech technology. *Communications of the ACM*,37(3):52-57.
9. Svendsen T., Paliwal K. K., Harborg E., Husy P. O. (1989). Proc. ICASSP'89, Glasgow
10. Tolba, H., and O'Shaughnessy, D., (2001). Speech Recognition by Intelligent Machines, *IEEE Canadian Review* (38).
11. Wilpon J.G., D.M.DeMarco,R.P.Mikkilineni (1988) "Isolated word recognition over the DD telephone network -Results of two extensive field studies", Proc. ICASSP,pp. 55-58

THE PROCESS OF SYNCHRONIZATION IN DUAL REDUNDANT FAULT-TOLERANT SYSTEM

Dong Liu, Chunyuan Zhang, Rui Li
Department of Computer, National University of Defense Technology, Changsha, Hunan 410073, P.R.China

Abstract: Synchronization is used in dual redundant fault-tolerant system to make two computers work jointly. It determines the work mode and controls the operations of the system. The paper presents a dual redundant fault-tolerant system and proposes its process of synchronization based on task. The synchronization treats task as the minimal operation unit. And it is implemented with the assist of dual-computer-controller and outer memory, the latter includes task buffer and global data region. Dual-computer-controller controls the input and output of tasks that are stored in task buffer. The switch in of backup computer is implemented by duplicating global data from global data region used by host computer. Additional resolutions for key points, such as the switch between two computers, are also put forward in conclusion. It is proved that the task-level synchronization can make two computers work in phase, and the system is applicable to critical fields requiring high dependability.

Key words: synchronization, dual redundant fault-tolerant system, task, dependability

1. INTRODUCTION

Computer systems, working in critical fields, such as bank and space, are commonly designed to be fault-tolerant to achieve high dependability, which generally increases exponentially by using linearly increasing redundant resources [1]. In engineering realizing, most of dual redundant systems are isomorphic redundant and classified to four elementary types, namely, cold backup, warm backup, hot backup and duplex. User applications in backup computer are suspended in the systems working in cold backup mode or

Please use the following format when citing this chapter:

Liu, D., Zhang, C., Li, R., 2006, in IFIP International Federation for Information Processing, Volume 228, Intelligent Information Processing III, eds. Z. Shi, Shimohara K., Feng D., (Boston: Springer), pp. 493–498.

warm backup mode, as a result of which there is no process of synchronization between two computers. And in the systems working in duplex mode, additional comparer, or arbitrator, is adopted to compare and output the results of two computers; more dependable as the systems are, high cost and complex structure limits their applications. Hot-backup systems own the advantages of easy realizing and quick switching; however, synchronization is required to ensure proper cooperation between two computers in different situation [2-3]. This paper presents a dual redundant fault-tolerant system, which works in hot backup mode. With the intercommunion between two computers in the system, its task based synchronization is introduced.

The paper is structured as follows: after the introduction, the architecture of the dual redundant fault-tolerant system is presented. Afterwards, the process of synchronization is analyzed, including task control of the system. Finally, in Section 4 the conclusions are stated.

2.   DESIGN FOR DUAL REDUNDANT FAULT-TOLERANT SYSTEM

For the purpose of decreasing the system complexity and weakening the coupling between two computers, intercommunion should be as little as possible [4-5]. As a result, the importing and exporting of one computer should be processed without the participation of the other one. In this way, two computers can make coarsely granular synchronization, named *the process of synchronization based on task* or *task-level synchronization*. According to the above statement, we designed a prototype working in hot backup mode. The system architecture is shown in figure 1.

The architecture includes two CPU-boards, one control-board and one connection-backboard, and the former two boards can be inserted into the connecter-backboard. CPU-board contains CPU, inner memory, interface circuit, self-detecting circuit and reset circuit. Therefore, one CPU-board, or computer-set, can be used as the minimal computer system that makes transactions independently. Control-board is used to administer two computer-sets and it consists of device interface, interface circuit, two outer memories and dual-computer-controller. Connection-backboard provides the channel of communications between CPU-boards and control-board; it comprises power circuit, protection circuit and bus of the system.

Outer memory is visible for outer devices and computer-sets. As one part of outer memory, task buffer stores the commands sent to the system by outer devices; and at the same time, it can be accessed by its corresponding computer-set. Since outer devices send commands to two outer memories at the same time, the contents contained in two task buffers should be same when the system works in dual-computer-working state. Another part of outer memory is called global data region, which stores global data, such as system parameters or temporary results. Device-communication-controller controls the direction of data stream, which means that only one computer-set can export its results to outer devices, and that two computer-sets can import transaction, or task, at the same time. CPU 0/1 resets watchdog 0/1 periodically, which locates in dual-computer-controller and monitors the work state of computer-set. When both computer-sets are in well state, task-input-controller determines when tasks in task buffer are read by computer-set. If one computer-set fails, only the working computer-set can import tasks from task buffer, as is also handled by task-input-controller.

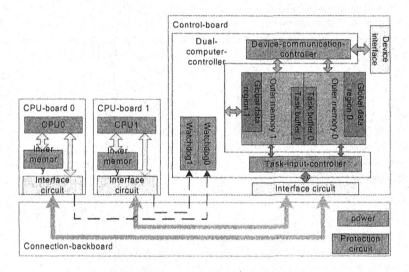

Figure 1. The architecture of the dual redundant fault-tolerant system

3.   PROCESS OF SYNCHRONIZATION BASED ON TASK

If host computer fails, the system should switch from dual-computer-working state to single-computer-working state smoothly. Then, original backup computer should take over the transactions of the system with the status of new host computer. As a prerequisite, the process of switch should be invisible to outer devices, which are unaware of the architecture of the system. Therefore, two computer-sets must synchronize when they are both in well state, so as to realize the smooth switch if host computer fails.

In single-task dual redundant systems, such as dual SCMs system, the synchronization can be achieved easily, because two computers' input and output is simultaneous. However, it is different to our system, which runs multi-tasks operating system, since its data input and output is asynchronous. Moreover, with smaller data granularity, it gets more cost and worse extension ability [6-8]. In this paper, we present the task-level synchronization, which uses coarsely granular, different to signal-level synchronization and instruction-level synchronization.

For system users, task is a command sent to the system by outer devices. And it determines the anticipant operation and behavior. For the system itself, task is data with specific format, saved in the task buffer. Each task possesses its own unique signification; and there is no explicit affiliation between two different tasks. Task number or time stamp marks a task. Furthermore, task is provided with a priority, which means task with higher priority owns higher authority to be solved. Besides, task also has task head, task tail and task content. The format of task is shown in figure 2.

Figure 2. Task format

a) **Task input.** Outer devices send tasks as commands to the system through the device interface. Then, tasks are stored in task buffer temporarily, waiting for the read-requests sent by computer-set. It is the dual-computer-controller that controls when tasks are read from task buffer by computer-set.

b) **Task output.** If task has finished, computer-set write data, with given format, to outer memory accessed by outer devices.

c) **Task synchronization.** If two computer-sets run single-task operating system, own the same working frequency and import tasks simultaneously, they will complete the same task at the same time. However, in the system we present, with multi-tasks operating system running on both computer-sets, they are not likely to export their results simultaneously despite that they import a task at the same time. To tackle this problem, outer memory is divided into many blocks, each of which is used by a specific application in computer-set. In this way, there will be no interfering between two computer-sets; and the order of executing applications becomes unimportant.

d) **Switch out.** Once watchdog detects the failure of host computer, it will inform the dual-computer-controller to connect outer devices with backup computer, leading the system into the single-computer-working state. Besides, a reset signal is sent to the failed computer-set by watchdog. The signal is also captured by dual-computer-controller to change the work state of the system. However, if backup computer fails, nothing occurs except that backup computer restarts.

e) **Switch in.** Supposing computer-set zero is in well state and computer-set one fails, watchdog one judges whether computer-set one has restarted by the periodical signals sent from CPU one. Affirming that computer-set one has restarted, dual-computer-controller will not permit computer-set zero to read new task from task buffer after the current tasks in computer-set zero finishes. Then, dual-computer-controller notifies computer-set zero to store global data to global data region zero, so that computer-set one could duplicate global data from global-data-region zero. Finally, dual-computer-controller permits both computer-sets to import and export tasks, leading the system into the state of synchronization between two computer-sets. In order to improve efficiency, the switch in of backup computer should arise at the time when host computer is in low workload; however, the system's dependability will decrease if it keeps on working in single-computer-working state for a long time.

The proposed synchronization is based on task and realized with the aids of dual-computer-controller and outer memory. And there is no monitor application running in computer-set and no communication between two computer-sets. Accordingly, with low overhead in operating system, the time of context switch decreases, as is favorable to improve the system efficiency.

4.   CONCLUSIONS

It is a challenge to design dual-computer-controller for its bottle-neck position and complex functions. Therefore, in our system, dual-computer-controller is realized in FPGA with particular ability of reprogramming and reconfiguring [9]. TMR is also used to increase the reliability of key components in dual-computer-controller.

As mentioned above, once backup computer begins switching in and duplicates global data from global data region, used by host computer, to global data region, used by backup computer, host computer will stop importing new tasks. In this process, if outer devices send tasks with higher priority to the system, the system should stop duplicating data and respond to the tasks before switching in completes. Furthermore, if this kind of tasks comes forth frequently, backup computer would not complete switching in, holding the system in the state of single-computer-working for a long period, which brings the hidden trouble of system crash. However, the appearance of that kind of tasks generally indicates emergencies of the system, so they come forth infrequently. Besides, global data occupies little storage space, which decreases the time of duplicating and expedites the process of switching in.

Watchdog being used to monitor computer-set, the count time of watchdog is distinctly the longest time that dual-computer-controller will take to become aware of computer-set's failure. In this period, dual-computer-controller believes that the system is in dual-computer-working state, but the fact is quite the reverse; as a result, the accesses from outer devices to outer memory fail and backup computer cannot export data to outer devices. However, the problem can be solved after original backup computer takes over the system.

It has been proved that our system, based on task-level synchronization, can make smooth switching between two computers. And, at the same time, high performance and reliability are preserved. It is applicable to the critical fields requiring high dependability. Furthermore, if a little change is made to the synchronization definition, it can also be used in duplex systems.

REFERENCES

1. MA Xiu-juan, CAO Xi-bin, MA Xing-rui, Reliability analysis and design of on-board computer system for small stereo mapping satellite, *Journal of Harbin Institute of Technology (New Series)*, 9(1), 79-81 (2002)
2. Surajit Dutta1, Sudip Dutta2, Riddhi Burman, et al., Design and Implementation of a Soft Real Time Fault Tolerant System, *S.K. Das and S. Bhattacharya (Eds.)*, IWDC 2002, LNCS 2571, 319-328 (2002)
3. Xiong-Fu Liu, Arthur Dexter, Fault-tolerant supervisory control of VAV air-conditioning systems, *Energy and Buildings*, 33, 379-389 (2001)
4. Vittoria de Nitto Personè, Vincenzo Grassi, An analytical model for a parallel fault–tolerant computing system, *Performance Evaluation*, 38, 201-218 (1999)
5. J.C. Campelo, F. Rodri'guez, A. Rubio, etc., Distributed industrial control systems --- a fault-tolerant architecture, *Microprocessors and Microsystems*, 23, 103-112 (1999)
6. R. Al-Omari, A.K. Somani, G. Manimaran, An adaptive scheme for fault-tolerant scheduling of soft real-time tasks in multiprocessor systems, *J. Parallel Distrib. Comput.*, 65, 595-608 (2005)
7. Koji Hashimoto , Tatsuhiro Tsuchiya, Tohru Kikuno, A new approach to fault-tolerant scheduling using task duplication in multiprocessor systems, *The Journal of Systems and Software*, 53, 159-171 (2000)
8. Douglas W. Caldwell, David A. Rennels, A Minimalist fault-tolerant Microcontroller Design for Embedded Spacecraft Computing, *The Journal of Supercomputing*, 16, 7-25 (2000)
9. John M. Emmert, Dinesh K. Bhatia, A Fault Tolerant Technique for FPGAs, *Journal of Electronic Testing, Theory and Applications*, 16, 591-606 (2000)

APPLICATION OF ASSOCIATION RULES FOR EFFICIENT LEARNING WORK-FLOW

Sylvia Encheva
Stord/Haugesund University College
Bjornsonsg. 45, 5528 Haugesund, Norway
sbe@hsh.no

Sharil Tumin
University of Bergen
IT-Dept., P. O. Box 7800, 5020 Bergen, Norway
edpst@it.uib.no

Abstract   This paper describes application of association rules in education. To make everything more clearly visible a graphic display of objects and attributes in a lattice structure is provided. Vectors and matrices are used to reduce the computational complexity while searching for association rules in the case when at least one attribute included in the 'if' part of the statement is known.

Keywords: E-learning, data mining

Introduction

Association-rule mining is a technique for finding association and/or correlation relationships among data items in large databases. Association rules are probabilistic in nature and show attribute value conditions that occur frequently together in a given dataset. The information association rules provide is a statement in an antecedent/consequent format. The probabilistic approach deals with statements of the form 'the presence of attributes $\aleph$ and $\Re$ often also involves attribute $\Im$'. This approach has an application in different fields such as market basket analysis [5], medical research [9] and census data [12].

In this paper we show an application of association rules in education. A graphic display of objects and attributes in a lattice structure is also provided.

The rest of the paper is organized as follows. Related work is described in Section 1. Some definitions and statements from formal concept analysis and rule mining may be found in Section 1. The main results of the paper are placed in Section 2. The paper ends with a conclusion in Section 3.

Please use the following format when citing this chapter:

Encheva, S., Tumin, S., 2006, in IFIP International Federation for Information Processing, Volume 228, Intelligent Information Processing III, eds. Z. Shi, Shimohara K., Feng D., (Boston: Springer), pp. 499–504.

1.   Related Work

Formal concept analysis [10], [16] started as an attempt of promoting better communication between lattice theorists and users of lattice theory. Since 1980's formal concept analysis has been growing as a research field with a broad spectrum of applications. Various applications of formal concept analysis are presented in [11]. An excellent introduction to ordered sets and lattices and to their contemporary applications can be found in [8].

The complexity of mining frequent itemsets is exponential and algorithms for finding such sets have been developed by many authors such as [4], [6], [15] and [18].

Mining association rules is addressed in [1]. Algorithms for fast discovery of association rules have been presented in [2], [3], and [14].

Preliminaries

A *concept* is considered by its *extent* and its *intent*: the *extent* consists of all objects belonging to the concept while the *intent* is the collection of all attributes shared by the objects [8].

A *context* is a triple (G, M, I) where G and M are sets and $I \subset G \times M$. The elements of G and M are called *objects* and *attributes* respectively.

For $A \subseteq G$ and $B \subseteq M$, define $A' = \{m \in M \mid (\forall g \in A)\ gIm\}$ and $B' = \{g \in G \mid (\forall m \in B)\ gIm\}$; so A' is the set of attributes common to all the objects in A and B' is the set of objects possessing the attributes in B. Then a *concept* of the context (G, M, I) is defined to be a pair (A, B) where $A \subseteq G$, $B \subseteq M$, $A' = B$ and $B' = A$. The *extent* of the concept (A, B) is A while its intent is B. A subset A of G is the extent of some concept if and only if $A'' = A$ in which case the unique concept of the which A is an extent is (A, A'). The corresponding statement applies to those subsets B of M which are the intent of some concept.

The set of all concepts of the context (G, M, I) is denoted by $\mathfrak{B}(G, M, I)$. $\langle \mathfrak{B}(G, M, I); \leq \rangle$ is a complete lattice and it is known as the *concept lattice* of the context (G, M, I).

An association rule $Q \rightarrow R$ holds if there are sufficient objects possesing both Q and R and if there are sufficient objects among those with Q which also possess R [7].

A context (G, M, I) satisfies the association rule $Q \rightarrow R_{minsup, minconf}$, with $Q, R \in M$, if $sup(Q \rightarrow R) = \frac{|(Q \cup R)'|}{|G|} \geq minsup$, and $conf(Q \rightarrow R) = \frac{|(Q \cup R)'|}{|Q'|} \geq minconf$ provided $minsup \in [0, 1]$ and $minconf \in [0, 1]$.

The ratios $\frac{|(Q \cup R)'|}{|G|}$ and $\frac{|(Q \cup R)'|}{|Q'|}$ are called, respectively, the *support* and the *confidence* of the rule $Q \rightarrow R$. In other words the rule $Q \rightarrow R$ has support $\sigma\%$ in the transaction set T if $\sigma\%$ of the transactions in T contain $Q \cup R$. The rule

Table 1. Context for students groups

	Preliminary knowledge			Chapter 1		Chapter 2		Chapter 3	
	sufficient	some	none	can	cannot	can	cannot	can	cannot
Gr. 1	×			×		×		×	
Gr. 2	×			×			×	×	
Gr. 3		×			×	×		×	
Gr. 4			×		×	×			×
Gr. 5	×			×		×		×	
Gr. 6	×			×			×	×	
Gr. 7		×			×	×		×	
Gr. 8			×		×	×			×
Gr. 9	×				×	×			×

has confidence $\psi\%$ if $\psi\%$ of the transactions in $\mathcal{T}$ that contain Q also contain R.

2. Application of Association Rules

Students taking a course are divided in groups according to gender and results from a test. The goal is to find the association rules that relate attributes, chosen by a lecturer, to students' results from the test.

Group 1 (Gr. 1) - male students with score above 80% on the test
Group 2 (Gr. 2) - male students with score between 60% and 80% on the test
Group 3 (Gr. 3) - male students with score between 40% and 59% on the test
Group 4 (Gr. 4) - male students with score between 20% and 39% on the test
Group 5 (Gr. 5) - female students with score above 80% on the test
Group 6 (Gr. 6) - female students with score between 60% and 80% on the test
Group 7 (Gr. 7) - female students with score between 40% and 59% on the test
Group 8 (Gr. 8) - female students with score between 20% and 39% on the test
Group 9 (Gr. 9) - students with score less than 20% on the test.

The corresponding Hasse diagram is shown in Fig. 1.

Based on this context a binary matrix G with rows and columns corresponding to the rows and columns in Table 1 is generated. The rows in the context are denoted by $g_i, i = 1, ..., 9$. An element in the matrix is set equal to 1 if the corresponding entry in the context is marked and to 0 otherwise.

Suppose we are interested in the association rules that involve the attribute 'has sufficient preliminary knowledge'. We then choose all vectors that have 1 as their first coordinate. The obtained matrix is denoted by $G_{i,j}$ (in this

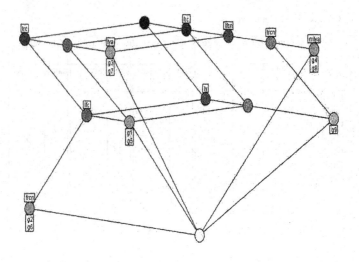

Figure 1.   Hasse diagram for students' results from an implicit differentiation test

particular case $G_{6,1}$), where the value of i shows the number of rows in $G_{i,j}$ and the value of j shows which attribute has been chosen.

This way we considerably reduce the number of any other following operations that involve the attribute 'has sufficient preliminary knowledge' in the 'if' part of our search. We then add g_1 to each of the remaining vectors in $G_{6,1}$ and thus obtain $G'_{6,1}$.

Advantage: At this point we can again reduce the number of rows in $G'_{6,1}$ by deleting all rows with 0's and 2's only. They are a repetition of the first vector in $G_{6,1}$ and only their number is of importance for our further work. Such a row reduction applied in our example leads to a matrix $G'_{5,1}$ with five rows only.

The next step is to look for positions in $G'_{6,1}$ (or in its redused version if applicable, in this case $G'_{5,1}$) with value 2, beginning with the first row. Those positions indicate association rules.

The association rules that have the attribute 'has sufficient preliminary knowledge' as an antecedent are

- If a student has sufficient preliminary knowledge then he/she can work with the material in Chapter 1 and Chapter 3 with a probability 79%.

- If a student has sufficient preliminary knowledge and can work with the material in Chapter 2 fractions then he/she can work with the material in Chapter 1 and Chapter 3 with a probability 66%.

- If a student has sufficient preliminary knowledge then he/she can work with the material in Chapter 2 with a probability 59%.

- If a student has sufficient preliminary knowledge and can work with the material in Chapter 1 and Chapter 3 then he/she can work with the material in Chapter 2 with a probability 50%.

Similar inquires will show any other association rule.

3.   Conclusion

In this paper association rules in education have been used for finding correlations among students' preliminary knowledge in a course and their abilities to work with the material in three chapters from the curriculum.

References

[1] R. Agrawal, T. Imielinski and A. Swami. Mining association rules between sets of items in large databases. *Proceedings of ACM SIGMOD international conference on management of data*, Washington, DC, USA, 207-216, 1993.

[2] R. Agrawal, H. Mannila, R. Srikant, H. Toivonen and A.I. Verkamo. Fast discovery of association rules. (Uthurusamy, F., Piatetsky-Shapiro, G., Smyth, P. eds) *Advances in Knowledge discovery of association rules*, MIT Press, 307–328, 1996.

[3] R. Agrawal, and R. Srikant. Fast algorithm for mining association rules. *Proceedings of the 20th very large data base conference*, Santiago, Chile, 487-489, 1994.

[4] T. Bastide,R. Taouil, N. Pasquier, G. Stumme and L. Lakhal. Mining frequent patterns with counting inference. *SIGKDD explorations*, Special issue on scalable algorithms, 2(2):71–80, 2000.

[5] S. Brin, R. Motwani, J.D. Ullmann and S. Tsur. Dynamic itemset counting and implication rules for market basket data. *Proceedings of the ACM SIGKDD international conference on management of data*, Tuscon, AZ, USA, 255–264, 1997.

[6] D. Burdick, M. Calimlim and J. Gehrke. MAFIA: a maximal frequent itemset algorithm for transactional databases. *Proceedings of the 7th international conference on data engineering*, IEEE Computer Society, Heidelberg, Germany, 443-452, 2001.

[7] C. Carpineto and G. Romano. *Concept Data Analysis: Theory and Applications*. John Wiley and Sons, Ltd., 2004.

[8] B. A. Davey and H. A. Priestley. *Introduction to lattices and order*. Cambridge University Press, Cambridge, 2005.

[9] M. Delgado,D. Sanchez, M.J. Martin-Bautista and M.A. Vila. Mining association rules with improved semantics in medical databases. *Artificial Intelligence in Medicine*, 21(1-3):241-5, 2001.

[10] B. Ganter and R. Wille. *Formal Concept Analysis - Mathematical foundations*. Springer Verlag, Berlin Heidelberg, 1999.

[11] B. Ganter, G. Stumme and R. Wille. *Formal Concept Analysis - Foundations and Applications*. Springer Verlag, LNCS, 3626, 2005.

[12] D. Malerba, F.A. Lisi, A. Appice and F. Sblendorio. Mining spatial association rules in census data: a relational approach. *Proceedings of the ECML/PKDD '02 workshop on mining official data*, University Printing House, Helsinki, 80–93, 2002.

[13] N. Pasquier, T. Bastide, R. Taouil and L. Lakhal. Discovering frequent closed itemsets for association rules. *Proceedings of the 7th international conference on database theory*, Jerusalem, Israel, 398–416, 1999.

[14] N. Pasquier, T. Bastide, R. Taouil and L. Lakhal. Efficient mining of association rules using closed itemset lattices. *Journal of Information Systems*, 24(1):25-46, 1999.

[15] J. Pei, J. Han, and R. Mao. Closet: An efficient algorithm for mining frequent closed itemsets. *Proceedings of the ACM SIGKDD international workshop on research issues in data mining and knowledge discovery*, Dallas, USA, 21–31, 2000.

[16] R. Wille. Concept lattices and conceptual knowledge systems. *Computers Math. Applic.* 23(6-9):493–515, 1992.

[17] M.J. Zaki. Generating non-redundant association rules. *Proceedings of the 6th ACM SIGKDD international conference on knowledge discovery and data mining*, Boston, USA, 34–43, 2000.

[18] M.J. Zaki and C.-J Hsiao. CHARM: An efficient algorithm for closed itemset mining. *Proceedings of the 2nd SIAM international conference on data mining*, Arlington, VA, USA, 34–43, 2002.

APPLICATION OF MACHINE TRANSLATION IN CHINA-AMERICA DIGITAL ACADEMIC LIBRARY

Huang Chen   Chen Haiying
Zhejiang University Libraries, Hangzhou, 310027, PR.China

Abstract: This paper briefly introduces the main ideas of Machine Translation
(MT) techniques, then discusses the application of MT in the China-
America Digital Academic Library (CADAL)

Key words: CADAL, machine translation, digital library

1.   INTRODUCTION

The China-America Digital Academic Library (CADAL) Project was launched by China-US scientists (http://www.cadal.cn), aiming at digitizing one million books for the digital library. The project is also one of the key projects of the China Education Ministry for the "Tenth Five-year Plan", intended to provide digitized resources for teaching and research, and to prompt the sharing of those resources.

The aim of the digital library is to provide information service. Nowadays users are no longer satisfied with the information retrieved though the internet; what they need is the integrated and processed information in different media. The service may even contain the knowledge and solution to the problem users have. CADAL therefore not only provides

Please use the following format when citing this chapter:

Chen, H., Haiying, C., 2006, in IFIP International Federation for Information Processing, Volume 228, Intelligent
Information Processing III, eds. Z. Shi, Shimohara K., Feng D., (Boston: Springer), pp. 505–511.

digitized books, replacing traditional printed ones, but also process the digitized resources to extract relevant information, and provides more services to the users. Machine Translation (MT) is a service that CADAL intends to adopt to provide bilingual or multi-lingual translations.

2.   MACHINE TRANSLATION THEORY AND TECHNOLOGY

As one of the earlier research branches of Natural Language Understanding (NLU), MT is a process to translate one natural language into another one. The software fulfilling such task is named Machine Translation System.

Warren Weaver, director of Natural Sciences Department of Association of America Rockefeller Fund, published a memorandum entitled "Translation" to raise the issue of Machine Translation in 1949. With the development of both classical linguistic theory and modern computational linguistic theory, some commercial MT systems appeared later 80's, such as the American SYSTRAN System, the METAL System by Texas University and Siemens Company, ATLAS by HITACHI Company and the CETA System by Grenoble University.

MT research in China was listed in the governmental "Science Development Compendium" as "MT/Natural Language Mathematics Theory" in 1956. In the later 80's and early 90's, two MT systems of practical value appeared: the "KY-1" English-Chinese MT System by the Academy of Sciences of Military Affairs and the "863-IMT" English-Chinese MT System by the Institute of Computing Technology, a division of the Chinese Academy of Sciences.

In recent years, MT systems are usually installed with professional dictionaries, run on the internet and have a user-friendly interface. MT research for new applications, such as speech translation systems, is also underway.

Traditional MT belongs to Knowledge Based MT (KBMT) [1], also called the Rule-based Method. Linguistic rules, which cover a wider domain than the training corpus, are constructed by specialists. These rules and their resulting systems tend to make more sense for human beings and can be adjusted quickly. However, they suffer from the following drawbacks:

(1). Rule-based Methods are too labor-intensive, and rule construction requires extensive linguistic training.

(2). Rule consistency is difficult to maintain, even for the same designer. Furthermore, common sense is often difficult to encode.

(3). Rules designed by different experts can sometimes contradict each other and thus affect the overall system performance.

Facing challenges of KBMT, Professor M. Nagao at Tokyo University proposed an analogy-based MT method in 1984 [2]. Many researchers extended Nagao's method to form a so-called Example-based MT (EBMT). The basic idea of EBMT is simple: given an input passage S in a source language and a bilingual text archive, where text passages S' in the source language are stored, aligned with their translations into a target language, T', S is compared with the source-language "side" of the archive. The "closest" match for passage S' is selected and the translation of this closest match, the passage T' is accepted as the translation of S.

Statistical MT [3, 4, 5] can be seen as one variant of EBMT. The basic idea in statistical MT is that the translation is based on the statistical probabilities of the words of the same text in two languages (parallel corpora). When such texts in two languages exist, the probabilities of the words can be counted and the translation system can be "taught to translate" by using the probabilities.

3.   APPLICATIONS OF MT IN CADAL

3.1   The goal

CADAL is making use of MT in a number of ways:

(1) Important information, such as a book's title or authors is translated manually, or first translated by MT systems and then verified manually;

(2) As the cornerstone of CADAL's system, MT provides instant service such as translation of contents indexed by XML;

(3) Integrating MT with other services, such as multilingual information retrieval and special words retrieval.

In the CADAL server (http://www.cadal.zju.edu.cn/), we applied a bilingual service engine to support the metadata retrieval between English and Chinese. This engine provides instant translation of book profiles. On the left of Figure 1 is a book profile in Chinese. When the user clicks the "English Profile"(link words in pink below the image of the book's cover), the system displays its English profile translated by the MT engine. The result is shown on the rightof Figure 1.

Figure 1. A book profile in both Chinese and English

3.2   MT evaluation in CADAL

Based on the goal of CADAL, we evaluated a number of existing MT systems. These included systems developed by IBM, Carnegie Mellon University, USC/ISI, RWTH Aachen University, Microsoft (Redmond) and the Institute of Computing Technology, a division of the Chinese Academy of Sciences.

Results show that the performance of MT Systems created by RWTH Aachen University, CMU and ISI is superior to even that by SYSTRAN, but strategies of MT vary from system to system. RWTH Aachen University adopted the SBMT model, and improved the traditional noise channel based paradigm into the maximum entropy model [6], Their MT System also further enhanced the words- based alignment model to a phrase-based alignment model. Mega2RADD by CMU integrates SBMT with EBMT though a translation engine, and provides the optimized translation result. Re2Write by ISI takes IBM-4 statistical model as the prototype, the translation quality is improved by adding grammar analysis and KBMT. The models used and the improvement of quality in those systems show that a single translation strategy, whether rule-based or based on statistical data, is only a partial solution, and integration of multiple translation strategies is the common feature of those systems.

3.3   MT strategy in CADAL

In light of the foregoing evaluation and current research in MT, we believe that the hybrid translation strategy is the most appropriate for MT in CADAL.

Firstly, we intend to collaborate with CMU by using their Mega2RADD system as the basic framework, and adopting the idea of RWTH Aachen University, which is to improve the source-channel based paradigm into the maximum entropy model. In this model, the parameters are estimated by large-scale samples. Among them, $P(E)$, the priori probability that E happens, can be estimated by constructing appropriate English linguistic model, while P(F/E), the conditional probability of F given E, can be estimated by the text-allied source text and corresponding target text. To this end, in addition to the hardware and software (natural language parsing and synthesis), MT in CADAL involves a dictionary, grammar rules, and dynamic correlation between texts.

Secondly, under the framework of multiple engines, CADAL will take mtSDK (http://lan.cpip.net.cn/) as the standard to provide translation services at different levels. CADAL will use different engine for different tasks. For instance, the translations of the author, book title, sentences, paragraphs, abstract, full text are carried out through different translation strategies, CADAL allows users to ask for the translation service and highlight the text that they would like translated. The translation engine of course must "understand" the individual words to translate in this way.

Thirdly, from automatic machine translation to human translation, there are human-assisted machine translations and machine-assisted human translations, to which CADAL will pay more attention. Under the framework of level translation, human intervention is allowed to improve the translation quality in CADAL.

4.   CONCLUSIONS

CADAL will make full use of the advantages of different MT systems to provide MT services to its users. The system will adopt multiple translation strategies, including rule-based, example-based and statistics-based strategies; manage various information used during the translation by employment of an object-oriented multiple type database; and provide a user interface which allows manual intervention to the resultant translation of MT. In order to obtain the linguistic resources required by KBMT, CADAL will also pay attention to the construction of its word library based on ontology, drawing on the research of Semantic Web.

As a digital library shared globally, CADAL will make use of state-of-the-art information technology to provide users of different levels with appropriate services, and let users study and work with digitized resources effectively. With the development of computer technology, we cherish the hope that MT can not only translate the textual information into the language with which the user is most familiar, but also achieve semantic information retrieval between different languages.

REFERENCES

1. Sergei Nirenburg, Jaime Carbonell, Masaru Tomita, and Kenneth Goodman , Machine Translation: A Knowledge-Based Approach, San Mateo, CA: Morgan Kaufmann Publishers, 1992.
2. Nagao, M. (1984), A framework of a mechanical translation between Japanese and English by analogy principle, *in* 'Artificial and Human Intelligence: edited review papers at the International NATO Symposium on Artificial and Human Intelligence sponsored by the Special Programme Panel held in Lyon, France, October, 1981', Elsevier Science Publishers, Amsterdam, chapter 11, pp. 173-180.
3. Peter F. Brown, John Cocke, Stephen A. Della Pietra, Vincent J. Della Pietra, Fredrick Jelinek, John D. Lafferty, Robert L. Mercer, Paul S. Roossin, A Statistical Approach to Machine Translation, Computational Linguistics,1990
4. Peter. F. Brown, Stephen A. Della Pietra, Vincent J. Della Pietra, Robert L. Mercer, The Mathematics of Statistical Machine Translation: Parameter Estimation, Computational Linguistics, Vol 19, No.2 ,1993
5. F. J. Och, C. Tillmann, and H. Ney. Improved alignment models for statistical machine translation. In Proc. of the Joint SIGDAT Conf. On Empirical Methods in Natural Language Processing and Very Large Corpora, pages 20-28, University of Maryland, College Park, MD, June 1999.
6. Franz Josef Och, Hermann Ney, Discriminative Training and Maximum Entropy Models for Statistical Machine Translation, ACL2002
7. Kishore Papineni, Salim Roukos, Todd Ward, Wei-Jing Zhu, Bleu: a Method for Automatic Evaluation of Machine Translation, IBM Research, RC22176 (W0109-022) September 17, 2001
8. LIU Qun, Survey on Statistical Machine Translation, Journal of Chinese language information, No. 4, 2003. (In Chinese)

IIP2006 PROCEEDINGS
The Study of ECA Rules System Model Based on Petri Nets

AI DiMing1, GAO XiuFeng2

1Ordnance Technology Institute, Ordnance Engineering College，
shijiazhuang 050003 China
2Department of Computer, Ordnance Engineering College，shijiazhuang
050003 China
Email：{ Aiyangmei,Gaoxiufeng}@vip.sina.com

Abstract:The active functions of aDBS (active Database System) are currently achieved by
ECA rule system. But it is difficult for ECA rules system to be analyzed and
validated. And there is no perfect model today. Based on the Petri Net, This paper
thinks over the character of rules system, and establishes a system model. And some
behaviors are analyzed in this paper.

Key words:aDBS, ECA rules, Petri Nets

1. INTRODUCTION

Usually active database system adopts active rules to realize active function, while typically active rule uses ECA rules modeling[1,2].Complexity of ECA rule system is due to its complicated behavior. When rule is active and action is executed depends on coupling mode and coordination of rules.

At present, rule execution diagram analysis method is applied to ECA rule system, such as trigger diagram, activation diagram, and etc[3]，however, it can only plot trigger and activation relation between rules, and cannot materialize trigger and activation procedure of each rule. Therefore, this method cannot reflect feature of ECA rule itself, and cannot show complexity of rule system behavior indeed. On the other hand, Petri net possesses good formalization basis, it can describe change of system states, and has quite mature analysis theory. Although there are already similar references that use Petri net technology to analyze ECA rule system

Please use the following format when citing this chapter:

Ai, D., Gao, X., 2006, in IFIP International Federation for Information Processing, Volume 228, Intelligent Information Processing III, eds. Z. Shi, Shimohara K., Feng D., (Boston: Springer), pp. 513–518.

modeling, for instance, reference 4 put forward Constraint Place/Transit Net, (shortened as CP/T Net), and use the Net to make modeling analysis on active rule, however, it did not consider coupling relation of event-condition-action.

This paper, on basis of Petri net, make modeling research on ECA rule, it puts forward a kind of extension Petri net system, and with which it builds ECA rule modeling, it can reflect feature of ECA rule modeling itself fully.

2.   BASIC PETRI NET MODEL OF ECA RULE

2.1   Basic principle of Petri net

Petri net, brought forward firstly in his doctoral thesis by Mr. C.A. Petri in 1962, is used for describing the relationship between computer events and the precedence, parallel and a synchronism relationships between complex events in discrete event system and can easily be used for describing the following events, such as resource conflicts, deadlock and buffer size in manufacturing system.

Definition 2.1 Petri net is a 3-tuple group

$$N = (S, T; F),$$

in which S and T are known as the place set and the transition set respectively and, F is the flow relation. The necessary and sufficient conditions are5:

$$S \cap T = \Phi$$
$$S \cup T \neq \Phi$$
$$F \subseteq S \times T \cup T \times S$$
$$dom\ (F) \cup cod\ (F) = S \cup F$$

Here:

$$dom(\ F) = \{x \mid \exists y : (x,\ y) \in F\},$$

$$cod(\ F) = \{y \mid \exists x : (x,\ y) \in F\}$$

are domain of definition and value

The place and transition are known as S_element and T_element, or S_meta and T_meta. X=S $\cup$ T is known as the element set of N.

The implemental rule of transition of basic Petri net is as follows: when t is given, if all p $\in$ t, M (p) $\geq$ 1 (M is the distribution function of Token in the place), then t is implemental, written as M[t>. i.e. if any input location of transition t has one Token at least, the transition can be implemental. The implementation of transition means that the preconditions under which the event represented by transition occurs are met in the current system status.

The inherent feature of transition in the net system is: that its scope (extension) is inherent, whether the transition occurs or not depends on its extension only, regardless of the global state, which is so called local determinacy. In the net system, there is no forms of global control which can describe not only the dependency (sequencing relationship) but also independency (concurrency relationship) between events. The security and progressively of the net system have general applicability.

2.2   Basic concept of ECA rule

Definition 2.2: Active rule is a 3-tuple <E, C, A>, E—event, C—condition, A—action, which has structure feature and behavior feature. When the trigger event occurs, the action is executed on basis of true or false of condition[6]. The basic denotation of ECA is as follows:

RULE <rule name>[(<parameters>,···)]
WHEN <event>
IF <condition 1> THEN <action 1>;
······
IF <condition n> THEN <actions N>; (n⩾1)
END-RULE [<rule name>].

2.3   Basic Petri net model

This paper makes use of Petri net to create model, place set mainly consists of three parts: S=SE ∪ SC ∪ SA ∪ others, in which SE is trigger event set, SC is condition set, SA is action set; transition set mainly consists of two parts: T=TEC ∪ TCA ∪ others, in which TEC is the trigger process of rule, by means of evaluating event, if success, then trigger rule. TCA is the evaluation process of conditions, if conditions are met, the rule will be active, then corresponding action will be executed. Since event, condition and action has atomicity which means it will occur or it will not occur at one time, the capacity of place in Petri net can be defined as 1.

For example, ECA rule is:
on e1
if c1 then a1;
if c2 then a2.
In this rule, it does not set coupling way between event and condition, condition and action, which can be regarded as immediate mode, in case that use Petri net to express, it can be omitted. The model is more complex regarding to simple ECA rule, but it's reasonable if the coupling relationships between E, C and A are considered.

3.   PETRI NET REPRESENTATION OF COMPOUND EVENT

The event of ECA rule can be classified into primitive and compound ones. Petri net representation of compound event is researched specially in this paper.

Definition 3 compound event: the system uses requested event operators to connect several component events (atomic or compound) and handles it as a single event, which is known as compound event.

Provided that e and e' are two component events, there are several compound event definitions:

1) $e \wedge e'$, means compound event when e and e' concur;

2) $e|e'$, means that in period of occurrence there is only one compound event from e and e', i.e. choose one occurred event;

3) $e \vee e'$, means there is compound event occurrence if there is only one (from e and e') compound event;

4) $e \bullet e'$, means that e' occurs when e is end, makes e and e' be compound event together;

5) $< e$, means one event that is terminated when e starts to occur;

6) $> e$, means one event starts to occur when e is terminated;

7) $\neg e$, means event that e does not occur.

Occurrence of compound event is same as atomic one, it has "atomicity", i.e., at one time, it occurs completely, or does not occur at all, there is no the 3rd state. Compound event Petri net is as the following Fig. 1.

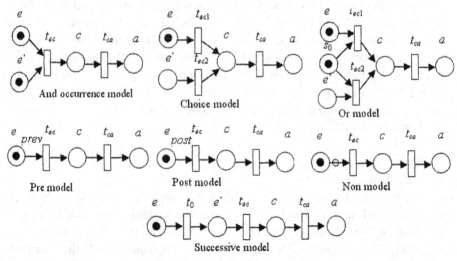

Fig. 1 composite events Petri net expression.

4.   ECA RULE EXTENSION PETRI NET MODEL AND BEHAVIOR ANALYSIS

Execution of ECA rule is related to coupling mode, there are 2 kinds of modes: one is coupling between event and condition (E-C coupling);the other is coupling between condition and action(C-A coupling). Most active database system support the following 3 modes:

Immediate mode: when trigger event occurs(conditions are met), it executes condition decision immediately(execute action);

Deferred mode: when trigger event occurs(conditions are met), it does not execute condition decision (execute action) until "Y" of the event is terminated (execute action);

Detached mode: Condition decision (action executes) and trigger event (condition decision) run in a detached event rather than in a same one.

Due to complexity of compound event expression and complicated coupling relation of ECA rules, when modeling is made for ECA rule system, this paper puts forward a extended Petri net system on basis of Petri net principle.

Definition 4 Extended Petri net system

$$\Sigma = (S, T; F, U, V, A_{FU}, H_{FV}, M_0),$$

in which:

1) (S,T;F) is basic net;

2) U is set of coupling relation,U={immediate, deferred, detached};

3) V is set of 1-tuple ordering operators:V={at, prev, post};

4) AFU is F '—>U binding, in which

$$F' \subseteq T_{EC} \times S_C \cup T_{CA} \times S_A, \forall f \in F', A_{FU}(f)$$

Corresponds to a kind of coupling relation;

5) HFV is F '—>V binding, in which

$$F' \subseteq S_E \times T_{EC}, \forall f \in F, H_{FV}(f) \in V$$

6) M is initial identity of Σ. Definition 3.2 ECA rule set R={$r_1, r_2, \cdots,$ rn}, in which ER={$e_1, e_2, \ldots e_m$} is event set of rule set R ,AR={$a_1, a_2, \cdots a_m$} is action set that are executed by rule set R. . Assume rule $r_i, r_j \in R$, in which r_{ie} ,$r_{je} \in ER \cup OE$, OE is compound event that is formed by events in ER, r_{ia}, r_{ja} $\in AR$, when $r_{ia} = r_{je}$, it can be replaced by rje.

Assume $r_1, r_2 , r_3, r_4 , r_5 \in R$, and expression form of such rules is:

r_1: On $e_1 \wedge e_2$, *immediate, if r_1.c then e_3,immediate*

r_2: On $e_4 \vee e_5$, *deferred, if r_2.c then e_6,immediate*

r_3: On e_3, *immediate, if r_3.c then r_3.a,immediate*

r_4: On e_6, *detached, if r_4.c then r_4.a,immediate*

r_5: On $e_3 | e_6$, *deferred, if r_5.c then r_5.a,immediate*

Taking it as an example, the corresponding ECA rule Petri net model is shown as Fig. 2:

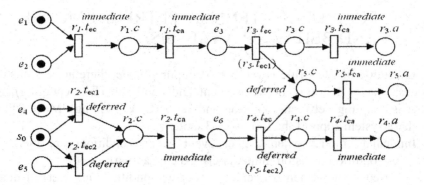

Fig. 2 ECA rule system Petri net.

From Fig. 2, it can know about event trigger and operation procedure of ECA rule straightly, and know about trigger relation between rules. Meanwhile, it can use relevant theory of Petri net to analyze dynamic behavior of ECA rule system.

5.   CONCLUSION

This paper, on basis of Petri net theory, makes modeling research on ECA rules, establishes basic Petri net model; meanwhile makes special research that how to use Petri net express compound event ECA rules; put forward extended Petri net system, and considers its feature of ECA rules in general, reflects system feature of ECA rules in all aspects. As a matter of course, This paper makes analysis on simple system action of ECA rules, it still need further research how to use Petri net technology to make analysis on system action of rules, like terminability and parallelism.

REFERENCES

1   Ullman.J," Principles of Database and Knowledge-Base Systems," Computer Science Press, Rockville ,vol.1, 1988.
2   Jennifer Widom, "The Starburst Active Database Rule System," Knowledge and Data Engineering, pp: 583-595, March 1996.
3   Kantere, V., Kiringa, "Coordinating peer databases using ECA rules," DBISP2P ,2003.
4   U. Dayal," Active Database Management Systems," In Proceedings of the Third International Conference on Data and Knowledge Bases, 1988.
5   Zimmer , A. Meckenstock and R. Unland ," Using Petri nets for rule termination analysis," In Proceedings of the Workshop on Databases: Active and Real-Time 1996 (CIKM'96), Rockville, Maryland, 1996.
6   Chang, L. & Moskowitz, "A Study of Inference Problem in Distributed Database Systems," to appear in Proc. of IFIP WG 11.3 2002, Cambridge, UK.

A FORMAL DESCRIPTION OF AGENTS' EPISTEMIC STATES AND ENVIRONMENTS*

Yu Sun,[1,2] Cungen Cao[2] and Yuefei Sui[2]

[1] *School of Computer Science and Information Technology*
Yunnan Normal University, Kunming 650092
sunyu_km@hotmail.com

[2] *Key Laboratory of Intelligent Information Processing*
Institute of Computing Technology
Chinese Academy of Sciences, Beijing 100080
cgcao,yfsui@ict.ac.cn

Abstract   To reason the interaction between agents' epistemic states and environments, the agents' epistemic states should include ontologies of agents (the agents' assumptions about environments), what the agents know, believe and desire, and also should include the agents' interpretations about these symbols in ontologies onto the environments. A formal description of such agents' epistemic states and several examples are given to show how such a description can be used to explain the puzzles in reasoning the modal sentences. For example, a sentence holding in a structure may have different consequences reasoned by different agents, because of the different epistemic states.

Keywords: Agent, Ontology, Epistemic state, Environment, Modality

1.   Introduction

Multi-agent VSK logic ([1],[2]) is a multi-modal logic for reasoning about the epistemic states of agents in some environment. The logic is used to represent information visible, perceived and known to agents in an external environment and an agents' internal environment (epistemic state). Because the VSK logic is based on the propositional logic, it cannot express the interaction between agents' epistemic states and environments in which the agents are. What the agents perceive may change what the agents believe, know and

*This work is supported by the NSF (grant no. 60273019, 60496326, 60573063, and 60573064), the National 973 Programme (grants no. 2003CB317008 and G1999032701) and the Foundation of Yunnan Province (grants no. 04F00062, 2004YX42, 2004F0017Q, 03Y312D and 2005F0022Q).

Please use the following format when citing this chapter:

Sun, Y., Cao, C., Sui, Y., 2006, in IFIP International Federation for Information Processing, Volume 228, Intelligent Information Processing III, eds. Z. Shi, Shimohara K., Feng D., (Boston: Springer), pp. 519–524.

desire; and what the agents' ontologies ([3],[4]) and interpretation of symbols in the ontologies may change the interpretation of statements holding in the environments.

An epistemic state of an agent in an environment includes statements about the real world, where the statements are interpreted in terms of the agent's own interpretation. It determines the interpretation of statements about the environment; and the environment changes what the agent perceives, hence, what the agent believes, knows and desires. Hence, an environment interacts with the epistemic states of the agent in the environment. Based on the above discussion, we shall give a logical description of agents' epistemic states and environments.

The paper is organized as follows: section 2 gives a formal definition of symbols representing the agents' epistemic states; in section 3, we give the interpretations of symbols and formulas in structures (environments), and the definition of inconsistency between what are true in structures and agents' epistemic states; section 4 uses examples to resolve the puzzles in modal logic. The last section concludes the paper.

2.   The Epistemic States

An epistemic state E_a of an agent a should include the following ingredients:

  • a logical language L which is sharable and common to every agent.

  • an ontology O_a of agent a, where O_a consists of a set $C_a \subseteq L$ of names (concepts, denoted by α, β, etc.), a binary relation $\sqsubseteq$ on C_a (the subsumption relation), and a function F^a such that every name (concept) α is associated with a frame F_α^a, where F_α^a contains statements (formulas in L) about α which are known or assumed by agent a. Define $\alpha \equiv \beta$ if $\alpha \sqsubseteq \beta$ and $\beta \sqsubseteq \alpha$.

  • a set $\mathbf{K}_a$ of statements known to agent a; $\mathbf{B}_a$ believed by agent a; $\mathbf{D}_a$ desired by agent a.

  • an interpretation function I_a such that for any structure M (an environment), there is an interpretation I_a maps a name in L onto M.

  • a set $\mathbf{W}$ of possible world (structure) names $\mathbf{M}$.

Assume that there is an ontology O and interpretation $\mathbf{I}$ independent of any agent.

Remark 2.1. The statements in F_α^a are different from these in $\mathbf{K}_a$ in that when agent a communicates with other agents, a assumes that F_α^a is known to other agents; but $\mathbf{K}_a$ may not be known to other agents.

Here, we assume that L and structures M are independent of agents. Any formula in L is called a statement.

The language $\mathcal{L}$ for representing epistemic states of agents consists of

  • L as a sub-language;

- a set $\mathcal{A}$ of agents;
- epistemic modals $\mathbf{K}_a, \mathbf{B}_a$ and $\mathbf{K}_a$ for every $a \in \mathcal{A}$;
- a symbol $\mathbf{I}_a$ for every $a \in \mathcal{A}$;
- a set $\mathbf{W}$ of possible world names.

Definition 2.2. A string t of symbols in $\mathcal{L}$ is a term if either
(i) t is a term in L, or
(ii) $t = \mathbf{I}_a(s)$, where s is a term in L, or
(iii) $t = \mathbf{M}$ for some $\mathbf{M} \in \mathbf{W}$.

For any $a \in \mathcal{A}$, a should be a term. Because a occurs only as a subscript of $\mathbf{K}_a, \mathbf{B}_a, \mathbf{D}_a$ or $\mathbf{I}_a$, a is not taken as a term any more.

Definition 2.3. A string φ of symbols is a formula in $\mathcal{L}$ if either

∘ φ is a statement in L (given a structure M and an interpretation I, φ is interpreted to be a property on M); or

∘ $\varphi = \mathbf{K}_a\psi, \mathbf{B}_a\psi, \mathbf{D}_a\psi$, where ψ is a statement in L or formula in $\mathcal{L}$ (given a structure M and an interpretation I_a, $\mathbf{K}_a, \mathbf{B}_a$ and $\mathbf{D}_a$ are interpreted to be sets of properties about M); or

∘ $\varphi = \mathbf{I}_a(t) = \mathbf{I}_a(s)$, or $\mathbf{I}_a(\psi)$, where t, s are terms in L and ψ is a formula in $\mathcal{L}$ (given a structure M, $\mathbf{I}_a$ is interpreted as an interpretation I_a, hence, $\mathbf{I}_a$ can be taken as a function from structures to interpretations); or

∘ $\varphi = \neg\psi, \psi_1 \rightarrow \psi_2$, where ψ, ψ_1 and ψ_2 are statements in L or formulas in $\mathcal{L}$.

We can list some axioms about modals, such as: $\mathbf{K}_a\varphi \rightarrow \mathbf{B}_a\varphi$, etc.

Remark 2.4. $\mathbf{K}_a, \mathbf{B}_a, \mathbf{D}_a$ are not taken as modalities as in the BDI logic, but as sets of sentences. There are two reasons: one is to avoid using the possible world semantics, which is not compatible very well with our intuition that what a believes is just a set of statements. Another reason is that there is no appropriate modal predicate logic for the multi-agent systems, because of the propositional attitude reports ([5]).

3. Interpretations I and I_a

Given a structure M, assume that agent a is among M, that is, a is an object in M. There is an interpretation I independent of any agents, and an interpretation I_a for an agent a, where I_a satisfies the following conditions:

(3.1) $I_a(\mathbf{K}_a), I_a(\mathbf{B}_a)$ and $I_a(\mathbf{D}_a)$ are consistent sets of formulas such that $I_a(\mathbf{K}_a) \subseteq I_a(\mathbf{B}_a)$;

(3.2) $I_a(\mathbf{I}_a) = I_a$.

Then, there is an interpretation $\mathcal{I}$ of $\mathcal{L}$ such that $\mathcal{I}(\mathbf{I}) = I$; and $\mathcal{I}(\mathbf{I}_a) = I_a$.

Let $Th^I(M)$ be the statements in L which are true in M under interpretation I, that is, $Th^I(M) = \{\varphi \in L : M, I \models \varphi\}$. For the convenience, we assume that $Th^{I_a}(M) = Th^{I_a}(P_{a,M})$, where $P_{a,M}$ is a sub-structure of M that agent a can perceive. I_a maps every concept α in C_a to be a set of objects in M, denoted by $I_a(\alpha)$, such that for any $a \in M$, if $a \in I_a(\alpha)$ then we say that a is an instance of α in M under interpretation I_a.

Definition 3.1. Given a sentence φ and a structure M, we define the satisfaction of φ in M as follows:

If φ is a statement in L then $M \models \varphi$ if $\varphi \in Th^I(M)$;

$M, I_a \models \alpha \sqsubseteq \beta$ if $I_a(\alpha) \subseteq I_a(\beta)$;

$M, I_a \models \mathbf{K}_a\varphi$ if $\varphi \in I_a(\mathbf{K}_a)$;

$M, I_a \models \mathbf{I}_a(t) = \mathbf{I}_a(s)$ if $I_a(t) = I_a(s)$;

$M, I_a \models \mathbf{I}_a(\varphi)$ if $I_a(\varphi) \in Th^{I_a}(M)$;

What a perceives should be represented in the agent's epistemic states. Hence, for any object $x \in P_{a,M}$, there is a new name $\mathbf{x}_{a,M}$ added in O_a, and $Th^{I_a}(P_{a,M})$ is added in $\mathbf{K}_a$ and O_a. Two agents a and b can communicate information about $\mathbf{x}_{a,M}$ if (1) $a, b \in P_{a,M}, P_{b,M}$; and (2) $x \in P_{a,M}, P_{b,M}$. In this case, $\mathbf{x}_{b,M}$ is added in O_b too.

Remark 3.2. Even when the universes in $P_{a,M}$ and $P_{b,M}$ are equal, $P_{a,M}$ may not be equal to $P_{b,M}$. Because a relation symbol $\mathbf{r}$ may have different interpretations $I_a(\mathbf{r})$ and $I_b(\mathbf{r})$ on $P_{a,M}$.

Let $I_a(\mathbf{x}_{a,M}, M) = x$; and assume that $I_a(\mathbf{x}_{a,M}, M')$ may be undefined.

Notice that $\mathbf{K}_a\varphi \to \varphi$ is not an axiom, because φ is to be interpreted by a common interpretation I and $\mathbf{K}_a\varphi$ is interpreted by I_a, and $\mathbf{K}_a\varphi$ being satisfied under I_a does not imply the satisfaction of φ under I.

Given a structure M, I_a interprets L onto M. What an agent should notice is the difference and consistency between $\mathbf{I}_a(\mathbf{K}_a)$ and $Th^{I_a}(M)$, where $\mathbf{I}_a(\mathbf{K}_a) = \{\mathbf{I}_a(\varphi) : \varphi \in \mathbf{K}_a\}$. An autonomic agent could revise $\mathbf{B}_a, \mathbf{K}_a$ and $\mathbf{D}_a$ according to the inconsistency of $\mathbf{I}_a(\mathbf{K}_a) \cup Th^{I_a}(P_{a,M})$. If a is retrospective then if $\mathbf{I}_a(\mathbf{K}_a)$ and $Th^{I_a}(M)$ are inconsistent then a revises $\mathbf{K}_a$ such that $\mathbf{I}_a(\mathbf{K}_a) \subseteq Th^{I_a}(M)$. If it is necessary then a may revise O_a.

Remark 3.3. Notice that the revision done by a is not based on the inconsistence of $\mathbf{I}_a(\mathbf{K}_a)$ and $Th^I(M)$, but on the inconsistence of $\mathbf{I}_a(\mathbf{K}_a)$ and $Th^{I_a}(M)$. Because a knows that there is an incorrect statement in $\mathbf{K}_a, \mathbf{B}_a$ or $\mathbf{D}_a$, not because of the inconsistence between $\mathbf{I}_a(\mathbf{K}_a)$ and $Th^I(M)$ (a does not know $Th^I(M)$), but because of the inconsistence between $\mathbf{I}_a(\mathbf{K}_a)$ and $Th^{I_a}(M)$. What a perceives in M is $Th^{I_a}(P_{a,M})$, not $Th^I(P_{a,M})$.

4.   Examples

In this section we give several examples to show how to use the description given above to reason what agents' know and what we know the agents' know.

Example 4.1. Let M_m be a snapshot of the real world in the morning, and M_e in the evening. Assume that $\alpha = morning\ star \in C_a$ and $\beta = evening\ star \in C_a$, and $\alpha \equiv \beta \notin O_a$. It is a basic fact that

$$M_m, I \models \alpha = \beta; \quad M_e, I \models \alpha = \beta.$$

For agent a, $I_a(\alpha)$ is defined in M_m and not defined in M_e; and $I_a(\beta)$ is defined in M_e and not defined in M_m. Hence, we have that

$$M_m, I_a \models \alpha \neq \beta; \quad M_e, I_a \models \alpha \neq \beta.$$

Because $I(\alpha) \in P_{a,M_m}$ and $I(\beta) \notin P_{a,M_m}$, agent a does not know $\alpha = \beta$ by perceiving α, so that agent a think that a need not revise $\mathbf{K}_a$ and O_a, because

$$\alpha \neq \beta \in \mathbf{K}_a, \quad \alpha \in \mathbf{M}_m \in \mathbf{K}_a, \quad \beta \notin \mathbf{M}_m \in \mathbf{K}_a.$$

In the common ontology O, we assume $\alpha, \beta \in C$, and $\alpha \sqsubseteq \beta, \beta \sqsubseteq \alpha \in O$. Notice that O may not be a perfect and complete ontology for the real world.

Even though the logical language L used to represent the real world is same to agents, conflicts and misunderstanding between agents may be resulted in by the difference in the following factors: (1) the statements about a concept; (ii) $\mathbf{K}_a, \mathbf{B}_a, \mathbf{D}_a$ and $\mathbf{I}_a$; and (iii) the environments perceived.

Because of the differences, a statement φ in L may be interpreted in different ways for different agents, i.e., it is possible that for some agents a and $b, M, I \models \varphi$; $M, I_a \models \varphi$ and $M, I_b \not\models \varphi$.

Example 4.2. Given a structure M and two agents a and b, it is possible that $P_{a,M} \neq P_{b,M}, O_a \neq O_b, I_a \neq I_b, F_\alpha^a \neq F_\alpha^b$ for some $\alpha \in L$. Hence, misunderstanding occurs between a and b.

Assume that α, β, M_m and M_e are the same as example 4.1; and $\alpha \equiv \beta \notin O_a, \alpha \equiv \beta \in O_b$. Let I_a and I_b be two interpretations such that $\mathcal{I}(\mathbf{I}_a) = I_a$ and $\mathcal{I}(\mathbf{I}_b) = I_b$. Then, I_a is a partial mapping and I_b is a total function, because $I_b(\alpha) \in M_e$ and $I_b(\beta) \in M_m$.

If agent b tells agent a in M_m that b perceives β in M_m, agent a does not believe in b, i.e.,

$$I_a(\alpha) \notin M_e; \qquad I_a(\beta) \notin M_m;$$
$$M_m, I_b \models S_b(\beta, \mathbf{M}_m); \quad M_m, I_a \not\models \mathbf{B}_a S_b(\beta, \mathbf{M}_m),$$

where $S_b(\beta, \mathbf{M}_m)$ means that b can see β in $\mathbf{M}_m$. Because agent a think it is impossible to perceive β in M_m.

Hence, the statement that b see the evening star in the morning is true in M_m for agent b, but false in M_m for agent a.

To explain that even when the universes in $P_{a,M}$ and $P_{b,M}$ are equal, as a structure, $P_{a,M}$ may not be equal to $P_{b,M}$, we use the following

Example 4.3. Let M be a structure consisting of a cubic object x which has one hole in three faces and no hole in other three faces. Assume that three faces with one hole, say x_1, x_2, x_3, are perceived only by agent a; and other three faces without hole, say x_4, x_5, x_6, are perceived only by agent b. Hence, defaultly, agent a think that every face of the cube has one hold on it, let $h_1, h_2, ..., h_6$ be the holes on $x_1, x_2, ..., x_6$ imaged by agent a; and agent b

think that there is no hole on any face of the cube. Hence,

$$x_{a,M} = x_{b,M}, x_{a,M} \in O_a, x_{b,M} \in O_b;$$
$$x_{1,a,M}, x_{2,a,M}, ..., x_{6,a,M} \in O_a; \quad x_{1,b,M}, x_{2,b,M}, ..., x_{6,b,M} \in O_b;$$
$$x_{1,a,M} \equiv x_{1,b,M}, x_{2,a,M} \equiv x_{2,b,M}, ..., x_{6,a,M} \equiv x_{6,b,M} \in L;$$
$$h_{1,a,M}, h_{2,a,M}, ..., h_{6,a,M} \in O_a, \notin O_b.$$

Let $on(x, y)$ denote a relation symbol that x is on y. Then,

$$on(h_{1,b,M}, x_{1,b,M}), ..., on(x_{6,b,M}, x_{6,b,M}) \in K_a;$$
$$on(h_{1,b,M}, x_{1,b,M}), ..., on(x_{6,b,M}, x_{6,b,M}) \notin K_b.$$

Notice that because $h_{1,b,M} \notin O_b$, it is meaningless to b that $on(h_{1,b,M}, x_{1,b,M})$.

5.   Conclusions

According to the difference of ontologies and interpretations of different agents, we can represent the agent' epistemic states in a more natural way which is similar to the way we perceive and revise our knowledge. The agents are in environments and perceive some properties holding in the environments, where the properties are interpreted by the agents under their own interpretations. Such a representation of epistemic states gives a natural way to describe the belief revision. An agent realizes to revise its belief set when the agent in some environment interprets its beliefs in an inconsistent way. Hence, the agent may not revise its belief set once when its belief set is inconsistent with the properties holding in a structure, as explained in the classical theory of belief revision, because the inconsistence may not be perceivable to the agent.

Further works should include the axiom systems for interpretations I and I_a; the theory of belief revision based on interpretations I and I_a; and the applications to emotional agents and the representation of speech acts.

References

[1] M. Wooldridge and A. Lomuscio, A computationally grounded logic of visibility, perception, and knowledge, *Logic Journal of the IGPL* 9(2001), 273-288.

[2] M. Wooldridge and A. Lomuscio, Multiagent VSK logic, in: *Proc. of the Seventh European Workshop on Logics in Artificial Intelligence (JELIAI-2000)*, Springer-Verlag.

[3] T. R. Gruber, Towards principles for the design of ontologies used for knowledge sharing, *International J. of Human-Computer Studies* 43(1995), 907-928.

[4] N. Guarino, Understanding, building, and using ontologies, *International J. of Human-Computer Studies* 46(1997), 293-310.

[5] G. E. Hughes and M. J. Cresswell, *A New Introduction to Modal Logic*, Routledge, London, New York, 1996.

Network Anomalous Intrusion Detection using Fuzzy-Bayes

Adetunmbi Adebayo.O[1,2]., Zhiwei Shi[1], Zhongzhi Shi[1] and
Adewale Olumide S.[2]

[1]Key Laboratory of Intelligent Information Processing

Institute of Computing Technology, CAS, Beijing 100080 China,

Tel: 86-10-62565533 ext. 5661 86-10-62565533 ext. 5688
{oluadetunmbi, shizw,shizz}@ics.ict.ac.cn

[2]Department of Computer Science,

Federal University of Technology, Ondo State, Nigeria.

adewale@ictp.it (+234-0803-361-6386)

Abstract: Security of networking systems has been an issue since computer networks became prevalent, most especially now that Internet is changing the facie computing. Intrusions pose significant threats to the integrity, confidentiality and availability of information for the internet users. In this paper, a new approach to real-time network anomaly intrusion detection via Fuzzy-Bayesian is proposed to detect malicious activity against computer network; the framework is described to demonstrate the effectiveness of the technique. The combination of fuzzy with Bayesian classifier will improve the overall performance of Bayes based intrusion detection system (IDS). Also, the feasibility of our method is demonstrated by the experiment performed on KDD 1999 IDS data set.

Key words: intrusion detection, fuzzy, naïve-Bayes

1.   INTRODUCTION

Developing an efficient and effective intrusion detection system to preserve data integrity and system availability has been the aim of researchers in computer security for almost three decades. Intrusion

Please use the following format when citing this chapter:

Adebayo.O, A., Shi, Z., Shi, Z., Olumide S., A., 2006, in IFIP International Federation for Information Processing, Volume 228, Intelligent Information Processing III, eds. Z. Shi, Shimohara K., Feng D., (Boston: Springer), pp. 525–530.

detection is a process of detecting security breaches by examining events occurring in a computer system.

Basically, there are two approaches to intrusion detection model as described in [3]: Misuse detection model refers to detection of intrusions that follow well-defined intrusion patterns. It is very useful in detecting known attack patterns. Anomaly detection Model refers to detection performed by detecting changes in the patterns of utilization or behavior of the system. It can be used to detect known and unknown attack.

Intrusion detection can also be classified as Network-based (NIDS) or host-based (HIDS) based on source of data used for analyses. The former collect raw network packets as the data source from the network and analyze for signs of intrusions [1, 4]. Host-based IDS operates on information collected from within an individual computer system such as operating system audit trails, C2 audit logs, and System logs [4].

Fuzzy is a novel classification technique that has been widely successfully applied in many applications, and it has been reported to perform well in detecting different attacks due to various reasons spelt out in [2 ,5, 7 and 8]. Ajith, et al [2] exploited fuzzy for intrusion detection and the results show an outstanding performance in terms of accuracy. Also, Naïve Bayes has been successfully applied in solving various problems [9].

Fuzzy is introduced to strengthen the detection ability of naïve bayes due to uncertainty nature of intrusions by recognizing anomalous events, consequently leading to reduction in false alarm rate. Fuzzy had been recognized to posses the following quality among others that makes it suitable for the subject matter: ability to readily combine inputs from widely varying sources, degree of alert that can occur with intrusions is often fuzzy because there is no clear distinction between normal and anomaly behavior in a networked computer.

We demonstrate the feasibility of our approach by carrying out experiments on KDD-cup 1999 intrusion detection dataset.

2.   THE FUZZYBAYESIAN CLASSIFIER

In naïve Bayes classifier, instances to be classified are described by attribute vectors $\vec{x} = (x_1,....,x_n)$. Bayes classifier assigns to instances most probable or maximum a posterior (MAP), classification from a finite set of c classes. Bayes classifier is given as:

$$c = \arg\max_{c_j \in C} P(c_j) \prod_{i=1}^{n} P(x_i \mid c_j)$$

Naïve Bayes classifier is trained by a set of labeled training data presented to it in relational form with desirable features because the strength of this model lies very much on the feature set used. In this work, the use of fuzzy is employed during the examination of network connection states to assign weight to various quantifiable variables in the selected features based on predefined fuzzy rules before presentation to the naïve bayes classifier. Weights are assigned with 0.0 representing absolute falseness and 1.0 representing absolute truth. Weights assigned to each features are then used to multiply the prior probability of each class during testing, and with a threshold set, normal and attack traffic can be classified.

3.   PROPOSED SYSTEM ARCHITECTURE

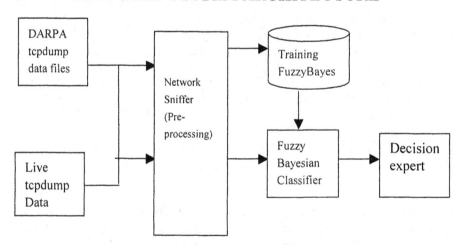

Fig. 1: proposed system architecture

Figure 1 shows the structure of our proposed architecture for real time intrusion detection system via fuzzy-bayes which are divided into two main phases: learning and testing. The network sniffer processes the tcpdump binary into a standard format putting into consideration both the temporal and spatial information of network connections. During the learning phase, two major parameters affecting machine learning are considered: the imbalance of data sets and identification of important features.

Class imbalance problem occurs when there are many more instances of some classes than others in a classification problem which results into suboptimal classification performance, which can have a detrimental effect on learner's behavior [10]. In order to balance the original training data with the utmost aim of improving the system performance, we adopt selective sampling method.

Often, output Y is only determined by the subsets of the input features X. Removing irrelevant features in learning process leads to reduction in computational cost, over fitting, model size and leads to increase in accuracy. In selecting important features, leave-one-out technique of deleting one feature at a time to rank input features and identify the most important features for intrusion detection is adopted [6].

The fuzzybayes technique is then used to obtain the optimal detection model for our system after the learning phase to classify new pattern samples in testing phase.

4.   EXPERIMENTAL SETUP

KDD cup 1999 dataset [11] was used for the experiment. The data set has five different classes namely Normal, Dos, R2L, U2R and Probes. In this work, the last four were combined into a class called Abnormal. The training and testing data comprised of 5,924 and 12,130 records respectively.

Frequency table for all the 41 variables were generated given class (normal and abnormal). From the analysis of the frequency table, it showed that some of the extracted attributes did not have any significance in detections of attacks. Attributes on columns 14, 18, 19 and 20 are good examples, while attribute on columns 0, 1, 8, 15, 16, 17, 21 and 36 made little or no impact.

Each variable (attribute) was partitioned into maximum of 20 membership functions except those with variations less than five which forms the basis for fuzzy rules and assigning of weights.

In cases where clear distinction could not be established amongst the variations of an attribute; two or more variables were combined to differentiate close cases and consequently in assigning of weights.   With all the 41 attributes, result obtained is shown in Table 1

Table. 1: Percentage accuracy of classified data

Class	No. of records	Correctly Classified.	Wrongly classified	Percentage Of accuracy
Normal	6514	6331	183	97.19
Abnormal	5616	5397	219	96.10
Total	12130	11728	402	96.67

Result obtained was the same when only 29 attributes were used (i.e, removing columns 0,1,8,14,15,16,17,18,19,20,21, and 36 from the experiment).

5 CONCLUSION

This paper proposed a light weight anomaly detection framework based on fusions of fuzzy and Bayes with the utmost aim of addressing large number of false alarms caused by incorrect classification of events in current system. We have demonstrated the effectiveness of our method on KDD-cup 99 intrusion detection datasets and accuracy is over 96%. And our method reveals redundant features, thereby minimizing the number of features the FuzzyBayes classifier should process and consequently increase IDS detection rate. We plan to conduct more experiments with real-life data using our proposed system.

ACKNOWLEDGMENT

This work is supported jointly by Third World Academy of Sciences (TWAS) and Chinese Academy of Sciences (CAS)

REFERENCES

1. Alan Bivens, Chandrika Palagiri, Raheda smith, Boleslaw Szymanski, Mark Embrechts, "Network-Based Intrusion detection using Neural Networks", www.cs.rpi.edu/~szymansk/paper/anie02.pdf
2. Ajith Abraham, Ravi Jainb, Johnson Thomas, and Sang Yong Han, "D-SCIDS: Distributed soft computing intrusion detection system", Journal of Network and Computer Applications, Elsevier, 2005.
3. Biswanath Mukherjee, Todd L. Heberlin, and Karl N. Levitt. Network intrusion detection. IEEE Network, 8(3):26-41, 1994.
4. Byunghae Cha, kyung Woo Park and Jaittyun Seo, "Neural Networks Techniques for Host Anomaly Intrusion Detection using Fixed Pattern Transformation. ICCSA 2005, LNCS 3481 pp. 254-263, 2005.
5. Susan M. Bridges and Rayford B. vaughnn, "Intrusion detection via fuzzy data mining", Twelfth annual Canadian Information Technology Security Symposium June 19-23. The Ottawa Congress Centre.
6. Andrew H. Sung and Srinivas Mukkamala, "Identifying important features for intrusion detection using support vector machines and neural networks". IEEE Proceedings of the 2003 Symposium on Application and the Internet (SAINT ' 03).
7. Jonatan Gomez and Dipankar Dasgupa "Evolving Classifiers for Intrusion Detection", Proceedings of the 2002 IEEE Workshop on

Information Assurance, United States Military Academy, West Point, NY, June 2001

8.   John E. Dickerson, Jukka Juslin, Uuramia Koukousoula, and Julie A. Dickerson, "Fuzzy intrusion detection (FIRE)", Electrical and Computer Engineering Department, IOWA state University, Ames, IA, USA. www.eng.iastate.edu/~julied/research.html

9.   Christopher Krungel, Darren Mutz, William Robertson and Fredik Valuer, "Bayesian Event classification for intrusion detection", Proceedings of the 19th Annual Computer Security Applications Conference (ACSAC'03), 2003

10. Miroslav Kubat and Stan Matwin, "Addressing the curse of Imbalanced Training Sets: One sided selection" Proc. 14th International Conference on Machine Learning, 1997

11. KDD Cup 1999 Data: http://kdd.ics.uci.edu/databases/kddcup99/

REFERENCE ALGORITHM OF TEXT CATEGORIZATION BASED ON FUZZY COGNITIVE MAPS

ZHANG Guiyun ,LIU Yang , ZHANG Weijuan,WANG Yuanyuan
*Computer and Information Engineering College, Tianjin Normal University, Tianjin 300384,
Email:dyxy1999@126.com, phone :013920736656*

Abstract: This paper introduces the reference theory and algorithm of text categorization
by using fuzzy cognitive map(FCM), which is based on value inference and
can be able to infer by combing rule and statistics. This method is flexible and
robust, and we do not need train the corpus time after time， it is suitable to the
text categorization of insufficiency training, new subject and multi-
classification.

Key words: text categorization; fuzzy cognitive map; reference algorithm

1.   INTRODUCTION

The technology of text automatic categorization has gone through the rule-based technology, statistics-based technology, and to the combination of rule and statistics. Recently there are Rocchio classical algorithm, Naïve Bayes probability algorithm, decision tree matching algorithm, K-nearest neighbor method based on similarity, Support Vector Machine (SVM)suggested by Vapnik, Linear Least Square Fitting (LLSF), Neural Network， maximum entropy categorization method rough set method[1] [10] [12] [13] [14] [15] and so on. This paper introduces a reference algorithm of text categorization based on fuzzy cognitive map for making the text categorization become the result of FCM reference which is based on weight of text term, term and category, and category and relevancy.

Please use the following format when citing this chapter:

Zhang, G., Liu, Y., Zhang, W., Wang, Y., 2006, in IFIP International Federation for Information Processing, Volume
228, Intelligent Information Processing III, eds. Z. Shi, Shimohara K., Feng D., (Boston: Springer), pp. 531–536.

2.   CONSTRUCTION OF FCM IN TEXT CATEGORIZATION

The cognitive map (CM) is constituted by relations of concepts which are represented by nodes. The relation between concept is represented by an arc with arrow, its strength is represented by number value, namely, the weight of arc. FCM combines fuzzy logic and neural networks technology, the state space of an FCM is determined initially by an initial condition and then propagated automatically through the node function relative to a threshold until a static pattern is reached. A causal inference is achieved when the FCM reaches a stable limit cycle or fixed point.

The foundation of text term model and selection of categorization method are core problems. Now, although there are various categorization algorithms based on vector space model, most of which need training a large number of corpus. The method in this paper regards text term and classification as nodes of CM, the corresponding state values of node are weight values of terms, relevancy of term t_i and classification C_j and that of classification C_k and classification C_j are the weights of corresponding edges to realize the text categorization reference algorithm based on FCM.

Definition 1   A text categorization FCM is a quadruples ordered set $U=(T,C,E,W)$,where $T=\{t_1,t_2,\ldots,t_n\}$ represents the term set in text, $C=\{C_1,C_2,\ldots,C_n\}$ represents classification set, $E=\{<t_i,C_j>,<C_k,C_j>\mid t_i\in T,\ C_k,C_j\in C\}$,directed arc $<t_i,C_j>$ represents that term t_i relates to classification C_j, $<C_k,C_j>$ represents that classification C_k relates to classification C_j,$W=\{W_{ij},P_{kj}\mid W_{ij}$ is weight of directed arc $<t_i,C_j>$, P_{kj} is weight of directed arc $<C_k,C_j>\}$. $V_{ti}(0)$, $V_{Ck}(0)$ represent initial value of term t_i and classification C_k (weight value).The weight of corresponding edge is 0 if there is no any relevancy.

Therefore, the adjacency matrix of text categorization FCM can be simplified as a (n+m) ×m matrix:

$$W_U = \begin{pmatrix} \cdots & \cdots & \cdots \\ \cdots & w_{ij} & \cdots \\ \cdots & \cdots & \cdots \\ \cdots & \cdots & \cdots \\ \cdots & P_{kj} & \cdots \\ \cdots & \cdots & \cdots \end{pmatrix} \qquad (1)$$

Where W_{ij} denotes the relevancy of node v_i and classification C_j, P_{kj} denotes the relevancy of classification C_k and classification C_j.

The total input received by text categorization FCM at time t+1is
$$(v'_{c1}(t+1),...,v'_{cm}(t+1))=(v_{t1}(t),...,v_{tn}(t),v_{C1}(t),...,v_{Cm}(t))\times w_U \qquad (2)$$
Therefore, the output received by text categorization FCM at time t+1is
$$(v_{c1}(t+1),...,v_{cm}(t+1))=(f(v'_{c1}(t+1)),...,f(v'cm(t+1))). \qquad (3)$$
The input received by text categorization FCM at time t+1is determined by equ (4)as follows:
$$(v_{t1}(t),...,v_{tn}(t),v_{c1}(t+1),...,v_{cm}(t+1))=(v_{t1}(t),...,v_{tn}(t),f(v'_{c1}(t+1)),...,f(v'cm(t+1))). \qquad (4)$$
Namely, the weight of term is not changed, values of classification nodes are updated.

3. REFERENCE ALGORITHM OF TEXT CATEGORIZATION BASED ON FUZZY COGNITIVE MAP

3.1 Decision of term weight and edge weight in text categorization FCM

Many weight functions about term weight such as Boolean weight function, TF-IDF weight function, ITC weight function, Okapi weight function, the algorithm of TF·IDF·IG (information gain) come out. In addition, the algorithm[10] by assigning weight value for the regions of term words is considered. Term frequency*inverse document frequency(TF·IDF) is a basic one.Assume that the term frequency t_i in document d_j is $tf_{ij}=freq_{ij}$, inverse document frequency $idf_i=\log(N/n_i)$, where N is the number of texts in data corpus, n_i is the sum of texts which comprise term t_i, and the base-number of log can be 10,e or 2. Initially, the weight of term t_i in document d_j is:

Vt_i （0） $= tf_{ij} \cdot idf_i$ （5） , then normalize it, the basic way is maximum normalization (others see paper[6]): $tf_{ij} = \dfrac{freq_{ij}}{\max_k\{freq_{kj}\}}$ (6).The relevancy of term t_i and classification C_j is weight W_{ij} in text categorization cognitive map. The common methods are Mutual Information, IG, and Expected Cross Entropy etc. Many researches show that Mutual Information algorithm is much better than others[12] .The mutual information of term t_i and classification C_j is: $MI(t_i,C_j)=\log(\dfrac{P(t_i/C_j)}{P(t_i)})$ (7), where $P(t_i/C_j)=\dfrac{1+\sum_{k=1}^{N}tf_{ik}}{|V|+\sum_{l=1}^{|V|}\sum_{k=1}^{N}tf_{lk}}$ and

$P(t_i)$ denote the specific weight of term t_i in classification C_j and word frequency in corpus, |V| and N denote sum of all term and the amount of documents, respectively.

3.2 Reference algorithm of text categorization based on fuzzy cognitive map

The reference algorithm of text categorization based on fuzzy cognitive map is as follows:

Input: weight of term, relevancy of term and text classification, relevancy among classifications.

Output: classification of text

Step1 Calculate weight of term t_i through equ(5), and normalize it e by using equ(6);

Step2 Calculate relevancy of term t_i and classification C_j, W_{ij}through equ(7), read relevancy of classification C_k and C_j which are specified by experts as weight P_{kj},and then decide the adjacency matrix through equ (1).

Step3 Calculate the output of C_j at time t+1 through equ(2) and equ(3),mostly f is a sigmoid function: $f(x)=1/(1+e^{-cx})$;

Step4 Whether $Vc_j \geq P_T$ (threshold),if yes, output C_j, and if there are many S_j ,then output the maximum; if no, goto step1(or terminate iterated algorithm by limiting its degree) .The output C_j is text classification.

4.   EXPERIMENTS AND ANALYSIS

Recall and precision are classical performance evaluate standards of text classification, where the precision reflects the proportion of correct text classification. We randomly choose 30,50,100,150,200,250,300,500 pieces of documents concerning economy, politic, computer, physical, education and law to train and carry out experiments from corpus in Fudan university, disk edition of *People Daily* corpus in 1999 and web. tf_{ij} is calculated by using the simplest word frequency, C is 0.5, C_j is the biggest output weight after 300 iterative. Table 1 indicates relationships weights between classifications.

Table2-1 and table2-2 describe the result of test, and the recall and precision of different pieces of texts，the calculated formulas are seed by reference 1.

Table1 Relationships weights between classifications

	economy	politic	computer	physical	education	law
economy	1	0.7	0.4	0.5	0.5	0.7
politic	0.7	1	0.2	0.3	0.6	0.8
computer	0.4	0.2	1	0.1	0.6	0.2
physical	0.5	0.3	0.1	1	0.3	0.3
education	0.5	0.6	0.6	0.3	1	0.5
law	0.7	0.8	0.2	0.3	0.5	1

Table 2-1 The recall (%)and precision(%) of different pieces of texts

evaluate / classification	50 pieces		100 pieces		150 pieces		200 pieces	
	Pi	Ri	Pi	Ri	Pi	Ri	Pi	Ri
economy	60	100	70	100	69	91	72.3	97.1
politic	85.7	85.7	100	80	98.3	84.6	91.7	91.7
computer	100	100	100	93.3	100	88	100	87.9
physical	100	75	100	77.8	88.9	76.2	96	78.1
education	100	71.4	90.5	90.5	93.3	90.3	88.2	85.7
law	100	87.5	81.3	86.7	88	91.7	93.1	90

Table 2-2 The recall (%)and precision(%) of different pieces of texts

evaluate / classification	250 pieces		300 pieces		500 pieces	
	Pi	Ri	Pi	Ri	Pi	Ri
economy	74.6	97.6	74.2	98	75.4	98.9
politic	93.5	89.6	95	89.8	92.4	90.1
computer	77.6	86.4	98	87.3	96.6	89.4
physical	96.9	81.6	97.2	83.3	100	81.4
education	88.1	90.2	92	92	86.7	87.8
law	88.0	86.5	91.1	89.1	90.8	83.1

5.   CONCLUSION

Text categorization is the basis of passage-chapter level text process, but different information demands will produce different categorization requirements. This paper suggests a reference theory and algorithm of text categorization based on fuzzy cognitive map which is derived from the weight of text term , the relevancy of term and classification and the relevancy of classification and classification. Although it is a new attempt, the results indicate its effect. The merits of using FCM to categorize text are:①It is a number value reference based on iterative calculation.②This method emphasizes feedback so that it is suitable to insufficiently training or new subject classification.③Considering the relevancy between classifications and the relevancy between terms.④Merging statistics and number value reference , so it overcomes the shortcoming of depending on experts' knowledge.⑤When FCM reaches stable, a unitary classification is received, while when FCM converges a limit cycle, then multi-classification is received, so it is suitable to the classification of cross science and synthetical science.⑥ The method is open. It can be added, deleted or combined, and it's suitable for real-time different requirement.

REFERENCE

1.   PANG Jianfeng , BU Dongbo, BAI Shuo Research and Implementation of Text Categorization System Based on VSM Application research of computers 2001,9:23-26
2.   CHEN Ruifen Chinese text categorization algorithm combined with feedback Computer Applications 2005 Vol. 25 No. 12
3.   Axelrod R. Structure of Decision: the Cognitive Maps of Political Elites. Princeton, NJ:Princeton University Press, 1976.
4.   Kosko B. Fuzzy cognitive maps. Int. J. Man-machine Studies, 1986, 24: 65-75
5.   Kosko B. Adaptive inference in fuzzy knowledge networks. In: Proc. 1st Int. Conf. Neural Networks. 1987. 2: 261-268
6.   Wang Xiaolong, Guan Yi Compter Natural Language Processing Tsinghua Press 2005 ,pp.146-154
7.   YE Hao, WANG Mingwen, ZENG Xueqiang Automatic text multi-classification model based on latent semantic Tsinghua Univ (Sci & Tech), 2005, Vol. 45, No. S1: 1818-1822
8.   Luo Xiangfeng, Cognitive map theory and its applications in image analysis and understanding ,dissertation of Ph. D,Hefei University of Technology, P. R. China, April 2003
9.   LuSong LiXiaoli ,BaiShuo, Wang Shi An Improved Approach to Weighting Terms in Text JOURNAL OF CHINESE INFORMATION PROCESSING Vol. 14 No. 6:8-13,20
10. Zhang Dong li, Wang Dongsheng, Zheng Weimin Chinese text classification system based on VSM J T singhua Univ (Sci & Tech) ,2003, Vo l. 43, No. 9:1288-1291
11. Liu Yunfeng , QiHuan , Xiangen Hu , Zhiqiang Cai A Modif ied Weight Function in Latent Semantic Analysis JOURNAL OF CHINESE INFORMATION PROCESSING Vol119 No16:64-69
12. Chen Zhigang He Pilian Research and Implementation of Text Categorization System Based on VSM Computer Applications 2004,Vol . 24.277-279
13. LU Jiaoli , ZHENGJiaheng The Research of Text Categorization Based on Rough Set JOURNAL OF CHINESE INFORMATION PROCESSING Vol119 No12:66-69
14. Sheng Xiaowei Jiang Minghu Automatic Classification of Chinnese Documents Based on Rough Set and Improved Quick-Reduce Algorithm Journal of Electronics & Information Technology 2005, Vol27 No7: 1047-1052
15. Demetrius A.Georgiou, Despina Makry. A Learner' s Style and Profile Recognition via Fuzzy Cognitive Map. Proceedings of the IEEE International Conference on Advanced Learning Technologies (ICALT'04) 2004 0-7695-2181-9/04

AN ONTOLOGY-BASED AND COOPERATIVE ANNOTATION SYSTEM

Wenjuan Wu, Xiaoyong Du, He Hu, Ning Ma
Information School, Renmin University of China, Beijing, P.R. China 100872

wendywood@ruc.edu.cn, duyong@ruc.edu.cn, hehu@ruc.edu.cn

Abstract: The Semantic Web is charming but not easy to realize, since one of the prerequisite steps is to create semantic and precise data adhere to traditional web pages. We provide an annotation system ConAnnotator, which is an ontology-based annotation system and allows cooperative working. It aims at supporting the annotation process as well as the evolvement of the ontology. By semi-automatically creating ontology-based annotations and managing the statistic information about the annotation history, it facilitates the annotation process, makes the annotated documents connected to the ontology and further constructs the Semantic Web, and ultimately helps the users to evolve the ontology itself.

Key words: ontology-based annotation, domain ontology, collaborative annotation, ontology evolvement.

1. INTRODUCTION

The semantic web [1] is more prominent for it contains information that is not only readable for human but also can be understood by the computer. Therefore, to make the semantic web come true, the first and the most important step is to add semantic and precise data to traditional web pages. The data is added is called "annotation". However, this is an arduous, time consuming and error-prone task [9]. In this paper, we mainly introduce our

Please use the following format when citing this chapter:

Wu, W., Du, X., Hu, H., Ma, N., 2006, in IFIP International Federation for Information Processing, Volume 228, Intelligent Information Processing III, eds. Z. Shi, Shimohara K., Feng D., (Boston: Springer), pp. 537–542.

ConAnnotator - an Ontology-based annotation system bundling role-based cooperation function.

In this paper, we first introduce related work in brief. We describe the structure of Cooperative Ontology Developing Environment and Repository System (CODERS) [2] in which our ConAnnotator plays an important role respectively in section 3. In section 4, we describe the framework of ConAnnotator[3] in detail. Finally, we discuss the future work and draw a conclusion.

2.   RELATED WORK

There are several tools used to create semantic annotation, such as SHOE, Annotea[13], Ontomat, SMORE and so on. [4][5] SHOE [10] was one the earliest systems for adding semantic annotations to web pages. SHOE Knowledge Annotator allows users to mark up pages in SHOE guided by ontologies available locally or via a URL. These marked up pages can be reasoned about by SHOE-aware tools such as SHOE Search. Such tools are described in [11, 12]. Annotea is a W3C tool (and protocol) that enhances collaboration via shared metadata but it does not support information extraction nor is it linked to an ontology server; Ontomat is quite meaningful for the future HTML editors; SMORE is a tool that allows users to markup their documents in RDF using web ontologies in association with user-specific terms and elements.

ConAnnotator improves the annotation efficiency by introducing a fully automotive method. The other mentioned systems provide useful tools in annotation processes; but they all lack automatic features in their implementations and hinder the large scale deployment. Further more, it applies itself to Chinese resource.

3.   COOPERATIVE ONTOLOGY DEVELOPING ENVIRONMENT AND REPOSITORY SYSTEM (CODERS)

We have been applying ourselves to building a demo Economics Semantic Web, which is a subject –oriented semantic web described in [2].

Cooperative ontology developing environment and Repository System (CODERS) is based on role-based collaborative development method (RCDM) [2]. Our ConAnnotator plays an important role in it.

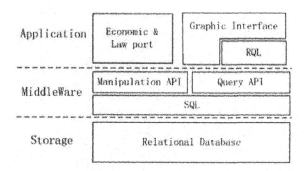

Figure 1. Hierarchy of CODERS

4.   FRAMEWORK OF CONANNOTATOR

Figure 2 depicts the architecture of ConAnnotator. The Google Web API is used to crawl resource from WWW, the resource, maybe web page or other formatted files, are moved to the Crawled Repository, then the domain filters act on them, resource focus on the domain is saved in the domain repository. Next step comes the ConAnnotator, it will automatically annotate the resources using the domain ontology after tokenizing and doing Part-Of-Speech (POS) tagging on resources.

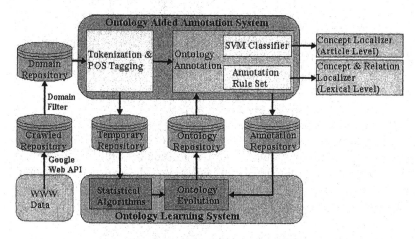

Figure 2. Framework of ConAnnotator

4.1   Semi-automatic Annotation

The semi-automatic process contains 2 levels:
1. Classification at Article Level
    Article level annotations describe the semantic linking between a
    particular resource and the domain ontology concepts. We use SVM
    (Support Vector Machine) as the classifier. SVM has been proven to
    be both precise and effective in solving text classify problem [7]. In
    the user interface, we use different color to show the confidence for
    the classification result, by this means we facilitate the annotate
    process.
2. Information Extraction at Lexical Level
    The IE function offers two ways to support semi-automatic annotate:
    a) Extract "°basi"¡ ±info rmt i o n abœt t h e doc umnt l i ke tit le
        author, abstract, keyword, and class number. We take advantage
        of Regular Expressions to describe the characters of the "basic"
        information.
    b) Extract keyword candidates.
        We use a free Chinese lexical analysis system ICTCLAS
        developed by Institute of Computing Technology, Chinese
        Academy of Sciences. Details are in [3]. We provide an
        algorithm to find keyword candidates based on word frequency.

4.2   Evolution of Ontology

We maintain a Post-controlled word repository which stores the Post-
controlled vocabulary and the statistic information about the "concept" term
of annotations, and an Ontology Repository to store the ontologies what
underpin the system. The structure of the Post-controlled vocabulary is as
same as that of ontology.

Repositories maintenance module helps in building the mapping between
the Post-controlled repository and the ontology repository, and showing the
statistic data of one given keyword. Users can decide which concept in the
ontology the keyword should relate to, according to their understanding,
experience, or type of the document, and so on. The statistic information is
used to help annotators to decide if they should add a keyword to the
ontology. In this way, we support the evolution of ontology.

4.3   User Interface of ConAnnotator

The user interface of ConAnnotator is divided into 5 parts: Function Bar,
Concept Browser (including the Keyword Browser), Resource Annotation

Editor, Resource Browser, and Resource List. The interface is showed in Figure 3.

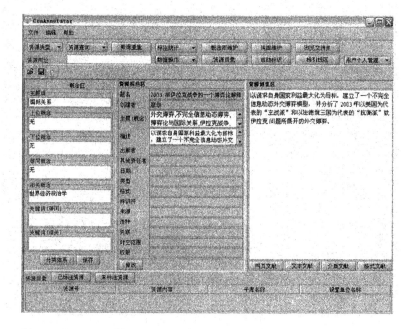

Figure 3. User Interface of ConAnnotator

5.   FUTURE WORK

In the future, firstly we will develop a content annotation module. This module will help us create annotation at the content level and save them, thereby provide more information about not only the whole document but also its content, and then these documents can support applications more freely and adequately. Secondly, we will improve our IE algorithm and try to make it more intelligent.

6.   CONCLUSIONS

ConAnnotator is an annotation system for facilitating the annotation process. It helps users, Digital Library Team members at present, to create annotation easily and efficiently. The annotated documents are connected to the domain ontology, thus they can support applications based on Semantic Web. It plays an important role in the CODERS, and has been proven to be practical. We will improve ConAnnotator both in function and efficiency in future, to make it more universal and perfect.

REFERENCES

1. T. B. Lee, J. Hendler and L. Ora, *The Semantic Web*, The Scientific American, May 200.
2. M. Li, D. Wang, X. Du, S. Wang, "° Ot d ogy Constr ucti o for Semantic Web: A Role-based Collaborative Development Method"∓*Proceedings of the 7th Asia Pacific Web Conference (APWeb 2005), Lecture Notes in Computer Science series 3399*, Shanghai, China, 2005, pp.609-619.
3. He Hu and Xiaoyong Du, ConAnnotator: Ontology-aided Collaborative Annotation System, Proc. Of the 10th International Conference on CSCW in Design (CSCWD 06), IEEE Press, Nanjing, China, 2006
4. M. Vargas-Vera, E. Motta, J. Domingue, etc., MnM: Ontology Driven Semi-Automatic and Automatic Support for Semantic Mark-up. The 13th International Conference on Knowledge Engineering and Management (EKAW 2002), 2002, pp379-391
5. S. Mukherjee, G.Z. Yang, and I. V. Ramakrishnan. Automatic Annotation of Content-Rich HTML Documents: Structural and Semantic Analysis. In *Proceedings of the Second International Semantic Web Con-ference (ISWC 2003)*, Sanibel Island, Florida, October, 2003. pp. 533-549.
6. K. Crammer, Y. Singer, "° Ont he al garit h rhci ngl c nert ati o of multi-class kernel-based vector machines"∓*Machine Learning Research*, 2:265-292, 2001.
7. J. Frank, M. Radermacher, P. Penczek, etc,. SPIDER and WEB: Processing and Visualization of Images in 3D Electron Microscopy and Related Fields. J. *Structural Biol.*, 116, 190-199 (1996)
8. M. Erdmann, A. Maedche, H. Schnurr, and S. Staab. From manual to semi-automatic semantic annotation: About ontology-based text annotation tools. In P. Buitelaar and K. Hasida, editors, Proceedings of the COLING 2000 Workshop on Semantic Annotation and Intelligent Content, August 2000.
9. J. Heflin and J. Hendler. Searching the web with shoe. In AAAI-2000 Workshop on AI for Web Search, 2000.
10. T. Leonard and H. Glaser. Large scale acquisition and maintenance from the web without source access. http://semannot2001.aifb.unikarlsruhe.de/positionpapers/Leonard.pdf, 2001.
11. M. Vargas-Vera, E. Motta, J. Domingue, M. Lanzoni, A. Stutt, and F. Ciravegna. MnM: Ontology driven semi-automatic and automatic support for semantic markup. In The 13th International Conference on Knowledge Engineering and Management (EKAW 2002), 2002.
12. J. Kahan, M. R. Koivunen, E. P. Hommeaux, and R. Swickd. Annotea: An Open RDF Infrastructure for Shared Web Annotations. In *Proceedings of the Tenth International World Wide Web Conference*, Hong Kong, China, May, 2001. pp. 623-632.

SIMULATING AGENT EMOTION IN A VIRTUAL SUPER MARKET
Utility Function Based Approach

Qing Yu [1], WenJie Wang [1], ZhongZhi Shi [2], Fen Lin [1,2]

1. Graduate School of Chinese Academy of Science, Beijing 100039 ,yuq@ics.ict.ac.cn

2. Key Laboratory of Intelligent Information Processing, Institute of Computing Technology,Chinese Academy of Sciences, Beijing 100080, China

Abstract: This paper reports a method of simulate an Agent emotion in a Virtual Super Market environment. Utility Function is the key to depict people's emotion especially in the satisfaction feelings. This method finished the process from the emotion to the decision. Agent will act emotionally according to the Utility.

Key words: Virtual Super Market, Utility Function, Lagrange Interpolating Polynomial

1.   INTRODUCTION

Our project is a multi-agent system – agent based virtual super market, what we try our best to do is to make all the agents act as the real person who cares about the financial situation and also we aim to simulate a smart manager agent. The manager's decision is based on the huge and exact history data. On some level, agent's emotion is a crucial factor affected his behavior. Although we simplified the emotion calculating, you can see that it does its work very well.

Please use the following format when citing this chapter:

Yu, Q., Wang, W., Shi, Z., Lin, F., 2006, in IFIP International Federation for Information Processing, Volume 228, Intelligent Information Processing III, eds. Z. Shi, Shimohara K., Feng D., (Boston: Springer), pp. 543–548.

2.   THE VIRTUAL SUPER MARKET

The Virtual Super Market[10][12] gives birth to three different kinds of Agents[9][11], customer agents, employee agents and manager agents. In this project, we use the utility function and the interpolation formula to simulate the Employee Agents' Emotion in the salary satisfaction feelings.

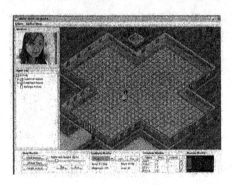

3.   SIMULATING EMPLOYEE'S EMOTION

The employee concerns himself with the pay level. Firstly, we will talk about his salary utility function. Then we will talk about the behavior affected by the utility function. Generally speaking, we follow two steps to get the emotion simulating.

3.1   Step one: salary utility function.

According to Daniel Bernoulli's solution of St. Petersburg Paradox[6][7]: (i) that people's utility from wealth, u (w), is not linearly related to wealth (w) but rather increases at a decreasing rate - the famous idea of diminishing marginal utility, $u'(y)>0$ and $u''(y)<0$; (ii) that a person's valuation of a risky venture is not the expected return of that venture, but rather the expected utility from that venture. This is shown as Figure 1.

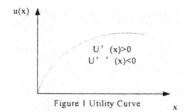

Figure 1 Utility Curve

We can see that the employs satisfaction feeling function can be defined according to the following consideration:

1) We shall talk about the values between [a, b].

2) How can we get the Utility Function? Firstly, we know that the curve can be approach a parabola[1]. Secondly, we will ask the employee many questions like:

- How about $c a month? $c \in [a, b]$
- How much money could satisfy you? Maybe the answer is d, $d \in [a, b]$

The answer should be formed into percent format. Then we get a set of numbers:

X	a	c	d	b
Y	U(a)	U(c)	U(d)	U(b)

Then we use the Lagrange Interpolating Polynomial [1][2][13]. The Lagrange interpolating polynomial is the polynomial $P(x)$ of degree $n-1$ that passes through the n points $(x_1, y_1 = f(x_1))$, $(x_2, y_2 = f(x_2))$, ..., $(x_n, y_n = f(x_n))$, and is given by

$$P(x) = \sum_{j=1}^{n} P_j(x) \quad \text{where} \quad P_j(x) = y_j \prod_{\substack{k=1 \\ k \neq j}}^{n} \frac{x - x_k}{x_j - x_k}$$

Given a triplet (a, c, d) and the respective functional values (U (a), U(c), U(d)), If currently the employee's pay is $e a month, then we can figure out the utility value by calculating:

$$u(e) = \frac{(e-c)(e-d)}{(a-c)(a-d)} \times u(a) + \frac{(e-c)(e-d)}{(c-a)(c-d)} \times u(c) + \frac{(e-c)(e-d)}{(d-a)(d-c)} \times u(d)$$

Finally, we can get the employee happiness degree u(e).

3.2   Step two: Behaviors affected by the emotion.

So, what will happen if the salary does not satisfy the employee? Asking for giving a raise or not, what is his choice?[8]

We firstly turn to the concept of "risk aversion"[3][4][5] which, intuitively, implies that when facing choices with comparable returns, agents tend to choose the less-risky alternative, a construction we owe largely to Milton Friedman and Leonard J. Savage (1948).

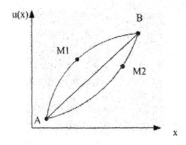

Figure 3 New Utility Function

Point M1 shows the agent is Risk-Averse, on the contrary, point M2 is Risk-Loving, and this agent loves risk. In this case, he will ask for raises. If M2 is chosen, he will not ask for it.

In this project the happiness degree can be calculated by the Lagrange Interpolating Polynomial mentioned above. The angry degree is caused by comparing with other's salary degree. In this project, the angry degree is simplified by the following formula:

Given the angry degree, $f(x_0, x_1, ...x_n)$, x_i represent the employee's salary, x_0 represents his own salary.

$$f(x_0, x_1, ...x_n) = \frac{\sum_{i=1}^{n}(x_i - x_0)}{(n-1)x_0}$$

If $f(x_0, x_1, ...x_n)$ >0.4 this employee will reset his salary utility. Then according to his risk attitude, he will ask for raises or not.

Suppose that we have three real people playing the employee. We can see their faces through the camera shown in the up-left corner to recognize who he is. They should answer two questions:

a) How about $600 a month? $600 \in [500, 1000.]$

b) How about $800 a month?

The answer is shown below:

questions	Employee A	Employee B	Employee C
(i) $600	0.55	0.7	0.5
(ii) $800	0.8	0.9	0.7

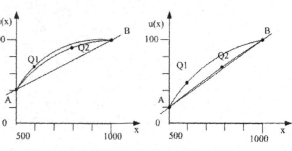

Employ A's utility   Employ B's utility   Employee C's utility

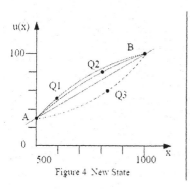

Figure 4 New State

Currently the salary set is (510, 850, 600), f_A (510,850,600)=0.435. His angry degree is 0.435 > 0.4, He will think about his new salary amount he wants, suppose that it is 825, the satisfaction degree is 60%. Let's look at his utility curve:

Now his new state is Q3, He has changed into a risk loving people, so he will ask the manager to give him a raise.

4.   FUTURE WORK

Here we build up the employee's emotion model, and there are other factors affecting the emotion like the workload, the existing emotion model is too simple to depict a real people. And the customer's emotion model is another import part in this project. This is what we will try to do in our future work.

5.   REFERENCES

1.   ChengSen Lin. *Numerical Implementation.* Science Press. P122-126
2.   Abramowitz, M. and Stegun, I. A. (Eds.). *Handbook of Mathematical Functions with Formulas, Graphs, and Mathematical Tables, 9th printing.* New York: Dover, pp. 878-879 and 883, 1972.

3.   M. Friedman and L.P. Savage (1948) "The Utility Analysis of Choices involving Risk", *Journal of Political Economy*, Vol. 56, p.279-304

4.   H. Markowitz (1952) "The Utility of Wealth", *Journal of Political Economy*, Vol. 60, p.151-8.

5.   K.J. Arrow (1965) *Aspects of the Theory of Risk-Bearing*. Helsinki: Yrjö Hahnsson Foundation.

6.   "Specimen Theoriae Novae de Mensara Sortis", 1738, *Commentarii Academiae Scientiarum Imperialis Petropolitanae*. (trans. in 1954, *Econometrica*).

7.   "Diiudicatio maxime probabilis plurium obferuation um difcrepantium atque verificillima inductio inde form anda", *Acta Scientarium Imperialis Petropolitanae* (trans. in 1961, *Biometrika*).

8.   Lin Padgham, Guy Taylor,"A System for Modeling Agents having emotion and Personality", Department of Computer Science ,RMIT University, Melbourne, Australia.

9.   Zhongzhi Shi, Haijun Zhang, and Mingkai Dong. Mage: Multi-agent environment. In ICCNMC-03, 2003.

10. Intelligent Science Website http://www.intsci.ac.cn

11. AgentCities, http://www.agentcities.net/.

12. N.R.Jennings and M.J.Wooldridge. Applications of intelligent agents. In Agent Technology, Foundations, Applications, and Markets, pages 3-28.

13. Eric W. Weisstein et al. "Lagrange Interpolating Polynomial." From MathWorld--A Wolfram   Web   Resource. http://mathworld.wolfram.com/LagrangeInterpolatingPolynomial.html

DIGGING HIGH RISK DEFECTS OUT IN SOFTWARE ENGINEERING

Jin-Cherng Lin, Kuo-Chiang Wu

Abstract: Data mining implies "digging through tons of data" to uncover implicit information. Software defect is an essential characteristic of software development process, offering much information about software quality assurance. Based on the information supplied by defects, it can help a software team with capability of software quality assurance. In order to dig through lots of defects to uncover implicit information of defects, this paper integrates PCA and DA, combined with the relationship among each defect attribute index, and then we can dig critical factor out of software defects. These critical factors are the vital few defects affecting software quality, warning programmer to stress concentration on getting rid of these vital few defects.

Key words: Prime Components Analysis (PCA) and Discriminate Analysis (DA)

1.   INTRODUCTION

The earlier defect is discovered in software, the lower the developing cost is. The higher the software quality is, the lower the maintenance cost after software released is.

Defect is the byproduct in software development process. Usually, defect may result in software products not satisfying requirement of user. Defect indicates error existed in program, for example, syntax error, spelling error or wrong program statement. Defect may be also errors existed in design, even in requirement and specification or other documentations. However, software defect is an elemental feature of software development process, offering much information about software quality. Based on the information supplied by defects, it can help a team with capability of SQA (Software

Please use the following format when citing this chapter:

Lin, J.-C., Wu, K.-C., 2006, in IFIP International Federation for Information Processing, Volume 228, Intelligent Information Processing III, eds. Z. Shi, Shimohara K., Feng D., (Boston: Springer), pp. 549–554.

Quality Assurance). SQA is an important strategy for safeguarding the design, production and support of software. It is imperative that all defects to be dug out for SQA.

Data mining is the process of analyzing data from different perspectives and summarizing it into useful information. Data Mining can be defined as "The nontrivial extraction of implicit, previously unknown, and potentially useful information from data" [1] and "The science of extracting useful information from large data sets or databases" [2]. Data mining, also referred to Knowledge Discovery in Database (KDD), is a pivotal step involving the extraction of interesting patterns (such as knowledge rules, constraints, and regularities) from a set of data sources. The patterns obtained are used to describe concepts, analyze associations, build classification and regression models, cluster data, model trends in time-series, and detect outliers. Likewise, the goal of this paper is to construct defects mining for software quality to analysis all defects, indicating the critical factors that affect the software quality.

The software development process is complicated and uncertain. Of factors all, the most are surrounded by defect problems, and therefore it is necessary to collect data of defect and have statistical analysis, especially in defect mining. This paper is trying to solve issues relating to the defect mining for software quality. This paper employs PCA and DA as techniques of defects mining in order to dig out vital few defects affecting software quality assurance, warning programmer to stress concentration on getting rid of these vital few defects.

2.   EXISTENCE OF DEFECTS DEPENDENCY IN COLLECTING DATA

If testers do not care about accuracy at classifying defects, programmer will not precisely find location of defects. Consequently, in software testing process, tester will classify found defects so as to effectively manage defects.

Perhaps testers classify defects according to their subjective judgment, which causes dependency among different defect attributes. In other words, testers sometimes classify a certain kind of defects into different defect attributes. A certain kind of defects is classed as class A, but the same kind defect is classed as class B in another instances. The reason why they mistake is tester forgets or mistakes the judging rule of classifying in different instance; that is to say, tester is busy at working in searching and classifying defects, so it is unavoidable for tester sometime cannot see where they went wrong. In short, too many classifying rules of defect attributes will bring about many mistaking chance. Consequently, defects classifying is too complex (many) to easily manage them, but too rough (few) to precisely locate them.

Another problem is that different defect attributes are caused by the same error and different defect attributes have the same defect frequency. This puzzling situation is like a ripple effect; for instance, defect in called subprogram introduced new defects to calling program. Besides, many other conditions also cause ripple effect Maybe only one source defect exists in source program, but they introduce a lot of new born defects. Repeated calculation of defect frequency will cause redundant information, while redundant information will cause errors in subsequent statistical analysis.

Dependency and redundant information should be overcome at once. PCA is a multivariate statistical analysis, which can reduce dependency (or collinear) and redundant information among different defect attributes (refer to [3]). Furthermore, PCA is able to transform many indexes to few independent comprehensive indexes. The nature of PCA is to make the high dimension system best integrated and to avoid objectively determining weight of each index (refer to [3]). Considering many factors affecting defect attribute, PCA is a relatively feasible method, especially for handling data dependency.

DA is also a multivariate statistical analysis, which a classified and predicate original data (refer to [4-6]). DA is classified and predicated by discriminate function, and the discriminate coefficient of discriminate function reflects the importance of the factor in discriminate function (refer to [4-6]). For example, the discriminate coefficient of erroneous logic is much greater than other factors, which is the major factor to evaluate the whole software quality. The discriminate coefficient of erroneous specification is much smaller than other factors, and no consideration can be made in evaluating the whole software quality. We can effectively find vital few defect attributes by discriminate coefficient of DA.

3.   CASE STUDY OF DEFECT MINING

This case is a plan for defects management, whose goal is to design an approach, indicating the key factor affecting software quality. Vital few defects are the key factor of software quality; therefore concentration should be stressed on vital few defects. First we will study how to standardize the gathered defect data and find out five prime components of defect through

PCA. Then establish discriminate function by five prime components of defect differentiates the importance of each defect attribute, and then vital few defects attributes can be found through discriminate function. Furthermore, vital few components were found by helps of vital few defects attributes. In vital few components, we will dig higher risk class out in OO environment (see section 4).

In the first column of table 1 is an acronym of defects attributes, which will be explained in table 2. In other words, there is a correspondence of abbreviation between table 1 and table 2. The other columns are the value of standardized original data (see section 3.1).

3.1   Standardized original data

In Table 1, the original data is obtained by number of defect density (defects/KLOC), complexity, or other method. A method for collection of data was determined by tester. In other words, different measuring methods will apply different dimensions, so we should pay attention to eliminating the effects of different dimensions. Therefore, we need to standardize original data. This case achieved normalization of original data by **Z-score**, which has an expression like:

$$Z = \frac{X - \bar{X}}{\hat{\alpha}}$$

Where X =original data $\bar{X}$ =mean value $\hat{\alpha}$ =standard deviation. Before the following PCA and DA treatment, original data should be calculated by Z-score first (see Table 1).

3.2   Prime Component Analysis of Defect Attributes

Originally there are 43 defect attributes in this case. However, some defect attributes rarely happen, so they are not listed in statistical analysis, with only 29 defect attributes listed in statistical analysis (see Table 1).

Then, based on correlation matrix of evaluation index, PCA can be conducted after VARIMAX rotation. The communalities of each index in defect type got from factor loading matrix indicate the total variance contribution that each index has made to defect attribute, and from this we can get index weights. Calculating the percentage of communalities in total communalities and then transforming the weight to number value between 0 and 1, we get the index weight.

PCA for the defect attribute in this project demonstrates that eigenvalues of five primary components are greater than 1, and is maintained for its explanation to most of total variances (75%)(see Table 2). From communalities in each defect attributes, we can see five primary components can explain the variance of LE, IOLE, MLT, BTSUI, DIDI, LSI and VIFNP, whose variance is greater than 90%; it can explain the variance of BTI, LPO, MCT, LAOS, WAOP and ID, whose variance is greater than 80%; it can explain the variance of IVT, VRWN, LPWI and DIND, whose variance is greater than 70%; it can explain the variance of DCII, DHE, ODW, MSL, VEWL, CPWS and ASD, whose variance is greater than 60%; while the variance explanation of five prime component FSWDW, IPS, AD, RLWD and WVBC is less than 60%. It is thus clear that five prime component can explain the variance of most defect attribute index.

Prime components arranged in order according to eigenvalues. The first prime component (PCA1), together with LE, IOLE, LAOS, LSI, MLT, MCT, BTI, BTSUI, DIDI, VIFNP, IVT,VRWN, LPWIS, DHE,DIDN,CPWS and WVBC, has relatively high factor loading (greater than 0.6), moreover, these indexes have obvious relevance with erroneous logic. Therefore, we call the first prime component erroneous logic factor. The second prime component (PCA2), together with IPS and MSL, has relatively high positive loading, and it has negative loading with DCII. All these indexes demonstrates erroneous specifications index, therefore, we call the second prime component (PCA2) as erroneous specifications factor. The third prime component (PCA3), together with FSWDN, VEWN, DDW and RLWD, has relatively high factor loading, of which VEWL, RLW, FSWDW and ODW have obvious relevance with erroneous data accessing. Therefore, we call this prime component erroneous data accessing. The forth prime component (PCA4), together with WAOP and LPO, has relatively high factor loading, which demonstrates erroneous arithmetic. Therefore, we call it as erroneous arithmetic factor. The fifth prime component (PCA5), together with ID and AD, has relatively high factor loading, and is called erroneous documentation.

We can get the scores of each measurement factor based on coefficient of factor scores of PCA and standardization of original variable. Table 3 (the second phase of our case) shows prime component scoring of defect types under different milestones. Variance analysis demonstrates that in five prime components only erroneous arithmetic factor doesn't have obvious differences under different milestones, while the other four primary components have obvious differences under different milestones.

3.3   Discriminate Analysis of Defect Type

Stepwise discriminate analysis in discriminate analysis goes to discriminate function by the smallest Wilks statistic. The variable in discriminate function F is used as the criterion of screening variables. When F>3.84, the variable is introduced; or when F<2.71, the variable is removed [4][5][6].

Stepwise discriminate analysis of five primary components demonstrates that erroneous arithmetic factor <2.71 among different milestones, therefore factor of erroneous arithmetic is removed from discriminate function, and the whole software quality discriminate function is:

LSI, VIFNP, MCT, ODW and ASD can be screened as software quality evaluation index, of which LE, BTSUI and LSI are key indexes to indicate software quality.

$Y_{TOTAL\ QUALITY}$ =1.9298* erroneous logic -0.0589* erroneous specification -0.4699* erroneous data accessing -0.4498* erroneous documentation

Discriminate coefficients of a certain factor demonstrate its importance in discriminate function. Discriminate coefficients of erroneous logic are far greater than other factors, and it is the major factor to evaluate the whole software quality. Discriminate coefficients of erroneous specification are much less than other factors, and no consideration can be made in evaluating the whole software quality.

Stepwise discriminate analysis of defect attributes index that composes erroneous logic factors demonstrates that the discriminate coefficient of LE, BTSUI and LSI is relatively high and can be regarded as erroneous logic evaluation index, and discriminate function is as follows:
Y_{LOGIC} =-3.47880* LE+1.6776* BTSUI + 1.2477* LSI + 0.5385*VFFNP + 0.3766* MCT + 0.3037* DIDN + 0.2578* DHE + 0.1586* LSI

Stepwise discriminate analysis of defect attributes index that composes erroneous data accessing factors demonstrates that OWD has relatively high discriminate coefficient and can be regarded as erroneous data accessing evaluation index, and discriminate function is as follows:
$Y_{DATA\ ACCESS}$ =0.9087* OWD + 0.3178* VEWL

Stepwise discriminate analysis of defect attributes index that composes erroneous documentation factors demonstrates that ASD has relatively high discriminate coefficient and can be regarded as erroneous documentation evaluation index, and discriminate function is as follows:
$Y_{DOCUMENTATION}$ =0.8978* ASD + 0.4187* AD + 0.2379* ID

You can get the full paper from us by e-mail (d9206006@ms2.ttu.edu.tw).

VISUAL CLUSTERING OF COMPLEX NETWORK BASED ON NONLINEAR DIMENSION REDUCTION

Jianyu Li[1], Shuzhong Yang[2]
[1]School of Computer and Software, Communication University of China, 100024, Beijing, China
[2]School of Computer and Information Technology, Beijing Jiaotong University, 100044, Beijing, China

Abstract: In this paper, we present a new visual clustering algorithm inspired by nonlinear dimension reduction technique: Isomap. The algorithm firstly defines a new graph distance between any two nodes in complex networks and then applies the distance matrix to Isomap and projects all nodes into a two dimensional plane. The experiments prove that the projected nodes emerge clear clustering property which is hidden in original complex networks and the distances between any two nodes reflect their close or distant relationships.

Key words: complex network, visual clustering, Isomap, graph distance.

1. INTRODUCTION

In recent years, there is a growing interest in evolving complex networks. Small world characteristic [1] and scale-free characteristic [2] are the two most important characteristics of complex networks. Many networks in real world not only have small world characteristic and scale-free characteristic, but also have community structure property. The description of the community structure of complex networks has also been one of the focuses of attention in recent years [3, 4, 5]. Visual clustering of complex networks can help us find the community structure hidden in the networks, understand the networks better and predict the behavior of networks in future. Since complex networks are usually characterized by various graphs, we can realize the visual clustering of complex networks by using the similar methods of graphs.

Please use the following format when citing this chapter:

Li, J., Yang, S., 2006, in IFIP International Federation for Information Processing, Volume 228, Intelligent Information Processing III, eds. Z. Shi, Shimohara K., Feng D., (Boston: Springer), pp. 555–560.

To realize the visual clustering of a graph, we must firstly define an effective measurement of distances between nodes. So how to define effective distances becomes a crucial issue for the visual clustering of graph. Then we need choose an appropriate projection technique to layout the result of visual clustering in a plane or a three dimensional space. Dimension reduction techniques have been widely developed as the projection techniques up to now [6, 7, 8, 9]. Since Isomap [9] can keep the global geometric property through estimating geodesic distances between pairwise nodes, we will choose it to realize the layout of visual clustering of complex works in this paper.

The rest of the paper is organized as follows. In Section 2, we show how to realize the visual clustering of complex works using nonlinear dimension reduction technique Isomap. In Section 3, some performance experiments are presented. Finally, discussions and future work are given in Section 4.

2.   VISUAL CLUSTERING ALGORITHM

2.1   Quantification of Distances in Graph

A graph $G = (V, E)$ consists of a finite set V of nodes and a finite set E of edges with $E \in V^{(2)}$, where $V^{(2)}$ is the set of all subsets of V which have exactly two elements.

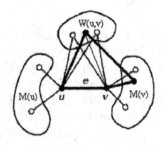

Figure 1. Dividing neighbors of edge (u, v)

According to the above graph definition and edge strength definition in [10], the pairwise distances between nodes can be computed through the following steps. Given an edge $(u, v) \in E$(Figure.1), we can compute its strength by dividing neighbors of u or v into three distinct subsets. Firstly, denote by $M(u)$ the set of neighbors of u that are not neighbors of v (excluding v). Secondly, denote by $M(v)$ the set of neighbors of v that are not neighbors of u (excluding u). Finally, denote by W(u, v) the set of common neighbors to u and v. Denote by r(A, B) the number of edges linking nodes in the set A to nodes in the set B such that s(A, B)=r(A, B)/|A||B| (|A| is the number of nodes in A) defines the proportion of existing edges among all possible edges connecting nodes of A and B. By above definition, any edge connecting two of the subsets M(u), M(v) or W(u, v) is part of a cycle of length 4 going through the edge (u, v) (see Figure. 1, the cycle labeled by thick lines). Note that all cycles of length 4 are captured this way. Finally, we define the ratio |W(u, v)|/(|M(u)|+|W(u, v)|+|M(v)|) as a ratio related to the proportion of cycles of length 3 containing the edge (u, v). Note that there are as many of these cycles as there are nodes in W(u, v). Then the strength of an edge is given by computing:

$$strength(u,v) = s(M(u), W(u, v)) + s(W(u, v), M(v)) + s(W(u, v)) +$$
$$s(M(u), M(v)) + |W(u, v)|/(|M(u)|+|W(u, v)|+|M(v)|) \tag{1}$$

(Note: we need to set s(A) = 2r(A,A)/(|A|(|A|-1)) when computing the proportion of edges connecting a set to itself). Then we can use the inverse of strength to define the pairwise distances between nodes. If the strength between two nodes is zero, the distance between them is infinity; otherwise the distance equals to $1/strength(u,v)$.

2.2   Visual Clustering Using Isomap

The main idea behind the Isomap (isometric feature mapping) algorithm is to perform classical MDS [7] to map data points from their high-dimensional input space to low-dimensional coordinates of a nonlinear manifold. The key contribution is to compute the MDS pairwise distances not in the input Euclidean space, but in the geodesic space of the manifold. The actual geodesic distances are approximated by a sequence of short hops between neighboring sample points. Finally, MDS is applied to the geodesic distances to find a set of low-dimensional points with similar pairwise distances. We use Isomap to visualize the complex networks because it can keep the global structural properties hidden in them.

Now we list the whole visual clustering algorithm as follows:

1. Quantify the distances between any two nodes according to equation (1) and get the distance matrix D= { $d(i, j)$ };

2. Using Isomap technique to projected all nodes into a plane. The detailed procedure is:

1) Suppose the quantified distances as the distances of some points on high dimensional manifold M;

2) Determine which points are neighbors on the manifold M by identifying their K nearest neighbors, based on the distances $d(i, j)$ between

pairs of points (i, j) in manifold M. These neighborhood relations are represented as a weighted graph, **G**, over the data points, with edges of weight $d(i, j)$ between neighbors;

3) Estimate the geodesic distances $d_M(i, j)$ between all pairs of points on the manifold, M, by computing approximations as the shortest path distances $d_G(i, j)$ in the graph G. Then the final matrix of graph distances $D_G = \{d_G(i, j)\}$ will contain the shortest path distance between all pairs of points in G;

4) Apply classical MDS to the matrix D_G to construct an embedding of the data in a two dimensional plane;

5) Draw the embedding data points in a plane.

3.   EXPERIMENTAL ANALYSIS

In the literature [11] the authors presented an energy model for visual graph clustering and proved that their LinLog model had better results than previous models. In this paper we will compare our model with LinLog model. Since lack of real world data only two typical kinds of artificial complex networks are used: structured complex network and non-structured complex network (WS small world network). The structured complex network is produced by the model presented in [12] and includes 4 communities and every community has 40 nodes. The non-structured complex network is produced by the WS small world model in [1] and includes 200 nodes. Fig. 2 and Fig. 3 list the visual clustering results of two methods, respectively.

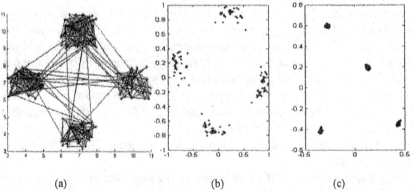

(a)   (b)   (c)

Figure. 2. Visual clustering of constructed complex network. (a) Original network; (b) The result of our model; (c) The result of LinLog model

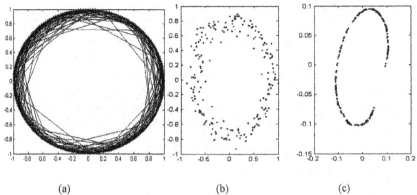

(a)   (b)   (c)

Figure. 3. Visual clustering of WS small world network. (a) Original network; (b) The result
of our model; (c) The result of LinLog model

In Fig.2 (a) original network consists of four communities. Our model
and LinLog model both visualize the network into four communities (Fig.2
(b) and (c)). But it is easy to see that our model can make clustering structure
of complex network clearer and project the nodes more uniformly. In
contrast to our model, LinLog model overlaps the nodes in the same
community after projection so that we can't distinguish them. However,
when applied to WS small world networks (Fig. 3), our method emerges
distinct advantages compared with LinLog model: our model can keep both
the local and global clustering property of small world networks but LinLog
model can not. That is to say that the visual clustering result of our model
not only preserves the adjacency between nodes but also preserves the
original circular distribution. Compared to our model, LinLog model can not
keep the circular distribution because its visual clustering result emerges
split. The phenomenon can be explained as: the distance of LinLog model
between two nodes is only proportional to the coupling, but our distance also
considers the neighborhood of two nodes and the following estimation of
geodesic distance extends the Euclidean distance. So when the clustering
structure of complex networks is less distinct, our visual clustering model
has more advantage than LinLog model.

In addition, regular and random network based on ER model are also
used to compare the performance between our model and LinLog model.
Our model also has better performance in node distribution after projection
than LinLog model. But the advantage is less distinctive because of degree
homogeneity of network nodes.

4.   DISCUSSIONS

In this paper we present a new visual clustering method. Our contribution includes two aspects: introducing a new measurement of distances between nodes in a graph and using nonlinear dimension reduction technique Isomap to realize the layout of complex networks. The experimental analysis shows that our method has better performance than other visual clustering methods and the resultant nodes in graph have more clear clustering property.

ACKNOWLEDGEMENTS

The research is supported by the National Natural Science Foundation of China under Grant Nos. 60373029 and the National Research Foundation for the Doctoral Program of Higher Education of China under Grant Nos. 20050004001.

REFERENCES

1. Watts, D., and Strogatz, S.: Collective dynamics of 'small-world' networks. Nature 393 (1998) 440-442.
2. Albert-Laszlo Barabasi, Reka Albert.: Emergence of scaling in random networks, Science 286 (1999) 509-512.
3. Girvan, M. and Newman, M. E. J.: Community structure in social and biological networks. Proceedings of the National Academy of Sciences of the United States of America (PNAS) 99(12) (2002) 7821-7826.
4. MEJ Newman and M. Girvan.: Finding and Evaluating Community Structure in Networks. Phys. Rev. E 69, 026113 (2004).
5. MEJ Newman.: Detecting Community Structure in Networks. Eur. Phys. J. B 38, (2004) 321-330.
6. J. Karhunen, J. Joutsensalo.: Generalizations of principal component analysis, optimization problems, and neural networks. Neural Networks, Vol. 8, No. 4, (1995) 549-562.
7. T.F. Cox, M.A.A. Cox.: Multidimensional Scaling. Chapman & Hall, (2000).
8. S.T. Roweis, L.K. Saul.: "Nonlinear Dimensionality Reduction by Locally Linear Embedding". Science 290 (2000) 2323-2326.
9. J.B. Tenenbaum, V.d.Silva, J.C. Langford.: "A Global Geometric Framework for Nonlinear Dimensionality Reduction". Science 290 (2000) 2319-2323.
10. Auber, D., Chiricota, Y., Jourdan, F., and Melancon, G.: Multiscale visualization of small world networks. In Proceedings of the 2003 IEEE Symposium on Information Visualization (2003) 75-81.
11. Noack, A.: An energy model for visual graph clustering. In Proc. 11th International Symposium on Graph Drawing, LNCS 2912 (2004) 425-436.
12. Chunguang Li and Philip K. Maini.: An evolving network model with community structure. Journal of Physics A: Mathematical and General. 38 (2005) 9741-9749.

REDUCED ATTRIBUTE ORIENTED HANDLING OF INCONSISTENCY IN DECISION GENERATION

Yucai Feng, Wenhai Li and Zehua Lv
Department of Computer Science,
Huazhong University of Science and Technology,
Wuhan 430074, Hubei, China,
lwhaymail@21cn.com

Abstract   Due to the discarded attributes, the effectual condition classes of the decision rules are highly different. To provide a unified evaluative measure, the derivation of each rule is depicted by the reduced attributes with a layered manner. Therefore, the inconsistency is divided into two primary categories in terms of the reduced attributes. We introduce the notion of joint membership function wrt. the effectual joint attributes, and a classification method extended from the default decision generation framework is proposed to handle the inconsistency.

Keywords: reduced attributes, reduced layer, joint membership function, rough set

1. Introduction

Classification in rough set theory [1] is mainly composed of two components: *feature extraction* and *decision synthesis*. Many researches focus on the construction of classification algorithm, such as probabilistic method [2], decision trees[3] and parameterized rule inducing method [4]. The purpose of these methods is to generate rules with high precision and simple expression. In view of the comprehensiveness and conciseness of the training rules, many discernibility matrices based rule extracting methods [5] concerning both approximate inducing and accurate decision are proposed to classify the objects previously unseen. We would like to point out the dynamic reduct [6], variable thresholds based hierarchical classifier [7]. The synthesis methods place emphasis on how to efficiently resolve the conflicts of training rules for the test objects, such as the stable coverings based synthesis [6], hierarchical classifier [7] and lower frequency first synthesis [8].

This paper, based on the default rule extracting framework [5], analyzes the conflicts [9] with two categories of inconsistent rules, and a synthesis stratagem with the notion of joint membership function is proposed to resolve the inconsistency [10]. In the sequel, a report from our experiments with the medical data sets is given to indicate the availability of our classification method.

Please use the following format when citing this chapter:

Feng, Y., Li, W., Lv, Z., 2006, in IFIP International Federation for Information Processing, Volume 228, Intelligent Information Processing III, eds. Z. Shi, Shimohara K., Feng D., (Boston: Springer), pp. 561–568.

2.   Rough set preliminaries

The starting point of rough set based data analysis is an *information system* denoted by IS, which is a pair $\mathcal{A}(U, A)$ [1]. An IS is a *decision system* when the attributes A can be further classified into disjoint sets of condition attributes C and decision attributes D. With every subset of attributes $B \subseteq A$ in $\mathcal{A}$, the *indiscernibility relation* denoted by $IND(B)$ is defined as follows:

$$IND(B) = \{(x, y) \in U \times U | \forall_{a \in B}, (a(x) = a(y))\}. \tag{1}$$

By $U/IND(B)$ we indicate the set of all equivalence classes in $IND(B)$. Two objects $x, y \in U$ with equation (1) held are indistinguishable from each other. In other words, each object in the universe can be expressed by its own equivalence class $E_i \in U/IND(B)$. For a set of objects $X \subseteq U$, based on $U/IND(B)$, the lower and upper approximations denoted by $\underline{B}X$ and $\overline{B}X$ are $\cup \{E \in U/IND(B) | E \subseteq X\}$ and $\{E \subseteq U/IND(B) | E \cap X \neq \emptyset\}$ respectively. For an information system $\mathcal{A}(U, A)$, the *discernibility matrix* denoted by $M_D(\mathcal{A})$ is expressed as an $n \times n$ matrix $\{m_D(i, j)\}$, where $n = |U/IND(A)|$ and

$$m_D(i, j) = \{a \in A | \forall_{i,j=1,2...n}, (a(E_i) \neq a(E_j))\}, \tag{2}$$

which implies the set of attributes of A which can distinguish between the two classes $E_i, E_j \in U/IND(A)$. For a decision system $\mathcal{A}(U, C \cup \{d\})$, the *relative discernibility matrix* $M'_D(\mathcal{A})$ is composed of $m'_D(i, j) = \emptyset$ if $d(E_i) = d(E_j)$ and $m'_D(i, j) = m_D(i, j) \backslash \{d\}$, otherwise.

Following this, a unique boolean variable $\overline{a}$ is associated with each attribute a, and $\overline{m}_D(i, j)$ is transformed from $m_D(i, j)$ in terms of $\overline{a}$. Therefore, the *discernibility function* of the attribute set A in an information system $\mathcal{A}(U, A)$ is defined by:

$$f(A) = \bigwedge_{i,j \in \{1...n\}} \vee \overline{m}_D(E_i, E_j), \tag{3}$$

where $n = |U/IND(A)|$, and the *relative discernibility function* $f'(C)$ in $\mathcal{A}(U, C \cup \{d\})$ is constructed from $\overline{M}'_D(\mathcal{A})$ like equation (3). Similarly, for $n = |U/IND(C)|$, the *local discernibility function* of any $E_i \in U/IND(C)$ is given as:

$$f'(E_i, C) = \bigwedge_{j \in \{1...n\}} \vee \overline{m}'_D(E_i, E_j). \tag{4}$$

For $\mathcal{A}(U, A)$, a *dispensable* attribute a of A implies $IND(A) = IND(A \backslash \{a\})$, and its counterpart called the *indispensable* has an opposite implication. A *reduct* of A denoted by $RED(A)$ is *a minimal set* of attributes $A' \subseteq A$ so that all attributes $a \in A \backslash A'$ are dispensable, namely $IND(A') = IND(A)$. For $\mathcal{A}(U, C \cup \{d\})$, the *relative reducts* $RED(C, d)$ of C to d are judged by $f'(C)$ similarly with the determination of $f(A)$ on $RED(A)$ [6]. Accordingly, we entitle an attribute (set) $C_{Cut} \subseteq C$ *relatively indispensable* to d iff $\forall_{c \in C_{Cut}} \vee c$ can construct a conjunct of $f'(C)$, and the *prime implicants* of $f'(E_i, C)$ is utilized to determine the *local reduct* of a condition class E_i in $\mathcal{A}$. For $X \subseteq U$ and $B \subseteq A$, the *rough membership* function of X with respect to any class $E_i \in U/IND(B)$ is

$$\mu_B(E_i, X) = \frac{|E_i \cap X|}{|E_i|}, \quad 0 \leq \mu_B(E_i, X) \leq 1. \tag{5}$$

3. Rule extracting from training tables

Though not entirely correct wrt. the classical relative reducts oriented rule extracting methods [1, 5, 7], the *default rule extracting* framework proposed in [5] provides at lest two advantages, namely *simplicity and generalization*. Therefore, we will use this framework as a basis to validate our research under a restriction of vast rules generation.

For a given *training* table $\mathcal{A}(U, C \cup \{d\})$, taking the prime implicants of $f'(E_i, C)$ of each class $E_i \in U/IND(C)$ for the *predecessor* while regarding the prime implicants of d of each $\{X_j \in U/IND(\{d\}) \mid E_i \cap X_j \neq \emptyset\}$ as the *successor*, all the simpler rules can be expressed as $R : Des(E_i, C) \rightarrow Des(X_j, \{d\})$ with $\mu_C(E_i, X_j)$ no less than a filtering threshold μ_{tr}. By introducing an iterative reduct stratagem, thereby, new training rules by deserting the relatively indispensable attributes are generated as much as possible to handle *test* objects. Accepting $\mathcal{A}$ and a given threshold μ_{tr} as the input, the primary extracting framework can be described as the following four steps:

Step 1 $INIT(\Psi)$. Calculate $U/IND(C)$, $U/IND(\{d\})$ and $M'_D(\mathcal{A})$. For each $E_i \in U/IND(C)$, calculate $f'(E_i, C)$ and generate the rule $R : Des(E_i, C) \rightarrow Des(X_j, \{d\}) \mid \mu_C(E_i, X_j)$ with each $X_j \in U/IND(d)$ if $\mu_C(E_i, X_j) \geq \mu_{tr}$. Let $C_{Pr} = C$ and goto Step 4.

Step 2 Exit if $ISEND(\Psi)$; let $\mathcal{A}'(U, C' \bigcup \{d\})$ equal to $NEXT(\Psi)$ and let $C_{Pr} = C'$. Calculate $U/IND(C_{Pr})$ and $M'_D(\mathcal{A}')$.

Step 3 For any $E_{(k,C_{Pr})} \in U/IND(C_{Pr})$, calculate $f'(E_i, C_{Pr})$ and generate a rule $\Delta : Des(E_{(k,C_{Pr})}, C_{Pr}) \rightarrow Des(X_j, \{d\}) \mid \mu_{C_{Pr}}(E_{(k,C_{Pr})}, X_j))$ for each $X_j \in U/IND$ (d) if $\mu_C(E_{(k,C_{Pr})}, X_j) \geq \mu_{tr}$, while the blocks to this rule $\mathcal{F} : Des(E_i, C_{Pr}) \rightarrow \neg Des(X_j, \{d\})$ are made if $\forall_{E_i \in U/IND(C)}, E_i \subseteq E_{(k,C_{Pr})} \wedge E_i \cap X_j = \emptyset$.

Step 4 Calculate $f'(C_{Pr})$. For each attribute set C_{Cut} emerging in the conjuncts of $f'(C_{Pr})$, select the projections $C'_{Pr} = C_{Pr} \backslash C_{Cut}$, then $INSERT(\Psi)$ with $\mathcal{A}'(U, C'_{Pr} \cup \{d\})$. Goto step2.

Where the *cursor queue* Ψ composed of all the *subtable* $\mathcal{A}'$ has four main operations $\{INIT; INSERT; ISEND; NEXT\}$. Different from the *classical queue*, $ISEND$ judges if the *cursor* is pointing to a $NULL$ subtable, and $NEXT$ is utilized to get the subtable pointed by cursor and move the cursor to the next subtable. To elucidate the generation of the *rule set*(denoted by $RUL(\mathcal{A})$), an illustrative sample displayed in figure 1 results from having observed a total of one hundred objects that were classified according to the condition attributes $C = \{a, b, c\}$ and decision attributes $\{d\}$. Furthermore, the decision classification followed with the cardinality of each $U/IND(C \cup \{d\})$ is represented as $D = \{d\}$.

| *Figure 1.* | An illustrative example | | | | | *Figure 2.* | Flow graph of reduct |

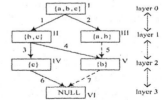

V	a	b	c	d
E_1	1	2	3	1 (50×)
E_2	1	2	1	2 (5×)
E_3	2	2	3	2 (30×)
E_4	2	3	3	2 (10×)
$E_{5,1}$	3	5	1	3 (4×)
$E_{5,2}$	3	3	1	4 (1×)

The real line with the executing sequence number in figure 2 illustrates the projection order of the default algorithm on figure 1, and the dashed denotes the duplicate projection prevented by the cursor queue. The node represents condition attribute set derived from the corresponding projection. Furthermore, the partial relation exists in the nodes which are in different layers and connected by the bidirectional line.

4. Inconsistency classifying based on Reduced Layer

The *default decision generation* method [5] extracts the rules measure up to a membership threshold as much as possible, also, it employs the membership as the interface to resolve the synthesis of the training rules for the test objects. Unfortunately, the conflict of the decision generation can not be resolved completely under this framework. Wang developed a rule-choosing stratagem named *lower frequency first* [8] to quantificationally dispose the *inconsistency* in view of a standpoint that a decision derived from the class with few test objects can represent some special cases, and the precondition of this stratagem is the rules obtained from training set with poor relativity to the test objects, but this stratagem can not work well under the situation in which the training table provides enough reliability for the universe. To parse the causation of the conflict, a notion of *reduced layer* is defined recursively as follows:

DEFINITION 1 *For a given training decision table* $A(U, C \cup \{d\})$, *the reduced layer* L *of each subtable* $A'(U, C' \cup \{d\}) \in \Psi$ *denoted by* $L(A')$ *is*
- *0   iff* $IND(C) = IND(C')$;
- *k+1   iff* $\exists_{A''(U,C''\cup\{d\})\in\Psi}, L(A'') = k \wedge C''\backslash C' \in CON(f'(C''))$.

Where $CON(f'(C''))$ accepts the attribute sets emerging in all the conjuncts of $f'(C'')$ as its elements, and each element corresponding to a *conjunct* in $f'(C'')$ includes all the attributes emerging in this conjunct. We call A'' the *parent* of A' (i.e $A''\mathcal{P}A'$) iff $C''\backslash C' \in CON(f'(C''))$. Simultaneously, P is used to depict the partial relation between C'' and C'. If $A_1\mathcal{P}A_2$ and $A_2\mathcal{P}A_3$, due to the transitivity of $\subseteq$, subtable A_1 is called the *forefathers* of A_3 (i.e. $A_1\mathcal{F}A_3$ or C_1FC_3). From the above, obviously, the original table $A(U, C \cup \{d\})$ is with the reduced layer 0. Any subtable $A'(U, C' \cup \{d\})$ in Ψ with reduced layer larger than 0 is homogenous with A except for $C' \subseteq C$, where C' is called *reduced attributes*. Let us now assume that the considered original table had no condition attributes with the same equivalence classes, i.e. $\forall_{c_1,c_2\in C}, IND/\{c_1\} \neq IND/\{c_2\}$, and it is commonly satisfied in the large-scale environments.

PROPOSITION 2 *For two reduced attributes* C'' *and* C' *which belong to* A'' *and* A' *respectively,* $U/IND(C') \subseteq U/IND(C'')$ *exists iff* $C''FC'$, *namely* $A''\mathcal{F}A'$.

When considering the necessity, due to the transitivity of relation $\mathcal{P}$ among all the middle subtables between A' and A'', $U/IND(C') \subseteq U/IND(C'')$ can be easily proven. When considering the sufficiency, we suppose there exists another subtable $B(U, B \cup \{d\})$ with $L(B) = L(A'') \wedge B\mathcal{F}A'$ held, and due to the greedy manner of the default rule extracting framework discussed in [5], we assert $U/IND(B) = U/IND(C'')$; also because both B and A'' root in the original table A with several indispensable attributes deserted, $B = C''$ can be obtained. And thus $C''FC'$ and $A''\mathcal{F}A'$ are proven.

As discussed in section 3, a set of rules with the form of $r_k : Pred(r_k) \rightarrow Succ(r_k)|\mu(r_k)$ can be generated by applying the four steps to a given training table

$\mathcal{A}(U, C \cap \{d\})$. For the universe W, each object $u \in W$ can be classified to a decision class $CLS(Succ(r_k))$ iff any attribute $a \in A$ emerging in $Pred(r_k)$ is supported by u, and it's denoted by $Mat(r_k, u) : \forall_{a \in A}, a(Pred(r_k)) \neq \emptyset \rightarrow a(u) = a(Pred(r_k))$. Therefore, the inconsistency consists in $RUL(\mathcal{A})$ iff

$$\exists_{r_i, r_j \in RUL(\mathcal{A})}, Mat(r_i, u) \wedge Mat(r_j, u) \wedge CLS(Succ(r_i)) \neq CLS(Succ(r_j)), \quad (6)$$

where $Mat(r_i, u)$ denotes $Pred(r_i)$ is supported by u, and $CLS(Succ(r_i))$ denotes the decision class determined by $Succ(r_i)$. Therefore, $RUL(\mathcal{A})$ is inconsistent due to the existence of any $r_i, r_j \in RUL(\mathcal{A})$ with both $\forall_{a \in A}, a(Pred(r_i)) \neq \emptyset \wedge a(Pred(r_j)) \neq \emptyset \rightarrow a(Pred(r_i)) = a(Pred(r_j)))$ and $CLS(Succ(r_i)) \neq CLS(Succ(r_j))$ held. To distinguish the rules derived from different subtables, each $r \in RUL(\mathcal{A})$ is expressed by $Des(E_i^r, C^r) \rightarrow Des(X_j, \{d\})$, where $Des(E_i^r, C^r)$ implies $Pred(r)$ comprising the local reduct of E_i^r in subtable $\mathcal{A}^r(U, C^r \cup \{d\})$. Based on the correlative notions of reduced layer, the inconsistency among the rules can be divided into two cases according to their condition class.

COROLLARY 3 *For two inconsistent rule r_1 and r_2 derived respectively from $\mathcal{A}^{r_1}$ and $\mathcal{A}^{r_2}$, suppose $L(\mathcal{A}^{r_2}) \geq L(\mathcal{A}^{r_1})$, we shall say that this inconsistency is:*

$$\begin{cases} \text{inherited} & \text{iff } C^{r_2} \subseteq C^{r_1}, & (7b) \\ \text{varietal} & \text{iff } C^{r_2} \not\subseteq C^{r_1}. & (7c) \end{cases}$$

The *inherited* inconsistency can be ulteriorly divided into two cases, i.e. $L(\mathcal{A}^{r_2}) = L(\mathcal{A}^{r_1}) \rightarrow C^{r_2} = C^{r_1}$ and $L(\mathcal{A}^{r_2}) > L(\mathcal{A}^{r_1}) \rightarrow C^{r_2} \subset C^{r_1}$, and the *varietal* inconsistency has two similar cases. In figure 2, the consistency between the rules from node II and the rules from node IV belongs to the inherited, and the consistency arising from node III and node IV is varietal. With little consideration of the difference among the subtables, many researches focus on the inconsistency of the rules derived from the same subtable, hence the rule certainty is converted into the cardinality-based evaluation measures for the sake of achieving high-frequency rule.

5.   Methods of inconsistency handling

In this paper, to complement the default decision generation method, we mainly discuss the inconsistency from different layers and suppose $L(\mathcal{A}^{r_2}) > L(\mathcal{A}^{r_1})$. For two inconsistent rules $r_1 : Des(E_{i_1}^{r_1}, C^{r_1}) \rightarrow Des(X_{j_1}, \{d\})$ and $r_2 : Des(E_{i_2}^{r_2}, C^{r_2}) \rightarrow Des(X_{j_2}, \{d\})$, if $C^{r_2} \subset C^{r_1}$ exists, it's obvious that the condition classes could hold either $E_{i_1}^{r_1} \subset E_{i_2}^{r_2}$ or $E_{i_1}^{r_1} \cap E_{i_2}^{r_2} = \emptyset$. Being comparable with the condition class determined by r_1, the *effectual set* covered by r_2 is only composed of the classes which leads to $Succ(r_2)$ while belonging to $U/IND(C^{r_1})$, namely:

$$ES(E_{i_2}^{r_2}, C_{r_1}) = \{E_i^{r_1} \in IND/C^{r_1} | E_i^{r_1} \cap X_{j_2} \neq \emptyset \wedge E_i^{r_1} \subseteq E_{i_2}^{r_2}\}. \quad (8)$$

When measuring the rules r_1 and r_2 with the relation $C^{r_2} \subset C^{r_1}$ held, due to the desertion of the relatively indispensable attributes $C^{r_1} \backslash C^{r_2}$, the condition classes in $U/IND(C^{r_1})$ which could not lead to the decision $Succ(r_2)$ are taken into account, and it may depress the rule r_2. Hence, for disposing the inherited inconsistency, the notion of *joint membership function* can be determined by the cardinality-based evaluation measure of the effectual set.

DEFINITION 4 *For two inconsistent rules r_1, r_2 with $C^{r_2} \subset C^{r_1}$ held, the joint membership function of r_2 with respect to C^{r_1} is defined as:*

$$\mu_{C^{r_1}}(E_{i_2}^{r_2}, X_{j_2}) = \frac{\sum_{E_k \in ES(E_{i_2}^{r_2}, C_{r_1})} |E_k \cap X_{j_2}|}{\sum_{E_k \in ES(E_{i_2}^{r_2}, C_{r_1})} |E_k|}, \quad 0 \le \mu_{C^{r_1}}(E_{r_2}, X_{j_2}) \le 1. \quad (9)$$

Where the denominator denotes the cardinality of the effectual set for r_2 under the condition attributes C^{r_1}, and the numerator denotes the cardinality of the objects which support r_2. Clearly, one can perceive that the rough membership function is a special case of the joint membership function, i.e. $\mu_{C^{r_1}}(E_{i_2}^{r_2}, X_{j_2}) = \mu_{C^{r_2}}(E_{i_2}^{r_2}, X_{j_2}))$ iff $C^{r_1} = C^{r_2}$. As shown in equation (9), on the assumption that both r_1 and r_2 are under the same condition restriction, $ES(E_{i_2}^{r_2}, C_{r_1})$ depicts the object sets contained by r_2 comparable with the ones determined by r_1, and $\mu_{C^{r_1}}(E_{i_2}^{r_2}, X_{j_2})$ is more equitable than $\mu_{C^{r_2}}(E_{i_2}^{r_2}, X_{j_2})$ for inherited inconsistency.

When considering the varietal inconsistency, for the above two rules r_1 and r_2, $C^{r_2} \not\subseteq C^{r_1}$ comes into existence as discussed in corollary 3. Similarly with the analysis of the inherited case, it can be divided into two subcases, i.e. $L(A^{r_2}) = L(A^{r_1}) \rightarrow C^{r_2} \ne C^{r_1}$ and $L(A^{r_2}) > L(A^{r_1}) \rightarrow C^{r_2} \not\subseteq C^{r_1}$. In figure 2, one may conclude the inconsistent rules from node II and node III to be the former and the ones from III and IV the latter. Due to the necessity of proposition 2, the condition attribute set $C^{r_1} \cup C^{r_2}$ is the forefather of the both subset, denoted by $(C^{r_1} \cup C^{r_2})FC^{r_1}$ and $(C^{r_1} \cup C^{r_2})FC^{r_2}$. Therefore, $C^{r_1} \cup C^{r_2}$ can be utilized to evaluate the rule certainty, and called by the *effectual joint attributes*.

PROPOSITION 5 *For two inconsistent rules r_1, r_2 with $L(A^{r_2}) = L(A^{r_1}) \rightarrow C^{r_2} \ne C^{r_1}$ held, we shall say that the rule certainty can be evaluated by the joint membership function $\mu_{C^{r_1} \cup C^{r_2}}(E_{i_1}^{r_1}, X_{j_1})$ and $\mu_{C^{r_1} \cup C^{r_2}}(E_{i_2}^{r_2}, X_{j_2})$.*

It's obvious that $C^{r_1} = C^{r_1} \cup C^{r_2}$ iff $C^{r_2} \subseteq C^{r_1}$, thus proposition 5 provides a unified evaluative condition attributes for the both rules, and the both categories of inconsistency can be disposed by choosing the rules with higher joint membership function. All the above accounts for the inconsistency between two rules, but when two rules r_1, r_2 are consistent with both the predecessor and the successor (denoted by $r_1 Cst\ r_2$), i.e. $\forall_{a \in A}; a(Pred(r_1)) \ne \emptyset \wedge a(Pred(r_2)) \ne \emptyset \rightarrow a(Pred(r_1)) = a(Pred(r_2)) \wedge CLS(Succ(r_1)) = CLS(Succ(r_2))$, to compete with any $r_3 \in RULA$ which is inconsistent with (denoted by $r_3 Inc\ r_1$) the both rules, all the consistent pairs of each rule must be treated like the inconsistent pairs for obtaining the most credible rule. To achieve the forementioned, the rule is constructed by a header followed with an array of consistent rule descriptions and an array of inconsistent rule descriptions, and the header include six members:

$$Idt : Rule : Block : Strength : Layer : Pds : CstArray : IncArray. \quad (10)$$

For any $r_a \in RUL(A)$, the symbol Idt denotes the identifier of r_a and $Strength(r_a) = |E_{i_a}^{r_a} \cap X_{j_a}|$ denotes the cardinality of the r_a supported objects. $Layer$ denotes the reduced layer of A_a^r. Pts points to the r_a related decision subtable in the cursor queue Ψ, and r_a is also pointed by its related subtable. During the rule extracting phase, as discussed in definition 1, these four members are obtained from Step 2 of the extracting framework with a layer marker in A'. Each element in the last two arrays is composed of an identifier $Idt(r_b)$ and a pair of joint membership function value $(\mu_{C^{r_a} \cup C^{r_b}}(E_{i_a}^{r_a}, X_{j_a}), \mu_{C^{r_a} \cup C^{r_b}}(E_{i_b}^{r_b}, X_{j_b}))$, in which $CstArray$ records all the consistent rules to r_a and $IncArray$ includes all the inconsistent ones.

Following Step 3, according to the established subtables in Ψ, each *generated rule* is fetched to compare with r_a. And then, as discussed in definition 4, join $Idt(r_b) : (\mu_{C^{r_a} \cup C^{r_b}}(E_{i_a}^{r_a}, X_{j_a}), \mu_{C^{r_a} \cup C^{r_b}}(E_{i_b}^{r_b}, X_{j_b}))$ into $CstArray$ if $r_a Cst\ r_b$ and join $Idt(r_b) : (\mu_{C^{r_a} \cup C^{r_b}}(E_{i_a}^{r_a}, X_{j_a}), \mu_{C^{r_a} \cup C^{r_b}}(E_{i_b}^{r_b}, X_{j_b}))$ into $IncArray$ if $r_a Inc\ r_b$. The generated rule implies that the both arrays only record the corresponding rules which are generated from the subtable with the reduced layer smaller than $\mathcal{A}^{r_a}$, due to the reflexivity of both Cst and Inc, this can reduce the complexity of extracting and synthesis. From all above, we assert the time and space complexity of reduced attributes oriented rule extracting algorithm are of order $O(n^4 \cdot m^2)$ and $O(n \cdot m + m^2)$, respectively.

According to the above structures, suppose several rules $M = (r_1...r_k)$ are supported by a test object u, then the most credible rule can be obtained by:

1. Classify $\forall r_a \in M$ into several consistent subsets (Suppose the number is K) according to X_{j_a}.

2. For each consistent subset, with a dimidiate manner, chose the rule with the maximal joint membership value by $CstArray$; if the result is not unique, chose the rule with the largest $Strength$, and $M' = (r^1...r^K)$ is obtained.

3. For $\forall r^a, r^b \in M'$, with a dimidiate manner, chose the one with the maximal joint membership value by $IncArray$; if the result is not unique, chose the rule with the largest $Strength$, and the most credible rule for u is found.

In Step 2 and 3, for comparing rules pairs, fetch the $CstArray$ or $IncArray$ of the rule with the larger $Layer$. The random selection is applied if both the joint membership value and $Strength$ of any pair are the same.

6.   Computational experiments

To indicate the validity of our method, three medical data from the UCI Machine Learning Repository is used in our experiments. Let us notice that the data sets used in our experiments are assumed to be complete. To achieve this, the data were slightly modified by removing a few attributes which result in vast incompleteness, and the other missing values with a ratio of 8% were made out by a statistic method. To insure the comparability, 10 fold cross-validation reclassification technique was performed.

In order to indicate the availability of our method, three synthesis methods based on vast rules generation algorithm [5] are given for comparison. In which, Std is the standard discernibility applying a random rule selection to the rules with equal membership, HFF uses the high frequency first strategy of inconsistenct rule-choosing and LFF is it's opposite. The Reduced Attributed oriented Rule Generation is denoted by RARG. Moreover, we consult two popular rough sets based rule induction systems, i.e. new version of LERS (New LERS) and the classification coefficient oriented synthesis system based on the object-oriented programming library (RSES-lib). For the purpose of comparison, the membership value threshold for Std, HFF, LFF and RARG are all 0.55 and the coefficient threshold for RSES-lib is 0.75, which are quoted by the corresponding authors.

568

IIP 2006

Table 1. Computational result with the medical datasets

Algorithm	Lymphography			Breast cancer			Primary tumor		
	Rule number	Error rate Train	Test	Rule number	Error rate Train	Test	Rule number	Error rate Train	Test
New LERS	984	0.000	0.233	1163	0.063	0.342	8576	0.245	0.671
RSES-lib	427	0.000	0.195	756	0.152	0.277	6352	0.136	0.687
Std	1321	0.000	0.320	2357	0.060	0.361	7045	0.175	0.764
HFF	1321	0.000	0.267	2357	0.042	0.338	7045	0.147	0.742
LFF	1321	0.000	0.341	2357	0.245	0.470	7045	0.360	0.720
RARG	1321	0.000	0.207	2357	0.051	0.292	7045	0.125	0.598

As shown in table 1, since HFF refined the default decision generation framework, its performance exceeds the later in all the three datasets. Due to the different granularity distribution of both classes, LFF works well in the first and the third datasets while falling across a sharply decrease in the breast cancer dataset. Because RARG provides a unified evaluation criterion for conflicts, with the irrelevant condition classes filtered, it guarantees the decision with the largest ratio of the sustaining decision objects to the effectual condition objects. For the tested objects, it refers to the most accordant rule with respect to other conflict ones. Therefore, RARG is particularly outstanding in the applications with voluminous inconsistency, such as the Primary tumor dataset displayed in the result. In conclusion, RARG takes on a comparatively high performance in the above four methods. The results also show that RARG is comparable with the other two systems, and especially, it exceeds them in the Primary tumor dataset.

References

1. Pawlak Z., Skowron A. (1993) A rough set approach to decision rules generation, In *Research Report 23/93, Warsaw University of Technology.* 1-19.
2. Michie D., Spiegelhalter D. J., C. Taylor C. (1994) Machine learning, neural and statistical classification. Ellis Horwood, New York.
3. Quinlan J. R. (1986) Induction of decision trees. *Machine Learning.* 1:81-106.
4. Grzymala-Busse, J. W. (1997) A new version of the rule induction system LERS. *Fundamenta Informaticae.* 31:27-39.
5. Mollesta T., Skowron A. (1996) A rough set framework for data mining of propositional default rules, In *9th Int. Sym. Proc. On Found. of Intelligent Systems.* 448-457.
6. Bazan J., Nguyen H. S., Synak P., Wróblewski J. (2000) Rough set algorithms in classification problems. In *Rough set methods and applications. New Developments in Knowledge Discovery in Information Systems, Studies in Fuzziness and Soft Computing.* 49-88.
7. Skowron A., Wang H., Wojna A., Bazan J. G. (2005) A hierarchical approach to multimodal classification. In *RSFDGrC.* 2:119-127.
8. Wang G. Y., Wu Y., Liu F. (2000) Generating rules and reasoning under inconsistencies, In *2000 IEEE Int. Conf. on Industrial Electronics, Control and Instrumentation.* 2536-2541.
9. Jerzy W., Grzymalao-Busse, Ming L. (2001) A comparison of several approaches to missing attribute values in data mining. In Ziarko W. and Yao Y. (ed.), *RSCTC2000.* 378-385.
10. Dzeroski S. (2000) Normalized decision functions and measures for inconsistent decision tables analysis. In *Fundamenta Informaticae.* 44(3):291-319.

MESSAGE RETRIEVAL AND CLASSIFICATION FROM CHAT ROOM SERVERS USING BAYESIAN NETWORKS

Debbie Zhang, Simeon Simoff and John Debenham
Faculty of Information Technology, University of Technology, Sydney

Abstract: Chat rooms and newsgroup on the internet is a valuable, and often free of charge, source of information. In this paper, a design of smart chat room bots that automatically retrieve and filter on line messages is proposed. The design is based on internet technology and Bayesian Networks. Technical details of connecting to and retrieving data from web based chat room servers are presented. A Naive Bayesian network classifier is implemented using frequency of the keywords that mostly appear in the selecting messages as input features. A prototype of such a message classification system has been implemented. It has been trialed on detecting investment related messages from four Australian chat room sites.

Key words: Information retrieval, Bayesian network, web mining

1.   INTRODUCTION

It is widely understood that much intelligence can be gathered from sources which are publicly available from internet. In particular, this raises the need for some organizations to surveillance the information on the internet, particular informal sources such as chat rooms. As the amount of traffic through chat rooms each day is large and occurs in real time, the process of monitoring internet messages is expensive and in some sense time critical. To assist the monitoring process, a data classification process is employed. The chat room messages are classified into selected class and

---

Please use the following format when citing this chapter:

Zhang, D., Simoff, S., Debenham, J., 2006, in IFIP International Federation for Information Processing, Volume 228, Intelligent Information Processing III, eds. Z. Shi, Shimohara K., Feng D., (Boston: Springer), pp. 569–574.

non-selected class. Messages in the selected class require further processing. While it is time consuming for humans, the classification process does not require deep understanding of the text and thus can be efficiently performed by computers.

Software robots, so-called bots, which are smart software tools for retrieving useful data from internet web sites, can be applied to search and categorize chat room messages in an efficient way [1]. Bots have great potential in text mining, which find patterns in enormous amounts of data. Bots can save labor as they persist in a search, refining it as they go along. Intelligent bots that can make decisions based on past experiences are the perfect way to perform the methodical searches to uncover information from internet. This paper presents the methods of design and implementation of smart chat room bots using Bayesian Networks for message filtering. Technical details of connecting to and retrieving data from chat room web servers are described. A case study of using the developed chat room bots to classify the messages retrieved from four Australian chat room sites is conducted.

This paper presents the methods of design and implementation of smart chat room bots using Bayesian Networks for message filtering. Technical details of connecting to and retrieving data from chat room web servers are described. A case study of using the developed chat room bots to classify the messages retrieved from four Australian chat room sites is conducted.

2.   DATA RETRIEVAL

2.1   Connecting to chat room web servers

The first step to develop a bot is to connect to the chat room web server that has been chosen. Java socket API is chosen to use to communicate to the web server since it is platform independent and comprehensive for network application development [2].

Java Sockets are a mechanism for communication over the Internet. Since web servers normally listen on TCP port 80, a socket with the IP address of the chat room can be constructed if the IP address of the chat room is know. Java encapsulates the concept of an ordinary TCP socket with the class Socket, and the concept of a server socket with the class ServerSocket. Data stream (document) that is input to or output from a socket is encapsulated in Java using the InputStream and OutputStream classes, respectively.

Documents on the Internet web server can also be retrieved by using Java URL class. The standard identifier for a document on the Internet is its Universal Resource Locator (URL). The URL object is constructed with the URL address of the chat room. Interacting with the URL requires that the connection is established with the Web server that is responsible for the document identified by the URL. The TCP socket for the connection is constructed by invoking the openConnection method on the URL object. This method also performs the name resolution necessary to determine the IP address of the Web server. This method returns an object of type URLConnection. The connection to the Web server is requested by calling connect on the URLConnection object. If the URL specifies the http protocol, then the URLConnection will actually be an object of the subclass HttpURLConnection which has additional methods specific to HTML documents.

2.2   HTML document analyzer

The documents retrieved from Web servers are HTML documents. The structure of the HTML document from each web site is different from each one. Therefore, retrieving messages from a chat room URL has to involve certain degree of customization. To minimize the customization level, a HTML document analyzer package is developed to allow bots to be built on top of it. Also, the difficulty of classifying a message increase dramatically if it contains HTML tags. The HTML document analyzer should provide the function to easily remove HTML tags in the document.

Sun provides a HTML parser package javax.swing.text.html.parser for parsing HTML documents. However, Swing's HTML parser fails to parse HTML documents into HTML objects. A similar approach presented by Somik Raha etc. was implemented to provide a fast real time parser for parsing HTML documents into HTML objects [3]. This HTML parser provides the following advantages:
- Handles formatted HTML as much as possible the way MS IE and Netscape do
- Dissects the document in an array of tag objects and string node objects
- Provides the value of a tag's attributes and comments, and
- Can also handle XML documents.

The HTML parser contains HTMLParser, HTMLReader, HTMLTag, HTMLTagScanner, HTMLTag and HTMLTagScanner six major classes.

The HTMLParser class is the access point to the package. It allows the user to register or remove the scanners for the type of tags. HTMLParser can be instantiated either with a string representing the URL to be parsed, or the html file on the hard disk. It can also be instantiated with a HTMLReader that constructed by an inputStream class. This flexibility is important for supporting two types of web server connections discussed in section 2.1.

HTMLReader builds on java.io.Bu? eredReader, providing methods to read text from a character-input stream. It analysis the HTML document line by line using the registered HTML tag scanners and creates an array of HTML tag objects and string node objects.

HTMLTag is the parent interface for the specific tags, which represents a generic tag entity. Each type of tag needs to develop a corresponding HTMLxxxTag that contains the methods to set and get attributes of the tag.

HTMLTagScanner is the abstract base class of specific tag scanner classes. It contains evaluate() method, which evaluates a tag, and scan() method that constructs the tag object if it can handle it. Again, each type of tag requires a HTMLxxxScanner to implement its own scan() and evaluate() methods.

3.   DATA FILTERING

The aim of this project is to categorize the chat room messages according to user requirements. Naive Bayesian classifier based on probabilistic learning method which is widely used for email message filtering is employed to classify the messages [4],[5].

A Bayesian network is a directed acyclic graph that compactly represents a probability distribution. The nodes in the graph represent random variables that associate with a conditional probability table. Network directed links signify direct causal influences between connected nodes. The posterior probabilities of nodes are computed in Bayesian networks [6][7][8].

A Naive Bayesian network is a simple structure Bayesian network that has the class node as the parent node of all other nodes. Naive Bayesian networks have been used as an effective classifier for many years. It is easy to construct. Also, the classification process is very efficient. To avoid the computational difficulty of exploring a previously unknown network and the speed requirement of this project, a Naïve Bayesian network is chosen for the message filtering algorithm.

Bayesian networks extend the concept of deterministic modeling by taking into account uncertainties. Outputs and inputs are not stated as fixed variables but whenever possible as probability distributions. This is particular suitable in the case of classifying messages where precise relationship between the message classes and message features of that class is difficult to achieve. In considering the specific problem of classifying certain type of messages, a database of the keywords that mostly appear in the selecting type of messages can be used as the feature variables. Langley et al.'s study shows Naive Bayesian network has surprisingly outperformed many sophisticated classifier when the features are not strongly correlated, which is the case in this application [9].

From Bayes' theorem and the theorem of total probability, the probability that a message m with vector $\vec{x} = \langle x_1,...,x_n \rangle$ belongs to class c is:

$$P(C = c \mid \vec{X} = \vec{x}) = \frac{P(C = c) \cdot P(\vec{X} = \vec{x} \mid C = c)}{\sum_{k \in \{c, \sim c\}} P(C = k) \cdot P(\vec{X} = \vec{x} \mid C = k)} \qquad (1)$$

As the Naïve Bayesian classifier assumes that $x_1,...,x_n$ are conditionally independent given the class C, which equation (1) can be simplified to:

$$P(C = c \mid \vec{X} = \vec{x}) = \frac{P(C = c) \cdot \prod_{i=1}^{n} P(X_i = x_i \mid C = c)}{\sum_{k \in \{c, \sim c\}} P(C = k) \cdot \prod_{i=1}^{n} P(X_i = x_i \mid C = k)} \qquad (2)$$

$P(X_i \mid C)$ and $P(C)$ can be estimate by the frequencies of the training data.

4.   CASE STUDIES

A prototype that implements the proposed methods has been built. Building a bot based on the HTML document analyser package described in section 2.2 is simple and straight forward. Adding a new chat room site only involves a few lines of coding. Thus the development time has been reduced to minimum.

Case studies using the prototype to classify on-line chat room messages into investment related category and non-investment related category were conducted. Data used in the experiments are real-world data collected from four Australian popular chat room sites. Two hundred messages were collected from each site. One fourth of the messages were used for testing and the remainder were used to build the network.

A database that contains 47 keywords such as "share", "price", "buy" etc. that mostly appear in investment related messages are used as feature variables. The frequencies of keywords occurred in the investment related messages and non-investment related messages are counted. The posterior probabilities of the test data were calculated using equation 2. A threshold value was chosen for the classifier. Preliminary results have proved that the above concept is feasible and e?ective in retrieving and classifying internet messages. It is also found the entire data retrieving and classification process very efficient and suitable for real-time implementation.

5.   CONCLUSIONS

This paper presents the methods to design and implement smart chat room bots using Bayesian Networks for message filtering. To reduce the level of customization of source code for retrieving data from different web site, a HTML document analyser has been implemented. This approach greatly increases the development efficiency. A prototype of the proposed system has been built. Case studies using the prototype were conducted. Experiment results show the proposed methods are feasible and efficient.

REFERENCES:

1. www.botspot.com
2. Hughes, M., Sho?ner, M., Hamner, D.: Java network programming: a complete guide to networking, streams, and distributed computing, Greenwich (1997).
3. http://htmlparser.sourceforge.net
4. Sahami, M., Dumais, S.,Heckerman, D., and Horvitz, E.: A Bayesian Approach to Filtering Junk E-mail. Proc. of the AAAI'98 Workshop on Learning for Text Categorization, Madison, Wisconsin (1998).
5. Androutsopoulos, I., Paliouras, G., Karkaletsis, V., Sakkis, G., Spyropoulos, C. and Stamatopoulos, P.: Learning to filter spam e-mail: A comparison of a naive Bayesian and a memory-based approach. Workshop on Machine Learning and Textual Information Access, 4th European Conference on Principles and Practice of Knowledge Discovery in Databases (2000) pp.1-13.
6. Cowell, R., Dawid, A., Lauritzen, S., and Spiegelhalter, D.: Probabilistic Networks and Expert Systems, Springer (1999).
7. Pearl J.: Probabilistic Reasoning in Intelligent System, Morgen Kaufmann (1988).
8. Jordan, M.: Learning in Graphical Models, MIT (1999).
9. Langley, P., Iba, W., and Thompson, K.: An Analysis of Bayesian Classifiers. Proceedings of AAAI-92 (1992) pp. 223-228.

OPERATIONAL SEMANTICS OF THE SEAL CALCULUS

Zhang Jing,[1] Zhang Li-Cui [2,*] Guo De-Gui[1]

[1] *College of Computer Science and Technology,*
Key Laboratory of Symbolic Computation and Knowledge Engineering
of Ministry of Education of P.R.China, Jilin University,Changchun,130012,P.R.China
zhangjing99@jlu.edu.cn,guodg@jlu.edu.cn

[2] *College of Communication Engineering, Jilin University, Changchun, 130012, P.R.China*
zlc6796@sohu.com

Abstract   As a distributed process calculus with localities and mobility of computational entities, Seal calculus is playing an important role in expressing key features such as security and mobility of Internet programming directly. However, little implementation technique proposed for the calculus, partly due to the complication of mobile computation, which fusions three important techniques: concurrency, distribution and mobility at the same time. The abstract machine PSN for a distributed implementation of the Seal calculus is presented. In PSN the logical structure of a seal system and its physical distribution are separated which induces a more simple and clear implementation. Moreover, an operational semantics description of the Seal calculus based on PSN is given.

Keywords: Mobile computation, Seal Calculus, abstract machine, operational semantics

1.   Introduction

The Seal calculus[1,2] is a mobile process calculus aims to model programming large scale distributed systems over open networks, with the goal of being able to express the essential properties of Internet programs. Seal can be seen as a framework for exploring the design space of security and mobility features[3,4]. However, at present the research on Seal calculus is still at the stage of perfecting its theory, less work has been done on its application and implementation, only one implementation is mentioned in [5]. Moreover, the existed formal semantics of the Seal all base on the reduction semantics, which is easy to understand but difficult to implement. The problems of implementa-

*Corresponding author: zlc6796@sohu.com

Please use the following format when citing this chapter:

Zhang, J., Zhang, L.-C., Guo, D.-G., 2006, in IFIP International Federation for Information Processing, Volume 228, Intelligent Information Processing III, eds. Z. Shi, Shimohara K., Feng D., (Boston: Springer), pp. 575–580.

tion have been a restraint to the development of programming languages based on Seal and to experimentation of Seals on concrete examples. In our opinion, implementation is one of the aspects of Seal that most need investigations.

One of the difficulties of a distributed implementation of a hierachical language such as Mobile Ambient[6] and Seal is that each movement operation involves ambients(or seals) on different hierachical levels. In [7,8] locks are used to achieve a synchronization among all ambients(or seals) affected by a movement. In a distributed setting, however, this lock-based policy can be expensive. Many programming languages and abstract calculi use abstract machine to describe their semantics. Abstract machine as an intermediate stage increases portability and maintainability of compilers[9,10]. [11] present a distributed abstract machine of SA(Safe Ambients Calculus), the main idea is to mode each seal as a network node, communication between these nodes base on asychcronous message transimission, which simulates the communication and mobility of seals. The contribution in [11] motivates our work. However, The Seal calculus differs from Ambients in two important ways. First, Ambients use subjective mobility(an agent moves itself) in Seal mobility is objective(an agent is moved by its context). Second, in Seal both communication and mobility between seals base on channels, which are named computational structures used to synchronize processes, in Ambients communication is local and mobility bases on capabilities. So neither the definition nor the implementation of the abstract machine of Seal will be defferent from the Ambients'. In [12], we give a simple distributed implementation of the Seal Calculus, which is the basis of this paper.

The paper is organized as follows. Section 2 introduces the formal syntax and relevant properties of the abstract machine PSN. Section 3 presents the operational semantics of Seal based on the states transition, finally, a transition example is proposed to verify the correctness of the semantics. The last section, concludes the paper with a discussion of future work.

2.   Abstract Machine

We call the abstract machine defined in this paper PSN(Pervasive Seal Network), which separates between the logical and the physical distribution of the seals. The logical distribution is given by the tree structure of the seal syntax(a seal can contain other seals). The physical distribution is given by the association of a location with each seal.

In PSN, a seal named s is represented as a located seal $(h : s[P], f, ss)$, where h is the location, or site, at which the seal runs, f is the location of the parent of the seal, and P is the proceses local to the seal and ss is the location set of the subseals. While the same name may be assigned to several seals, a location univocally identifies a seal; it can be thought of as its physical address.

A tree of seals is rendered, in PSN, by the parallel composition of the seals in the tree. In this sense, the physical and the logical topology are separated: the space of the physical locations is flat, and each location hosts at most one seal, each seal resides at a distinct physical location(this gives us the physical distribution), but each seal knows the location at which its parent and its sons reside(this gives us the logical topology). For instance, an Seal term $s_1[P_1 \parallel P_2 \parallel s_2[Q_1] \parallel s_3[Q_2]]$, where P_1 and P_2 are the local processes of s_1, and $Q_i(i = 1, 2)$ is a local process of m_i(i.e., m_i has no subseals), becomes in PSN:

$$h : s_1[P_1|P_2], root, \{k_1, k_2\}) \parallel (k_1 : s_2[Q_1], h, \{\}) \parallel (k_2 : s_3[Q_2], h, \{\})$$

where h, k_1, k_2 are different location names, root is a special name indicating the outermost location, and $\parallel$ is the parallel composition of located seals. Since seals may run at different physical sites, they communicate with each other by means of asynchronous messages.

We use $m, n, \ldots$ to range over names, $h, k, \ldots$ to range over locations, $p, q, \ldots$ to range over both names and locations. The syntax of PSN is shown as follows: A term of PSN, a net, is the parallel composition of agents and

---

Net $A ::= 0 \mid A_1 \parallel\mid A_2(\nu p)A \mid Agent \mid h(MsgBody)$
Agent $Agent ::= (h : n[P], k, SS)$
Process $P ::= 0 \mid P_1 \mid P_2 \mid (\nu n)P \mid M.p \mid M[P] \parallel wait.P \mid \{MsgBody\}$
Action $M ::= x \mid n \mid \bar{x}^n(\bar{y}) \mid x^n(\lambda\bar{y}) \mid \bar{x}^n \langle\bar{y}\rangle \mid x^n \langle\bar{y}\rangle$
Message $MsgBody ::= write(c, x) \mid Okwrite \mid send(c, \eta, n) \mid$
$\qquad\qquad\qquad moveAck \mid move(h) \mid Okmove(h)$

---

messages, with some names possibly restricted. An agent is a located seal. Located seal is the basic unit of PSN, and represent seals of Seal with their local processes. Messages include two kinds. One kind is the messages that the requestor sends to the receiver, to ask for services; Another kind is the acknowledgement messages that the services provider sends back to the requestor to notify the completion of services and to execute the next operation. The syntax of the processes inside located seals is similar to that of processes in Seal. The only additions are: the prefix wait.P, which appears in a seal when this has sent a request but has not received an answer yet; and the requests, which represent messages received from the requestors and not yet served. We use A to range over nets.

For example, for the following Seal program:

$$s_1[c^{s_3}(y).y^{s_2}(x).0 \parallel s_3[\bar{c}^\uparrow(c_1).0] \parallel s_2[\bar{c_1}^\uparrow(z).0]]$$

the PSN is:

$\{\langle r.r_n[0], rp, \{\ell_1\}\rangle ,$
$\langle \ell_1 : s_1[rcomm(c, y, son(s_3)).rcomm(y, x, son(s_2)).0], r, \{\ell_2, \ell_3\}\rangle ,$
$\langle \ell_2 : s_2[scomm(c_1, z, fath).0], \ell_1, \{\}\rangle ,$
$\langle \ell_3 : s_3[scomm(c, c_1, fath).0], \ell_1, \{\}\rangle\}$

3.   Operational Semantics

Operational Semantics Based On Transitions

Our operational semantics is based on a transition system. In this kind of formalism the semantics of a program is given in terms of the transitions which can make from one configuration to another. The execution of a program is then modeled by a sequence of configurations with transitions, starting from a suitable initial configuration. The transitions are given by a transition relation $\mapsto \subset Conf \times Conf$ (where $Conf$ is the set of configurations).

In transition systems, a configuration usually consists of something like the statement that is to be executed, plus some extra state information. The configuration that we shall use will have a rather complex structure. Formally we define the set of $Conf$ by:

$Conf\{\langle l_i : s_i[cl_i], f_i, SS_i\rangle\}, i \in 1 \ldots n$

Where l_i denotes the location of the seal, s_i denotes the name of the seal, cl_i denotes the actionlist of seal s_i, f_i denotes the location of the parent seal and SS_i denotes the location set of the subseals.

According to the above definition of configurationčňthe initial configuration is the final transformation result of Seal source program P to PSN, i.e,

$conf^0 = PSN(P) = \{\langle l_1 : s_1[cl_1], f_1, SS_1\rangle, \ldots, \langle l_n : s_n[cl_n], f_n, SS_n\rangle\}$

the terminal configuration is the state that all the parallel process' action queues become empty, i.e.,

$conf^\sharp = \{\langle l_1 : s_1[0], f_1, SS_1\rangle, \ldots, \langle l_n : s_n[0], f_n, SS_n\rangle\}$

Now, having an intuitive understanding of the meaning of the programming constructs, it is rather easy to give the corresponding transition rules.

Throughout this section, whenever we write $\langle \alpha \rangle \triangleright \rho$, we require that $\langle \alpha \rangle \notin \rho$.

(1) local communication

(T1) $(h : n[scomm(c, y, loc).cl_1' \triangleright rcomm(c, x, loc).cl_2' \triangleright cl], f, SS) \triangleright \rho'$
    $\mapsto (h : n[cl_1' \triangleright cl_2'\{y/x\} \triangleright cl], f, SS) \triangleright \rho'$

(2) local son to parent communication

(T2) $(l_1 : n_1[scomm(c, x, fath).cl_1' \triangleright cl_1, f_1, SS_1) \triangleright \rho'$
    $\mapsto (l_1 : n_1(wait.cl_1' \triangleright cl_1 \triangleright fath\{write(c, x)\}], f_1, SS_1) \triangleright \rho'$
        (if $fath = f_1$)

(T3) $(l_2 : n_2[rcomm(c, y, son(n_1)).cl_2' \triangleright \{write(c, x), l_1\}], f_2, SS_2) \triangleright \rho$
    $\mapsto (l_2 : n_2[cl_2'\{x/y\} \triangleright cl_2 \triangleright l_1\{Okwrite\}], f_2, SS_2) \triangleright \rho'$
        (if $l_1 \in SS_2$)

(T4) $(l_1 : n_1[wait.cl_1' \triangleright cl_1 \triangleright \{Okwrite, fath\}], f_1, SS_1) \triangleright \rho'$
    $\mapsto (l_1 : n_1[cl_1' \triangleright cl_1], f_1, SS_1) \triangleright \rho'$ (if $fath = f_1$)

(3) parent to son communication

(T5) $(l_1 : n_1[scomm(c, x, son(n_2)).cl_1' \triangleright cl_1], f_1, SS_1) \triangleright \rho'$
    $\mapsto (l_1 : n_1[wait.cl_1' \triangleright cl_1 \triangleright l_2\{write(c, x)\}], f_1, SS_1) \triangleright \rho'$
        (if $l_2 = Loc(n_2)$ and $n_2 \in SS_1$)

(T6) $(l_2 : n_2[rcomm(c, y, fath).cl_2' \triangleright cl_2 \triangleright \{write(c, y), l_1\}], f_2, SS_2) \triangleright \rho'$
$\mapsto (l_2 : n_2[cl_2'\{x/y\} \triangleright cl_2 \triangleright l_1\{Okwrite\}], f_2, SS_2) \triangleright \rho'$ (if $f_2 = l1$)

For space limitation, we omit the transition rules of process movement, which include local movement, parent to son movement and son to parent movement. These rules are similar to the above communication transition rules.

An Execution Sample of PSN

For the sample presented in section 3, we apply the transition rules in subsection 4.1, we get the following transition steps:

S1: Suppose $\rho = \rho_1 \triangleright \rho_2 \triangleright \rho_3$, there

$\rho_1 = \{\langle l_1 : s_1[rcomm(c, y, son(s_3)).rcomm(y, x, son(s_2)).0], r, \{l_2, l_3\}\rangle\}$,
$\rho_2 = \{\langle l_2 : s_2[scomm(c_1, z, fath).0], l_1, \{\}\rangle\}$,
$\rho_3 = \{\langle l_3 : s_3[scomm(c, c_1, fath).0], l_1, \{\}\rangle\}, then$

S2: After transition T2, ρ becomes

$\rho_1 \triangleright \{\langle l_2 : s_2[wait.0 \triangleright l_1\{write(c, z)\}], l_1, \{\}\rangle\} \triangleright \{\langle l_3 : s_3[wait.0 \triangleright l_1\{write(c, c_1)\}], l_1, \{\}\rangle\}$

S3: Using T3 transition, becomes

$\{\langle l_1 : s_1[rcomm(c_1, x, son(s_2)).0 \triangleright l_3\{Okwrite\} \triangleright \{write(c_1, z), l_2\}], r, \{l_2, l_3\}\rangle\} \triangleright \{\langle l_2 : s_2[wait.0]\}, l_1, \{\}\rangle\} \triangleright \{\langle l_3 : s_3[wait.0]\}, l_1, \{\}\rangle\}$

S4: Using T4 transition, becomes

$\{\langle l_1 : s_1[rcomm(c_1, x, son(s_2)).0 \triangleright \{write(c_1, z), l_2\}], r, \{l_2, l_3\}\rangle\} \triangleright \{\langle l_2 : s_2[wait.0]\}, l_1, \{\}\rangle\} \triangleright \{\langle l_3 : s_3[0]\}, l_1, \{\}\rangle\}$

S5: Using T3, T4 transition continuously, we get

$\{\langle l_1 : s_1[0], r, \{l_2, l_3\}\rangle\} \triangleright \{\langle l_2 : s_2[0], l_1, \{\}\rangle\} \triangleright \{\langle l_3 : s_3[0], l_1, \{\}\rangle\}$

4. Conclusion and future work

We have presented an abstract machine for the Seal calculus, and discussed briefly its operational semantics based on transition system. The main originality of our abstract machine lies in the fact that an operational semantics based on transition system is given not a reduction one, this work facilitates the implementation and constitutes the first step in a potential series of more and more refined abstract machies, getting us closer to a provably correct implementation of the Seal calculus.

Finally let us point out some directions in which further work could be done. First, it would certainly be worthwhile to see whether for this kind of language also a denotational semantics can be developed, and possibly proved equivalent to the current operational semantics. Maybe the representation used here for parallel processes could be adapted to denotational semantics in such a way that a clear description is possible. Also this kind of operational semantics could be a good basis to explore the possibility of automatic implementation of mobile computation languages by means of a interpreter.

References

[1] J.Vitek and G.Castagna. Seal: A Framework for secure Mobile Computations. *In Internet Programming Languages*, number 1686 in Lectures Notes in Computer Science, pages 47-77. Springer-Verlag, 1999.

[2] G.Castagna and F.Zappa. The Seal Calculus Revisited. *In Proceedings 22th FST-TCS*, number 2556 in LNCS. Springer, 2002.

[3] M.Bugliesi and G.Castagna. Secure safe ambients. *In Proc. of POPL'01*, pages 222-235. ACM Press, 2001.

[4] F.Nielson, H.Riis Nielson, R.R.Hansen, and J.G.Jensen. Validating firewall in mobile ambients. *In Proc.CONCUR'99*, number 1664 in Lecture Notes in Computer Science, pages 463-477. Springer-Verlag, 1999.

[5] J.Vitek and G.Castagna. Towords a calculus of secure mobile computations. *Proceedings Workshop on Internet Programming Languages*. Chicago, Illinois, USA, Lectures Notes in Computer Science 1686, Springer, 1998.

[6] L.Cardelli and A.D.Gordon. Mobile Ambients. *In M.Nivat, editor,Foundations of Software Science and Computational Structures*, number 1378 in LNCE, Springer-Verlag, 1998, 140-155.

[7] L.Cardelli, Ambit.http://www.luca.demon.co.uk/Ambit.html.1997.

[8] L.Cardelli. Mobile ambient synchronization, *Technical Report* 1997-013, Digital SRC, 1997.

[9] Stephan Diehl. A generative methodology for the design of abstract machines. *Science of Computer Programming*. 2000. 38. 125-142.

[10] G.Berry and G.Boudol. The chemical abstract machine. *Theoretical Computer Science*, vol.96,1992.

[11] D.Sangiorgi and A.Valente. A Distributed Abstract Machine for Safe Ambients. *In Proceedings of the 28th ICALP*, volume 2076 of LNCS. Springer-Verlag, 2001.

[12] Zhang Jing, Zhang Li-Cui and Jin Cheng-Zhi. A Distributed Implementation for the Seal Calculus. *To Appear in Proceedings of the First International Symposium on Pervasive Computations and Applications(SPCA06)*. Urumchi, Xin Jiang, P.R.China.